TIME
CHARTERS

TIME CHARTERS

THIRD EDITION BY

MICHAEL WILFORD
London, Solicitor
Clyde & Co.

TERENCE COGHLIN
Partner, Thos. R. Miller & Son

JOHN D. KIMBALL
New York, Attorney
Healy & Baillie

LLP

LONDON NEW YORK HAMBURG HONG KONG
LLOYD'S OF LONDON PRESS LTD.
1989

Lloyd's of London Press Ltd.
Legal Publishing and Conferences Division
One Singer Street, London EC2A 4LQ

U.S.A. AND CANADA
Lloyd's of London Press Inc.
Suite 523, 611 Broadway
New York, NY 10012 USA

GERMANY
Lloyd's of London Press GmbH
59 Ehrenbergstrasse
2000 Hamburg 50, West Germany

SOUTH EAST ASIA
Lloyd's of London Press (Far East) Ltd.
Room 1101, Hollywood Centre
233 Hollywood Road
Hong Kong

First edition, 1978
Second edition, 1982
Third edition, 1989

British Library Cataloguing in Publication Data
Wilford, Michael, *1930–*
Time charters.—3rd ed.
1. England. Freight transport. Shipping. Time charters. Law
I. Title II. Coghlin, Terence III. Kimball, John D.
344.203'968

ISBN 1–85044–185–5

Text set 10 on 12 pt Linotron 202 Times by
Promenade Graphics Ltd., Cheltenham, Glos.
Printed in Great Britain by
WBC, Bridgend, Mid Glam.

To Gerti, Claire and Astri

Acknowledgments

We would like to acknowledge our especial debt to Francis Reynolds of Worcester College, Oxford. His learning, criticism and comment have again been of immeasurable help in the preparation of this edition.

We would also like to thank our secretaries Helen Godel and Mavis Taylor without whom the accomplishment of the task of bringing out another edition of the book would not have been possible.

M.T.W.

T.G.C.

I wish to record my gratitude to Betty Waterman for her help in proofreading and to my secretary, Ann Roth, for her patience and constant assistance.

J.D.K.

Introduction to the Third Edition

Over the seven years since the last edition of this book, there have been, both in England and America, large numbers of decisions on, or relevant to, time charterparties. We have tried to cover these cases in as much detail as possible in the new edition.

As we emphasised in our introduction to the first edition, this book is primarily intended for those at the coal face of shipping law—charterers, owners, agents, brokers, P. and I. Club Managers and the lawyers who advise them on their day-to-day problems. For this reason we make no apology for continuing to give prominence to the judgments at first instance of the Commercial Court in England and to the decisions of arbitrators in New York.

The late Lord Diplock, in the House of Lords in *The Evia* (1982), castigated "the misuse of judgments given at first instance" and the "heresy" to which he considered this had led in the case in question. But it is with the current problems of the day that the shipping community is mainly concerned and it is upon these problems above all that it requires guidance. With the discouragement of appeals from arbitration awards in England, the decisions of the Commercial Court are often the only source of authoritative guidance available and the shipping community is fortunate that over the past two decades this guidance has been of such a high order, reflecting as it does the remarkable strength of the Commercial Court over that period.

As we pointed out in the introductions to the previous editions, the situation in New York is that very few charter disputes reach the courts. The vast majority are dealt with and finally resolved by arbitrators, from whose awards there is no appeal to the courts, except in those few cases where grounds may exist for vacating an award. By contrast to the position in London, the awards of New York arbitrators are published and indexed by the Society of Maritime Arbitrators and in *American Maritime Cases*; previous awards are cited to arbitrators and treated as having value as precedents for that purpose. Consequently the American sections of this book must, and do, continue to draw heavily on the awards of New York arbitrators. Throughout the book American law is, as before, distinguished from English law on each topic by a margin line against each American section.

Finally, we would be remiss indeed if we failed to acknowledge the contribution to our work of Nicholas J. Healy, Jr., who co-authored the first two editions of this book. Nick Healy retired from the field of maritime law in 1987 to devote his time to other endeavours involving the Catholic Church. Although he had no part in the preparation of the third edition, his prior contributions remain a vital part of *Time Charters*.

Contents

Table of Cases

(*Numbers in* **bold** *type refer to pages on which the details of a case are set out.*)

(*Numbers in* **bold** *type refer to pages on which the details of a case are set out.*)

(*Numbers in* **bold** *type refer to pages on which the details of a case are set out.*)

(*Numbers in* **bold** *type refer to pages on which the details of a case are set out.*)

(*Numbers in* **bold** *type refer to pages on which the details of a case are set out.*)

(*Numbers in* **bold** *type refer to pages on which the details of a case are set out.*)

(Numbers in **bold** *type refer to pages on which the details of a case are set out.)*

(*Numbers in* **bold** *type refer to pages on which the details of a case are set out.*)

(*Numbers in* **bold** *type refer to pages on which the details of a case are set out.*)

(*Numbers in* **bold** *type refer to pages on which the details of a case are set out.*)

(*Numbers in* **bold** *type refer to pages on which the details of a case are set out.*)

(*Numbers in* **bold** *type refer to pages on which the details of a case are set out.*)

(*Numbers in* **bold** *type refer to pages on which the details of a case are set out.*)

(*Numbers in* **bold** *type refer to pages on which the details of a case are set out.*)

(*Numbers in* **bold** *type refer to pages on which the details of a case are set out.*)

(*Numbers in* **bold** *type refer to pages on which the details of a case are set out.*)

(*Numbers in* **bold** *type refer to pages on which the details of a case are set out.*)

(*Numbers in* **bold** *type refer to pages on which the details of a case are set out.*)

(*Numbers in* **bold** *type refer to pages on which the details of a case are set out.*)

(*Numbers in* **bold** *type refer to pages on which the details of a case are set out.*)

(*Numbers in* **bold** *type refer to pages on which the details of a case are set out.*)

(*Numbers in* **bold** *type refer to pages on which the details of a case are set out.*)

(*Numbers in* **bold** *type refer to pages on which the details of a case are set out.*)

(*Numbers in* **bold** *type refer to pages on which the details of a case are set out.*)

(*Numbers in* **bold** *type refer to pages on which the details of a case are set out.*)

(Numbers in **bold** *type refer to pages on which the details of a case are set out.)*

(*Numbers in* **bold** *type refer to pages on which the details of a case are set out.*)

(*Numbers in* **bold** *type refer to pages on which the details of a case are set out.*)

(Numbers in **bold** *type refer to pages on which the details of a case are set out.)*

(Numbers in **bold** *type refer to pages on which the details of a case are set out.)*

(*Numbers in* **bold** *type refer to pages on which the details of a case are set out.*)

(*Numbers in* **bold** *type refer to pages on which the details of a case are set out.*)

(*Numbers in* **bold** *type refer to pages on which the details of a case are set out.*)

(*Numbers in* **bold** *type refer to pages on which the details of a case are set out.*)

(*Numbers in* **bold** *type refer to pages on which the details of a case are set out.*)

(Numbers in **bold** *type refer to pages on which the details of a case are set out.)*

(*Numbers in* **bold** *type refer to pages on which the details of a case are set out.*)

(Numbers in **bold** *type refer to pages on which the details of a case are set out.)*

(*Numbers in* **bold** *type refer to pages on which the details of a case are set out.*)

(*Numbers in* **bold** *type refer to pages on which the details of a case are set out.*)

(*Numbers in* **bold** *type refer to pages on which the details of a case are set out.*)

(*Numbers in* **bold** *type refer to pages on which the details of a case are set out.*)

(*Numbers in* **bold** *type refer to pages on which the details of a case are set out.*)

(*Numbers in* **bold** *type refer to pages on which the details of a case are set out.*)

(*Numbers in* **bold** *type refer to pages on which the details of a case are set out.*)

(*Numbers in* **bold** *type refer to pages on which the details of a case are set out.*)

Table of Legislation

New York Produce Exchange Form

Time Charter

GOVERNMENT FORM

Approved by the New York Produce Exchange

November 6th, 1913—Amended October 20th, 1921; August 6th, 1931; October 3rd, 1946

This Charter Party, made and concluded in .... day of .... 19.....

Between ....

Owners of the good .... {Steamship / Motorship} .... of .... of............ tons gross register, and............ tons net register, having engines of .... indicated horse power and with hull, machinery and equipment in a thoroughly efficient state, and classed .... at............ of about............ cubic feet bale capacity, and about............ tons of 2240 lbs. deadweight capacity (cargo and bunkers, including fresh water and stores not exceeding one and one-half percent of ship's deadweight capacity, allowing a minimum of fifty tons) on a draft of............ feet............ inches on .... Summer freeboard, inclusive of permanent bunkers, which are of the capacity of about .... tons of fuel, and capable of steaming, fully laden, under good weather conditions about............ knots on a consumption of about............ tons of best Welsh coal—best grade fuel oil—best grade Diesel oil, now .... and............ Charterers of the City of............

Witnesseth, That the said Owners agree to let, and the said Charterers agree to hire the said vessel, from the time of delivery, for about .... within below mentioned trading limits. Charterers to have liberty to sublet the vessel for all or any part of the time covered by this Charter, but Charterers remaining responsible for the fulfillment of this Charter Party.

Vessel to be placed at the disposal of the Charterers, at .... in such dock or at such wharf or place (where she may safely lie, always afloat, at all times of tide, except as otherwise provided in clause No. 6), as the Charterers may direct. If such dock, wharf or place be not available time to count as provided for in clause No. 5. Vessel on her delivery to be ready to receive cargo with clean-swept holds and tight, staunch, strong and in every way fitted for the service, having water ballast, winches and donkey boiler with sufficient steam power, or if not equipped with donkey boiler, then other power sufficient to run all the winches at one and the same time (and with full complement of officers, seamen, engineers and firemen for a vessel of her tonnage), to be employed, in carrying lawful merchandise, including petroleum or its products, in proper containers, excluding .... (vessel is not to be employed in the carriage of Live Stock, but Charterers are to have the privilege of shipping a small number on deck at their risk, all necessary fittings and other requirements to be for account of Charterers), in such lawful trades, between safe port and/or ports in British North America, and/or United States of America, and/or West Indies, and/or Central America, and/or Caribbean Sea, and/or Gulf of Mexico, and/or Mexico, and/or South America............ and/or Europe and/or Africa, and/or Asia, and/or Australia, and/or Tasmania, and/or New Zealand, but excluding Magdalena River, River St. Lawrence between October 31st and May 15th, Hudson Bay and all unsafe ports; also excluding, when out of season, White Sea, Black Sea and the Baltic,

....

....

....

as the Charterers or their Agents shall direct, on the following conditions:

1. That the Owners shall provide and pay for all provisions, wages and consular shipping and discharging fees of the Crew; shall pay for the insurance of the vessel, also for all the cabin, deck, engine-room and other necessary stores, including boiler water and maintain her class and keep the vessel in a thoroughly efficient state in hull, machinery and equipment for and during the service.

2. That the Charterers shall provide and pay for all the fuel except as otherwise agreed, Port Charges, Pilotages, Agencies, Commissions, Consular Charges (except those pertaining to the Crew) and all other usual expenses except those before stated, but when the vessel puts into a port for causes for which vessel is responsible, then all such charges incurred shall be paid by the Owners. Fumigations ordered because of illness of the crew to be for Owners account. Fumigations ordered because of cargoes carried or ports visited while vessel is employed under this charter to be for Charterers account. All other fumigations to be for Charterers account after vessel has been on charter for a continuous period of six months or more.

Charterers are to provide necessary dunnage and shifting boards, also any extra fittings requisite for a special trade or unusual cargo, but Owners to allow them the use of any dunnage and shifting boards already aboard vessel. Charterers to have the privilege of using shifting boards for dunnage, they making good any damage thereto.

3. That the Charterers, at the port of delivery, and the Owners, at the port of re-delivery, shall take over and pay for all fuel remaining on board the vessel at the current prices in the respective ports, the vessel to be delivered with not less than .... tons and not more than ....tons and to be re-delivered with not less than........................tons and not more than.........................tons.

4. That the Charterers shall pay for the use and hire of the said Vessel at the rate of ....United States Currency per ton on vessel's total deadweight carrying capacity, including bunkers and stores, on.....................................summer freeboard, per Calendar Month, commencing on and from the day of her delivery, as aforesaid, and at and after the same rate for any part of a month; hire to continue until the hour of the day of her re-delivery in like good order and condition, ordinary wear and tear excepted, to the Owners (unless lost) at ....unless otherwise mutually agreed. Charterers are to give Owners not less than.........................days notice of vessel's expected date of re-delivery, and probable port.

5. Payment of said hire to be made in New York in cash in United States Currency, semi-monthly in advance, and for the last half month or part of same the approximate amount of hire, and should same not cover the actual time, hire is to be paid for the balance day by day, as it becomes due, if so required by Owners, unless bank guarantee or deposit is made by the Charterers, otherwise failing the punctual and regular payment of the hire, or bank guarantee, or on any breach of this Charter Party, the Owners shall be at liberty to withdraw the vessel from the service of the Charterers, without prejudice to any claim they (the Owners) may otherwise have on the Charterers. Time to count from 7 a.m. on the working day following that on which written notice of readiness has been given to Charterers or their Agents before 4 p.m., but if required by Charterers, they to have the privilege of using vessel at once, such time used to count as hire.

Cash for vessel's ordinary disbursements at any port may be advanced as required by the Captain, by the Charterers or their Agents, subject to $2\frac{1}{2}\%$ commission and such advances shall be deducted from the hire. The Charterers, however, shall in no way be responsible for the application of such advances.

6. That the cargo or cargoes be laden and/or discharged in any dock or at any wharf or place that Charterers or their Agents may direct, provided the vessel can safely lie always afloat at any time of tide, except at such places where it is customary for similar size vessels to safely lie aground.

7. That the whole reach of the Vessel's Hold, Decks, and usual places of loading (not more than she can reasonably stow and carry), also accommodations for Supercargo, if carried, shall be at the Charterers' disposal, reserving only proper and sufficient space for Ship's officers, crew, tackle, apparel, furniture, provisions, stores and fuel. Charterers have the privilege of passengers as far as accommodations allow, Charterers paying Owners .... per day per passenger for accommodations and meals. However, it is agreed that in case any fines or extra expenses are incurred in the consequence of the carriage of passengers, Charterers are to bear such risk and expense.

8. That the Captain shall prosecute his voyages with the utmost despatch, and shall render all customary assistance with ship's crew and boats. The Captain (although appointed by the Owners), shall be under the orders and directions of the Charterers as regards employment and agency; and Charterers are to load, stow, and trim the cargo at their expense under the supervision of the Captain, who is to sign Bills of Lading for cargo as presented, in conformity with Mate's or Tally Clerk's receipts.

9. That if the Charterers shall have reason to be dissatisfied with the conduct of the Captain, Officers, or Engineers, the Owners shall on receiving particulars of the complaint, investigate the same, and, if necessary, make a change in the appointments.

10. That the Charterers shall have permission to appoint a Supercargo, who shall accompany the vessel and see that voyages are prosecuted

with the utmost despatch. He is to be furnished with free accommodation, and same fare as provided for Captain's table, Charterers paying at the rate of $1.00 per day. Owners to victual Pilots and Customs Officers, and also, when authorized by Charterers or their Agents, to victual Tally Clerks, Stevedore's Foreman, etc., Charterers paying at the current rate per meal, for all such victualling.

11. That the Charterers shall furnish the Captain from time to time with all requisite instructions and sailing directions, in writing, and the Captain shall keep a full and correct Log of the voyage or voyages, which are to be patent to the Charterers or their Agents, and furnish the Charterers, their Agents or Supercargo, when required, with a true copy of daily Logs, showing the course of the vessel and distance run and the consumption of fuel.

12. That the Captain shall use diligence in caring for the ventilation of the cargo.

13. That the Charterers shall have the option of continuing this charter for a further period of .... on giving written notice thereof to the Owners or their Agents .... days previous to the expiration of the first-named term, or any declared option.

14. That if required by Charterers, time not to commence before .... and should vessel not have given written notice of readiness on or before .... but not later than 4 p.m. Charterers or their Agents to have the option of cancelling this Charter at any time not later than the day of vessel's readiness.

15. That in the event of the loss of time from deficiency of men or stores, fire, breakdown or damages to hull, machinery or equipment, grounding, detention by average accidents to ship or cargo, drydocking for the purpose of examination or painting bottom, or by any other cause preventing the full working of the vessel, the payment of hire shall cease for the time thereby lost; and if upon the voyage the speed be reduced by defect in or breakdown of any part of her hull, machinery or equipment, the time so lost, and the cost of any extra fuel consumed in consequence thereof, and all extra expenses shall be deducted from the hire.

16. That should the Vessel be lost, money paid in advance and not earned (reckoning from the date of loss or being last heard of) shall be returned to the Charterers at once. The act of God, enemies, fire, restraint of Princes, Rulers and People, and all dangers and accidents of the Seas, Rivers, Machinery, Boilers and Steam Navigation, and errors of Navigation throughout this Charter Party, always mutually excepted.

The vessel shall have the liberty to sail with or without pilots, to tow and to be towed, to assist vessels in distress, and to deviate for the purpose of saving life and property.

17. That should any dispute arise between Owners and the Charterers, the matter in dispute shall be referred to three persons at New York, one to be appointed by each of the parties hereto, and the third by the two so chosen; their decision or that of any two of them, shall be final, and for the purpose of enforcing any award, this agreement may be made a rule of the Court. The Arbitrators shall be commercial men.

18. That the Owners shall have a lien upon all cargoes, and all sub-freights for any amounts due under this Charter, including General Average contributions, and the Charterers to have a lien on the Ship for all monies paid in advance and not earned, and any overpaid hire or excess deposit to be returned at once. Charterers will not suffer, nor permit to be continued, any lien or encumbrance incurred by them or their agents, which might have priority over the title and interest of the owners in the vessel.

19. That all derelicts and salvage shall be for Owners' and Charterers' equal benefit after deducting Owners' and Charterers' expenses and Crew's proportion. General Average shall be adjusted, stated and settled, according to Rules 1 to 15, inclusive, 17 to 22, inclusive, and Rule F of York-Antwerp Rules 1924, at such port or place in the United States as may be selected by the carrier, and as to matters not provided for by these Rules, according to the laws and usages at the port of New York. In such adjustment disbursements in foreign currencies shall be exchanged into United States money at the rate prevailing on the dates made and allowances for damage to cargo claimed in foreign currency shall be converted at the rate prevailing on the last day of discharge at the port or place of final discharge of such damaged cargo from the ship. Average agreement or bond and such additional security, as may be required by the carrier, must be furnished before delivery of the goods. Such cash deposit as the carrier or his agents may deem sufficient as additional security for the contribution of the goods and for any salvage and special charges thereon, shall, if required, be made by the goods, shippers, consignees or owners of the goods to the carrier before delivery. Such deposit shall, at the option of the carrier, be payable in United States money and be remitted to the adjuster. When so remitted the deposit shall be held in a special account at the place of adjustment in the name of the adjuster pending settlement of the General Average and refunds or credit balances, if any, shall be paid in United States money.

In the event of accident, danger, damage, or disaster, before or after commencement of the voyage resulting from any cause whatsoever, whether due to negligence or not, for which, or for the consequence of which, the carrier is not responsible, by statute, contract, or otherwise, the goods, the shipper and the consignee, jointly and severally, shall contribute with the carrier in general average to the payment of any sacrifices, losses, or expenses of a general average nature that may be made or incurred, and shall pay salvage and special charges incurred in respect of the goods. If a salving ship is owned or operated by the carrier, salvage shall be paid for as fully and in the same manner as if such salving ship or ships belonged to strangers.

Provisions as to General Average in accordance with the above are to be included in all bills of lading issued hereunder.

20. Fuel used by the vessel while off hire, also for cooking, condensing water, or for grates and stoves to be agreed to as to quantity, and the cost of replacing same, to be allowed by Owners.

21. That as the vessel may be from time to time employed in tropical waters during the term of this Charter, Vessel is to be docked at a convenient place, bottom cleaned and painted whenever Charterers and Captain think necessary, at least once in every six months, reckoning from time of last painting, and payment of the hire to be suspended until she is again in proper state for the service.

....

....

22. Owners shall maintain the gear of the ship as fitted, providing gear (for all derricks) capable of handling lifts up to three tons, also providing ropes, falls, slings and blocks. If vessel is fitted with derricks capable of handling heavier lifts, Owners are to provide necessary gear for same, otherwise equipment and gear for heavier lifts shall be for Charterers' account. Owners also to provide on the vessel lanterns and oil for night work, and vessel to give use of electric light when so fitted, but any additional lights over those on board to be at Charterers' expense. The Charterers to have the use of any gear on board the vessel.

23. Vessel to work night and day, if required by Charterers, and all winches to be at Charterers' disposal during loading and discharging; steamer to provide one winchman per hatch to work winches day and night, as required, Charterers agreeing to pay officers, engineers, winchmen, deck hands and donkeymen for overtime work done in accordance with the working hours and rates stated in the ship's articles. If the rules of the port, or labor unions, prevent crew from driving winches, shore Winchmen to be paid by Charterers. In the event of a disabled winch or winches, or insufficient power to operate winches, Owners to pay for shore engine, or engines, in lieu thereof, if required, and pay any loss of time occasioned thereby.

24. It is also mutually agreed that this Charter is subject to all the terms and provisions of and all the exemptions from liability contained in the Act of Congress of the United States approved on the 13th day of February, 1893, and entitled "An Act relating to Navigation of Vessels, etc.," in respect of all cargo shipped under this charter to or from the United States of America. It is further subject to the following clauses, both of which are to be included in all bills of lading issued hereunder:

U.S.A. Clause Paramount

This bill of lading shall have effect subject to the provisions of the Carriage of Goods by Sea Act of the United States, approved April 16, 1936, which shall be deemed to be incorporated herein, and nothing herein contained shall be deemed a surrender by the carrier of any of its rights or immunities or an increase of any of its responsibilities or liabilities under said Act. If any term of this bill of lading be repugnant to said Act to any extent, such term shall be void to that extent, but no further.

Both-to-Blame Collision Clause

If the ship comes into collision with another ship as a result of the negligence of the other ship and any act, neglect or default of the Master, mariner, pilot or the servants of the Carrier in the navigation or in the management of the ship, the owners of the goods carried hereunder will indemnify the Carrier against all loss or liability to the other or non-carrying ship or her owners in so far as such loss or liability represents loss of, or damage to, or any claim whatsoever of the owners of said goods, paid or payable by the other or non-carrying ship or her owners to the owners of said goods and set off, recouped or recovered by the other or non-carrying ship or her owners as part of their claim against the carrying ship or carrier.

25. The vessel shall not be required to enter any ice-bound port, or any port where lights or light-ships have been or are about to be withdrawn by reason of ice, or where there is risk that in the ordinary course of things the vessel will not be able on account of ice to safely enter the port or to get out after having completed loading or discharging.

26. Nothing herein stated is to be construed as a demise of the vessel to the Time Charterers. The owners to remain responsible for the navigation of the vessel, insurance, crew, and all other matters, same as when trading for their own account.

27. A commission of $2\frac{1}{2}$ per cent is payable by the Vessel and Owners to

....

on hire earned and paid under this Charter, and also upon any continuation or extension of this Charter.

28. An address commission of $2\frac{1}{2}$ per cent payable to .... on the hire earned and paid under this Charter.

By cable authority from

The original Charter Party in our possession. As..For Owners

BROKERS.

Baltime Form

THE BALTIC AND INTERNATIONAL MARITIME CONFERENCE

(Formerly The Baltic and White Sea Conference)

UNIFORM TIME-CHARTER

....19...........

IT IS THIS DAY MUTUALLY AGREED between .... Owners of the Vessel called .... of......... tons gross/tons net Register, classed .... of............................indicated horse power, carrying about ....tons deadweight on Board of Trade summer freeboard inclusive of bunkers, stores, provisions and boiler water, having as per builder's plan ....cubic-feet grain/bale capacity, exclusive of permanent bunkers, which contain about........tons, and fully loaded capable of steaming about....................... knots in good weather and smooth water on a consumption of about .... tons best Welsh coal, or about......................tons oil-fuel, now................... and .... of .... Charterers, as follows:

1. The Owners let, and the Charterers hire the Vessel for a period of.................................... calendar months from the time (not a Sunday or a legal Holiday unless taken over) the Vessel is delivered and placed at the disposal of the Charterers between 9 a.m. and 6 p.m., or between 9 a.m. and 2 p.m. if on Saturday, at.. ....in such available berth where she can safely lie always afloat, as the Charterers may direct, she being in every way fitted for ordinary cargo service.

The Vessel to be delivered ....

2. The Vessel to be employed in lawful trades for the carriage of lawful merchandise only between good and safe ports or places where she can safely lie always afloat within the following limits:

....

....

....

....

....

....

....

No live stock nor injurious, inflammable or dangerous goods (such as acids, explosives, calcium carbide, ferro silicon, naphtha, motor spirit, tar, or any of their products) to be shipped.

3. The Owners to provide and pay for all provisions and wages, for insurance of the Vessel, for all deck and engine-room stores and maintain her in a thoroughly efficient state in hull and machinery during service.

The Owners to provide one winchman per hatch. If further winchmen are required, or if the stevedores refuse or are not permitted to work with the Crew, the Charterers to provide and pay qualified shore-winchmen.

4. The Charterers to provide and pay for all coals, including galley coal, oil-fuel, water for boilers, port charges, pilotages (whether compulsory or not), canal steersmen, boatage, lights, tug-assistance, consular charges (except those pertaining to the Master, Officers and Crew), canal, dock and other dues and charges, including any foreign general municipality or state taxes, also all dock, harbour and tonnage dues at the ports of delivery and re-delivery (unless incurred through cargo carried before delivery or after re-delivery), agencies, commissions, also to arrange and pay for loading, trimming, stowing (including dunnage and shifting boards, except any already on board), unloading, weighing, tallying and delivery of cargoes, surveys on hatches, meals supplied to officials and men in their service and all other charges and expenses whatsoever including detention and expenses through quarantine (including cost of fumigation and disinfection).

All ropes, slings and special runners actually used for loading and discharging and any special gear, including special ropes, hawsers and chains required by the custom of the port for mooring to be for the Charterers' account. The Vessel to be fitted with winches, derricks, wheels and ordinary runners capable of handling lifts up to 2 tons.

5. The Charterers at port of delivery and the Owners at port of re-delivery to take over and pay for all coal or oil-fuel remaining in the Vessel's bunkers at current price at the respective ports. The Vessel to be re-delivered with not less than............tons and not exceeding............tons of coal or oil-fuel in the Vessel's bunkers.

6. The Charterers to pay as hire:.. per 30 days, commencing in accordance with clause 1 until her re-delivery to the Owners.

Payment of hire to be made in cash, in .... without discount, every 30 days, in advance.

In default of payment the Owners to have the right of withdrawing the Vessel from the service of the Charterers, without noting any protest and without interference by any court or any other formality whatsoever and without prejudice to any claim the Owners may otherwise have on the Charterers under the Charter.

7. The Vessel to be re-delivered on the expiration of the Charter in the same good order as when delivered to the Charterers (fair wear and tear excepted) at an ice-free port in the Charterers' option in

....

....

between 9 a.m. and 6 p.m., and 9 a.m. and 2 p.m. on Saturday, but the day of re-delivery shall not be a Sunday or legal Holiday.

The Charterers to give the Owners not less than ten days' notice at which port and on about which day the Vessel will be re-delivered.

Should the Vessel be ordered on a voyage by which the Charter period will be exceeded the Charterers to have the use of the Vessel to enable them to complete the voyage, provided it could be reasonably calculated that the voyage would allow re-delivery about the time fixed for the termination of the Charter, but for any time exceeding the termination date the Charterers to pay the market rate if higher than the rate stipulated herein.

8. The whole reach and burthen of the Vessel, including lawful deck-capacity to be at the Charterer's disposal, reserving proper and sufficient space for the Vessel's Master, Officers, Crew, tackle, apparel, furniture, provisions and stores.

9. The Master to prosecute all voyages with the utmost despatch and to render customary assistance with the Vessel's Crew. The Master to be under the orders of the Charterers as regards employment agency, or other arrangements. The Charterers to indemnify the Owners against all consequences or liabilities arising from the Master, Officers or Agents signing Bills of Lading or other documents or otherwise complying with such orders, as well as from any irregularity in the Vessel's papers or for overcarrying goods. The Owners not to be responsible for shortage, mixture, marks, nor for number of pieces or packages, nor for damage to or claims on cargo caused by bad stowage or otherwise.

If the Charterers have reason to be dissatisfied with the conduct of the Master, Officers, or Engineers, the Owners, on receiving particulars of the complaint, promptly to investigate the matter, and, if necessary and practicable, to make a change in the appointments.

10. The Charterers to furnish the Master with all instructions and sailing directions and the Master and Engineer to keep full and correct logs accessible to the Charterers or their Agents.

11. (A) In the event of drydocking or other necessary measures to maintain the efficiency of the Vessel, deficiency of men or Owners' stores, breakdown of machinery, damage to hull or other accident, either hindering or preventing the working of the vessel and continuing for more than twentyfour consecutive hours, no hire to be paid in respect of any time lost thereby during the period in which the Vessel is unable to perform the service immediately required. Any hire paid in advance to be adjusted accordingly.

(B) In the event of the Vessel being driven into port or to anchorage through stress of weather, trading to shallow harbours or to rivers or ports with bars or suffering an accident to her cargo, any detention of the Vessel and/or expenses resulting from such detention to be for the Charterers' account even if such detention and/or expenses, or the cause by reason of which either is incurred, be due to, or be contributed to by, the negligence of the Owners' servants.

12. Cleaning of boilers whenever possible to be done during service, but if impossible the Charterers to give the Owners necessary time for cleaning. Should the Vessel be detained beyond 48 hours hire to cease until again ready.

13. The Owners only to be responsible for delay in delivery of the Vessel or for delay during the currency of the Charter and for loss or damage to goods onboard, if such delay or loss has been caused by want of due diligence on the part of the Owners or their Manager in making the Vessel sea-worthy and fitted for the voyage or any other personal act or omission or default of the Owners or their Manager. The Owners not to be responsible in any other case nor for damage or delay whatsoever and howsoever caused even if caused by the neglect or default of their servants. The Owners not to be liable for loss or damage arising or resulting from strikes, lock-outs or stoppage or restraint of labour (including the Master, Officers or Crew) whether partial or general.

The Charterers to be responsible for loss or damage caused to the Vessel or to the Owners by goods being loaded contrary to the terms of the Charter or by improper or careless bunkering or loading, stowing or discharging of goods or any other improper or negligent act on their part or that of their servants.

14. The Charterers or their Agents to advance to the Master, if required, necessary funds for

ordinary disbursements for the Vessel's account at any port charging only interest at 6 per cent p.a., such advances to be deducted from hire.

15. The Vessel not to be ordered to nor bound to enter: a) any place where fever or epidemics are prevalent or to which the Master, Officers and Crew by law are not bound to follow the Vessel b) any ice-bound place or any place where lights, lightships, marks and buoys are or are likely to be withdrawn by reason of ice on the Vessel's arrival or where there is risk that ordinarily the Vessel will not be able on account of ice to reach the place or to get out after having completed loading or discharging. The Vessel not to be obliged to force ice. If on account of ice the Master considers it dangerous to remain at the loading or discharging place for fear of the Vessel being frozen in and/or damaged, he has liberty to sail to a convenient open place and await the Charterers' fresh instructions.

Unforeseen detention through any of above causes to be for the Charterers' account.

16. Should the Vessel be lost or missing, hire to cease from the date when she was lost. If the date of loss cannot be ascertained half hire to be paid from the date the Vessel was last reported until the calculated date of arrival at the destination. Any hire paid in advance to be adjusted accordingly.

17. The Vessel to work day and night if required. The Charterers to refund the Owners their outlays for all overtime paid to Officers and Crew according to the hours and rates stated in the Vessel's articles.

18. The Owners to have a lien upon all cargoes and sub-freights belonging to the Time-Charterers and any Bill of Lading freight for all claims under this Charter, and the Charterers to have a lien on the Vessel for all moneys paid in advance and not earned.

19. All salvage and assistance to other vessels to be for the Owners' and the Charterers' equal benefit after deducting the Master's and Crew's proportion and all legal and other expenses including hire paid under the charter for time lost in the salvage, also repairs of damage and coal or oil-fuel consumed. The Charterers to be bound by all measures taken by the Owners in order to secure payment of salvage and to fix its amount.

20. The Charterers to have the option of subletting the Vessel, giving due notice to the Owners, but the original Charterers always to remain responsible to the Owners for due performance of the Charter.

21. (A) The Vessel unless the consent of the Owners be first obtained not to be ordered nor continue to any place or on any voyage nor be used on any service which will bring her within a zone which is dangerous as the result of any actual or threatened act of war, war hostilities, warlike operations, acts of piracy or of hostility or malicious damage against this or any other vessel or its cargo by any person, body or State whatsoever, revolution, civil war, civil commotion or the operation of international law, nor be exposed in any way to any risks or penalties whatsoever consequent upon the imposition of Sanctions, nor carry any goods that may in any way expose her to any risks of seizure, capture, penalties or any other interference of any kind whatsoever by the belligerent or fighting powers or parties or by any Government or Ruler.

(B) Should the Vessel approach or be brought or ordered within such zone, or be exposed in any way to the said risks, (1) the Owners to be entitled from time to time to insure their interests in the Vessel and/or hire against any of the risks likely to be involved thereby on such terms as they shall think fit, the Charterers to make a refund to the Owners of the premium on demand; and (2) notwithstanding the terms of clause 11 hire to be paid for all time lost including any lost owing to loss of or injury to the Master, Officers, or Crew or to the action of the Crew in refusing to proceed to such zone or to be exposed to such risks.

(C) In the event of the wages of the Master, Officers and/or Crew or the cost of provisions and/or stores for deck and/or engine room and/or insurance premiums being increased by reason of or during the existence of any of the matters mentioned in section (A) the amount of any increase to be added to the hire and paid by the Charterers on production of the Owner's account therefor, such account being rendered monthly.

(D) The Vessel to have liberty to comply with any orders or directions as to departure, arrival, routes, ports of call, stoppages, destination, delivery or in any other wise whatsoever given by the Government of the nation under whose flag the Vessel sails or any other Government or any person (or body) acting or purporting to act with the authority of such Government or by any committee or person having under the terms of the war risks insurance on the Vessel the right to give any such orders or directions

(E) In the event of the nation under whose flag the Vessel sails becoming involved in war, hostilities, warlike operations, revolution, or civil commotion, both the Owners and the Charterers may cancel the Charter and, unless otherwise agreed, the Vessel to be redelivered to the Owners at the port of destination or, if prevented through the provisions of section (A) from reaching or entering it, then at a near open and safe port at the Owners' option, after discharge of any cargo on board.

(F) If in compliance with the provisions of this clause anything is done or is not done, such not to be deemed a deviation.

22. Should the Vessel not be delivered by the..........................day of ....19.........., the Charterers to have the option of cancelling.

If the Vessel cannot be delivered by the cancelling date, the Charterers, if required, to declare within 48 hours after receving notice thereof whether they cancel or will take delivery of the Vessel.

23. Any dispute arising under the Charter to be referred to arbitration in London (or such other place as may be agreed) one Arbitrator to be nominated by the Owners and the other by the Charterers, and in case the Arbitrators shall not agree then to the decision of an Umpire to be appointed by them, the award of the Arbitrators or the Umpire to be final and binding upon both parties.

24. General Average to be settled according to York/Antwerp Rules, 1974. Hire not to contribute to General Average.

25. The Owners to pay a commission of..............to...

....

on any hire paid under the Charter, but in no case less than is necessary to cover the actual expenses of the Brokers and a reasonable fee for their work. If the full hire is not paid owing to breach of Charter by either of the parties the party liable therefor to indemnify the Brokers against their loss of commission.

Should the parties agree to cancel the Charter, the Owners to indemnify the Brokers against any loss of commission but in such case the commission not to exceed the brokerage on one year's hire.

STB Form of Tanker Time Charter

CODE WORD FOR THIS CHARTER PARTY
STB TIME

....
Vessel Name

TANKER TIME CHARTER PARTY

....
Place Date

IT IS THIS DAY MUTUALLY AGREED between .... as Owner/Chartered Owner (herein called "Owner") of the .... (herein called "Vessel") and .... herein called "Charterer") that the Owner lets and the Charterer hires the use and services of the Vessel for the carriage of ...., in bulk, and such other lawful merchandise as may be suitable for a vessel of her description, for the period and on the terms and conditions hereinafter set forth.

TERM

1. (a) The term of this Charter shall be for a period of about (hereinafter "Original Period") plus any extensions thereof as provided in (b) below. The Original Period shall commence at the time when the Vessel is placed at the Charterer's disposal as provided in Clause 5. The word "about" as used above shall mean "14 days more or less" and shall apply to the term of this Charter consisting of the Original Period plus any extensions as hereinafter provided.

EXTENSIONS

(b) Charterer shall have the option of extending the term of this Charter for a period of .... (hereinafter "Extended Period") by written notice to Owner at least 30 days previous to the expiration of the Original Period. The term of this Charter may be extended by Charterer also for periods (hereinafter "Off/Hire Extensions") of all or any part of the time the Vessel is off hire during the Original Period and/or Extended Period, if any, by giving written notice to Owner at least 30 days before the expiration of the Original Period or Extended Period, as the case may be, and, if Charterer so elects and gives a further written notice to Owner at least 30 days before the expiration of any such Off-Hire Extension, all or any part of the time the Vessel is off hire following the previous notice shall be added to the term of this Charter.

VESSEL PARTICULARS

2. The following are particulars and capacities of the Vessel and her equipment:

A. Cargo Carrying Capacity

I. Total cargo tank capacity when 100% full .... US Barrels

II. Weight of stores, etc., permanently deducted from cargo carrying capacity .... L.T.

III. a. Fresh water consumption per day .... L.T.
b. Capacity of evaporators per day .... L.T.
c. Quantity of fresh water deductible from cargo carrying capacity on a daily basis .... L.T.

IV. Estimated loss of cargo carrying capacity due to "sag" when fully loaded with light, medium, heavy cargo

Light ..................................L.T.
Medium .... L.T.
Heavy .... L.T.

V. The vessel can carry .... tons (of 2,240 lbs.) total deadweight (as certified by Classification Society) of cargo, bunkers, water, and stores on an assigned summer mean draft of ....ft.....................in. and an assigned freeboard of ....ft.....................in.

B. Other Tank Capacities

I. Total capacity of fuel tanks for propulsion .... US Barrels
II. Total capacity of fresh water tanks .... L.T.
III. Total capacity of segregated ballast tanks .... L.T.

C. Capacity of Pumps

I. **Cargo Pumps**
a. Number ....
b. Make ....
c. Type ....
d. Design rated capacity of each pump in U.S. Barrels per hour and corresponding head in feet .... US Bbls/Hr. .... Feet/Head

II. **Stripping Pumps**
a. Number ....
b. Design capacity of each pump in U.S. Barrels per hour for the guaranteed discharge head of .... US Bbls/Hr. .... Feet/Head

III. **Segregated Ballast Pumps**
a. Number ....
b. Design capacity each pump .... US Bbls/Hr.

D. Cargo Loading/Discharge Manifold

The whole manifold is made of steel or comparable material and is strengthened and supported to avoid damage from loading and discharge equipment and to withstand a maximum load from any direction equivalent to the safe working load of the cargo hose lifting equipment.

I. a. Number of manifold connections ....
b. Diameter of manifold connections ....
c. Distance from centers of manifold connections ....
d. Distance from manifold connections to ship's side ....
e. Distance center of manifold connection to deck ....
f. Distance bow/center of manifold ....
g. Safe working load of cargo hose lifting equipment .... tons.

II. **Cargo Manifold Reducing Pieces**
Vessels from 16 to 60 MDWT are equipped with a sufficient number of cargo manifold reducing pieces of steel or a comparable material to permit presenting of flanges of 8″, 10″ and 12″ (ASA) cargo hoses/arms at all manifold connections on one side of the vessel.
Vessels over 60 MDWT are equipped with a sufficient number of cargo manifold reducing pieces of steel or a comparable material to permit presenting of flanges of 10″, 12″ and 16″ (ASA) cargo hose/arms at all manifold connections on one side of the vessel.

E. Heating Coils

I. Type of coils and material of which manufactured ....
II. Ratio heating surface/volume
a. Center Tanks Ft.^{2}/40 Ft.^{3}
b. Wing Tanks Ft.^{2}/40 Ft.^{3}

F. Cargo Loading/Performance

Vessel can load homogeneous cargo at maximum rate of .... B/H.

G. Vessel Particulars

I. Length overall...................ft....................In.
II. Fully loaded summer draft in salt water of a density of 1.025 ....ft...................inches on an assigned freeboard of ....
III. Fresh Water allowance....................In.
IV. Light ship draft Forward...................Ft....................In.
Aft ....Ft....................In.
Mean ....Ft....................In.
V. Moulded Depth ....
VI. Light ship freeboard...................Ft....................In.
VII. TPI on light ship draft ....
VIII. TPI on summer draft ....
IX. Extreme beam ....
X. Gross Reg. Tons ....
XI. Net Reg. Tons ....
XII. Suez Canal Tonnage ....
XIII. Panama Canal Tonnage ....
XIV. Flag of Registry ....
XV. Call letters ....
XVI. Classification Society ....
XVII. Maximum bunkers aboard when vessel is placed at Charterer's disposal to be ....

XVIII. Owner shall provide Charterer with copies of the Vessel's plans upon Charterer's request therefor, provided, in the case of a newbuilding, that Owner need not provide same until such plans are available to him from the building yard.

XIX. Vessel is equipped with a fresh water evaporator which will be maintained in good operating condition. Owners warrant that this evaporator is capable of making sufficient fresh water to supply the vessel's needs.

XX. Owner warrants vessel is capable of heating cargo to 135°F. and of maintaining same throughout entire discharge. Should vessel fail to heat cargo in accordance with Charterer's instructions, Charterer shall have the option to:

a) Delay discharge of the cargo

b) Delay berthing of the Vessel

c) Discontinue discharge and remove vessel from berth until cargo is heated in accordance with Charterer's instructions.

All time lost to be considered as off-hire and for Owner's account. In addition any expenses incurred in moving vessel from berth will be for Owner's account.

HIRE

3. (a) The Charterer shall pay hire for the use of the Vessel at the rate of .... in .... currency per ton (of 2,240 lbs.) on Vessel's deadweight as shown in Clause 2. A. per calendar month, payment to be made in advance monthly at .... by check without discount commencing with the date and hour the Vessel is placed at Charterer's disposal hereunder and continuing to the date and hour when the Vessel is released to Owner at the expiration of this Charter except as otherwise expressed in this Charter. Any hire paid in advance and not earned shall be returned to the Charterer at once. In no event will initial payment of hire be made until Charter Party is signed and Vessel placed at Charterer's disposal as herein provided.

DEDUCTIONS

(b) The Charterer shall be entitled to deduct from hire payments: (1) any disbursements for Owner's account and any advances to the Master or Owner's agents, including commissions thereon, (2) layup savings calculated in accordance with Clause 17, (3) any previous overpayments of hire including offhire and including any overpayments of hire concerning which a bona fida dispute may exist but in the latter event the Charterer shall furnish an adequate bank guarantee or other good and sufficient security on request of the Owner, (4) any Clause 8 and 9 claims, and (5) any other sums to which Charterer is entitled under this charter. The Charterer shall be entitled to $2\frac{1}{2}$% commission on any sums advanced or disbursements made for the Owner's account. However, the Owner shall have the option of making advances to the Charterer or its designated agent for disbursements (provided such advances are deemed adequate and reasonable by the Charterer), and, in such event, no commissions shall be paid.

FINAL VOYAGE

(c) Should the Vessel be on her final voyage at the time a payment of hire becomes due, said payment shall be made for the time estimated by Charterer to be necessary to complete the voyage and effect release of the Vessel to Owner, less all deductions provided for in sub-paragraph (b) of this Clause which shall be estimated by Charterer if the actual amounts have not been received and also less the amount estimated by Charterer to become payable by the Owner for fuel and water on release as provided in Clause 19. (b). Upon redelivery any difference between the estimated and actual amounts shall be refunded to or paid by the Charterer as the case may require.

LOSS OF VESSEL

(d) Should the Vessel be lost or be missing and presumed lost, hire shall cease at the time of her loss or, if such time is unknown, at the time when the Vessel was last heard of. If the Vessel should become a constructive total loss, hire shall cease at the time of the casualty resulting in such loss. In either case, any hire paid in advance and not earned shall be returned to the Charterer. If the Vessel should be off hire or missing when a payment of hire would otherwise be due, such payment shall be postponed until the off-hire period ceases or the safety of the Vessel is ascertained, as the case may be.

REDUCTION IN HIRE

(e) If the Vessel shall not fulfill the Owner's Warranty or any other part of her description as warranted in Clause 4, Charterer shall be entitled without prejudice to a reduction in the hire to correct for the deficiency and to any other rights the Charterer may have.

DEFAULT

(f) In default of punctual and regular payment as herein specified, the Owner will notify .... at .... whereupon the Charterer shall make payment of the amount due within ten (10) days of receipt of notification from the Owner, failing which the Owner will have the right to withdraw the Vessel from the service of the Charterer without prejudice to any claim the Owner may otherwise have against the Charterer under this Charter.

INCREMENT

(g) The rate of hire set forth in sub-paragraph (a) of this Clause includes an increment of $ .... to cover in full any expenses for Charterer's account for extra victualling by the Master, telephone calls, radio messages, telegrams and cables and all overtime worked by the Vessel's officers and crew at Charterer's request.

(h) The rate of charter hire set forth in this Clause 3 is equivalent to $ .... per hour.

WARRANTIES

4. Owner warrants that at the time the Vessel is placed at Charterer's disposal, the Vessel shall fulfill the descriptions, particulars and capabilities set forth in Clause 2 above, and shall be tight, staunch, and strong, in thoroughly efficient order and condition and in every way fit, manned, equipped, and supplied for the service contemplated, with holds, cargo tanks, pipelines, and valves clear, clean, and tight and with pumps, heating coils, and all other equipment in good working order. Such description, particulars, and capabilities of the Vessel shall be maintained by Owner throughout the period of the Vessel's service hereunder so far as possible by the exercise of due diligence.

HIRE

5. (a) The use and services of the Vessel shall be placed at the disposal of the Charterer at .... (hereinafter "Port of Delivery") at such readily accessible dock, wharf, or other place as the Charterer may direct. Charter hire shall commence when the Vessel is at such dock, wharf, or place and in all respects ready to perform this Charter and ready for sea and written notice thereof has been given by the Master to the Charterer or its Agents at the Port of Delivery.

LAYDAYS

(b) Hire shall not commence before ...., except with Charterer's consent, and the Vessel shall be placed at Charterer's disposal in accordance with the provisions hereof no later than ....in default of which Charterer shall have the option to cancel this Charter declarable not later than the day of the Vessel's readiness. Cancellation by Charterer or acceptance of the use of the Vessel's services shall be without prejudice to any claims for damages Charterer may have for late tender of the Vessel's services.

USE OF VESSEL

(c) The whole reach and burthen of the Vessel (but not more than she can reasonably stow and safely carry) shall be at the Charterer's disposal, reserving proper and sufficient space for Vessel's Officers, Crew, Master's cabin, tackle, apparel, furniture, fuel, provisions, and stores.

TRADING LIMITS

6. (a) The Vessel may be employed in any part of the World trading between and at ports, places, berths, docks, anchorages, and submarine pipe-lines in such lawful trades as the Charterer or its agents may direct, subject to Institute Warranties and Clauses attached hereto but may be sent to ports and places on the North American Lakes, the St. Lawrence River and tributaries between May 15 and November 15 and through the Straits of Magellan and around Cape Horn and The Cape of Good Hope at any time of the year without payment of any extra premium. Notwithstanding the foregoing restrictions, the Vessel may be sent to Baltic Sea ports not North of Stockholm, and to Helsingfors and Abo, Finland, and other ports and places as set forth in the Institute Warranties and Clauses, provided, however, that Charterer shall reimburse Owner for any additional premia properly assessed by Vessel's underwriters and payable by Owner for breach of such trade warranties.

BERTHS

(b) The Vessel shall be loaded, discharged, or lightened, at any port, place, berth, dock, anchorage, or submarine line or alongside lighters or lightening vessels as Charterer may direct. Notwithstanding anything contained in this Clause or any other provisions of this Charter, Charterer shall not be deemed to warrant the safety of any port, berth, dock, anchorage, and/or submarine line and shall not be liable for any loss, damage, injury, or delay resulting from conditions at such ports, berths, docks, anchorages, and submarine lines not caused by Charterer's fault or neglect or which could have been avoided by the exercise of reasonable care on the part of the Master or Owner.

FUEL

(c) The Charterer shall accept and pay for all fuel in the Vessel's bunkers at the time the vessel is placed at Charterer's disposal not exceeding the maximum quantity in Clause 2 above. Any excess quantity shall be removed by the Owner at its expense before such time unless the

Charterer elects to accept such excess at the price determined as hereinafter provided or at such other price as may be mutually agreed. Payment for such fuel shall be in accordance with The Exxon International Contract Price List current for the date when and the port or place where the vessel is placed at Charterer's disposal under the Charter or the nearest port to which such list applies.

CARGO

7. The Charterer shall have the option of shipping any lawful dry cargo in bulk for which the Vessel and her tanks are suitable and any lawful merchandise in cases and/or cans and/or other packages in the Vessel's forehold, 'tween decks, and/or other suitable space available, subject, however, to the Master's approval as to kind and character, amount and stowage. All charges for dunnage, loading, stowing, and discharging so incurred shall be paid by the Charterer.

SPEED, FUEL AND PUMPING WARRANTIES

8. The Owner warrants that the Vessel is capable of maintaining and shall maintain throughout the period of this Charter Party on all sea passages from Seabuoy to Seabuoy a guaranteed average speed under all weather conditions of .... knots in a laden condition and ....knots in ballast (speed will be determined by taking the total miles at sea divided by the total hours at sea as shown in the log books excluding stops at sea and any sea passage covered by an off-hire calculation) on a guaranteed daily consumption of .... tons (of 2,240 lbs.) of Diesel/Bunker C/High Viscosity Fuel Oil maximum .... seconds Redwood No.1 at 100 degrees F. for main engine, and .... tons (of 2,240 lbs.) of Diesel for auxiliaries for propulsion.

For each day that heat is applied to cargo the guaranteed daily consumption is ....bbls. of Diesel/Bunker C/High Viscosity Fuel Oil maximum .... seconds Redwood No. 1 at 100 degrees F. per tank day. For each hour that tank cleaning is required, the guaranteed consumption is ....bbls. of Diesel/Bunker C/High Viscosity Fuel Oil maximum ....seconds Redwood No. 1 at 100 degrees F. per machine hour.

The Charterer is entitled to the full capabilities of the Vessel and the Owner warrants that the Vessel is capable of discharging a cargo of petroleum at the following minimum rates:
Light petroleum (viscosity less than 320 SSU at 100°F.) ....bbls/hr
Medium petroleum (viscosity of 320 to 3200 SSU at 100°F.) ....bbls/hr
Heavy petroleum (viscosity above 3200 SSU at 100°F.) ....bbls/hr
or of maintaining a pressure of 100 PSI at ship's rail should the foregoing minimum rates not be met.

Charterer is to be compensated at $ .... per hour or pro rata for each part of an hour that Vessel takes in excess of the pumping rates as stipulated above. The owner understands and agrees that he will receive no credit or compensation if the Vessel is able to discharge at a rate greater that those specified above. Any delay to Vessel's discharge caused by shore conditions shall be taken into account in the assessment of pumping performance. Pumping performance shall be reviewed in accordance with Clause 9.

ADJUSTMENT OF HIRE

9. (a) The speed and consumption guaranteed by the Owner in Clause 8 will be reviewed by the Charterer after three calendar months counting from the time of delivery of the Vessel to the Charterer in accordance with this Charter Party and thereafter at the end of each three (3) calendar month period. If at the end of each twelve (12) calendar month period (or at any time during the term of this charter) it is found that the Vessel has failed to maintain as an average during the proceeding twelve (12) calendar month period (or for any other twelve month period during the term of this Charter) the speed and/or consumption warranted, the Charterer shall be retroactively compensated in respect of such failings as follows:

(b) Speed—Payment to Charterer of $...................................... per hour or pro rata for each part of an hour that Vessel steams in excess of the equivalent time Vessel would have taken at the guaranteed speed warranted in Clause 8 as calculated in accordance with Attachment 1—"Performance Calculations".

(c) Consumption—the Owner to reimburse the Charterer for each ton of 2,240 lbs. or pro rata for part of a ton in excess of the guaranteed daily consumption for main engine and/or auxilliaries and/or heating and/or tank cleaning including any excess not borne by the Owner in accordance with the off hire clause of this Charter Party at the average price for the particular grade of oil as set forth in the then current Exxon International Contract Price List at...................for the total period under review provided that Vessel's actual speed is in accordance with Clause 8. To the extent the Vessel's speed is less than that warranted, fuel consumption allowed will be determined in accordance with Attachment 1—"Performance Calculations".

(d) The basis for determining the Vessel's performance (a) and (b) above shall be the statistical data supplied by the Master in accordance with Clause 14. (b).

(e) Owner to have similar privileges under this Clause for receiving compensation as Charterers do should Vessel performance as concerns speed be in excess or consumption for propulsion be below the descriptions outlined herein.

(f) The Charterer shall provide Owner with an opportunity to review any claim submitted by Charterer under this Clause, and the Owner shall complete such review, and provide Charterer with the results thereof within 30 days from the date such claim was mailed by Charterer to Owner.

Charterer may deduct from hire any amount to which it is entitled under this Clause after the expiration of 40 days from the date of Charterer's mailing of a claim relating thereto to Owner.

In the event of Charterer having a claim in respect of Vessel's performance during the final year or part of the Charter period and any extension thereof, the amount of such claim shall be withheld from hire in accordance with Charterer's estimate made about two months before the end of the Charter period and any necessary adjustment after the end of the Charter shall be made by the Owner to the Charterer or the Charterer to the Owner as the case may require.

LIENS

10. The Owner shall have a lien on all cargoes for all amounts due under this Charter, and the Charterer shall have a lien on the Vessel for all moneys paid in advance and not earned, all disbursements and advances for the Owner's account, for the value of any of Charterer's fuel used or accepted for Owner's account, for all amounts due to Charterer under Clause 9, and other provisions of this Charter and for any damages sustained by the Charterer as a result of breach of this Charter by the Owner.

OFF HIRE

11. (a) In the event of loss of time from breakdown of machinery, interference by authorities, collision, stranding, fire, or other accident or damage to the Vessel, not caused by the fault of the Charterer, preventing the working of the Vessel for more than twelve consecutive hours, or in the event of loss of time from deficiency of men or stores, breach of orders or neglect of duty by the Master, Officers, or Crew, or from deviation for the purpose of landing any injured or ill person on board other than any person who may be carried at Charterer's request, payment of hire shall cease for all time lost until the Vessel is again in an efficient state to resume her service and has regained a point of progress equivalent to that when the hire ceased hereunder; cost of fuel consumed while the Vessel is off hire hereunder, as well as all port charges, pilotages, and other expenses incurred during such period and consequent upon the putting in to any port or place other than to which the Vessel is bound, shall be borne by the Owner; but should the Vessel be driven into port or to anchorage by stress of weather or on account of accident to her cargo, such loss of time, shall be for Charterer's account. If upon the voyage the speed of the Vessel be reduced or her fuel consumption increased by breakdown, casualty, or inefficiency of Master, Officers, or Crew, so as to cause a delay of more than twenty-four hours in arriving at the Vessel's next port or an excess consumption of more than one day's fuel, hire for the time lost and cost of extra fuel consumed, if any, shall be borne by the Owner. Any delay by ice or time spent in quarantine shall be for Charterer's account, except delay in quarantine resulting from the Master, Officers, or Crew having communications with the shore at an infected port, where the Charterer has given the Master adequate written notice of infection, which shall be for Owner's account, as shall also be any loss of time through detention by authorities as a result of charges of smuggling or of other infraction of law by the Master, Officers, or Crew.

(b) If the periods of time lost for which hire does not cease to be payable under the foregoing provisions of this Clause because each such period or delay is not of more than twelve (12) hours duration exceed in the aggregate one hundred and forty-four (144) hours in any charter party year (and pro rata for part of a year), hire shall not be payable for the excess and any hire overpaid by the Charterer shall be repaid by the Owner.

(c) In the event of loss of time by detention of the Vessel by authorities at any place in consequence of legal proceeding against the Vessel or the Owner, payment of charter hire shall cease for all time so lost. Cost of fuel and water consumed as well as all additional port charges, pilotages, and other expenses incurred during the time so lost shall be borne by the Owner. If any such loss of time shall exceed thirty consecutive days, the Charterer shall have the option to cancel this Charter by written notice given to the Owner while the vessel remains so detained without prejudice to any other right Charterer may have in the premises.

DRYDOCKING

12. (a) Owner, at its expense, shall drydock, clean, and paint Vessel's bottom and make all overhaul and other necessary repairs at reasonable intervals not to exceed twenty-four (24) months for which purpose Charterer shall allow Vessel to proceed to an appropriate port. Owner shall be solely responsible therefor, and also for gasfreeing the Vessel, upon each occasion. All towing, pilotage, fuel, water and other expenses incurred while proceeding to and from and while in drydock, shall also be for Owner's account. Fuel used during such drydocking or repair as provided in this Clause or Clause 15 or in proceeding to or from the port of drydocking or repair, will be charged to Owner by Charterer at the price charged to Charterer by its bunker supplier at such port if bunkers are obtained there or at the next replenishment port.

(b) In case of drydocking pursuant to this Clause at a port where Vessel is to load, discharge or bunker, under Charterer's orders, hire shall be suspended from the time the Vessel received free pratique on arrival, if in ballast, or upon completion of discharge of cargo, if loaded, until Vessel is again ready for service. In case of drydocking at a port other than where Vessel loads, discharges, or bunkers, under Charterer's orders, the following time and bunkers shall be deducted from hire: total time and bunkers including repair port call for the actual voyage from last port of call under Charterer's orders to next port of call under Charterer's orders, less theoretical voyage time and bunkers for the direct voyage from said last port of call to said next port of call. Theoretical voyage will be calculated on the basis of the seabuoy to seabuoy distance at the warranted speed and consumption per Clause 8.

OWNER PROVIDES

13. The Owner shall provide and pay for all provisions, deck and engine room stores, galley and cabin stores, galley and crew fuel, insurance on the Vessel, wages of the Master, Officers, and Crew, all certificates and other requirements necessary to enable the Vessel to be employed throughout the trading limits herein provided, consular fees pertaining to the Master, Officers, and Crew, all fresh water used by the Vessel and all other expenses connected with the operation, maintenance, and navigation of the Vessel.

MASTER'S DUTIES

14. (a) The Master, although appointed by and in the employ of the Owner and subject to Owner's direction and control, shall observe the orders of Charterer in connection with Charterer's agencies, arrangements, and employment of the Vessel's services hereunder. Nothing in this Clause or elsewhere in this Charter shall be construed as creating a demise of the Vessel to Charterer nor as vesting Charterer with any control over the physical operation or navigation of the Vessel.

(b) The Master and the Engineers shall keep full and correct logs of the voyages, which are to be patent to the Charterer and its agents, and abstracts of which are to be mailed directly to the Charterer from each port of call.

(c) If the Charterer shall have reason to be dissatisfied with the conduct of the Master or Officers, the Owner shall, on receiving particulars of the complaint, investigate it and if necessary, make a change in the appointments.

FUEL, PORT CHARGES, ETC.

15. (a) The Charterer (except during any period when the Vessel is off hire) shall provide and pay for all fuel except for galley and Crew as provided in Clause 13. The Charterer shall also pay for all port charges, light dues, dock dues, Panama and other Canal dues, pilotage, consular fees, (except those pertaining to Master, Officers, and Crew), tugs necessary for assisting the Vessel in, about, and out of port for the purpose of carrying out this Charter, Charterer's agencies and commissions incurred for Charterer's account and crew expense incurred for connecting and disconnecting cargo hoses and arms. The Owner shall, however, reimburse the Charterer for any fuel used or any expenses incurred in making a general sacrifice or expenditure, and for any fuel consumed during drydocking or repair of the Vessel.

TUGS AND PILOTS

(b) In engaging pilotage and tug assistance, Charterer is authorized by Owner to engage them on behalf of Owner on the usual terms and conditions for such services then prevailing at the ports or places where such services are engaged, including provisions there prevailing, if any, making pilots, tug captains, or other personnel of any tug the borrowed servants of the Owner.

(c) Neither the Charterer nor its agents nor any of its associated or affiliated companies, nor any of their agents or employees, shall be under any responsibility for any loss, damage, or liability arising from any negligence, incompetence, or incapacity of any pilot, tug captain, or other personnel of any tug, or arising from the terms of the contract of employment thereof or for any unseaworthiness or insufficiency of any tug or tugs, the services of which are arranged by Charterer on behalf of Owner, and Owner agrees to indemnify and hold Charterer, its agents, associated and affiliated companies and their employees harmless from and against any and all such consequences.

(d) Charterer shall have the option of using its own tugs or pilots, or tugs or pilots made available or employed by any associated or affiliated companies, to render towage or pilotage services to the Vessel. In this event, the terms and conditions relating to such services prevailing in the port where such services are rendered and applied by independent tugboat owners or pilots, shall be applicable, and Charterer, its associated or affiliated companies and their pilots shall be entitled to all exemptions from and limitations of liability, applicable to said independent tugboat owners or pilots and their published tariff terms and conditions.

ADDITIONAL EQUIPMENT

16. The Charterer, subject to the Owner's approval not to be unreasonably withheld, shall be at liberty to fit any additional pumps and/or gear for loading or discharging cargo it may require beyond that which is on board at the commencement of the Charter, and to make the necessary connections with steam or water pipes, such work to be done at its expense and time, and such pumps and/or gear so fitted to be considered its property, and the Charterer shall be at liberty to remove it at its expense and time during or at the expiry of this Charter; the Vessel to be left in her original condition to the Owner's satisfaction.

LAY-UP

17. The Charterer shall have the option of laying up the Vessel for all or any portion of the term of this Charter, in which case hire hereunder shall continue to be paid, but there shall be credited against such hire the whole amount which the Owner shall save (or reasonably should save) during

such period of layup through reduction in expenses, less any extra expenses to which the Owner is put as a result of such layup.

Should the Charterer, having exercised the option granted hereunder, desire the Vessel again to be put into service, the Owner will, upon receipt of written notice from the Charterer to such effect, immediately take steps to restore the Vessel to service as promptly as possible. The option granted to the Charterer hereunder may be exercised one or more times during the currency of this Charter or any extension thereof.

18. (a) In the event that title to the Vessel shall be requisitioned or seized by any government authority (or the Vessel shall be seized by any person or government under circumstances which are equivalent to requisition of title), this Charter shall terminate automatically as of the effective date of such requisition or seizure.

REQUISITION

(b) In the event that the Vessel should be requisitioned for use or seized by any government authority on any basis not involving, or not equivalent to, requisition of title, she shall be off hire hereunder during the period of such requisition, and any hire or any other compensation paid in respect of such requisition shall be for Owner's account, provided, however, that if such requisition continues for a period in excess of 90 days, the Charterer shall have the option to terminate this Charter upon written notice to the Owner. Any periods of off-hire under this Clause shall be subject to the Charterer's option for off-hire extension set forth in Clause 1 (b) hereof.

REDELIVERY

19. (a) Unless the employment of the Vessel under this Charter shall previously have been terminated by loss of the Vessel or otherwise, the Charterer shall release the Vessel to the Owner's use, free of cargo, at the expiration of the term of this Charter stated in Clause 1 (including any extension thereof provided in said Clause or elsewhere in this Charter), at ....
....(herein called "Port of Redelivery") and shall give written notice of the date and hour of such release. At the Charterer's option, the vessel may be released to the Owner with tanks in a clean or dirty condition.

(b) The Owner shall accept and pay for all fuel in the Vessel's bunkers when this Charter terminates. Payment for such fuel shall be made in accordance with the Exxon International Company Contract Price List current for the date when and the port or place where the Vessel is redelivered by Charterer to Owners under this Charter, or the nearest port to which such list applies.

BILLS OF LADING

20. (a) Bills of Lading shall be signed by the Master as presented, the master attending daily, if required, at the offices of the Charterer or its Agents. However, at Charterer's option, the Charterer or its Agents may sign Bills of Lading on behalf of the Master. All Bills of Lading shall be without prejudice to this Charter and the Charterer shall indemnify the Owner against all consequences or liabilities which may arise from any inconsistency between this Charter and any bills of lading or other documents signed by the Charterer or its Agents or by the Master at their request or which may arise from an irregularity in papers supplied by the Charterer or its Agents.

(b) The carriage of cargo under this Charter Party and under all Bills of Lading issued for the cargo shall be subject to the statutory provisions and other terms set forth or specified in subparagraphs (i) to (vi) of this Clause and such terms shall be incorporated verbatim or be deemed incorporated by the reference in any such Bill of Lading. In such subparagraphs and in any Act referred to therein, the word "carrier" shall include the Owner and the Chartered Owner of the Vessel.

(i) *Clause Paramount.* This bill of lading shall have effect subject to the provisions of the Carriage of Goods by Sea Act of the United States, approved April 16, 1936, except that if this Bill of Lading is issued at a place where any other Act, ordinance, or legislation gives statutory effect to the International Convention for the Unification of Certain Rules relating to Bills of Lading at Brussels, August 1924, then this Bill of Lading shall have effect subject to the provisions of such Act, ordinance, or legislation. The applicable Act, ordinance, or legislation (hereinafter called "Act") shall be deemed to be incorporated herein and nothing herein contained shall be deemed a surrender by the Owner or Carrier of any of its rights or immunities or an increase of any of its responsibilities or liabilities under the Act. If any term of this Bill of Lading be repugnant to the Act to any extent, such term shall be void to that extent but no further.

(ii) *New Jason Clause.* In the event of accident, danger, damage, or disaster before or after the commencement of the voyage, resulting from any cause whatsoever, whether due to negligence or not, for which, or for the consequences of which, the Carrier is not responsible, by statute, contract or otherwise, the cargo shippers, consignees, or owners of the cargo shall contribute with the Carrier in General Average to the payment of any sacrifices, losses, or expenses of a General Average nature that may be made or incurred and shall pay salvage and special charges incurred in respect of the cargo. If a salving ship is owned or operated by the Carrier, salvage shall be paid for as fully as if the said salving ship or ships belonged to strangers. Such deposit as the Carrier or its Agents may deem sufficient to cover the estimated contribution of the cargo and any salvage and special charges thereon shall, if required, be made by the cargo, shippers, consignees or owners of the cargo to the Carrier before delivery.

(iii) *General Average.* General Average shall be adjusted, stated, and settled according to

York/Antwerp Rules 1950, as amended, and, as to matters not provided for by those rules, according to the laws and usages at the Port of New York. If a General Average statement is required, it shall be prepared at such port by an Adjuster from the Port of New York appointed by the Carrier and approved by the Charterer of the Vessel. Such Adjuster shall attend to the settlement and the collection of the General Average, subject to customary charges. General Average Agreements and/or security shall be furnished by Carrier and/or Charterer of the Vessel, and/or Carrier and/or Consignee of cargo, if requested. Any cash deposit being made as security to pay General Average and/or salvage shall be remitted to the Average Adjuster and shall be held by him at his risk in a special account in a duly authorized and licensed bank at the place where the General Average statement is prepared.

(iv) *Both to Blame*. If the Vessel comes into collision with another ship as a result of the negligence of the other ship and any act, neglect or default of the Master, mariner, pilot, or the servants of the Carrier in the navigation or in the management of the Vessel, the owners of the cargo carried hereunder shall indemnify the Carrier against all loss or liability to the other or noncarrying ship or her owners in so far as such loss or liability represents loss of, or damage to, or any claim whatsoever of the owners of said cargo, paid or payable by the other or recovered by the other or noncarrying ship or her owners as part of their claim against the carrying ship or Carrier. The foregoing provisions shall also apply where the owners, operators, or those in charge of any ships or objects other than, or in addition to, the colliding ships or object are at fault in respect of a collision or contract.

(v) *Limitation of Liability*. Any provision of this Charter to the contrary notwithstanding, the Carrier shall have the benefit of all limitations of, and exemptions from, liability accorded to the Owner or Chartered Owner of vessels by any statute or rule of law for the time being.

(vi) *Deviation Clause*. The Vessel shall have liberty to sail with or without pilots, to tow or be towed, to go to the assistance of vessels in distress, to deviate for the purpose of saving life or property or of landing any ill or injured person on board, and to call for fuel at any port or ports in or out of the regular course of the voyage.

21. *War Risks*. (a) No contraband of war shall be shipped, but petroleum and/or its products shall not be deemed contraband of war for the purposes of this Clause. Vessel shall not, however, be required, without the consent of Owner, which shall not be unreasonably withheld, to enter any port or zone which is involved in a state of war, warlike operations, or hostilities, civil strife, insurrection or piracy whether there be a declaration of war or not, where it might reasonably be expected to be subject to capture, seizure or arrest, or to a hostile act by a belligerent power (the term "power" meaning any de jure or de facto authority or any other purported governmental organization maintaining naval, military, or air forces).

(b) For the purposes of this Clause it shall be unreasonable for Owner to withhold consent to any voyage, route, or port of loading or discharge if insurance against all risks defined in Article 21 (a) is then available commercially or under a Government program in respect of such voyage, route or port of loading or discharge. If such consent is given by Owner, Charterer will pay the provable additional cost of insuring Vessel against Hull war risks in an amount equal to the value under her ordinary hull policy but not exceeding.................... In addition, Owner may purchase war risk insurance on ancillary risks such as loss of hire, freight disbursements, total loss, etc., if he carries such insurance for ordinary marine hazards. If such insurance is not obtainable commercially or through a Government program, Vessel shall not be required to enter or remain at any such port or zone.

(c) In the event of the existence of the conditions described in Article 21 (a) subsequent to the date of this Charter, or while vessel is on hire under this Charter, Charterer shall, in respect of voyages to any such port or zone assume the provable additional cost of wages and insurance properly incurred in connection with Master, Officers and Crew as a consequence of such war, warlike operations or hostilities.

EXCEPTIONS

22. (a) The Vessel, her Master and Owner shall not, unless otherwise in this Charter expressly provided, be responsible for any loss or damage to cargo arising or resulting from: any act, neglect, default or barratry of the Master, Pilots, mariners or other servants of the Owner in the navigation or management of the Vessel; fire, unless caused by the personal design or neglect of the Owner; collision, stranding, or peril, danger or accident of the sea or other navigable waters; or from explosion, bursting of boilers, breakage of shafts, or any latent defect in hull, equipment or machinery. And neither the Vessel, her Master or Owner, nor the Charterer, shall, unless otherwise in this Charter expressly provided, be responsible for any loss or damage or delay or failure in performing hereunder arising or resulting from: act of God; act of war; perils of the seas; act of public enemies, pirates or assailing thieves; arrest or restraint of princes, rulers or people, or seizure under legal process provided bond is promptly furnished to release the Vessel or cargo; strike or lockout or stoppage or restraint of labor from whatever cause, either partial or general; or riot or civil commotion.

NUMBER OF GRADES

(b) The Owner warrants the Vessel is constructed and equipped to carry .... grades of oil. If for any reason the Vessel, upon arrival at a loading port, is unable to load the required number of grades, the Charterer will do its utmost to provide a suitable cargo consistent with Vessel's capabilities. However, if this is not possible the Vessel is to proceed to the nearest repair port in ballast and will there repair all bulkhead leaks necessary, any time and expense being for Owner's account.

(c) The exceptions stated in subparagraph (a) of this Clause shall not affect the Owner's undertakings with respect to the condition, particulars and capabilities of the Vessel, or the provisions for payment and cessation of hire or the obligations of the Owner under Clause 20 in respect of the loading, handling, stowage, carriage, custody, care and discharge of cargo.

23. All salvage moneys carried by the Vessel shall be divided equally between the Owner and the Charterer after deducting Master's, Officers' and Crew's share, legal expenses, hire of Vessel during time lost, value of fuel consumed, repairs of damage, if any, and any other extraordinary loss or expense sustained as a result of the service, which shall always be a first charge on such money.

24. Owner warrants that the Vessel is entered in TOVALOP and will remain so entered during the currency of this Charter, provided, however, that if Owner acquires the right to withdraw from TOVALOP under Clause VIII thereof, nothing herein shall prevent it from exercising that right.

OIL POLLUTION

Where an escape or discharge of oil occurs from the Vessel and threatens to cause pollution damage to coastlines, Charterer may, at its option, and upon notice to Owner or Master, undertake such measures as are reasonably necessary to prevent or mitigate such damage, unless Owner promptly undertakes same. Charterer shall keep Owner advised of the nature of the measures intended to be taken by it. Any of the aforementioned measures actually taken by Charterer shall be at Owner's expense (except to the extent that such escape or discharge was caused or contributed to by Charterer), provided that if Owner considers said measure should be discontinued, Owner may so notify Charterer and thereafter Charterer shall have no right to continue said measures under the provisions of this Clause and all further liability to Charterer thereunder shall thereupon cease.

If any dispute shall arise between Owner and Charterer as to the reasonableness of the measures undertaken and/or the expenditure incurred by Charterer hereunder, such dispute shall be referred to arbitration as herein provided.

The provisions of this Clause are not in derogation of such other rights as Charterer or Owner may have under this Charter, or may otherwise have or acquire by law or any International Convention.

CLEAN SEAS

25. The Owner agrees to participate in the Charterer's program covering oil pollution avoidance. Such program aims to prevent the discharge into the sea anywhere in the world of all oil, oil water or ballast, chemicals or oily waste material in any form if the said material is of a persistent nature, except under extreme circumstances whereby the safety of the Vessel, cargo or life would be imperiled.

The Owner agrees to adhere to the oil pollution avoidance instructions provided by the Charterer in the Charterer's Vessel Instruction Manual together with any amendments which may be issued in writing or by radio to cover special cases or changes in International and National Regulations or Laws. The Master will contain on board the Vessel all oily residues from consolidated tank washings, dirty ballast, etc. Such residues shall be contained in one compartment after the separation of all possible water has taken place by safe methods employing the use of settlement and decanting or mechanic separation to approved and recognized standards.

The oily residue will be pumped ashore at the loading or discharge terminal either as segregated oil, dirty ballast, commingling with cargo or as is possible for Charterer to arrange with each cargo.

If the Charterer requires that demulsifiers be used for the separation of oil and water, the cost of such demulsifiers will be at the Charterer's expense.

Owner will also arrange for the Vessel to adhere to Charterer's oil pollution program during off-hire periods within the term of this Charter including the preparing of cargo tanks for drydocking and repairs. In the latter case, the Charterer agrees to bear costs for the disposal of oil residues.

Vessel will take all necessary precautions while loading and discharging cargo or bunkers as well as ballast to ensure that no oil will escape overboard.

Nothing in the Charterer's instructions shall be construed as permission to pollute the sea by the discharge of oil or oily water etc. The Owner agrees to instruct the Master to furnish Charterer with a report covering oil pollution avoidance together with details of the quantity of oil residue on board on arrival at the loading port.

PRODUCTS

26. Owner hereby agrees to receive sales representatives of affiliates of Charterer which market marine products. However, Owner is under no obligation to purchase from said affiliates, and said affiliates are under no obligation to sell to Owner any of such products. Owner designates the following as the appropriate persons or organizations with whom said affiliates should deal:

Name ....

Address ....

CHANGE OF OWNERSHIP

27. Owner's rights and obligations under this Charter are not transferable by Sale or Assignment without Charterer's consent. In the event of the Vessel being sold without its consent in addition to its other rights, Charterer may, at its absolute discretion, terminate the Charter, whereupon the Owner shall reimburse Charterer for any hire paid in advance and not earned, the cost of bunkers, for any sums to which Charterer is entitled under the Charter, and for any damages which Charterer may sustain.

ARBITRATION

28. Any and all differences and disputes of whatsoever nature arising out of this Charter shall be put to arbitration in the City of New York pursuant to the laws relating to arbitration there in force, before a board of three persons, consisting of one arbitrator to be appointed by the Owner, one by the Charterer, and one by the two so chosen. The decision of any two of the three on any point or points shall be final. Until such time as the arbitrators finally close the hearings either party shall have the right by written notice served on the arbitrators and on an officer of the other party to specify further disputes or differences under this Charter for hearing and determination. The arbitrators may grant any relief which they, or a majority of them, deem just and equitable and within the scope of the agreement of the parties, including, but not limited to, specific performance. Awards pursuant to this Clause may include costs, including a reasonable allowance for attorney's fees, and judgments may be entered upon any award made hereunder in any Court having jurisdiction in the premises.

ASSIGNMENT

29. (a) Charterer, upon notice to Owner, may assign this Charter Party to any of its affiliates.

SUBLET

(b) Charterer shall also have the right to sublet the Vessel, but in the event of a sublet, Charterer shall always remain responsible for the fulfillment of this Charter in all its terms and conditions.

LAWS

30. The interpretation of the Charter and of the rights and obligations of the parties shall be governed by the laws applicable to Charter Parties made in the City of New York. The headings of Clauses are for convenience of reference only and shall not affect the interpretation of this Charter. No modification, waiver or discharge of any term of this Charter shall be valid unless in writing and signed by the party to be charged therewith.

IN WITNESS, WHEREOF, THE PARTIES HAVE CAUSED THIS CHARTER TO BE EXECUTED IN DUPLICATE THE DAY AND YEAR HEREIN FIRST ABOVE WRITTEN.

....

WITNESS TO SIGNATURE OF

....

WITNESS TO SIGNATURE OF

Formation of the Contract

THE NEW YORK PRODUCE EXCHANGE TIME CHARTER (1946)

"1. This Charter Party, made and concluded in .... day of .... 19 ...."

No need for special form

No special form is needed for a charter contract. The ordinary rules of the law of contract determine whether the parties have or have not made a binding charter. Accordingly a charter may be binding although it is not signed by the parties and though the agreement has not been drawn up on a printed form. Even an oral agreement to charter a ship, if proved, is binding: see observations of Wigram, V.C., in *Lidgett* v. *Williams* (1845) 14 L.J. Ch. 459. If the owners and charterers (or brokers on their behalf) have agreed all the essential terms of the charter in correspondence or by telex (or cable) and if there is nothing in the exchanges to indicate an intention not to be bound until a charter is formally drawn up and signed, the court will regard the agreement as concluded. There will then be, in chartering language, a fixture.

Necessity for clear agreement upon all essential terms

The fundamental rule is that there can be no contract until the parties have reached clear agreement on all essential terms. Lord Blackburn, in *Rossiter* v. *Miller* (1878) 3 App. Cas. 1124, said, at page 1151: "If some particulars essential to the agreement still remain to be settled afterwards, there is no contract." Obviously, if the parties have failed or omitted to agree on an important term, for example the rate of hire to be paid, there can be no contract. More difficult are cases in which the parties have agreed on an important term but in such vague or ambiguous words that upon examination it is hard to attribute a certain meaning to their agreement.

The courts will generally strive in such cases to discover a certain meaning in the words the parties have used, for example by reference to previous dealings between the parties or to the usual meaning given to the relevant words in the particular trade, so as to preserve an apparent contract, particularly where the parties themselves believed they had reached full agreement. In the words of Viscount Maugham in *Scammell* v. *Ouston* [1941] A.C. 251, at page 255: "In commercial documents connected with dealings in a trade with which the parties are perfectly familiar the court is very willing, if satisfied that the parties thought that they made a binding contract, to imply terms and in particular terms as to the method of carrying out the contract which it would be impossible to supply in other kinds of contract: see *Hillas & Co.* v. *Arcos Ltd.*" The facts of the case referred to by Viscount Maugham were as follows:

Timber merchants entered into an agreement to buy "22,000 standards of softwood goods of fair specification" of Russian origin during 1930. The agreement gave them an option to purchase in 1931 "100,000 standards" at a stated discount from the sellers' official price list for that year, but gave no details as to the kind, size or quality of those standards nor as to the manner of shipment. No problems arose with regard to the purchases in 1930, but the sellers sought to avoid liability under the option for 1931 on the ground that it was too uncertain in its terms to constitute a binding agreement. The House of Lords held the option for 1931 enforceable: the gaps in its terms could be filled by reference to the terms of the agreement for 1930, and where those terms were themselves vague (as in describing the softwood goods merely as "of fair specification") their meaning could be ascertained by implying what was just and reasonable.

Hillas v. *Arcos* (1932) 43 Ll.L.Rep. 359.

(See also *Shamrock* v. *Storey* (1899) 81 L.T. 413.)

Where, however, the courts cannot establish such certain meaning for an important term they will declare that no contract exists at all.

An agreement to purchase a van stated that "this order is given on the understanding that the balance of purchase price can be had on hire-purchase terms over a period of two years". It was held by the House of Lords that there was no contract. As there were many different types of hire-purchase terms this stipulation was so uncertain in meaning that agreement was lacking on what was clearly a material point. Viscount Maugham said: "In order to constitute a valid contract the parties must so express themselves that their meaning can be determined with a reasonable degree of certainty. It is plain that unless this can be done it would be impossible to hold that the contracting parties had the same intention; in other words the consensus *ad idem* would be a matter of mere conjecture." Lord Wright said: "It is a necessary requirement that an agreement in order to be binding must be sufficiently definite to enable the court to give it a practical meaning. Its terms must be so definite, or capable of being made definite without further agreement of the parties, that the promises and performances to be rendered by each party are reasonably certain."

Scammell v. *Ouston* [1941] A.C. 251.

On the other hand, meaningless words or phrases may be ignored if they add nothing to an otherwise complete contract (see *Nicolene* v. *Simmonds* [1953] 1 Q.B. 543), and a self-contradictory clause will not destroy a contract from which it can be severed without affecting the important rights and duties of the parties.

The arbitration clause in a contract for the sale of timber provided for "Any dispute" to be referred to arbitration in London and for "Any other dispute" to be arbitrated in Moscow.

The Court of Appeal held that the whole clause was meaningless and that it should be disregarded altogether. The clause being severable from the rest of the contract, the dispute between the parties as to non-delivery and defective quality would be dealt with by the courts.

Lovelock v. *Exportles* [1968] 1 Lloyd's Rep. 163.

As a general rule an agreement that provides for the parties to negotiate subsequently upon an essential term is not an enforceable contract; *Courtney & Fairbairn* v. *Tolaini Bros.* [1975] 1 W.L.R. 297, and *Mallozzi* v. *Carapelli* [1976] 1 Lloyd's Rep. 407. But this does not necessarily invalidate an agreement that leaves the determination to a person or persons to be nominated by the parties, so long as the determination is to be in accordance with an objective standard expressed or implied. In *Sudbrook Trading Estate* v. *Eggleton* [1983] 1 A.C. 444, the House of Lords upheld a clause in a lease giving the lessee an option to purchase the freehold reversion at a price to be "agreed upon by two valuers one to be nominated by the lessor and the other by the lessee and in default of such agreement by an umpire appointed by the . . . valuers". When the lessee sought to exercise this option the lessor refused to nominate a valuer, thus preventing agreement on the price. The House of Lords held that by referring in their contract to valuers the parties had imported an objective standard, namely that the price should be fair and reasonable (by contrast to the subjective decision of an individual named in the contract); thus they had agreed to a sale at a fair and reasonable price and the machinery laid down for arriving at the exact price was not itself an essential part of the contract but was subsidiary to its main purpose; consequently it was permissible for the court to step in when that machinery broke down and to make the assessment of the price in accordance with the objective standard laid down by the contract. The Court of Appeal applied this decision to a contract which, while laying down an objective standard, left the assessment to the parties themselves. In *Didymi Corporation* v. *Atlantic Lines and Navigation* (*The Didymi*) [1988] 2 Lloyd's Rep. 108 an additional clause in the New York Produce form charter provided that if the ship achieved a better average performance than the stipulated speed and consumption the owners were to be indemnified by an increase in hire calculated "equitably . . . by an amount to be mutually agreed between owners and charterers". The Court of Appeal upheld the judgment of Hobhouse, J., [1987] 2 Lloyd's Rep. 166, that the indemnity agreement was enforceable. The essential agreement was that in the circumstances the owners should be indemnified and the procedure for calculating the exact amount merely a matter of machinery. But the stipulation for an objective standard, by use of the word "equitably", was a necessary element in the court's decision. Nourse, L.J., said: "Accordingly, the parties having agreed upon an objective standard, it seems to me that the identity of those to whom the agreement is referred, albeit that they are the parties themselves, is of no real importance . . . I desire to emphasise that my view of this case depends wholly on the parties having prescribed a standard by reference to which their agreement . . . was to be made. I do not intend to suggest that an agreement for sale, lease, charter or whatever at a price, rent, hire or other sum 'to be agreed' between the parties to the agreement could be one to which the law would give effect. It is to this category of case that *Mallozzi* v. *Carapelli S.p.A.* . . . must be assigned."

The Court of Appeal had also been prepared to uphold a contract that left an important matter to be agreed subsequently by the parties, but provided, by an arbitration clause, a mechanism for resolving any failure to do so; *Sykes* v. *Fine Fare* [1967] 1 Lloyd's Rep. 53. In that case Lord Denning, M.R., said: "I am quite satisfied that this phrase '[after the first year] such other figures as may be agreed between the parties hereto', does not introduce such uncertainty into the contract as to render it no contract. Effect can be given to this agreement by saying that in default of agreement, the number . . . shall be such reasonable number as may be ascertained by an arbitrator under the arbitration clause."

Although the Court of Appeal in *Didymi Corporation* v. *Atlantic Lines and Navigation*, above, cited *Sykes* v. *Fine Fare* with approval and said that, if necessary, it could have afforded another ground for their decision, the merits were unusually strong as the disputed contract had already been performed in part at considerable expense to the parties; it should be treated with some caution, but it illustrates that the courts are likely to be more ready to give effect to provisions of this type if the contract has been partly performed.

Fixture before formal charter signed

Where the parties intend that their eventual agreement shall be set out in a formal charter the question may arise whether this formal charter is merely to record the terms of a contract already agreed or whether there is to be no binding contract at all until it is drawn up and approved (or signed). This is a matter which must be resolved by construing the communications that are claimed by one party to have created the contract. Parker, J., said in *Von Hatzfeldt-Wildenburg* v. *Alexander* [1912] 1 Ch. 284, at page 288: "It appears to be well settled by the authorities that if the documents or letters relied on as constituting a contract contemplate the execution of a further contract between the parties, it is a question of construction whether the execution of the further contract is a condition or term of the bargain or whether it is a mere expression of the desire of the parties as to the manner in which the transaction already agreed to will in fact go through. In the former case there is no enforceable contract either because the condition is unfulfilled or because the law does not recognize a contract to enter into a contract. In the latter case there is a binding contract and the reference to the more formal document may be ignored." For recent decisions on this point see *Okura* v. *Navara* [1981] 1 Lloyd's Rep. 561, [1982] 2 Lloyd's Rep. 537 (C.A.), and *The Blankenstein* [1983] 2 Lloyd's Rep. 522, [1985] 1 Lloyd's Rep. 93 (C.A.).

It is normal for a binding agreement to have been made before the formal charter is drawn up and signed, but sometimes important terms are not finally agreed upon until after the charter has been drawn up or reservations are made that one party will not regard himself as bound until the charter is signed. The following case is an example:

Negotiations for a long term time charter of the *Polarsol* were terminated by a direction of the Portuguese Government prohibiting the charterers from fixing any new charters. The owners contended that a binding agreement had already been reached. While it was acknowledged by McNair, J., that charters were fixed daily on an informal basis he held that in this particular case the parties had made it clear in their written exchanges that they did not intend to be bound until the charter was signed. It was further held that one material term relating to a bank guarantee had not been agreed at the date the direction of the Government was notified. It was accordingly held by McNair, J., and by the Court of Appeal, affirming his decision, that there was no binding contract.

Sociedade Portuguesa de Navios Tanques v. *Polaris* [1952] 1 Lloyd's Rep. 71 and 407 (C.A.). (See also *Zarati Steamship* v. *Frames Tours* [1955] 2 Lloyd's Rep. 278.)

"Subject to contract"

In non-charter cases references in negotiations to "subject to contract" or similar words have repeatedly been held to show an intention not to be bound until a formal contract is subsequently entered into. They can be expected to have the same effect in negotiations for a charter contract: see the remarks of Somervell, L.J., in *Sociedade Portuguesa de Navios Tanques* v. *Polaris*, above, at page 417.

But in *Howard Marine* v. *Ogden* [1978] 1 Lloyd's Rep. 334, an offer to charter barges was made "subject to availability and charterparty"; although terms were thereafter agreed no charter was ever signed, but it was held that when the barges were delivered to and employed by the charterers a contract came into being on the agreed terms. This follows the authority of *Brogden* v. *Metropolitan Railway* (1877) 2 App. Cas. 666.

Subject to survey, permission or approval

When the parties have in their negotiations used such phrases as "subject to survey", "subject to Government permission" or "subject to shippers' approval", it is a matter of construction of all the exchanges in their contexts to decide whether there is (*a*) no binding contract at all; or (*b*) a contract which binds immediately but whose main obligations come into operation only if and when the survey has been carried out or the permission or approval has been given; or (*c*) a contract which binds immediately but will cease to do so if the requirement is not fulfilled. In the case of construction (*b*), although the main obligations of the contract will not come into operation until the survey is carried out or the permission or approval is given, there may, meanwhile, be an obligation on one or both of the parties not to prevent the fulfilment of the requirement or even to do what is reasonable to try to fulfil it: see *Brauer* v. *Clark* [1952] 2 Lloyd's Rep. 147, and *Hargreaves Transport* v. *Lynch* [1969] 1 W.L.R. 215.

In *Astra Trust* v. *Adams* [1969] 1 Lloyd's Rep. 81, construction (*a*) was adopted and the words "subject to a satisfactory survey" were held to prevent any binding contract for the sale of a ship coming into existence for the time being. Megaw, J., held that neither side was bound by the terms provisionally agreed until the buyers had received a survey report which they found satisfactory. Up to that time either party could freely withdraw. The decision would have been the same had the phrase been simply "subject to survey". The effect of this decision is to give to "subject to (a satisfactory) survey" the same effect as to "subject to contract" above.

Lord Denning, M.R., expressed some doubt about the correctness of Megaw, J's decision in a subsequent sale contract case, *The Merak* [1976] 2 Lloyd's Rep. 250, and remarked that in some circumstances there might be an immediately binding contract despite such a phrase. The buyer would be obliged to make the survey and the seller to permit it and the contract would come to an end only if the survey were unsatisfactory, presumably on an objective view.

The use of the phrase "subject superficial inspection" in telex negotiations for a sale contract intended throughout to be based on the Norwegian Saleform was held by the Court of Appeal in *The Merak*, above, not to prevent the conclusion of an immediately binding contract (including, however, the usual printed provisions of the Norwegian Saleform for rejection by the buyers after inspection).

But in the case which follows it was held that the words "subject to satisfactory completion of two trial voyages" meant that there was not to be any binding charter unless and until these trial voyages had been satisfactorily completed and the parties had then agreed to enter into the contract.

Starch manufacturers agreed to take the *John S. Darbyshire* on time charter to bring starch to their factory, but only "Subject to satisfactory completion of two trial voyages", as they wanted to be sure that a compressed air piping system which they paid to have fitted to the ship would activate the starch sufficiently during transport to keep it in slurry form. After the second trial voyage they said they were not going ahead with the time charter. Before the Commercial Court they argued that no binding time charter had been made. Mocatta, J., agreed. He said that the effect of the relevant words was that the terms of the time charter "had been prepared and agreed, so to speak, in escrow, to use if and when it was further agreed between the parties that they should be bound contractually by them."

The John S. Darbyshire [1977] 2 Lloyd's Rep. 457.

There are many cases on conveyancing contracts in which clauses beginning "subject to" have been used, some of which contain more complicated analyses of the contractual position. Care should be exercised in applying the decisions in these cases to charter disputes, as many have been influenced by the special conveyancing practices in the countries from which they come, in particular by the potential existence in England of a period between agreement and exchange of contracts in which neither party is normally bound; see Coote, *Agreements subject to finance*, 40 Conv. (N.S.) 37 (1976).

"Subject details"

The expression commonly used in charterparty negotiations "subject to details" or simply "sub details" will usually prevent the formation of a binding contract under English law. It should be noted that there are American cases to a contrary effect (see page 30 below) but in the case which follows it was suggested by Steyn, J., that in this respect the United States courts were out of step with the way in which the shipping trade works.

Following negotiations for a voyage charter of the *Junior K*, the owners' broker sent a telex to the charterers' broker setting out the terms agreed which began "Confirm telcons here recap fixture sub details" and ended "sub dets Gencon CP". The telex contained all the essential terms of a charterparty and no matters had been specifically raised in the negotiations which remained unresolved. The owners contended that there was a binding contract. It was held by Steyn, J., on an interlocutory application, that the owners' contention had no realistic prospect of success. He said: "It is plain that the parties had in mind a contract on the Gencon form but that they had not yet considered the details of it. By the expression, 'subject to details of the Gencon charterparty' the owners made clear that they did not wish to commit themselves contractually until negotiations had taken place about the details of the charterparty. Such discussions might have covered a number of clauses. It does not follow that the owners were willing to accept all the detailed provisions of the standard form document. After all, it is a common occurrence for some of the detailed provisions of the Gencon form to be amended during the process of negotiation. In any event, the Gencon standard form contains within it alternative provisions which require a positive selection of the desired alternative . . . No discussion whatever had taken place about these options . . . Against this background it seems to me clear that the stipulation 'subject to details of the Gencon charterparty' conveys that the fixture is conditional upon agreement being reached on the details of the Gencon form, which had not yet been discussed."

The Junior K [1988] 2 Lloyd's Rep. 583.

(See also the views expressed by Staughton, J., in *The Solholt* [1981] 2 Lloyd's Rep. 574, at page 576, and by Leggatt, J., in *The Intra Transporter* [1985] 2 Lloyd's Rep. 158, at page 163.)

In *The Nissos Samos* [1985] 1 Lloyd's Rep. 378, a case on a ship sale contract, Leggatt, J., remarked at page 385: " 'Subject details' is a well-known expression in broking practice which is intended to entitle either party to resile from the contract if in good faith either party is not satisfied with any of the details as discussed between them." But Steyn, J., in *The Junior K*, above, considered that, insofar as he was referring to the qualification of good faith, Leggatt, J., was simply recording and stating a broking view and not the strict legal position. Ordinarily, if no binding contract has been formed, the reason for a party's withdrawal from negotiations is irrelevant.

Further, matters which, in the ordinary practice of broking are, it seems, regarded as "details", may be of essential contractual importance. So, in *The Winner* [1986] 1 Lloyd's Rep. 36, at page 38, evidence was given by a broker that "the style" of the charterers, by which was meant the description or naming of the charterers in the charterparty, was one of the matters regarded as a detail which had to be established before the fixture was finally concluded.

On the other hand, as Parker, J., said in *The Samah* [1981] 1 Lloyd's Rep. 40, at page 42: "It is undoubtedly possible to contract when much is left outstanding and for a party to commit himself to the acceptance of certain conditions which he has not seen". But the trend of current English authority clearly supports the view that the use of the qualification "subject to details" indicates that the parties do not yet intend to be bound. In *The Samah*, there had been negotiations for the chartering of two ships. At a certain stage telexes were sent stating that the ships were fixed "subject to satisfactory modifications" which were to be discussed with the charterers; and the telexes ended "NYPE TC sub charts proforma details . . . ". It was held that there was no binding contract at that stage, although there was a binding charterparty entered into at a subsequent stage. See generally Ball [1984] LMCLQ 250 and Debattista [1985] LMCLQ 241 and [1988] LMCLQ 439.

Other uses of "subject to"

The words "subject to" may be used by a party merely to introduce into negotiations a particular term or clause, as in "subject to war risks clause". The use of these words does not prevent a binding agreement if the other party assents to the proposal; but the whole phrase must identify with sufficient clarity the particular clause intended, for otherwise it may be read as meaning "subject to our being able to agree upon a suitable war risks clause" and prevent the formation of a binding contract. For example, in *Love & Stewart* v. *Instone* (1917) 33 T.L.R. 475 terms were agreed for the sale of a quantity of coal "subject to strike and lock-out clauses"; it was held by the House of Lords that there was no contract because although the parties had agreed that there should in their contract be such a clause they had not agreed what it should say. The following case also illustrates this point:

Agents for the prospective purchasers of the steamer *Ring* made a "firm offer of £22,000, less 1 per cent., subject to drydocking clause". The agents of the owners of the ship replied: " . . . I have to inform you that the offer is accepted by the sellers, and we shall try to send you contract on Monday." Bailhache, J., held that there was not a concluded contract, saying: "It is sufficient to say, as far as I know, there is no drydocking clause which can be said is the usual drydocking clause and invariable in its terms. This offer and acceptance, which are bound together, were subject to a drydocking clause undetermined in terms, and it prevents a concluded contract between the parties in this case. There is a reference to a contract and both parties contemplated a contract, but the mere fact that a contract is contemplated is not sufficient."

Svenska Lloyd v. *Niagassas* (1921) 8 Ll.L.Rep. 500.

By what law formation is determined

The question whether a binding contract has been entered into may not be determined by the law the parties intended should govern their contract once made. The English court and the foreign court will apply their own conflict of law rules, which may involve application of the putative proper law (see *The Parouth* [1982] 2 Lloyd's Rep. 351), the objective proper law or the *lex fori*, even though one of the parties may have had no intention of subjecting himself to that law (see *Great Circle Lines* v. *Matheson & Co.* 1982 AMC 567 (S.D.N.Y. 1981), *aff'd*, 681 F.2d 121, 1982 AMC 2321 (2d Cir. 1982). For comments on the proper law of the charter see page 363 below.

American Law

Applicable law

In American jurisprudence, maritime cases are given specific recognition as a proper subject of federal jurisdiction. (Article III, United States Constitution.) Hence, those causes of action which are deemed maritime in nature are governed by the general maritime law of the United States, which is paramount to the statutes and case precedents of the various states. *Southern Pacific Co.* v. *Jensen*, 244 U.S. 205 (1917). This is true even though under the "Savings to Suiters" Clause of the Judiciary Act of 1789 (1 U.S. Stat. 76–77) any claimant in a maritime case may seek a common law remedy in a state court or in a federal court exercising civil (i.e., non-admiralty) jurisdiction, such as diversity jurisdiction. Whenever the cause of action is maritime, federal substantive law is supreme even if the case is brought in a state court. *Kossick* v. *United Fruit Co.*, 365 U.S. 731 (1961).

Charters have long been considered maritime contracts. *The Ada*, 250 F. 194 (2d Cir. 1918). As such, they are not subject to such state enactments as the Statute of Frauds or the Uniform Commercial Code. *Union Fish Co.* v. *Erickson*, 248 U.S. 308 (1919). Rather, the governing law is that body of judicial precedents which comprises the general maritime law, together with those federal statutes (e.g., The Federal Maritime Lien Act, 46 U.S.C. §§971–975) which affect the rights and duties of the parties to the charter. *The Ada*, above. The federal maritime law governing charters embraces ordinary contract principles and principles of agency. *Kirno Hill Corp.* v. *Holt*, 618 F.2d 982, 985 (2d Cir. 1980); *Navieros Oceanikos S.A.* v. *S.T. Mobil Trader*, 554 F.2d 43, 47 (2d Cir. 1977).

The vast majority of charter disputes in the United States are settled by arbitration at New York. However, if the making of the contract is at issue, that question must first be heard by a court otherwise having jurisdiction. *Pollux Marine Agencies Inc.* v. *Louis Dreyfus Corp.*, 455 F.Supp. 211 (S.D.N.Y. 1978), aff'd 595 F.2d 1209 (2d Cir. 1979). The federal court in New York sitting in admiralty is deemed to have jurisdiction once it is alleged that there is a maritime contract providing for arbitration at New York. If the existence of the contract and its arbitration provision is upheld, then the issues of breach of charter and damages normally will be referred to arbitrators.

Rules of construction

The general rule of construction applied in admiralty cases is to construe contract language most strongly against its drafter. This rule only applies, however, where the language contained in the charter is ambiguous, or "susceptible of two reasonable and practical interpretations". *Navieros Oceanikos S.A.* v. *S.T. Mobil Trader*, above.

Under ordinary contract principles as applied in the federal maritime law, charter language is to be interpreted to give full effect to the plain meaning of the words used. If these words are ambiguous, the court will consider such factors as whether a particular interpretation creates or avoids a redundancy; the existence of limiting definitions in the charter; the breadth of the language of the disputed provision; and the surrounding provisions of the whole contract. *Capozziello* v. *Lloyd Brasileiro*, 443 F.2d 1155, 1159, 1971 AMC 1477 (2d Cir. 1971). Moreover, the disputed provision will be construed in the light least favorable to the party who drafted it, and will be given the meaning the other party believed it would have. These rules of construction are discussed at length in *Restatement (Second) of Contracts*, §§201–208.

Formation of the contract

A charter comes into existence when the parties agree to its essential terms. *Christman* v. *Maristella Compania Naviera*, 349 F.Supp. 845 (S.D.N.Y. 1971), aff'd on opinion below, 468 F.2d 620 (2d Cir. 1972); *Interocean Shipping Co.* v. *National Shipping and Trading Corp.*, 523 F.2d 527, 534 (2d Cir. 1975), *cert.* denied 423 U.S. 1054 (1976); *Pollux Marine Agencies Inc.* v. *Louis Dreyfus Corp.*, above; *The Cielo Rosso*, 1980 AMC 2088 (Arb. at N.Y. 1980). An oral charter is valid and enforceable. *Kossick* v. *United Fruit Co.*, 365 U.S. 731 (1961); *Interocean Shipping Co.* v. *National Shipping and Trading Corp.*, above. At the same time, an oral maritime contract may refer to and incorporate by reference the terms of a written document. *Sun Oil Co.* v. *Dalzell Towing Co. Inc.*, 55 F.2d 63 (2d Cir. 1932). aff'd 287 U.S. 291 (1932). In *Central Marine Service Inc.* v. *Ocean Marine Contractors Inc.*, 1984 AMC 1730 (5th Cir. 1982) (*per curiam*), the court stated that the admiralty parol evidence rule does not bar proof that a written agreement was later orally altered.

The parties may, of course, agree that the charter will be subject to specified conditions. If conditions are agreed, they must either be satisfied or waived before the charter will come into existence. The parties have a duty to act reasonably with respect to the fulfillment of conditions. In *The Zakynthos*, S.M.A. No. 2097 (Arb. at N.Y. 1985), the fixture telex included the following condition in favor of charterer: "subject to favorable report after inspection of vessel at Curacao on present voyage." After inspecting the vessel, the charterer rejected her and deemed the charter cancelled. The arbitrators ruled, however, that a standard of reasonableness was implicit in the clause and "did not give charterer a blank check to reject the ship without reasonable cause". The panel found that charterer acted capriciously in rejecting the vessel and held that this was a breach of the contract which permitted owner to recover damages.

Essential terms

Whether a term is by its nature "essential" is often difficult to determine. In *Uninav* v. *Molena Trust*, 1973 AMC 1386 (S.D.N.Y. 1973), aff'd 490 F.2d 1406 (2d Cir. 1974), it was held that there was no binding contract where the parties never agreed on the issue of crew overtime, which was considered to be an essential element of the charter. In *Interocean Shipping Co.* v. *National Shipping and Trading Corp.*, above, agreement on delivery range, insurance terms, and a dry-docking clause was considered essential to the charter. Similarly, in *Orient Mid-East Great Lakes Service* v. *Int'l Export Lines Ltd.*, 315 F.2d 519, 1964 AMC 1810 (4th Cir. 1963), the court held that there was no charter because the parties had not reached agreement on the quantity of stores and bunkers owner would be allowed to maintain. In *Himoff Indus.* v. *Seven Seas Shipping Corp.*, 1976 AMC 1030 (N.Y. Sup., 1976), the court held that there was no charter where there was never any meeting of the minds on the cancellation date and redelivery notice period, as well as other material terms of the fixture. See also *Bulk Charters (Pty) Limited* v. *Korea Shipping Corporation*, 1981 AMC 2877 (S.D.N.Y. 1981), holding that because of a disagreement over a proposed clause providing for a lump sum payment in lieu of hold cleaning, no meeting of the minds had taken place on a "main term" and therefore a charter was not concluded.

Normally the parties may stipulate that agreement on particular charter terms, otherwise minor, is a precondition to a "fixture" coming into being. Thus, in *The Toxon*, S.M.A. No. 913 (Arb. at N.Y. 1974), the charterer proposed a charter on a new Mobiltime charter form neither the owner nor its brokers had ever seen. The owner expressly reserved the right to review the new form before committing itself to the fixture, and once it had reviewed the form, requested a number of changes. The charterer never responded to this request, and it was held that there was no charter. See also *The Harpagus*, S.M.A. No. 323 (Arb. at N.Y. 1968), holding that there was no fixture where the owner's telex accepting the charterer's offer also stated: "Accept except details mutually agreed and delivery area to be declared latest 5 Oct." According to the panel, this was, in fact, a counter offer: "Any alteration in an offer constitutes a counter, no matter what wording is used."

"Sub details"

The widespread practice of fixing "sub details" ordinarily will not be construed as requiring agreement on each and every charter term before a binding contract is created. Once there has been agreement on essential terms, a contract is deemed to exist and the negotiation of remaining details becomes a ministerial task. As the court stated in *Interocean Shipping Co.* v. *National Shipping and Trading Corp.*, 523 F.2d 527, 535 (2d Cir. 1975), *cert.* denied 423 U.S. 1054 (1976): " . . . 'sub details' meant filling in the blanks—not reviewing the whole negotiations again." A similar result was obtained in *Atlantic & Great Lakes S.S. Corp.* v. *Steelmet Inc.*, 74 Civ. 5048 (S.D.N.Y., Feb. 22, 1977), aff'd 565 F.2d 848, 1978 AMC 107 (2d Cir. 1977), where the court held that the words "Genjascrap sub details" did not create a condition precedent for a meeting of the minds and the execution of a written contract.

These principles are illustrated by *Pollux Marine Agencies Inc.* v. *Louis Dreyfus Corp.*, above. There, brokers began negotiations for a three-year time charter of a bulk carrier. One of the early points that was specifically traded was an "ITF Clause" and at one point negotiations were broken off because of the parties' inability to agree on such a clause. A few days later, however, a compromise was suggested and a provision in substitution of a standard ITF Clause was found acceptable. Trading of other terms then resumed in earnest and later on a Friday all essential terms were agreed. The broker thereupon sent the customary fixture telex setting out all the terms agreed and adding the usual qualification "sub details". On the following Monday the parties began working out the details, using as agreed the charterer's *pro forma* time charter form. While these negotiations were in progress the charterer sought to modify the substitute ITF Clause which previously had been agreed. The owner objected. "Without prejudice" to its position that a fixture had been concluded, however, the owner did attempt to agree on a redraft of the wording. In the meantime, negotiations continued on "details" and, by the close of business on Monday, all details had been agreed. This left only the substitute ITF Clause. After several attempts to work out a compromise, negotiations ceased, with the charterer maintaining that no fixture had been agreed.

Ultimately, however, the owner made a claim for damages for repudiation and demanded arbitration. Since it denied that a charter had been agreed, the charterer refused to arbitrate and the issue was thereupon referred to the court in New York. After a trial, the court found that the parties had in fact reached agreement on all essential terms on Friday, that the term "sub details" was not a condition precedent to a binding fixture, and that charterer's insistence on reopening negotiations on the substitute ITF clause on Monday was a repudiation. The decision was affirmed by the Court of Appeals for the Second Circuit.

A similar result obtained in *Great Circle Lines Ltd.* v. *Matheson & Co. Ltd.* 1982 AMC 567 (S.D.N.Y. 1981), *aff'd.*, 681 F.2d 121, 1982 AMC 2321 (2d Cir. 1982). Again negotiations of main terms were concluded on a Friday and a "fixture recap" was sent by the brokers, "subject details". Subsequently both parties proposed changes in various clauses, including some of the "main terms" previously agreed. The defendant shipowner sought to insist, however, on plaintiff charterer agreeing to London arbitration. Under the agreed charter form, the New York Produce form, the place of arbitration was New York. The court found that the place of arbitration was a detail not specifically traded. The court then held that, since a binding contract already existed, the owner could not properly demand changes in its terms. Although the charterer had proposed modifications, they were no more than suggestions: a contract had been concluded and neither party could unilaterally insist on changes. See also *Cobec Brazilian Trading and Warehousing* v. *H. & J. Isbrandtsen*, 79 Civ. 3833 (S.D.N.Y. 1979).

In *Great Circle Lines*, above, the Second Circuit stated that main terms "include the name of the charterer, name of owner, ship and its characteristics, time and place of delivery, duration of the charter, place of redelivery, hire rate, printed form upon which the contract is based, and any other term that a party deems important". 1982 AMC at 2326. The court further noted that minor terms include "fuel used, speed of vessel, exact time of ship's delivery to charterer, brokerage, breakdown, option to extend the charter, cargo capacity, demurrage, and whatever else is deemed by the parties to be of minor importance". 1982 AMC at 2327. Clearly, however, many of the items the Second Circuit labeled as "minor" will frequently be very material "main" terms in most time charters. The fact that the court referred to them as "minor" does not mean that they will not be deemed to be main items if one or both of the parties indicates that the term is important.

In *J. Lauritzen A/S* v. *Korea Shipping Corporation*, 1986 AMC 2450 (S.D.N.Y. 1986), a dispute arose concerning the alleged fixture of a contract of affreightment to carry four separate grain shipments from the United States to Japan. A telex recap which was labeled "fixture sub-details" was sent by owner to charterer, but a disagreement subsequently arose concerning a freight payment clause contained in the pro forma charter referred to in the fixture telex. The court held that the question of whether the freight payment clause was a main term or a minor detail presented a genuine issue of material fact which had to be resolved by a trial.

Fixture before formal charter signed

In the usual case, an oral agreement to charter a vessel is subsequently confirmed in writing by a fixture letter or telex, and all of the details agreed to are ultimately set forth in a final typewritten or printed charter signed by both parties. The final written charter then becomes the evidence of the contract, and all prior oral or written agreements on details are deemed to have been merged therein. *Interocean Shipping Co.* v. *National Shipping and Trading Corp.*, above. This principle is especially important where there are differences between the fixture telex and the final charter. In *Interocean*, for example, there were a number of differences between the fixture telex and the final charter on details such as trading limits, speed, performance, penalties and method of payment. The court held that this disparity did not vitiate the agreement, and stated that the terms of the telex: "should be viewed as having merged in the subsequent written document, whether favorable to one side or the other. The party that wanted a provision which was omitted or altered could have pressed for its inclusion in the final written instrument." (523 F.2d at 535.)

In *Compania Naviera Aisgiannis S.A*. v. *Holt*, 1984 AMC 2228 (E.D. Pa. 1983), however, the final written charter named a non-existent corporation as charterer, so the court instead inserted the name used in the fixture telex.

Parties to the Contract

"2. Between ....

3. Owners of the good .... { Steamship / Motorship } ....

12. ....and .... Charterers of the City of ...."

General

The Parties named as owners and charterers in the preamble to the time charter are usually, but not necessarily, the parties entitled to claim under the charter or the parties against whom claims can be brought. In order to establish who may sue and be sued it is often necessary because of the intervention of brokers to apply the general rules of the law of agency. As Pickford, J., said in *Harper* v. *Vigers* [1909] 2 K.B. 549, "a shipbroker is only an agent to make a charter, just as anyone else may be an agent to make a charter". (For the right of the charterer to sue for the broker's commission see *Les Affréteurs Réunis* v. *Walford* [1919] A.C. 801, and page 451 below.)

The effect of agency is considered under four heads.

Where an authorised agent makes the contract for a principal of whose existence the other contracting party is aware ("disclosed principal")

Basic rule

Where a duly authorised agent makes a contract for his named principal and, if he signs the contract at all, does so in such a way as to show that he is acting only as agent for that principal, the principal but not the agent will in general be the party to that contract. It is said that "the agent drops out". See, for an example of the failure of an action brought by a broker in such circumstances, *Fairlie* v. *Fenton* (1870) L.R. 5 Ex. 169.

When agent liable

The agent may, however, become liable under a contract himself, where an intention to that effect is shown by the contract or by the mode of its signature. This intention may well be shown if the agent signs the contract and does so without suitably qualifying his signature. Indeed, Scrutton, L.J., in *Brandt* v. *Morris* [1917] 2 K.B. 784, at page 797, referred to this as a "strong *prima facie* presumption". This has been held to be so even where the other party knows that he was acting as agent: *Basma* v. *Weekes* [1950] A.C. 441. There is no such strict rule with regard to oral contracts. In *Vlassopulos* v. *Ney Shipping* [1977] 1 Lloyd's Rep. 478, the Court of Appeal held that Baltic Exchange brokers, who were known to be acting as agents for others, were not personally liable on a bunker supply contract made by telephone with other Baltic brokers, although they had not expressly stated on this occasion that they were agents only.

Where the agent is liable, older cases assume that he is liable instead of his principal; but it is also possible for him to be liable as well as his principal and this possibility is becoming increasingly recognised, especially where his principal is unnamed: see below. (There is, however, authority (although of uncertain standing) that here, as in the case of an undisclosed principal, the liability of one party is extinguished by judgment against, or perhaps even an "election" to sue, the other (see *Debenham's* v. *Perkins* (1925) 133 L.T. 252, 254).)

Where a party opens negotiations describing himself as agent for a named principal, but ultimately enters into a binding contract without reference to agency and without signing any formal charter, the question whether he is personally liable under the contract will be determined by an examination of the statements made in negotiations leading up to the charter and of all the surrounding circumstances.

Negotiations for a part charter of the owners' ship *Rab* were conducted, through brokers, with prospective charterers described as B. & S. "on account of Indonesian Government". Subsequently the business for the *Rab* lapsed but the owners offered their ship *Primorje* for the same cargo subject to the terms being negotiated afresh. A fixture was concluded and a charter was drawn up naming B. & S. as charterers. There was no mention of B. & S. acting as agents for any principals either in the fresh negotiations or in the charter, which was signed by the owners but not by B. & S. It was only after the charter had been performed and claims made under it that B. & S. contended that they acted only as intermediaries. It was held that B. & S. contracted as principals despite the reference in the original negotiations to them chartering "on account of" the Indonesian Government.

The Primorje [1980] 2 Lloyd's Rep. 74.

Signature "as agents"

But to sign a contract "for and on behalf of" or "on account of" the principal or to sign "as agent" shows a clear intention to avoid the rights and obligations attaching to a principal to the contract and so, in the absence of some exceptionally clear term of the contract to the contrary, displaces this presumption of personal liability.

A charter was entered into by T. H. S. & Co., agents for owners of the *Ariadne Irene*, and "J. McK. & Co., Charterers". The charter was signed "For and on behalf of J. McK. & Co. (as Agents), J. A. McK". The owners were aware at the time the charter was signed that J. McK. & Co. were acting for others.

The owners brought a claim under the charter against J. McK. & Co. who pleaded that they were not principals. It was held by the House of Lords that by signing "as Agents" J. McK. & Co. were relieved of personal liability under the charter. Lord Shaw said: " . . . in my opinion the appending of the word 'agents' to the signature of a party to a mercantile contract is, in all cases, the dominating factor in the solution of the problem of principal or agent. A highly improbable and conjectural case (in which this dominating factor might be overcome by other parts of the contract) may by an effort of the imagination be figured, but, apart from that, the appending of the word 'agent' to the signature is a conclusive assertion of agency, and a conclusive rejection of the responsibility of a principal . . . ".

Universal Steam Navigation v. *McKelvie* [1923] A.C. 492.

In this case, the words "as Agents" after the signature had the effect of excluding any personal liability of the agents despite their being described as "Charterers" in the body of the charter.

Other words following signature

Other words added after a signature may be less effective to prevent the agent from being a party to the contract or suable upon it. The case which follows illustrates this. It also shows that the court may look not only at the particular words used but also at the surrounding circumstances in order to discover the intention of the parties.

The owner of a motor boat, the *Swan*, hired it to a company of which he was a director. He placed a repair order for the boat which was written on the company's paper and signed by him with the word "Director" after his name. The repairers knew that he was the owner of the boat. It was held by Brandon, J., that the owner had made the resulting contract as agent for the company, but that he could also be sued personally under the contract (which was partly oral and partly in writing) as he had failed to displace the reasonable assumption of the repairers that as the owner of the boat he would pay for the repairs to it.

Brandon, J., said: "Where A contracts with B on behalf of a disclosed principal C, the question whether both A and C are liable on the contract or only C depends on the intention of the parties. That intention is to be gathered from (1) the nature of the contract, (2) its terms and (3) the surrounding circumstances . . . ".

The Swan [1968] 1 Lloyd's Rep. 5.

Agency indicated in body of contract

Not only may an agent exclude personal liability under the contract by suitably qualifying his signature; alternatively, he may make it clear in the body of the contract that his legal status is to be that of agent alone. Archibald, J., in *Gadd* v. *Houghton* (1876) 1 Ex.D. 357, said, at page 361: "The usual way in which an agent contracts so as not to render himself personally liable is by signing as agent. That, however, is not the only way, because, if it is clear from the body of the contract that he contracted only as agent, he would save his liability."

Whether the principal alone, the agent alone, or both the principal and the agent are liable is therefore a matter of construction of the contract as a whole, taking into account the surrounding circumstances (as to which see *Brandt* v. *Morris* [1917] 2 K.B. 784, and *The Swan* [1968] 1 Lloyd's Rep. 5, above). The two cases which follow illustrate this and show also that the courts will not give undue weight to particular clauses.

In a charter of the *Virgo* the charterers were stated in Line 7 to be "Tradax Export S.A." and the charter was signed by "Greenwich Marine Incorporated As Agents for: Tradax Export S.A." However, Clause 31, in the "Rider" to the charter, provided: "This vessel was chartered on behalf and for account of General Organisation for Supply Goods Cairo." Tradax Export S.A. sought to rely on the words of Clause 31 to establish that they themselves were agents only and not charterers.

The Court of Appeal held that the overall sense of the charter was that Tradax Export S.A. were principals and had the liabilities of charterers and that Clause 31 did not show a sufficiently clear intention to the contrary to alter that position.

Megaw, L.J., said: " . . . the law requires that all relevant contractual provisions, wherever they may appear in the written contractual documents, shall be looked at and taken into account when a question arises whether a person named in a contract—charter-party or otherwise—is a principal party to the contract, or is an agent; and, if an agent, whether he also has in law liabilities under the contract. You do not look at one part of the contract only: for example, the signature. You weigh anything that may be relevant in any part of the contractual provisions and documents."

Tudor Marine v. *Tradax Export S.A. (The Virgo)* [1976] 2 Lloyd's Rep. 135.

(See also *The Sun Happiness* [1984] 1 Lloyd's Rep. 381.)

The *Scaplake* was chartered to C.D.M. "as charterers". Clause 29 of the charter provided: "Freight and demurrage will be guaranteed by actual charterers D. & K. . . . or personally by their director." The charter was signed by C.D.M. and also by D. & K. in two places. One of the addenda was signed by both C.D.M. and D. & K., the other addenda being signed by C.D.M. alone.

It was argued by the owners that D. & K. were liable under the charter as principals of C.D.M. Mocatta, J., held that as D. & K. had signed both the charter and an important addendum and were described as "actual charterers" they could not be regarded only as guarantors of freight and demurrage. These features and the surrounding commercial circumstances showed that both C.D.M. and D. & K. were parties to the charter and liable under it.

The Scaplake [1978] 2 Lloyd's Rep. 380.

(See also *The Primorje* [1980] 2 Lloyd's Rep. 74, above, and *The Yanxilas* [1982] 2 Lloyd's Rep. 445, "as operating Owners".)

Principal unnamed

The position is in principle the same where a duly authorised agent professedly makes a contract for a principal whose name is not mentioned. In such cases, however, it may be easier for the court to hold the agent personally liable under the contract than where the principal is named: see the judgment of Diplock, L.J., in *Teheran-Europe* v. *Belton (Tractors)* [1968] 2 Lloyd's Rep. 37, at page 38 below.

Foreign principal

Formerly there was a presumption that where an English agent contracted on behalf of a foreign principal, the agent was personally liable under the contract. No such presumption exists today (*Teheran-Europe* v. *Belton (Tractors)* [1968] 2 Lloyd's Rep. 37). But on the facts of a particular case it may be the correct inference that the agent in such circumstances is personally responsible: *Fraser* v. *Equitorial Shipping (The Ijaola)* [1979] 1 Lloyd's Rep. 103, 111.

Rights of agent

Generally an agent who is liable to the other party is entitled to sue; "the existence of the liability on the one hand involves the existence of the correlative right on the other" (*Repetto* v. *Millar's Karri & Jarrah Forests* [1901] 2 K.B. 306, 310). But this is not necessarily so, for on a proper construction of the contract the agent may have assumed a liability without a corresponding right, or, in exceptional circumstances, a right without a corresponding liability.

Where a person, although describing himself as an agent, is in fact the principal

Such a person is generally liable under the contract; whether he has rights under it may depend on whether the supposed principal is named or not.

Named principal

Where the person making the contract intends to be the principal, but describes himself in the contract as agent for a named principal, he cannot sue under the contract as principal if the other party entered into the contract in reliance on the status or reputation of the named principal. Indeed, it is doubtful if he can ever sue where the principal is named, save where the other party becomes aware of the truth and nevertheless affirms the contract: *Rayner* v. *Grote* (1846) 15 M. & W. 359.

Afrab, a subsidiary of Librekcem, entered into a charter with Gewa for shipment of a cargo of bitumen on the basis of a named vessel or substitute. The named vessel was not available at the required time and Gewa therefore negotiated for a charter of the *Remco* to meet their commitment to Afrab. It was found as a fact that Gewa represented to the owners' brokers that Gewa were chartering as agents for Afrab or another subsidiary of Librekcem, whereas in fact Gewa were chartering on their own account. It was held that Gewa could not enforce the charter with the owners of the *Remco* since:

(*a*) the owners of the *Remco* had shown that the identity of the party they believed to be the principal was material; they knew the Librekcem group was a large group to whom they were happy to charter, whereas they would have required some sort of guarantee for the freight had they known that Gewa were the charterers; and

(*b*) the owners of the *Remco* had never affirmed the contract with knowledge of the true state of affairs.

The Remco [1984] 2 Lloyd's Rep. 205.
(See also *Rayner* v. *Grote* (1846) 15 M. & W. 359).

Unnamed principal

Where, on the other hand, the purported principal is not named the other party cannot have placed importance on his identity and the person making the contract as agent has been held entitled to sue upon it as principal. But these decisions have been criticised (see *Hill Steam Shipping* v. *Stinnes*, 1941 S.C. 324, and *Bowstead on Agency*, 15th edition, pages 478 to 479) and should be treated with caution.

G. Schmaltz & Co. chartered a ship as "agents of the freighter" and stipulated as follows: "This charter being concluded on behalf of another party, it is agreed that all responsibility on the part of G. Schmaltz & Co. shall cease as soon as the cargo is shipped." In an action by them against the owners, Schmaltz & Co. were allowed to prove that they were in fact the freighters in their own right, and were held to be entitled to sue as principals under the contract. Patterson, J., cited with approval a passage from the judgment delivered by Alderson, B., in *Rayner* v. *Grote* (1846) 15 M. & W. 359, 365, reading in part: "In many such cases, such as, for instance, the case of contracts in which the skill or solvency of the person who is named as the principal may reasonably be considered as a material ingredient in the contract, it is clear that the agent cannot then shew himself to be the real principal, and sue in his own name; and perhaps it may be fairly urged that this, in all executory contracts, if wholly unperformed, or if partly performed without the knowledge of who is the real principal, may be the general rule." He then continued: "With this passage we entirely agree; but it is plain that it is applicable only to cases where the supposed principal is named in the contract: if he be not named, it is possible that the other party can have been in any way induced to enter into the contract by any of the reasons suggested."
Schmaltz v. *Avery* (1851) 16 Q.B. 655.

Harper & Co. entered into a charter "as agents for owners" of a ship to be nominated and signed the charter "By authority of and as agents for owners." In fact they were not acting for any principals but entered into the charter on a speculative basis on their own account. The charterers gave evidence that, had they been aware of this fact at the time, they would not have entered into the charter. It was nevertheless held by Pickford, J., following *Schmaltz* v. *Avery*, that, there being no principals other than Harper & Co. themselves, Harper & Co. could sue the charterers under the charter.
Harper v. *Vigers* [1909] 2 K.B. 549.

Where an authorised agent makes the contract in his own name, but does so for a principal of whose existence the other contracting party is unaware ("undisclosed principal")

The principal is here said to be "undisclosed". The general rule is that either the principal or the agent (at least until the principal intervenes) may sue under the contract. Likewise either one or the other may be sued under it, although the other party may lose his right to sue one by obtaining judgment against the other; and possibly also if he can be regarded as having "elected" to look to one of them only.

Diplock, L.J., said in *Teheran-Europe* v. *Belton (Tractors)* [1968] 2 Lloyd's Rep. 37, at page 41: "In determining who is entitled to sue or liable to be sued on a contract, a useful starting point, where the contract is in writing, is to look at the contract. In doing so a number of elementary principles should be borne in mind. The first is that a person may enter into a contract through an agent whom he has actually authorized to enter into the contract on his behalf or whom he has led the other party to believe he has so authorized. But we are concerned here only with actual authority. Where an agent has such actual authority and enters into a contract with another party intending to do so on behalf of his principal, it matters not whether he discloses to the other party the identity of his principal, or even that he is contracting on behalf of a principal at all, if the other party is willing or leads the agent to believe that he is willing to treat as a party to the contract anyone on whose behalf the agent may have been authorized to contract. In the case of an ordinary commercial contract such willingness of the other party may be assumed by the agent unless either the other party manifests his unwillingness or there are other circumstances which should lead the agent to realize that the other party was not so willing."

Agent describes himself as "owner"

But there are situations in which the terms of the contract or the surrounding circumstances may exclude the intervention of the undisclosed principal. It has held in *Humble* v. *Hunter*, below, that an undisclosed principal might not sue where the agent had described himself as "owner", because that expression effectively excluded the possibility of agency and thus of the undisclosed principal proving that he was indeed the true owner. The decision should, it is suggested, be regarded as of doubtful validity (see, for example, the judgment of Scott, L.J., in *Epps* v. *Rothnie* [1945] K.B. 562). It was based on an application of the rule excluding parol evidence to contradict or vary the terms of a written contract which would, if followed widely, greatly restrict the intervention of the undisclosed principal.

A charter was made between "C. J. Humble, Esq. owner of the good ship or vessel called the *Ann*" and Hunter as charterer. C. J. Humble was in fact the son of the real owner. It was held that evidence was not admissible to show that the person who described himself as owner contracted merely as agent, because such evidence would contradict an express statement in the charter, namely that C. J. Humble was the owner. The expression "owner" was not, it was held, capable of bearing the connotation of agency.

Humble v. *Hunter* (1848) 12 Q.B. 310.

Agent describes himself as "charterer" or "disponent"

Even if the above decision is correct and the description "owner" does exclude the possibility of agency, the descriptions "charterers" and "disponents" do not exclude it.

A time charter was entered into between "Messrs. Fred. Drughorn, Ltd., Owners of the screw steamship called the *England*" and "Wilh. R. Lundgren, of Gothenburg, Charterer". The charter party was headed "Swedish South African Line. Wilh. R. Lundgren, Manager" and signed by agents "by telegraphic authority of and as agents for Wilh. R. Lundgren". Lundgren was in fact chartering as agent for Red. Transatlantic. It was held by the House of Lords that evidence of the agency was admissible because the description of a party as "charterer" does not exclude the possibility that they are chartering as agents for others.

Drughorn v. *Red. A/B Transatlantic* [1919] A.C. 203.

A charter was entered into by N.V. Stoomschip "Hannah" as "disponent owners of the good steamer called the *Elle*" and was signed by brokers "under telephonic authority from and as agents for disponents." The charter referred in various clauses to "owners". It was held by Morris, J., that, construing the charter as a whole, the phrase "disponent owners" indicated someone other than the owners of the ship. Evidence that O/Y Wasa Steamship Co. were the owners of the ship and the real principals was not inconsistent with the terms of the charter and was admissible.

O/Y Wasa Steamship v. *Newspaper Pulp & Wood Export* (1949) 82 Ll.L.Rep. 936.

But in the case which follows it was held that even though the person described as "disponent owner" was an employee of the owners' managing agents, the owners could not enforce the charter as undisclosed principals; the evidence showed that in regard to the particular charter in question the relationship between the owners and the "disponent owner" was inconsistent with agency.

Negotiations for a voyage charter of the *Astyanax* were concluded between authorised brokers acting for owners and charterers. But it was agreed that for the purposes of avoiding an Argentinian tax on freight, the owners should be named in the charter as P.S. of Piraeus "as disponent owner". P.S. was an employee of the owners' managing agents who, being Greek, was eligible to take advantage of a double taxation agreement with Argentina. It was envisaged in the exchanges between the brokers that there should then be a head time charter between the owners, who were a Cypriot company, and the disponent owner P.S. The owners, however, sought to enforce the voyage charter as undisclosed principals on the basis that P.S. was a mere nominee. It was held by the Court of Appeal, reversing Leggatt, J., that since it was not intended that the proposed head time charter should be a mere sham, the position of P.S. as a head charterer, sub-chartering as disponent owner, was inconsistent with his acting merely as agent for the owners as principals, even though ultimately he stood neither to gain nor to lose personally. He was himself a principal.

The Astyanax [1985] 2 Lloyd's Rep. 109.

(See also *The Scaplake* [1978] 2 Lloyd's Rep. 380 and page 35 above ("actual charterers"); *The Yanxilas* [1982] 2 Lloyd's Rep. 445 ("as operating Owners") and *Bowstead on Agency*, 15th edition, pages 312 to 325.)

Where a person acts as agent but without authority from the alleged principal

It has so far been assumed that the agent who signs for a principal is authorised to do so. But he may not be. Questions then arise whether the principal has ratified the contract or whether the agent had apparent or ostensible authority. If not, the agent may be liable for breach of warranty of authority.

Ratification

A principal may cure any lack of authority in the agent by subsequently ratifying what he has done, for example by adopting a charter which the agent has without authority concluded. This power to ratify is not possessed by the "undisclosed" principal, discussed above: see *Keighley, Maxted* v. *Durant* [1901] A.C. 240. It is also subject to certain limits to prevent its being used unfairly. Ratification may likewise render a principal liable on a contract originally made by the agent without authority.

Apparent or ostensible authority

A principal may also be, and frequently is, liable under the doctrine of apparent or ostensible authority, by which a principal may be bound by the act of an agent who has no actual authority but who has been held out by the principal as having authority.

Ostensible authority cannot be established by the statements or conduct of the agent alone. The principal must, by his own statements or conduct, or by those of a suitably authorised agent (see *British Bank of the Middle East* v. *Sun Life Assurance Co. of Canada* [1983] 2 Lloyd's Rep. 9), have given the other party reasonably to understand that the agent had authority to act as agent on his behalf. This will occur, for instance, where he entrusts his affairs to an agent who would normally have the appropriate authority.

Lord Keith said, in *The Ocean Frost* [1986] 2 Lloyd's Rep. 109 at page 112: "Ostensible authority comes about where the principal, by words or conduct, has represented that the agent has the requisite actual authority, and the party dealing with the agent has entered into a contract with him in reliance on that representation. The principal in these circumstances is estopped from denying that actual authority existed. In the commonly encountered case, the ostensible authority is general in character, arising when the principal has placed the agent in a position which in the outside world is generally regarded as carrying authority to enter into transactions of the kind in question. Ostensible general authority may also arise where the agent has had a course of dealing with a particular contractor and the principal had acquiesced in this course of dealing and honoured transactions arising out of it." (See also the judgment of Diplock, L.J., in *Freeman & Lockyer* v. *Buckhurst Park Properties* [1964] 2 Q.B. 480, at page 505, for the specific conditions which have to be satisfied to establish the existence of ostensible authority.)

In *The Ocean Frost* it was common ground by the time the case reached the Court of Appeal that a vice-president (transportation) and chartering manager of the intended charterers had, in the particular circumstances of the case, no actual or ostensible general authority to enter into a three-year charter agreement on their behalf. But it was argued that he had ostensible specific authority to bind the charterers, in that by appointing him to his positions, the charterers had represented him as having authority to notify their approval of the charter to the owners. It was held by the Court of Appeal and the House of Lords that since, admittedly, the vice-president (transportation) and chartering manager had no ostensible authority to enter into a three-year charter—the owners being aware that a charter for such a period required the charterers' approval—his appointment to those positions could not amount to a representation by the charterers that he had authority to notify their approval of such a charter.

In *The Rhodian River* [1984] 1 Lloyd's Rep. 373, a chartering manager for two separate one-ship companies, having the same shareholders and directors, was held to have neither actual nor ostensible authority from one of the companies to let the other company's ship out on charter. As a result of an error, the Rhodian River Company was named as owner in a charter of the other company's ship, the *Rhodian Sailor*. The actual authority which he had as chartering manager of each company to charter that company's ship could not be construed as embracing incidental authority to charter the other company's ship; nor was there any evidence at all to justify the conclusion that such a chartering manager would usually have such authority. (For cases in which chartering brokers were held to have had ostensible authority to bind their principals see *The Samah* [1981] 1 Lloyd's Rep. 40 and *The Wave* [1981] 1 Lloyd's Rep. 521. See also *The Nea Tyhi* [1982] 1 Lloyd's Rep. 606, at page 273 below and *The Saudi Crown* [1986] 1 Lloyd's Rep. 261.)

Breach of warranty of authority

But where the principal is not liable, the agent may be sued by the other party to the contract for damages for breach of an implied warranty (see page 56 below) that he had the authority he claimed. See *Collen* v. *Wright* (1857) 8 E. & B. 647 and

V/O Rasnoimport v. *Guthrie* [1966] 1 Lloyd's Rep. 1 (liability of loading broker signing bill of lading). The warranty is absolute in nature, so honest belief that he had authority does not give the agent any defence to such a claim.

"By telegraphic authority"

It has been held in this context that an agent signing "by telegraphic authority" of the principal warrants no more than that he has a telegram seemingly authorising him to sign the relevant charter.

Brokers signed as agents for charterers a charter for the *Pocklington*, preceding their signature by the words "by telegraphic authority" of the charterers. The rate of freight in the charter was in accordance with that authorised in the telegram from the charterers but that telegram had been wrongly transmitted by the telegraph company and stated a rate higher than the charterers were actually offering. On being sued by the shipowners for warranting an authority they did not possess, the brokers produced evidence which was accepted by Denman, J., that the words "by telegraphic authority" were "well understood in the trade as meaning to negative the implication of a warranty by the charterer's agent, at all events, to a greater extent than warranting that he has had a telegram which, if correct, authorises such a charter as that which he is signing." It was accordingly held that the absolute warranty of authority had been effectively displaced by the use of these words.

Lilly, Wilson v. *Smales, Eeles* [1892] 1 Q.B. 456.

It is hard, however, to reconcile that decision with the following decision of the House of Lords in the next year.

A London broker received from a Bombay firm a telegram apparently authorising him to sign a charter for the *Eastbourne* on behalf of Colombo charterers. He accordingly effected a charter, showing as charterers the Bombay firm as agents for the Colombo charterers, and signed it as agent "By telegraphic authority of" the Bombay firm. In fact the Colombo charterers had not authorised the Bombay firm to act as they had. The shipowners brought an action for breach of warranty against the broker, who argued that the particular words they had used made it clear that there was to be no contract unless the Colombo firm had in fact given authority. The House of Lords rejected this argument and held the broker liable. Lord Watson said: "I am of opinion that the words upon which the appellants rely are not sufficient to indicate that the validity of the contract between the shipowners and the charterers was to be dependent upon an unascertained condition. Taken in their natural sense they appear to me to do no more than describe the source from which the appellants derived their authority to represent the charterers."

Suart v. *Haigh* (1893) 9 T.L.R. 488.

American Law

Ordinary contract principles as applied under the federal maritime law determine who is a party to a charter. The federal maritime law embraces agency principles. *Interocean Shipping Co.* v. *National Shipping and Trading Corp.*, 523 F.2d 527, 539 (2d Cir. 1975), *cert.* denied 423 U.S. 1054 (1976); *Kirno Hill Corp.* v. *Holt*, 618 F.2d 982, 985 (2d Cir. 1980).

Agents

A person acting as agent for a disclosed principal is not himself a party to the charter. *Interocean Shipping Co.* v. *National Shipping and Trading Corp.*, above. The crucial test in determining whether an agent can be bound to the contract is not whether a principal is named, but whether a principal is identified. It is common practice for a broker or other person to sign the charter "as agents for Owners of the good ship [Victory]", without further identifying the name of the owner. It has been held that this is sufficient to identify the principal. *Instituto Cubano de Estab.* v. *S.S. Theotokos*, 153 F.Supp. 85 (S.D.N.Y. 1957) (before trial), 155 F.Supp. 945 (S.D.N.Y.) (after trial); *Tubos de Acero de Mexico* v. *Dynamic Shipping Inc.*, 249 F.Supp. 583, 1966 AMC 1903 (S.D.N.Y. 1966); *Hudson Trading Co.* v. *Hasler & Co. Inc.*, 11 F.2d 666, 667 (S.D.N.Y. 1926). It is essential in this context, however, that the vessel be clearly named. For example, if the broker were to sign "as agents for owners of vessels to be named", there would not be a sufficient identification of a principal and the broker/agent could be held as a party to the charter. See *Hidrocarburos y Derivados C.A.* v. *Lemos*, 453 F.Supp. 160, 171 (S.D.N.Y. 1978). As Judge Haight noted in that case, there is no recognition in the law of agency of the "potential principal". In the example cited, of course, the principal would become sufficiently disclosed once the vessel is nominated and thus identified.

The question of whether a person is in fact an authorized agent often can be far from simple. An agency may be created by either actual or apparent authority. In certain circumstances, a principal will be estopped from denying the existence of an agency relationship.

Actual authority

Actual authority will exist only if there has been a manifestation by the principal to the agent that the agent may act on his behalf, and consent by the agent so to act. An agency relationship need not be contractual; however, it is always consensual. A broker who is authorized by the owner or charterer to negotiate and fix a charter will be deemed an agent of that party. In *Interocean Shipping Co.* v. *National Shipping and Trading Corp.*, above, the Court of Appeals for the Second Circuit held that a broker through whom the charter terms were negotiated by both parties, and who sent telexes to both parties confirming the fixture, was an agent for the owner and charterer, even though he viewed himself solely as a broker, and the charterer did not intend to make him an agent. According to the court: "Agency is a legal concept which depends on the manifest conduct of the parties, not on their intentions or beliefs as to what they have done." (523 F.2d at 537.)

Unless express limiting instructions are given to the agent, a grant of actual authority will carry with it the power to take such actions as the agent considers are reasonably necessary to carry out his duties. This includes the power to enter into contracts on behalf of the principal which are incidental to accomplishing the original assigned task. Thus, where the agent of the cargo owner was authorized to arrange for the delivery of the cargo by barge, it was inferred from the nature of the agency relationship that the agent was also invested with the authority to enter into a barge charterparty, the making of which was a necessary incident to the fulfillment by the agent of his delegated task. *Alamo Chemical Transportation Co.* v. *M/V Overseas Valdes*, 469 F.Supp. 203, 1979 AMC 2033 (E.D.La. 1979).

Apparent authority

Apparent authority rests on a different foundation, and will be found to exist where the principal's actions are reasonably perceived by the third party as indicating that the agent has authority to bind the principal. Apparent authority was succinctly defined in *Dr. Beck & Co.* v. *General Electric Co.*, 210 F.Supp. 86, 90 (S.D.N.Y. 1962) as follows:

> Apparent authority results from a manifestation by a principal that another is his agent, the manifestation being made to a third person and not, as when actual authority is created, to the agent . . . Where apparent authority exists, the third person has the same rights with reference to the principal as where the agent is actually authorized . . . The appearance of authority must be created by the principal. While agents are often successful in creating an appearance of authority by their own acts and statements, such an appearance does not create apparent authority. . . .
>
> It remains . . . a basic proposition of the law of agency that the third party takes the risk of being misled by the unauthorized misrepresentations of the agent and that the principal is only liable where he has either authorized the representations or done something from which reasonable people would draw the inference that the agent had authority. (210 F.Supp. at 90.)

Reliance on the perceived authority of the agent must be reasonable in light of all the circumstances. A good illustration of the problems which can arise is *Karavos Compania Naviera S.A.* v. *Atlantica Export Corp.*, 588 F.2d 1, 1978 AMC 2634 (2d Cir. 1978). The owner claimed that the named charterer, Atlantica, breached an alleged agreement to charter the vessel when it declined to take delivery. The owner argued that Atlantica was bound by the agreement of its alleged agent, Alfred Repetti, who purportedly had negotiated and fixed the charter on Atlantica's behalf. Repetti carried out the charter negotiations from Atlantica's offices, and, at times, received telephone calls and telexes concerning the proposed charter while he was in those offices. Repetti did not have actual authority to bind Atlantica, however, and the court found that nothing Atlantica had done gave the owner sufficient reason to believe that he had authority to fix a charter on its behalf. According to the court, the fact that Atlantica permitted Repetti to work in its office and use its communication facilities did *not* justify the owner in believing that he had authority to commit Atlantica to a charter or relieve it of the duty to make reasonable inquiry as to Repetti's status. The court further stated that, even if the owner had been justified in believing that Repetti was an Atlantica employee, it was bound to inquire what his authority was. As the court noted, "not every employee of a trading company has authority to fix a time charter, let alone a series of such charters". (588 F.2d at 10.)

See also *P. D. Marchessini & Co. (New York) Inc.* v. *H. W. Robinson & Co.*, 287 F.Supp. 728, 1968 AMC 2084 (S.D.N.Y. 1967), where the court held that a vessel owner was not justified in relying on the apparent authority of an employee of a shipping concern to sign a contract for the shipment of cargo.

A party may be estopped from denying an agent's authority if third persons have changed their positions because they believed there was an agency if the principal intentionally or carelessly caused such a belief, or failed to take reasonable steps to notify the third parties of the true facts even though he knew the others believed he was a principal to the transaction and might change their positions because of it. *Restatement (Second) of Agency* § 8(B). See generally *Karavos Compania Naviera S.A.* v. *Atlantica Export Corp.*, above, 588 F.2d at 11.

However, it was stated in *Golden Chase Steamship Inc.* v. *Valmar de Navegacion S.A.*, 724 F.2d 129, 1984 AMC 2040 (5th Cir. 1984) (*per curiam*) that persons dealing with agents are presumed to know the customs of the industry, and therefore, cannot hold the principal liable for unauthorized acts not customarily permitted to agents in the industry. The court reasoned: "By custom among New York ship brokers, each broker must have a separate and express grant of authority from the principal each time a firm offer is made or confirmed on behalf of the principal . . . The very limited nature of the authority to fix the charter is inconsistent with the creation of apparent authority." (1984 AMC at 2042.)

Ratification

A person may elect to become a party to an act or transaction which was done or purported to be done for him without prior authorization. Thus, an unauthorized act performed by an agent may be ratified by the principal, with the result that the act will be deemed to have been authorized when it was carried out. See *Restatement (Second) of Agency* §§82–104.

Undisclosed principals

An undisclosed principal may enforce its rights under a charter, or may be the subject of an action by the other party to the charter to enforce its rights. *Kirno Hill Corp.* v. *Holt*, 618 F.2d 982, 984 (2d Cir. 1980); *Philippine Bulk Shipping Inc.* v. *International Minerals & Chemical Corp.*, 376 F.Supp. 654 (S.D.N.Y. 1973). At the same time, an agent acting for an undisclosed principal is a party to the charter, and will thus have all the rights and liabilities of its principal. See, e.g., *Hidrocarburos y Derivados C.A.* v. *Lemos*, 453 F.Supp. 160, 168 (S.D.N.Y. 1978).

An action against either the agent or the undisclosed principal will not be deemed an election of remedies which precludes an action against the other unless, of course, a judgment has been satisfied. Under New York law, this principle is embodied in CPLR §3002(*b*).

Agent's liability to principal

An agent is under a duty to act competently and carefully, and may be subject to liability to the principal for errors or omissions resulting from his failure to have the standard knowledge or to use the standard care required of one in his position. *Restatement (Second) of Agency* §379. For example, if a broker were to prepare and sign a charter which varied from the language authorized by the principal, he could be subject to liability to the principal for any damages which might result. Agents are by no means expected to perform according to a standard of perfection, and minor errors or carelessness ordinarily will not expose them to liability to the principal. They are obliged, however, to act in accordance with the standard of care one can reasonably expect of a charter broker.

Agents are also required to act within the scope of authority given by the principal. An agent may be liable to his principal for acts in excess of his authority which nonetheless bind the principal. As indicated above, an agent need not have each and every act he is to perform spelled out precisely. Indeed, unless specific instructions to the contrary are given, the agent is expected to exercise his discretion in carrying out his duties and is entitled to take the steps he considers appropriate to fulfill his task.

There is a broad range of remedies available to a principal whose agent has violated or threatens to violate his duty. The most important remedies include an action in contract for failure to carry out contract obligations; an action in tort for negligence in carrying out agency duties; an action for restitution; an action for an accounting; and an action for an injunction. See *Restatement (Second) of Agency* §399.

"Piercing corporate veils"

In an appropriate case, a party's "corporate veil" may be pierced and it may be held a party to the charter as the signatory's *alter ego*. See *Fisser* v. *International Bank*, 282 F.2d 231, 233–34 (2d Cir. 1960). There an action was brought by coal importers to compel International Bank to submit to arbitration a claim for breach of a contract of affreightment signed by the plaintiff and a third company, Allied Transportation. The court stated that, as a matter of law, International Bank could be held bound by the arbitration clause of the contract even though it had not signed the contract if the court found that the Bank was the *alter ego* of Allied. According to the court:

> [T]he consequence of applying the alter ego doctrine is that the corporation and those who have controlled it without regard to its separate entity are treated as but one entity, and, at least in the area of contracts, the acts of one are the acts of all . . . There is no reasonable basis for distinguishing between the parent's obligation to respond in damages for its instrumentality's breach of contract and its obligation to arbitrate the measure of those damages . . . We have heretofore held that the obligation to respond in damages arises from a contract to which the alter ego theory binds that parent which as "puppeteer" had "directed his marionette" to sign . . . We hold now that if the parent is bound to the contract then like its marionette it is bound to submit to arbitration. (282 F.2d at 234–35.)

The court went on to find, however, that on the facts before it, plaintiff failed to prove that Allied was a mere instrumentality of International, and held that International was not required to submit to arbitration. (282 F.2d at 235–41.)

It is difficult to set down precise guidelines for piercing corporate veils. Indeed, as Judge Mulligan aptly wrote in *Brunswick Corp.* v. *Waxman*, 599 F.2d 34, 35 (2d Cir. 1979): "New York law in this area is hardly as clear as a mountain lake in springtime." The same comment certainly can be made with respect to the prerequisites for piercing a corporate veil under the Federal maritime law.

The guiding concept for corporate veil piercing was set out in *Mull* v. *Colt Co.*, 31 F.R.D. 154, 162 (S.D.N.Y. 1962):

> The rule is well established that where corporations are organized, controlled and utilized so as to make them merely instrumentalities, agencies or conduits of another corporation, the corporate entity will be disregarded.

In *Brunswick Corp.* v. *Waxman*, above, the court adopted the comment of a leading commentator in the field, who stated: " 'what the formula comes down to, once shorn of verbiage about control, instrumentality, agency and corporate entity, is that liability is imposed to reach an equitable result.' Latty, *Subsidiaries and Affiliated Corporations 191* (1936)."

The Court of Appeals for the Second Circuit has specifically avoided making any attempt to lay down a precise formula, and instead, has set out factors to be considered on a case by case basis. The factors which count most include ownership, complete control and use of the corporation as an instrument to achieve the ends of the alleged *alter ego*. It is settled, however, that there must be a showing that the control by the *alter ego* was used to carry out a fraud or something akin to a fraud, or that the corporation was used without regard to its corporate form primarily as a conduit for purposes of the *alter ego*. *Interocean Shipping Co.* v. *National Shipping & Trading Corp.*, above.

Kirno Hill Corp. v. *Holt*, 618 F.2d 982 (2d Cir. 1980) provides a useful example of what facts must be proved in order to pierce a corporate veil. There it was alleged that an individual named Thomas J. Holt was the *alter ego* of Waterside-Pennsylvania, a corporation of which he was the sole owner, and, therefore, liable for charter hire payments owed by Waterside-Pennsylvania to the vessel owner. The court found that the facts did not meet the requirements for disregarding the corporate entity of Waterside-Pennsylvania:

> The prerequisites for piercing a corporate veil are as clear in federal maritime law as in Shoreside law: Holt must have used Waterside-Pennsylvania to perpetrate a fraud or have so dominated and disregarded Waterside-Pennsylvania's corporate form that Waterside-Pennsylvania primarily transacted Holt's personal business rather than its own corporate business . . . That Holt is the sole owner of Waterside-Pennsylvania does not alone justify piercing the corporate veil . . . ; indeed, individuals may incorporate for the very purpose of avoiding personal liability. (618 F.2d at 985.) (Citations omitted.)

There are a number of arbitration awards in which, contrary to well-settled law, commercial arbitrators have permitted a company to pierce its own corporate veil in order to assert a claim that belongs to an affiliate. In *The Baron Venture*, S.M.A. No. 2138 (Arb. at N.Y. 1985), the panel allowed a parent company which had chartered the vessel to prosecute a cargo loss claim which belonged to a subsidiary. The subsidiary was not a party to the charter or any arbitration agreement. Similar decisions were rendered in *The Volere*, S.M.A. No. 1885 (Arb. at N.Y. 1983); *The Trade Greece*, S.M.A. No. 1643 (Arb. at N.Y. 1982); and *The Velma*, S.M.A. No. 958 (Arb. at N.Y. 1975). While some arbitrators apparently see commercial equity in allowing such "short-cuts ", it is submitted that these decisions are manifestly in error as a matter of law.

A motion to vacate the award in *The Baron Venture* was brought by the charterer who was held liable for the cargo loss. The District Court agreed with the charterer that the award was legally incorrect, but concluded that it was not in manifest desregard of the law since "the arbitrators explicitly understood their outcome to be grounded in established precedent and practice". *Fried, Krupp GmbH* v. *Solidarity Carriers Inc.*, 674 F. Supp. 1022, 1027, 1988 AMC 1383 (S.D.N.Y. 1987), aff'd w.o. opinion, 838 F.2d 1202 (2d Cir. 1987). See discussion below, at page 390.

Guarantors

A guarantor of one party's obligations under a charter is not a party to the contract. *Interocean Shipping Co.* v. *National Shipping and Trading Corp.*, above. Unless the charter provides otherwise, a guarantor may be looked to only after there has been a default in the performance of the obligations he has undertaken to guarantee.

Ordinarily, the guarantor will not be deemed to be bound by the arbitration clause in the charter. See, e.g., *Cordoba Shipping Co. Ltd.* v. *Maro Shipping Ltd.*, 494 F.Supp. 1183, 1980 AMC 1945 (D.Conn. 1980), holding that a guarantor was not bound by the arbitration clause where its performance contract was silent as to how disputes were to be resolved and the charter provided for arbitration of disputes between "owners and charterers".

There have been instances, however, where a guarantor was held to be bound by the arbitration clause. In *Coastal States Gas Corp.* v. *Atlantic Tankers Ltd.*, 546 F.2d 15, 1976 AMC 2337 (2d Cir. 1976), the charterer's guarantor was held to be bound by the arbitration clause. There the charter provided that: "Any and all differences and disputes of whatsoever nature arising out of this charter shall be put to arbitration." According to the court, the guarantor "could have protected itself by coupling its guarantee . . . with a clause limiting arbitration to disputes between the original owner and [charterer] . . . Not having bargained for such protection, [it] cannot now obtain it from this court". (1976 AMC at 2340.)

The fact that the guarantor was bound into the arbitration provided the owner with substantial procedural advantages. The reason for this is that an agreement to act as a surety for obligations under a charter ordinarily is not a maritime contract and will, for example, be subject to state statutes of frauds. See *Interocean Shipping Co.* v. *National Shipping & Trading Corp.*, 462 F.2d 673, 678 (2d Cir. 1972). But see *Eagle Transport Ltd.* v. *O'Connor*, 449 F.Supp. 58 (S.D.N.Y. 1978), for an example of a guarantee that was held to be a maritime contract. In addition, the issuance of an award against a guarantor would save the owner from the necessity of bringing a separate action to establish its liability.

Arbitration agreements

The issue of whether a person is a party to an arbitration agreement in a charter is determinable by the court under the Federal Arbitration Act, 9 U.S.C. §4, by an action to compel arbitration. See *Interocean Shipping Co.* v. *National Shipping and Trading Corp.*, 462 F.2d 673, 676–77 (2d Cir. 1972); *In re Kinoshita & Co.*, 287 F.2d 951, 953 (2d Cir. 1961); *Almacenes Fernandez S.A.* v. *Golodetz*, 148 F.2d 625, 1961 AMC 1974 (2d Cir. 1945). See Discussion below at pages 375 to 376.

Description of the Ship

"4. of .... tons gross register, and .... tons net register, having engines of .... indicated horse power
5. and with hull, machinery and equipment in a thoroughly efficient state, and classed ....
....
6. at .... of about .... cubic feet bale capacity, and about .... tons of 2240 lbs.
7. deadweight capacity (cargo and bunkers, including fresh water and stores not exceeding one and one-half percent of ship's deadweight capacity,
8. allowing a minimum of fifty tons) on a draft of .... feet .... inches on .... Summer freeboard, inclusive of permanent bunkers,
9. which are of the capacity of about .... tons of fuel, and capable of steaming, fully laden, under good weather
10. conditions about .... knots on a consumption of about .... tons of best Welsh coal—best grade fuel oil—best grade Diesel oil,
11. now ...."

Introduction

In order to appreciate the effect of the description of the chartered ship in Lines 4 to 11 of the New York Produce form or the equivalent words in other time charter forms, it is necessary to consider the general principles of English law on the effect of statements and promises. Therefore an account of these principles is given at this point, which will be referred to throughout the book. The application of these principles to Lines 4 to 11 is discussed after this general section, under the following headings:

When the ship must comply with the description: page 60.
Delivery of ship not meeting her description: page 61.
Name of the ship: page 61.
Substitution and sale of the ship: pages 62 and 63.
Flag: page 64.
With hull, machinery and equipment in a thoroughly efficient state: page 64.
Statement as to class: page 69.
Bale and deadweight capacity: page 69.
Speed and fuel consumption: page 72.
Present position: page 74.

Statements made in the course of negotiations

(1) Statements giving rise to no liability

Vague or extravagant commendations (mere "puffs"), statements of pure opinion, and statements of intention in respect of which nothing is promised by the other party in return so that they lack "consideration", have no legal effect. See, for example, *Ecay* v. *Godfrey* (1947) 80 Ll.L.Rep. 286. But in a commercial context the courts will be slow to place statements into this category.

(2) Misrepresentations

A misrepresentation is a false statement (representation) of fact. A pure statement of opinion or of intention cannot amount to a misrepresentation. But a statement of opinion made during negotiations may involve an implied statement that there exist facts supporting such an opinion, or that the opinion is honestly held: then it may be a misrepresentation if there are no such facts or the opinion is not honestly held. Thus in *Cremdean Properties* v. *Nash* (1977) 244 E.G. 547, at page 551, Bridge, L.J., said: "I cannot see why one should not be making a representation when giving information or when stating one's opinion or belief."

In negotiations leading to a contract, silence, even about a material fact, will not amount to a representation: *Turner* v. *Green* [1895] 2 Ch. 205. But a statement which is only half true, in the sense that it discloses parts of the truth but conceals other parts, may be a misrepresentation: *Oakes* v. *Turquand* (1867) L.R. 2 H.L. 325. If a statement is made which is true at that time but subsequently becomes untrue to the knowledge of the party who made it and before the contract is concluded, failure to correct the statement is a misrepresentation: *With* v. *O'Flanagan* [1936] Ch. 575.

A misrepresentation gives remedies to the party to whom it is made only if it actually induced him to enter into the contract: see, for example, *The Lucy*, below. The misrepresentation need not be the sole inducement, but it must have been one inducement: see *Barton* v. *Armstrong* [1976] A.C. 104, at page 118. However, if the party to whom the misrepresentation is made knows, or discovers before relying on it, that it is untrue, then, provided he has full knowledge of the untruth, he will have no remedy for misrepresentation: *Begbie* v. *Phosphate Sewage* (1875) L.R. 10 Q.B. 491.

Rescission for misrepresentation

A party who has been induced to enter into a contract by a misrepresentation will usually have the right to rescind that contract, whether the misrepresentation was made fraudulently, negligently or innocently. Rescission means that he may refuse to perform (or perform further) and may take proceedings to recover money paid or property transferred: see, for example, *Goldsmith* v. *Rodger* [1962] 2 Lloyd's Rep. 249. But this right may be affected by the operation of Section 2(2) of the Misrepresentation Act 1967, and it may also be lost in some other circumstances which are summarised below.

The *Lucy* was sub-time chartered on the basis that, with certain stated exceptions, the terms of the sub-charter should be exactly in accordance with the existing head time charter, a copy of which was sent to the sub-charterers during the negotiations. In fact, in regard to trading outside Institute Warranty Limits the head time charter did not reflect the actual agreement between the owners and the head charterers. When, after the sub-charter had been running for about nine months, the sub-charterers learned of this they purported to rescind. It was held by Mustill, J., that the sending of the copy of the head charter to the sub-charterers, without disclosing (innocently) the actual agreement, amounted to an implied misrepresentation which was capable of justifying rescission; but that on the evidence the sub-charterers had not relied on the terms as to trading outside Institute Warranty Limits in entering into the charter. They were, therefore, not entitled to rescind.

Mustill, J., observed at page 202, *obiter*, that had he reached a different conclusion on the evidence, he would have been disposed to hold that "in the case of an innocent misrepresentation inducing a contract for the performance of services, it is not a bar to rescission that the contract has been partially performed, although the imposition of some order for the payment of money as an adjunct to the order for rescission (or a declaration that a prior rescission was valid) will often be required, in order to bring about a full adjustment of the equitable rights of the parties". It would, therefore, have been open to the court to have ordered rescission and he would then have been concerned with the exercise of a discretion under Section 2(2) of the Misrepresentation Act 1967 to order damages as an alternative to rescission (as to which see below).

The Lucy [1983] 1 Lloyd's Rep. 188.

Misrepresentation Act 1967, Section 2(2)

This provision confers upon the court or arbitrator the power to award damages instead of rescission "if of opinion that it would be equitable to do so, having regard to the nature of the misrepresentation and the loss that would be caused by it if the contract were upheld, as well as to the loss that rescission would cause to the other party". In effect it gives a discretion to the court or arbitrator to remove the right to rescind and replace it with damages when this seems fair. It does not, however, apply where the misrepresentation was fraudulent (see below).

Mustill, J., in *The Lucy*, above, remarked that although in his view Section 2(2) of the Act must entitle the court to annul retrospectively a rescission that has taken place in the past the exercise of the discretion in such circumstances gave rise to formidable difficulties. The difficulties had been reduced in the case of *The Lucy* because the sub-charterers' purported rescission had not been accepted as a repudiation and the charter had continued until the ship was redelivered under a without prejudice agreement. He would have exercised the discretion in favour of an award of damages instead of rescission because the damage to the head charterers which would ensue from having the ship returned to them by the sub-charterers on a collapsing spot market would be great; there was no evidence that there would have been any material differences in the rate of sub-charter hire consequent upon the special agreement between the owners and the head charterers; and even if the misrepresentation had induced the charter, it was of quite a trivial nature.

Loss of the right to rescind in other circumstances

The right to rescind may also be lost, (*a*) where the party originally entitled to rescind knows the relevant facts but nevertheless expressly or impliedly declares that he will go on with the contract: see the judgment of Sellers, L.J., in *Car and Universal Finance* v. *Caldwell* [1965] 1 Q.B. 525, at page 550, and *Long* v. *Lloyd* [1958] 1 W.L.R. 753; or (*b*) where that party can no longer restore the other party to substantially the same position he was in before the contract: see *Spence* v. *Crawford* [1939] 3 All E.R. 271, and *The Lucy* [1983] 1 Lloyd's Rep. 188, above; or (*c*) where an innocent third party has in the meantime acquired an interest in the subject matter of the contract: see *Clough* v. *L. & N.W.R.* (1871), L.R. 7 Exch. 26; or (*d*) where a party originally entitled to rescind for innocent misrepresentation fails for a long time to do so: see *Leaf* v. *International Galleries* [1950] 2 K.B. 86. Where the right to rescind has been lost, it seems that the power to award damages under Section 2(2) of the Misrepresentation Act cannot be exercised (although damages may be available under Section 2(1)).

Damages for misrepresentation

Damages may be claimed by the party to whom the misrepresentation has been made in the following cases.

(1) *Fraudulent misrepresentation*

A party who suffers loss through relying on a fraudulent misrepresentation is entitled not only to rescind the contract (see above) but also to claim damages in tort for deceit. A fraudulent misrepresentation is one "made (1) knowingly, or (2) without belief in its truth, or (3) recklessly, careless whether it be true or false": Lord Herschell in *Derry* v. *Peek* (1889) 14 App. Cas. 337.

(2) *Negligent misrepresentation as a tort*

A party to whom a negligent misrepresentation has been made may be entitled to recover damages in tort: see *Hedley Byrne* v. *Heller* [1963] 1 Lloyd's Rep. 485. But the circumstances in which the misrepresentation was made must have been such as to impose a duty of care upon the party making it, and it is not entirely clear when such a duty arises: see *Esso Petroleum* v. *Mardon* [1976] 2 Lloyd's Rep. 305. It is difficult to envisage a negligent misrepresentation made prior to contract by a person who becomes a party to that contract which would not be covered by Section 2(1) of the Misrepresentation Act 1967: and, as it is in any case easier for a claimant to succeed under that section because of its reversal of the burden of proof, the importance of the remedy in tort now seems slight—save where the misrepresentation has been made by a person who does not become a party to the contract, or where no contract is subsequently made.

(3) *Negligent misrepresentation under the Misrepresentation Act, Section 2(1)*

Where a party has entered into a contract after a misrepresentation has been made to him and he has suffered loss as a result, he may recover damages from the party making the misrepresentation, unless that party "proves that he had reasonable ground to believe and did believe up to the time the contract was made that the facts represented were true": Misrepresentation Act 1967, Section 2(1). For a case in which the owner of barges was held not to have had reasonable ground for his misstatement of their deadweight capacity (but it was not clear that the other party could have proved negligence), see *Howard Marine* v. *Ogden* [1978] 1 Lloyd's Rep. 334.

Only a principal can be held liable under Section 2(1) of the Act; the wording of the section is not apt to include an agent: *The Skopas* [1983] 1 Lloyd's Rep. 431.

(4) *Misrepresentation as a breach of a collateral contract*

Sometimes a representation can be treated as part of a separate and "collateral" contract—the truth of the statement is promised in return for the other party's entering into the main contract. Where this is so the promise will usually be treated as absolute, and so liability for the misrepresentation will not depend on proof of negligence. Sometimes, however, the party making the representation is treated as promising only that he has exercised reasonable care in making the representation, or in the investigations preceding it: in such a case the liablity will be very similar to that in negligence and (save that there is no requirement that the person making the representation become a party to the contract) to that under Section 2(1) of the Misrepresentation Act 1967: see *Esso Petroleum* v. *Mardon* [1976] 2 Lloyd's Rep. 305, where both liabilities were found to exist in respect to predictions as to the likely throughput of a petrol station.

For an example of a case in which statements (as to the "estimated speed" of a motor cruiser) were held not to amount to promises, see *Savage* v. *Blakney* (1970) 119 C.L.R. 435. See also *Howard Marine* v. *Ogden*, above, where no collateral contract was found.

In all the above situations the damages awarded would in general be such as to compensate the other party for loss suffered in reliance upon the misrepresentation, but not for loss of profits expected on the main contract as these can be recovered only in an action for breach of that contract. But damages for fraud might in appropriate cases go somewhat further than those for negligence (see *Doyle* v. *Olby* [1969] 2 Q.B. 158), and the special wording of Section 2(1) of the Misrepresentation Act 1967 suggests that the rules for fraud may also apply to the calculation of damages under that Section: see *André & Cie. S.A.* v. *Ets. Michel Blanc & Fils* [1977] 2 Lloyd's Rep. 166, 181 (affirmed without reference to this point [1979] 2 Lloyd's Rep. 427); see also *Archer* v. *Brown* [1985] Q.B. 401.

(5) *Damages under Section 2(2) of the Misrepresentation Act 1967*

A court or arbitrator may refuse rescission for misrepresentation under this provision (see above) and award damages instead. There is no indication as to how these are to be calculated, save that Section 2(3) implies that the calculation would not be the same as under Section 2(1). A more limited award, perhaps compensating only for the fact that the contract is not rescinded, seems to be contemplated.

Clauses excluding liability for misrepresentation

By Section 3 of the 1967 Act, as amended by Section 8(1) of the Unfair Contract Terms Act 1977, if a contract contains a provision excluding or restricting liability for any misrepresentation made before the contract was made or any remedy for such misrepresentation, that provision shall be of no effect except in so far as it is held to have been a fair and reasonable one to be included, having regard to the circumstances which were, or ought reasonably to have been, known to the parties when the contract was made. Unlike the Unfair Contract Terms Act itself (see Section 27 and Schedule 2), this provision is applicable to charterparties and other maritime and international contracts; it applies, therefore, whenever the proper law of the charter is English (for the proper law of a charter, see page 363 below). A clause indicating that statements should not be relied upon is caught by it: *Cremdean Properties* v. *Nash* (1977) 244 E.G. 547, but a clause denying authority to agents to make representations is not: *Overbrooke Estates* v. *Glencombe Properties* [1974] 1 W.L.R. 1335. See also *Waller* v. *Boyle* [1982] 1 W.L.R. 495. A shipping case in which it was applied in its original, slightly different, form is *Howard Marine* v. *Ogden* [1978] 1 Lloyd's Rep. 334.

Misrepresentation becoming part of a contract

Normally a misrepresentation is made before the contract is concluded and cannot be regarded as incorporated into it, either because of its distance in time from the contract or because of the rule that oral evidence cannot be given to contradict or vary the terms of a written contract (the "parol evidence rule"). But sometimes a misrepresentation made during negotiations is repeated as part of the eventual contract itself. Also, such a misrepresentation may occasionally be treated as a term of the contract because the contract is held to be partly in writing and partly oral, so that the parol evidence rule does not apply: see *The Ardennes* (1950) 84 Ll.L.Rep. 340, and *Evans* v. *Merzario* [1976] 2 Lloyd's Rep. 165. Further, a misrepresentation may be treated as one side of a collateral contract, see page 51 above, in which case an action will lie (notwithstanding inconsistency with the main written contract) upon the collateral but not upon the main contract: see *City and Westminster Properties* v. *Mudd* [1959] Ch. 129.

Where a misrepresentation has been incorporated into the contract, the normal remedies for breach (see page 54 below) will be available and will usually be adequate. But it seems likely that any right to sue in tort remains, which, subject to proof of negligence, may occasionally be of advantage, for example in connection with assessment of damages, jurisdiction and time limits on actions: see *Midland Bank Trust* v. *Hett, Stubbs and Kemp* [1979] Ch. 384. Moreover, it is provided by statute that the fact that the misrepresentation has become a contractual term does not prevent rescission of the contract by a party to whom the misrepresentation has been made: Section 1 of the 1967 Act. For example, a charterer may be entitled to throw up the charter because of some misdescription of the ship by the owners during the negotiations, despite the fact that the corresponding particular term of the charter is not a condition and the breach insufficiently serious to go to the root of the contract. However, arbitrators or the courts might well, in practice, use their discretion under Section 2(2) to award damages in lieu of rescission. In the case of a fraudulent misrepresentation the charterer has, as before, a right to throw up the charter despite the incorporation of the misrepresentation into the charter, and Section 2(2) has no application.

Terms of the contract

Some terms of a charter are clearly promises that certain events will come about. For example, Clauses 1 to 5 of the New York Produce form are promises of this type. Other terms are not expressed as promises but as statements, such as those in Lines 4 to 11 of the same form. But these terms may nevertheless be treated as contractual promises, in that the party making the statements may be taken to promise that they are true. Thus, for example, the statement "expected ready to load under this charter" was held, in *The Mihalis Angelos* [1970] 2 Lloyd's Rep. 43, to contain a promise that such an expectation was reasonably held.

"De minimis" rule

In considering whether any contractual obligation in a commercial contract has been broken, any divergence from the performance required by the contract which is negligible will be disregarded: *Margaronis Navigation* v. *Peabody* [1964] 2 Lloyd's Rep. 153.

In that case, Sellers, L.J., said: "It seems to me that in all cases the Court is called upon to consider the substance of the matter and will not regard or give effect to what are undoubtedly, in the view of the Court, trivialities, matters of little moment, of a trifling and negligible nature." Diplock, L.J., said: "It seems to me that the law has always regarded a contract to deliver or load a specified quantity of goods as satisfied if that quantity has been delivered within the margin of error which it is not commercially practicable to avoid . . . "

Remedies for breach of contract

Damages

The basic remedy for breach of contract in English law is an action for damages.

Orders for specific performance and injunctions

Specific performance of a time charter will not be granted, although the position may be different in the case of a demise charter: *De Mattos* v. *Gibson* (1858) 4 De G. & J. 276; *The Scaptrade* [1983] 2 Lloyd's Rep. 253, 256.

Further, the courts have no jurisdiction to grant an injunction restraining an owner from exercising his right of withdrawal from the service of the charterers under a withdrawal clause in a time charter, although again the position may be different under a demise charter. Lord Diplock so stated, *obiter*, in the House of Lords in *The Scaptrade* [1983] 2 Lloyd's Rep. 253 in holding that the equitable remedy of relief from forfeiture was not applicable to withdrawal under a time charter withdrawal clause: see page 209 below. He said, at page 256 of the report: "A time charter, unless it is a charter by demise, with which your Lordships are not here concerned, transfers to the charterer no interest in or right to possession of the vessel; it is a contract for services to be rendered to the charterer by the shipowner through the use of the vessel by the shipowner's own servants, the master and the crew, acting in accordance with such directions as to the cargoes to be loaded and the voyages to be undertaken as by the terms of the charter-party the charterer is entitled to give to them . . . To grant an injunction restraining the shipowner from exercising his right of withdrawal of the vessel from the service of the charterer, though negative in form, is pregnant with an affirmative order to the shipowner to perform the contract; juristically it is indistinguishable from a decree for specific performance of a contract to render services; and in respect of that category of contracts, even in the event of breach, this is a remedy that English Courts have always disclaimed any jurisdiction to grant."

Nevertheless the practice of granting temporary injunctions restraining the owners or other parties interested in the ship from employing the ship in such a way as to prevent performance of the charter, has a long history: see *De Mattos* v. *Gibson* (1858) 4 De G. & J. 276, 299; *Sevin* v. *Deslands* (1860) 30 L.J. (Ch.) 457; *Whitwood Chemical Co.* v. *Hardman* [1891] 2 Ch. 416, 431 and page 63 below. So owners have been restrained from employing their ship otherwise than in accordance with the charter where they have withdrawn or threatened to withdraw their ship from the charter and the charterers have disputed their right to do so. Interim injunctions have been granted in such cases until the dispute could be heard and decided; the object being to preserve the *status quo* pending resolution of the dispute. See *The Georgios C* [1971] 1 Lloyd's Rep. 7; *The Oakworth* [1975] 1 Lloyd's Rep. 581 and *The Balder London* (*No. 2*) [1983] 1 Lloyd's Rep. 492. It is not thought that the power to grant temporary injunctions in such terms is affected by the pronouncement of Lord Diplock in *The Scaptrade*, above. But it now seems that injunctions in terms "restraining the owners from withdrawing the vessel from the service of the charterers" (see for example *The Chrysovalandou Dyo* [1981] 1 Lloyd's Rep. 159, 162), are not within the court's power to grant.

Right to treat contract as discharged

Where the breach is sufficiently serious the innocent party may also be entitled to "treat the contract as discharged" or "repudiated", refuse to perform or perform further, and sue for recovery of money paid or property transferred. This process is sometimes also referred to as "termination", "cancellation" or "rescission" of the contract: but this is not the same as rescission for a misrepresentation made during negotiations for a contract, as to which see above; nor is it the same as termination or cancellation in accordance with specific rights agreed to in and conferred by the contract itself where the rights of the innocent party depend not on general principles but on the precise terms of the contract itself (for the right of cancellation under a charter see page 287 below and for charter withdrawal clauses see page 206 below).

It should be noted that the right to treat the contract as discharged does not affect the right to damages for the breach. Indeed, the exercise of the former right may well increase the damages payable, which will cover the loss of all or the remaining part of the contract and not merely the loss that would have arisen from the breach had the contract continued. If the innocent party purports to treat the contract as discharged when in law the breach is not sufficiently serious to give him this right, he himself becomes in breach and may be exposed to extensive damages: see *The Hongkong Fir* [1961] 2 Lloyd's Rep. 478, page 65 below. There is in general no right at common law to suspend performance merely because it is uncertain whether the other party will be able to perform or to continue performance. (But particular clauses may give a right to suspend performance: see the off-hire clause, page 295 below.)

Classification of contractual terms

In determining whether the innocent party has the right to treat the contract as discharged it seems that regard must first be had to the nature of the contractual term that has been breached: see *Bunge* v. *Tradax* [1981] 2 Lloyd's Rep. 1. For this purpose the breached term may be placed in one of three categories, namely *conditions*, *warranties* and *intermediate* (or *innominate*) *terms*. This classification is carried out by construing the particular term and the contract in which it appears, rather than by consideration of the seriousness of the breach of that term that has taken place in the instant case; see *Bunge* v. *Tradax*, above.

Conditions

A condition in this context (see below for other uses of this word) is a term of the contract that is of such importance that *any* breach of it will entitle the innocent party to treat the whole contract as discharged. It will arise where, in the words of Lord Diplock in *Photo Production* v. *Securicor* [1980] 1 Lloyd's Rep. 545, at page 553, "the contracting parties have agreed, whether by express words or by implication of law, that *any* failure by one party to perform a particular . . . obligation . . . , irrespective of the gravity of the event that has in fact resulted from the breach, shall entitle the other party to elect to put an end to all . . . obligation[s] of both parties remaining unperformed". For comment on the circumstances in which contractual terms will be so classified, see below.

Warranties

A warranty in this context (see below for other uses of the word) is a term of the contract of such minor importance that *no* breach of it will entitle the innocent party to treat the whole contract as discharged. For breach of such a term the innocent party can make only a claim for damages.

Intermediate (or innominate) terms

Any term of the contract which cannot be classified as a condition or a warranty will be classified as an intermediate (or innominate) term. Whether a breach of such a term does or does not entitle the innocent party to treat the contract as discharged depends on the nature and consequences of the particular breach that has occurred. The court will enquire, in the words of Lord Diplock in *Photo Production* v. *Securicor*, above, at page 553, whether "the event resulting . . . has the effect of depriving the other party of substantially the whole benefit which it was the intention of the parties that he should obtain from the contract". If the event has this effect, the innocent party may treat the contract as discharged; otherwise he can make only a claim for damages.

Other uses of the word "condition"

It may be noted that the use of the word "condition" as a label for a particular term, explained above, is, although well established as a special usage of English law, somewhat unsatisfactory, as it confuses the notions of "promise" and "condition". It is actually the *performance* of the contractual promise (or willingness to perform it) that is the condition of the other party's duty to proceed with the contract.

Since the word "condition" can be used in other senses, it is important that judgments and contracts using the word be read with care. This is particularly so because a contractual term may exist as a "condition" in the more accurate sense of the word. That is to say that no promise is made that it will happen; if it does not then no cause of action arises, but the obligation of the other party to perform his part of the bargain does not arise.

Other uses of the word "warranty"

In the sense used here a warranty simply means an unimportant contractual promise. Its use in contracts of marine insurance is quite different. It is also used, particularly in earlier cases, to describe contractual obligations which certainly are not so classified in this context; the expression "the warranty of seaworthiness" is particularly misleading as terms relating to seaworthiness are in this context intermediate (or innominate) terms, see *The Hongkong Fir* [1961] 2 Lloyd's Rep. 478, *The Ymnos* [1982] 2 Lloyd's Rep. 574 and page 65 below.

It may be argued that there is little value in maintaining a category of warranties separate from intermediate (or innominate) terms, for, if it can be determined in advance that no breach of a contractual term would be sufficiently serious to justify the innocent party treating the contract as discharged, the correct result would be achieved equally well if that term had been classified not as a warranty but as an intermediate (or innominate) term. The judgment of Ormrod, L.J., in *The Hansa Nord* [1975] 2 Lloyd's Rep. 445, at page 466, suggested that the separate category of warranties might indeed be fading away. But the House of Lords in *Bunge* v. *Tradax* [1981] 2 Lloyd's Rep. 1, assumed the existence of this separate category and it remains important to appreciate the meaning attributed to the word "warranty" in this context.

Conflict between the desires for commercial certainty and for equity

It is apparent from the leading cases, from *The Hongkong Fir* [1961] 2 Lloyd's Rep. 478 to *Bunge* v. *Tradax* [1981] 2 Lloyd's Rep. 1, that the courts are seeking to strike a balance between the sometimes conflicting principles that there should be certainty in the relationships of parties to commercial contracts and that justice between those parties should not be prevented by over-rigid rules. The knowledge (available in advance) that any breach of certain terms of a contract will allow the innocent party to treat the contract as discharged, without the necessity for examination of the seriousness of the breach or its consequences, promotes certainty and is the justification for maintaining the concept of conditions.

On the other hand, the fact that a party may escape from what has turned out to be a disadvantageous contract because a condition has been broken, despite the fact that the breach may be technical and may not really have prejudiced him, suggests that as many terms as possible should be classed as intermediate rather than as conditions. As Roskill, L.J., said in *The Hansa Nord* [1975] 2 Lloyd's Rep. 445 at page 457: "In principle contracts are made to be performed and not to be avoided according to the whims of market fluctuation." This approach does not allow escape from the contract unless the results of the breach are sufficiently serious to justify it. The test applied (see page 55 above) is not at all favourable to treating the contract as discharged. Thus in *The Hongkong Fir* (see below page 65) under a 24-month time charter the ship was by reason of her unseaworthiness unavailable to the charterers for some 20 weeks out of the first six months, yet it was held that the breach was not serious enough (the unseaworthiness having been rectified at the end of that period) to justify the discharge of the charter. This approach is also open to the criticism that whether the breach was sufficiently serious to allow discharge may not be known for some time, and even when the facts are clear a lengthy process of arbitration or litigation may be necessary to determine the rights of the innocent party.

The balance between these principles that the courts now seek is illustrated by the comments of Lord Roskill in *Bunge* v. *Tradax* [1981] 2 Lloyd's Rep. 1, at page 14: "In short, while recognizing the modern approach and not being over ready to construe terms as conditions unless the contract clearly requires the Court so to do, none the less the basic principles of construction for determining whether or not a particular term is a condition remain as before, always bearing in mind on the one hand the need for certainty and on the other the desirability of not, where legitimate, allowing rescission where the breach complained of is highly technical and where damages would clearly be an adequate remedy."

When terms will be treated as conditions

In *Bunge* v. *Tradax*, above, the House of Lords made it clear that, in the words of Lord Wilberforce at page 6, "the Courts should not be too ready to interpret contractual clauses as conditions". But terms will be so classified, it seems, in the following cases:

1. Where the obligation is designated as a condition in a statute. This is not relevant in

time charter law; but as examples see Sections 13, 14 and 15 of the Sale of Goods Act 1979.

2. Where the obligation is specifically designated in the contract as a condition. But this is not conclusive, and the context of the whole contract may suggest that the word "condition" should not be read in its technical sense: see *Wickman* v. *Schuler* [1973] 2 Lloyd's Rep. 53.

3. Where the obligation has been held to be a condition in another case. The "expected ready to load" provision in a voyage charter was held to be a condition, partly on this ground, in *The Mihalis Angelos* [1970] 2 Lloyd's Rep. 43. But in *The Diana Prosperity* [1976] 2 Lloyd's Rep. 621, at page 626, Lord Wilberforce suggested that some of the earlier cases on sale of goods might require reconsideration, and, although he did not refer to other types of contract, it is clear that the conclusiveness of earlier case law on this point cannot be taken entirely for granted.

4. Where the supposed intention of the parties, as indicated from the terms and general background of the contract, so indicate. In *Bunge* v. *Tradax*, above, Lord Wilberforce suggested that this is usually so in cases of "time clauses in mercantile contracts": and Lord Roskill said that the same is true "where a term has to be performed by one party as a condition precedent to the ability of the other party to perform another term" (in that case, an f.o.b. buyer's statement of his ship's e.t.a. in the U.S. Gulf as a condition precedent to the seller's duty to nominate a loading port). See also *The Mavro Vetranic* [1985] 1 Lloyd's Rep. 580 (nomination of ship under contract of affreightment to be made "twenty days prior to ETA") and *Gill & Duffus* v. *Société pour l'Exportation des Sucres S.A.* [1986] 1 Lloyd's Rep. 322 (port of shipment to be specified by a given date "at latest"). The fact that performance of other contracts depends on the performance of the contract under consideration (as in "string" sales) is another indication.

In a case prior to *The Hongkong Fir* where particular details as to a tanker's cargo lines and heating coils (of great importance in connection with the charterers' intended use of the ship) were "guaranteed" by the owners, it was held that this part of the description was a condition of the charter.

The tanker *Vendémiaire* was chartered for a period of 12 months with a cancelling date of 15 July. Statements which had been made in the course of negotiations as to the diameter of the ship's cargo lines and as to the position of heating coils were embodied in the charter as "guaranteed" by the owners. These matters were of great importance to the charterers because of their intended use of the ship for the carriage of molasses. On 11 and 12 June, the ship's cargo lines and heating coils were inspected by the charterers' superintendent and found not to conform with the description given. The charterers thereupon informed the owners that they were not bound to take delivery but were prepared to do so if the ship was made to conform with the description. The owners did not effect the alteration and on 25 June tendered delivery. Delivery was refused by the charterers on the ground that the ship did not tally with the description. Finally, when the owners continued to insist on the charterers taking delivery (but without effecting any alterations) the charterers on 30 June cancelled the charter.

It was held by Branson, J., that they were entitled to do so. He said: "I think that the word 'guarantee' . . . shows an intention to lay a special emphasis upon the obligations assumed under these clauses and to treat them as conditions of the contract as distinguished from mere warranties."

Pennsylvania Shipping v. *Cie. Nationale de Navigation* (1936) 55 Ll.L.Rep. 271.

If a similar case were before the courts today, the clauses containing the guaranteed particulars of the ship's cargo lines and heating coils which were categorised in the *Pennsylvania Shipping* case as conditions might well be put in the category of intermediate terms, although no doubt the result would be the same. In *The Ymnos* [1982] 2 Lloyd's

Rep. 574, which was time-chartered for the charterers' container services, the charter contained a term: "Owners guarantee the loading of the containers . . . without any stability problem". In fact there were stability problems, but they were related to the closing stages of loading or the early stages of discharge and might be slight or serious in effect. They could be remedied by the use of shore cranes or, if these were not available, might result in a smaller or larger number of containers being shut out. It was held by Robert Goff, J., on the authority of *The Hongkong Fir*, that since the term was one of which there might be breaches of varying degrees of seriousness, it was not properly to be classified as a condition. The use of the word "guarantee" meant no more, in the clause in question, than that any stability problem during loading of the contractual number of containers would result in a breach of contract by the owners. It did not require the provision to be construed as a condition rather than an intermediate term.

It is not clear to what extent the fact that a stipulation is reinforced by a clause allowing one party to terminate the contract (for example a withdrawal or cancelling clause) indicates that it is a condition. In *The Mihalis Angelos* [1970] 1 Lloyd's Rep. 118 at first instance Mocatta, J., treated the presence of a cancelling clause as tending towards the conclusion that the "expected ready to load" provision was *not* a condition. The decision was reversed by the Court of Appeal. In principle, however, it is clear that such a clause is a specific facility for the party benefited and does not by implication determine the basis of the contractual obligations: see *The Heron II* [1967] 2 Lloyd's Rep. 457, at page 486 (a cancelling clause in a voyage charter does not set a time scale so as to displace the obligation of reasonable dispatch). For the nature of a time charter withdrawal clause, see page 194 below.

Where the term broken is one which can be broken in many ways leading to great potential variety of consequences, it is unlikely to be interpreted as a condition. In the leading case of *The Hongkong Fir*, the stipulation as to seaworthiness in a time charter was on such grounds interpreted as an intermediate term: see below, page 65; and see the explanation of this case by Donaldson, J., in *Toepfer* v. *Lenersan-Poortman* [1978] 2 Lloyd's Rep. 555 (affirmed [1980] 1 Lloyd's Rep. 143).

Waiver and affirmation

A party who has become entitled, by breach of the contract by the other party, to treat the contract as discharged may lose the right to do so if he "waives" the breach. Similarly, an owner who has become entitled to exercise his option to withdraw his ship under Clause 5 of the New York Produce form because the charterer has failed to make timely payment of hire may lose the right to do so if he is held to have waived that right; see pages 211 to 214 below.

It is possible for the innocent party to waive his right to damages for the breach as well as his right to treat the contract as discharged. This may occur where he represents to the party in breach that he will not enforce these rights; the court may prevent him from going back on this representation "where it would be inequitable having regard to the dealings which have thus taken place between the parties" (*per* Lord Cairns in *Hughes* v. *Metropolitan Railway* (1877) 2 App. Cas. 439, at page 448; see also *Birmingham & District Land Co.* v. *L.N.W.R.* (1888) 40 Ch.D. 268). Although the law in this area is still developing, it seems that for the innocent party to lose both his right to treat the contract as discharged and his right to damages, (*a*) he must be shown to have known or to have had obvious means of knowing of the breach, (*b*) he must make a clear representation that he will not enforce those rights (although this need not involve actually saying "we hereby waive"), and (*c*) the other party must, in reliance upon this representation, act or fail to act in such a way as to make it inequitable for the innocent party to go back on his representation. Requirement (*c*) will clearly be satisfied if it has become impossible for the other party to fulfil his obligation: but the contrary will be true if, upon notice that the innocent party intends to resume his full rights, the other party can recover his position in full. See *Bremer* v. *Vanden* [1978] 2 Lloyd's Rep. 109, *Bremer* v. *Mackprang* [1979] 1 Lloyd's Rep. 221 and *The Post Chaser* [1981] 2 Lloyd's Rep. 695.

Where the party in breach makes a more restricted allegation than that so far considered, namely that the innocent party has waived only his right to treat the contract as discharged (keeping open his right to claim damages), less is demanded of him by the courts. Waiver in this more limited sense is also referred to as "affirmation", that is to say affirmation of the contract's continued existence but with no waiver of any right to damages. This type of waiver may be seen as arising from an "election" to maintain or terminate the contract which, once made, cannot be revoked. In *The Mihalios Xilas* [1979] 2 Lloyd's Rep. 303 (see page 214 below) Lord Scarman approached in this way the question of whether owners had waived their right to withdraw under the Baltime Clause 6 for non-payment of hire: "The present case is concerned with the process of election. The consequence of the election, if established, is the abandonment, i.e., the waiver, of a right . . . When a man, faced with two alternative and mutually exclusive courses of action, chooses one and has communicated his choice to the person concerned in such a way as to lead him to believe that he has made his choice, he has completed his election."

In a helpful analysis of this type of waiver in *The Athos* [1981] 2 Lloyd's Rep. 74, approved by the Court of Appeal [1983] 1 Lloyd's Rep. 127, Neill, J., said: "there is no need to show that the other party acted to his detriment or changed his position in reliance on the election"; compare requirement (*c*) above.

But a party who has the right to treat the contract as discharged will not usually be held to have elected to waive that right unless he had actual knowledge of the breach and knowledge of his right of choice; see *Peyman* v. *Lanjani* [1985] Ch.457 and *The Uhenbels* [1986] 2 Lloyd's Rep. 294, at page 298. It is, however, sometimes possible that a party who did not know of his rights may be estopped from alleging that he has not elected; see the difficult and controversial cases of *Panchaud Frères* v. *Etablissements General Grain* [1970] 1 Lloyd's Rep. 53 and *Peyman* v. *Lanjani*, above.

The particular items of description

When the ship must comply with the description

In general, the descriptive details of the ship inserted in the charter have to be correct at the time the charter is entered into. In the case of speed, however, it has been said that the ship must accord with her description at the time of delivery (see "Speed and fuel consumption" below). It is suggested that the preferable view is that the obligation on the owners is to provide a ship which has the characteristics described at the time the charter is entered into; but a term is to be implied that after that date the owners will not so alter the characteristics of the ship as to render services to the charterers substantially different or less valuable than those contracted for: see *Isaacs* v. *McAllum* (1921) 6 Ll.L.Rep. 289 and page 64 below.

Delivery of ship not meeting her description

If the ship is misdescribed by the owners in the charter and the misdescription is discovered by the charterers before or upon delivery, the question arises whether delivery may be refused or whether the charterers must accept delivery and claim damages for any loss suffered as a result of the misdescription. The answer, it seems, depends in part on which element of the description is inaccurate and in part on the seriousness of the misdescription.

It was argued in *The Diana Prosperity* [1976] 2 Lloyd's Rep. 60 and 621, the facts of which are set out below, that by analogy with certain contracts for the sale of goods, any inaccuracy in any part of the description of the ship entitled the charterers to refuse delivery and to treat the contract as discharged. On this analogy each element of the description must be assumed to be vital and thus must be a condition of the contract, breach of which entitles the charterers (irrespective of the seriousness of the breach) to reject.

Neither Lord Denning, M.R., in the Court of Appeal, nor Lord Wilberforce in the House of Lords, was prepared to accept this argument. Lord Wilberforce (with whom Lord Simon and Lord Kilbrandon agreed) expressed the opinion that the earlier sale of goods cases might have to be reviewed and that in any event they were not applicable in the case of time charters. In their view only those parts of the description of the ship which could be said to be "substantial ingredients" of the ship's "identity" could be regarded as conditions of the contract: see [1976] 2 Lloyd's Rep. at page 626. (For the meaning of "conditions" see page 55 above.)

Insofar as the elements of the description of the ship are not conditions the charterers will, it seems, only have the right to refuse delivery and to treat the charter as terminated if either:

(1) the total effect of the misdescription is so serious that it goes to the root of the contract and deprives the charterers of substantially the whole benefit of the contract (see *The Diana Prosperity* [1976] 2 Lloyd's Rep. at pages 72 and 627 and *Cargo Ships El-Yam* v. *Invotra* [1958] 1 Lloyd's Rep. 39, at page 52); or

(2) the owners refuse or fail to take steps to make the ship comply with the description in such manner that their refusal or failure shows an intention no longer to be bound by the contract and so amounts to a repudiation of the charter (see page 66 below); or

(3) the misdescription is such that the owners are unable by the cancelling date to satisfy the requirements of readiness or fitness, for the purposes of the cancelling clause, and the charterers thereupon cancel (see page 287 below).

Name of the ship

The charter is for the named ship alone and the charterers cannot be required to accept delivery under it of another, even of identical characteristics. But where the charter is for a ship which has yet to be built and named, the ship tendered for delivery will be regarded as complying with the contract if she can be readily identified as the ship chartered from the words or number used in the charter to identify the ship.

Disponent owners of a ship to be built, time chartered her on the Shelltime 3 form, describing her in the charter as "to be built by Osaka Shipbuilding Co. Ltd. and known as Hull No. 354 until named". The charterers sub-chartered her on the same form, describing her in the sub-charter as "Newbuilding motor tank vessel called Yard No. 354 at Osaka Zosen". The Osaka yard had in their books a ship bearing that number, but she had been too large for them to build and had, therefore, been sub-contracted to another Japanese yard, Oshima. This yard was 300 miles away, but the Osaka yard had a substantial financial and management involvement in it and they were to supervise the building of this ship. This arrangement was in accordance with the usual practice in Japan. The ship continued on the Osaka books as No. 354 but was also given an Oshima number, 004. The House of Lords held that neither the head charterers nor the sub-charterers could refuse to accept delivery of that ship. If (which the majority considered was not the case) it was a condition that the ship should comply strictly with the description, the relevant words in the two charters were not intended as an essential part of the description but only as a means of identifying the ship. Lord Wilberforce said: "So the question becomes simply whether, as a matter of fact, it can fairly be said that—as a means of identification—the vessel was yard no. 354 at Osaka Zosen or 'built by Osaka Shipbuilding Co. Ltd. and known as Hull No. 354 until named'. . . . The fact is that the vessel always was Osaka Hull no. 354—though also Oshima no. 4—and equally it can fairly be said to have been 'built' by Osaka Shipbuilding Co. Ltd. as the company which planned, organized and directed the building. . . . For the purpose of the identificatory clause, the words used are quite sufficient to cover the facts. No other vessel could be referred to: the reference fits the vessel in question."

The Diana Prosperity [1976] 2 Lloyd's Rep. 621.

(See also *The Sanko Steamship* v. *Kano Trading* [1978] 1 Lloyd's Rep. 156.)

Substitution

It is open to the parties to agree that another ship may be (or must be) substituted for the originally named ship or to agree to more than one substitution.

The tanker *Driade* was chartered for as many consecutive voyages as could be performed over a period of about 13 months, the owners having the liberty of "substituting a coiled vessel of similar size and position at any time before or during this charterparty . . . ". The owners substituted a similar sistership, the *Nayade*, for the *Driade* before the beginning of the first voyage. Subsequently during the currency of the charter the *Nayade* had to undertake repairs and the owners proposed to substitute the *Driade* for her. The charterers refused to accept the substitution, contending that the liberty clause allowed only one substitution. It was held by Devlin, J., and the Court of Appeal that, although the liberty clause could be construed either way, if regard was had to the length of the charter and the commercial purpose of the clause, the intention was clear that the owners should be entitled to substitute whenever it might become convenient to do so.

Société Anonyme Maritime et Commerciale v. *Anglo-Iranian Oil* [1953] 2 Lloyd's Rep. 466, [1954] 1 Lloyd's Rep. 1 (C.A.).

(See also *Société Navale de L'Ouest* v. *Sutherland* (1920) 4 Ll.L.Rep. 58, 185—obligation to substitute "reasonably similar" ship for chartered ship.)

The parties may also agree that the substitution be made at any time, whether before the start of the charter period, during it, or after the loss of the named or any substituted ship. But if it is intended to give a right of substitution after loss, particularly clear words must be used; for otherwise the charter will be held to have been frustrated by the loss and the right to substitute will terminate with the termination of the charter.

The *Badagry* was demise chartered for a period of eight years, the charter providing by Clause 33: "Owners have the option to substitute the vessel with a similar vessel type/size during the period of this charter party." The charter further provided, by Clause 3(*d*): " . . . If the Vessel should become a constructive total loss, hire shall cease at the time of the casualty resulting in such loss . . . ". The *Badagry* became a constructive total loss on or about 27 September. On

17 October the owners purported to substitute the *Bonny* for the *Badagry*. It was held by the Court of Appeal that Clause 3(*d*) was not consistent with a continuation of the charterparty after a constructive total loss, that the charter was frustrated before 17 October and that with the termination of the charter the right to substitute perished.
The Badagry [1985] 1 Lloyd's Rep. 395.

For a case on the right to substitute "subject to charterers' approval", see *Niarchos (London)* v. *Shell Tankers* [1961] 2 Lloyd's Rep. 496, and page 325 below.

Sale of the ship

It seems from *Sorrentino* v. *Buerger* [1915] 3 K.B. 367 (C.A.) and *Isaacs* v. *McAllum* (1921) 6 Ll.L.Rep. 289, that it is not of itself a breach of the charter for her owners to sell the ship during the period of the charter. (For the effect of a consequent change of flag, see page 64 below.) The original owners will however continue to be responsible to the charterers for the performance of all the obligations assumed by them under the charter.

If the purchasers of the ship have acquired it with actual knowledge of the existence of the charter it may be that the charterers have the right to an injunction to restrain them from using the ship otherwise than in accordance therewith. A decision of the Privy Council to this effect in *Lord Strathcona* v. *Dominion Coal* (1925) 23 Ll.L.Rep. 145, was said to be wrong by Diplock, J., in *Port Line* v. *Ben Line* [1958] 2 Q.B. 146: but in a more recent case, *Swiss Bank* v. *Lloyds Bank* [1979] Ch. 548, Browne-Wilkinson, J., expressed the view that the Privy Council had been correct, although his decision on the case was reversed by the Court of Appeal on other grounds, [1980] 3 W.L.R. 457. Browne-Wilkinson, J., relied particularly on the principle laid down by Knight Bruce, L.J., in *De Mattos* v. *Gibson* (1858) 4 De G. & J. 276 (itself concerning the grant of an injunction to restrain interference with a charter by a person to whom the ship had been charged) who said, at page 282:

> Reason and justice seem to prescribe that, at least as a general rule, where a man, by gift or purchase, acquires property from another, with knowledge of a previous contract, lawfully and for valuable consideration made by him with a third person, to use and employ the property for a particular purpose in a specified manner, the acquirer shall not, to the material damage of the third person, in opposition to the contract and inconsistently with it, use and employ the property in a manner not allowable to the giver or seller.

Browne-Wilkinson, J., saw this equitable principle as the counterpart of the tort of knowing interference with contractual rights, requiring actual and not merely constructive knowledge of the contract on the part of the purchaser, and leading not to an order to the purchaser positively to perform the charter but to an injunction restraining him from dealing with the ship in such a way as to cause a breach of the continuing charter. It is submitted that this view is likely to be followed in future cases—always subject to the two restrictions mentioned in the previous sentence, which Diplock, J., said in *Port Line* v. *Ben Line*, above, would apply even if the *Strathcona* case, above, had been correctly decided and which were supported by the authorities relied upon by Browne-Wilkinson, J., in *Swiss Bank* v. *Lloyds Bank*, above. It may be noted that this conclusion is not based upon the charterers having any interest in the time chartered ship (they have none, see page 54 above and page 440 below), and thus avoids a step in the reasoning of the Privy Council in the *Strathcona* case which has correctly been subjected to much criticism.

Flag

It is submitted that the statement as to the ship's flag will usually be an intermediate term (as to which see page 56 above). But where the flag of the ship has a vital bearing on her safety or on her trading opportunities—as in wartime, when the flag of the ship may determine her neutrality or otherwise—the statement may be treated as a condition (see page 55 above), so that any breach will allow the charterers to treat the contract as discharged.

A term will generally be implied that the flag of the ship will not be changed without the charterers' agreement.

The *City of Hamburg* was time chartered for 12 months. She was a British ship, but this fact was not set out in the charter. Shortly after the time charter period began, the owners sold her and this involved a change of flag. The charterers objected but continued to use the ship. It was accordingly not necessary to decide whether the nationality of the ship was a condition, breach of which would have given the charterers the right to terminate the charter. However, on the charterers' claim for damages, Rowlatt, J., held (1) that the sale itself was not a breach of the charter, but (2) that a term was to be implied into the charter that the ship should not be so altered during the period of the charter as to render services to the charterers substantially less valuable or different from those contracted for; and that the change of flag was a breach of such implied term.

Isaacs v. *McAllum* (1921) 6 Ll.L.Rep. 289.

With hull, machinery and equipment in a thoroughly efficient state

This constitutes an absolute undertaking of seaworthiness and applies to the state of the ship at the time the charter is entered into. There is a further absolute undertaking of seaworthiness in Line 22 of the New York Produce form in the requirement that on delivery the ship is to be "tight, staunch, strong and in every way fitted for the service". There is also an absolute undertaking of seaworthiness on delivery in the Baltime form. Clause 1 provides that on delivery the ship is to be "in every way fitted for ordinary cargo service," which was held in *The Madeleine* [1967] 2 Lloyd's Rep. 224 (see page 68 below) to mean that the ship must be seaworthy in the widest sense.

In the absence of express undertakings of seaworthiness on delivery, an undertaking of seaworthiness will be implied: *Giertsen* v. *Turnbull*, 1908 S.C. 1101. This is also absolute in nature.

Standing on their own these undertakings of seaworthiness on delivery are not continuing obligations (see *Giertsen* v. *Turnbull* above). But where the Hague Rules are incorporated into the charter, as by Clause 24 of the New York Produce form, it seems that the absolute obligations of seaworthiness on delivery (whether express or implied) are replaced by an undertaking that due diligence to make the ship seaworthy must be exercised before and at the beginning of each voyage under the charter. This is discussed at pages 425 to 428 below.

The following statement as to the meaning of "seaworthiness" in *Carver on Carriage by Sea* was approved by Scrutton, L.J., in *F.C. Bradley & Sons* v. *Federal Steam Navigation Co.* (1926) 24 Ll.L.Rep. 446: "The ship must have that degree of fitness which an ordinary careful owner would require his vessel to have at the commencement of her voyage having regard to all the probable circumstances of it. Would a prudent owner have required that it should be made good before sending his ship to sea, had he known of it?"

There are, in Lines 37 and 38 of the New York Produce form and Lines 24 and 25 of the Baltime form separate provisions as to the maintenance of the ship in a thoroughly efficient state during the service. These are clearly continuing obligations. Comment upon them will be found at page 165.

Seaworthiness obligations not conditions

Neither the undertaking of seaworthiness at the time the charter is made nor the undertaking as to seaworthiness at the time of delivery are conditions (as to which see page 55 above). They are intermediate terms and whether breach of them allows the charterers to treat the charter as discharged depends on the nature and consequences of the breach. Since the obligation of seaworthiness is so wide-reaching, it may easily be breached in comparatively trivial ways and it would be unreasonable that for minor breaches the charterers should have the right to terminate the charter.

The *Hongkong Fir* was chartered on the Baltime form for 24 months, one month more or less. Her engines at the time of delivery were in a reasonable condition but, because of their age, required careful attention. The engineers employed by the owners on delivery were insufficient in number and also incompetent. Consequently, there was, on the very first charter voyage, a succession of serious engine failures. That voyage, from Liverpool to Osaka, included five weeks off hire for repairs and was followed by 15 further weeks of repairs at Osaka. Before the ship was again ready for sea, the charterers repudiated the charter and the owners claimed damages on the ground that the repudiation was wrongful. It was held by Salmon, J., and the Court of Appeal that:

(1) the owners were in breach of the undertaking of seaworthiness having regard to the incompetence of the engine room staff;
(2) the owners were not protected by the Baltime exceptions Clause (13) since the incompetence of the engine room staff was attributable to the owners' want of due diligence in their selection;
(3) seaworthiness was not a condition and breach of the undertaking of seaworthiness did not in itself give the charterers the right to repudiate;
(4) the charterers could only justify their repudiation if the breach of the undertaking of seaworthiness went to the root of the contract;
(5) the breach of the undertaking had resulted in considerable delays, but this could not be regarded as going to the root of the contract or as depriving the charterers of substantially the whole benefit of the contract unless the delays were such as to frustrate the charter;
(6) having regard to the length of the charter (24 months) and to the fact that off-hire periods could by its terms be added to extend the period, the delays were not such as to frustrate the charter and therefore the charterers' repudiation was wrongful.

The Hongkong Fir [1961] 1 Lloyd's Rep. 159 and [1961] 2 Lloyd's Rep. 478 (C.A.).

Delivery of unseaworthy ship

The charterers are not obliged to accept delivery of a ship which is found to be unseaworthy. They may require that the relevant defects be made good first.

In *The Hongkong Fir*, above, Sellers, L.J., said: "By Clause 1 of the [Baltime] charter-party, the shipowners contracted to deliver the vessel at Liverpool 'she being in every way fitted for ordinary cargo service'. She was not fit for ordinary cargo service when delivered because the engine-room staff was incompetent and inadequate and this became apparent as the voyage proceeded. It is common-place language to say that the vessel was unseaworthy by reason of this inefficiency in the engine-room . . . If, in the present case, the inadequacy and incompetence of the engine-room staff had been known to them, the charterers could have complained of the failure by the shipowners to deliver the vessel at Liverpool in accordance with Clause 1 of the charter-party and could have refused to take her in that condition." Until the ship was "in every way fitted for ordinary cargo service" as required by Clause 1 of the Baltime charter the charterers could have refused to accept delivery. Moreover, if this requirement had not been met by the time stipulated in the cancelling clause (see pages 287 to 292 below) then the charterers would have the right to bring the charter to an end by virtue of that clause.

Quite apart from the cancelling clause the charterers have, at common law, the right to treat the charter as discharged if at the time of delivery the ship is unseaworthy and cannot be made seaworthy within such time as will prevent the charter from being frustrated. In the leading voyage charter case of *Stanton* v. *Richardson* (1875) 45 L.J.C.P. 78 the charterers were held by the House of Lords to be released from all obligation to load a ship which was unfit to receive the contractual cargo and, as found by the jury, could not be made fit within such a time as would not have frustrated the object of the venture. See also the judgment of Brett, J., to the same effect in the subsequent time charter case of *Tully* v. *Howling* (1877) 2 Q.B.D. 182. But unless the unseaworthiness complained of is so serious that it goes to the root of the contract, depriving the charterers of substantially the whole benefit of the charter, or cannot be corrected within such time as will prevent the charter from being effectively frustrated, the charterers will be obliged to continue with the charter and to seek their remedy in damages. As explained above, the seaworthiness obligations are not conditions and only breaches having the consequences described allow the charterers to refuse to perform their part of the contract. As Diplock, L.J., explained in *The Hongkong Fir* [1961] 2 Lloyd's Rep. 478, at page 495:

> . . . the mere occurrence of the events that the vessel was in some respect unseaworthy when tendered or that such unseaworthiness had caused some delay in performance of the charter-party would not deprive the charterer of the whole benefit which it was the intention of the parties he should obtain from the performance of his obligations under the contract—for he undertakes to continue to perform his obligations notwithstanding the occurrence of such events if they fall short of frustration of the contract . . .

(See also *Photo Production* v. *Securicor* [1980] 1 Lloyd's Rep. 545, 553 and page 55 above.)

Where therefore the ship is found to be unseaworthy on or before delivery but the unseaworthiness does not go to the root of the contract, the charterers may not (unless there is a repudiation, see below) refuse delivery and treat the whole contract as discharged. They may only call upon the owners to make the ship fit for delivery in accordance with the requirements of the charter; and if the owners do so by the cancelling date, the charterers must accept her.

Refusal or failure to remedy unseaworthiness

Although the unseaworthiness may not be sufficiently serious to allow the charterers to treat the charter as discharged, a refusal or failure on the part of the owners to make the ship seaworthy or otherwise fit for delivery in accordance with the requirements of the contract may show an intention no longer to be bound by the charter. Then the owners' refusal or failure to remedy the deficiency would probably amount to a repudiation giving the charterers the right to terminate. Sellers, L.J., in *The Hongkong Fir* continued after the passage in his judgment quoted at page 65 above:

> If the shipowners had refused or failed [to bring the engine-room staff into suitable strength and competency], their conduct and not the unseaworthiness would have amounted to a repudiation of the charter-party and entitled the charterers to accept it and treat the contract as at an end.

This statement should however be treated with caution. Although, as has been stated, the owners' conduct might in some circumstances amount to a repudiation by evincing an intention no longer to be bound by the contract, a failure to remedy a breach which does not itself go to the root of the contract will not without more amount to a repudiation.

The *Hermosa* was chartered on the New York Produce form for a period of two years with options to extend the period for a further four months in certain circumstances. She was sub-chartered by the head charterers on the same form for a similar period. Following delivery in December 1974 there was serious damage to the cargo carried on her first voyage, as a result of unseaworthiness. Because of the repairs which were then carried out, and which took from mid January to the end of March 1975, the sub-charterers lost their next employment for the ship. On the subsequent ballast voyage in April the ship was in collision and had to put into Curacao for repairs. The owners had refused to allow the sub-charterers to survey the ship after the first voyage, but since the sub-charterers could obtain no satisfactory reassurances as to the time the further repairs would take to complete, or as to their efficacy, they obtained a court order to survey the ship on 9 August 1975. This survey revealed that deficiencies in the ship's hatch covers, which were the cause of the damage to the cargo on the first voyage, still remained unrepaired and that the ship was in bad condition in other respects. Having received no firm assurances from the head charterers (who were without information from the owners) that these defects were being satisfactorily dealt with, the sub-charterers purported to terminate the sub-charter on 29 August 1975. Unknown to the sub-charterers the owners had arranged for the repair of these defects prior to 29 August and the repairs were properly completed by 22 October. It was held by Mustill, J., and the Court of Appeal that:

(1) the sub-charterers were not justified in treating the charter as discharged by reason of the ship's unseaworthiness because the remaining defects were capable of being put right within a relatively short time and thereafter the sub-charter would still have had 16 to 20 months to run;
(2) there was no repudiation of the charter by the head charterers, because their conduct was not such as to lead a reasonable person to conclude that they did not intend to fulfil their part of the contract. The sub-charterers were justifiably suspicious that the hatch covers might not be properly repaired; but that was not enough, and their action was premature.

The Hermosa [1980] 1 Lloyd's Rep. 638 and [1982] 1 Lloyd's Rep. 570.

(See generally on repudiation *Decro-Wall* v. *Practitioners in Marketing* [1971] 1 W.L.R. 361, *The Nanfri* [1979] 1 Lloyd's Rep. 201 and *Woodar* v. *Wimpey* [1980] 1 W.L.R. 277.)

The Court of Appeal in *The Hermosa* held further that where, as in that case, the question is whether the contract between head charterers and sub-charterers has been repudiated, it is the conduct of the head charterers which has to be considered and whether they themselves have evinced an intention no longer to be bound by the charter. The conduct of the owners is not necessarily to be regarded as the conduct of the head charterers.

Unseaworthiness frustrating the contract

Where the initial unseaworthiness cannot be or is not corrected by the owners within such a time as will frustrate the commercial object of the charter, the charterers may treat the contract as discharged.

The *Yuri Maru* was time chartered for nine months. She was, when delivered, to be in every way fitted for ordinary cargo service. Although a new ship, her propeller was insufficiently strong and it began to lose blades after less than three months of the charter. After the owners had spent over two months trying without success to remedy this defect, the charterers cancelled the charter. It was held by the Court of Appeal that the unseaworthiness of the ship had prevented performance of the contract for such time as to frustrate the charter and that the charterers were entitled to act as they did. Bankes, L.J., said:

> "I think it is impossible to contend that, in a case like this of a time-charter, the charterer, simply because the vessel is off-hire, is bound to wait an interminable time (if I may use that expression) without getting his vessel, and yet have no right to terminate the contract under circumstances which make it not only absolutely impossible for him to use the vessel, but quite conclusively certain that he never will be able to make use of it for the purpose contemplated by both parties at the time they entered into the contract."

Snia v. *Suzuki* (1924) 18 Ll.L.Rep. 333.

Commenting on this case in *The Hongkong Fir* [1961] 1 Lloyd's Rep. 159, Salmon, J., said: "The facts of that case were exceptional. The charterers, after the failure of repeated efforts of the owners to make the vessel seaworthy, had good reason to believe that the shipowners would never be able to do so." (See also *Stanton* v. *Richardson* (1874) L.R. 9 C.P. 390 and *The Hermosa*, above.)

Cancelling clause

Again, although the unseaworthiness may not be sufficiently serious to entitle the charterers to treat the charter as discharged, if the deficiency or condition cannot be made good before the cancelling date, the charterers may be entitled to cancel under the cancelling clause. Under Clause 14 of the New York Produce form the charterers may cancel if the ship has not given a valid written notice of readiness before the cancelling date. Under Clauses 1 and 22 of the Baltime form the right arises if the ship is not delivered by the due date, "in every way fitted for ordinary cargo service". These words mean that the ship must, on her delivery, be seaworthy in its widest sense and capable of performing the charter service.

The *Madeleine* was time chartered on the Baltime form. The ship was tendered for delivery without a deratisation certificate. Attempts were made to fumigate the ship but a certificate could not be obtained before the cancelling date. In holding that the charterers were entitled to cancel, Roskill, J., said: " . . . There was here an express warranty of seaworthiness and unless the ship was timeously delivered in a seaworthy condition, including the necessary certificate from the port health authority, the charterers had the right to cancel."

The Madeleine [1967] 2 Lloyd's Rep. 224.

(A fuller summary of the facts of this case appears at page 288 below.)

But the cancelling clause does not depend upon breach. If the ship is not ready by the due date the charterers may cancel even if the unreadiness of the ship is not attributable to any breach of charter on the part of the owners (provided it is not attributable to anything for which the charterers are responsible).

Reference should be made to the chapters on the cancelling clause (page 287) and readiness (page 114) for fuller discussion of this subject. The doctrine of frustration is dealt with at page 322.

Effect of Clause Paramount on seaworthiness obligations

See pages 425 to 428 below.

Statement as to class

A statement that the ship is classed will usually be a condition (see page 55 above) so that the charterers will be entitled to treat the charter as discharged, if at the date of the charter the ship was not classed as stated: see *Routh* v. *MacMillan* (1863) 9 L.T. 541 and *The Apollonius* [1978] 1 Lloyd's Rep. 53, at page 61.

The description will be correct if the class stated in the charter is the class assigned to the ship in the register of the classification society at the date of the charter. The statement does not import any undertaking that the ship is rightly classed; nor does it import any undertaking that the ship will remain so classed.

The *William Jackson* was chartered on 4 September to load a cargo of cotton at New Orleans, the ship being described in the charter as "A1½, Record of American and Foreign Shipping Book". At the date of the charter the ship was so classed. After the ship arrived at New Orleans in November her class was cancelled because it was discovered that when the ship had been surveyed for class in August it had been thought, wrongly, that she had recently been remetalled. The charterers refused to perform the charter, but it was held by the Court of Appeal that since the ship was classed as described at the time the charter was entered into, the charterers' refusal was wrongful.

French v. *Newgass* (1878) 3 C.P.D. 163.

Furthermore, the owners do not warrant, by stating the ship's class, that they will omit no act necessary to retain her class. In *Hurst* v. *Usborne* (1856) 18 C.B. 144, Crowder, J., said: "The statement in the charterparty that the *Elizabeth* was A.1., applied, I apprehend, only to the time of entering into the contract. It clearly does not amount to a warranty that the vessel should continue A.1. during the whole time covered by the charterparty, or that the owners would omit no act necessary to be done to retain her in that class."

Most time charters (as in the case of the New York Produce form in Line 37) impose on the owners an obligation to maintain the class of the ship. It is suggested that in the absence of such an express provision a term will be implied that the owners will not so alter the ship after the date of the charter that she loses her class as a result: see, by way of analogy, *Isaacs* v. *McAllum* (1921) 6 Ll.L.Rep. 289.

Bale and deadweight capacity

Statements of bale and deadweight capacity usually constitute intermediate terms. Thus, as explained at page 56 above, the consequences of a misdescription depend upon the nature and consequences of the breach. In *Cargo Ships El-Yam* v. *Invotra* [1958] 1 Lloyd's Rep. 39, Devlin, J., said that in principle a misdescription would have to be "sufficient to make a fundamental difference to that which the party has contracted to take" to entitle the charterers to treat the charter as discharged because of it.

The deadweight figure is normally an abstract measurement of lifting capacity.

The *Freden* was voyage chartered to load a full cargo of maize. The charter provided: "The owners guarantee the ship's dead-weight capacity to be 3,200 tons and freight to be paid on this quantity." The clause was construed by the Court of Appeal as referring to the ship's abstract lifting capacity and it was held that there was no breach in her inability to lift more than 3,081 tons of maize because of insufficient cubic capacity.

Millar v. *Freden* [1918] 1 K.B. 611.

If, as might occasionally happen, a ship were time chartered for a trip to carry one particularly described cargo, the deadweight capacity figure in the charter might, as a matter of construction, be held to relate to the particular cargo. But it is in general less likely that the deadweight capacity would be construed as referring to a particular cargo in time charter forms such as the New York Produce and Baltime, because in these forms the cubic capacity and the deadweight capacity are separately described.

In the New York Produce form the deadweight capacity is defined as "cargo and bunkers, including fresh water and stores not exceeding one and one-half percent of ship's deadweight capacity, allowing a minimum of fifty tons". It is suggested that this means that the fresh water and stores together are not to exceed either 50 tons or one and one-half per cent. of the deadweight capacity, whichever is the larger.

It was held in a voyage charter case that a deadweight cargo capacity guarantee included the weight of dunnage which the owners were obliged to use in proper stowage of the cargo.

The *Benledi* was chartered to load "a full and complete cargo of unobjectionable merchandise". The charter provided "Owners guarantee to place 5,600 tons dead-weight cargo capacity and 300,000 cubic feet (bale space), as per builders' plan, at disposal of charterers". It was held by Atkin, J., that there was no breach of the deadweight cargo capacity guarantee when the cargo actually lifted was less than the weight guaranteed by reason of the dunnage that the owners were obliged to use in proper stowage of the cargo.

Thomson v. *Brocklebank* [1918] 1 K.B. 655.

"About"

Both the New York Produce form and Baltime form qualify the deadweight capacity figure by the word "about". This allows the owners a margin of accuracy: if the figures are within this margin, there will be no breach of the term as to deadweight capacity.

No general rule can be laid down as to the margin allowed by "about". It is a question of fact and will depend on the accuracy with which the deadweight can reasonably be measured and on what margin is regarded as reasonable in the particular trade: see by analogy *The Al Bida* [1986] 1 Lloyd's Rep. 142 and [1987] 1 Lloyd's Rep. 124 (C.A.), summarised under "Speed and fuel consumption", below. In one early case concerning a ship with a small deadweight capacity, a margin of five per cent. was allowed, but this is not a reliable guide to the smaller margins which would today be allowed by courts or arbitrators in respect of far bigger ships.

The *Resolven* was chartered to carry "2,000 tons or thereabouts". Sir Francis Jeune said, in giving judgment: "I think that the word 'thereabouts' must be taken as qualifying the figure of 2,000 tons to some extent . . . I take it that words of elasticity are elastic, and this extensiveness runs with the subject matter they refer to. I think that in this instance 5 per cent. may be taken as a fair margin in this case . . . "

The Resolven (1892) 9 T.L.R. 75.

(See also *Morris* v. *Levison* (1876) 1 C.P.D. 155—three per cent. allowed for a cargo of about 1,100 tons—and *Rederiaktiebolaget Urania* v. *Zachariades* (1931) 41 Ll.L. Rep. 145—three per cent. allowed on "about 80,000 grain cubic ft." capacity.)

Although decisions in cases in which the figures qualified by "about" are matters of estimation rather than measurement may be of some assistance on the margin to be allowed, they should be applied with caution to cases relating to description of capacity. In *The Pantanassa* [1958] 2 Lloyd's Rep. 449, a time charter provided that the ship was to be delivered with bunkers as aboard expected "about 6/700 tons". It was considered that this meant between 575 and 725 tons.

The *Dominator* was voyage chartered to load "a full and complete cargo of not more than 10450 tons and not less than 8550 tons wheat in bulk, quantity in owners' option, to be declared by the master". The master declared that the "approximative" amount the ship would load would be 10,400 tons. It was held by the Court of Appeal that "approximative" meant the same as "about" and that a 331 tons deficiency in a cargo of 10,400 tons (just over three per cent.) fulfilled the obligation to ship about 10,400 tons. Sellers, L.J., said: "I would regard 331 tons of deficiency in a cargo of 10,400 tons, a deficiency of just over 3 per cent., as fulfilling the obligation to ship about 10,400 tons: see *Morris* v. *Levison* (1876) 1 C.P.D. 155, and *The Resolven* (1892) 9 T.L.R. 75. In the absence of any trade evidence on the matter, it is, in my opinion, within a reasonable commercial margin in respect of such a cargo".

Dreyfus v. *Parnaso* [1960] 1 Lloyd's Rep. 117.

In a case relating to bale capacity under a charter on the New York Produce form, the importance of trade evidence was again emphasised.

The *Tel Aviv* was time chartered on the New York Produce form and was described as "of about 478,000 cubic feet bale capacity . . . ". In fact, her total bale capacity was 484,000 cubic feet or 1.2 per cent. in excess of the figure described. Dealing with the meaning to be given to the word "about", Devlin, J., said: "If I had to determine whether the margin of 1.2 per cent. was within the phrase 'about', it might be a point on the evidence that I have had which would require some careful consideration. *Prima facie*, I must say that I should have thought it was a small percentage and might well have been within the phrase 'about' but [counsel for the charterers] rightly relies upon the evidence on this point . . . as showing that 1000 cu. ft. or thereabouts would be the sort of margin as a matter of business so contemplated within the meaning of the word 'about' . . . "

Cargo Ships El-Yam v. *Invotra* [1958] 1 Lloyd's Rep. 39.

The court in that case did not, in the event, have to decide finally what the margin should be, but the passage demonstrates that with large figures the percentage likely now to be allowed by "about" will be lower than the percentages allowed in the earlier cases.

Measure of damages

Prima facie the measure of damages for misdescription of a ship's cubic capacity is the difference between the hire agreed and the hire that would have been payable for a ship of the actual capacity.

The *Tibermede* was described in a time charter as having a certain deadweight capacity and a certain cubic capacity. In fact, her deadweight capacity was greater and her cubic capacity less. The charterers claimed damages for the deficiency in cubic capacity on the difference between the agreed hire and the hire they would have paid for a ship of the actual cubic capacity. This method of assessing damages was disputed by the owners who contended that the charterers should prove their actual losses. In upholding the charterers' contention, Shearman, J., said: "If you buy a ship of a certain cubic capacity, and one of less cubic capacity is tendered, you can deduct the difference in value from the price. I am unable to see that there is a difference in the case of a hiring."

Tibermede v. *Graham* (1921) 7 Ll.L.Rep. 250.

(See also *Sterns* v. *Salterns* (1922) 12 Ll.L.Rep. 385.)

In some cases, however, the *prima facie* rule may not compensate the injured parties and if they can prove that they have suffered loss during the currency of the charter as a result of the difference in deadweight or cubic capacity, they may, as an alternative, put their claim on that basis: see *The TFL Prosperity* [1982] 1 Lloyd's Rep. 617.

Speed and fuel consumption

It seems that statements as to speed and fuel consumption will usually constitute intermediate terms. The consequences of misdescription will then depend upon the nature and consequences of the breach as explained at page 56 above. Usually, a lack of speed or an excess of consumption can be compensated for by damages alone. However, a serious discrepancy in either respect may be so fundamental to the charter as to entitle the charterers to treat it as being discharged. This could be the case where speed is obviously an essential attribute for the service contemplated by the parties as, for example, where the ship is being chartered in to supplement an express container service.

When the ship must comply

There is a divergence of view on the question whether the ship has to comply with the description as to speed at the time the charter is entered into or at the time of delivery, or whether it is a continuing warranty.

The *Adderstone* was time chartered for a period of seven to nine months and was described in the charter as being capable of steaming fully laden in good weather conditions at about 10 knots on a consumption of about 13 tons of best grade fuel oil. A month after the commencement of the charter, the owners sold the ship. The charterers filed a claim against the buyers for poor speed and excessive consumption. On the trial of a preliminary point of law in a dispute between the original owners and the buyers, the question arose whether, assuming the ship was not capable of the performance described, the original owners were liable. It was said by Atkinson, J. (*obiter*) that the warranty as to speed and consumption was a warranty that at the date of the charter the ship was capable of the described performance and not that the ship should continue to be so capable.
Lorentzen v. *White Shipping* (1943) 74 Ll.L.Rep. 161.

Mocatta, J., in *The Apollonius* [1978] 1 Lloyd's Rep. 53, declined to follow Atkinson, J., in *Lorentzen* v. *White Shipping* and held that the description of the ship's speed in a time charter applied at the date of delivery.

The *Apollonius* was time chartered for a trip on the Baltime form. In the charter she was described as " . . . fully loaded capable of steaming about $14\frac{1}{2}$ knots in good weather and smooth water on a consumption of about 38 tons oil fuel". The time charter was entered into on 28 August and the ship was to be delivered not before 25 September, the cancelling date being 15 October. By a subsequent addendum, the cancelling date was extended to 31 October. Among a large number of additional clauses was Clause 50, reading, "Owners to have the option of dry-docking vessel prior to delivery". Between 7 September and 26 October the ship was discharging at Whampoa. While there her bottom became badly fouled. Consequently she was able to average only 10.61 knots on the charter voyage, which was from Japan to Argentina. The owners did not dispute that upon delivery the ship was not capable of the described speed, but they argued that their obligation related not to the time of delivery but only to the time the charter was made.

Mocatta, J., disagreeing with what had been said by Atkinson, J., in *Lorentzen* v. *White*, considered that there were "overwhelming commercial considerations" favouring the charterers' contention that the obligation as to speed applied at the time of delivery. He left open whether it might also apply at any earlier or later date.
The Apollonius [1978] 1 Lloyd's Rep. 53.

The view expressed in *Lorentzen* v. *White* was, however, generally accepted for a number of years and it seems more consistent with the wording of the preamble to the charter that the characteristics described should be those which the ship has at the date the contract is entered into rather than those which the ship will have at the date of delivery. The commercial considerations relied upon by Mocatta, J., in *The Apollonius,* above, would largely be met by the express obligation to deliver the ship "in every way fitted" for the service and by implying a term that subsequent to the date of the charter the owners will not so alter the ship as to reduce her speed or increase her consumption: see, by analogy, *Isaacs* v. *McAllum* (1921) 6 Ll.L.Rep. 289, and the term implied by Denning, L.J., in *Karsales* v. *Wallis* [1956] 1 W.L.R. 936; also the Court of Appeal judgments in *Robertson* v. *Amazon Tug* (1881) 7 Q.B.D. 598.

In *The Al Bida* [1986] 1 Lloyd's Rep. 142, at page 150, Evans, J., doubted whether a speed warranty was a continuing warranty, save insofar as one might arise from an implied undertaking that the specification of the ship would not be changed. See also the observations of Parker, L.J., in the Court of Appeal [1987] 1 Lloyd's Rep. 124, at page 129 on the meaning of the words "capable of maintaining" the warranted speed and consumption.

Moreover, although the obligation to maintain the ship in an efficient state probably does not apply until after delivery, the standard of efficiency to which the ship is to be maintained should, so far as concerns speed and consumption, be set by the description in the preamble.

"About"

The word "about" when qualifying the warranty as to speed allows a margin either side of the stated speed; the extent of the margin is a matter of fact, not one of law: *The Al Bida* [1987] 1 Lloyd's Rep. 124, at page 129 (C.A.).

It was argued in *The Al Bida* (in which the warranted speed was "about 15.5 knots") that there were only two possible margins that could be allowed for the word "about", half a knot or five per cent. The Court of Appeal rejected this contention, agreeing with the arbitrators that it "must be tailored to the ship's configuration, size, draft and trim, etc." (See also *The Ioanna* [1985] 2 Lloyd's Rep. 164 in which the parties agreed that the margin to be allowed by "about" on a warranted speed of "about 13 knots" was half a knot.)

Average speed and consumption

Questions as to the assessment of averages and the consequent calculations of damages or adjustments of hire were considered in *The Al Bida* and *The Didymi* below.

The *Al Bida* was chartered for two consecutive one-year periods on the Standime form of tanker time charter. Both charters provided in the preamble that the ship was "capable of maintaining under normal working conditions an average sea speed of about 15.5 knots in moderate weather when fully laden, on an average consumption of 53 metric tons IFO 1500 fully laden and 50 metric tons in ballast . . . per 24 hours". Form C.Gas, attached to and forming part of the charters, provided as follows: "Guaranteed sea speed on a year period abt. 15.5 knots. *Consumption*. At sea. IFO average consumption 53 m/tons . . . fully laden and 50 m/tons in ballast . . . "

Arbitrators found that the ship's bottom was foul on delivery and that for a period following delivery, until underwater cleaning took place, and for a further period before a subsequent drydocking, the owners did not comply with the consumption warranty. This was due to their failure to make the ship fit on delivery and to comply with their maintenance obligations. However, the ship did comply with the guarantee in Form C. Gas as to her average speed over one year. The owners contended that they were entitled to credit for periods when the ship under-consumed to be set against the over-consumption during the periods the ship was in breach of the consumption warranty in the preamble. In other words, they contended that the consumption over the whole one-year period should be taken into account.

It was held by Evans, J., and the Court of Appeal that what the preamble required was an assessment of the ship's average capability at the time of delivery and at any time thereafter when the question arose whether the owners had maintained the ship in that state required by the preamble. Parker, L.J., said at page 129: "The preamble does not require an actual average to be taken over the period of the charter, or indeed any period. It may be that actual performance in the early period of the charter would be good evidence as to whether, on delivery, the vessel had the required capability, but it is no more than that. A shortfall from the required capacity might easily be otherwise proved, for example, by the fact that in the three weeks before delivery she had, in ideal conditions, to consume more than the stated figure to reach the lowest of the speeds embraced in the range of 'about' 15.5 knots". At certain times the ship had, in breach of charter, been incapable of maintaining the average consumption stipulated and this was so despite overperformance at other times. That Form C. Gas required the guaranteed speed "on a year period" supported that construction of the preamble. The absence of a similar provision in relation to consumption indicated that the parties intended the average to be taken over a year in the case of speed, but not in the case of fuel consumption.

The Al Bida [1986] 1 Lloyd's Rep. 142 and [1987] 1 Lloyd's Rep. 124 (C.A.)

The *Didymi* was time chartered on the New York Produce form for five years. An additional clause provided that the ship was capable of maintaining and should maintain throughout the periods of the charter "a guaranteed average speed of 15.5 knots in good weather conditions (smooth seas, wind less than 3 on the Beaufort scale) on a guaranteed daily consumption of 35 long tons . . . ". The clause also provided that should the ship fail to perform in accordance with these guarantees, the charterers should be entitled to a decrease in hire and that if the ship maintained a better speed and/or consumption, the owners should be indemnified in like manner.

The charterers contended that in calculating the amount by which the owners were to be compensated for better than guaranteed performance, the periods when conditions were not "good" could be excluded. The owners contended that the whole period of the charter should be taken into account. It was held by Hobhouse, J., in upholding the charterers' contention, that over the period of the five-year charter there would be a sufficient number and spread of periods of good conditions to enable a reasonable assessment of average performance to be made, but that the resultant gain should be applied appropriately over the whole period of the charter. The decision and reasoning of Hobhouse, J., were approved and adopted by the Court of Appeal.

Didymi Corporation v. *Atlantic Lines and Navigation (The Didymi)* [1987] 2 Lloyd's Rep. 166 and [1988] 2 Lloyd's Rep. 108 (C.A.).

(For consideration of the provision in this case that for better performance than that guaranteed the hire was to be equitably increased "by an amount to be mutually agreed between owners and charterers", see page 23 above.)

For two cases on the application of the escalation of hire provisions in Clause 24 of the Shelltime 3 tanker time charter form to fuel consumption, see *The Evanthia M* [1985] 2 Lloyd's Rep. 154 (application of an amended clause 24 to periods when the ship was used for storage) and *The Larissa* [1983] 2 Lloyd's Rep. 325 (maximum guaranteed fuel oil consumption inserted into Clause 24 at figure in excess of actual maximum consumption of ship).

Present position

It is this statement which should follow the word "now" in Line 11 of the New York Produce form and Line 8 of the Baltime form. It seems that it may sometimes amount to a condition: see *Bentsen* v. *Taylor* [1893] 2 Q.B. 274. In *Behn* v. *Burness* (1863) 3 B. & S. 751, it was held by the Exchequer Chamber that charterers were entitled to refuse to load when a ship, described as "now in the port of Amsterdam", did not in fact reach Amsterdam until four days later. But comments on that decision in *The Diana Prosperity*, by Lord Denning in the Court of Appeal and by Lord Wilberforce in the House of Lords, cast doubt on whether it can be regarded today as a reliable authority: see [1976] 2 Lloyd's Rep. pages 73 and 626. It is probable that a statement of the ship's position would today be regarded as a condition only if it constituted a "time clause" (as to which, see page 58 above), as it might do in view of its relevance to calculations as to the ship's probable time of arrival at the delivery port.

"Expected ready to load"

If the owners describe the ship as "trading", but state that she is "expected ready to load" on or about a certain date, the statement of expectation will probably be regarded as a condition. If the statement is made without belief in its truth or without reasonable grounds, the charterers may treat the contract as discharged. This sort of provision is, of course, more common in voyage than in time charters, but its effect is likely to be the same in both. When expressed, there is an obligation that the stated expectation shall be both honest and reasonably based.

The *Mihalis Angelos* was described in a voyage charter as "now trading and expected ready to load under this Charter about 1st July 1965". There was, in fact, no reason at the time the charter was made, 25 May of that year, to expect that the ship would be ready to load about 1 July. The Court of Appeal held, following previous authority, that the term was a condition so that breach of it entitled the charterers to treat the charter as discharged.

The Mihalis Angelos [1970] 2 Lloyd's Rep. 43.

American Law

There has been in the American decisions a struggle to give the appropriate legal label to the various statements of a ship's characteristics in the preamble of the charter. Thus, such statements may be called "representations", "warranties" or "conditions", although the term invoked may well not dispose of the underlying issue, i.e., whether the ship's failure to comply entitles the charterer to treat the contract as terminated or merely to recover damages resulting from the breach. Rather than focus on the proper terminology applicable to a representation or undertaking, it is more useful to consider the inherent materiality of the representation or undertaking in question, the point in time at which a breach or default occurs, and the consequences thereof to the charter.

Under the American precedents, it is important to distinguish between cases involving a misdescription determined prior to delivery of the vessel and one occurring after delivery. In the former a refusal to accept the vessel has been held justified even where the deviation from the represented characteristic is relatively small. In *The Maria Lemos*, S.M.A. No. 74 (Arb. at N.Y. 1963), it was held that charterer had the right to reject the vessel because the amount of fuel oil on board did not comply with the minimum stipulated in the charter and there was water ballast in the No. 3 deeptank when the vessel was tendered as being ready. See also *The Augvald*, 1965 AMC 1614 (Arb. at N.Y. 1965); *The Grand Explorer*, S.M.A. No. 551 (Arb. at N.Y. 1963).

Once delivery of the vessel has been accepted, however, the charterer is entitled to refuse to perform the charter only if there is a material breach on the part of the owner which frustrates the essential purpose of the contract. See *Aaby* v. *States Marine Corp.* (*The Tendo*), 181 F.2d 383, 1950 AMC 947 (2d Cir. 1950), *cert.* denied, 340 U.S. 829 (1950); *United States* v. *The Marilena P*, 433 F.2d 164, 1969 AMC 1155 (4th Cir. 1969); *Petroleum Export Corp.* v. *Kerr S.S. Co.*, 32 F.2d 969, 1929 AMC 905 (9th Cir. 1929); *Massari* v. *Forest Lumber Co.*, 290 F. 470, 1923 AMC 1111 (S.D. Fla. 1923); *Davison* v. *Von Lingen*, 113 U.S. 40 (1885); *Romano* v. *West India Fruit and S.S. Co.*, 151 F.2d 727, 1946 AMC 90 (5th Cir. 1945); *The Leslie*, S.M.A. No. 1341 (Arb. at N.Y. 1979); *The Eastern Street*, S.M.A. No. 1352 (Arb. at N.Y. 1979). See generally, Healy, Jr., *Termination of Charter Parties*, 49 Tul. L. Rev. 845, 846–47 (1975).

Two arbitrations illustrate some of these points. In *The Fu Chiao*, S.M.A. No. 1089 (Arb. at N.Y. 1977), the panel unanimously held that charterer was justified in cancelling the charter because the owner had misdescribed the vessel's characteristics. Although the charter did not contain an express requirement that the vessel be vertically ventilated, the charterer had received assurances to this effect during the negotiations that led to the fixture, and would not otherwise have entered into the charter. According to the panel:

> The Panel is unanimous in its opinion that where there has been misrepresentation of the vessel's characteristics, innocent or otherwise, which induces a charterer to enter into a contract and this misrepresentation strikes down or otherwise seriously prejudices the very purpose of charterers' intended use of the vessel then charterers are within their rights to cancel the contract and claim damages if any are sustained.

In *The Tordenskjold*, S.M.A. No. 1091 (Arb. at N.Y. 1977), the charter provided that the vessel "shall be maintained according to U.S. Coast Guard regulations and always maintain and carry valid U.S. Coast Guard letter of compliance". The vessel had completed three voyages when the owner was advised by the Coast Guard that three sets of flanges had to be replaced if he intended to load propylene at Houston. The vessel went off-hire for three days while the repairs were accomplished. Coast Guard approval was received upon completion of the repairs, but the charterer then decided to cancel the charter and declared it commercially frustrated because the vessel had not been ready to load. In addition, the vessel had been without a Coast Guard letter of compliance since the outset of the charter. The panel held, however, that these circumstances did not justify cancellation and were not "such a fundamental and pervasive breach of the charter party as to destroy the commercial purpose of the contract". According to the panel:

> The law, in our opinion, is relatively clear and convincing in a line of decisions which declare that the charterer must sustain a different burden if it wishes to cancel a charter party once a vessel is delivered and has performed in part than it would have at the time of delivery.

Name of the ship

American law no doubt requires the owner to deliver the ship named in the charter. In *Compania Naviera Asiatic* v. *Burmah Oil*, 1977 AMC 1538 (S.D.N.Y. 1977), the court construed a charter for "Hull #2283" as requiring delivery of that precise vessel, and owner's obligation could not be satisfied by the delivery of a sister ship designated as "Hull #2284". *Cf. The Christina Pezas*, 149 F. Supp. 678, 1958 AMC 240 (S.D.N.Y. 1957), concerning an arbitration award holding that under a consecutive voyage charter for the "vessel CHRISTINA PEZAS, or at owner's option Liberty substitute in same position on any voyage", the owner had the right to freely substitute other Liberty type vessels.

Flag

It is probable that American courts and arbitrators would follow the test of materiality in determining whether a misdescription of the ship's flag would constitute a breach of the charter which would give the charterer a right to terminate or merely a claim for damages.

In *The Penta*, 1981 AMC 532 (Arb. at N.Y. 1980), the panel unanimously ruled that the owner was in breach of the charter by changing the vessel's registry from Liberia to the Republic of Philippines without the charterer's consent. The change of registry occurred some months after the vessel had been delivered to the charterer. The panel also ruled, however, that the breach was not so substantial that it gave the charterer the right to cancel the charter.

In *The Syra*, S.M.A. No. 297 (Arb. at N.Y. 1968), the vessel was initially represented as flying the Greek flag. When the charter was signed by the owner, it changed the flag of the vessel from Greek to Liberian. The charter was then sent on to the charterer, who executed it without protesting the change of flag. Subsequently, however, when extra grain fittings were required because of the Liberian flag, the charterer deducted the cost from hire, and alleged that the owner should be liable because it misrepresented the vessel's flag. The panel held for the owner, finding that since the change was known to the charterer before it executed the charter, there was no misrepresentation. *Cf. The Stolt Pam*, S.M.A. No. 1026 (Arb. at N.Y. 1976), where the owner was held entitled to change the vessel's flag in accordance with an express provision of the charter. See Vandeventer, *Analysis of Basic Provisions of Voyage and Time Charter Parties*, 49 Tul. L. Rev. 806, 832 (1975).

With hull, machinery and equipment in a thoroughly efficient state

American authorities view this statement in the charter as an express warranty of seaworthiness which must be satisfied both at the time of the making of the charter and delivery of the ship to the charterer. *The Caledonia*, 157 U.S. 124 (1895); *The Carib Prince*, 170 U.S. 655 (1898); *The Toledo*, 30 F.Supp. 93 (E.D.N.Y. 1939), aff'd 122 F.2d 255 (2d Cir. 1941), *cert.* denied 314 U.S. 689. The additional language in Lines 22 and 38 constitute further express undertakings as to the seaworthiness of the vessel, and are discussed in detail below. Where there is no express warranty of seaworthiness, the American decisions hold that there is an implied warranty of seaworthiness, unless the charter provides otherwise. *Work* v. *Leathers*, 97 U.S. 379 (1878); *The Edwin I. Morrison*, 153 U.S. 199, 210 (1893); *The Caledonia*, above.

In the absence of qualifying language in the charter, or the incorporation of the Carriage of Goods by Sea Act, the implied warranty of seaworthiness is an absolute one. The Supreme Court made this clear in *The Caledonia*:

> In our opinion, the shipowner's undertaking is not merely that he will do and has done his best to make the ship fit, but that the ship is really fit to undergo the perils of the sea and other incidental risks to which she must be exposed in the course of the voyage; and, this being so, that undertaking is not discharged because the want of fitness is the result of latent defects. (157 U.S. at 131.)

It has been held that the owner gives an implied warranty of seaworthiness of the chartered vessel at the commencement of every voyage. *Coca-Cola Co.* v. *S.S. Norholt*, 333 F.Supp. 946, 1972 AMC 388 (S.D.N.Y. 1971).

An implied warranty may be found even where the charterer has accepted the vessel as being in good condition. In *Thomas Jordan Inc.* v. *Mayronne Drilling Mud Chem. & Eng'r Serv.*, 214 F.2d 410 (5th Cir. 1954), for example, it was held that a provision in the charter that the vessel had been inspected by the charterer and found to be in "first class condition" was not a waiver of the implied warranty of seaworthiness. In that case, a loaded barge sank due to an underwater defect that could not have been detected during the inspection conducted by the charterer.

Consequence of breach of warranty of seaworthiness

A breach of the warranty of seaworthiness must be a material one to entitle the charterer to treat the contract as repudiated. See *Aaby* v. *States Marine Corp.*, above, where the Court of Appeals for the Second Circuit held that unseaworthiness alone does not entitle the charterer to cancel and that repudiation is justified only where the unseaworthiness frustrates the essential purpose of the contract. In that case, the court held that the charterer was not justified in repudiating a 12-month charter beacuse of a two-day delay at the outset of the charter period.

In *The M/V Pacsea and M/V Pacsun*, S.M.A. No. 746 (Arb. at N.Y. 1972), the arbitrators held that the charterer was not justified in terminating the charter because of apparent deficiencies in the vessel and her crew, and the owner's failure to repair. The panel found that the defects were not of "sufficient importance to warrant the termination of the charter party". According to the panel:

> The Panel realize from the testimony given, both convincingly in oral form and subsequently by documentation, that Charterers were under terrific pressures from their cargo receivers to make sure that the vessels arrived at fixed times, and in June when both vessels were delayed by weather conditions causing them both to lose their berths to other vessels, this apparently caused Charterers to feel that the weight of problems they had encountered and the number of various small

items which had been allowed to weigh heavily in their minds, all were the cause of their difficulties with their customers. As stated, however, no one single item—nor the continuity of the small annoyances that Charterers were indeed suffering—was in the opinion of the Panel sufficient to permit Charterers to terminate their commitment to Owners ahead of the contracted period.

Charterers maintained that they were able to anticipate a continuation of non-performance by the vessels' crews and the vessels' performance and also non-cooperation from Owners and that this would have made their working arrangement with their own clients absolutely unworkable. This was also put forward by Charterers as a prime reason for termination of the ships' Charters, but once again the majority of the Panel view this position as conjectural resulting in anticipatory breach of contract.

In *The Serena*, S.M.A. No. 1159 (Arb. at N.Y. 1977), the charterer claimed that it was justified in cancelling a five-year time charter after one voyage during which the vessel was delayed because of boiler problems caused primarily by crew negligence. The charterer contended that any breach of the performance warranties contained in the charter justified cancellation. The panel rejected this argument, however, and held that in view of the charter provisions concerning delays and vessel deficiencies, the cancellation was wrongful:

Charterers have requested us to consider that performance was a fundamental commitment by Owners and that it was agreed to be the very essence of the Contract and that any breach thereof permitted cancellation. We find it hard to believe that either party contemplated that a vessel almost 17 years old upon delivery would not breach a warranted condition. The Contract itself provided an elaborate and comprehensive formula to deal with such breaches when and if they occurred . . . We did not consider the non-performance Charterers demonstrated occurred during vessel's actual performance under the Contract or would have occurred had they continued performance, substantial enough to be considered fundamental breaches of this Contract, permitting cancellation.

See also *Hildebrand* v. *Geneva Mill Co.* (*The Edward R. Smith*), 32 F.2d 343, 348, 1929 AMC 962, 972–73 (M.D. Ala. 1929), holding that "the right of cancellation of a charter party does not arise out of any breach. In order to justify the rescission of a charter party, the character of the breach must be such as to defeat the purpose of the contract; otherwise recovery is confined to damages sustained"; *The Navigator*, S.M.A. No. 287 (Arb. at N.Y. 1968), holding that "unseaworthiness as such does not entitle the charterers to repudiate the charter"; *The S.S. Angelica*, S.M.A. No. 504 (Arb. at N.Y. 1970), holding that while the vessel did not conform to the charter, "the discrepancies, percentagewise, are not sufficient to make the continuation of the venture commercially impracticable"; *Tug Diane*, S.M.A. No. 819 (Arb. at N.Y. 1973), holding that the owner's failure to repair the tug's engines justified cancellation by the charterer; *The Warm Springs*, S.M.A. No. 134 (Arb. at N.Y. 1966), holding that the charterer was not entitled to cancel the charter because the owner refused to follow its voyage directions to undertake a deviation.

COGSA and the Harter Act

The incorporation by reference of the Carriage of Goods by Sea Act or the Harter Act in the charter constitutes an agreement by the owner and charterer to have their respective rights and duties controlled by these Acts to the extent they are applicable by their own terms, except insofar as the charter expressly modifies them. *Hartford Fire Insurance Co.* v. *Calmar S.S. Corp.*, 404 F.Supp. 442, 1976 AMC 2636 (W.D.Wash. 1975). As the court held in that case, where the charter incorporates COGSA, "the applicable COGSA provisions become a part of the parties' contract with the same force and effect as ordinary contract terms". (1976 AMC at 2639.) See also *The Westmoreland,* 86 F.2d 96, 1936 AMC 1680 (2d Cir. 1936). But see *Bunge Corp.* v. *Republic of Brazil,* 353 F.Supp. 64, 1973 AMC 1219 (E.D.La 1972), holding that in the event of a conflict between a provision of the charter and COGSA, the latter would prevail.

The most important effect of incorporating COGSA in the charter is that the implied warranty of seaworthiness is modified and reduced from an absolute warranty to an undertaking by the owner to exercise due diligence to render the vessel seaworthy. *Horn* v. *Cia de Navegacion Fruco S.A. (The Heinz Horn),* 404 F.2d 412 (5th Cir. 1968), *cert.* denied 394 U.S. 943 (1969); *Iligan International Corp.* v. *John Weyerhaeuser,* 372 F.Supp. 859, 1974 AMC 1719 (S.D.N.Y. 1974), aff'd 507 F.2d 68 (2d Cir. 1974), *cert.* denied 421 U.S. 956.

It has been held, however, that where the charter contains an express absolute warranty of seaworthiness, the incorporation of COGSA in the charter will not abrogate it. In *John Weyerhaeuser,* above, the vessel was chartered by Weyerhaeuser to New York Navigation on the New York Produce form. New York Navigation, in turn, entered into an agreement with Iligan whereby it agreed to provide ships for the transport of machinery and parts of a steel mill. Cargo was damaged on the voyage, and Iligan commenced an action against New York Navigation and Weyerhaeuser for the loss.

The agreement between Iligan and New York Navigation contained both an express warranty of seaworthiness and incorporated by reference the provisions of COGSA. The court held that, as between New York Navigation and Iligan, there were two obligations in force: first, the absolute duty under the express warranty to provide seaworthy vessels, and, second, an implied warranty of seaworthiness modified by COGSA to a duty to exercise due diligence. The court held that New York Navigation was liable to cargo under the express warranty, but not liable for the alleged breach of its duty to exercise due diligence.

The same analysis was applied to the charter between Weyerhaeuser and New York Navigation. The court held that Weyerhaeuser's express agreement to furnish a vessel "tight, staunch, strong and in every way fitted for service" was an absolute warranty of seaworthiness which was not modified by COGSA. This express warranty superseded the implied warranty so far as it extended, the express warranty remaining in force only until the time of delivery in the absence of charter language imposing a continuing absolute obligation to maintain the vessel in seaworthy condition. The court noted that where the charter does not provide for a continuing obligation to maintain the vessel in seaworthy condition, the express warranty having lapsed upon delivery, the implied warranty would then operate at the time of sailing.

In *John Weyerhaeuser,* the court found that Weyerhaeuser breached both its express warranty as well as the implied warranty, which, as modified by COGSA, constituted a duty only to exercise due diligence before the loading of the cargo.

Statement as to class

There do not appear to be any American cases on the question whether a statement in the charter as to the vessel's class constitutes a warranty. In view of the importance of class in terms of the charterer's ability to trade with the vessel, it seems likely the statement would be held to constitute a warranty, the breach of which would entitle the charterer to recover damages and possibly to cancel the charter if the consequences were serious enough to frustrate its purposes.

Bale and deadweight capacity

Statements in the charter as to the vessel's deadweight and cubic capacity are generally held to be warranties, although this depends on the circumstances of the case. As the court stated in *Romano* v. *West India Fruit & Steamship Co.,* 151 F.2d 727, 731 (5th Cir. 1945):

> What is important is whether the warranty was positively and unequivocally made as a statement of fact and whether the natural tendency of its making was to induce the chartering of the ship.

A warranty with respect to deadweight capacity does not necessarily constitute a warranty that the vessel will actually lift that particular tonnage. Thus, where the charter provided that the vessel merely be capable of "loading 5500 MT" cargo, and where the vessel demonstrated such capacity by loading 5,500 metric tons on its third voyage, the panel denied the charterer's deadweight deficiency claim for two earlier voyages. *The Robertina,* S.M.A. No. 1151 (Arb. at N.Y. 1977).

It is well established, however, that the charter need not expressly refer to the description as a "warranty" or "guaranty" if the intent of the parties that the statement be so understood is clear. *Denholm Shipping Co.* v. *W. E. Hedger Co.,* 47 F.2d 213, 1931 AMC 297 (2d Cir. 1931); *Metropolitan Coal Co.* v. *Howard,* 155 F.2d 780, 783 (2d Cir. 1946).

Breach of the warranty may give the charterer the option of cancellation prior to acceptance of the vessel. In the alternative, he may accept the vessel and claim damages resulting from the misdecription. See, e.g., *Dominica Mining Co.* v. *Port Everglades Towing Co.,* 318 F.Supp. 500, 1970 AMC 123 (S.D. Fla. 1969); *The Aghia Marina,* S.M.A. No. 1236 (Arb. at N.Y. 1978). In *The Atlantic Glory,* S.M.A. No. 76 (Arb. at N.Y. 1962), the panel held that since the vessel's deadweight tonnage was less than that described in the charter, the charterer was penalized by having to pay hire on a deadweight that was not available to them. Once the charterer accepts the vessel, however, he has no right to repudiate the charter unless the misrepresentation is material in the context of the intended trading of the vessel.

In *Watts* v. *Camors,* 115 U.S. 353 (1885), the vessel was described as "of the burthen of 1100 tons, or thereabouts, registered measurement". The charter provided that the charterer would provide "a full and complete cargo, say about 11,500 quarters of wheat in bulk . . .". When the vessel was delivered to the charterer, it refused to accept her or to furnish cargo, for the reason that her tonnage exceeded 1,100 tons, and was in fact about 1,203 tons. Her actual carrying capacity, however, was 11,500 quarters of wheat. The owner commenced an action to recover its damages resulting from the rejection of the vessel. The court held for the owner, concluding that the charterer had bargained for a vessel that could carry 11,500 quarters of wheat, and had got what it bargained for. Since the ship was capable of loading this amount, the misdescription of her registered tonnage was not material and would not justify termination of the charter.

In *The Neptune Kiku,* S.M.A. No. 2102 (Arb. at N.Y. 1985), charterer was held entitled to recover damages caused by the owner's failure to make a complete description of the vessel, including "any and all obstructions that existed to prevent the full reach of the holds and decks being available". There were car decks on the vessel which reduced the deck capacity for containers. The containers which could not be loaded on deck had to be shipped by ground transport to an alternate port and shipped on another vessel to the discharge port. In the charter description of the vessel, nothing was said about the presence of the car decks. The panel found that owner was in breach of the charter by having obstructions on deck which were not described in the negotiations or referred to in the charter.

Gross/net tonnage

A misdescription of the vessel's registered tonnage does not give the charterer the right to reject the vessel, except in a case where there is a very large discrepancy, although it could give rise to a claim for damages by the charterer. *Watts* v. *Camors,* 115 U.S. 353 (1885), discussed above. See also *Ashburner* v. *Balchen,* 7 N.Y 262 (1852), holding that a representation in the charter as to the vessel's registered tonnage was not a warranty; *The Emily S. Malcolm*, 278 F. 943 (3d Cir. 1922), holding that a charter provision estimating the vessel's carrying capacity was not a warranty, and that the owner was entitled to the full freight provided in the charter even though the vessel's capacity was substantially less than as described; *Ontario Paper Co.* v. *Neff,* 261 F. 353 (7th Cir. 1919), holding that the owner was entitled to rescind the charter where the parties had made a mutual mistake as to the vessel's paper-carrying capacity; *S. O. Stray and Co.* v. *Trottier, Ide and Co.*, 280 F. 249 (D. Mass. 1922), holding that a statement of the vessel's bale capacity as to which there was a mutual mistake of fact was not a warranty, but was intended only to be an estimate.

"About"

Where the charter provides that the deadweight capacity is "about" a specified amount, an allowance of 5 per cent more or less has been permitted. See *J. E. Hurley Lumber Co.* v. *Compania Panamena Maritima San Gerassimo S.A.*, 1958 AMC 2502 (Arb. at N.Y. 1958); *The North Hills,* 1973 AMC 2318 (Arb. at N.Y. 1972). The use of the term "about" in describing the vessel's deadweight, however, does not in the absence of qualifying language in the charter permit a reasonable allowance on the vessel's actual carrying capacity for which the charterer has bargained and paid. In *The Aghia Marina,* S.M.A. No. 1236 (Arb. at N.Y. 1978), the vessel's deadweight was given as "about 17,593 long tons" and the owner warranted that stores and fresh water would not exceed 300 tons. The panel rejected the owner's contention that the "about" provision should apply to actual carrying capacity. The charterer called for a cargo of 16,800 tons. Since only 16,467.78 tons were loaded, the charterer was held entitled to a hire reduction for a shortloading of 293.92 long tons for the applicable period of the voyage.

Speed and fuel consumption

A description of the vessel's speed and fuel consumption constitutes a warranty by the owner that the ship will be able to attain the stated speed at the stipulated rate of consumption under the described weather conditions. The statement is a warranty even though it is not expressly described as such in the charter. *Denholm Shipping Co.* v. *W. E. Hedger Co.*, 47 F.2d 213, 1931 AMC 297 (2d Cir. 1931). Under American law the vessel must be capable of attaining the stated speed at the stipulated rate of consumption on the date of delivery to the charterer. It is not, however, a continuing warranty. As the court stated in *Denholm Shipping*:

> The meaning of the warranty is however another matter; it spoke from the time of delivery, and was satisfied if the ship was at that time 'capable' of making the prescribed speed under the stipu-

lated conditions. It did not follow that she would make it uniformly; that depended upon how she was driven, and whether she had become foul or disabled, even though the conditions were fulfilled. On the other hand, the charterer might assume that it meant something of practical use to him; that it spoke of ordinary service at sea; and it is not relevant whether she later made the required speed under a test by the owner, as apparently she did. We are to inquire whether when laden as intended, she could steam at the stipulated speeds in good weather and smooth seas. If the charterer showed that she could not, he proved a breach, and the best test is what she actually did during the voyage in question on such days as fulfilled the requirements. (47 F.2d at 215.)

The warranty does not mean that the owner guarantees the vessel will average the described speed throughout the period of the charter, unless the contract so provides. See *Cargo Ships El-Yam Ltd.* v. *Stearns & Foster Co.,* 149 F.Supp. 754, 770 (S.D.N.Y. 1955); *The Ceres,* 72 F. 936 (2d Cir. 1896), *cert.* denied 163 U.S. 706 (1896); *The Astraea,* 124 F. 83 (E.D.N.Y. 1903). It is clearly inapplicable in bad weather or when the vessel is in confined waters, such as harbors or rivers. See *The Mini Lap,* S.M.A. 1077 (Arb. at N.Y. 1976) and *The Medita,* S.M.A. No. 1150 (Arb. at N.Y. 1977). See also *The Drosia,* S.M.A. No. 1303 (Arb. at N.Y. 1979), where the charterer was granted damages for owner's breach of his performance warranties in good weather, but no allowance was made for failure to meet the charter warranties in bad weather.

In determining whether the vessel is in conformity with the speed warranty, however, the practice generally followed in arbitrations is to consider the vessel's performance throughout the period of the charter. As the panel stated in *The Seamaid,* 1967 AMC 1362, 1364–1365 (Arb. at N.Y. 1966):

There are two established methods of determining a speed claim. The first is . . . did the vessel make the Charter Party warranty of speed on the days when good weather conditions prevailed?

Second . . . was the average speed that the vessel made on the entire voyage, taking weather conditions into consideration as well as currents, reasonable in relation to the Charter Party description?

The majority of the Panel is of the opinion that both criteria should normally be used.

In *The Stove Vulkan,* S.M.A. No. 292 (Arb. at N.Y. 1968), the panel held that the method it should follow in determining whether there was a breach of the speed warranty was as follows:

It was decided by the Panel that the average speed attained by the vessel on only those days when she was fully loaded and the weather was force 4 or less, coupled with a few other days when force 5 and 6 winds were generally following this ship, should be truly indicative of her capability made evident during this charter.

In *The Penta,* S.M.A. No. 1603 (Arb. at N.Y. 1981), the charter was on the Baltime 1939 form and stated "and fully loaded capable of steaming about 16 1/2 knots in good weather and smooth water". The arbitrators held that in evaluating the charterer's speed claim, the criterion to be used was to review the vessel's actual performance under the described weather conditions. They found that the vessel had actually met her warranted speed at these times and proved her ability to comply with the speed warranty. See also *The Mount Athos,* S.M.A. No. 1570 (Arb. at N.Y. 1981).

The "distance/speed" theory, by which the vessel's performance is evaluated by dividing the distance traveled by the time required for the voyage, has been repudiated in some arbitrations as a means of determining whether there is a speed deficiency. See *The Bedeburn,* 1931 AMC 1678 (Arb.); *The Cape Palmas,* S.M.A. No. 440 (Arb. at N.Y. 1964).

Once a speed deficiency has been determined, any charter hire reduction should apply only to those periods when speed was an essential component. This was the view expressed in *The Olympic Garland,* S.M.A. No. 1209 (Arb. at N.Y. 1978), where the vessel failed to maintain its guaranteed average speed of 15.75 knots in moderate weather and the resulting hire deduction was neither based on the entire period of the contract including port time, nor limited only to the moderate weather steaming period, but was based on the period it would have taken the vessel to cover the charter distance at the vessel's actual moderate weather speed of 14.83 knots.

The speed warranty must also be considered in connection with the owner's undertaking under Clause 1 to maintain the vessel in a thoroughly efficient state during the service. This undertaking requires that the vessel be maintained throughout the charter in substantially the same condition as she is in at the commencement of the charter, insofar as the performance warranties are concerned. If a defect in the hull, machinery or equipment arises after delivery and adversely affects the vessel's speed and fuel consumption, the charterer may have a basis for asserting a claim against the owner under that clause, even if it is unable as a practical matter to show a breach of the speed warranty on the date of delivery. See *Hellenic Bulk Transport S.A.* v. *Burmah Oil Tankers Ltd.*, S.M.A. No. 1086 (Arb. at N.Y. 1976); *Compania Venetico de Navegacion S.A.* v. *Presthus Chartering A/S,* S.M.A. No. 1110 (Arb. at N.Y. 1977); *Romano* v. *West India Fruit & S.S. Co.,* 151 F.2d 727 (5th Cir. 1945); *The Astraea,* 124 F. 83 (E.D.N.Y. 1903).

In *The Grace V,* S.M.A. No. 1760 (Arb. at N.Y. 1982), the panel refused to accept a charterer's speed claim based upon a report prepared by a weather routing service:

> Arbitration panels have consistently held in the past that a speed claim based upon actual time consumed on a voyage, adjusted for assumed weather conditions derived from inconclusive sources, fails.
>
> Further, the method employed by Charterer in its speed claim presentation based upon the findings of the weather service utilized, effectively converts the speed evaluation under the charter party to an *all weather* computation, whereas the language of the contract and commercial interpretation exclude heavy weather periods from consideration. (Emphasis in original.)

Arbitration panels have preferred to rely upon ship's logbooks over reports prepared by independent weather routing services. Panels will generally rely on the vessel's records unless there is proof that the records are "so at variance with any conceivable prevailing condition that they lack integrity or that no reliance whatsoever should be given to them". *The Manila Enterprise,* S.M.A. No. 2060 (Arb. at N.Y. 1983). See *The Georgios,* S.M.A. No. 2005 (Arb. at N.Y. 1984); *The Trade Endeavor,* S.M.A. No. 1916 (Arb. at N.Y. 1983); *The Spray Cap,* S.M.A. No. 1706 (Arb. at N.Y. 1982). In some cases, the weather routing service report has been found to be more reliable than the ship's logs. See, e.g., *The United Bounty,* S.M.A. No. 2040 (Arb. at N.Y. 1984), discussed below at page 284.

"About"

The speed description is usually modified by the word "about". This frequently has been held to give the owner an allowance of half a knot below the described speed. See, e.g., *The Northern Clipper,* 1967 AMC 1557 (Arb. at N.Y. 1967); *The Ghikas,* S.M.A. No. 686 (Arb. at N.Y. 1972); *Byzantine Maritime Corp.* v. *Matthew Shipping Co. Ltd.*, S.M.A. No. 972 (Arb. at N.Y. 1975); *The Skadi,* S.M.A. No. 789 (Arb. at N.Y. 1973); *Hellenic Bulk Transport S.A.* v. *Burmah Oil Tankers Ltd.*, S.M.A. No. 1086 (Arb. at N.Y. 1976); *The Panagiotis Xilas,* S.M.A. No. 1035 (Arb. at N.Y. 1976); *The Grand Integrity,* S.M.A. No. 671 (Arb. at N.Y. 1971); *The Stove Vulkan,* S.M.A. No. 292 (Arb.

at N.Y. 1968); *The Aghia Marina,* S.M.A. No. 1236 (Arb. at N.Y. 1978); *The Argo Master,* S.M.A. No 1489 (Arb. at N.Y. 1980). However, the interpretation of the "about" provision may depend upon the facts of each case and the intent of the parties as expressed in the entire charter. See *Cargo Ships El-Yam Ltd.* v. *Stearns & Foster Co.,* 149 F.Supp. 754, 1957 AMC 668 (S.D.N.Y. 1955). Thus, it is possible the panel would find that the parties intended a greater or smaller allowance should be applicable. For example, in *The Seamaid,* 1967 AMC 1362 (Arb. at N.Y. 1966), nine knots was held to be a reasonably average all-weather speed for a 20-year-old vessel described in the charter as capable of "about 10 knots". In *The Adelfoi,* 1972 AMC 1742 (Arb. at N.Y. 1972), the panel held that the warranty of 13 knots on the stated consumption of 26 tons would have been satisfied if the vessel had made 12.6 knots, based on an allowance of .5 knot for "about" and adding .1 knot for the fact that the vessel was not always fully laden. In *The Chris,* S.M.A. No. 199 (Arb. at N.Y. 1958), "about" was held to permit an allowance of .33 knot, against the warranty of "about 10 knots".

"Good weather"

"Good weather" is generally held to mean winds of Force 4 or below on the Beaufort Scale. *The Northern Clipper,* above; *The Miami,* S.M.A. No. 240 (Arb. at N.Y. 1967); *The Costa Rican Trader,* S.M.A. No. 203 (Arb. at N.Y. 1967); *The Argo Sky,* S.M.A. No. 627 (Arb. at N.Y. 1971); *The Adelfoi,* 1972 AMC 1742, 1743 (Arb. at N.Y. 1972); *The Alma,* S.M.A. No. 261 (Arb. at N.Y. 1964); *The Union Mariner,* S.M.A. No. 89 (Arb. at N.Y. 1960). In *The Stove Vulkan,* S.M.A. 292 (Arb. at N.Y. 1968), the panel held that "good weather" is inclusive of Force 4 and can even be Force 5 or 6 when such winds are following or on the vessel's quarter.

Bottom fouling

A common problem that has arisen in connection with the speed warranty and the collateral undertaking to maintain the vessel in a thoroughly efficient state is that of bottom fouling which slows the vessel down. Who bears this risk?

The earlier cases approached the problem in conjunction with the owner's obligation to drydock. Thus, where the charterer failed to bargain for a drydocking clause, fouling in the ordinary course of tropical trading was held not a breakdown or defect of hull within the meaning of Clause 15. *Glasgow Shipowner's Co.* v. *Bacon,* 139 F. 541 (2d Cir. 1905); *Damps. Norden* v. *Isbrandtsen-Moller Co. (The Katonia),* 43 F.2d 560, 1930 AMC 1441 (S.D.N.Y. 1930). As stated in *The Katonia:*

> The charterer knew the use to which the vessel was to be put, and the waters through which she would travel, and if it wished to protect itself against the consequences of marine growths encumbering the hull, specific provision for that contingency should have been made. It will not do to take chances with marine growths, and then at a later date seek to hold the owner to liability under a provision of general fitness contained in the agreement, which was designed to cover an entirely different subject matter. (43 F.2d at 562.)

Where the charter contains a drydocking clause, it has been held that the owner is under a duty to drydock the vessel to remove bottom growth if the bottom fouling is readily discernible. Thus, in *The Praxiteles,* S.M.A. Nos. 104, 600 (Arb. at N.Y. 1964), the owner was held liable for a speed deficiency resulting from bottom fouling where the growth could have been detected and he had failed to drydock the vessel. Clause 21 of the New York Produce form requires drydocking every six months in tropical trade, even if there is no reason to suspect bottom growth and drydocking appears to be unnecessary. *Munson S.S. Line* v. *Miramar S.S. Co.,* 166 F.722 (2d Cir. 1908), *cert.* denied 214 U.S. 526; *Noyes* v. *Munson S.S. Line,* 173 F. 814 (S.D.N.Y. 1909); *Falls of Keltie S.S. Co.* v. *United States & A.S.S. Co.,* 108 F. 416 (S.D.N.Y 1901).

Some cases have tended to ignore the question of responsibility for fouling, and have simply treated the resulting slow speed as a deficiency like any other under the off-hire clause. See *The Northern Clipper,* 1967 AMC 1557 (Arb. at N.Y. 1967); *The Panagiotis Xilas,* S.M.A. No. 1035 (Arb. at N.Y. 1976). See discussion of the off-hire clause at page 315.

Where fouling exists before delivery, the owner must, of course, bear the responsibility. *The Atlanta,* 82 F.Supp. 218, 1948 AMC 1769 (S.D.Ga. 1948). Similarly, in *The Pomona,* S.M.A. No. 118 (Arb. at N.Y. 1966), the owner was held liable for delays caused by bottom fouling which developed while the vessel was off-hire for an extended period of time.

On the other hand, bottom growth during the charter period has been held to be the charterer's responsibility. In *The Stove Vulkan,* S.M.A. No. 292 (Arb. at N.Y. 1968), the charterer was held to be responsible for contributing to the speed deficiency on inward and outward voyages resulting from bottom growth during the term of the charter. The panel deducted 25 per cent. of the award for a speed deficiency to account for bottom growth. In *The Mount Athos,* S.M.A. No. 1570 (Arb. at N.Y. 1981), the arbitrators applied to their speed computations an allowance for speed reduction occasioned by the presence of bottom growth.

In *The Milly Gregos,* S.M.A. No. 2190 (Arb. at N.Y. 1986), the panel denied charterer's claim for a speed deficiency attributable to bottom growth which grew during the vessel's prolonged stay in the Philippines. The panel noted that charterer had the right to have the problem removed by cleaning the bottom at its expense. Similarly, in *The Mykali II,* S.M.A. No. 2240 (Arb. at N.Y. 1986), the panel held that bottom and propeller fouling during the vessel's prolonged stay at Durban "was a natural and foreseeable consequence of the vessel's complying with charterer's orders". The panel declined charterer's claim that the vessel was off-hire, as well as its claim for excess consumption.

Fuel consumption

The speed description is followed immediately by a representation as to the amount of fuel the vessel will consume to maintain that speed. This statement is also a warranty which must be satisfied on delivery of the vessel to the charterer. One panel of arbitrators held that the speed and fuel consumption warranties are not independent guarantees, but are to be read together. As the panel stated in *The Vendelso,* S.M.A. No. 663 (Arb. at N.Y. 1971): "Compliance means satisfaction of both—not one in deference to the other". However, in *The Olympic Garland,* S.M.A. No. 1209 (Arb. at N.Y. 1978), the arbitrators held otherwise. After noting that the combined consumptions of diesel fuel and high viscosity fuel oil determined the net consumption for which the owner was liable, and after finding that the combined overconsumption of the one fuel and under consumption of the other resulted in a net underconsumption the panel denied the owner's request that the value of the net balance for underconsumption of fuel be deducted from the damages for speed deficiency, holding flatly that "the speed and consumption guarantees of the contract are independent of each other and cannot be used to adjust the value of the other".

In *The Panamax Venus,* S.M.A. No. 1979 (Arb. at N.Y. 1984), however, the panel found that owner's claim for fuel underconsumption could be set-off against a charterer's claim for speed deficiency.

As with the speed warranty, the word "about" does modify the owner's duty, although the allowance that will be permitted depends upon the facts of each case. In *The Medita,* S.M.A. No. 1150 (Arb. at N.Y. 1977), the ship was given an allowance of 3 per cent. for the word "about" in the charterparty description. In *The Areti S,* 1965 AMC 2116 (Arb. at N.Y. 1965), the panel held there was no breach of the warranty of about 10 knots on a consumption of 26/27 tons of fuel, where the vessel made 9.5 knots on an average consumption of 24.35 tons. See also *The Atlantic Master,* S.M.A. No. 510 (Arb. at N.Y.); *The Panagiotis Xilas,* S.M.A. No. 1035 (Arb. at N.Y. 1976), *The United Bounty*, S.M.A. No. 2040 (Arb. at N.Y. 1984).

Like the speed warranty, the consumption warranty normally applies only to the vessel's performance in the open sea. *The Eurytan,* S.M.A. No. 289 (Arb. at N.Y. 1968). But see *The Alma,* S.M.A. No. 261 (Arb. at N.Y. 1964), where in-port consumption was extraordinarily high and the warranty was held to have been breached.

Present position

A statement as to the vessel's position may constitute a warranty depending upon the importance of the statement in the circumstances. Compare *Davison* v. *Von Lingen,* 113 U.S. 40, 41 (1885) (warranty) and *Lovell* v. *Davis,* 101 U.S. 541 (1879) (no warranty).

In *Davison,* the court found that the "time and situation of the vessel were material and essential parts of the contract". Thus, according to the court, the statement as to the vessel's position was a warranty, the breach of which justified cancellation or a claim for damages. According to the court:

> That the stipulation in the charter-party, that the vessel is "now sailed or about to sail from Benizaf, with cargo, for Philadelphia" is a warranty, or a condition precedent, is, we think, quite clear. It is a substantive part of the contract, and not a mere representation, and is not an independent agreement, serving only as a foundation for an action for compensation in damages. A breach of it by one party justifies a repudiation of the contract by the other party, if it has not been partially executed in his favor. (113 U.S. at 49–50.)

See also *Himoff Indus* v. *Seven Seas Shipping Corp.,* 1976 AMC 1030, 1032–33 (N.Y. Sup. 1976), holding that an innocent misrepresentation by the owner as to the vessel's position permitted cancellation of the charter, inasmuch as the position was material because of approaching ice conditions on the St. Lawrence Seaway.

In *Lovell,* on the other hand, the court held that the statement as to the vessel's position was not a warranty, but a representation, which the charterer apparently knew to be incorrect and upon which it therefore did not rely. The vessel was represented in the charter to be lying in the harbor of New Orleans, when she was in fact at sea. The vessel was delayed in arriving at New Orleans, and the charterer cancelled the charter. The court held that the representation as to the vessel's position should be given no significance since the charterer did not rely on it, and held for the owner.

The result in *Lovell* would probably have been quite different, however, had the charterer not known the vessel's true position and had it in fact been induced to charter the vessel on the basis of the owner's misrepresentation as to her position. In these circumstances, under general principles of contract law, the charterer would have had a basis for an action for damages.

Charter Period

"13. Witnesseth, That the said Owners agree to let, and the said Charterers agree to hire the said vessel, from the time of delivery, for
14. about ...."

Delivery

The period begins with "delivery". This word on its own means no more than the placing of the ship and her crew at the disposal of the charterers at the place stipulated in Line 18. Roskill, J., said in *The Madeleine* [1967] 2 Lloyd's Rep. 224, at page 238: "An owner delivers a ship to a time charterer under this form of charter-party [the Baltime] by placing her at the charterers' disposal and by placing the services of her master, officers and crew at the charterers' disposal, so that the charterers may thenceforth give orders (within the terms of the charter-party) as to the employment of the vessel to the master, officers and crew, which orders the owners contract that their servants shall obey."

For other requirements which must be met before the hire period can start, see pages 113 to 121 below. See also pages 228 and 229, below, as to when time starts to count for the purpose of payment of hire.

"Let" and "hire"

The use of these words in the New York Produce form and other similar forms of time charter is misleading. Despite these words and the words "delivery" and "redelivery", the owners neither hire the ship nor part with possession of it. Their obligation under this type of contract is to render to the charterers the agreed services with the ship, master and crew: see pages 440 to 441 below.

Charter period (overlap/underlap)

Unless the parties have used exceptionally strong words to impose upon the charterers an absolute obligation to redeliver the ship by a certain date (see page 94 below), the charterers will not be in breach in sending the ship on a final voyage which may be expected to allow redelivery within the charter period, including any express margin, or any margin implied by law, as to which see pages 91 to 94 below, even if in fact redelivery takes place outside that period.

Legitimate final voyage

If the charterers send the ship on a final voyage which is legitimate in the sense that it may reasonably be expected to allow redelivery by the end of the charter period, including any express or implied margin, the owners must comply with the charterers' orders.

If, despite the reasonableness of that expectation, the ship cannot in fact be redelivered until the charter period (including any express or implied margin) has expired, the charterers will be obliged to continue to pay hire at the rate agreed in the charter until the date of actual redelivery. Upward or downward differences between the charter rate and the market rate of hire during this overlap period are ignored in this situation. In the New York Produce form the continuity of the obligation in such circumstances to pay hire at, but not above or below, the rate agreed in the charter is emphasised by the words in Line 54 (Clause 4), "hire to continue until the hour of the day of her re-delivery". (The sometimes different effect of the corresponding clause in the Baltime charter (Clause 7) is recorded below.) In *The Dione* [1975] 1 Lloyd's Rep. 115, Lord Denning, M.R., said: "If [after being sent on a legitimate final voyage] the vessel is afterwards delayed by matters for which neither party is responsible, the charter is presumed to continue in operation until the end of that voyage, even though it extends beyond the charter period. The hire is payable at the charter rate until redelivery, even though the market rate may have gone up or down."

The *London Explorer* was chartered under the New York Produce form for "12 months 15 days more or less in Charterers option", the preceding printed word "about" in Line 14 having been deleted. She was sent on a final voyage that should have allowed redelivery well within this period but which was extended by unforeseen strikes until considerably after its expiry. The freight market had fallen and the charterers sought to establish that they were in breach and, therefore, obliged to pay damages for the period of "overlap" at the then market rate instead of continuing throughout that period to pay hire at the (higher) rate stipulated in the charter. The House of Lords rejected this argument, holding that there was no breach of contract. The orders for the final voyage were good and did not cease to be so because of unexpected delays thereafter. In any event, the hire was payable at the charter rate until redelivery under Line 54 (whether or not supplemented by damages for breach of contract).

Lord Reid said: "It seems to me that, unless the parties agree otherwise, it must be presumed because it is business-like that the charter is intended to continue in operation until the end of a legitimate last voyage—unless of course one of the parties was responsible for the delay."

The London Explorer [1971] 1 Lloyd's Rep. 523.

(See also *Hector* v. *Sovfracht* (1945) 78 Ll.L.Rep. 275.)

It should be noted that certain *obiter* comments of Lord Morris in *The London Explorer,* above, have been taken to mean that where the charterers have sent the ship on a legitimate final voyage they may nevertheless be in breach if in fact that voyage continues, even without their fault, for an unreasonable time beyond the end of the charter period. It is suggested that this interpretation of those comments is inconsistent with the test of the legitimate final voyage, which is now generally accepted as correct, as well as with the approach of Lord Reid in the same case, and should be rejected. Thus, once the final voyage has been characterised as legitimate, the charterers should not be regarded as in breach and obliged to pay a rate higher than that agreed in the charter merely because that voyage actually postpones redelivery well beyond the date agreed in the charter.

If, however, the charterers cause additional delay by a breach of another term of the charter (for example their obligation to send the ship only to safe ports) and the market rate has risen above the charter rate of hire, they will be liable to pay the excess as damages for the period of additional delay. It has not been decided whether the same is true where the charterers have caused the additional delay but without breaching any term of the charter; the use of the word "responsible" by Lord Reid in *The London Explorer* and by Lord Denning, M.R., in *The Dione,* above, is ambiguous (see also *The Mareva A.S.* [1977] 1 Lloyd's Rep. 368).

Baltime Clause 7

For the effect of the second paragraph of Clause 7 of the Baltime form (set out at page 464 below) see below at page 91.

Time at which the legitimacy of the final voyage is to be judged

The relevant time for considering the question of the reasonableness of an estimate as to the length of the last voyage is immediately prior to the last voyage.

The *Democritos* was chartered for a trip on the New York Produce form for "duration about 4 to 6 months". Allowing a margin of five days, this meant the ship had to be redelivered by 23 June 1970. It was argued that the time for testing the legitimacy of the last voyage was the date when the charterers first gave orders for the ship's last voyage, namely 13 May; but it was held by the Court of Appeal that the relevant date was when the ship started on the ballast leg of her last voyage and it was plain that, at that time, 6 June, there was no reasonable prospect whatever of the ship reaching her redelivery port by 23 June.
The Democritos [1976] 2 Lloyd's Rep. 149.

In the above case Lord Denning, M.R., disapproved of suggestions by Donaldson, J., in *The Berge Tasta* [1975] 1 Lloyd's Rep. 422, that attention should be paid to the overall voyage planning of the charterers rather than to the last voyage on its own. But Staughton, J., in *The Matija Gubec* [1983] 1 Lloyd's Rep. 24, speculated (without having to decide) whether it was still open to him on the authorities to determine the legitimacy of the last voyage by reference to the date of the order, rather than by reference to the date of the beginning of that voyage. A case can certainly be made for preferring the date of the order if the order is not given unreasonably early, but such a qualification would introduce an undesirable element of uncertainty. Further, it is submitted that on the balance of the authorities as they stand the relevant time is, as stated above, immediately prior to the last voyage. If the first leg of that voyage is in ballast, the relevant time would be immediately prior to sailing; if cargo is to be loaded on the last voyage, the relevant time would be immediately prior to the commencement of loading.

Bridge, L.J., in *The Democritos,* forecast difficulties in deciding in some cases what was the last voyage. He pointed out that the Court of Appeal had assumed in *The Dione* that the last voyage was the round trip from Europe to the River Plate and back, but without hearing argument on the point. Lord Denning, M.R., referred to "the last full voyage".

The legitimacy or otherwise of whatever is to be regarded as the ship's last voyage must also be judged by reference to what the charterers actually order her to do. In *The Mareva A.S.,* the charterers argued that there was an implication or joint expectation that the ship would perform a final loaded passage to the redelivery area, but that they had been deprived of that opportunity by delays on the last voyage for which the owners were responsible. It was held that as no orders had been given for that passage at any time when it would have been wrongful for the owners to refuse them, no claim could be made in respect of it. Kerr, J., recognised that, had such orders been given along with the last voyage orders that were given, difficult questions would have arisen, particularly as to whether the orders would then have been for a larger last voyage or, in effect, for two—a penultimate and then a last voyage: see [1977] 1 Lloyd's Rep. 368, at page 379.

In *The Matija Gubec* above, Staughton, J., held that the legitimacy of a last voyage was not to be judged at the date when the charterers formed a firm intention to send the ship on a particular voyage if that intention was not at the time communicated to the owners.

Illegitimate last voyage

If the charterers send the ship on a final voyage which is illegitimate in the sense that it cannot reasonably be expected to allow redelivery by the end of the charter period (including any express or implied margin), then the owners are entitled to refuse their orders and call for fresh orders for a final voyage that is legitimate. If no such orders are then forthcoming, the owners may treat the charter as discharged, seek other employment and claim damages.

Mere compliance with an illegitimate order, without more, will probably not amount to a waiver of the owners' rights either to refuse further compliance with the order subsequently or to claim damages for the breach: see *The Kanchenjunga* [1987] 2 Lloyd's Rep. 509, [1989] 1 Lloyd's Rep. 354 (C.A.) and page 148 below. But if, with full knowledge of the facts and the consequent illegitimacy of the order, the owners allow the ship to proceed on the voyage, they will usually be held to have waived the right to refuse further compliance with the order subsequently, although probably not their right to damages for the breach: see the general comments on waiver, page 59 above. If the ship undertakes the illegitimate voyage, and there has been no waiver of the owners' right to claim damages for the breach, the owners will be entitled to hire at the rate agreed in the charter up to the end of the charter period and, where the market rate has risen, to the market rate from then until redelivery: see *The Dione* [1975] 1 Lloyd's Rep. 115 and particularly the judgment of Lord Denning, M.R., at page 118. If at the end of the charter period the market rate is below the charter rate, it is submitted that the owners will still be entitled to hire at the charter rate until redelivery. This is in accordance with the decision of the House of Lords in *The London Explorer,* above, that regardless of breach by the charterers the charter hire continues to be payable until actual redelivery, particularly where the charter contains a provision such as that in Clause 4 of the New York Produce form.

Baltime Clause 7

The last paragraph of Clause 7 of the Baltime form expressly allows the charterers to send the ship on a final voyage "by which the Charter period will be exceeded" provided "it could be reasonably calculated that the voyage would allow re-delivery about" the end of the charter period (see page 465 below). For the period of any actual overlap the market rate of hire is to be paid if it exceeds the charter rate. But this provision applies only where the final voyage "will" overrun the charter period as at the time the orders for it are given; so it does not displace the general rule, above, that where a legitimate voyage is ordered which unexpectedly overruns the charter period the charterers pay only at the charter rate until redelivery; see *Hector* v. *Sovfracht* (1945) 78 Ll.L.Rep. 275.

Charter period extended by express or implied margin

In order to determine the legitimacy or otherwise of the final voyage in accordance with the above rules, it is necessary to know whether the charter period will be extended by an additional margin. This depends upon the words in which the parties have defined the charter period: see generally the judgment of Lord Denning, M.R., in *The Dione* [1975] 1 Lloyd's Rep. 115.

(1) *Where margin may be implied*

Where the charter is for a simple stated period, such as "six months" or "two years", the courts will imply a reasonable margin. This is the result of a recognition that it is not commercially practicable for the charterers in making their voyage planning to calculate exactly the day on which the final voyage will end and the ship be ready for redelivery. Where such a margin is implied the charterers, as explained above, are not in breach if they send the ship on a final voyage which can reasonably be expected to end beyond the stated period itself but within the implied margin.

The *Blytheville* was chartered for three calender months from 26 June 1880. The charterers ordered a final voyage which was then expected to allow redelivery four days after 26 September, but which, in the event, resulted in redelivery only on 13 October. Mathew, J., held that the charterers were not in breach and the owners were not entitled to damages at the (higher) market rate from 26 September.
Gray v. *Christie* (1889) 5 T.L.R. 577.

A margin will also be implied where the period of the charter is stated as a range—such as "four to six months"—or where a range of dates is given for redelivery.

The *Democritos* was chartered on the New York Produce form for a trip, "duration about 4 to 6 months". It was held by the Court of Appeal that a margin should be allowed beyond six months. The margin allowed by the arbitrators was five days.
(It seems that a margin would still have been allowed even if the stated period had not been preceded by the word "about".)
The Democritos [1976] 2 Lloyd's Rep. 149.

As to a range of dates for redelivery, see *Watson Steamship* v. *Merryweather* (1913) 18 Com. Cas. 294, below.

The presumption in favour of an implied margin is reinforced when the charter period is preceded by the word "about", as in Line 14 of the New York Produce form.

(2) *Where margin may not be implied*

Where the parties have in their charter expressed the charter period as being between a certain "minimum" and a certain "maximum" time, the court will not imply an additional margin beyond the stated "maximum".

The *Mareva A.S.* was chartered under the New York Produce form for a trip. By addendum No. 1 the charter was extended to "five (5) months, twenty (20) days more or less in Charterers' option". Subsequently, a further addendum was concluded providing "Charterers are to keep the vessel on Time Charter for a further period of 2 months minimum, 3 months maximum, in direct continuation from the end of the full period of 5 months and 20 days". It was held by Kerr, J., that no margin beyond the further three months was to be allowed.
The Mareva A.S. [1977] 1 Lloyd's Rep. 368.
(See also for a minimum/maximum period, *The Johnny* [1977] 2 Lloyd's Rep. 1, and page 465 below.)

Similarly, no additional margin will be implied where the parties have themselves expressed a margin in their definition of the charter period, for example by adding to the basic period "20 days more or less". From certain observations in the House of Lords in *The London Explorer* [1971] 1 Lloyd's Rep. 523, it had seemed that in such a case an additional margin might still be implied by the court, but it was subsequently decided otherwise by a majority of the Court of Appeal in the case which follows.

The *Dione* was time chartered on the Baltime form "for a period of 6 (six) months time charter 20 days more or less in Charterers' option". The period of six months from the date of delivery ended on 8 September 1970, and 20 days more than six months on 28 September. On 24 July while the ship was discharging at Ancona, the charterers declared their intention of sending her on another round voyage to the River Plate—a voyage which could reasonably be expected to take about 73 days. Despite the owners' protests, the charterers sent the ship on 2 August to the Plate and she was not redelivered until 7 October. It was found as a fact by arbitrators that, if a margin was to be allowed over six months and 20 days, the actual overlap of 8.4 days was reasonable. It was held by a majority of the Court of Appeal that:

(1) the clause expressly defined the margin as "20 days more or less" and left no room for any implied margin beyond this; and consequently,
(2) the charter period expired on 28 September and the orders given by the charterers to the ship to sail for the Plate on 2 August were illegitimate in the sense that it was not expected that the voyage could be completed within the charter period; and
(3) the charterers were liable to pay the higher market rate of hire for the ship from 28 September to 7 October.

The Dione [1975] 1 Lloyd's Rep. 115.

Whether the courts will be influenced against allowing an implied margin where the printed form of charter includes the word "about" before the description of the charter period (see Line 14 of the New York Produce form) and this word has been deleted by the parties, is not finally decided. In *The London Explorer,* above, Lord Reid was clearly of the view that he was entitled to take note of the deletion of the word "about" from a standard printed charter form, as opposed to the deletion of words from an earlier draft drawn up by the parties themselves, but he refrained from expressing a final opinion on the point as it had not been argued before him.

In *The Matija Gubec* [1983] 1 Lloyd's Rep. 24, where the charter period was expressed to be for 12 months "45 days more or less in Charterers' option", Staughton, J., did not consider that it mattered whether "about" was originally in the printed form of charter and had been deleted, or whether the word "about" was absent altogether; in either case the express tolerance ousted any margin that would otherwise have been implied. However, the deletion of "about" from the printed form might affect the construction of less clear wording. See also on the general problem of deletions from standard forms of charter, the judgment of Diplock, J., in *Dreyfus* v. *Parnaso* [1959] 1 Lloyd's Rep. 125, at page 130.

For a case on the delayed exercise of a contractual right (held also to be a duty) to narrow a redelivery margin where the original margin was expressed as "five years time charter with three months more or less in charterer's option", see *The Didymi and The Leon* [1984] 1 Lloyd's Rep. 583 (C.A.).

Extent of the margin that the court may imply

The extent of any margin that the court or arbitrators may imply under (1) above depends on the circumstance of each case, but is likely to be influenced by the length of the basic charter period. In *The Democritos* [1975] 1 Lloyd's Rep. 386, Kerr, J., said, in regard to the arbitrators' findings in the case of a charter for "duration about 4 to 6 months": " . . . perhaps because of the word 'about', and no doubt also because dates for redelivery in time charters are generally to be regarded as approximate only and as permitting some reasonable overrun, the arbitrators extended the period of six months by a further five days. Whether I would have reached the same conclusion or made some greater allowance is not an issue before me and I therefore say nothing about it. They have added what they regarded as a reasonably additional period . . . "

In *The Berge Tasta* [1975] 1 Lloyd's Rep. 422, Donaldson, J., considered that under a consecutive voyage charter for 30 months from 25 April 1969, redelivery within 10 or 11 days of 25 October 1971, was just within a reasonable margin, and in *The Dione* [1975] 1 Lloyd's Rep. 115, London arbitrators considered as reasonable an overlap (if an overlap were to be allowed) of 8.4 days beyond a period of six months 20 days. See also *Meyer* v. *Sanderson* (1916) 32 T.L.R. 428.

Interaction with Clause 13 of the New York Produce form

A problem may arise in calculating the maximum total charter period where, in addition to an expressed allowance beyond the basic period, the charterers have an option to extend that basic period under Clause 13 of the New York Produce form: see page 285.

Absolute obligation to redeliver by end of charter period

In exceptional cases it may be held that the parties have used words which impose on the charterers an absolute obligation to redeliver the ship by the end of the charter period and thus exclude the flexibility in their favour which is introduced by the concept of the legitimate final voyage considered above. Where this is so, the charterers will be in breach simply by failing, for whatever reason other than a causative breach by the owners, to make redelivery on or before the relevant date.

The *Hugin* was time chartered for a period "from May 15/31 1912, until 15/31 October, 1912". The charter contained printed words similar to Lines 54 and 55 of the New York Produce form "hire to continue . . . until her redelivery to owners (unless lost) at a port on east coast of the United Kingdom", after which there were the handwritten words "between 15th and 31st October, 1912". On 18 October 1912, the charterers ordered the ship on a voyage which could not have been performed in time to allow redelivery by 31 October. In a claim for hire at the market rate from 31 October, it was held by Atkin, J., that:

(1) had the handwritten words not been added, a reasonable margin beyond 31 October would have been allowed for redelivery;
(2) the addition of the handwritten words imposed an obligation on the charterers to redeliver by 31 October and the market rate was claimable from that date.

Atkin, J., said: "I think the proper inference to draw is that [the parties] expressly intended to negative the right to continue the contract beyond October 31, in other words, they used these words for the express purpose of making the time mentioned in the charterparty as of the essence of the contract, so that the hire should terminate on October 31, and that the ship should be delivered by that date".

Watson Steamship v. *Merryweather* (1913) 18 Com. Cas. 294.

Early redelivery

In the converse situation of a purported redelivery by the charterers to the owners prior to the expiry of the charter period, the question arises whether the owners may refuse to accept the redelivery and continue to claim hire. The general rule of contract is that where there has been a repudiation, the innocent party has a choice whether to accept the repudiation and claim damages or to reject it and hold the other party to the contract: see *White & Carter* v. *McGregor* [1962] A.C. 413, and *Decro-Wall* v. *Practitioners in Marketing* [1971] W.L.R. 361. But in *The Puerto Buitrago* [1976] 1 Lloyd's Rep. 250, see page 189 below, the Court of Appeal held that where damages were an adequate remedy and it would be wholly unreasonable to refuse to accept the redelivery, the owners were bound to accept it and claim damages. However, Kerr, J., in *The Odenfeld* [1978] 2 Lloyd's Rep. 357 held that in the special circumstances of that case the owners were entitled for a certain period to hold the ship at the charterers' disposal and claim hire—although he indicated that with the passage of time they might have lost their right to treat the contract as continuing. It seems that once it becomes clear that there is no room for a change of mind by the charterers, the courts are likely to insist that the owners accept the redelivery and sue for damages—assuming that damages will be an adequate remedy.

The *Alaskan Trader* was chartered on the New York Produce form for 24 months and delivered in December 1979. In October 1980 she suffered a serious engine breakdown which it was clear would take several months to repair. The charterers indicated that they had no further use for the ship but the owners nevertheless proceeded with the repairs. The repairs were completed in April 1981 but the charterers declined to give the master any orders and said they regarded the charter as at an end. The owners did not treat the charterers' conduct as a repudiation but continued to hold the ship at the charterers' disposal, fully crewed and ready to sail, until the charter expired in December 1981. She was then sold for scrap. Hire was paid throughout by the charterers on a without prejudice basis. The charterers claimed to recover the hire they had paid on the basis that the owners should have accepted their repudiation and claimed damages.

It was held by an arbitrator that the owners were not obliged to accept the charterers' repudiation in October 1980, but that they should have done so in April 1981 as the finality of the charterers' refusal to accept the ship made it "clear that the Charter was dead". The arbitrator held further that the owners had no legitimate interest in holding the charterers to their contract rather than claiming damages, rejecting the various grounds upon which it was argued that the owners were justified in continuing to claim hire: the requirements of their bank, the difficulty in assessing damages and the difficulty in finding other employment.

Lloyd, J., upheld the award, saying that he could find no fault with the arbitrator's approach in law and that the findings of fact were a matter for him.

The Alaskan Trader (*No. 2*) [1983] 2 Lloyd's Rep. 645.

In *The Alaskan Trader* it was also argued for the charterers that a time charter is a contract which calls for such a degree of cooperatioon between the parties that it is more in the nature of a contract for services, breach of which can only give rise to a remedy in damages; as with a servant wrongly dismissed by his master, the shipowner cannot claim his contractual remuneration by holding himself at the disposal of the charterer but is confined to his remedy in damages. Lloyd, J., while declining to decide this issue thought that, *prima facie,* there was much to be said for the argument. However, a similar argument failed to impress Kerr, J., in *The Odenfeld* [1978] 2 Lloyd's Rep. 357; at page 374 he said: "When the freight market is at one extremity or the other, as at present, there are many and often bitter disputes between charterers and owners which come before the Courts; but they do not prevent the operation of the vessels under the charters."

(For a case in which there was special provision in the charter for the continuation of the payment of hire, apparently up to the termination date of the charter and hire was thus payable from the date of early redelivery until such termination date, see *Reindeer Steamship* v. *Forslind* (1908) 13 Com. Cas. 214.)

Definition of the period of hire by reference to the duration of a specified trip or voyage

It has become a frequent practice to time charter for a period measured by the duration of a certain voyage instead of a stated number of months or days; see page 441 below. It seems that the voyage is then not merely the measure of the duration of the charter, but becomes the subject-matter of the contract, so that the charterers must send the ship on that particular voyage.

The *Temple Moat* was chartered on an amended Baltime (1920) form, with delivery in the Bristol Channel and redelivery in the Cape Town/Lourenço Marques range "for a period of one round voyage to the Kara Sea". The charter also specified that she should be employed within certain wide limits which included the United Kingdom. She sailed in ballast to Igarka (in the Kara Sea) and there, in August 1939, loaded a cargo of timber for Durban. She was, however, ordered by the Russian Government to proceed to Murmansk and discharge the timber there, which order the charterers were bound to obey. After some unexplained delay at Murmansk, the ship was loaded with pitprops for Garston and was requisitioned at the latter port by the British Government. Had she proceeded instead to South Africa, it was unlikely that she would have been requisitioned there. The owners argued that the charterers were in breach in delaying at Murmansk and in reloading for and proceeding to Garston instead of South Africa. The charterers replied that the period of the voyage described was only a way of determining how long the ship was to be available to them for trading within the permitted limits and that although, after the Kara Sea, the ship had to proceed substantially in the direction of South Africa, it was permitted to trade to other places on that general route.

The House of Lords held that the described voyage was paramount. The charter was thus for a voyage first to the Kara Sea and thence to South Africa. The trading limits in the charter limited rather than extended the confines of that voyage. Therefore, the charterers were in breach and liable in damages for the owners' losses caused by the requisition of the ship.

(The obedience of the master to these orders did not prejudice the owners' claim as he was, by Clause 8, under the orders of the charterers as to employment.)

Temple Steamship v. *Sovfracht* (1945) 79 Ll.L.Rep. 1.

Variations on this method of fixing the duration of a charter may present problems. In *The Democritos* [1976] 2 Lloyd's Rep. 149, the duration of a charter on the New York Produce form was described as "for about a trip via port or ports via the Pacific, duration about 4 to 6 months". It was argued for the charterers that these words had made the contract a voyage or at least a hybrid between a voyage and a time charter, so that the owners could not, on the ordinary principles set out above, claim damages for overrun beyond the six months. The Court of Appeal rejected that argument as they considered the contract was still clearly a time charter. It is suggested, however, that had the contemplated trip been precisely defined, by contrast to the very vague words actually used, the decision might have been different—not because the charter would have ceased to be a time charter but because the specific trip might have been held paramount and the stated months merely an indication of the likely length of that trip. But such a case is unlikely because with a precisely defined trip an indication of duration would normally be superfluous. See also *The Aragon* [1975] 1 Lloyd's Rep. 628.

American Law

Overlap/underlap: implied margin

Under American law the rule is that a reasonable overlap is permitted if the charter is for a "flat" period of time. Thus, prior to redelivery the charterer may send the vessel on the shortest commercially practicable voyage possible under the charter, even if it appears redelivery may be late, provided that the anticipated overlap will be shorter than the underlap which would result if the voyage was not made. An early redelivery, or underlap, will be a breach of the charter if another voyage could have been made with an expected overlap shorter than the period of underlap.

In the leading case of *Straits of Dover Steamship Co.* v. *Munson,* 99 F.690 (S.D.N.Y. 1899), aff'd 100 F. 1055 (2d Cir. 1900), the court held that redelivery two months 23 days after the expiration of the charter period was excused. The charter provided for a flat period of three months from the time of delivery. The vessel was delayed as the result of causes for which the charterer was not responsible. The court concluded that the parties must have understood that redelivery on a given day could not be promised, and that since the charterer had sent the vessel on a reasonable voyage which could have been performed within the three-month period except for the delays, the charterer was not in breach. The rule enunciated is that the propriety of the final voyage is to be determined as of the date the voyage commences, based on the overlap which can be reasonably anticipated at that time.

In *Anderson* v. *Munson,* 104 F. 913 (S.D.N.Y. 1900), redelivery 49 days late was excused, despite the fact that the word "about" was deleted. In *Trechman S.S. Co.* v. *Munson S.S. Line,* 203 F. 692 (2d Cir. 1913), the charterer was not permitted to redeliver 29 days before expiration of the term because an additional voyage with a reasonable overlap could have been performed. The court held, however, that the owner was entitled to damages only up to the end of the flat period.

In *Britain S.S. Co.* v. *Munson S.S. Line,* 31 F.2d 530 (2d Cir. 1929), the charter was to be "from the time of delivery, for *about* two (2) to *about* three (3) consecutive calendar months." The ship was delivered on 20 March at Cuba. She was to be redelivered at a U.S. Atlantic port north of Cape Hatteras. Charterer tendered redelivery at New York on 7 May or 13 days before the expiration of two months from the date of delivery. The court held that redelivery was premature and ineffective, because the vessel could reasonably have made another voyage between Cuba and New York and redelivered within the "about three (3)" month period. According to the court:

> [T]he use of the word "about" is interpreted as signifying an intention to allow the charterer a reasonable leeway in respect to the date on which the vessel shall be surrendered . . . Hence, if a voyage terminates in a port of redelivery before the end of the stated term, the charterer may require the vessel to make another "reasonable" voyage, even though it is certain to overlap the stated term. If, however, the time remaining before the end of the stated term is so short as to render another voyage "unreasonable", then the vessel may be surrendered by the charterer, or withdrawn by the owner, thus creating an underlap. (31 F.2d at 531.)

The court further held, however, that since the charterer could have made a valid redelivery on 20 May, the owner's damages should be limited accordingly. The court reasoned that although the charterer had an option to use the vessel beyond 20 May, the owner could not insist that the option be exercised.

Minimum/maximum

Where the charter provides for minimum and maximum periods, redelivery is proper at any time in between the two. *Tweedie Trading Co.* v. *Sangstand,* 180 F. 691 (2d Cir. 1910). It is customary and, of course, logical to delete the word "about" where there is a minimum/maximum range of redelivery dates. When this occurs, no overlap will be permitted. Thus, principles of underlap and overlap as such are inapplicable where the charter is for a fixed "minimum" or "maximum" period and there is a range of redelivery dates.

In *The Romandie,* S.M.A. No. 1092 (Arb. at N.Y. 1977), the printed word "about" in the New York Produce form was deleted from the charter, which provided for a period of a minimum of 35 months to a maximum of 38 months, at the charterer's option. The vessel was redelivered eight days beyond the maximum flat term of 38 months. The panel held that the owner was entitled to recover damages resulting from the late redelivery. According to the panel:

> The Panel considers that the deletion of the word "about" preceding the time period for which the ROMANDIE was to be chartered, coupled with the minimum/maximum phraseology, are expressions of clear intent that the parties contemplated specific minimum and maximum dates of redelivery. There can be no other sensible interpretation of the words. We were not unmindful of the references that had been made to the uncertainties of navigation and that ships do not run on rails. Neither could we disregard the rights of the parties to make any arrangements they chose and to express their intent as they deemed proper.
>
> We are of the opinion that this Charter Party, by its very terms and conditions, is an absolutely fixed period charter, allowing no overlap. A redelivery of the vessel prior to the 35th month or after the 38th month would be a breach of the contract for which Charterers would become liable in damages, unless the breach was the result of an Owners' breach. Here Charterers took a calculated risk that they could perform their contemplated voyage within the maximum period for redelivery, although we consider that the possibility of success was marginal at best. The risk failed, not due to any fault of the Owners, and Charterers are, therefore, liable for the reasonable and forseeable damages of Owners.

Similar results were reached in *The Scaldia,* S.M.A. No. 905 (Arb. at N.Y. 1975), where the panel held that "the maximum employment period of seven months [was] inflexible and absolute" in a charter providing "for a minimum of six months/maximum seven months", and in *The Elizabeth Entz,* S.M.A. No. 588 (Arb. at N.Y. 1971), where the panel held that no overlap or underlap would be allowed where the charter provided "for fourteen (14) months, one month more or less." See also *The Themis,* 244 F. 545 (S.D.N.Y. 1917); *Tweedie Trading Co.* v. *Sangstand,* 180 F. 691 (2d Cir. 1910); *Schoonmaker-Conners Co. Inc.* v. *Lambert Transp. Co.*, 269 F. 583 (2d Cir. 1920).

But see *Ropner* v. *Inter-American S.S. Co.,* 243 F. 549 (2d Cir. 1917), where the court held that the maximum period should be treated as a flat period, and allowed a reasonable overlap. As the cases cited above show, however, this case has not been followed in arbitration decisions.

Express margin

Where the charter states an express range of redelivery dates no additional overlap will be permitted. In *The Themis,* 244 F. 545 (S.D.N.Y. 1917), the charter provided for redelivery "between December 15th and January 5th" at the charterer's option. The court held that this clause imposed a duty on charterer to surrender the vessel no later than Jan. 5. According to the court:

> The period of 16 days was thought enough to give commercial latitude for the enterprises to be

undertaken, and the event of unforeseen contingencies was amply provided for by the exceptions to be considered later. That period of 16 days was the "overlap" or "twilight" zone which gave the charterer a sufficient leeway against ordinary vicissitudes, beyond which he engaged himself not to go. Such a plan was altogether reasonable. (244 F. at 552.)

In *Tweedie Trading Co.* v. *Sangstand,* 180 F. 691, 692 (2d. Cir. 1910), the court found that the provision for an express margin distinguished the charter from ones providing for a flat period. There the charter provided "for a period of about twelve months, charterers guaranteeing to redeliver steamer within three weeks more or less of this period". According to the court, by this clause the charterer had the right if it chose to keep the vessel for 11 months and one week or for 12 months and three weeks. At the same time, the charterer had the duty to redeliver the vessel within the precise dates specified.

In *Tweedie,* the charterer was also given the option to extend the charter for another term with a fixed margin which was to end on 9 April. On 28 March, the vessel lay at Hampton Roads. When the charterer directed the master to sail to Cuba for a cargo of sugar, the owner withdrew her and returned the hire the charterer had paid for the period 29 March to 6 April. The charterer brought an action for damages based on wrongful withdrawal. The court held that the withdrawal was a breach of the charter, since the charterer had the right to keep the vessel until 9 April. Since the vessel could not have made the voyage and been redelivered by 9 April, however, it was held that the return of hire for that period, plus payment for bunkers put aboard by the charterer, was full compensation.

In *The Medita,* S.M.A. No. 1150 (Arb. at N.Y. 1977), the owner was awarded damages based on the market rate for the period of the overlap. The panel stated:

Shortly expressed, a charterer has an absolute obligation to ensure redelivery within the maximum period allowed, or must pay for the daily hire at a rate commensurate with the existing overlap. This Panel considered carefully whether there is sufficient or any evidence of poor performance of the ship on the last voyage that might permit an exception of the stated rule to be applied. In fact the evidence shows no undue delays that may be attributed to "non-performance" of the ship. The delays were all weather related . . . A charterer has to take all such matters into consideration when deciding upon the final voyage of a vessel, and even whether a last voyage may reasonably be undertaken. The absolute obligation to redeliver within the maximum period is exactly that. It may not be considered as an option for a charterer to overlap, even by a few days against payment of an increased hire.

In *The Har Rai,* S.M.A. No. 1868 (Arb. at N.Y. 1983), charterer attempted to fix the vessel for a voyage which could not reasonably have been completed prior to a stated range of redelivery dates (the date had already been extended once). The panel ruled that charterer had committed an anticipatory breach of the charter by such action, and that owner was entitled to refuse charterer's use of the ship for any employment likely to exceed the maximum period of the charter. However, owner was not entitled to withdraw the vessel because hire had been paid in advance for a period after the vessel was withdrawn.

"About"

Where the charter describes the term as "about" a given period, a margin will be permitted, although the duration of the margin will depend on the facts of each case. As the court stated in *Britain S.S. Co.* v. *Munson S.S. Line,* 31 F.2d 530 (2d Cir. 1929):

When a charter party is for a term of "about six months" . . . the use of the word "about" is interpreted as signifying an intention to allow the charterer a reasonable leeway in respect to the date on which the vessel shall be surrendered. (31 F.2d at 531.)

In *The Rygja,* 161 F. 106 (2d Cir. 1908), a leading American case, the charter was for a period of "about six months", and gave the charterer the option to extend the period for a further period of "about six months". The vessel was delivered on 13 July 1905. On 12 December 1905, the charterer exercised its option for a further six-month period. On 12 June 1906, the charterer declared its option to redeliver the vessel in Europe. The owner, however, ordered the master to refuse to perform the voyage, and the charterer commenced an action for damages. The issue presented was when the second six-month period began. The last voyage under the original six-month period terminated on 4 March 1906, and the charterer contended that it was at this time that the extended term commenced. The owner argued that it began on 13 January or six months after delivery. The court held for the charterer, stating:

In this charter the term is not an absolutely fixed period, but is "about six calendar months". The district judge restricted the effect of the word "about" to the underlap. Doubtless in a charter containing a clause like No. 4 the word is not necessary because that clause accomplishes the same thing. Still we think the word "about" applicable to the term whether it be over or under six calendar months, and that, if the last voyage terminates so near the end of the fixed time as to make another voyage unreasonable, the charterer may deliver and the owner may withdraw the vessel, or, if any voyage is reasonable, the charterer may require it at the charter rate of freight. This leaves room for dispute in the case of an underlap as to what voyage is reasonable, but that is a difficulty which cannot be avoided where a fixed term is not agreed upon. In this case, if there were no question of a second term, it could not be denied that the charter terminated March 4th. The charterer having declared its option for a second term, we think the further period began to run from March 4th. (161 F. at 108.)

In *Prebensens Damps. A/S* v. *Munson S.S. Line,* 258 F. 227 (2d Cir. 1919), "about" was held to allow a one-month overlap on a charter for 36 months. For any overlap beyond 36 months, the charterer was required to pay hire at the market, rather than the charter, rate.

In *The Adelfoi,* 1972 AMC 1742 (Arb. at N.Y. 1972), however, while accepting the principle that an additional voyage is permitted where the charterer, acting in good faith, calculates that the projected overlap will be no greater than the existing underlap, the arbitrators limited the permissible overlap to 14 days. The vessel was chartered for "about 21 to about 24 months, period at Charterer's option". The charterer opted for the 24-month period. According to the panel, "a normal overlap for the word 'about' on this 2-year charter, expiring under the circumstances, should only be about 2 weeks beyond the flat term". (1972 AMC at 1745.)

In *The Derrynane,* 1954 AMC 1015 (Arb. at N.Y 1954), the panel held that under a New York Produce form charter providing for "about six (6) to about eight (8) consecutive calendar months, period at Charterers' option", the charterer was entitled to a leeway of at least two weeks more or less because of the broad trading limits, and that the charterer was justified in sending the vessel on a voyage before redelivery which it reasonably believed would take two weeks.

In *The Federal Voyager,* 1955 AMC 880 (Arb. at N.Y. 1953), "about" was held to allow an overlap of 11 days on a seven-month charter. In that case, the charter was for "about four to about seven consecutive calendar months, period at Charterers' option". Owner contended that since the charter contained two "about" periods, ordinary rules of overlap and underlap were inapplicable, and that no overlap should be allowed. The panel rejected this argument, and held that the charterer was permitted to make a voyage that would result in a reasonable overlap.

In *The Trade Yonder,* S.M.A. No. 2435 (Arb. at N.Y. 1987), the charter called for a time charter trip of "about 80 days without guarantee". The panel held that redelivery after a voyage which lasted 97 days did not give rise to a claim by owner for overlap.

In some charters, the provision for "about" a given period is modified to state an agreed limitation on the period of leeway that will be allowed the charterer. Thus, in *The Aretusa,* S.M.A. No. 835 (Arb. at N.Y. 1973), the panel held that the words "about eighteen months, fifteen days more or less" gave the charterer the option to redeliver 15 days before or after the 18-month period.

Extent of reasonable margin

The test for determining whether the underlap or overlap is reasonable is set out in *Britain S.S. Co.* v. *Munson S.S. Line,* see above at page 97.

Redelivery after end of charter period

Is hire payable until redelivery or only until the end of the charter period?

Although the New York Produce form provides that hire is to continue until redelivery, where redelivery is made after the allowed period, the owner is also entitled to damages based on the market rate. *Constantine & Pickering S.S. Co.* v. *West India S.S. Co.,* 231 F. 472 (S.D.N.Y. 1914); *Munson S.S. Line* v. *Elswick Steam Shipping Co.,* 207 F. 984 (S.D.N.Y. 1913), aff'd *per curiam* 214 F. 84 (2d Cir. 1914).

In general, damages in an underlap or overlap case will be based on the market rate. As Judge Learned Hand wrote in *Constantine & Pickering S.S. Co.,* above, the owner is to be awarded damages on a basis which will "produce, so far as money can", the same result as if the vessel had been redelivered at the time and place provided in the charter. Thus, if there is an underlap, damages usually will be based on the difference between the charter rate and the lower market rate for the period of underlap. In an overlap situation, damages are usually based on the difference between the higher market rate and the charter rate for the overlapping period. The application of these general principles in the cases, however, will always depend on the particular factual situation presented.

In *The Jagat Padmini,* S.M.A. No. 1097 (Arb. at N.Y. 1977), where the charter contained an express margin, the panel held that the vessel should have been surrendered to the owner on 11 May 1973. She was actually redelivered on 1 June. Accordingly, the owner was awarded damages based on the substantially higher market rate for the period 11 May to 1 June. The panel rejected the owner's contention that he should be awarded damages from the date the vessel could have been redelivered prior to the last voyage which caused the overlap.

This same formula for determining the owner's damages was applied by the panels in *The Julia,* S.M.A. No. 552 (Arb. at N.Y.) and *The Romandie,* S.M.A. No. 1092 (Arb. at N.Y. 1977). In the latter case, the charterer breached a "minimum/maximum" redelivery provision. It is noteworthy that the owner sought to recover "special damages" in that case, based on a profitable transatlantic voyage it claimed could have been completed had the vessel not been redelivered late. The panel held that the evidence did not support this claim for "special damages", but clearly indicated they would have awarded them had the owner proved that "Charterers either had been forewarned or had other independent knowledge of the financial consequences of overlapping the maximum 38 months."

In *The Thorgerd,* 1926 AMC 160 (Arb. at N.Y. 1925), the owner was awarded a form of special damages, consisting of profits it would have earned under a charter that was cancelled as a result of the late redelivery. In that case, the charterer had been given notice of the cancelling date under the new charter.

See also *The Rygja,* 161 F. 106, 107 (2d Cir. 1908), where, in describing the method of computing damages where the charter provides for an express margin, Judge Ward stated:

> Charters for a fixed period involve from the nature of things considerable difficulties because of the uncertainty as to the time voyages are likely to occupy. At the expiration of a fixed term the charterer is no longer entitled to possession. If in the employment of the ship he overruns the term, he is certainly liable at the charter rate of freight for the overlap, and, if freights have risen, to the difference between the market rate and the charter rate in addition. If the last voyage of the vessel terminates so near the expiration of the fixed term that another voyage cannot be made, the charterer either loses that time entirely, or if he employs the vessel on another voyage, he does so at the risk of being liable for the increase of the market rate of freight for the overlap.

In *The Scaldia,* S.M.A. No. 905 (Arb. at N.Y. 1975), the panel declined to base damages for an overlap on the market rate. There, the charterer was held to have breached its charter with disponent owner by making a late redelivery. The redelivery was made to the disponent owner simultaneously with the redelivery to the actual owner, and the disponent owner was not required to pay any overlap penalty to the actual owner. In addition, the overlap amounted to only 10 days, and the panel doubted that the disponent owner actually could have used the vessel advantageously during that period. The charterer, however, had made profits on its own sub-charter during the 10-day overlap. The panel held that while in the circumstances it would be unrealistic to award the disponent owner damages based on the market rate, fairness dictated that it recover the profits made by the charterer during the overlap.

This issue was also considered in *The Hans Sachs,* S.M.A. No. 1493 (Arb. at N.Y. 1980). It was conceded by the charterer that the vessel was redelivered eight days and 20 hours beyond the allowed period, and the only issue before the panel concerned the quantum of damages the owner was entitled to recover. The owner sought damages based upon the prevailing charter market rates during the overlap period. The charterer, on the other hand, contended that the proper measure of damages was the difference between the existing charter rate and the rate for the vessel's subsequent employment under a charter which was fixed by the owner prior to the commencement of the overlap voyage. According to the charterer, since the owner was committed to another charter when the vessel was redelivered, it would be inappropriate to base owner's damages on a market rate which exceeded that charter rate. The panel agreed with the charterer and held that the rule generally followed in overlap situations whereby the owner is awarded compensation based upon the difference between the existing charter hire and the prevailing market rate was not applicable because the vessel was not in fact available to enter the market. According to the panel, since the vessel was previously committed to a specific charter, it was the difference between the rate under that charter and the existing charter that formed the basis of owner's damages.

Is the last voyage a legitimate voyage?

The test for determining whether the last voyage is a legitimate one is set out in *Britian S.S. Co.* v. *Munson S.S. Line,* 31 F.2d 530 (2d Cir. 1929). Under American law, however, this question will only be considered where the charter is for a flat period, or if the period is modified by the word "about". Where there is an express margin, or a "minimum/maximum" term, it is generally held irrelevant whether the last voyage is reasonable, if redelivery is made after the cut-off date. See *The Romandie,* above; *The Scaldia,* above; *The Elizabeth Entz,* above.

Early redelivery

If there is an underlap, the owner is entitled to damages based on its loss of earnings until the end of the minimum charter term. In *The Itel Taurus,* S.M.A. No. 1220 (Arb. at N.Y. 1977), for example, the charterer redelivered the ship 10 days before the earliest date allowed under the charter. The panel held that the owner was entitled to recover its provable damages for the 10-day period, and stated:

> Specifically, the Owners are entitled to charter hire less the amount of any earnings received in the mitigation of this loss.

The owner, of course, remains under a duty to mitigate damages if there is an underlap. Thus, the owner cannot refuse a wrongful redelivery, but must accept the vessel and seek substitute employment for the period of the underlap. In *The Lamyrefs,* 1970 AMC 1966 (Arb. at N.Y. 1970), the vessel was redelivered four days early. The panel held that redelivery prior to the redelivery date the charterer had given notice of was a breach of the charter. The owner, however, re-employed the vessel almost immediately. The panel held that the re-employment was in mitigation of damages, and that the owner's damages consisted only of hire it would have earned after redelivery up to the date the vessel was again employed.

Place of redelivery

The owner is entitled to a redelivery of the vessel at the place or in the range stated in the charter. The owner, however, may waive this right if it is to his benefit to do so. For example, in *Munson S.S. Line* v. *Elswick Steam Shipping Co.,* 207 F. 984 (S.D.N.Y. 1913), aff'd *per curiam,* 214 F. 84 (2d Cir. 1914), the time charter called for redelivery at a European port. The vessel lost a significant amount of time en route to the discharge port, Buenos Aires, by a series of unexpected and unforeseen delays, however, and did not complete discharging until some three weeks after the end of the agreed charter period had passed. In these circumstances, the owner was held to be entitled to insist on redelivery of the vessel at Buenos Aires. See discussion below at page 111.

The charterer, of course, is entitled to make redelivery at any place within the specified range. In *The Federal Voyager,* 1955 AMC 880 (Arb. at N.Y. 1953), the charterer had the option of redelivering the vessel within a range of areas, including the United Kingdom, Continent, U.S. Gulf, U.S.N.H. or British North America. Near the end of the charter period, the charterer entered into a sub-charter which called for redelivery at a U.S.N.H. port, and so advised the owner. The owner then fixed employment for the vessel on the assumption that she would be redelivered at a U.S.N.H. port. Subsequently, the sub-charter was cancelled, and the charterer in fact made redelivery in Holland. The arbitrators held that the charterer was justified in making redelivery in Holland, and that the owner acted at its own risk in arranging a future charter on the assumption redelivery would be made at a U.S.N.H. port.

Trading Limits

15. .... within below mentioned trading limits."

Purpose of the trading limits

In *Temple Steamship* v. *Sovfracht* (1944) 77 Ll.L.Rep. 257, a case of a time charter for a round voyage, Scott, L.J., said of the trading limits clause in time charters: "It originated in and belongs to pure time charters. In such a charter-party there is nothing to limit the geographical range of the voyages on which the charterer is free to send the ship: he may send it to any navigable waters in the wide world that he likes (apart from navigation and trading dangers). That is the fundamental distinction from a voyage charter, which *ipso facto* defines the geographical employment of the ship. The object of a trading limit clause in time charter-parties is obvious. It is not to grant a liberty (because *ex hypothesi* the charterer already has it), but to impose a limit or restriction, by cutting down the otherwise unlimited and universal liberty of the charterer and excluding him from certain areas." (For the decision of the House of Lords in this case, see below; and for comments on the distinction between time and voyage charters see pages 440 and 441 below.)

Orders to trade outside the limits

Master may refuse

It is a breach of the contract for the charterers to employ the ship outside the limits stated and the master may properly refuse an order from the charterers to proceed outside them. Devlin, J., said in *The Sussex Oak* (1950) 83 Ll.L. Rep. 297, at page 307: "I cannot think that the clause in a time charter-party which puts the master under the orders of the charterers as regards employment is to be construed as compelling him to obey orders which the charterers have no power to give". Nor is the master obliged to sign a bill of lading which names a port of discharge outside the trading limits. MacKinnon, L.J., said in *Halcyon Steamship* v. *Continental Grain* (1943) 75 Ll.L. Rep. 80: "The limits of trading . . . are Institute Warranty limits, not north of Holland. If the charterers shipped a cargo in America and then tendered bills of lading to the captain under which he was to deliver to Copenhagen or Danzig, of course he would rightly refuse to sign . . . "

Charter for trip defined more narrowly than trading limits

Where a voyage is specified and wider trading limits are also stated, the description of the voyage will be regarded as paramount.

The *Temple Moat* was chartered on an amended Baltime (1920) form, with delivery in the Bristol Channel and redelivery in the Cape Town/Lourenco Marques range "for a period of one round voyage to the Kara Sea". The charter also specified that she should be employed within certain wide limits which included the United Kingdom. The charterers argued that the period of the voyage described was only a way of determining how long the ship was to be available to them for trading within the permitted limits and that although after the Kara Sea the ship had to proceed substantially in the direction of South Africa, it was permitted to trade to other places on that general route.

The House of Lords held that the described voyage was paramount. On the facts found as to the meaning of "one round voyage to the Kara Sea" (which were not to be regarded as a precedent as to the meaning of "round voyage") the charter was for a voyage to the Kara Sea and thence to South Africa. The trading limits in the charter did not extend but rather limited the confines of that voyage.

Temple Steamship v. *Sovfracht* (1945) 79 Ll.L.Rep.1.

(For further comments on "time charters for a trip", see page 95 above and page 441 below.)

Effect of obedience to charterers' orders

Mere compliance, without more, with the charterers' order to proceed outside the trading limits will probably not amount to a waiver of the owners' rights either to refuse further compliance subsequently or to claim damages for the breach: see by analogy *The Kanchenjunga* [1987] 2 Lloyd's Rep. 509, [1989] 1 Lloyd's Rep. 354 (C.A.) and page 148 below. Nor will the master's obedience to such an order usually amount to a waiver as he is under the charterers' orders and directions as regards employment.

In *Temple Steamship* v. *Sovfracht* (1945) 79 Ll.L.Rep. 1, above (and see also page 96 above), the charterers argued that the master's acceptance of an order to proceed to Garston and the owners' failure to protest amounted to a waiver. Lord Porter dealt with this argument in the following terms, at page 11: "The ship had been detained in Murmansk for over five weeks and the owners may well have thought it advisable to make no protest against a sailing to Garston, lest the charterers should be guilty of a worse deviation. In these circumstances the failure to protest is easily comprehensible and even the receipt of chartered hire under such conditions might well take place without being held to excuse the deviation, and, deviation or no deviation, there still remains the breach of the obligation to prosecute the voyage with the utmost despatch as required by Clause 8 and to send the ship direct to South Africa. No doubt the master obeyed the charterers' orders in sailing to Garston, but under Clause 8 of the charter-party he was under their orders as regards employment, and in accordance with the principles adopted in *Tyrer* v. *Hessler*, 7 Com. Cas. 166, his obedience would not constitute a waiver of his employers' rights."

But if the owners, in circumstances less unusual than those in *Temple Steamship* v. *Sovfracht*, above, and with full knowledge of the breach, allow the ship to proceed outside the trading limits, they will probably be held to have waived their right to refuse further compliance with the order subsequently, although not necessarily their right to damages. Further comments on waiver in general will be found at page 59 above.

Measure of damages for trading outside limits

If the charterers order the ship outside the trading limits and the owners instruct the master to comply with the order under protest, the owners may claim from the charterers the difference between the charter rate and the market rate (if higher) for the voyages performed outside the trading limits even if that exceeds the additional costs to which the owners have been put by those voyages: *Rederi Hansen* v. *Van Ommeren* (1921) 6 Ll.L.Rep. 193.

Agreement that trading limits may be broken

It is not unusual for the parties to agree in the charter that the charterers may order the ship outside the specified trading limits, the charterers paying any extra premium consequently required by the ship's underwriters. It does not follow from their assumption of such extra premium that the charterers are relieved from their obligation as to the safety of the ports to which they order the ship outside those limits.

The New York Produce form charter for the *Helen Miller* contained an additional clause defining the trading limits as being "between safe ports within Institute Warranty Limits including St. Lawrence up to and including Montreal, but excluding Cuba . . . Guinea, and all unsafe ports, but Charterers have the liberty of breaking limits, they paying extra insurance, if any, . . . ". The charterers ordered the ship to ports outside the Institute Warranty Limits and she suffered ice damage on voyages to these ports, which were found to have been unsafe at the relevant time. Mustill, J., held that the charterers were liable for this damage: the owners had given general consent to trading outside the Limits but this did not detract from the charterers' duty to select ports which were safe, and this was not affected by the charterers' payment of extra insurance premium; "by paying the premium the charterer does obtain a benefit—the benefit of being able to send the ship on a voyage which the owner would not otherwise allow her to perform. But this is not at all the same as saying that the charterer thereby obtains the right to send her on such a voyage risk-free".

The Helen Miller [1980] 2 Lloyd's Rep. 95.

In *The Evia (No. 2)* [1982] 2 Lloyd's Rep. 307, the House of Lords held that in respect of the war risks referred to in Clause 21 (A) of the Baltime form the charterers were relieved of their safe port obligation under Clause 2. But in arriving at this decision Lord Roskill drew attention to several special features of Clause 21. As Bingham, J., emphasised in *The Concordia Fjord* [1984] 1 Lloyd's Rep. 385, at pages 387 and 388, everything depends on the construction of the detailed terms of the particular charter. In the case before him Bingham, J., upheld the decision of an arbitrator that the charterers under an amended New York Produce form were liable for the damages suffered by the ship at a port which was unsafe because of war, despite a clause putting upon them the costs of additional war risk insurance premiums, to which the relevant port was then subject. The charter terms in *The Helen Miller*, above, were equally distinct from those in *The Evia (No. 2)* and the facts more so; consequently there seems no reason to suppose that the validity of the decision has been undermined by the latter case, unless it be by a general comment of Lord Roskill that, as by Clause 21(B)(1) of the Baltime charter the charterers were to refund the owners' war risks insurance premiums, it would be unjust that they should remain exposed to a subrogated claim by the war risk underwriters under the safe port provision, Clause 2. As to this comment of Lord Roskill, Bingham, J., in *The Concordia Fjord*, above, recorded with approval the arbitrator's rejection of any general principle exempting charterers from a liability merely because they have assumed a contractual obligation to put the owners into funds to insure themselves against the relevant damage. It seems that there is no such principle.

For a case on misrepresentation of the extent of trading limits see *The Lucy* [1983] 1 Lloyd's Rep. 188 and page 49 above.

American Law

Trading limits

The broad trading limits generally available under a time charter are one of the distinctive features of that type of charter. Whereas under a voyage charter the vessel normally is chartered for a trip to one or more specified places, under a time charter the vessel is under the charterer's orders as to which ports she shall visit. The geographical limitations found in time charters usually are dictated by safety or political considerations.

The charterer is in breach of its obligations under the charter if it orders the vessel to go outside the specified trading limits. The master is free to refuse such orders. Indeed, it has been held that the owner is justified in withdrawing the vessel from the charterer's service if the charterer persists in a demand that the vessel trade outside the agreed limits. In *The Central Trust*, 1971 AMC 200 (Can. Exch. 1970), the court held that the owner was entitled to withdraw the vessel where the charter excluded "communist and communist satellite ports" from the permitted trading areas and the charterer nominated Yugoslavian ports for discharge. *Cf. The New Way*, 1977 AMC 88, 95 (Arb. at N.Y. 1976); *The Arietta Venizelos*, 1973 AMC 1012 (Arb. at N.Y. 1972), discussed below at page 160.

In *The Andros Mentor*, S.M.A. No. 2125 (Arb. at N.Y., 1985), charterer's routing directions called for the vessel to travel in the Bering Sea, an area outside Institute Warranty Limits (IWL), even though the charter explicitly limited trading to areas within IWL. The panel held that the master was not bound by the charterer's instructions, noting:

> Owner argued that it would have incurred an additional insurance premium of about $15,000 in so doing, and Charterer argued that it would have gained Owner's permission before so doing. While the panel notes that permission to proceed via the Bering Sea is frequently granted by insurance companies without additional premium, such permission (with or without added premium) is granted upon application, and is not necessarily automatic. In this case, there was no contemporaneous evidence that any such permission had been applied for, or even discussed.

In *The Universe Explorer*, 1985 AMC 1014 (Arb. at N.Y. 1984), a dispute under the Texacotime form, the panel stated that owner had indirectly limited the ship's eligibility to engage in worldwide trading by calling for stores at South Africa. The panel held that charterer was entitled to off-hire during the time when Nigerian authorities refused to allow loading because of the call at South Africa.

Liberty to Sublet

"16. Charterers to have liberty to sublet the vessel for all or any part of the time covered by this Charter, but Charterers remaining responsible for
17. the fulfillment of this Charter Party."

Effects of sub-charter

Line 16 gives the charterers the express right to sub-charter the ship during the currency of the head time charter. A sub-time charter (or a sub-voyage charter) does not create any contractual relationship between the owners and the sub-charterers. The owners may not, therefore, sue the sub-charterers, or be sued by them, under or by virtue of the head charter or the sub-charter. This is in accordance with the principle that a contract cannot, generally, confer rights or impose obligations on persons who are not parties to that contract: see *Dunlop* v. *Selfridge* [1915] A.C. 847.

A sub-charterer may however be in direct contractual relationship with the owners under bills of lading issued under the sub-charter, if both the owners and the sub-charterers are parties to such bills. In these circumstances the owners may sue (and be sued) under the bills of lading, although they have no rights or obligations under the sub-charter and are not entitled to enforce the terms of the head charter against the sub-charterers.

The *Bombay* was time chartered for six months with an option to sublet and was sub-chartered for a round voyage. The head charter provided that bills of lading were to be signed at any rate of freight the charterers or their agents might direct, without prejudice to the head charter. The head charter further provided that the owners were to have a lien "upon all cargoes for freight or charter money due under this charter". Bills of lading were issued to the sub-charterers and the owners sought to exercise a lien on the sub-charterers' cargo for hire due under the head charter. It was held that the owners had no right of lien for the time charter hire; that was a right enforceable only against the head charterers. Under the bills of lading, which constituted contracts between the owners and the sub-charterers, the owners had a lien only for the freight due under those bills.

Turner v. *Haji Goolam* [1904] A.C. 826.

The owners may also be responsible to sub-charterers in tort as bailees if the owners, through their servants or agents, are in possession of the sub-charterers' cargo: see *The Termagant* (1914) 19 Com. Cas. 239, and *Lee Cooper* v. *Jeakins* [1964] 1 Lloyd's Rep. 300. The owners may however be entitled to rely on exceptions in the contract under which the cargo is carried: see page 270 below.

Sub-charterers' authority to sign bills of lading for master

Where there is a liberty to sublet in the head time charter, sub-charterers will generally be authorised to sign bills of lading (either personally or by their agents) in such a way as to bind the owners. Browne, L.J., said in *The Vikfrost* [1980] 1 Lloyd's Rep. 560, at page 567: " . . . the charterers had the option of sub-letting and no restrictions are imposed as to the terms of the sub-letting. In my view, the owners must have contemplated that, if there was a sub-letting, the sub-charterers would be entitled to require the master to sign bills of lading, and to sign themselves such bills of lading as they were entitled to require the master to sign, and so create a contract between the owners and the holders of the bills of lading."

In that case the owners of a ship, which was trading under a time charter that was subject to Norwegian law and jurisdiction, contended that sub-agents of sub-charterers had no authority to issue, on behalf of the master, bills of lading containing an English jurisdiction clause. It was held that since the head charter contained an option to sublet and permitted the inclusion of a demise clause in bills of lading, the sub-charterers and their agents had implied authority to issue such bills of lading. (See further on the question of bills of lading pages 268 and 272.)

Payment of freight under sub-charter

For the circumstances in which the owners are entitled to bill of lading freight in respect of cargo shipped under a sub-charter see page 399 below.

American Law

Liberty to sublet

Under the New York Produce form, the charterer has the right to sub-charter the vessel. The charterer, however, remains responsible for the performance of its obligations under the head charter. The sub-charter does not create a contractual relation between the owner and the sub-charterer, and will not relieve the charterer of any of its duties to the owner under the head charter.

These principles are illustrated by the decision in *Dampskibs Akt. Thor.* v. *Tropical Fruit Co.*, 281 F. 740 (2d Cir. 1922). The head charter was for a period of "about three years", with redelivery of the vessel to be made "at a port in the United States, Atlantic or Gulf of Mexico". The charterer exercised its right to sub-charter, although the sub-charter was not on identical terms with the head charter and called for redelivery "at a port in the United States-Atlantic North of Hatteras".

The head charter commenced on 11 May 1915; consequently the charter was to expire "about" 11 May 1918. On 10 May 1918, the vessel was in New Orleans, empty of cargo. Instead of making redelivery, however, the charterer allowed a voyage to Cuba and thence to New York which ended on 24 May 1918. The owner then brought a claim for hire at the market rate (which was greater than the rate under the head charter) for the period 11–24 May and the claim was granted. The court found that the voyage to Cuba was an unreasonable overlap, and that as a matter of law the head charter terminated at New Orleans on "about" 11 May 1918. The sub-charter did not set up any contractual relation between the owner and sub-charterer, and did not vary in any way the owner's rights under the head charter.

In *The Banes*, 221 F. 416, 418 (2d Cir. 1915), the court held that a sub-charterer was not entitled to a direct recovery from the owner for cargo damage on the ground that the vessel was unseaworthy. As stated by the court:

> A subcharter, even on the same terms as the original charter, would not constitute any contract relation between the subcharterers and the owners.

See also *Saxis S.S. Co.* v. *Multifacs International Traders Inc.*, 375 F.2d 577, 582n.7 (2d Cir. 1967), where the court stated that "the subcharter relationship normally gives the subcharterer no rights against the general owner of a vessel . . . "; *Flat-Top Fuel Co. Inc.* v. *Martin*, 85 F.2d 39, 1936 AMC 1296 (2d Cir. 1936); *Perez* v. *Cia Tropical Exportadora*, 182 F.2d 874, 1950 AMC 1264 (5th Cir. 1950).

A sub-charterer may have a lien on the vessel in certain circumstances. See discussion below at page 412.

Sub-charterers' authority to sign bills of lading for master

See discussion below at page 276.

Time to count

See discussion under Clause 5 of the New York Produce form at pages 228 to 230 below.

Place of Delivery

"18. Vessel to be placed at the disposal of the Charterers, at ....
19. ....
20. in such dock or at such wharf or place (where she may safely lie, always afloat, at all times of tide, except as otherwise provided in clause No. 6), as
21. the Charterers may direct. If such dock, wharf or place be not available time to count as provided for in clause No. 5 . . ."

Safely lie, always afloat

Clause 6 modifies the obligation that the ship is to be placed at the charterers' disposal at a dock, wharf or place where she can safely lie afloat, by allowing the ship to take the ground "where it is customary for similar size vessels to safely lie aground". Clause 6 itself provides that loading and discharging of cargo is to take place in similar docks, wharves or places selected by the charterers. Line 27 restricts the employment of the ship under the charter to "lawful trades, between safe port and/or ports" in various areas. The combined effect of these provisions is dealt with at pages 136 to 155 below, the comments on page 152 being particularly relevant to Lines 18 to 21. For American law see page 156.

From when time is to count

The part of Clause 5 referred to in Line 21 of the New York Produce form is clearly the last sentence of its first paragraph, Lines 62 to 64:

"Time to count from 7 a.m. on the working day following that on which written notice of readiness has been given to Charterers or their Agents before 4 p.m., but if required by Charterers, they to have the privilege of using vessel at once, such time used to count as hire."

For comments on the relationship between Line 21 and Lines 62 to 64 see page 228 below.

State of the Ship on Delivery

"21. . . . Vessel on her delivery to be
22. ready to receive cargo with clean-swept holds and tight, staunch, strong and in every way fitted for the service, having water ballast, winches and
23. donkey boiler with sufficient steam power, or if not equipped with donkey boiler, then other power sufficient to run all the winches at one and the same
24. time (and with full complement of officers, seamen, engineers and firemen for a vessel of her tonnage),"

General

If the ship is not in the state required by Lines 21 to 24 of the New York Produce form, a valid notice of readiness cannot be given under Clause 14, the cancelling clause; and upon the expiry of the time allowed in Line 95 the charterers may exercise their option to cancel the charter. The charterers have the same right under Clause 22 of the Baltime form if by the end of the agreed day the ship has not been delivered "in every way fitted for ordinary cargo service" as required by Line 16 of Clause 1. This right of the charterers arises irrespective of any fault or breach of contract by the owners. It is discussed in detail at pages 287 and 292 below.

Quite separately from the potential operation of the cancelling clause, other consequences may follow from the failure of the owners to have the ship in the state required for delivery, as where they are in breach of the obligation as to seaworthiness or where the ship does not meet her description in the charter.

It may be helpful, therefore, to summarise here the potential consequences of such defects in the state of the ship:

(1) The charterers may become entitled to cancel the charter under the cancelling clause; see above and page 288 below.
(2) Time may not start to count for the purposes of the payment of hire; in the New York Produce form the starting of time under Clause 5 depends upon the giving of a (valid) notice of readiness, see page 228 below, and time will not start to run under the Baltime form until the ship is "in every way fitted for ordinary cargo service" under Line 16 of Clause 1, below.
(3) If the state of the ship is due to a breach of any of the owners' obligations under the charter, the charterers will normally be entitled to damages if they have suffered loss as a result: see *Thomas Nelson* v. *Dundee East Coast Shipping* 1907, S.C. 927 and *The Democritos* [1975] 1 Lloyd's Rep. 386.
(4) The charterers may decline to accept delivery until the defects have been made good (see page 65 above); and if this is not or cannot be done without such delay as will frustrate the object of the contract the charterers may treat the charter as discharged (see pages 66 and 67 above).

(5) The charterers may also be entitled to treat the contract as discharged if the state of the ship constitutes a breach of condition by the owners or amounts to a breach which deprives the charterers of substantially the whole benefit of the contract (see pages 65 to 68 above).

Tight, staunch, strong and in every way fitted for the service

The words "tight, staunch, strong" and "in every way fitted for the service" which both appear in Line 22 of the New York Produce form, constitute, either separately or together, an express obligation of seaworthiness. The words in Clause 1 of the Baltime form "in every way fitted for ordinary cargo service", which stand alone, also impose an obligation of seaworthiness on delivery: see *The Hongkong Fir* [1961] 2 Lloyd's Rep. 478, *The Madeleine* [1967] 2 Lloyd's Rep. 224, and pages 64 to 68 above. In the absence of an express undertaking of seaworthiness on delivery, such an undertaking will be implied: *Giertsen* v. *Turnbull*, 1908 S.C. 1101. These obligations of seaworthiness may require to be distinguished from the requirements of readiness and fitness for the purposes of the cancelling clause. For the effect on the obligations of seaworthiness of the incorporation of the Hague Rules, see pages 425 to 428 below.

Readiness for purposes of cancelling clause

The cancelling clause in the New York Produce form (Clause 14) which requires notice of readiness to be given before the cancelling date, does not refer to the requirements of Lines 21 to 24. But it is considered that, on a proper construction of these provisions, a valid notice of readiness cannot be given under Clause 14 unless the requirements of Lines 21 to 24 have been complied with: see page 288. In the Baltime form the cancelling clause refers expressly to Clause 1. The requirement of being "in every way fitted" for service means that the ship must be seaworthy in the widest sense of the word: see *The Hongkong Fir* and *The Madeleine*, above, and *The Derby* [1985] 2 Lloyd's Rep. 325. But the concepts of seaworthiness and fittedness for service are not necessarily synonymous; while an unseaworthy ship can hardly be fitted for service, a ship may be seaworthy yet not so fitted: see the judgments of Sir Denys Buckley in *The Derby*, above, at page 333, and of Webster, J., in *The Arianna* [1987] 2 Lloyd's Rep. 376, at page 390.

Absolute nature of requirement

It is considered that the requirement of readiness and fittedness on delivery in the New York Produce form (like the similar requirement in the Baltime form) is, for the purposes of the cancelling clause in the charter, an absolute requirement. The requirement is not for this purpose modified by Section 4(1) of the United States Carriage of Goods by Sea Act (incorporated by Clause 24 of the New York Produce form), which relates only to liability for loss or damage arising or resulting from unseaworthiness; see pages 425 to 428 below. Thus it is not sufficient that the owners shall have exercised due diligence to make the ship ready or fit; the ship must in fact be ready and fitted (see pages 68 above and 287 below).

Ready to receive cargo with clean-swept holds

Readiness for the receipt of cargo is a concept much developed in cases under voyage charters, particularly in relation to the commencement of laytime. It is considered that the general propositions developed in these voyage charter cases apply also to time charters which, like the New York Produce form, require that on delivery the ship shall be ready to load or ready to receive cargo.

The meaning of readiness in this sense was defined by Lopes, J., in the voyage charter case of *Groves, Maclean* v. *Volkart* (1884) C. & E. 309 as follows:—"A ship to be ready to load must be completely ready in all her holds . . . so as to afford the merchant complete control of every portion of the ship available for cargo."

The holds must at the relevant time be in a fit state to receive cargo.

The *Tres Flores* gave notice of readiness under a voyage charter. At the time notice was given, the ship's holds were infested. Fumigation was ordered by the local authorities. Although the fumigation process would only have taken a matter of a few hours to complete, it was held that the ship was not "ready" so as to be able to give a valid notice of readiness for the purpose of the commencement of laytime.

The Tres Flores [1972] 2 Lloyd's Rep. 384 and [1973] 2 Lloyd's Rep. 247 (C.A.).

Cargo gear and equipment

In the case of voyage charters, a distinction has been drawn between the state of readiness of the ship's holds and the state of readiness of gear and equipment. It has been held that, for the purposes of the cancelling clause, gear and equipment may not necessarily have to be in the same state of readiness as the ship's holds.

The *San George* was chartered for a voyage with grain under the Centrocon form, the charterers being obliged to bring the cargo alongside and the shipowners to load it. The charterers had the option of cancelling if the ship was not ready to load by 6 p.m. on 27 December. The ship gave notice of readiness on 27 December at 10.30 a.m. At that time, the ship was without her mainmast and after derricks. However, the ship's gear was not needed for the loading of the cargo, unless some bags had to be taken on board from lighters (a "somewhat remote contingency") in which event there was nothing to suggest that some temporary equipment could not have been devised. The charterers cancelled. It was held that they acted wrongfully in doing so. Devlin, J., held that they were entitled to no more than the reasonable cooperation of the shipowners in selecting and working the most convenient method of loading, and the evidence of the absence of mainmast and after derricks was inadequate to discharge the onus on the charterers of showing that the defects in the ship's equipment were such that she would probably be unready or unable, when the time came, to employ any reasonable method of loading which might then be decided upon. This judgment was affirmed by the Court of Appeal.

Noemijulia Steamship v. *Minister of Food* (1950) 83 Ll.L.Rep. 500 and (1950) 84 Ll.L.Rep. 354.

Devlin, J., in the above case explained why he considered ship's gear should be treated differently from the condition of the holds. He said at page 507: "The ship's gear is different; some of it may not be required at all; some of it may not be needed until an advanced stage of the loading, and the keeping of it in constant readiness from the first moment to the last may involve labour and expense unnecessarily. *Vaughan and Others* v. *Campbell, Heatley & Co.*, 2 T.L.R. 33, *Grampian Steamship Company* v. *Carver & Co.*, 9 T.L.R. 210, and *Armement Adolf Deppe* v. *John Robinson & Co. Ltd.* [1917] 2 K.B. 204, have been cited to me; and though none is directly in point, each in its own way shows, I think, that outside the clear rule about the condition of the holds, some elasticity is permissible . . . a test which produces a sensible result in the case of the holds may not work equally well in respect to gear."

However this distinction cannot so easily be drawn under a time charter on the New York Produce or similar form, where there is an express requirement that the ship is upon her delivery to be in every way fitted for service. Devlin, J., himself added the following remarks, which seem to modify the application of his decision to the usual forms of time charter (at 83 Ll.L.Rep. page 507): "I have not here to deal with a charterparty which expressly gives to the charterer the right to use any part of the ship's gear: in such a case it might well be argued that all such gear must be in readiness. Nor have I to deal with a charter-party which prescribes any particular method of loading or allows the charterer to select a method; in such a case it might be argued that any ship's gear required for such method must be in readiness."

But even where there is an express requirement that the ship shall be in every way fitted for service, some latitude may, it seems, be allowed. Hobhouse, J., in *The Derby* [1984] 1 Lloyd's Rep. 635 (affirmed [1985] 2 Lloyd's Rep. 325), said, in considering the relationship between readiness and fitness, at page 641: "When one is concerned, as here, with a charter-party which is going to run for a considerable period of time and gives to the charterer very wide options as to the orders he may give to the owners, questions arise as to the extent to which the owners are required, at the time of delivery, to anticipate and provide in advance for every contingency. The Baltime charter-party escapes from this problem by referring to 'ordinary cargo service' and in connection with the word 'ready' the Courts have held (e.g., *Noemijulia Steamship Co. Ltd.* v. *Minister of Food* (1950) 84 Ll.L.Rep. 354) that readiness does not require immediate readiness for every alternative cargo. With regard to 'fitness for the service', as used in the NYPE form, the fitness must be fairly generally construed as otherwise one may be laying the owners open to having to fulfil conflicting and inconsistent obligations, depending on which contingency is taken into account. So, while I do not accept owners' argument that to be unfit the vessel must be foredoomed to being unable properly to carry out the charter-party obligations (e.g., the *Ciampa* case and *The Nizeti* [1960] 1 Lloyd's Rep. 132) I do not accept either charterers' argument that any subsequent delay or any necessity to make some alteration to the vessel or its equipment, etc., automatically shows an initial lack of fitness."

Readiness to be judged commercially

The question of readiness and fittedness (at least as applied to matters other than the condition of the ship's holds) has to be looked at in a business sense. Thus in the context of a long term time charter, a deficiency in tank-cleaning equipment which might never, or only seldom, give rise to a problem—and then only of a minor nature—may not render the ship unready or unfitted, even though the deficiency constitutes a breach of one of the express terms of the charter.

The *Arianna* was time chartered for a period of 10 years on the Essotime form for worldwide trading with general products. The charter provided by one of its additional clauses that six tank-cleaning machines should be capable of being run simultaneously at a given temperature and pressure. The charterers had the right to cancel if the ship was not ready and in every way fitted for the service by the cancelling date. In fact the ship could not run six tank-cleaning machines simultaneously while in port and while at the same time heating cargo destined for other ports. But the pattern of trading under the charter might have been such that this situation would never have arisen and, even if it did, the ship could always run four cleaners simultaneously so that the only consequence of the deficiency would have been some minor delay.

The charterers purported to cancel on the ground that the ship did not comply with the charter requirements. Arbitrators held that, despite the breach of the charter term regarding tank-cleaning machines, the ship was fitted for the service and the cancellation was unjustified. Webster, J., upheld the award. He said that a deficiency which had no effect on the safety of the ship or the security or integrity of the cargo did not necessarily, as a matter of law, render the ship unfit; whether it did so or not depended upon the significance of the defect and it was implicit in the arbitrators' award that they regarded the deficiency in this case as of no real significance in a commercial sense.

The *Arianna* [1987] 2 Lloyd's Rep. 376.

Again, looking at the matter in a business sense, the ship may not have to be ready at the very instant notice of readiness is given or delivery is tendered, with the charterers able to have immediate access to the ship's holds.

The *Elizabeth Van Belgie* arrived at her discharge port under a voyage charter but no discharging berth was available and she moored at buoys to wait. The question arose whether the ship could there give a valid notice of readiness before removing her hatches and rigging her unloading gear. It was held by the Court of Appeal that the ship was ready in a business sense and that the removal of hatches and the rigging of gear at the buoys would have been an "idle formality".

Scrutton, L.J., said, at page 212: "I should be surprised to find that in practice it was ever thought necessary for the ship as soon as she entered the dock to rig her discharging gear, and get men to do her part of the discharging on board, before her time could begin to run, though it was well known that, at the place where she was, discharging would not take place. Such a requirement would be quite unbusinesslike."

Armement Adolf Deppe v. *Robinson* [1917] 2 K.B. 204.

Likewise insignificant defects which do not delay loading and can be corrected before sailing may sometimes be disregarded. In the case which follows, where the defects were in fact substantial, Greer, J., gave an indication of the sort of defects he considered might be ignored.

The *Waco* was chartered for a voyage under a charter which provided that the ship should be "tight, staunch and strong, and in every way fitted for the intended voyage" and that "should the steamer not be ready to load by 6 p.m. on Nov. 25, 1920, charterers shall have the option of cancelling this charterparty." At the time the master gave notice of readiness to load, 4 p.m. on 25 November, the ship's boilers were in need of repairs which would take at least 10 days to effect. It was held by Greer, J., that the express provision amounted to an undertaking of seaworthiness; that the ship was unseaworthy at the time the notice of readiness was given, and that the charterers were entitled to cancel.

Greer, J., said: "She is to be fit to commence her chartered enterprise which consists of going to her loading berth, loading, sailing and unloading. If she be, in fact, fit to lie afloat and take in cargo, but has some small defects, which can, with reasonable certainty, be made right during the loading and without interfering with the due course of loading, she would, in my judgment, be in every way fitted for the intended voyage, notwithstanding those small defects; but if she is in such a condition that she cannot be made ready by her cancelling day, and there is no reasonable certainty that she will be ready by the time her loading is finished (as was the case here) she cannot be said to be 'tight, staunch and strong and in every way fitted for the intended voyage' ".

New York and Cuba Mail Steamship v. *Eriksen & Christensen* (1922) 27 Com. Cas. 330.

In *The Tres Flores* [1972] 2 Lloyd's Rep. 384, the facts of which are set out at page 115 above, it was argued on behalf of the owners that because of the shortness of the time it would have taken to complete fumigation of the ship's holds, the deficiency should be ignored on the *de minimis* principle. But this argument was dismissed by Mocatta, J., who said at page 394 of the report of the case at first instance:

It is the duty, in my judgment, of the shipowner to make his ship fit to carry cargo. If he does not do this, he is not in a position, as long as his ship is unfit, to give a valid notice of readiness. No doubt to certain facts, as in all branches of the law, the maxim *de minimis* would apply, but I do not consider that the facts here fall within that maxim at all.

It is suggested that this case is an example of the stricter interpretation of readiness and fittedness which is applied to the condition of a ship's holds; see pages 114 and 115 above.

Special equipment

The general rule is that, while the ship must be fitted to deal with the ordinary cargo work of a ship of her type, the owners do not have to be ready to deal with any cargo which the charterers may have liberty to load under the charter.

The voyage charter for the *Rowland Hill* provided for the shipment of a full cargo of "wheat and (or) flour in bags and (or) other lawful merchandise". The charterers were given an option to cancel if the ship was not, by sundown on the specified date, at Portland and "ready to receive cargo". At the stipulated time the ship was at Portland but was not lined in the manner necessary for wheat or flour cargoes. It was held by the Court of Appeal that the charterers were not entitled to cancel: by Lord Esher, M.R., apparently on the ground that the charter required the ship to be "ready" but not "fit" to load, but by the other two Lords Justices on the ground also that the charter left it open to the charterers to load any kind of cargo that they wished and that many kinds of cargo they might load would not require the ship to be lined.
Vaughan v. *Campbell, Heatley* (1885) 2 T.L.R. 33.

Tucker, L.J., in *Noemijulia Steamship* v. *Minister of Food* (1950) 84 Ll.L.Rep. 354, see above, commented that the latter ground for the decision in this case, "negatives the idea that, so far as equipment is concerned, the shipowner has got to be ready from the outset to deal with any kind of cargo which the charterer is entitled under the charter-party to call upon him to take on board". (For two cases concerning the obligation to provide shifting boards under earlier forms of time charter, see *Rederi Unda* v. *Burdon* (1937) 57 Ll.L.Rep. 95, "every way fitted to carry bulk and general cargoes", and *Skagerak* v. *Saremine* (1939) 64 Ll.L.Rep. 153, "in every way fitted for ordinary cargo service"; and for a case on equipment supplied from the shore, see *The Demosthenes V* [1982] 1 Lloyd's Rep. 275.)

But problems may occur where an unusual cargo has been specially mentioned in the charter and that cargo requires special equipment on the ship. Without such equipment, it seems that the ship is not "in every way fitted for the service" (although she may well be "fitted for ordinary cargo service" under the Baltime form) and the owners are in breach. On the other hand, Lines 45 and 46 of the New York Produce form appear to relieve the owners from this obligation. It is suggested that where there is in the charter special mention of a particular cargo, the obligation remains with the owners and that Lines 45 and 46 are applicable only where the charterers opt for a special trade or unusual cargo not expressly specified in the charter.

In every way fitted; extending beyond physical state of ship

While the words "tight, staunch, strong and in every way fitted for the service" in the New York Produce form and "in every way fitted for ordinary cargo service" in the Baltime form relate primarily to the physical state of the ship, in at least two cases their scope is wider. They include the requirement that the ship must have certain kinds of documents, and they also include the requirement that the ship must be provided with a sufficient and competent crew.

Documents

Kerr, L.J., in *The Derby* [1985] 2 Lloyd's Rep. 325, said at page 331 that: "the vessel must carry certain kinds of documents which bear upon her seaworthiness or fitness to perform the service for which the charter provides. Navigational charts which are necessary for the voyages upon which the vessel may be ordered from time to time are an obvious illustration. For present purposes, however, we are concerned with certificates bearing upon the seaworthiness of the vessel. The nature of such certificates may vary according to the requirements of the law of the vessel's flag or the laws or regulations in force in the countries to which the vessel may be ordered, or which may lawfully be required by the authorities exercising administrative or other functions in the vessel's ports of call pursuant to the laws there in force". Thus, in *Levy* v. *Costerton* (1816) 4 Camp. 389, it was held that the owners under a voyage charter requiring the ship to be "tight, staunch and strong . . . and furnished with everything needful and necessary for such a ship, and for the voyage" from England to Sardinia, were in breach because the ship did not have a "bill of health" which, as was well known to persons engaged in the trade, was required by the law of Sardinia, even though it was not required by English law. See also *Ciampa* v. *British India Steam Navigation* [1915] 2 K.B. 774 (ship unfumigated and lacking clean bill of health after calling at a plague port held to be unseaworthy).

A similar conclusion was reached in a case under the Baltime form.

The *Madeleine* was time chartered for three months on the Baltime form which required her, upon delivery at Calcutta, to be "in every way fitted for ordinary cargo service". Roskill, J., held that the lack of a deratisation certificate prevented a good delivery being made at Calcutta as, without that document, the ship could not sail to a port outside India. Thus the charterers were given the opportunity to exercise their right under the cancelling clause in the charter.

Roskill, J., said, at page 241: "There was here an express warranty of seaworthiness and unless the ship was timeously delivered in a seaworthy condition, including the necessary certificate from the port health authority, the charterers had the right to cancel."

The Madeleine [1967] 2 Lloyd's Rep. 224.

It is, however, suggested that this scope of this decision in *The Madeleine* may be less wide than at first appears. In *The Derby*, below, Hobhouse, J., pointed out that essentially the *Madeleine* was unfit because she needed to fumigate rather than because she lacked the relevant certificate.

Moreover, where the obtaining of an official document or permit is a mere formality and where the absence of such document or permit does not interfere with the ship's ability to perform the charter service, the lack of it will not prevent the ship being "ready" under a voyage charter nor "in every way fitted for the service" under a time charter.

The *Aello* was required, under local law, to have a police permit. It was held by the House of Lords that the ship could give a valid notice of readiness before obtaining one, since it was "little more than a formality" and its absence would not delay the loading of the ship.

The Aello [1960] 1 Lloyd's Rep. 623.

The *Delian Spirit* had not obtained free pratique at the time she gave notice of readiness under her voyage charter. It was held by the Court of Appeal that since there was no reason to suppose that the ship would have any difficulty or delay in getting free pratique on reaching her berth, the fact that she had not obtained free pratique did not prevent her being "ready".

The Delian Spirit [1971] 1 Lloyd's Rep. 506.

The *Pencarrow* was time chartered on the Baltime form for a Baltic round voyage from the United Kingdom. She was obliged to be "in every way fitted for ordinary cargo service". However, she did not have a Swedish measurement certificate and on her arrival to discharge in Stockholm the charterers obtained and paid for this certificate. There was no evidence that such a certificate was usually obtained prior to sailing on a Baltic round voyage or that the lack of one in this case had caused delay to the ship at or off Stockholm. Acton, J., held that there had been no breach by the owners in not having this certificate at the start of this voyage.

Chellew Navigation v. *Appelquist* (1933) 45 Ll.L.Rep. 190.
(See also *Wilson* v. *Rankin* (1865) L.R. 1 Q.B. 162.)

In *The Delian Spirit*, above, Lord Denning, M.R., distinguished, as "a very special case", *The Austin Friars* (1894) 10 T.L.R. 633. There charterers under a voyage charter had the right to cancel if the ship had not arrived at the port of loading and was not ready to load by midnight on 10 October. The ship arrived at 23.00 hours on 10 October, but the health officer did not visit the ship until the following day, and, in the meantime, the charterers had no access to the ship at all. It was held that the charterers were entitled to cancel.

It was also held in *The Derby*, below, that a ship did not have to have an I.T.F. blue card or certificate in order to be "in every way fitted for the service" under a New York Produce form charter, on the ground that it was not a document required by the law of the ship's flag or by the laws, regulations or lawful administrative practices of governmental or local authorities at the ship's ports of call. Further, there was no evidence that it was customary for owners to obtain an I.T.F. blue card or certificate.

Crew

It was held by the Court of Appeal in *The Hongkong Fir* [1961] 2 Lloyd's Rep. 478, that a ship was not "fitted for ordinary cargo service" under the Baltime form in a case where it was found that the engine room crew were both incompetent and inadequate in number. See pages 65 to 68 for a fuller discussion of this case. It was accepted by the Court of Appeal in *The Derby*, below, that the words "in every way fitted for the service" in the New York Produce form should in this respect be construed in the same way as the words in the Baltime form.

But the owners do not thereby undertake that the rates of pay and conditions of employment of the crew will comply with the requirements of a self-appointed and extra-legal organisation such as the International Transport Workers Federation ("I.T.F.").

The Cypriot flag *Derby* was chartered under the New York Produce form for a period of 11 to 13 months. She carried a Filipino crew on terms which were normal for such crews but which did not meet with the approval of the I.T.F. Certain countries were excluded from the charter's trading limits because they were known to be countries where the I.T.F. was specially active. It was provided by an additional clause that if the ship was delayed by labour stoppages due to flag or crew or payment of crew, any time lost was to be for the owners' account. In the course of the charter the ship called at Leixoes in Portugal, which country was not among those excluded from the trading limits. However, an I.T.F. representative there made enquiries which revealed that the ship did not hold an I.T.F. blue card and the stevedores refused to discharge the ship. By the time a settlement had been negotiated with the I.T.F. and work had resumed, a total of 21 days' work had been lost. The owners acknowledged that the ship was off hire for these 21 days under the additional labour stoppages clause, but the charterers claimed that they were entitled, in addition, to damages arising from the consequent cancellation of a sub-charter.

It was held by Hobhouse, J., and the Court of Appeal that, although the obligation in Lines 21 to 24 amounted to a warranty of seaworthiness and included an obligation to have the documents necessary for proper performance of the charter service and a competent and adequate crew, this did not extend to having an I.T.F. blue card or to complying with I.T.F. manning or crew pay requirements. The I.T.F. intervention affected the working of the ship by the stevedores and they were the charterers' responsibility: there was no failure on the part of the owners to perform any of the services they were obliged to perform. Further, there was no evidence that it was customary for owners to obtain an I.T.F. blue card. Consequently the owners were not liable for any of the damages claimed.

The Derby [1984] 1 Lloyd's Rep. 635 and [1985] 2 Lloyd's Rep. 325 (C.A.).

Prima facie question of fact

The question whether the ship is "fitted" for service is, *prima facie*, one of fact. Webster, J., in *The Arianna* [1987] 2 Lloyd's Rep. 376, dealing at page 390 with the charterers' argument that it was a question of law, summarised his conclusions as being: "... first, questions of seaworthiness and fittedness, etc., are *prima facie* questions of fact; secondly, that although the factual element in the determination of questions of seaworthiness may have been significantly diminished, seaworthiness and fittedness are not necessarily synonymous, and there is still a significant factual element in the determination of a question of fittedness; thirdly, that a defect in the vessel which has no effect on the safety of the vessel or the security or integrity of its cargo does not, as a matter of law, necessarily render the vessel unseaworthy or unfitted; fourthly, that whether or not it does so is a question of fact, the answer to which depends upon the significance of the effect of the defect ..."

Acceptance of delivery

If delivery of the ship is accepted by the charterers in circumstances in which they would have been entitled to refuse delivery, to cancel or to treat the contract as discharged, they will not necessarily lose the right to claim damages, even if they accept delivery without protest. In *The Democritos* [1975] 1 Lloyd's Rep. 386 (the facts of which are set out at page 290 below) Kerr, J., said at pages 397 and 398:

> In my judgment the question whether or not there was a waiver of any claim for damages is a question of mixed fact and law, but predominantly one to be decided by inference from the facts ... the mere fact of accepting the vessel amounts to no more than a waiver of the right to cancel; viewed in isolation it cannot, or at any rate does not by any means necessarily, carry with it a waiver of the right to claim damages. Such waiver can only be implied from something in the nature of an agreement on the part of the charterers to give up their potential claims for damages.

(For a fuller discussion of the circumstances in which rights under the charter may be waived see page 59 above.)

Clearly the right to damages will not be lost if the deficiency which constitutes the breach is not reasonably apparent on delivery or does not manifest itself until after delivery. In such circumstances acceptance of delivery will not even prevent the charterers from subsequently treating the contract as discharged if the breach is such as to deprive them of substantially the whole benefit of the charter: see *Snia* v. *Suzuki* (1924) 18 Ll.L.Rep. 333, *The Hongkong Fir* [1961] 2 Lloyd's Rep. 478 and *The Hermosa* [1980] 1 Lloyd's Rep. 638, [1982] 1 Lloyd's Rep. 570 and also pages 64 to 68 above.

American Law

Readiness to load

To be ready to load, all of the vessel's holds must be ready in all respects. *Crow* v. *Myers*, 41 F. 806 (E.D. Va. 1890). In *Rudolf A. Oetker* v. *Koninklijke Nederlandsche Stoomboot-Maatschappij N.V.*, S.M.A. No. 508 (Arb. at N.Y. 1970), unknown to the owner, the vessel was infested with Khapra beetles when she was delivered to the charterer. The panel held that notwithstanding its lack of knowledge of the latent condition, the owner was in breach of its duty to provide a "cargoworthy" vessel. According to the panel: "The Owner is bound to make the holds of the vessel fit for the reception of the cargo to be carried under the Charter." The panel held that the owner was obligated to fumigate the vessel once the condition was discovered, and that the vessel went off-hire while the fumigation was performed. The owner's contention that its duty to fumigate was waived by the charterer's acceptance of a delivery certificate was rejected.

In *The Endeavor*, 1978 AMC 1742 (Arb. at N.Y. 1977), the panel held that the owner was obliged to install new ladders in the cargo holds to meet the local requirements of an Australian trade union. The charterer had the right to direct the vessel to Australia, and this right would have been impeded if the vessel was not fitted with the special ladders. See further discussion below at page 168.

The holds need be ready only for general cargo, however, and unless the charter contains an express provision to the contrary, the owner need not have the holds ready for cargoes that require special treatment. See *Disney* v. *Furness*, 79 F. 810, 815 (D.Md. 1897), holding that "the readiness required was a reasonable readiness, and not a special readiness to gratify particular requirements established by the [charterer]". Similarly, in *Greenwell* v. *Ross*, 34 F. 656 (E.D. La. 1888), the court held that where the vessel was in all respects ready to load "lawful merchandise", as required by the charter, the charterer was not justified in cancelling the charter because the vessel was not ready to load a cargo that required special preparations where the charterer had not given the owner any advance notice of the cargo it intended to load, and the vessel could easily be prepared to load it. See also *The Stolt Lion*, S.M.A. No. 1188 (Arb. at N.Y. 1977).

In *The Emmanuel C*, S.M.A. No. 1575 (Arb. at N.Y. 1981), the panel held that the vessel was not ready within the meaning of Lines 21/22 of the charter when a routine preloading inspection by the National Cargo Bureau inspector revealed rust in all the cargo compartments. The cargo the charterer intended to load was bulk diammoniam phosphate, which was a permissible cargo under the charter. The cargo would have been contaminated by exposure to rust and the vessel, therefore, was not ready to receive permissible cargo. The vessel was held to be off-hire while the rust was removed.

If it is comtemplated that the vessel will be transporting goods that require special care, such as perishable cargo, the vessel must be equipped to do so. The leading American case is *Martin* v. *The Southwark*, 191 U.S. 1 (1903). In that case, a bill of lading was issued for a cargo of meat for shipment from Philadelphia to Liverpool. The meat arrived in damaged condition because the refrigeration apparatus had broken down prior to the vessel's departure from Philadelphia. The court held for the cargo owner, finding that the owner had failed to exercise due diligence to make the vessel seaworthy when she broke ground on the voyage.

The bill of lading in *Martin* v. *The Southwark* was governed by the Harter Act.

According to the court, the test of seaworthiness was whether the vessel was fit to carry the cargo of meat:

> As seaworthiness depends not only upon the vessel being staunch and fit to meet the perils of the sea, but upon its character in reference to the particular cargo to be transported, it follows that a vessel must be able to transport the cargo which it is held out as fit to carry or it is not seaworthy in that respect. But for the special appliances furnished by the vessel, perishable cargoes, such as dressed beef, could not be shipped on long voyages in hot weather. (191 U.S. at 9.)

Material defects may preclude an effective delivery. In *Oneida Nav. Co.* v. *L. Richardson & Co.*, 282 F. 241 (2d Cir. 1922), the vessel was described in the charter as an auxiliary schooner, or a schooner with auxiliary engines. On the cancelling date, her auxiliary engines were inoperative, and it was uncertain how soon they could be repaired. While recognizing that cancellation would probably not have been allowed if it had been known at the time that the necessary repairs could have been completed in eight or nine days, the court held that the charterer's cancellation was proper. According to the court, on the cancellation date, the "vessel chartered as an auxiliary schooner [was] not an auxiliary schooner . . . ". See discussion above at page 76.

With clean-swept holds

In *The Van Hawk*, 1975 AMC 254 (Arb. at N.Y. 1975), the panel held that the owner was not liable for extra cleaning expenses incurred by the charterer to make the holds ready to load a cargo of sulphur where under the New York Produce form the charter required the vessel's holds to be "swept-clean" and the vessel had been accepted by the charterer after an on hire survey.

See also *The Augvald*, 1965 AMC 1614 (Arb. at N.Y. 1965), holding that the charterer was entitled to reject the owner's tender of the vessel because the owner had not obtained "weevil free certificates" and the ship was therefore not in all respects ready to load. The owner knew that the charterer intended to load a cargo of grain. According to the panel:

> The Arbitrators are of the opinion that Owners were obligated to tender the vessel to the charterers with all cargo spaces clean and ready to receive a cargo of bulk and/or bagged grain . . . In the panel's opinion it was incumbent upon the Owners to tender the vessel with all cargo spaces free of live insects or weevils injurious to a grain cargo. (1965 AMC at 1616–1617.)

Tight, staunch, strong

These words state an express warranty that the vessel will be seaworthy at the time of delivery to the charterer. *Work* v. *Leathers*, 97 U.S. 379 (1878); *Munson S.S. Line* v. *S.S. Miramar S.S. Co.*, 166 F. 722, 724 (2d Cir. 1908); *Iligan Int'l. Corp.* v. *S.S. John Weyerhaeuser*, 372 F.Supp. 859, 1974 AMC 1719 (S.D.N.Y. 1974), aff'd 507 F.2d 68 (2d Cir. 1974), *cert.* denied 421 U.S. 956. In the absence of language such as that contained in Clause 1 of the New York Produce form, which imposes on the owner a continuing obligation to maintain the ship in a seaworthy condition, the warranty will be satisfied if the vessel is in a seaworthy condition at the time of delivery.

In *The Captain John*, 1973 AMC 2005 (Arb. at N.Y. 1973), where the charter stated that the vessel would be "tight, staunch and strong so far as these can be attained by the exercise of due diligence", it was held that the owner was under a duty to exercise due diligence throughout the charter term. As stated by the panel:

We interpret this as an express undertaking that due diligence would be exercised to make the vessel seaworthy at the commencement of each voyage. (1973 AMC at 2009.)

In *The Grand Explorer*, S.M.A. No. 551 (Arb. at N.Y. 1963), the charterer was held entitled to refuse to accept the vessel because the No. 5 hold had not been floored over with a sugar platform, as required by the charter. Similarly, in *Coca-Cola Co.* v. *S.S. Norholt*, 333 F.Supp. 946, 1972 AMC 388 (S.D.N.Y. 1971), the court stated:

The charter party specifically provided that Owner warranted that the vessel's deep tanks were suitable for dry or liquid cargo. A vessel owner gives an implied warranty of seaworthiness of the chartered vessel at the commencement of every voyage . . . The owners must provide a vessel with equipment and tanks to safely store and transport the various cargoes, or the warranty has been breached. (333 F.Supp. at 948–49.)

A vessel may be unseaworthy, i.e., not reasonably fit for the service, if she is not properly equipped to perform the safe carriage of the cargo under normal reasonably expected conditions. In *Demsey & Assoc.* v. *S.S. Sea Star*, 461 F.2d 1009 (2d Cir. 1972), the court held that a vessel chartered to carry steel was unseaworthy because her 'tween deck hatch boards were not capable of supporting the weight of the cargo.

Lawful Merchandise

"24. . . . to be employed, in carrying lawful merchan-
25. dise, including petroleum or its products, in proper containers, excluding ....
....
26. (vessel is not to be employed in the carriage of Live Stock, but Charterers are to have the privilege of shipping a small number on deck at their risk,
27. all necessary fittings and other requirements to be for account of Charterers), in such lawful trades,"

Unlawful cargoes

Lawful merchandise may include military stores and munitions. But goods will not be lawful merchandise if their loading amounts to a breach of the local law nor if they cannot lawfully be discharged at the nominated discharge ports. Presumably they must also be lawful under the law of the ship's flag and the proper law of the charter.

The *Dodecanese* was chartered on the Baltime 1920 form for employment "in lawful trades for the conveyance of lawful merchandise". She was loaded at various Mediterranean ports with ammunition and other explosives and ordered to discharge these to the British forces at Adabiya in Egypt, although the charterers knew this was prohibited by the Egyptian authorities. Having obeyed these orders and been black-listed by the Egyptian authorities for so doing, the ship loaded again, at Port Tewfik, with military stores for Aqaba, but she broke down before sailing. Because she was black-listed, the authorities delayed her repairs so that they took 26 days longer than they should have done. Pilcher, J., held that, as the goods loaded for Adabiya could not be discharged at the nominated port without a breach of local law, they were not "lawful merchandise" and the charterers were, therefore, liable to pay damages for the delay caused (effectively restoring the loss to the owners from the ship being off-hire during the 26 days).

Leolga v. *Glynn* [1953] 2 Lloyd's Rep. 47.

(See also *Vanderspar* v. *Duncan* (1891) 8 T.L.R. 30, described by Pilcher, J., in the case above as "only an authority upon 'usage' applied to its own particular facts".)

Shipment of cargo excluded under the charter

It is a breach of the contract for the charterers to ships goods excluded by the charter and the master may properly refuse an order to load such cargo. In *The Sussex Oak* (1950) 83 Ll.L.Rep. 297, Devlin, J., said at page 307: "I cannot think that the clause in a time charter-party which puts the master under the orders of the charterers as regards employment is to be construed as compelling him to obey orders which the charterers have no power to give."

The circumstances may be such that the shipment of excluded cargo is to be regarded as a fundamental breach of the charter, as to which generally, see pages 354 and 355 below.

The *Evgenia Chandris* was chartered for a voyage, the charter providing: "Cargo to consist of lawful general merchandise, excluding acids, explosives, arms, ammunition or other dangerous cargo." The charterers shipped turpentine, which was a dangerous cargo, and the discharge was delayed as a result. It was held that this cargo was excluded under the above clause and that the charterers were accordingly in breach of a "fundamental term". However, since the shipowners had affirmed the contract, they were entitled to demurrage only and not to damages for detention. Devlin, J., construed the demurrage clause as applicable to excluded as well as permitted cargo.

Chandris v. *Isbrandtsen-Moller* [1951] 1 K.B. 240.

It was argued in *Chandris* v. *Isbrandtsen-Moller* that the shipment of any quantity of excluded cargo (unless so small a quantity as to be *de minimis*) would entitle the owners to treat the charter as repudiated. Devlin, J., recognised the problems that such a contention presented when he said, at page 251: "If it be the law that an owner who at the end of a voyage discovers that a small portion of cargo (enough to be above *de minimis*) outside the contract description has been shipped, albeit with the knowledge of the master, can tear up the whole contract, it may result in some practical inconvenience. No such question arises for my consideration here, since the owner himself chose to affirm."

It is suggested that a court today would not regard the term as to excluded cargo as a term such that *any* breach of it would entitle the owners to treat the contract as discharged. Only those breaches which are so serious as to go to the root of the charter should be regarded as having that consequence.

Effect of acceptance of excluded cargo

If the charterers order the master to load excluded cargo and the owners either are unaware of this or instruct the master to accept it under protest, the owners may be entitled to additional remuneration based on the current market rate for carriage of the excluded cargo, either as damages or under an implied promise by the charterers.

The *Strathcona* was sub-chartered for a voyage to load steel billets. Unknown to the disponent owners, the sub-charterers loaded her partly with steel billets and partly with general cargo, for which the market rate of freight was much higher. It was held that the disponent owners (who did not seek to terminate the charter) were entitled to the market rate of freight for the general merchandise, the master, though having accepted the general cargo, having no authority to vary the original charter. By tendering excluded cargo the sub-charterers had impliedly promised to pay reasonable remuneration if it were carried.

Steven v. *Bromley* [1919] 2 K.B. 722.

Dangerous cargo

The New York Produce form contains no provision which forbids the shipment of dangerous cargo, by contrast to the Baltime form, Lines 21 and 22 of which read: "No live stock nor injurious, inflammable or dangerous goods (such as acids, explosives, calcium carbide, ferro silicon, naphtha, motor spirit, tar, or any of their products) to be shipped." It is, however, usual for the parties to agree some such exclusion in the space provided in Line 25 of the New York Produce form.

Implied obligation of charterers

A particular cargo may be dangerous despite the fact that cargoes of its type are not usually so classified if its own peculiar characteristics, including where relevant its own packaging, endanger the ship or other cargoes on board.

The charterers will be in breach of an undertaking implied at common law if they load such goods without notice of these peculiar characteristics, unless the owners or their crew knew or ought reasonably to have known of them. This rule originated in early cases dealing with the obligations of shippers of goods to common carriers; but Mustill, J., in *The Athanasia Comninos* [1981] COM LR 132 said: "It has been established for more than a century than a shipper, party to a contract of carriage, is under certain contractual obligations as to the suitability for carriage of the goods which he ships, and as to the giving of warnings concerning any dangerous characteristics of the goods: *Williams* v. *East India Co.* (1802) 3 East 192; *Brass* v. *Maitland* (1856) 6 E. & B. 470. These obligations are not confined to cases where the goods are tendered to a common carrier, but are capable of applying, in appropriate circumstances, to all contracts for the carriage of goods by sea." It seems, therefore, that under a time charter these common law obligations fall upon the charterers. Mustill, J., went on to express his view that the weight of authority supported the proposition that the obligation of the shipper was absolute, that is to say not depending upon whether he himself knew or should have known of the dangerous characteristics of the relevant cargo. Again, it seems that this should also be true of the obligation when it is placed upon the charterers.

The principle discussed above becomes more difficult to apply where the type of cargo concerned cannot simply be classified as "dangerous" or as "safe". As Mustill, J., pointed out in *The Athanasia Comninos*, it is not possible to say in the abstract that coal is either a dangerous or a safe cargo. It is well known that coal may emit methane gas which can combine with air to produce an explosive mixture. The shipowner may, however, argue that while he appreciated this danger and took appropriate precautions, he could not be expected to anticipate or to accept the risk of the particular shipment being gassy to an unexpected and quite extraordinary degree. Mustill, J., said that, in such a case: "I consider that it is not correct to start with an implied warranty as to the shipment of dangerous goods and try to force the facts within it; but rather to read the contract and the facts together, and ask whether, on the true construction of the contract, the risks involved in this particular shipment were risks which the [owners] contracted to bear." He went on to suggest that the risks which the owners should be regarded as having contracted to bear were those which would be avoided by appropriate methods of carriage for goods of the relevant type—the owners being expected to take reasonable steps to keep up to date with the correct methods but not to have the knowledge of an expert chemist. He said: "This approach will be sufficient to deal with most problems relating to dangerous cargoes, for in respect of the great majority of goods, the 'normal' precautions will suffice to eliminate the risk of carrying normal goods of the description stated in the contract. Leaving aside casualties from wholly extraneous causes, one can say that proper carriage and 'dangerous' nature are opposite sides of the same coin." Of course, the appropriate or "normal" methods of carriage might turn out in practice to be inadequate to prevent an accident, despite the normality of the cargo, and this risk Mustill, J., considered fell upon the owners. Where, however, the risks produced by the particular cargo were "of a totally different kind (whether in nature or degree) from those attached to the carriage of the described cargo", they should fall on the shippers or charterers rather than upon the owners. See also *The Atlantic Duchess* [1957] 2 Lloyd's Rep. 55.

In the New York Produce form, the common law obligations of the charterers are supplemented by the provisions of the United States Carriage of Goods by Sea Act.

United States Carriage of Goods by Sea Act

Clause 24 of the New York Produce form incorporates the United States Carriage of Goods by Sea Act, 1936, and Section 4(6) of this Act provides as follows:

Goods of an inflammable, explosive, or dangerous nature to the shipment whereof the carrier, master or agent of the carrier, has not consented with knowledge of their nature and character, may at any time before discharge be landed at any place or destroyed or rendered innocuous by the carrier without compensation, and the shipper of such goods shall be liable for all damages and expenses directly or indirectly arising out of or resulting from such shipment. If any such goods shipped with such knowledge and consent shall become a danger to the ship or cargo, they may in like manner be landed at any place, or destroyed or rendered innocuous by the carrier without liability on the part of the carrier except to general average, if any.

This Section 4(6) falls into three parts. *The first part* allows the owners to land, destroy or render innocuous inflammable, explosive or dangerous goods to the shipment of which they have not consented with knowledge of their nature. *The second part* makes "the shipper" liable for all damages and expenses arising out of such shipment. *The third part* concerns shipment of such cargoes to which the owners have consented with knowledge of their nature but which become a danger to their ship or its cargo, and gives the owners the rights listed in the first part.

Applying the principles set out at pages 424 to 428 below, there is no reason why the first and third parts of Section 4(6) should not have full effect as between owners and charterers under the New York Produce form. It is not so clear that the second part should be equally effective, because this involves reading "the shipper" as "the charterer": but it is submitted that in the context of the New York Produce form this is the correct approach (see page 426) and that consequently the second part of Section 4(6) does have effect in that context.

Some doubt exists as to whether the second part of Section 4(6) can be used by owners in relation to claims by them as well as in relation to claims against them. Although Mustill, J., in *The Athanasia Comninos* [1981] COM LR 132, see page 240 below, reserved his position on this point, there is support for owners' right to use this provision in relation to claims by them from the American cases cited at page 132 below and from the Canadian case of *The Erwin Schroder* [1970] Ex. C.R. 426.

It is also open to question whether the liability to owners that may be imposed by the second part of Section 4(6) is reduced from an absolute obligation to an obligation of due diligence by Section 4(3) of the same Act, which provides: "The shipper shall not be responsible for loss or damage sustained by the carrier or the ship arising or resulting from any cause without the act, fault, or neglect of the shipper, his agents, or his servants." The American cases cited at page 133 below suggest that the obligation is so reduced, but it is doubtful whether the same conclusion would be reached in English law. Mustill, J., reserved his position on this point also in *The Athanasia Comninos*.

The words in Section 4(6) "with knowledge of their nature and character" may include knowledge which the owners and their crew ought reasonably to have had, even if they did not. In *The Athanasia Comninos*, above and page 240 below, Mustill, J., said, *obiter*: "I consider that if the Rule [the identical provision in the Hague Rules] is concerned at all with claims by, rather than against, the carrier, the words quoted must include knowledge which the carrier and crew ought to have, as well as that which they actually have: otherwise, there would be a premium on ignorance."

It does not follow from the fact that the second part of Section 4(6) applies to the first part (which depends on lack of consent) and not to the third part (which depends on consent) that the shippers cannot be held liable for damage resulting from the shipment of dangerous goods to which the master consented. Devlin, J., rejected this argument in *Chandris* v. *Isbrandtsen-Moller* [1951] 1 K.B. 240 and page 125 above, where the master had consented to the shipment of prohibited dangerous cargo, but without, it was held, waiving the rights of the owners in respect thereof. The judge pointed out that the silence of the third part of Section 4(6) as to liability of the shipper (or, by incorporation, the voyage charterer) could not be used as a defence to the claim of the owners for breach by the voyage charterers of the express exclusion in the charter of such cargo; the Act was not intended as a comprehensive code altogether supplanting the contract of carriage, rather it controlled certain topics and remained silent on others, including the consequences of shipping such cargo with the consent of the master, which the parties remained free to regulate for themselves by the terms of their contract.

The owners' indemnity under Clause 8 of the New York Produce form

The owners may sue the charterers for damages caused by an order to load dangerous cargo on the basis of the indemnity implied under Clause 8 of the New York Produce form, see page 237 below. This action is not dependent on any fault on the part of the charterers, see page 239 below, and thus is an easier route for the owners as it avoids the possibility that the charterers' implied obligation at common law and under the second part of Section 4(6) of the United States Carriage of Goods by Sea Act may be held to be one of due diligence and not to be absolute in nature (see the comments at page 127 and page 128 above). Moreover, in order for owners to succeed on the basis of this indemnity in the case of a cargo of a type not automatically classified as dangerous, they will not necessarily have to prove that the particular cargo was unusual; see page 240 below.

Lack of warning

A cargo may be dangerous through lack of information given to the master.

The *Agios Nicolas* was chartered on the Baltime form, excluding the shipment of "dangerous goods". A cargo of iron ore concentrate was loaded, but the master was misled as to the moisture content and was not informed (despite all reasonable enquiries made by him) that the moisture content was such that shifting boards should have been fitted. Shifting boards were not fitted and, as a result of the cargo shifting, the ship developed a list and had to put into a port of refuge. The time charterers were held to be in breach for shipping dangerous cargo.

Donaldson, J., said: "In a word, what [the master] was being offered was a wet wolf in a dry sheep's clothing and there was nothing to put him on notice that the cargo was something radically and fundamentally different from that which it appeared to be. In those circumstances it seems to me that the cargo was dangerous beyond all argument."

Micada v. *Texim* [1968] 2 Lloyd's Rep. 57.

Baltime form

Lines 21 and 22 of the Baltime form provide: "No live stock nor injurious, inflammable or dangerous goods (such as acids, explosives, calcium carbide, ferro silicon, naphtha, motor spirit, tar or any of their products) to be shipped." The words in brackets beginning "such as" do not restrict the full and natural meaning of the words that precede them; "such as" in this clause means "for example" and not "namely": *Micada* v. *Texim* [1968] 2 Lloyd's Rep. 57, and above.

Extra remuneration

In *Steven* v. *Bromley* [1919] 2 K.B. 722, above, Atkin, L.J., discussed the possibility, on which he reserved opinion, of the shipowner who charters his ship for non-dangerous work and finds it used instead for dangerous work claiming as part of his damages for breach of contract reasonable extra remuneration for the dangerous work.

In such lawful trades

It is thought that "lawful trades" should be construed similarly to "lawful merchandise". Presumably a trade would be unlawful not only if unlawful by the law of the proposed port of shipment or of discharge, but also if it was unlawful by either the law of the ship's flag or by the law governing the charter.

American Law

Lawful merchandise

It is customary to include in the charter a clause concerning the type of cargoes to be carried. If such a clause is included, the owner is obliged to load only cargoes of the type provided for. In the absence of a cargo exclusion clause, the only limitation on the charterer's right to ship cargo is that it be "lawful merchandise".

In *The Wismar*, S.M.A. No. 1454 (Arb. at N.Y. 1980), the charter included a cargo exclusion clause which provided in relevant part:

Clause 45A: Excluded Cargoes
Asphalt and pitch in bulk, acids, nuclear and radioactive material, livestock, hides, turnings, and motorblocks. Arms, ammunition and explosives and any other injurious and inflammable and dangerous cargo unless packed, labelled, loaded, stowed and discharged according to IMCO Regulations/U.S. Coast Guard Regulations.

The vessel was sub-chartered on identical terms, and the sub-charterer directed the master to load a cargo of direct reduced iron ore pellets ("DRIP"). The owner instructed the master to refuse to load the cargo because of reports that DRIP gives off hydrogen gas and generates heat when it comes in contact with water, and was, therefore, dangerous within the meaning of the cargo exclusion clause quoted above. The panel majority concluded that in determining whether DRIP was in fact a dangerous cargo, IMCO [now IMO] and United States Coast Guard regulations were especially relevant since those were the regulatory bodies expressly referred to in the charter. DRIP was not then listed in the IMCO Dangerous Goods Code, and was not classified by the United States Coast Guard as a dangerous cargo, although precautions were prescribed for the loading of DRIP by the Coast Guard. Moreover, the Canadian Coast Guard had approved the loading of DRIP provided certain guidelines were followed. Because the cargo was not officially classified as "dangerous", the panel majority held that it was not dangerous under Clause 45A of the charter, notwithstanding a considerable body of expert testimony to the effect that the material was explosive and inflammable in the presence of water.

In *The Witfuel*, S.M.A. No. 1381 (Arb. at N.Y. 1979), the vessel was chartered under a tanker time form for the carriage of "crude oil and/or dirty petroleum products". The panel held that the charterer was in breach of the charter for loading a clean or refined product, and was liable for damages resulting therefrom, including the cost of repairs, and a pollution fine. The panel noted that in deciding whether the cargo was excluded under the charter, it: "was guided by the general understanding of clean and dirty products, i.e., refined on the one hand, and crude or residual on the other, in the industry, as distinct from elaborate definitions, founded on criteria of which vessel operating and chartering personnel usually have little knowledge."

The Maria K., S.M.A. No. 1324 (Arb. at N.Y. 1979), involved the question of whether petroleum coke ("Petcoke") was an excluded cargo. The charter was on the New York Produce form and Line 22 contained no express reference to Petcoke. The panel held that Petcoke was a lawful cargo, and that the owner's refusal to load it was a breach of charter.

See also *The Fernglen*, 1971 AMC 213 (Arb. at N.Y. 1970), discussed below at page 186.

In *The Mercandian Supplier II*, S.M.A. No. 2509 (Arb. at N.Y. 1988), arbitrators noted that marijuana is not lawful merchandise.

Controlled substances

In 1986, the Maritime Drug Law Enforcement Act was enacted 46 U.S.C. §§ 1901–1904. Among other things, the act makes it unlawful for any person on board a United States flag vessel or a vessel otherwise subject to the jurisdiction of the United States to manufacture or distribute a controlled substance. The penalties provided for include the seizure and forfeiture of any vessel on which illegal controlled substances are found. 46 U.S.C. §§ 1904.

Dangerous cargo

Under the general maritime law, a cargo owner is under a duty to advise the carrier of any dangers in the cargo of which it is or ought to be aware and of which the carrier is not and cannot reasonably be expected to be aware. *International Mercantile Maritime Co.* v. *Fels*, 170 F. 275, 277 (2d Cir. 1909). The cargo owner, however, is not considered to warrant absolutely that the cargo contains no inherent dangers. Rather, the cargo owner's duty is based on either its actual or constructive knowledge of danger. See *Sucrest Corp.* v. *Jennifer*, 455 F.Supp. 371, 1978 AMC 2520 (D.Me. 1978); *William J. Quillan*, 180 F. 681, 682–84 (2d 1910), *cert.* denied 218 U.S. 682; *Akt. Fido* v. *Lloyd Brasileiro*, 267 F. 733 (S.D.N.Y. 1919), aff'd 283 F. 62 (2d Cir. 1922), *cert.* denied 260 U.S. 737 (1922).

In *Sucrest Corp.* v. *Jennifer*, above, the vessel developed a severe list because the cargo of sugar shifted and was intentionally stranded for the safety of the vessel and the cargo. The cargo shifting resulted from a biological degradation of the sugar. The court found that the casualty marked "the first instance in which the maritime or scientific community learned of the thixotropic properties of raw sugar". The sugar was owned by a voyage charterer, whom the owner alleged was liable for damages caused by the grounding. The court held, however, that the cargo owner had neither actual nor constructive knowledge of the inherent dangers of the cargo and therefore was not liable for the casualty.

It also has been held that there is an implied warranty given by the shipper of cargo that the shipment is reasonably fit and safe for carriage. *Pierce* v. *Winsor*, F.Cas. Nos. 11,150 and 11,151 (D.C.D. Mass. and C.C.D. Mass. 1861). The carrier in that case was held to be entitled to indemnity for damage done by a bulk stowage of mastic which melted other cargo. See also *The Santa Clara*, 281 F. 725, 736 (2d Cir. 1922); *Cf. Luckenbach S.S. Co.* v. *Coast Mfg. & Sup. Co.*, 185 F.Supp. 910, 1960 AMC 2076 (E.D.N.Y. 1960). It would seem correct that this warranty would apply to a charterer under a time charter, particularly if the charterer owns the cargo.

The implied warranty does not apply where the owner knows or ought to know the dangerous character of the goods. *Westchester Fire Insurance Co.* v. *Buffalo Housewrecking & Salvage Co.*, 40 F.Supp. 378, 381–82, 1941 AMC 1601 (W.D.N.Y. 1941), aff'd 129 F.2d 319, 1942 AMC 1052 (2d Cir. 1942). In that case, the court held that the implied warranty by the shipper of a cargo of metal turnings and borings was not applicable where the owner had been given a full opportunity to observe the cargo before it was loaded.

In *Pitria Star Navigation Co.* v. *Monsanto Co.*, 1986 AMC 2966 (E.D.La. 1984), claims were asserted by the shipowner against a voyage charterer and the manufacturer and shipper of a cargo of parathion, a poison, liquid insecticide. The cargo was packaged in 55 gallon steel drums, each of which contained prominently displayed warning labels. Three seamen died during the voyage as a result of an accident which resulted in the parathion contaminating the ship's bilges. Several of the drums of parathion leaked when the discharging stevedores mishandled the drums. The parathion found its way into the ship's bilges and, subsequent to redelivery of the vessel by the voyage charterer, the three crew members were exposed to the parathion when they were cleaning the bilges. The court found that the deaths of the seamen did not give rise to a claim against the manufacturer of the cargo because there was no showing of any negligence in the manufacture or packaging of the insecticide. The court also dismissed the shipowner's claim against the charterer on the basis of its finding that the direct cause of the deaths was the negligence of the stevedores at the discharge port and, under the voyage charter, such negligence was imputed to the owner. The court also found that there had been no negligence on the part of any of the defendants with respect to giving required warnings of the dangerous nature of the cargo. As to the duty of the charterer and the shipper to warn, the court applied *Restatement (Second) of Torts*, Section 388 which states:

Sec. 388. *Chattel Known to be Dangerous for Intended Use*
One who supplies directly or through a third person a chattel for another to use is subject to liability to those whom the supplier should expect to use the chattel with the consent of the other or to be endangered by its probable use, for physical harm caused by the use of the chattel in the manner for which and by a person for whose use it is supplied, if the supplier

(*a*) knows or has reason to know that the chattel is or is likely to be dangerous for the use for which it is supplied, and
(*b*) has no reason to believe that those for whose use the chattel is supplied will realize its dangerous condition, and
(*c*) fails to exercise reasonable care to inform them of its dangerous condition or of the facts which make it likely to be dangerous.

Because the shipowner knew that the parathion was a poison, the court found that the defendants had "no reaon to believe" that the shipowner and the crew would not realize the dangerous condition of the cargo.

In *Serrano* v. *U.S. Lines Co.*, 238 F.Supp. 383 1965 AMC 1038 (S.D.N.Y. 1965), the court held that this implied warranty was not operative where COGSA is applicable. According to the court, Section 1304(3) of the COGSA would govern the shipper's liability. That section states:

The shipper shall not be responsible for loss or damage sustained by the carrier or the ship arising or resulting from any cause without the act, fault, or neglect of the shipper, his agents, or his servants.

Serrano illustrates how broad the reach of COGSA can be. The case involved a claim for personal injuries caused by the explosion of a tire on a trailer that had been loaded abroad the vessel. The owner claimed a right of indemnity for any sums it was held liable to pay to the injury claimant from the space charterer and owner of the trailer. The court held that the owner's indemnity claim was governed by COGSA; while the claim was not one for cargo damage: "COGSA [defines] the rights and obligations *inter sese* arising out of the carriage of goods relation." Because there was no actual fault on the shipper's part, the owner's claim was denied.

So also in *The Stylianos Restis*, 1974 AMC 2343 (S.D.N.Y. 1972), the owner's claim for fire damage against the shipper of a cargo of fishmeal was denied under Section 4(3) where it failed to prove actual negligence on the part of the shipper. See also *Williamson* v. *Compania Anonima Venzolana de Navegacion*, 446 F.2d 1339, 1971 AMC 2083 (2d Cir. 1971).

If the charter incorporates COGSA, as the New York Produce form does, the charterer's liability to the owner for damages arising from defects or inherent dangers in the cargo would be governed by Section 4(3) of COGSA.

Section 4(6) of COGSA would also affect the charterer's responsibilities. That section states:

Goods of an inflammable, explosive, or dangerous nature to the shipment whereof the carrier, master or agent of the carrier, has not consented with knowledge of their nature and character, may at any time before discharge be landed at any place or destroyed or rendered innocuous by the carrier without compensation, and the shipper of such goods shall be liable for all damages and expenses directly or indirectly arising out of or resulting from such shipment. If any such goods shipped with such knowledge and consent shall become a danger to the ship or cargo, they may in like manner be landed at any place, or destroyed or rendered innocuous by the carrier without liability on the part of the carrier except to general average, if any.

To obtain a recovery from the charterer under Section 4(6), the owner must show that the cargo was dangerous within the meaning of COGSA.

The basic question whether a given cargo is dangerous is one of fact and will depend entirely on the circumstances arising in a given case. For example, in *Westchester Fire Ins. Co.* v. *Buffalo Housewrecking & Salvage Co.*, above, a barge was destroyed by fire when its cargo of turnings and borings overheated. The bill of lading for the shipment contained the provision that the shipper should be liable in the event that the cargo was dangerous, unless full written disclosure of its character were made to the barge owner. In dealing with the threshold issue of whether the cargo was "dangerous", the court stated that turnings, as such, are not explosives or dangerous goods. The court noted, however, that turnings may become dangerous if they contain an excessive amount of moisture or waste material such as oily waste and rags. On the facts before it, the court held that the turnings were dry and free of waste materials when loaded, and, therefore, not "dangerous".

In *The Kapetan Antonis*, 1989 AMC 551 (Arb. at N.Y. 1988), a case involving a voyage charter, it was held that charterer was liable for damages resulting from a fire in a cargo of turnings. The arbitrators ruled that charterer had a duty to owner "to furnish a safe and transportable cargo" (1989 AMC at 561), and breached that duty by negligently loading unsafe turnings. But see *The Gyda*, 1971 AMC 2070, 406 F.2d 1039 (6th Cir. 1969), holding that the shipper of a cargo of turnings was not liable to owner under Section 4(6) of COGSA where the master was aware of the hazard presented by turning prior to loading.

In *Poliskie Line Oceanic* v. *Hooker Chemical Corp.*, 499 F.Supp. 94, 1980 AMC 1748 (S.D.N.Y. 1980), it was held that the shipper of a cargo of sulphur dichloride was liable to the owner for damages resulting from its improper stowage of the hazardous material in a sealed container without complying with government regulations.

In *The Wismar*, above, a majority of the panel held that a cargo of direct reduced iron ore pellets was not "dangerous" because it was not officially classified as such by either the United States or Canadian Coast Guards or IMCO [now IMO].

See also *International Mercantile Marine Co.* v. *Fels*, 170 F. 275 (2d Cir. 1909), involving an explosion caused by vapor emitted from a cargo of soap. The court held that while the soap was dangerous when stored in a poorly ventilated place, the owner was at fault since the charterer had made the required full disclosure of its nature and qualities.

In *The Stylianos Restis*, above, the vessel suffered damage when spontaneous combustion of the cargo of fishmeal caused a fire in the holds. The court found that the cargo's susceptibility to spontaneous combustion was an inherent vice of the commodity. The cargo was being shipped under a voyage charter which expressly stated that fishmeal would be the cargo and contained warranties as to the conditions of shipment. The court found that the master had full knowledge of the inherent characteristics of fishmeal. Moreover, since the master had consented to the loading of the cargo with the express approval of the owner, the court held that there was no basis for holding the shipper or voyage charterer liable under Section 4(6) of COGSA.

Whether a cargo can be carried safely is an issue committed to the sound discretion of the master, upon whom the responsibility for safe carriage rests. *Boyd* v. *Moses*, 74 U.S. 192 (1869). As stated in *A & D Properties Inc.* v. *M.V. Volta River*, 1984 AMC 464, 471 (E.D. La. 1983):

> when the master rejects a cargo based on a well-founded concern for the safety of the vessel, after due consideration of all of the circumstances, his decision will not be judged with hindsight.

To the same effect, *see also Drummond Coal Co.* v. *Interocean Shipping Co.*, 1985 AMC 1152, 1162 (S.D. Ala. 1985).

In *The Kartini*, S.M.A. Nos. 1958 and 2196 (Arb. at N.Y. 1984 and 1985), charterer was held responsible for damages arising from the spontaneous heating and fire in a coal cargo. Charterer had loaded an amount of "pond solids", a coal by-product which is highly flammable, along with the regular coal. However, the master had not been warned of the propensities of the "pond solids". The panel rejected charterer's contention that the master was acting for the owner regarding this cargo because it affected the safety and seaworthiness of the vessel. Instead, the panel held that charterer was responsible for loading and those acts performed by the master in this respect were as agent of the charterer. See, generally, the discussion below at page 256 concerning Clause 8.

Other United States legislation

The "Carriage of Explosives or Dangerous Substances Act", 46 U.S.C. §170 (1970) was repealed in 1983 by Pub. L. 98–89, §4(6), 97 Stat. 600–605. The repeal of Section 170 was part of a partial overhaul of numerous maritime laws. New provisions were adopted to cover the carriage of dangerous or hazardous materials and are codified at 45 U.S.C., §§2101, 3701–3718.

In addition, Coast Guard regulations govern the loading of dangerous cargo and hazardous materials. See 46 C.F.R. §§30–40, 98, 146–154, 171–176. The Coast Guard regulations are extensive, and cover the transportation and storage of military explosives on board vessels, the use of dangerous articles as ship's stores and supplies, dangerous solids in bulk, and dangerous liguid and gas cargoes.

Safe Ports and Berths

"27. [Vessel......to be employed] . . . . between safe port and/or ports in British North
28. America, and/or United States of America, and/or West Indies, and/or Central America, and/or Caribbean Sea, and/or Gulf of Mexico, and/or
29. Mexico, and/or South America .... and/or Europe
30. and/or Africa, and/or Asia, and/or Australia, and/or Tasmania, and/or New Zealand, but excluding Magdalena River, River St. Lawrence between
31. October 31st and May 15th, Hudson Bay and all unsafe ports; also excluding, when out of season, White Sea, Black Sea and the Baltic,
32. ....
33. ....
34. ....
35. as the Charterers or their Agents shall direct, on the following conditions:"

General

The primary obligation on the charterers is to order the ship only to ports which, at the time when their order is given, are prospectively safe. The elements of safety are discussed in this and the following pages; the concept of prospective safety at page 145, below.

The elements of safety

The classic definition of a "safe port" is that of Sellers, L.J., in *Leeds Shipping* v. *Société Française Bunge* (*The Eastern City*) [1958] 2 Lloyd's Rep. 127, at page 131: " . . . a port will not be safe unless, in the relevant period of time, the particular ship can reach it, use it and return from it without, in the absence of some abnormal occurrence, being exposed to danger which cannot be avoided by good navigation and seamanship . . . ."

Roskill, L.J., in agreeing with this statement in the Court of Appeal in *The Hermine* [1979] 1 Lloyd's Rep. 212 remarked: " . . . it is now quite unnecessary, in these unsafe port or unsafe berth cases, to refer back to the multitude of earlier decisions . . . There is the law clearly stated. What has to be determined by the tribunal of fact in each case is whether, on the particular facts, the particular warranty of safety has or has not been broken". But Mustill, J., in *The Mary Lou* [1981] 2 Lloyd's Rep. 272 drew attention to the fact that points of law could arise which were not covered by the general principles laid down by Sellers, L.J., and that it might then be helpful to consult the earlier authorities, albeit that the conclusion of the court on such points of law should be consistent with those general principles.

The relevant period of time

The prospective safety of the port is to be judged as at the time of the charterers' order to it; see *The Evia* (*No. 2*) [1982] 2 Lloyd's Rep. 307 and pages 145 and 146 below. The relevant period of time, during which it is to be prospectively safe, is the time when the ship will be using it (or, where relevant, approaching or departing from it; see pages 139 to 142 below). A port may be unsafe for the particular ship at all times or only at certain times.

The *Eastern City* was chartered for a winter voyage from "one or two safe ports in Morocco" to Japan. The charterers ordered the ship to load at Mogador, where she arrived and anchored on 26 December. Two days later the weather deteriorated and the master, fearing that his anchor was dragging, tried to put to sea. But the ship was caught by a strong gust of wind and driven on to rocks adjacent to the anchorage.

It was held by the Court of Appeal that the port was unsafe because, during the winter, it was exposed to sudden southerly gales which could not be predicted and which were liable to cause the ship to drag her anchors in the unreliable holding ground of the restricted anchorage area.

The Eastern City [1958] 2 Lloyd's Rep. 127.

The fact that for tidal, meteorological or other reasons, the ship may have to wait for a time before entering the port does not, in itself, make that port unsafe. For example, a ship may have to wait for high water to clear a bar in the approach to the port or for a storm to abate before entering, but as Devlin, J., said in *The Stork* [1954] 2 Lloyd's Rep. 397, at page 415: "The law does not require the port to be safe at the very time of the vessel's arrival. Just as she may encounter wind and weather conditions which delay her on her voyage to the loading port, so she may encounter similar conditions which delay her entry into the port, and the charterer is no more responsible for the one than for the other."

Indeed, the port may be safe even if at certain times or during certain conditions ships already in it have to put to sea for safety.

Burriana in Spain was found as a matter of fact to be a safe loading place although it was necessary for ships which loaded in the roadstead there to keep up steam so as to be ready to put to sea in certain weather conditions.

Smith v. *Dart* (1884) 14 Q.B.D. 105.

Temporary dangers

It is sometimes said that purely temporary dangers will not make a port unsafe. But temporary dangers may be an important element of unsafety particularly if the existence of the danger is not known to the master of the ship. Thus, the temporary failure or temporary absence of navigational aids in a port, such as lights or buoys, may very well render the port unsafe if, because of the temporary nature of the deficiency, the master is unaware of the failure or absence of the navigational aids. (See generally on this point, the judgment of Mustill, J., in *The Mary Lou* [1981] 2 Lloyd's Rep. 272, at page 279.) In this context the time at which safety is to be judged may be particularly important, as to which see pages 143 to 145 below.

Weather conditions may also render a port unsafe even though of short duration. For example, a port may be unsafe if ships are liable to be trapped inside it and damaged by unpredictable storms even if the storms are of short duration: *The Eastern City* above.

Therefore, the proposition that temporary dangers will not make a port unsafe is only accurate in the limited sense that known or evident dangers which temporarily delay the ship in reaching the port, while remaining in it or in leaving it, will not make the port unsafe.

Delays

Delays caused by patent dangers or obstructions may, however, render a port unsafe if the delays are of sufficient duration.

In *Knutsford* v. *Tillmanns* [1908] A.C. 406, a ship on a voyage from Middlesbrough was held up 40 miles from Vladivostock by ice. She tried to get through the ice but, after three days, went to Nagasaki and discharged her cargo there. The owners sought to rely on a term in the bill of lading that if a port should be inaccessible on account of ice, or if a port should be deemed by the master unsafe, it should be competent for the master to discharge the goods at some other safe port or place. Lord Loreburn, dealing with the meaning of "unsafe", said that it "does not mean unsafe at the moment, but it means unsafe for a period which would involve inordinate delay". It was accordingly held by the House of Lords that the owners were not justified in discharging the cargo at an alternative port after a delay of only three days on such a long voyage.

An argument was advanced in *The Sussex Oak* (1950) 83 Ll.L.Rep. 297, that the exceptionally heavy ice encountered by the *Sussex Oak* on a voyage up the Elbe to Hamburg was only a temporary danger. The ship in that case was time chartered on the Baltime form and Devlin, J., in supporting the arbitrators' decision against the charterers on this point, said: "It is the law that the danger must be operative for a period which, having regard to the nature of the adventure and of the contract would involve inordinate delay: see in particular *S.S. Knutsford Ltd.* v. *Tillmanns & Co.* [1908] A.C. 406 . . . The period of the ice danger compared with the duration of the charter-party and the shortness of the voyage to Hamburg clearly justifies [the arbitrators'] conclusion." The ship was on a voyage from London and the arbitrator had found that ice conditions in the Elbe that winter were of exceptional severity and duration.

The meaning of "inordinate delay" was explained by the Court of Appeal in *The Hermine*, below. It must be such a period of delay as would frustrate the charter: a danger or obstruction which resulted in a delay to the ship of any shorter duration would not render the port unsafe.

A charter was entered into on the Baltimore Form C, for ships to be nominated, for three voyages from the U.S. Gulf to north Europe. The *Hermine* was nominated for one of the voyages and was ordered to Destrehan, a port on the Mississippi River about 140 miles from the open sea. Having proceeded safely up river to Destrehan, loaded there and departed again without suffering any damage, the *Hermine* was held up about 115 miles down river from Destrehan because of silting at the Southwest Pass. The usual time to reach the open sea from Destrehan was 10–12 hours, but because of the silting the ship was held up for about 30 days.

It was held by the Court of Appeal that, assuming a port could be regarded as unsafe because of an obstruction more than 100 miles from it (a question which was left undecided), delay caused by an obstruction could only constitute unsafety if it was so long as to frustrate the adventure. The delay suffered by the *Hermine* was acknowledged to be insufficient to amount to frustration.

Unitramp v. *Garnac Grain* (*The Hermine*) [1979] 1 Lloyd's Rep. 212.

(See also on the question of frustration pages 326 to 329 below and on the question of an obstruction a long distance from the port, *The Mary Lou* [1981] 2 Lloyd's Rep. 272 and page 142 below.)

The particular ship

The fact that the port would be safe for ships of different size or characteristics is not relevant. The port must be safe for the particular ship chartered.

The *Sagoland* was ordered under a voyage charter to discharge at Londonderry. She was the largest ship ever to go there and because of the narrow winding approach to the port was unable to enter without tugs. There were no tugs at Londonderry and the ship was obliged to call for tugs from the Clyde. The owners claimed to recover the cost from the charterers. Roche, J., in holding that the cost was recoverable, affirmed the finding of the umpire that Londonderry was unsafe for that particular ship, but he added:

> "Let not the findings of the umpire be misunderstood. It was not a finding that the Port of Londonderry was not an entirely safe port for 99 out of 100 or an even larger proportion of the

ships which may seek to resort thereto, but merely that it was not a safe port for the ship in question, the *Sagoland*."

Brostrom v. *Dreyfus* (1932) 44 Ll.L.Rep. 136.

The port must also be safe for the particular ship, laden as she is at the relevant time. Roche, J., in *Brostrom* v. *Dreyfus*, above, said: "The test of whether a port is safe in the physical sense or in the political sense is whether it is safe for the particular ship (laden as it is contemplated that she will be laden and as she is in fact laden under the particular contract of carriage in question) to enter and load or unload in the port in question." (See also *Hall* v. *Paul* (1914) 19 Com. Cas. 384 (laden) and *Limerick* v. *Stott* (1920) 5 Ll.L.Rep. 190 (light).)

Safety of approach

The ship must be able to reach the port in safety.

The *Sussex Oak* was time chartered under the Baltime form and was ordered to proceed to Hamburg in January 1947. On her passage up the Elbe ice was encountered, but the pilot considered it safe to proceed. When the ship was nearing the approaches to Hamburg she was stopped by a large ice flow. The ship was then in a part of the river in which she could neither turn, go astern nor anchor in safety and on the advice of the pilot forced her way through the ice, sustaining damage in consequence. It was found as a fact that the master acted properly in proceeding without ice breaker assistance and held that the charterers were liable for the damage on the ground that Hamburg was then an unsafe port. Devlin. J., said: "In my judgment, there is a breach of Clause 2 if the vessel is employed upon a voyage to a port which she cannot safely reach. It is immaterial in point of law where the danger is located, though it is obvious in point of fact that the more remote it is from the port the less likely it is to interfere with the safety of the voyage. The charterer does not guarantee that the most direct route or any particular route to the port is safe, but the voyage he orders must be one which an ordinarily prudent and skilful master can find a way of making in safety."

Grace v. *General Steam Navigation* (*The Sussex Oak*) (1950) 83 Ll.L.Rep. 297.

So a port will be unsafe if the approach to it is such that the ship cannot reach the port in safety without dismantling part of her structure.

The *Vanduara* was time chartered for the period of a voyage to a safe port in the United Kingdom. It was held by the Court of Appeal that Manchester was an unsafe port for the *Vanduara* because she could not reach Manchester without passing Runcorn Bridge (24 miles from the port) and to do that she would have to dismantle her masts.

Re Goodbody and Balfour, Williamson (1899) 5 Com. Cas. 59.

It has also been held that a port is unsafe if, in order to enter it, the ship must lighten some of her cargo.

The *Peerless* was employed under a voyage charter which required that she should discharge at a safe port. She was ordered to discharge at King's Lynn but her draft was too great to allow her to enter on any tide with her full cargo of maize. Sankey, J., held that the port was unsafe for her and that the owners were entitled to recover the cost of lighters.

Hall v. *Paul* (1914) 19 Com. Cas. 384.

(See also *The Alhambra* (1881) 6 P.D. 68.)

The risk of hostile seizure or attack en route to the port nominated may make the port unsafe.

The *Frankby* was time chartered under a charter which provided that the ship should be employed between safe ports within a certain limited area. The ship was ordered to Newcastle at a time when the German Government had declared that hostile merchant ships would be sunk in the waters around Great Britain. It was held that the risk of being sunk by submarines was a matter to be taken into account in considering whether Newcastle was a safe port. But, on all the facts, the port was safe at the material time.

Sankey, J., said " . . . the port must be both physically and politically safe, and I think that the action either of nature or man may render a port unsafe."

Palace Shipping v. *Gans Line* [1916] 1 K.B. 138.

(See also *The Teutonia* (1872) L.R. 4 P.C. 171.)

Safety in use

The port must be physically safe in its location, size and layout for the particular ship to use at the relevant time, having regard to both its natural and artificial aspects. The fact that it is safe to enter is not enough if the port may become unsafe for the ship to remain at.

The *Saxon Queen* was employed under so time charter "between any safe ports between Hamburg and Brest and the United Kingdom". The ship was ordered to Craster in the United Kingdom which was safe to enter in the weather conditions then prevailing. The port was one, however, which was liable to become dangerous if a change of wind altered the conditions and it was held that it was not a safe port.

Johnston v. *Saxon Queen Steamship* (1913) 108 L.T. 564.

The port does not have to be safe for uninterrupted use, so long as ships can leave in safety when the port becomes dangerous. So in *Smith* v. *Dart* (1884) 14 Q.B.D. 105, it was held that Burriana in Spain was a safe port, although it was necessary for ships to keep up steam so as to be ready to put to sea in certain weather conditions. But the port will only be safe if the necessity to depart is predictable and the ship is able to take the required action in safety and in good time.

The *Eastern City* was chartered for a winter voyage from "one or two safe ports in Morocco" and was ordered to Mogador. Ships of her size could not, in certain winter weather conditions, safely remain there as the holding was unreliable, and departure to sea was itself hazardous once such conditions had arisen. Furthermore, the onset of these conditions was sudden and unpredictable. In holding that the port was unsafe, Pearson, J. said, at page 172: "Be it supposed that a port can be safe for a ship even though the ship may have to leave it when certain weather conditions are imminent, nevertheless such a port is not safe for the ship unless there is reasonable assurance that the imminence of such weather conditions will be recognised in time and that the ship will be able to leave the port safely."

The Eastern City [1957] 2 Lloyd's Rep. 153 (upheld on appeal at [1958] 2 Lloyd's Rep. 127).

(See also *The Khian Sea* [1979] 1 Lloyd's Rep. 545, below.)

In his judgment in *The Eastern City* Pearson, J., remarked, at page 172, that "it might be necessary, on the true construction of a particular charter-party, that the port should be safe for uninterrupted loading".

Local warnings

If it is necessary at the onset of adverse weather for the ship to leave the port, there must be arrangements to provide the master with adequate warning.

The *Dagmar* was chartered for the period of a trip from Canada to Italy on the Baltime form. She was ordered to load timber at Cape Chat, a small port on the Saint Lawrence River. The pier at which she was berthed afforded the ship little protection from wind and sea and in certain weather conditions it was necessary for her to leave to seek safety in open water. The charterers neither made arrangements for the warnings of adverse weather which were available locally to be passed to the master, nor made it clear to the master that it was up to him to keep a wireless watch.

Mocatta, J., held that the port was unsafe and that the charterers were liable for the damage caused to the ship when she broke her moorings to the pier and ran aground following the sudden onset of adverse weather.

The Dagmar [1968] 2 Lloyd's Rep. 563.

Adequate warning to depart because of the onset of bad weather will not suffice if the ship may nevertheless be trapped by lack of the searoom necessary to do so.

The *Khian Sea* was chartered on the New York Produce form for a round voyage via safe ports including Valparaiso. She was ordered by the charterers to a berth at Valparaiso which was outside the breakwater. Upon the onset of bad weather the master was advised to put out to sea but, although a pilot and tug arrived promptly, it was impossible for him to leave the berth for several hours until two other ships which had anchored nearby had moved. Meanwhile the *Khian Sea* suffered ranging damage. Donaldson, J., and the Court of Appeal held that the charterers were liable for the damage to the ship. The berth was unsafe in that there was no system to ensure that ships needing to leave it hurriedly upon the onset of bad weather would have adequate searoom in which to do so.

Lord Denning, M.R., said at page 547: " . . . the following requirements must be satisfied when a vessel has to leave its berth. First, there must be an adequate weather forecasting system. Secondly, there must be adequate availability of pilots and tugs. Thirdly, there must be adequate searoom to manoeuvre. And, fourthly, there must be an adequate system for ensuring that the searoom and room for manoeuvre is always available."

The Khian Sea [1979] 1 Lloyd's Rep. 545.

Berthing and mooring facilities

A port may be unsafe for reasons other than its geographical and meteorological characteristics. Navigational aids within the port may be defective or missing. Pilots may be incompetent or unavailable in a port in which pilotage is essential to safe berthing. Mooring facilities may be inadequate or the berth to which the ship is directed within the port may be dangerous because of some obstruction. Any such factor might make the port unsafe for the particular ship at the time she is using it.

The *Houston City* was ordered under a voyage charter to proceed to one or two safe ports in Western Australia and there load at a safe wharf as ordered. She was ordered to a berth at Geraldton which was exposed to northerly winds but which ordinarily would have been safe for a ship of the size of the *Houston City*. To reduce danger from northerly winds there were two hauling off buoys and a fender on the wharf. However, one of the buoys had been removed for repair, although the master was told that its return was imminent. A 50-ft. section of the fender on the wharf was also missing. The ship was damaged in a northerly gale as a result of the absence of the hauling off buoy and the missing section of fender, and it was held by the Privy Council that Geraldton was unsafe for the ship because of these deficiencies.

Reardon Smith Line v. *Australian Wheat Board* (*The Houston City*) [1956] 1 Lloyd's Rep. 1.

It is the system that must be adequate: an error by a competent individual in an adequate system will not make the charterers liable; see the judgment of Lord Denning, M.R., in *The Evia* (*No. 2*) [1982] 1 Lloyd's Rep. 334.

A port may also be unsafe by reason of the risks to which the ship might be exposed other than from purely physical causes—for instance, because of political risks (see below under Danger). Risks to the crew may also be a relevant factor in determining whether a port is safe for the ship to use.

Safety in departure

The port will not be safe if the ship is endangered in departing from it.

The *Innisboffin* in laden condition reached the port of Manchester by the Ship Canal without difficulty. But after discharging she could not clear the canal bridges on her outward passage owing to her decreased draft. It was held that Manchester was, for her, an unsafe port.

Limerick v. *Stott* (1920) 5 Ll.L.Rep. 190.

After encountering ice on her passage up the Elbe to Hamburg (see page 139 above) the *Sussex Oak* was further damaged by the exceptional ice on her way out down river. The charterers were held liable for this damage also.

The Sussex Oak (1950) 83 Ll.L.Rep. 297.

(See also *The Eastern City* [1958] 2 Lloyd's Rep. 127 and *The Khian Sea* [1979] 1 Lloyd's Rep. 545.)

It is not clear from the authorities how far the warranty of safety extends after the ship has departed from the port. In *The Hermine* [1979] 1 Lloyd's Rep. 212 (see page 138 above) all three Court of Appeal judges expressed doubt whether an up-river port could be regarded as unsafe in a case where the ship had reached and departed from the port in safety and without delay, but had encountered an obstruction about 100 miles down river in the course of her passage to the sea.

But logically the distance between an up-river port and the place in the river where the condition of unsafety exists should not be relevant, given that there is no alternative route which will enable the particular ship to reach the port and depart from it in safety.

The voyage charter for the *Mary Lou* provided that she was to sail for loading to "one safe port U.S. Gulf (excluding Brownsville) New Orleans/Ama/Reserve/Myrtle Grove/Destrehan counting as one port". The charterers nominated the New Orleans area. A ship of this size has no route to the sea from New Orleans other than the Mississippi and eventually the Southwest Pass of that river, which lies about 100 miles from New Orleans and is subject to silting in a manner which cannot accurately be forecast. While outward bound through the Pass the *Mary Lou* grounded and was damaged, despite the fact that her draft was slightly less than the maximum recommended at that time by the river pilots. Arbitrators found that at the relevant time there was a significant risk that ships such as the *Mary Lou* might ground in the Pass and that her grounding had not been caused by negligence on the part of the pilot or the master in navigating the ship; as to the choice of draft, they found that the master had acted reasonably in relying on the recommendation of the river pilots and made no finding as to whether the pilot should have checked further to ensure that this recommendation was still up to date (by, for example, examining the latest hydrographic survey of the Pass by the Corps of Engineers).

Mustill, J., held that the charterers were in breach. He said, at page 283: "In my judgment the dangers of the navigable channel were such as to amount to a characteristic of the port which would make it unsafe within the meaning of the warranty, unless the system [of recommended maximum drafts provided by the river pilots] was actually operating effectively at the relevant time. On this occasion it was not. In my opinion, the arbitrators were right to decide that this amounted to a breach of contract, from which flowed (on their findings of fact) the loss and damage suffered by the shipowners." In rejecting the charterers' argument that the unsafety of the Pass was too distant to make New Orleans an unsafe port, he said, at page 280: "Certainly it is not easy to accept at first sight the idea that hazards existing nearly one hundred miles away can be treated as features of the port. But logically the distance should make no difference, although the further away the obstacle, the less likely it will be that there is no alternative route which will enable the ship to reach the port in safety. In the present case, however, there was no such alternative; the Southwest Pass provided the only means of access. Notwithstanding the doubts tentatively expressed by the Court of Appeal in *The Hermine*, I would regard any unsafe feature of the Pass as a breach of the warranty."

The Mary Lou [1981] 2 Lloyd's Rep. 272.

(It should be noted that the House of Lords in *The Evia* (*No. 2*) disagreed with that part of Mustill, J.'s, judgment in which he said that the charterers' obligation of safety was absolute and continuing; see page 145 below.)

Abnormal occurrences

Charterers will not be responsible for damage to the ship which is unrelated to the prevailing characteristics of the particular port. Thus a port is not unsafe because a ship within it is damaged by a wholly exceptional storm or by another ship being negligently navigated. Such causes of damage do not arise from the qualities or attributes of the port itself: in the words of Lord Roskill in *The Evia* (*No. 2*) [1982] 2 Lloyd's Rep. 307 at page 317 the port is not "inherently unsafe". In the same case Lord Denning, M.R., in the Court of Appeal [1982] 1 Lloyd's Rep. 334, said: "if the set-up of the port is good but nevertheless the vessel suffers damage owing to some isolated, abnormal or extraneous occurrence—unconnected with the set-up—then the charterer is not in breach of his warranty. Such as when a competent berthing-master makes for once a mistake, or when the vessel is run into by another vessel . . . ".

In *The Mary Lou* [1981] 2 Lloyd's Rep. 272, Mustill, J., pointed out that a particular cause of unsafety is not to be regarded as abnormal in this sense merely because it is out of the ordinary when looked at over the whole history of the port. He said, at page 278: "Changed circumstances may make a port unsafe if the new circumstances can be regarded as an attribute of the port." Referring to *The Houston City* [1956] 1 Lloyd's Rep. 1, above, he said: "The port was unsafe, not because it was prone to suffer this kind of defect . . . but because the defects were of sufficiently long standing to be, for the time being, a characteristic of the port."

Thus to say that abnormal occurrences will not make a port unsafe may be seen as another way of saying that a port will be unsafe only if the danger flows from its own qualities or attributes.

In *The Evia* (*No. 2*), the facts of which are set out at page 146 below, the question arose whether the outbreak of a local war while the ship was discharging at Basrah under a Baltime charter was a characteristic of the port or, by contrast, an abnormal occurrence at an otherwise safe port. Reversing Robert Goff, J., the Court of Appeal (Lord Denning, M.R., and Sir Sebag Shaw, with Ackner, L.J., dissenting) held that the outbreak of war was not connected with the characteristics or attributes of the port but was an isolated and abnormal occurrence, so that the charterers were not thereby in breach of their safe port obligation. Lord Denning, M.R., said: "When the full-scale war erupted on 22 September 1980 that was an utterly abnormal and extraneous occurrence. It rendered the port unsafe, but this unsafeness was not a breach of the warranty of a 'safe port'. If the vessel had been hit by shell-fire, the owners would have had to bear the damage themselves and recover from their insurers. They could not have recovered it from the charterers. When she was prevented from leaving—and ordered not to leave—that too was an utterly abnormal and extraneous occurrence." The House of Lords took the same approach to this aspect of the case; giving the decision of the House, Lord Roskill said, " . . . since Basrah was prospectively safe at the time of nomination [see page 145 below], and since the unsafety arose after her arrival and was due to an unexpected and abnormal event, there was at the former time no breach of Clause 2 by the [charterers] . . . "

The possibility of the ship being damaged by an abnormal occurrence must naturally be disregarded when considering whether the owners must accept orders from the charterers to go to a particular port: see the judgment of Mustill, J., in *The Mary Lou*, above. In the words of Ackner, L.J., in *The Evia* (*No. 2*), above: "In such circumstances, the formation of a test of whether a port is safe must assume normality and must therefore exclude danger from some abnormal occurrence."

But if at the time the ship is ordered to the port it is unsafe due to risks caused by a certain situation, the subsequent increase in those risks due simply to a worsening of that situation should not amount to an abnormal occurrence. Looked at in terms of causation, the consequent damage to the ship arises from the same risks that made the port unsafe at the time of the order to go there, albeit that their extent and gravity have subsequently increased. Had the damage arisen from some different risk then the concept of abnormal occurrence might have been relevant. See *The Lucille* [1983] 1 Lloyd's Rep. 387, [1984] 1 Lloyd's Rep. 244 (C.A.).

If after orders have been given under a time charter to a prospectively safe port, that port subsequently becomes unsafe (as a result of an abnormal occurrence) at a time when the ship can still avoid the danger by stopping short of or leaving the port, the charterers come under a new obligation to order her to do so. See *The Evia* (*No. 2*), at page 147 below.

Danger and political unsafety

The most common dangers are those of topography, such as shallows and sandbanks, and of exposure to certain weather conditions such as high winds, swell and ice. But a port may also be unsafe because of danger created by a political situation or an existing state of war.

A voyage charter provided that the ship was to proceed with cargo to a safe port in Chile. The charterers ordered the ship to discharge at Carrisal Bago, which the Chilean Government had declared closed because of a rebellion. So far as concerned its marine characteristics, Carrisal Bago was a safe port, but had the ship proceeded there she would have been liable to confiscation. Blackburn, J., said, in holding that the port was unsafe: "Now, in the absence of all authority, I think that, on the construction of this charter-party, the charterers are bound to name a port which, at the time they name it, is in such a condition that the master can safely take his ship into it: but, if a certain port be in such a state that, although the ship can readily enough, so far as natural causes are concerned, sail into it, yet, by reason of political or other causes, she cannot enter it without being confiscated by the Government of the place, that is not a safe port within the meaning of the charter-party."

Ogden v. *Graham* (1861) 1 B. & S. 773.

(See also *Palace Shipping* v. *Gans Line* [1916] 1 K.B. 138, above, *The Teutonia* (1872) L.R. 4 P.C. 171 and *The Lucille* [1984] 1 Lloyd's Rep. 244).

In *The Evaggelos Th* [1971] 2 Lloyd's Rep. 200 a ship was chartered for trading in the Red Sea which was, at all material times during the period of the charter, a war zone. A term as to safety was nevertheless implied in the charter by the court, the charter containing no express obligation as to safety.

In *The Evia* (*No. 2*), below, the House of Lords rejected an argument by the charterers that Clause 2 of the Baltime form applied only to physical unsafety; the obligation applied to political unsafety as well.

Dangers avoidable by good navigation and seamanship

Dangers which are avoidable by ordinary good navigation and seamanship do not render a port unsafe. In *The Eastern City* [1958] 2 Lloyd's Rep. 127, Sellers, L.J., said, at page 131: "Most, if not all, navigable rivers, channels, ports, harbours and berths have some dangers from tides, currents, swells, banks, bars or revetments. Such dangers are frequently minimised by lights, buoys, signals, warnings and other aids to navigation and can normally be met and overcome by proper navigation and handling of a vessel in accordance with good seamanship." But if more than ordinary skill is required to avoid the dangers the port will not be safe.

The tanker *Polyglory* while employed under time charter was ordered to Port La Nouvelle. While taking on ballast the master and the compulsory pilot decided to leave the berth because of increasing wind forces. In leaving, difficulties were experienced because the ship was still light and one of her anchors dragged, damaging an underwater pipeline. The owners settled a claim in respect of the damage to the pipeline and sought to recover the amount from the charterers on the ground that the port was unsafe. In awarding in favour of the owners the arbitrator held that (1) the port was unsafe, (2) the pipeline was damaged as a result of the pilot's negligence, but (3) the negligence did not break the chain of causation between the order to proceed to the port and the damage. In upholding the award Parker, J., said that the principle to be applied in deciding whether the port was unsafe was that: " . . . if the only dangers to which a properly manned and equipped vessel of the size and type in question will be exposed are dangers which can be avoided by the exercise of ordinary reasonable care and skill that port is not, as a matter of law, unsafe and the order to proceed to it is not therefore a breach . . . "

He held that the arbitrator was justified (1) in finding the port unsafe, because the dangers could only be avoided by very high standards of navigation and seamanship and (2) in finding that the pilot's negligence did not break the chain of causation, because it was not the effective cause, even though, chronologically, it was the immediate cause.

Kristiandsands Tankrederi v. *Standard Tankers* (*Bahamas*) (*The Polyglory*) [1977] 2 Lloyd's Rep. 353.

It does not necessarily follow from proof that the ship suffered damage despite the exercise by her officers of reasonable skill and care that the port was unsafe. As Mustill, J., pointed out in *The Mary Lou* [1981] 2 Lloyd's Rep. 272; " . . . care and safety are not necessarily the opposite sides of the same coin. A third possibility must be taken into account, namely that the casualty was the result of simple bad luck." See also *The Apiliotis* [1985] 1 Lloyd's Rep. 255.

Fact and law

Safety is a question of fact (see, for example, *The Apiliotis* [1985] 1 Lloyd's Rep. 255), but the criteria which have to be applied in determining whether a port is a "safe port" are matters of law: *The Polyglory* [1977] 2 Lloyd's Rep. 353.

Charterers' primary obligation arises when they order the ship to the port

The obligation of the charterers, under either a time or a voyage charter, with regard to the safety of the port to which they order the ship arises at the time they give that order and it is at that time that their compliance with the obligation is to be judged. At that time the port need only be *prospectively* safe for the ship at the appropriate time in the future, to reach, use and leave. Thus the obligation will not be broken by a state of unsafety prevailing at the time of the order which will have been cured before the ship's arrival. Nor will the obligation be broken if the port is prospectively safe at the time of the order but a state of unsafety subsequently arises from some unexpected and abnormal event occurring after the order has been given; in this sense the obligation is not a continuing obligation.

The *Evia*, time chartered on the Baltime form, was ordered in March 1980 to load cargo in Cuba for discharge at Basrah. She reached the Shatt-al-Arab on 1 July, berthed on 20 August and completed discharge on 22 September, on which day war broke out between Iran and Iraq. The ship was trapped for a time sufficient to frustrate the charter (see page 333 below), being unable to sail because of the danger to navigation in the Shatt-al-Arab. The umpire found that: "Basrah was a safe port for the vessel both when she was ordered to proceed there and when she got there. It did not become unsafe until the 22nd September, and by then it was impossible for the vessel to leave."

The owners claimed that in these circumstances the charterers were in breach of their safe port obligation in Clause 2: "The vessel to be employed . . . between good and safe ports . . . ". This was accepted by Robert Goff, J., but rejected by a majority of the Court of Appeal and unanimously by the House of Lords. The House of Lords held that the charterers were not in breach of Clause 2 because at the time they gave their order to go there Basrah was prospectively safe and the state of unsafety arose after the ship's arrival and was due to an unexpected and abnormal event, namely the outbreak of the local war.

Giving the decision of the House, Lord Roskill said: "The charterer's contractual promise must, I think, relate to the characteristics of the port or place in question, and in my view, means that when the order is given that port or place is prospectively safe for the ship to get to, stay at, so far as necessary, and in due course, leave. But if those characteristics are such as to make that port or place prospectively safe in this way, I cannot think that if in spite of them, some unexpected and abnormal event thereafter suddenly occurs which creates conditions of unsafety where conditions of safety had previously existed and as a result the ship is delayed, damaged or destroyed, that contractual promise extends to making the charterer liable for any resulting loss or damage, physical or financial. So to hold would make the charterer the insurer of such unexpected and abnormal risks which in my view should properly fall upon the ship's insurers under the policies of insurance the effecting of which is the owner's responsibility under Clause 3 unless, of course, the owner chooses to be his own insurer in these respects. . . . My Lords, on the view of the law which I take, since Basrah was prospectively safe at the time of nomination, and since the unsafety arose after her arrival and was due to an unexpected and abnormal event, there was at the former time no breach of Clause 2 by the respondents."

Lord Diplock said: "It is with the prospective safety of the port at the time when the vessel will be there for the loading or unloading operation that the contractual promise is concerned and the contractual promise itself is given at the time when the charterer gives the order to the master or other agent of the shipowner to proceed to the loading or unloading port."

An alternative ground for the decision of the House of Lords was that, even if there would otherwise have been a breach by the charterers of Clause 2, the war clause of the Baltime charter, Clause 21 (see page 491 below), fixed upon the owners all risks of unsafety arising from the war risks referred to in Clause 21(A). In respect of those risks Clause 21 displaced Clause 2; it thereby freed the charterers in the present case from any liability that might otherwise have been placed upon them by Clause 2, in respect of the results of the local war.

Lord Roskill said: "My Lords, whether Clause 21 is a complete code and thus exhaustive of the owners' rights depends upon the construction of the time charter-party as a whole. But if the owners are right that Clause 21 leaves the time charterers' obligations under Clause 2 in full force and effect, one remarkable result follows. The time charterers are to repay to the owners the premiums for the extra insurance, including extra war risk insurance premiums. But if the dangers, against the risks on which they have paid those premiums materialise and cause loss or damage to the ship, then war risk insurers, upon payment of the relevant claim, become subrogated to the owners' rights against the time charterers for the assumed breach of Clause 2. My Lords, this result would no doubt be highly attractive to war risk insurers but the less fortunate time charterers would have paid the premiums not only for no benefit for themselves but without shedding any of the liabilities which Clause 2 would, apart from Clause 21, impose upon them." (But not every clause obliging charterers to pay war risk premiums will have this effect; see *The Concordia Fjord* [1984] 1 Lloyd's Rep. 385.)

The Evia (No. 2) [1981] 2 Lloyd's Rep. 613, [1982] 1 Lloyd's Rep. 334 (C.A.) and [1982] 2 Lloyd's Rep. 307 (H.L.).

Port becomes unsafe after nomination; charterers' secondary obligation

If the charterers have complied with their obligation by ordering the ship to a prospectively safe port but the port subsequently becomes unsafe while the ship is en route to it, the charterers come under a new obligation to cancel the original order and, if they wish to continue to trade the ship, to issue fresh orders to another port which is then prospectively safe. Similarly if a subsequent state of unsafety arises when the ship is at the port but while she may still avoid the danger by leaving, the charterers come under a new obligation to order the ship to leave and, if they wish to continue to trade the ship, to issue fresh orders to another port which is then prospectively safe. See the speech of Lord Roskill in *The Evia* (*No. 2*), above. On the particular facts of that case no such new obligation arose, because by the time the war broke out and endangered the ship it was too late for the ship to avoid the danger by leaving Basrah. But the new obligation did arise and was broken in *The Lucille* [1983] 1 Lloyd's Rep. 387, [1984] 1 Lloyd's Rep. 244; the port, prospectively safe when nominated, became unsafe while there was still time for the charterers to cancel their orders.

The House of Lords in *The Evia* (*No. 2*) declined to consider whether similar new obligations were placed upon voyage charterers when the nominated port became unsafe after it had been nominated.

Unsafety not known to charterers

The charterers may be in breach despite their lack of knowledge as to the unsafety of the port or berth.

The *Terneuzen*, which was time chartered on the Baltime form, grounded at her berth in Leningrad. This was not expected by the charterers and their representatives or by those on board, particularly as the ship had safely loaded at the same place on an earlier voyage under the same charter. Despite the charterers' lack of knowledge of the unsafety of the berth, the Court of Appeal held the charterers liable for the damage caused.

Lensen Shipping v. *Anglo-Soviet Shipping* (1935) 52 Ll.L.Rep. 141.

It is not considered that the restatement of the law by the House of Lords in *The Evia* (*No. 2*), above, has changed this principle, at least so far as concerns the primary obligation upon the charterers; their order must be to a port which is in fact prospectively safe and not merely to a port which they have no reason to believe is prospectively unsafe. The position may however be different with regard to the secondary obligation of the charterers in the event of the port becoming prospectively unsafe after nomination. Although Lord Roskill did not draw this distinction when explaining the secondary obligation, it would seem more consistent with the way he described the obligation if it arises only where the charterers become aware of the fact that a state of unsafety has arisen. However, if knowledge is necessary before the secondary obligation can arise it will eventually be necessary for the courts to decide whether constructive as well as actual knowledge will suffice.

Consequences of order to a prospectively unsafe port

If the charterers order the ship to a prospectively unsafe port they are in breach: see *The Evia* (*No. 2*), above, and *The Stork* [1955] 1 Lloyd's Rep. 349. The owners will be entitled to damages if the master reasonably obeys the charterers' order and the ship is lost or damaged as a result of the unsafety of the port: *The Houston City* [1956] 1 Lloyd's Rep. 1.

Generally speaking, the owners and the master are entitled to assume that the charterers in making their nomination of a port are doing so in accordance with their contractual obligation; there is not usually any duty on the owners or the master to check the safety of the nominated port; see the judgment of Morris, L.J., in *The Stork* [1955] 1 Lloyd's Rep. 349 at page 372. In *The Kanchenjunga* [1987] 2 Lloyd's Rep. 509 Hobhouse, J., said at page 515: "Generally speaking a person is entitled to act in the faith that the other party to a contract is carrying out his part of it properly. Even if the breach of contract is clear it is vital to the proper conduct of business that the relevant party should be able if he considers the breach a minor one to proceed without sacrificing his right to be indemnified. But this does not mean that a master can enter ports that are obviously unsafe and then charge the charterers with damage done. It is also the rule that an aggrieved party must act reasonably and try to minimize his damage".

But the owners or the master may refuse an order to an unsafe port, both because it is "uncontractual" (see the judgment of Hobhouse, J., in *The Kanchenjunga*, above) and because to proceed to an unsafe port would take the ship outside the limits within which the owners agree she should be employed: *Lensen Shipping* v. *Anglo-Soviet Shipping* (1935) 52 Ll.L.Rep. 141. And, despite an inference to the contrary in the judgment of Greer, L.J., in the above case, the master may refuse to comply with such an order even though he is, by the terms of the charter, under the charterers' orders as regards employment. Devlin, J., said in *Grace* v. *General Steam Navigation* (*The Sussex Oak*) (1950) 83 Ll.L.Rep. at page 307: "I cannot think that the clause in a time charter-party which puts the master under the orders of the charterers as regards employment is to be construed as compelling him to obey orders which the charterers have no power to give".

Indeed, the owners or the master may be obliged, if they know the port to be unsafe, to refuse to obey the order. As with any other breach of contract, a breach of this obligation by the charterers places the owners under a duty to take reasonable steps to avoid or mitigate the loss they may suffer or are suffering. See the extract, above, from the judgment of Hobhouse, J., in *The Kanchenjunga*. Similarly, if they discover the port to be unsafe at some stage after having at first obeyed the charterers' order, they should refuse to enter the port or, if already within it, leave the port.

If the owners or their master do take reasonable action to avoid or mitigate the effects of any unsafety of the port, they may claim from the charterers the cost of so doing: for example, the cost of tugs in *Brostrom* v. *Dreyfus* (1932) 44 Ll.L.Rep. 136, and the cost of lightening in *Hall* v. *Paul* (1914) 19 Com. Cas. 384.

Although the owners may treat an order to a prospectively unsafe port as invalid, they may be held to have waived their right to do so if, knowing of the unsafety and the right that this gives them, they indicate unequivocally that they will nevertheless treat the order as valid and obey it; see the judgment of Hobhouse, J., in *The Kanchenjunga* [1987] 2 Lloyd's Rep. 509, in which case the owners, although aware of the unsafety of the nominated port, served a notice of readiness and called upon the charterers to nominate a priority berth. In affirming this judgment the Court of Appeal noted that the owners' waiver was of their right to refuse the order to go to the nominated port and not of their additional right to recover from the charterers if they obeyed the order and their ship was damaged by the unsafety of the port; [1989] 1 Lloyd's Rep. 354 and see page 60.

An order to proceed to an unsafe port, if persisted in, might in certain circumstances entitle the owners to terminate the charter: see, for example, *The Kanchenjunga*, above. (For comment on the various effects of breach see page 54.) Such an order might also, it seems, amount to a breach within the meaning of the words "any breach of this Charter"in Line 61 of the New York Produce form and give the owners the right to withdraw under Clause 5: see *The Tropwind* (*No. 1*) [1977] 1 Lloyd's Rep. 397 and page 215 below.

Effect of negligence by master or crew

It is frequently argued by charterers that although the port is unsafe, the damage suffered by the owners has been caused by or contributed to by the negligence of the master and crew. It may be said that the master should have seen the danger for himself and refused to enter the port. It may be said that the damage was caused not by the unsafety of the port but by the negligent handling of the ship by her master or crew at the relevant time, or that this damage was caused partly by one and partly by the other.

Dealt with as a question of causation, not by apportionment of damage

Where the charterers' breach is of an express term as to the safety of the port, English law solves these problems by seeking the effective cause of the damage, rather than by apportioning liability between the parties by reference to each party's share of responsibility under the doctrine of contributory negligence. The crucial enquiry is whether in all the circumstances the charterers' breach of contract in ordering the ship to an unsafe port is the effective cause of the damage, in which event their liability will not be reduced on account of the negligence of master and crew, or whether that negligence has broken the chain of causation, in which event the charterers will not be liable at all. In *The Dagmar* [1968] 2 Lloyd's Rep. 563, at page 571, Mocatta, J., said: "If Cape Chat were unsafe for this vessel and if her master and crew were negligent, the difficult question arises whether in law the proper conclusion should be that the casualty was caused by such negligence in the sense that it constituted a break in the chain of causation between the unsafety of Cape Chat and the casualty, or whether the unsafety was, notwithstanding what may have been done by those on board or omitted to be done, nevertheless still the direct and effective cause of the casualty." (See also *The Polyglory* [1977] 2 Lloyd's Rep. 353, above; and the judgment of Mustill, J., in *The Mary Lou* [1981] 2 Lloyd's Rep. 272).

The concept of contributory negligence has no application where there has been a breach of an express term as to safety. As explained at page 250 below, the provisions of the Law Reform (Contributory Negligence) Act 1945 do not apply to a situation in which the defendant's liability arises from a contractual term which does not depend on negligence on the part of the defendant. The charterers' primary obligation to nominate a port that is prospectively safe does not depend on negligence; nor, is it believed, does their secondary obligation to issue new orders in the event of subsequent unsafety.

It follows that under a charter with express safe port provisions, such as the New York Produce and Baltime forms, the negligence of the master or crew is relevant only where:

(1) the negligence of the master or crew rather than the unsafety of the port is the effective cause of the loss or damage; or
(2) the unsafety of the port is the effective cause of some clearly defined part of the loss or damage, but the negligence of the master or crew is the effective cause of another distinct and separable part of the loss or damage.

The negligence of the master or crew is not relevant if it is only a contributing cause of the loss or damage and the unsafety of the port is the effective cause.

Negligence breaking the chain of causation

If the negligent act of the master or crew rather than the order of the charterers is the effective cause of the damage, there is no liability on the charterers. It is said that the chain of causation from the order of the charterers has been broken by the intervening act or default of the master or crew. But the dilemma in which a master is frequently placed, and the fact that it is the initial breach of contract by the charterers that has placed him in it, has to be taken into account in determining the effective cause. If the master acts reasonably in the situation confronting him it is unlikely that his actions will be held to have been the effective cause of the damage: see, for example, the judgment of Sellers, L.J., in *The Stork* [1955] 1 Lloyd's Rep. 349, at page 363. In the case of *The Houston City* the port of Geraldton was held to be unsafe because of the absence of a hauling off buoy and a section of fender on the wharf at which the ship was berthed. Dixon, C.J., in a dissenting judgment in the High Court of Australia (subsequently supported by the Privy Council), dealt with the argument that the chain of causation had been broken by the master's actions in the following terms (see [1954] 2 Lloyd's Rep. 148, at page 158): "It was then contended that the damage to the ship was not the natural or probable consequence of her being ordered to the berth. The chain of causation was broken, it was suggested, because the decision of the master to rely upon the fine weather and not to put out a stream anchor intervened. The master knew the berth to be unsafe, so it was said, or liable to become unsafe on a change of weather. His action in going to the berth with that knowledge, it was said, was the true cause of the damage. I do not think that this view can be supported. The purpose of requiring the charterer to choose a safe port or berth is to avoid danger to the ship. By ordering the ship to an unsafe berth the charterer placed the master in a dilemma, and the master's acquiescence in the order cannot relieve the charterer of his responsibility. If it is material the charterer may be taken to have known as much about the matter as the master. The charterer was represented by an agent who took charge of the loading and had the same opportunities for knowledge as the master. The master was guided by the harbour-master pilot who did not advise any other measures. In these circumstances, it is difficult to see why the course which was taken was not a direct and natural consequence of the breach of the provision of the charter in giving an order to go to the berth at Geraldton."

Where the master has fears about the safety of the port but eventually decides to enter it or remain in it, damage which is then caused to the ship may yet be regarded as the natural and probable result of the charterers' order—and thus caused by it. This is particularly likely to be so when the master's fears have been allayed by the charterers or their agents.

The Stork was chartered for a voyage to carry logs from Newfoundland and the charter provided that the ship was to load at "not more than two approved loading places as ordered". The loading place nominated by the charterers was a small rocky inlet called Tommy's Arm. It was too small to allow the ship to lay out sufficient anchor chain to prevent dragging and eventually she was damaged in one of the gales that occurred regularly at that place at that time of year. On first arriving there, the master of the *Stork* had expressed considerable concern for the ship's safety but had been reassured by an experienced local pilot whom the charterers had sent to meet him. It was held by the Court of Appeal, affirming Devlin, J., that the place was unsafe for the ship and that despite the master's awareness of danger, the damage was caused by the charterers' order to proceed there. Sellers, L.J., said of the master: "He is sometimes on the horns of a dilemma. The material question is, I believe, whether he acted reasonably. The learned Judge was of the opinion that the master, in accepting the assurances given to him, acted reasonably, and I share his view."

The Stork [1955] 1 Lloyd's Rep. 349, affirming [1954] 2 Lloyd's Rep. 397.

It seems that in this context a pilot will usually be identified with the port rather than the ship: see *The Stork*, above, and *The Mary Lou* [1981] 2 Lloyd's Rep. 272. See also *The Evia (No. 2)* [1982] 1 Lloyd's Rep. 334, at page 338.

Apportionment of damage under obligation of reasonable care

By contrast with the position under an express term as to safety, there may be apportionment of damage in accordance with the doctrine of contributory negligence where the charterers' liability under the charter contract is the same as it would be in negligence if no charter contract existed; see page 250 below.

This could be the case under a charter in respect of which the court implied a safe port obligation which was merely to exercise reasonable care when ordering the ship to a particular port. Assuming that the charterers would, in the circumstances, have been liable in negligence regardless of the charter, then it follows from the cases discussed at page 250 below that the Law Reform (Contributory Negligence) Act 1945 applies and introduces apportionment of damage as an option for the court.

The same may well be true where the charter expressly provides that the charterers' obligation in regard to the safety of ports is one of due diligence only. For example, the Shelltime 3 form of tanker time charter provides in Clause 3 that: " . . . Charterers shall not be deemed to warrant the safety of any port . . . and shall be under no liability in respect thereof except for loss or damage caused by their failure to exercise due diligence . . . " It is, however, right to be somewhat cautious about the application of the 1945 Act to every safe port term that includes a reference to due diligence, because it is doubtful whether it should be applied where liability arises under a contractual obligation which, although expressed in terms of taking care or similar words, does not correspond to the independent common law duty to take care. As explained on page 250 below, the law in this area is not yet fully developed.

Implied term as to safety

Where there is no express term as to safety it seems that the court may in certain circumstances imply a term as to safety.

The tanker *Evaggelos Th* was time chartered in November 1968 for trading in the Red Sea and elsewhere, which was at all material times a war zone. The charterers agreed to contribute to the cost of the ship's war risks insurance. The charter contained no express term as to the safety of ports to which the ship might be ordered but provided that cargoes should be loaded or discharged at any place where the ship could "always lie safely afloat". The ship was ordered by the charterers to proceed to Suez at a time when there was a cease fire. But following the ship's arrival hostilities broke out again and the ship became a constructive total loss as a result of shell fire. It was held that:

(1) the words "always lie safely afloat" were concerned exclusively with the marine characteristics of the place of discharge (see page 154 below);
(2) a term should be implied that the nominated port of discharge was safe at the time of nomination and might be expected to remain so from the moment of the ship's arrival until her departure;
(3) since Suez was not unsafe at the time of nomination, nor at that time expected to become so, the charterers were not in breach of the implied term as to safety.

(For the owners' alternative claim under the employment and indemnity clause see page 155 below.)

The Evaggelos Th [1971] 2 Lloyd's Rep. 200.

In *The Evia* (*No. 2*), above, Lord Roskill said that he agreed with the decision in *The Evaggelos Th*. but questioned the reasoning.

But the court will not imply a term as to safety unless it takes the view that this is necessary to give business efficacy to the charter.

The *A.P.J. Priti* was voyage chartered during the Iran/Iraq war for a voyage from Damman to "1/2 Safe berths" at one of three named Iranian ports, from which the charterers selected Bandar Khomeini. There was no express term as to the safety of the ports themselves. An elaborate war risks clause gave the master the right to discontinue the voyage if the ship became endangered by war. During the approach to Bandar Khomeini the ship was damaged by a hostile missile.

The Court of Appeal approved the owners' concession that it was inappropriate to seek to imply a promise as to the safety of the discharge port. Bingham, L.J., said: "There is no ground for implying a warranty that the port declared was prospectively safe because the omission of an express warranty may well have been deliberate, because such an implied term is not necessary for the business efficacy of the charter and because such an implied term would at best lie uneasily beside the express terms of the charter."

The court went on to reject the owners' argument that they could rely instead on the term as to the safety of the berth or berths. In the absence of a safe port term, the safe berth obligation could not be extended to the approach to the port but was restricted to movements within the port. Moreover, it related only to safety from risks that did not affect the port as a whole or all the berths within it. Bingham, L.J., said: "There will be no breach by the charterers even if a berth nominated is prospectively unsafe, if every berth or the port as a whole is prospectively unsafe in the same way and to the same extent."

The A.P.J. Priti [1987] 2 Lloyd's Rep. 37.

Named ports

It is not clearly decided whether charterers can be liable for the unsafety of a port which is named in the charter, either on its own, or as one of a list of named ports from which the charterers may select. If there is no express term in the charter as to safety of ports, it is suggested that the charterers would generally not be responsible for the safety of a named port. If there is an express term as to safety, it is suggested that it will be a matter of construction of the particular charter whether the term applies to the named port or only to ports which the charterers nominate in the course of the ship's employment under the charter.

In *The Houston City* (High Court of Australia) [1954] 2 Lloyd's Rep. 148—a voyage charter case—Dixon, C.J., said at page 153: "When the charterer is prepared at the time of taking the charter to specify the place where the cargo will be available or the place at which he desires it delivered, the shipowner must take the responsibility of ascertaining whether he can safely berth his ship there or will take the risk of doing so. If he agrees upon the place, then, subject to excepted perils, his liability to have his ship there is definite." This statement was adopted by Devlin, J., in *The Stork* [1954] 2 Lloyd's Rep. 397, at page 415, but Mustill, J., in *The Helen Miller* [1980] 2 Lloyd's Rep. 95, 101, doubted whether it was any authority for the proposition that an express warranty of safety was restricted in some way by the naming of a port or range (see, however, the comments of the same judge in *The Mary Lou* [1981] 2 Lloyd's Rep. 272, at page 280).

The ports of delivery and redelivery are often agreed by the parties and inserted in the places left at Lines 18 and 55 of the New York Produce form. Whether or not the charterers are responsible for such named ports they may still be liable if the berth they select within the port of delivery is unsafe (Lines 20 and 21 of the New York Produce form, Line 15 of the Baltime form). The same is true of the redelivery berth if the berth has been used for cargo purposes (New York Produce form Clause 6, Baltime form Clause 2) and maybe in any event, see below. It is also possible that in such cases the obligation as to safety of the berth may be extended to cover the immediate approach to and departure from the berth, a point discussed but left undecided in *Stag Line* v. *Ellerman & Papayanni Lines* (1949) 82 Ll.L.Rep. 826—a case which concerned the alleged unsafety of a berth selected by charterers at a named port of redelivery. But it is clear from the judgments of the Court of Appeal in *The A.P.J. Priti* [1987] 2 Lloyd's Rep. 37 that the safe berth obligation, while capable of covering movements within the port, does not extend to the approach to or departure from the port; see page 152 above.

Safety of berth

Where charterers are subject to a safe port obligation they will also be responsible for the safety of docks, wharves, berths and other places within the port to which the ship is directed. This will probably be so whether or not there is an obligation, as in Clause 6 of the New York Produce form (Lines 68 to 70), to load and discharge at any place where the ship can "safely lie always afloat".

The *Terneuzen*, which was time chartered under the Baltime form, was damaged owing to the unsafety of the berth to which she had been ordered at Leningrad. The question arose as to the extent of the obligation imposed on the charterers by the words in Clause 1 of the charter "Steamer to be employed in lawful trades . . . between good and safe ports or places within the following limits . . . where she can lie safely always afloat or safe aground where steamers of similar size and draft are accustomed to lie aground in safety". It was held by a majority of the Court of Appeal that either these words meant, on their true construction, that the ship had to be directed to a safe berth within the port or, alternatively, that the words made it necessary to imply a term into the charter to that effect. Slesser, L.J., said: "In my view, the stipulation in Clause 1 in this case, implying the right of the owners to direct the ship to good and safe ports as there defined as a matter of business, requires an implication that the port or place should include good and safe berths therein."

Lensen Shipping v. *Anglo-Soviet Shipping* (1935) 52 Ll.L.Rep. 141.

(See also *Stag Line* v. *Ellerman & Papayanni Lines* (1949) 82 Ll.L.Rep. 826, and page 152 above.)

The duty of the charterers with regard to a "safe berth" is generally the same as with regard to a "safe port": *The Stork* [1955] 1 Lloyd's Rep. 349.

Where there is no term express or implied as to the safety of the port, an express term as to the safety of the berth or berths will not avail the owners if every berth in the port is prospectively unsafe in the same way and to the same extent; *The A.P.J. Priti* [1987] 2 Lloyd's Rep. 37 and page 152 above. It was also held by the Court of Appeal in that case that the safe berth term in such a charter could not be used to cover the safety of the approach to the port as opposed to movements within the port to and from a nominated berth.

As with a port, the prospective safety of a berth is to be judged as at the time of the order to go there. This order will not normally have to be given until the voyage to the port has been concluded (see the judgments of the Court of Appeal in *The A.P.J. Priti*, above).

Charterers may become liable in respect of orders to an unsafe berth given on their behalf by agents if either (a) the nomination of that berth was in breach of an express or implied safe berth obligation in the charter, or (b) the agent was negligent, in which case the charterers may be vicariously liable regardless of any safe berth obligation in the charter. But not everyone who gives orders to the ship to proceed to a particular berth or place within a port will be held to be doing so as agent for the charterers.

The *Mediolanum* was chartered on the New York Produce form. In the course of the charter, the charterers, through their agents, stemmed bunkers for the ship at Las Minas, itself a safe port for this ship. It was found as a fact by arbitrators that in stemming bunkers the charterers impliedly authorised the bunker suppliers to select the exact place where the ship was to bunker. The bunkering place actually selected by the suppliers was unsafe by reason of an uncharted reef and the ship was damaged in consequence.

The Court of Appeal expressed grave doubt as to whether the bunker suppliers were indeed acting as the charterers' agents in making the selection of bunkering place. In giving the judgment of the court, Kerr, L.J., suggested that the suppliers might instead be regarded as performing similar functions to those of a harbour master or port authority, whose actions would not be those of the charterers, following the judgment of Robert Goff, J., in *The Isabelle* [1982] 2 Lloyd's Rep. 81.

Assuming, "with the greatest misgivings", that the suppliers were the agents of the charterers for this purpose, the court found no liability on the charterers for there had been no breach of their safe port promise and no negligence on the part of the suppliers for which the charterers could be vicariously liable.

The Mediolanum [1984] 1 Lloyd's Rep. 136.

Despite the caution expressed by the Court of Appeal in *The Mediolanum*, above, and the court's adoption of the judgment of Robert Goff, J., in *The Isabelle*, Staughton, J., held in *The Erechthion* [1987] 2 Lloyd's Rep. 180 that an order of the Port Harcourt harbour authority to lighten at Dawes Island anchorage, where the ship was damaged, should be considered as the charterers' order for the purpose of the charterers' implied obligation to indemnify the owners for compliance with such orders under the New York Produce form charter (as to which obligation generally, see page 236 below). It may be noted, however, that the judge expressed a preference for treating the matter not as a question of agency but rather on the basis that the charterers' orders were to such discharging place at Port Harcourt as the port authorities might nominate. This approach, while presumably leaving charterers exposed to a claim for breach of any safe berth obligation under the relevant charter, would exclude claims based on vicarious liability for negligence of the harbour authority.

Safely lie always afloat

In *The Evaggelos Th* [1971] 2 Lloyd's Rep. 200, Donaldson, J., construed the phrase "where the vessel can always lie safely afloat" as being limited to the purely marine characteristics of a berth. But it was recognised expressly by Donaldson, J., that this phrase differed from phrases of the type used in the Baltime and New York Produce forms. These should not therefore be restricted in this way but should be read as a stipulation for safety in all the aspects discussed in these pages.

Voyage and time charters

In general the criteria applicable in the case of voyage charters are applicable also to time charters. Thus the Privy Council in *Reardon Smith Line* v. *Australian Wheat Board* (*The Houston City*) [1956] 1 Lloyd's Rep. 1, at page 9, said: "Where a time charter contains . . . an undertaking by the charterer that the vessel is to be employed between good and safe ports, the liability of the charterer is at any rate in all ordinary circumstances the same as where under a voyage charter-party the charterer undertakes to nominate a 'safe port'." (See also the judgments of the Court of Appeal in *The Stork*, above.)

But, as Bingham, L.J., pointed out in *The A.P.J. Priti* [1987] 2 Lloyd's Rep. 37 at page 40, the owners of a ship are more in need of protection from a safe port promise when operating under a time charter, in accordance with which they may be required to go to ports worldwide, than when operating under a voyage charter with named or listed loading and discharging ports. In his speech in *The Evia* (*No. 2*), Lord Roskill, mindful of distinctions in this area between time and voyage charters including the lack of a right to renominate under many voyage charters, declined to indicate whether the secondary obligation placed on time charterers when the nominated port became unsafe after nomination would apply equally to a voyage charterer; see page 147 above.

Alternative claim under employment clause

By Clause 8 the master is to be under the orders and direction of the charterers as regards employment. The court will imply a term that the charterers will indemnify the owners against the consequences of the master obeying their orders (as to which see page 237 below). Thus, if in consequence of the master obeying the charterers' orders to sail to a particular port the ship is damaged or other losses are suffered by the owners, they may claim to be indemnified by the charterers. The same questions of causation arise as are discussed above.

Where the charterers are in breach of the safe port obligation there would usually be no purpose in claiming under Clause 8. Under the New York Produce form it seems that if a claim for breach of the safe port obligation fails (for example because negligence of the master has broken the chain of causation) a claim under Clause 8 would normally fail for the same reason. An alternative claim under the Baltime employment and indemnity clause failed in *Stag Line* v. *Ellerman & Papayanni Lines* (1949) 82 Ll.L.Rep. 826. Morris, J., said at page 836: "In my judgment, if it is not shown that there is a breach of Clause 1['where she can lie safely always afloat'], the plaintiffs cannot claim that under Clause 8 [the employment and indemnity clause] they can recover against the defendants. The casualty, the happening after the ship had left a berth at which she could safely lie afloat, was not something, in my judgment, which can be regarded as a consequence or liability arising from the order to go to Berth 51."

But where the charterers' obligation as to the safety of ports is restricted—either because the charter expressly says so or because the courts have implied a limited obligation only—there may be a good claim under Clause 8 although there is none under the safe port obligation. In *The Evaggelos Th* [1971] 2 Lloyd's Rep. 200, page 151 above, Donaldson, J., held that the charterers had not broken the implied obligation, but went on to hold that they would nevertheless be liable under the employment and indemnity clause of the charter if the arbitrators found that compliance with the orders of the charterers was the cause of the damage to the ship. He said: "I am quite satisfied that the owner can recover under this clause if, but only if, he can prove that the proximate cause of the loss of the vessel was his, or his master's, compliance with the charterers' orders as to the employment of the vessel." In that case the employment and indemnity clause was worded similarly to the corresponding clause in the Baltime form, both containing an express indemnity against the results of complying with the orders of the charterers.

In *The Erechthion* [1987] 2 Lloyd's Rep. 180, arbitrators had held that charterers were liable to indemnify owners under Clause 8 of the New York Produce form for damage suffered by the ship from a submerged object while complying with charterers' order to a lightening anchorage, despite the lack of any breach of any safe port or berth obligation. Staughton, J., upheld this decision, subject only to confirmation from the arbitrators that the damage was proximately caused by the charterers' order.

American Law

Nomination of unsafe port or berth

If the vessel is damaged or delayed by reason of the nomination of an unsafe port or berth, the owner is entitled to recover its loss from the charterer. Moreover, the owner would be justified in refusing to accept the charterer's orders to proceed to an unsafe port or berth.

Safely lie, always afloat

The words "safely lie, always afloat" constitute an express warranty of safe port and safe berth. See, e.g., *Cities Service Transp. Co.* v. *Gulf Refining Co.*, 79 F.2d 521, 1935 AMC 1513 (2d Cir. 1935), holding that "the charter party was itself an express assurance on which the Master was entitled to rely, that at the berth 'indicated' the ship would be able to lie 'always afloat'". See also *Park S.S. Co.* v. *Cities Service Oil Co.*, 188 F.2d 804, 1951 AMC 851 (2d Cir. 1951), *cert.* denied 342 U.S. 802 (1951).

Between safe port and/or ports

The American and English authorities are in agreement that these words constitute an express warranty of safe port by charterer, the components of which are set forth in *Leeds Shipping* v. *Société Française Bunge* (*The Eastern City*) [1958] 2 Lloyd's Rep. 127 (see page 136 above). The warranty means that the port or berth nominated by the charterer must be completely safe for the particular vessel so that she can proceed there and leave in the normal course of operation without being exposed to the risk of physical damage. *Venore Transportation Co.* v. *Oswego Shipping Corp.*, 498 F.2d 469. 1974 AMC 827 (2d Cir. 1974), *cert.* denied 419 U.S. 998.

In *The Oceanic First*, S.M.A. No. 1054 (Arb. at N.Y. 1976), the panel summarized the safe port warranty in the following manner:

> There is no dispute that both Charters contain a warranty that the vessel will only be employed between "Safe Ports" and that she will only be loaded and/or discharged at "Safe Berths". We believe it is generally accepted that this warranty is an undertaking that this vessel could proceed to discharge her cargo and depart from the port and that in the absence of some abnormal and unforeseen occurrence and given good navigation and seamanship this could be done without undue risk of physical damage to the vessel. The warranty is expressly given for each period the vessel was ordered to discharge at Niigata and must be weighed in light of the known conditions which one could reasonably expect would prevail during each call of the vessel at the Port.

The charterer's duty to provide a safe port and berth is nondelegable. *Venore Transportation Co.* v. *Oswego Shipping Corp.*, above, 498 F.2d at 472. This principle flows quite naturally from the commercial purpose of the safe port clause. As Judge Swan wrote in *Park S.S. Co.* v. *Cities Service Oil Co.*, above:

> The charterer wishes to control the manner and place of discharging its cargo . . . Hence, the charterer bargains for the privilege of selecting the precise place of discharge and the ship surrenders that privilege in return for the charterer's acceptance of the risk of its choice. (188 F.2d at 806.)

Although the language in Line 27 expressly refers only to safe ports, the warranty has universally been held to encompass safe berths as well as safe ports. See *The Mozart Festival*, S.M.A. No. 2393 (Arb. at N.Y. 1987).

The particular ship

The American cases have adopted the rule that the port must be safe for the particular ship named in the charter. See *The Zaneta*, 1970 AMC 807 (Arb. at N.Y. 1968). In *The Pyrgos*, S.M.A. No. 896 (Arb. at N.Y. 1974), for example, the vessel went aground at the Mantua Creek Anchorage in the Delaware River. The panel held for the owner, stating "although Mantua Creek Anchorage is a safe anchorage for smaller and lighter draft vessels, it is not safe for vessels the length and depth of the 'Pyrgos' . . . ".

Safety in approach/safety in departure

The safe port warranty covers not only the immediate area of the port itself; it also means that adjacent areas the vessel must traverse to either enter or leave the port are to be safe.

In *The Gazelle*, 128 U.S. 474 (1888), the court found that the charterer had breached a safe port warranty because a sand bar at the mouth of the inlet made it impossible for the *Gazelle* to pass, either in ballast or with cargo. The court stated:

> By the express terms of the charter-party, the charterers were bound to order the vessel "to safe, direct, Norwegian or Danish port, or as near thereunto as she can safely get and always lay and discharge afloat". The clear meaning of this is that she must be ordered to a port which she can safely enter with her cargo, or which, at least, has a safe anchorage outside where she can lie and discharge afloat . . . The charterers, having refused to order the vessel to such a port as the charter-party called for, and having insisted on ordering her to a different one, were rightly held to be in default and answerable in damages . . . (128 U.S. at 485–86.)

In *Crisp* v. *United States & Australasia S.S. Co.*, 124 F. 748 (S.D.N.Y. 1903), the court said:

> A covenant for a safe loading or discharging place implies that a port to be named by the charterer shall be one where the vessel can safely get with her whole cargo and can discharge her whole cargo without touching the ground . . . and, of course, without being subject to obstructions, at any stage of the tide . . . (124 F. at 750.)

In *Crisp*, the court found that the words "always safely lie afloat" put the risk of a safe port on the charterer, and that the charterer was liable for damages even though they were caused when the vessel was under the control of a compulsory pilot.

In *Carbon Slate Co.* v. *Ennis*, 114 F. 260 (3d Cir. 1902), the court found that the owner was entitled to deadfreight, stating:

> [T]he contract was, in legal effect, that the vessel should proceed to Bilboa, or as near as she could safely get, and when loaded get away from, in order to proceed to the port of Philadelphia . . . and the fact is that she was directed to load at a berth where a full cargo, if taken aboard, would have made it impossible for her, at any state of water or at any time, to pass out over the harbor bar. (114 F. at 261.)

In *The Silvercove*, S.M.A. No. 813A (Arb. at N.Y. 1976), the charterer was held liable for damage to the vessel's rudder caused by contact with an underwater object in or immediately adjacent to the berth which prevented the vessel from safely departing therefrom.

See also *Mencke* v. *A Cargo of Java Sugar*, 187 U.S. 248 (1902), holding a berth above the Brooklyn Bridge unsafe for a vessel with masts too tall to allow the vessel to pass under the bridge; *The Caroline Horn*, S.M.A. No. 649 (Arb. at N.Y. 1971), where the panel stated: "We hold this warranty to mean that the port and its approaches must be safe for this vessel at the particular time Charterers order her there"; *The Magdalene*, S.M.A. No. 579 (Arb. at N.Y. 1957).

The safe port warranty has been held to be quite far-reaching in geographic scope. In *The Tropical Veneer*, S.M.A. No. 1172 (Arb. at N.Y. 1977), the vessel suffered ice damage as she made her way down the St. Lawrence River after departing from Montreal. The panel unanimously held that the charterer was liable for the damage, and, in so doing, rejected the charterer's argument that the safe port warranty was not intended to stretch as far as 225 miles down river from the port of Montreal. The panel stated:

> The Panel cannot accept Charterers' view that the established law and practice should be disregarded with respect to safe approach waters for entry and exit of a vessel as an integral part of the safe port warranty the Charterers granted the vessel and owners. Whether it be the Amazon or Mississippi or St. Lawrence Rivers, all are direct extensions of the ports they serve at their heads or at any intermediate point insofar as accessibility to the legal or geographical limits of their respective ports are concerned. We believe that indifference to the approach waters, if they were divorced from the port limits per se, would make a hollow mockery of the safe port warranty sort of in the vein of "it's a safe place if you can overcome the obstacles to get there or get out".

So also in *The Ross Isle*, S.M.A. No. 1340 (Arb. at N.Y. 1979), the panel held that the Mississippi River itself was within the coverage of the safe port warranty where the vessel was diverted to a port on that river.

Similarly, in *The Naiad*, S.M.A. No. 1177 (Arb. at N.Y. 1977), the panel concluded that owner was entitled to recover deadfreight for cargo shut out as the result of a seasonal draft restriction at the Southwest Pass of the Mississippi River. The panel held that the safe port warranty encompassed the entrance to the river, as well as the berths along the river at which the vessel loaded.

In *The Eastern Eagle*, 1971 AMC 236 (Arb. at N.Y. 1970), the panel held that the owner was justified in refusing the charterer's orders to send the vessel to Macapa, on the Amazon River. The vessel had stranded there on a previous voyage under the same charter. Moreover, the panel found that no accurate charts of the area were available, and that those navigational aids which did exist were "insufficient in number and functionally inadequate. There are no buoy markers, and there is no competent pilotage service available because no one really knows the varying depths of water in the approaches to Macapa." Accordingly, the port was held to be unsafe for the vessel.

The safe port warranty does not mean, however, that "every conceivable approach be free of hazards or even that every possible approach be risk-free". *H. Schuldt* v. *Standard Fruit & Steamship Co.*, 1979 AMC 2470, 2477 (S.D.N.Y. 1978). In that case, the court held that the presence of rocky shoals in shallow water near a berth did not render it unsafe so long as there was a safe approach open to the berth. See also *Trade Banner Line Inc.* v. *Caribbean Steamship Co.*, 521 F2d 229, 1975 AMC 2515 (5th Cir. 1975), holding that a berth was not unsafe because the vessel broke from her moorings after being safely berthed and went aground on nearby shoals.

Ice

Actual or expected ice conditions may render a port or berth unsafe. *The Banja Luka*, S.M.A. No. 1293 (Arb. at N.Y. 1979), holding that the berth was unsafe because ice conditions rendered it inaccessible; *The Bennington*, S.M.A. No. 940 (Arb. at N.Y. 1975), holding that the port was unsafe because of ice conditions. See also *The Tropical Veneer*, discussed above. See discussion below at page 447.

Safety in use

The safe berth warranty is quite simply a promise that the berth will be safe for the vessel. Perhaps the most important element of this warranty is the obligation of the charterer to provide a berth where there is sufficient water for the vessel in loaded condition. Thus, in *The Harding*, S.M.A. No. 959 (Arb. at N.Y. 1975), the charterer was held liable for damages to the vessel caused by insufficient water at the loading berth. The same result was reached in *The Federal Calumet*, S.M.A. No. 1667 (Arb. at N.Y. 1982), where the vessel touched bottom due to insufficient water at the berth. In *Appeal of U.S. Lines Inc.*, 1977 AMC 318, 338 (A.S.B.C.A. 1976), it was held that the charterer breached the warranty by directing the vessel to a berth that was obviously in disrepair and against which the vessel sustained damage because of the absence of vertical pilings and horizontal stringers.

Similarly, in *The Oceanic First*, S.M.A. No. 1158 (Arb. at N.Y. 1977), the arbitrators held that a berth was unsafe because of the presence of an unprotected sharp steel angle-iron concrete reinforcement bar in the northeast corner of the pier, as well as a submerged concrete platform. The panel noted that:

> Charterer's contention that the vessel would not have suffered damage had she entered the centerline of the slip, the usual and recommended procedure for vessels berthing there, misses the mark somewhat. The safe berth provision of the charter party places upon the charterer not only an obligation to provide a berth that is safe but one as well that permits safe ingress and egress. Considering the physical characteristics of the berth and the size of vessels entering it, such as the *Oceanic First*, it seems reasonable to conclude that under certain circumstances some vessels will be forced to lay up against or use the northeast edge of the pier for turning purposes. The absence of any sort of protection for the menacing aspects of this corner as well as the water level concrete platform adjacent to it constitutes hazards of significant proportion for vessels berthing there.

Where the dock is in good order and condition, and the vessel is damaged as the result of making contact with the bulkhead in heavy winds, it has been held that the charterer is not liable for the loss, on the theory that the damage was caused not by an unsafe berth, but by a danger of navigation as to which the owner undertook to bear the risk. *The Schiffbek*, 1934 AMC 713, 716 (Arb. at N.Y. 1934).

In general, poor weather conditions will not render a port or berth unsafe for purposes of the charterer's warranty. See *Esso Standard Oil S.A.* v. *The S.S. Sabrina*, 154 F.Supp. 720, 1957 AMC 691 (D.C.Z. 1957), where the court held:

> The Court does not think that the berth was proven unsafe in violation of the terms of the contract and is of the opinion that the same inevitable accident, the violent natural storm, one of the perils of the sea, that caused the damage to the 8-inch pipe of libelant, was responsible for the damage to the ship . . . (1957 AMC at 700.)

In *The Stadt Schleswig*, 1971 AMC 362 (Arb. at N.Y. 1970), the owner claimed the charterer was liable for hull damages sustained as the vessel was in the process of undocking from her berth at the port of Grindstone after she completed discharging cargo. The owner claimed the damages were the result of the charterer's breach of the safe port warranty. During the cargo operation, winds in the range of Force 6–7 had developed, and the vessel's lines had broken while she was in the process of undocking. The panel held for the charterer. The vessel, and many others of her size, had been to the port without incident on many occasions, and the master had also been there on several occasions. Moreover, the storm had built up over a period of hours, and there had been ample time for the master to leave the pier before it reached its full force. According to the panel:

It is the Panel's opinion that not even the safest port in the world is necessarily completely safe all the time. Major ports can become temporarily unsafe, as a result of storms and hurricanes, tidal waves and other acts of God. This does not *per se* make it unsafe or entitle that label at any given moment. Within the meaning of this charterparty, the Panel is concerned with the safety of the port of Grindstone for a vessel of the size and general characteristics of the *Stadt Schleswig*. The record and evidence shows that countless vessels of similar size and draft as the *Stadt Schleswig*, including over 20 calls by same Owners as in this charterparty had successfully made calls at Grindstone, during all navigable periods and that the record of the port is not one which entitles the Panel to believe that the port is unsafe during this season. The temporary and occasional problem of rising wind is a foreseeable hazard requiring prudence and in extreme cases the premature sailing of the vessel to a sheltered anchorage to ride out the weather. (1971 AMC at 365–366.)

Danger

In *The Arietta Venizelos*, 1973 AMC 1012 (Arb. at N.Y. 1972), the vessel was chartered on the Texacotime form. When the charterer nominated a loading port in Libya, which, because of threats of guerilla attacks on tankers, had been placed outside Institute Warranty limits by war risk underwriters, the owner withdrew the vessel. A majority of the panel found that the loading port nominated by the charterer was in a danger zone and that the owner was justified in withdrawing the vessel on the basis of the charterer's safe port warranty. According to the panel:

Under Clause 3 of this Charter Party, Charterer was under a fundamental obligation to "exercise due diligence to ensure that the vessel is only employed between and at safe ports". There can be little doubt that ordering a ship to an unsafe port is a breach of that fundamental charter party obligation . . . it is irrelevant to consider all the alternatives available to Owner following Charterer's breach. The alternative chosen, withdrawal of the vessel, was both permissible and justified. (1973 AMC at 1021–1022.)

See also *The Amoco Texas City*, 1979 AMC 690 (Arb. at N.Y. 1977).

Political dangers

In *Pan Cargo Shipping Corp.* v. *United States*, 234 F.Supp. 623, 1965 AMC 2649 (S.D.N.Y. 1964), aff'd 323 F.2d 525, 1967 AMC 850 (2d Cir. 1967), *cert.* denied 389 U.S. 836, the shipowner contended that the warranty meant that the port nominated by the charterer must be politically was well as physically safe. The vessel had been prevented from loading a cargo of oil at Ras Tanura as a result of the Arab boycott on vessels which had called at Israeli ports. While recognising that there was some authority for the shipowner's position, the court found that: "the danger to the ship apprehended in a port which is politically 'unsafe' seems to be something like seizure or 'certain risk of confiscation'." The court then held that, in the circumstances, the safe port warranty could not be stretched so far as to place liability for the loss of the voyage on the charterer. According to the court:

In the circumstances here "safe port" should not be given the meaning "without risk of loading interference from the Arab boycott". The parties never considered such a meaning; the Navy knew nothing about the *Memory I* voyage to Israel, and certainly was not put on notice by the entry in the Houston Custom House. The word "safe" was not part of the provisions to which the Navy agreed at the time the Charter was fixed. It was added by libelant's broker and ought not to be given such effect as to shift the risk from the owner to the charterer. Other portions of the charter . . . indicate that the word "safe" is used in the sense of physically safe. Moreover, with full knowledge of all the facts, including facts as to the Israel voyage not known to the Navy, libelant and the master accepted the nomination of Ras Tanura and proceeded there without protest. (234 F.Supp. at 638.)

A claim that a port was politically unsafe was raised in *The Universe Explorer*, 1985 AMC 1014 (Arb. at N.Y. 1984). The owner contended that charterer nominated a politically unsafe port when it directed the vessel to load a cargo of oil in Nigeria. The vessel had loaded stores off Cape Town, South Africa and was denied entry to Nigeria under a Nigerian law which prohibited contacts with South Africa in the six weeks preceding a port call. Both owner and charterer were aware of the Nigerian regulation. However, only owner had knowledge of the call at South Africa. The panel held that because owner alone knew of the call at South Africa, owner bore the risk that Nigeria would refuse permission to load.

Avoidability by good navigation and seamanship

A port or berth will not be unsafe if the dangers are avoidable by good navigation and seamanship on the part of the master. The test is whether in the exercise of reasonable care in the circumstances, a competent master would be expected to avoid the dangers present at the port or berth.

In *The Medita*, S.M.A. No. 2347 (Arb. at N.Y. 1986), the panel denied owner's claim for hull damage which occurred when the vessel hit the pier during heavy swells while discharging a cargo of fertilizer. The panel found that the pier in question was a safe berth and that whatever physical damage the vessel sustained was attributable to the master's failure to take reasonable steps to protect the vessel by removing it to the anchorage.

A master's refusal to load for fear of grounding must be reasonable. In *The Konkar Victory*, S.M.A. No. 1798 (Arb. at N.Y. 1983), the panel held that the master had acted unreasonably in refusing to load despite assurances by the harbor master, an uninterested and unbiased party, that the berth was safe. The panel noted that the master should have called in his own independent surveyor to help support his contentions and concerns.

Acceptance of named port or berth

Notwithstanding the "safe port" warranty, if the owner or master accepts the nomination of a loading or discharge port with full knowledge of local conditions which make it unsafe for that particular voyage, the charterer may be excused from any liability for damages for which he would otherwise be liable. *Tweedie Trading Co.* v. *New York & Boston Dyewood Co.*, 127 F.278 (2d Cir. 1903), *cert.* denied 193 U.S. 669 (1903); *Pan Cargo Shipping Corp.* v. *United States*, above; *The Breynton*, 1934 AMC 1473 (Arb. at N.Y. 1933). In *The Eva Borden*, S.M.A. No. 219 (Arb. at N.Y.), the panel held that the owner's claim that the anchorage was unsafe was unfounded "if only for the reason of the master's complete acceptance of charterers' berthing designation".

Where the charter is for a trip to a named port, the owner will be deemed to have accepted the port as being safe. See *The Naiad*, 1978 AMC 2049, 2056 (Arb. at N.Y. 1977); *The Challenger*, 1978 AMC 2037, 2044–45 (Arb. at N.Y. 1978).

Intervening negligence

The charterer may be relieved from any liability for its breach of the safe port warranty if it can demonstrate that the casualty was caused by intervening negligence on the part of the master. *American President Lines Ltd.* v. *United States*, 208 F.Supp. 573, 1968 AMC 830 (N.D.Cal. 1961). It must be shown, however, that the master's decision to follow the charterer's instructions was so imprudent as to entail an unreasonable risk.

In *Venore Transp. Co.* v. *Oswego Shipping Corp.*, 498 F.2d 469, 1974 AMC 827 (2d Cir. 1974), *cert.* denied 419 U.S. 998, the vessel owner was awarded damages resulting from a collision with a wharf as the vessel attempted to leave in a storm for an anchorage at sea. The charterer sought to avoid liability by contending that the collision was the result of intervening negligence on the part of the master, who had inspected the berth before docking and had been given assurances by the charterer's local agents that it would be safe to berth even though one pontoon was missing from the pier. The pontoon was designed to prevent the vessel from striking against the concrete pier. The court held that the charterer was liable for breach of its safe berth warranty, and that "being unfamiliar with conditions in the harbor, the master was entitled to rely on [the] assurances" he had received from the local agents.

In *The Sabrina*, 1957 AMC 691, 695 (D.C.Z., 1957), however, the court held that the grounding was caused by the master's failure to properly anchor and secure the vessel at the mooring. Similarly, in *Trade & Transport Inc.* v. *Caribbean S.S. Co.*, 384 F.Supp. 782, 1975 AMC 1065 (S.D. Tex. 1974), where the vessel was damaged when she broke her moorings during a hurricane, the owner was denied any recovery against the voyage charterer. The court held that the cause of the damage was the master's negligent decision, based on the wharf owner's suggestion, to shift to another berth which was not adequate to protect the vessel. See also *Nassau Sand & Gravel Co.* v. *Red Star Towing and Transp. Co.*, 62 F.2d 356 (2d Cir. 1932).

The Roman Bernard, S.M.A. No 1202 (Arb. at N.Y. 1978), involved a claim by the owner for losses resulting from the grounding of the vessel after she broke away from the pier during a storm. The berth in question was an open roadstead pier located on the eastern coast of Nicaragua. While the panel noted that as an open roadstead pier it was "precariously exposed to the elements of wind, sea and swell" and frequent sudden changes of weather, the majority held that it was not unsafe. Rather, as stated by the majority:

> . . . the Master of a vessel moored there bears a special burden of ensuring that his vessel is both properly secured and in a ready position to quickly depart should a sudden change of weather occur, a not uncommon event for the Puerto Isabel area. During periods of heavy squalls, the area about the Puerto Isabel pier is quickly and substantially affected because the relatively low depth of water is aggravated by the wind, thereby creating swells which cause vessels alongside to surge and often break lines. When such conditions arise it becomes the master's responsibility to immediately depart from the berth and seek a safe haven for his vessel in deep and open waters where he may employ his engines to maneuver and ride out the storm.

The panel majority found, however, that the master had negligently failed to secure the vessel at the pier in a manner which ensured his ability to leave quickly because he had not properly placed his starboard anchor. Moreover, when the storm arose, rather than immediately depart from the berth, the master decided to attempt to ride it out by remaining alongside the dock. The master's faulty decision in remaining at the pier, and his failure to properly locate the anchor, were held to have caused the loss, and the charterer was excused from liability.

In *The Zaneta*, 1970 AMC 807 (Arb. at N.Y. 1970), the shipowner was denied any recovery where, despite a grounding which should have put the master on notice that the berth was unsafe, he continued loading and the vessel grounded a second time.

Owner was also denied any recovery in *The Pyrgos*, S.M.A. No. 896 (Arb. at N.Y. 1974), for damages sustained as the result of a grounding at Pointe-a-Pierre. The panel held that the berth was a safe one, and that the grounding was the result of the master's negligence. According to the panel:

It is the opinion of this Panel that the Master could have done more to satisfy himself that the PYRGOS could safely load her cargo and then unberth at or near low tide. He was acquainted with the port, and the Texaco charts which were shown him indicated limited maneuvering area and some dangerous shoaling west of the berth. He could have taken soundings for himself. He need not have undocked at about the time of low water; this was a matter in which he could exercise his own discretion and for which he had sole authority.

See also *Cook Inlet* v. *Amer. T. & P.*, 1976 AMC 160 (S.D.N.Y. 1976), where the court held that the terminal was safe, and that the damage to the vessel was the result of negligence on the part of the master and the pilot during the vessel's departure from the berth.

Similarly, in *The Itel Taurus*, S.M.A. No. 1220 (Arb. at N.Y. 1977) the owner was denied a recovery for damage sustained by the grounding of the vessel at the berth. The panel found that the grounding was caused not by an unsafe condition, but by the master's disregard of principles of good seamanship when he chose to berth the vessel with a draft in excess of depth representations received from the authorities. See also *The Caribbean Nostalgia*, S.M.A. No. 1788 (Arb. at N.Y. 1983).

The cases cited above certainly do not mean that the master or pilot can be held to a standard of perfection. Rather, there must be a finding of intervening negligence to impose liability on the owner. As the panel observed in *The Oceanic First*, S.M.A. No. 1158 (Arb. at N.Y. 1977) in holding the charterer liable for damages sustained by the vessel when she made contact with an unfendered angle bar in the corner of the berth:

We do not consider that faulty navigation contributed materially to the casualty although it would be difficult to deny that a perfect or faultless berthing attempt would have averted the contact. Such a standard, without some margin, is not, however, required of masters or docking pilots.

Contributory negligence

If both the master and the charterer are at fault, damages may be divided proportionally. See *United States* v. *Reliable Transfer Co. Inc.*, 421 U.S. 397 (1975); *Cities Service Transp. Co.* v. *Gulf Refining Co.*, 79 F.2d 521, 1935 AMC 1513 (2d Cir. 1935); *Paragon Oil Co.* v. *Republic Tankers S.A.*, 310 F.2d 169, 1963 AMC 158 (2d Cir. 1962); *Ore Carriers of Liberia Inc.* v. *Navigen Corp.*, 332 F.Supp. 72, 1971 AMC 505 (S.D.N.Y. 1969), aff'd 435 F.2d 549, 1971 AMC 513 (2d Cir. 1970).

In *The Oceanic First*, S.M.A. No. 1054 (Arb. at N.Y. 1976), the panel held that damages sustained by the vessel during her ninth call at Niigata, Japan, were the joint responsibility of owner and charterer, and divided damages on a 50/50 basis. Because of the prior calls at the port, both owner and charterer knew or should have known the conditions which could reasonably be expected at the port, and chose to disregard a protest from the master about continued calls. According to the panel:

Both were guilty of taking a calculated risk which failed. Owners' right to rely upon the safe port, safe berth warranties of the Contract does not extend to their ignoring obvious unsafe and dangerous conditions that in all probability could exist. Likewise, the giving of such a warranty is an assurance that these obvious unsafe and dangerous conditions don't and won't exist. The damages which were sustained were brought about by a mutual lack of appreciation to the dangers that a call at this time of the year at Niigata would produce.

The same result was reached in *Appeal of U.S. Lines Inc.*, 1977 AMC 318, 343 (A.S.B.C.A. 1976), where the vessel docked despite the berth's obviously deteriorated condition, and with full knowledge that heavy winds and seas could be expected.

In *Board of Commissioners* v. *M/S Space King*, 1978 AMC 856 (E.D.La. 1978), the vessel grounded at a berth where she was loading cargo because of falling river conditions, and damaged the adjacent dock in being freed from the river bottom. The court held that the owner was 70 per cent. at fault since it was the responsibility of the master to prevent loading of cargo in a manner which would result in putting the ship aground. In addition, the master should have been aware of the danger to the vessel posed by the changing river conditions. The charterer was held 30 per cent. to blame because its agents failed to obtain available information concerning river conditions.

Maintenance Clause

"36. 1. That the Owners shall provide and pay for all provisions, wages and consular shipping and discharging fees of the Crew; shall pay for the
37. insurance of the vessel, also for all the cabin, deck, engine-room and other necessary stores, including boiler water and maintain her class and keep
38. the vessel in a thoroughly efficient state in hull, machinery and equipment for and during the service."

Wages

"Wages" in this context means the remuneration to which the crew is lawfully entitled for its services. It was so held in *The Manhattan Prince* [1985] 1 Lloyd's Rep. 140, by Leggatt, J., who rejected an argument by the charterers, on a similar provision in Clause 5 of the Shelltime 3 form, that owners were in breach of this provision by failing to pay the higher rates which the I.T.F. (International Transport Workers Federation) sought to impose on the owners by boycott. For a fuller summary of the facts of this case, see page 304 below.

Insurance of the vessel

The provision in Lines 36 and 37 of the New York Produce form that the owners are to pay for the insurance of the vessel is reinforced by Clause 26 which places on the owners the responsibility for insurance "same as when trading for their own account". As stated at page 441 below, these provisions require the owners to insure against war risks as well as against hull and machinery risks.

For comments on the effect of additional clauses providing for reimbursement of certain insurance premiums to the owners by the charterers see pages 443 to 446 below.

Maintenance clause

This obligation continues throughout the charter period, supplementing the initial warranty of seaworthiness in Lines 5 and 22, as to which see page 64 above.

The obligation of the owners under this provision is not an absolute one. Although they will be in breach if they fail to keep up a prudent programme of inspections and surveys, replacements and repairs, and as a result the ship, her machinery or equipment cease to be in good order, they will not automatically be in breach because breakdowns occur or the ship becomes unseaworthy. In *Tynedale Shipping* v. *Anglo-Soviet Shipping* (1936) 41 Com. Cas. 206, Lord Roche said that such a maintenance obligation does "not constitute an absolute engagement or warranty that the shipowners will succeed in so maintaining her whatever perils or causes may intervene to cause her to be inefficient for the purpose of her services". See also *Giertsen* v. *Turnbull*, 1908 S.C. 1101. (As to other types of maintenance clauses, see below.)

If the ship, her machinery or equipment do become inefficient during the charter period the owners are obliged by reason of this provision to take reasonable steps within a reasonable time to put them right. Greer, J., said in *Snia* v. *Suzuki* (1924) 17 Ll.L.Rep. 78, at page 88, that although the obligation of the owners "does not mean that she will be in such a state during every minute of the service, it does mean that when she gets into a condition when she is not thoroughly efficient in hull and machinery they will take within a reasonable time reasonable steps to put her into that condition.".

The obligation of the owners under this provision, like the initial warranty of seaworthiness, is an intermediate obligation not a condition, and so the charterers do not have the right to treat the charter as discharged for *any* breach of the obligation: see the judgment of Salmon, J., in *The Hongkong Fir* [1961] 1 Lloyd's Rep. 159, approved by the Court of Appeal at [1961] 2 Lloyd's Rep. 478 and pages 55 to 59 above. The charterers' remedy for breach of the obligation as to maintenance will lie only in damages unless they can show that the breach was so serious as to deprive them of substantially the whole benefit of the contract—for example a failure to remedy deficiencies in the engines which continued or were going to continue for such a time as would frustrate the contract, not merely for an unreasonable time: see the judgment of Sellers, L.J., in *The Hongkong Fir* [1961] 2 Lloyd's Rep. 478, at page 489. In that case Salmon, J., reconciled the decision in *Snia* v. *Suzuki* (1924) 18 Ll.L.Rep. 333, see page 67 above, with the view that delays in repair would have to be of a frustrating rather than an unreasonable duration to allow the charterers to rescind. He said: "The facts of that case were exceptional. The charterers, after the failure of repeated efforts of the owners to make the vessel seaworthy, had good reason to believe that the shipowners would never be able to do so": [1961] 1 Lloyd's Rep. 159, at page 174. See also *The Hermosa* [1982] 1 Lloyd's Rep. 570 and page 67 above.

Other types of maintenance clause

Although the maintenance clause in the New York Produce form imposes an obligation which is less than absolute, other forms of maintenance clause may be so worded that the obligation is absolute (subject to any applicable exceptions). For example, in *The Saxon Star* [1957] 1 Lloyd's Rep. 271, it was held by the Court of Appeal that an absolute obligation was created by a clause reading, "being tight, staunch and strong, and every way fitted for the voyage, and to be maintained in such condition during the voyage, perils of the sea expected". This maintenance provision was written as part of the initial warranty of seaworthiness; it also contained its own exception of perils of the sea, which would not have been necessary if it was intended to impose an obligation that was less than absolute. As Parker, L.J., said at page 280: "The nature of the obligation to maintain must depend on the exact words used."

(The facts of *Adamastos Shipping* v. *Anglo-Saxon Petroleum* (*The Saxon Star*) [1957] 1 Lloyd's Rep. 271 (C.A.) and [1958] 1 Lloyd's Rep. 73 (H.L.), are set out at page 425.

American Law

The maintenance clause reinforces the express warranty of seaworthiness provided in the preamble, and imposes on the owner the duty of maintaining the vessel in a seaworthy condition throughout the charter term. The warranty is satisfied only if the vessel is seaworthy at the outset of each voyage performed under the charter, or, if the charter so provides, the owner has exercised due diligence to make her seaworthy before each voyage. *Luckenbach* v. *McCahan Sugar Co.*, 248 U.S. 139 (1918). In that case, the Supreme Court explained the warranty as follows:—

It is also urged that, as between the owners and the Insular Line, the original warranty of seaworthiness was exhausted upon delivery of the ship to the charterers and that the maintenance clause relied upon does not import a warranty of seaworthiness at the commencement of each voyage under a time charter, but merely an obligation to pay the expense of keeping her hull and machinery in repair throughout the service. Neither the language of the clause nor the character of time charters afford support for this contention. The charter of the vessel states clearly that the vessel "being, on her delivery, tight, staunch, [and] strong", the owners will "maintain her in a thoroughly efficient state in hull and machinery for and during the service",—*not pay the expense* of maintaining her. This duty to maintain the vessel in an efficient state is imposed by the contract, because a time charter, like a charter for a single voyage, is not a demise of the ship. In both, the charterer is without control over her repair and maintenance. In operations under each the charterer becomes liable to shippers without limitation for losses due to unseaworthiness discoverable by the exercise of due diligence on the part of the owners; and in each case he requires for his protection a warranty, without limitation, of seaworthiness at the commencement of every voyage. (248 U.S. at 149–50.)

See also *The Fort Gaines*, 21 F.2d 865, 1927 AMC 1778 (D.Md. 1927); *Strong* v. *United States*, 154 U.S. 632 (1878); *Mondella* v. *S.S. Elie V.*, 223 F.Supp. 390 (S.D.N.Y. 1963); *The Captain John*, 1973 AMC 2005 (Arb. at N.Y. 1973).

While in respect of cargo there is thus imposed on the shipowner a nondelegable duty of due diligence, the maintenance clause will not ordinarily be interpreted as imposing a similar duty insofar as non-cargo matters are concerned. Thus, in *The Bjorneford*, 271 F. 682, 683 (2d Cir. 1921), the vessel was in dry dock and a crack was discovered in the propeller. The repair yard negligently damaged the spare propeller while it was being installed, and a new one had to be cast, causing a delay of two weeks. The charterer's suit to recover loss of earnings for that period was dismissed on the ground that the owner was not in breach of the charter because of the repair yard's negligence. In fulfillment of its duties under the charter, all the owner was "required to do was to exercise reasonable and ordinary care to restore the vessel to a thoroughly efficient state for her service". According to the court, by engaging a reputable and fully equipped repair yard, the owner complied with this obligation.

In *The Argo Leader*, S.M.A. No. 2065 (Arb. at N.Y. 1985), during the fourth year of a five-year time charter, the vessel suffered engine damage which required the vessel to be placed off-hire. Based upon surveyors' reports, charterer concluded that owner could not or would not restore the vessel to a seaworthy condition and cancelled the charter while the vessel was still undergoing repairs. The panel held that the cancellation was premature and improper. The panel stated that owner was entitled to an opportunity to comply with the seaworthiness and readiness requirements and that charterer was obligated to wait until owner gave notice of readiness before carrying out surveys to confirm the vessel's condition.

A ship is not seaworthy simply by virtue of the fact that she is in class and the owner will not be considered to have exercised due diligence merely by obtaining certificates of seaworthiness from a classification society. See *Ionian S.S. Co.* v. *United Distillers of America Inc.*, 236 F.2d 78 (5th Cir. 1956); *Petition of Southern Transp. Co.*, 211 F.Supp. 940 (E.D. Va. 1963).

A classification society certificate has been held to be *prima facie* evidence of seaworthiness, however, which shifts the burden of proving unseaworthiness to the charterer in a non-COGSA case. *The Seaford*, 1975 AMC 1553 (Arb. at N.Y. 1975), is an extreme example of the difficulties the charterer may face in meeting this burden where COGSA is not incorporated in the charter. In that case the shipper had chartered the vessel under a Gencon form of voyage charter to carry a cargo of steel. The vessel stranded and the panel, finding COGSA inapplicable, held that the charterer had the burden of proving that the grounding was caused by a "personal want of due diligence" on the shipowner's part. Moreover, the panel stated that while the existence of a classification society's certificate did not conclusively establish the vessel's seaworthiness, it did constitute *prima facie* proof sufficient to put the burden of proving the contrary on the charterer. The latter attempted to show that the grounding was caused by improper manning and the owner's failure to have the ship's radio direction finder properly calibrated. The panel held that the evidence did not support these contentions, and that the proximate cause of the stranding was an error in navigation for which the owner was not liable.

Changed legal requirements

A very difficult problem that has arisen, particularly where long-term time charters are involved, concerns the obligation of the owner to maintain the vessel in accordance with changed legal requirements of either the flag state or countries within the allowed trading limits. When laws come into force during the period of the charter which impose new requirements on vessels, how are the relations between owner and charterer affected? The question is particularly difficult when large costs or major capital improvements to the vessel are required to comply with the new requirements.

Cases involving these issues will always depend on the particular circumstances involved. In certain circumstances, principles of frustration may be applicable. This would be so where the parties had not anticipated or allocated the risk of the particular requirement and the cost of continued performance of the charter rendered the venture commercially impracticable. See discussion below at page 342.

Where the factors involved do not frustrate the charter, the main factors to be considered are whether the requirements of the law call, on the one hand, for substantial capital improvements or, on the other, for maintenance items which the owner would ordinarily expect might be required during the charter. In the former case, it would seem from the few cases which have been decided that the owner would not be under a duty under the charter to comply. This appears to be true especially where the owner is under a duty to exercise due diligence to maintain the vessel. In the latter case, the owner's duty to maintain the vessel would be clear.

In *The Endeavor*, 1978 AMC 1742 (Arb. at N.Y. 1977), the charterer successfully claimed that the owner was obligated under the charter to install special hold ladders required for trading in Australia. The charter was on the New York Produce form, and was for a period of five years. The vessel was delivered to the charterer in June 1973. In May 1977 the charterer demanded that the owner install "WWF Ladders" required by the Australian longshoremen's union. The majority of the panel held that the charterer was justified in its demand, and stated:

This controversy touches upon the sensitive albeit diversified subject of separation of duties and responsibilities as between Owners and Charterers in an era of constant technical evolution and universal concern over human safety and environmental protection. This written Award is for the purpose of formalizing and refining the decision rendered at the termination of the hearing session, a decision which was requested to be made at that time.

The majority of this Panel considers that, although the WWF ladder requirements evidently necessitate a modification or alteration of the existing shape, design and perhaps location of the present hold ladders fitted on board the *Endeavor*, these modifications do not constitute structural changes of such a nature and magnitude as to override Owners' duty of maintaining the Vessel in a state which imposes no restrictions on the ability of the Vessel to perform in the manner called for in the Charter Party. In this respect, the Vessel should be capable of trading within the geographic areas permitted by the Charter Party and carrying such lawful cargoes as are allowed by this agreement. The WWF ladder requirement, if unattended to, imposes such a restriction as respects Australian ports which are serviced by the WWF and on cargoes which require the presence of WWF longshoremen in the holds. (1978 AMC at 1764–47.)

See also *The Guldborg*, 1932 AMC 1206 (S.D.N.Y. 1932), holding that the owner was obligated to bear the cost of fire-extinguishing equipment as a maintenance item; *The Amerocean*, 1952 AMC 1559 (Arb. at N.Y. 1952), holding the owner liable for the cost of repairs to the vessel's tackle and gear necessary for compliance with regulations at the load port.

In *The Stolt Lion*, S.M.A. No. 1188 (Arb. at N.Y. 1977), the charterer contended that the owner was obligated to install a high level audio-alarm system required by a Ministerial Decree of the Netherlands which was based upon IMCO [now IMO] recommendations. The charterer based its claim on a provision in the charterparty which stated:

The vessel shall at all times satisfy the requirements for the carriage of solvents, chemicals as set forth by national or international authorities, etc. . . . Owners shall exercise due diligence to maintain the vessel and her equipment as on delivery on this Charter Party, normal wear and tear excepted.

The panel unanimously held, however, that this clause did not require that the owner bear the expense of what was in fact a capital improvement necessary for employment of the vessel in the Netherlands. According to the panel:

Under the provisions of the Time Charter, Owners had accepted the contractual obligation to furnish a specific vessel to the Charterers, a vessel which would be suitable for a specific trade contemplated by the Charterers. In the acceptance of the vessel into this Time Charter, coupled with the prior approval of the vessel based on the plans and specifications, Charterers confirmed vessel's suitability for their trade at the time of the delivery and vessel's compliance with the specifications and requirements for which they had bargained. Whereas Owners' warranty "to maintain her in such a state during the currency of this Charter" is a continuous one, the Panel does not consider the purchase and installation of the audio-alarm system to fall under this warranty. The careful reading of all other clauses relating to the condition of the vessel, do not, in the Panel's opinion, allocate the responsibility for the installation of any equipment such as the audio-alarm unto the Owners. The purchase and installation of such system, even if required under inter-governmental regulations, by its nature is a capital improvement and as such not a maintenance item but an upgrading of the vessel.

In *The Angantyr*, 1971 AMC 2503 (Arb. at N.Y. 1971), the vessel was without an approved grain loading plan as required under the 1960 SOLAS Convention, and the building of an additional bulkhead in the No. 1 hold was necessary to enable the vessel to load grain. The panel held that the owner was under no liability to the charterer for this expense:

> Quite apart from the question of the burden of proof of damages not being met by Charterers, the crux of the matter is there is nothing contained in the Time Charter on which Charterers can rely to render Owners liable for the failure to supply suitable documentation permitting the vessel to load under SOLAS rules. The arbitrators know of Time Charters specifically calling for this requirement. The mere fact that grain was not contemplated by Charterers (or Owners) at the time of entering into the Charter Agreement, cannot by any stretch of the imagination shift the burden of the grain fitting from Charterers to Owners when the Charter is silent on the point. (1971 AMC at 2507.)

These issues were also raised in *The Ultramar*, 1981 AMC 1831 (Arb. at N.Y. 1981). The vessel was an American flag OBO of about 82,000 dwt built in 1973. In that year, the vessel was chartered on the Mobiltime form to the charterer for a period of 10 years. During the performance of the charter, the United States Port and Tanker Safety Act entered into force. Under that Act, the vessel was required to be fitted with, among other things, an inert gas system by 1 June 1981. The arbitrators were asked to decide whether the owner was required to perform the changes required by the Port and Tanker Safety Act. The majority held that the owner was so obligated by reason of its duty to furnish and maintain a vessel capable of trading as a crude oil carrier. The panel majority noted that while there was no express wording in the charter requiring that the vessel be in compliance with the Port and Tanker Safety Act, under the charter terms the owner remained under a duty to exercise due diligence to maintain the vessel during the period of the charter "in every way fitted for the service and carriage of crude oil and/or dirty petroleum". Since the vessel would not have been permitted to carry crude oil if she were not in compliance with the Port and Tanker Safety Act, the owner would be in breach of its duty to maintain the vessel were it to fail to retrofit.

Charterers to provide and pay for

"39. 2. That the Charterers shall provide and pay for all the fuel except as otherwise agreed, Port Charges, Pilotages, Agencies, Commissions,
40. Consular Charges (except those pertaining to the Crew), and all other usual expenses except those before stated, but when the vessel puts into
41. a port for causes for which vessel is responsible, then all such charges incurred shall be paid by the Owners. Fumigations ordered because of
42. illness of the crew to be for Owners account. Fumigations ordered because of cargoes carried or ports visited while vessel is employed under this
43. charter to be for Charterers account. All other fumigations to be for Charterers account after vessel has been on charter for a continuous period
44. of six months or more.
45. Charterers are to provide necessary dunnage and shifting boards, also any extra fittings requisite for a special trade or unusual cargo, but
46. Owners to allow them the use of any dunnage and shifting boards already aboard vessel. Charterers to have the privilege of using shifting boards
47. for dunnage, they making good any damage thereto."

General nature of the charterers' duty to provide

In general the obligation cast upon the charterers by Lines 39 and 40 of the New York Produce form and by Clause 4 of the Baltime form is absolute, in the sense that they must actually provide the stipulated items rather than merely exercise due diligence towards that end. Thus, in a voyage charter case, where the charterers undertook to provide icebreaker assistance in the event of the loading port being inaccessible by reason of ice, it was held by the House of Lords that the charterers were under an absolute obligation to provide icebreakers: *Anastassia* v. *Ugleexport* (1934) 49 Ll.L.Rep. 1. Lord Wright in that case said: "the charterers have contracted to supply the assistance, and that, in my opinion, means either by themselves or by others, so that they cannot justify a failure to do so on the pretext that they had not the icebreakers under their control and could not get them supplied by those who controlled them. In that sense the obligation is absolute. The charterers assumed the obligation and the risk. It follows equally that the charterers' obligation is not limited to an obligation to do their best to supply".

But in some circumstances there may be a duty upon the owners to give information to the charterers to enable them to make proper provision and the owners cannot complain if the charterers fail to make such provision because of the inaccuracy of that information: see below.

Fuel

Provision is made in Clause 3 of the New York Produce form and Clause 5 of the Baltime form for the purchase by the charterers of fuel on board on delivery and by the owners of fuel on board on redelivery: see page 181 below. Fuel so purchased by the charterers becomes their property, together with fuel provided by them during the charter service: see page 173 below.

Quantity

Of necessity the ability of the charterers to provide the ship with the correct quantity of bunkers requires the cooperation of the owners and their officers, upon whom the charterers must largely rely for the provision of information as to previous and current consumption. The owners or their officers may also indicate the further quantities that will be required for safe completion of the next voyage or voyages ordered by the charterers. If the charterers reasonably rely upon such information and it turns out to be wrong they cannot be held responsible for the consequent losses.

The *Patapsco* was time chartered for a round voyage from Liverpool to the River Plate and back. Owing to a miscalculation by the ship's engineer, the ship did not take on sufficient bunker coals for the first stage of the homeward voyage and she had to deviate for additional bunkers. The owners contended that the extra expenses incurred were the charterers' responsibility since, under the terms of the charter, the charterers were to "provide and pay for all coal". But the Court of Appeal, affirming Kennedy, J., held that the obligation on the charterers to provide coal did not cut down the owners' initial warranty of seaworthiness which included the obligation to arrange for sufficient bunkers at each stage of the round voyage. Vaughan-Williams, L.J., said at page 128: "The argument based on this provision of the charterparty is that, the charterers being bound to 'provide' as well as to 'pay for' all the coal, all responsibility in respect of the coaling of the ship was put upon the charterers, and that the shipowners were therefore relieved from their duty of rendering the ship seaworthy in respect of coal, which, it was admitted, would have existed in the absence of such a special provision.

"In my opinion, this is to endeavour to give far too extensive an operation to the provision that the charterers are to 'provide and pay for all coal'; I think that it leaves untouched the duty of the shipowners to render the ship seaworthy by seeing that there is on board sufficient coal for the use of the ship when she starts on each stage of her voyage."

MacIver v. *Tate* (1903) 8 Com. Cas. 124.

Commenting on the above case in *The Captain Diamantis* [1977] 1 Lloyd's Rep. 362, at page 367, Ackner, J., said: "The provision [to provide and pay for fuel] does not relieve the shipowners from the obligation of seeing that the vessel is in a seaworthy condition in respect of the supply of fuel . . . Thus it is the duty of the master to give the charterers correct information, to enable them to provide the requisite quantity of fuel . . . "

Although the Court of Appeal in *MacIver* v. *Tate* based its decision on the ground that the owners were not relieved of their obligations in regard to seaworthiness by the charterers' obligation to provide and pay for fuel, the seaworthiness obligation is not overriding. Thus it would not, it is suggested, prevent the owners raising as a defence to a claim by the charterers a plea that the charterers were in breach of their obligation. Kennedy, J., whose decision at first instance in *MacIver* v. *Tate* (1902) 18 T.L.R. 379 was approved by the Court of Appeal, remarked that the position would have been different had the master asked for more coal and had the charterers failed to supply it. If in such circumstances the owners had discharged their obligation as to seaworthiness (for example, by obtaining the required fuel themselves, either prior to sailing or, if unavailable, at an intermediate port) the charterers would, it is thought, have been responsible for any losses or extra expenses which the owners thereby incurred.

Quality

The charterers must take care that the bunkers they provide are of reasonable general quality and suitable for the type of engines fitted to the particular ship. They will not be obliged to meet any unusual requirements of the engines, beyond those to be expected of their type, unless these have been drawn to their attention by the owners in advance. In view of declining quality in bunkers it has become more usual recently for the charter to include express requirements as to the type and grade of the fuel to be supplied: where such a stipulation exists the charterers must comply with it.

For a case concerning a fire in bunkers supplied by charterers, see *Nourse* v. *Elder Dempster* (1922) 13 Ll.L.Rep. 197, and page 308 below.

Property in bunkers

In *The Saint Anna* [1980] 1 Lloyd's Rep. 180 it was held by Sheen, J., that charterers under a Shelltime 3 form of charter retained the property in fuel which had been supplied and paid for by them and which was on board the ship. Referring to the provision in Clause 6 of that charter that the charterers "shall provide and pay for all fuel (except galley fuel)" he said: "It seems to me that if the charterers purchase fuel, that fuel is their property unless the parties clearly and unequivocally agree that the property shall vest in the owners." The decision in *The Saint Anna* was approved by the House of Lords in *The Span Terza* [1984] 1 Lloyd's Rep. 119, who held that the position was the same under the New York Produce form. There is a similar provision in Clause 4 of the Baltime form. For the effects on the property in bunkers of termination of the charter, see under "Bunkers" at page 182 below.

Safety of bunkering place

The charterers may in certain circumstances be responsible for damage done to the ship as a result of the unsafety of the bunkering place to which the ship is directed by bunker suppliers if the bunker suppliers are the charterers' agents for this purpose, or if the charterers' orders as to bunkering are properly to be construed as orders to bunker at such place as the bunkering suppliers may direct. See *The Mediolanum* [1984] 1 Lloyd's Rep. 136, *The Erechthion* [1987] 2 Lloyd's Rep. 180 and page 154 above, where these cases are discussed.

Port Charges

Port charges include all charges which a ship has to pay before she leaves a port, even if some of those charges relate to benefits which will accrue to the ship only after she has left the port.

The charterers of the *Apex* were obliged by a special clause to pay the port charges at Deptford if they ordered the ship to discharge deck cargo there, which they did. The port charges payable at Deptford included Trinity House dues in respect of lights to be passed during the remainder of the voyage to Leith where the under deck cargo was to be discharged. Had the ship gone straight to Leith without calling at Deptford these dues would have been payable by the owners. Mathew, J., held that the charterers were responsible for these dues. He said: "The ordinary meaning of the phrase seems to me to be those charges which a vessel must pay before she leaves a port."

Newman & Dale v. *Lamport & Holt* [1896] 1 Q.B. 20.

But it is only those charges which are payable during the period of the charter for which the charterers are responsible. Thus where light dues were paid at the delivery port shortly before delivery was made the owners could not recover these from the charterers, despite the Baltime form provision that the charterers were to provide and pay for "port charges" and "lights": *Scales* v. *Temperley Steam Shipping* (1925) 23 Ll.L.Rep. 312.

Baltime form

It should be noted with regard to the Baltime form that Clause 4 expressly provides that the charterers are to pay "all dock, harbour and tonnage dues at the ports of delivery and re-delivery (unless incurred through cargo carried before delivery or after re-delivery)". Thus these particular charges are made an exception to the general rule and will be payable by the charterers even if incurred or paid before delivery or after redelivery. As these words place on the charterers an obligation to pay for charges incurred or paid outside the period of the charter they are to be narrowly construed. Thus in *Scales* v. *Temperley Steam Shipping*, above, Roche, J., did not construe them as embracing the light dues, which had been mentioned earlier in the clause. No corresponding words appear in the New York Produce form.

Pilotages

Where pilots are necessary, either to meet local regulations or to ensure the safety of the ship, the charterers must provide and pay for them under Line 39 of the New York Produce form or Lines 29 and 30 of the Baltime form.

It seems that, in accordance with the general principle set out on page 171 above, such pilots must be provided and that the charterers do not discharge their obligation by trying but failing to provide them, even where their availability depends upon authorities over which the charterers have no control. It may also be that the charterers will be in breach if the pilots supplied lack a reasonable degree of competence; see, for a case referring to the competence of a stevedore appointed by charterers, *The Sinoe* [1972] 1 Lloyd's Rep. 201. It has been held that the pilots, although provided and paid for by the charterers, do not become the servants of the charterers so as to make the charterers vicariously responsible to the owners for their negligence.

The time charterers of the *Sir Bevis* were to provide and pay for pilotages. One of the pilots provided by them negligently put her aground and she was damaged. The owner argued that the off-hire clause did not excuse the charterers from paying hire during the repairs because the pilot was the servant of the charterers and they were therefore responsible for his negligence. Mathew, J., rejecting this "extraordinary contention", said: "The fact that the charterers had to pay the pilot did not make him their servant."

Fraser v. *Bee* (1900) 17 T.L.R. 101.

It should be noted that the owners' case in *Fraser* v. *Bee*, above, was put squarely on the assertion, which Mathew, J., rejected in a short judgment, that the pilot had been the servant of the charterers. An alternative argument for the owners could have been that, although the pilot was not the servant of the charterers, responsibility for his work had been shifted onto the charterers as between them and the owners. This argument would be consistent with the decision of Greer, J., in *Brys* v. *Drysdale* (1920) 4 Ll.L.Rep. 24, that the effect of a clause in a voyage charter reading "the Charterers . . . are to provide and pay a stevedore to do the stowing of the cargo under the supervision of the Master" was to "transfer the duty and obligation, which would otherwise rest on the shipowner, to the Charterer, of stowing the cargo in the way it ought to be stowed". This decision of Greer, J., was cited with approval by the House of Lords in *Court Line* v. *Canadian Transport* (1940) 67 Ll.L.Rep. 161, see pages 247 to 248 below, and must be regarded as authoritative. It is suggested, nevertheless, that the decision in *Fraser* v. *Bee* is correct and would be followed today. It is possible that a court faced with similar facts but an argument along the lines of that which succeeded in *Brys* v. *Drysdale* would distinguish the latter case on the basis that it dealt with the transfer of the work of stevedoring and its attendant risks which, save in the exceptional circumstances discussed in *Court Line* v. *Canadian Transport*, summarised at page 247 below, do not touch upon the shipowners' seaworthiness obligation, whereas the work of pilotage and its attendant risks bear inevitably and directly on that obligation.

Moreover, support for any argument against a transfer to the charterers of the risk of pilot negligence is provided by Lines 170 and 171 of the New York Produce form: "The Owners to remain responsible for the navigation of the vessel . . . , same as when trading for their own account".

Agencies

By Line 39 of the New York Produce form and Line 34 of the Baltime form, the charterers are obliged to provide and pay for agencies. It is suggested that a competent agent must be chosen, at least where such a firm or person exists in the particular port or area. Whether the charterers are responsible to the owners for the negligence of a generally competent agent whom they have appointed may depend upon the type of work being done and the extent, if at all, that it relates to the ship as opposed to her cargo.

In considering a similar provision in Clause 20 of the Beepeetime 2 form, Staughton, J., said in *The Sagona* [1984] 1 Lloyd's Rep. 194, at page 199: " . . . the agents, being appointed and paid by the charterers, are as between the owners and charterers to be considered the agents of the charterers for all the ordinary business of a ship in port. That solution avoids some difficulties which might arise if the charterers appoint incompetent or negligent agents. But there may be some business which, as between the owners and the charterers, the master ought to do himself, and not delegate to the agents. If the master does nevertheless entrust such a task to the agents, then it may be that the agents' omission to perform it would be an omission on behalf of the owners and not on behalf of the charterers". See also *Strathlorne Steamship* v. *Andrew Weir* (1934) 49 Ll.L.Rep. 306, 310.

All other usual expenses

There is a lack of judicial authority as to what is covered by these words from Line 40 of the New York Produce form. It seems probable, however, that they include "tug-assistance", which appears in the fuller list of charterers' items in Clause 4 of the Baltime form. Assuming that the charterers do have the obligation to provide tugs, it is suggested that the extent of that obligation should be similar to that in respect of pilots, discussed above.

Off-hire periods

The obligations of the charterers under this clause continue throughout the period of the charter, save only where there are express words to the contrary. Thus under the equivalent provision (Clause 4) of the Baltime form, the charterers remain liable to pay for fuel used even while the ship is off-hire.

The *Arild* was off-hire during certain periods of repair. Bunker coal was consumed during these periods. The charterers were obliged by the charter-party to "provide and pay for all the coals, fuel . . . ", but argued that this obligation should be suspended during off-hire periods. McCardie, J., held that the charterers' obligation continued.

Arild v. *Hovrani* [1923] 2 K.B. 141.

The position with regard to fuel used during off-hire periods would be the same under the New York Produce form in accordance with Line 39 were it not for the express provision to the contrary in Clause 20, Lines 133 and 134. The same effect can be achieved under the Baltime form by the frequently employed insertion at the very beginning of Clause 4 of the words "While on hire". This insertion shifts to the owners the responsibility for the other matters mentioned in Clause 4 as well as for fuel consumed. Although the insertion of similar words at the beginning of Line 39 of the New York Produce form is not necessary to protect the charterers so far as fuel is concerned, it is necessary to make the owners responsible for the other matters mentioned in Lines 39 and 40.

However, the obligations of the charterers do not commence before delivery nor extend beyond redelivery, save only where expressly provided (as in Clause 4 of the Baltime form). See further under "Port Charges" above.

American Law

Charterers to provide and pay for . . .

As stated above, Clause 2 allocates to the charterer the duty to pay for such items as fuel, port charges, pilotage, and agents' fees, unless these expenses are incurred by reason of a cause for which the vessel is responsible. The charterer remains responsible for these items for as long as the charter remains in force, unless there is a specific exception provided elsewhere in the charter. For example, under Clause 20 of the New York Produce form, the charterer is excused from the obligation to pay for fuel while the ship is off-hire.

The charterer will remain responsible for these costs even if, by reason of a material breach of charter on its part, the vessel is withdrawn from its service while cargo remains on board. This situation arose in *The Athenian Horizon*, S.M.A. No. 1197 (Arb. at N.Y. 1977). The charterer had defaulted in making its hire payment while the vessel was en route to the discharge port, and the owner sent the charterer a notice of withdrawal which the arbitrators held was justified. The vessel was loaded with cargo when the notice was sent, however, and the arbitrators held that the charter remained in effect until the cargo was discharged. Because the charter was still in force, notwithstanding the owner's notice of withdrawal, the charterer remained responsible for port charges at the discharge port.

Similarly, in *The Arizona*, S.M.A. No. 1259 (Arb. at N.Y. 1978), the charterer was held liable to pay for fuel consumed during the period between the time the notice of withdrawal was given and the cargo was discharged.

Bunkers

Quantity

It is the charterer's responsibility to supply and pay for bunkers. It is the master's responsibility, however, to determine what quantity of fuel shall be brought on board the vessel. Moreover, it is the master's obligation to make sure that there is an adequate supply of fuel for the voyage the charterer instructs him to make.

In *The Venetia*, S.M.A. No. 1351 (Arb. at N.Y. 1979), the vessel was held to be off-hire for time lost on the voyage when she had to put into Cape Town to load fuel oil. The unscheduled call was necessary because the master had miscalculated the bunkers required for the voyage given the vessel's speed and consumption. The charterer had supplied the quantity requested by the master at the outset of the voyage and, according to the panel, could not be held liable for hire for time lost by reason of the master's miscalculations.

Similarly, in *The Argentine Transport*, 1956 AMC 1772 (Arb. at N.Y. 1956), the owner was held responsible for the cost of excessive bunkers ordered by the master. The vessel arrived at the discharge port with 475 tons of bunkers remaining, having consumed 493 tons on the voyage. According to the panel, the safety margin of nearly 100 per cent required by the master was excessive; rather, "a 25 per cent. margin is customarily recognized as an equitable safety factor". Because the bunkers were more expensive at the loading port than at the discharge port, the owner was held liable for the price differential.

In *The Silver Hawk*, S.M.A. No. 1857 (Arb. at N.Y. 1983), the panel held that the charterer had grossly oversupplied the vessel with bunkers. However, because the master did not protest when the fuel was delivered, owner had no practical recourse against charterer. Nevertheless, the panel held that the charterer had injured owner by deprivation of cash flow.

In *The Mandolyna*, S.M.A. No. 2115 (Arb. at N.Y. 1985), the panel held that though charterer had accepted and paid for bunkers upon delivery in excess of the quantity stipulated in the charter, charterer was not required to redeliver the vessel with the same excess.

In *The Zannis*, S.M.A. No. 2074 (Arb. at N.Y. 1985), charterer redelivered the vessel with bunkers in excess of the amount stipulated in the charter. The panel awarded owner damages consisting of the difference between the charter rate and the market rate for the excess fuel which owner was forced to purchase.

Quality

The New York Produce form contains no express provisions as to the quality of the bunkers the charterer will provide during the period of the charter except to say that it must be "best grade". The absence of any detailed provisions concerning specifications for the fuel would seem to indicate that so long as the charterer supplies fuel which meets generally accepted standards for bunkers, the owner would not have a basis for claiming damages should problems arise because of the quality of the fuel. At the same time, it appears that if the parties agree to include in the charter specifications as to the type or quality of fuel to be used, the charterer would be liable for any losses resulting from the supplying of fuel which does not meet the charter description. The problems which may result from defective bunkers are quite serious, and include physical damage to the engines, reduced levels of performance, and loss of time.

In *The Royal Prince*, 1927 AMC 62 (S.D.N.Y. 1926), Judge Augustus Hand held the charterer liable for losses resulting from its failure to supply bunker coal of merchantable quality.

In *The Maro*, S.M.A. No. 2533 (Arb. at N.Y. 1988), the charter described the fuel charterer was to furnish as IFO 1550 SECS and MDO. Owner claimed that the fuel oil supplied by charterer was off specification, improperly blended or contained excessive contaminants. The panel agreed with the owner's argument that the charterer has a non-delegable duty to supply bunkers that meet the charter specifications:

> Clearly, it is the charterer and not the fuel merchant who bears the responsibility of furnishing bunkers which meet charter party standards. Essentially, the charterer orders and pays for the fuel and it is its obligation *vis-à-vis* the shipowner. The fuel merchant undertakes to supply fuel in accordance with industry standards and its instructions without guaranty that it will be suitable for the particular vessel's machinery. In addition to meeting the viscosity stated in the fuel purchase order, the bunkers should also meet current standards for compatibility and freedom from excessive levels of harmful contaminants.

The panel found, however, that owner had failed to meet its burden of proving that the bunkers supplied by charterer caused engine damage.

In *The Leslie*, S.M.A. No. 1341 (Arb. at N.Y. 1979), the owner made a claim for engine damage and reduced speed caused by off-specification bunkers. The preamble of the charter contained a reference to the vessel's fuel consumption, and stated: " . . . on a consumption of about nine tons intermediate fuel oil maximum viscosity 300 seconds

Redwood." The owner proved from samples taken from the vessel that the fuel oil supplied by the charterer had a viscosity of 750 seconds. The arbitrators unanimously held that "to the extent that the owner can demonstrate that the vessel was damaged having used this off-specification oil charterer is liable for the reasonable costs thereof".

The burden of proof on the owner is a heavy one. *The London Glory*, S.M.A. No. 1771 (Arb. at N.Y. 1982), is perhaps the best illustration of this. There, the panel found that the vessel's main diesel engine sustained excessive wear which was caused by contaminants, including catalytic fines, introduced into the engine through the fuel system. The panel further ruled, however, that owner failed to meet its burden of establishing by a preponderance of the evidence that the contaminants were in the fuel supplied by charterer rather than bunkers used by the vessel previously.

In *Antilles Shipping Co. Ltd.* v. *Texaco Inc.*, 321 F.Supp. 166, 1971 AMC 1291 (S.D.N.Y. 1970), the owner failed to establish that engine breakdowns were caused by the unsuitability of the vessel's lubricating oil. The court noted that to prove its case, the owner had to show that it used the fuel properly, that there was no crew negligence, and that the damage was not caused by other foreign substances in the vessel's lubricating system.

In *The Lumber Carrier*, S.M.A. No. 252 (Arb. at N.Y. 1955), the arbitrators held the charterer and the owner both to blame for losses resulting from fuel which had excessive water content. The owner was held to blame because the master and chief engineer had reason to know that the fuel was defective, and failed to take steps to correct the situation. The arbitrators concluded that the charterer was liable for damages directly caused by his breach of charter in supplying fuel which had excessive water content.

The charterer is not only required, but is entitled to supply the "best grade" fuel oil even over the owner's objections. In *The Derrynane*, 1954 AMC 1015 (Arb. at N.Y. 1954), for the last voyage the charterer supplied a high-priced fuel described by the oil company as "Marine Diesel Medium" and this was accepted by the master without objection. When the vessel was redelivered, the owner claimed that it was only obliged to pay charterer for the fuel at the lower price of a lesser grade fuel called "Marine Diesel" which would have been usable in the ship's engine. The panel held, however, that the charterer was fully justified in buying the highest quality fuel oil and that the owner was obliged to pay the actual cost of that fuel for the quantity remaining on board on redelivery.

Had the situation in *The Derrynane* been reversed, with the charterer desiring to supply a lower grade fuel over the owner's objection, there can be little doubt that the owner would have been entitled to insist on the highest quality or "best grade" available.

Pilotage

A voluntary pilot aboard a vessel under time charter is the borrowed servant of the owner and not the charterer even though the charterer is obliged to pay for pilotage. *H. Schuldt* v. *Standard Fruit & Steamship Co.*, 1979 AMC 2470, 2478 (S.D.N.Y. 1978); *California* v. *S/T Norfolk*, 435 F.Supp. 1039, 1046n.2, 1978 AMC 144, 153n.2 (N.D. Cal. 1977). The decision whether to employ a pilot remains the responsibility of the owner. The charterer is under an implied duty, however, to exercise due diligence to provide a pilot who is reasonably fit and qualified for the particular assignment. *California* v. *Norfolk*, above.

The charterer's obligation to provide and pay for pilotage does not give it authority to bind the owner to the terms and conditions of the pilotage contract. In *A/S Acadia* v. *Curtis Bay Towing Co.*, 304 F.Supp. 1050 (E.D. Pa. 1967), the *Acadia* collided with another vessel and a pier while in tow of two tugs. The owner commenced an action against the tug owners and the pilot whose negligence was claimed to have caused the accident. The towage company raised a defense based on the "pilotage clause" contained in the dockage contract. This provided in substance that when a pilot went on board the vessel he became the servant of the vessel, and that neither the towage company, the tugs, nor the pilot would be liable for any damage resulting from the pilot's handling of the vessel. The dockage contract was entered into by the charterer with the towage company. The vessel owner moved to strike the defense on the ground that the charterer had no authority to bind the owner to the terms of the dockage contract, arguing that the charter-party merely provided that the charterer was to "provide and pay for . . . pilotage". The court agreed with the owner and held that this clause did not give the charterer authority to commit the owner to the pilotage clause in the extraneous docking contract.

Bunkers

"48. 3. That the Charterers, at the port delivery, and the Owners, at the port of re-delivery, shall take over and pay for all fuel remaining on
49. board the vessel at the current prices in the respective ports, the vessel to be delivered with not less than .... tons and not more than
50. .... tons and to be re-delivered with not less than .... tons and not more than .... tons."

Quantity on delivery and redelivery

Sometimes there will be included within this clause an estimate of the amount of bunkers that will be on board at the time of delivery. It has been held that where the estimate is expressed as "expected about" so many tons there is an obligation on the owners to provide an estimate which is not only honest but is based on reasonable grounds, having regard to information which their responsible officials have or ought to have. This is by analogy with the authorities on the "expected ready to load" provisions, mentioned at page 75 above.

The *Pantanassa* was time chartered for a trip. The charter provided that the charterers were to pay for the bunkers on board at delivery, she "to be delivered with bunkers as aboard at the current Moji price, plus barging (expected about 6/700 tons) . . . ". On delivery she had on board 936 tons. The owners' London agents had inserted the figures in the charter-party in good faith but on the basis of erroneous figures cabled to them from the ship. Diplock, J., held that the owners were in breach of contract. Having acknowledged that the figures had been inserted honestly he said: "but, when I look to see whether [the owners] have reasonable grounds for their estimate, I see no reason why I should not take as the knowledge of the shipowners—and it is they who are proffering the estimate—such knowledge as their responsible officials have or ought to have."

The Pantanassa [1958] 2 Lloyd's Rep. 449.

The provision that the charterers shall provide and pay for fuel (see page 171 above) does not confer on the charterers a power to require the master to take on fuel which is clearly not required for the service under the charter.

The *Captain Diamantis* was chartered on the New York Produce form for three to four months. Clause 3 had been amended to read as follows: "That the Charterers, at the port of delivery, and the Owners, at the port of re-delivery, shall take over and pay for all fuel remaining on board the vessel at U.S.$85 per long ton for IFO and U.S.$120 per long ton for Diesel Oil, the vessel to be delivered with bunkers as on board but sufficient to reach nearest main bunkering port."

As the ship approached her redelivery port she had on board ample bunkers for the remainder of the service and to enable her to reach the nearest main bunkering port, but the charterers gave orders that she was before redelivery to bunker to her full capacity, they having found IFO at U.S.$56 and diesel at $103 per long ton. The master, on his owners' instructions, refused to obey these orders and the charterers sued for the loss of the profit that they would otherwise have made under Clause 3 as amended. Ackner, J., held that the charterers had no power to order that fuel be taken on which was "in no way required for charter-party purposes". His decision was affirmed by the Court of Appeal.

The Captain Diamantis [1977] 1 Lloyd's Rep. 362 and [1978] 1 Lloyd's Rep. 346 (C.A.).

Property in bunkers

The provision of Clause 2 of the New York Produce form that the charterers are to provide and pay for fuel (see pages 171 to 173 above) coupled with the provision of Clause 3 that the charterers shall take over and pay for all fuel at the port of delivery vests in the charterers the property in bunkers during the currency of the charter, the owners merely having the possession of bunkers on board the ship as bailees: *The Span Terza* [1984] 1 Lloyd's Rep. 119. The further provision of Clause 3 that the owners shall take over and pay for all fuel remaining on the ship at the port of redelivery has the effect, when read together with Clause 4 of the charter, of transferring the property in bunkers from the charterers to the owners upon redelivery of the ship at the end of the charter period at a port within the redelivery range. But Clause 3 does not apply where, during the currency of the charter, the charterers cancel the charter under a clause giving an option of cancellation upon the happening of a specific event. In such circumstances the property in the bunkers remains in the charterers following cancellation. The owners remain bailees of the bunkers, but any contractual right they had to retain possession against the charterers comes to an end. If, however, the charter were to be cancelled while the ship was at sea or at a time when she still had cargo on board, terms might have to be implied as to the right of the owners to continue to use fuel on board. See the House of Lords decision in *The Span Terza*, above.

Price

Where the charter—unlike the New York Produce or Baltime forms—makes no provision for the price to be paid for bunkers by the charterers on delivery or the owners on redelivery, the price will be the market price then prevailing, without regard to the price actually paid by the originally purchasing party: *The Good Helmsman* [1981] 1 Lloyd's Rep. 377, at page 419.

Quality

See page 173 above.

American Law

Quantity

See discussion above at page 177.

Price

It is customary for the owner and charterer to provide in the charter for a specific price for bunkers at delivery and redelivery. See, e.g., *The Efplia*, S.M.A. No. 1359 (Arb. at N.Y. 1979).

Under the New York Produce form, the price to be paid for bunkers by the charterer on delivery and the owner on redelivery is the current market price at the time and place these events occur. If the charter is silent on price, however, it would seem correct that the same rule should apply, even if the market price is different from the price actually paid.

Quality

See discussion above at page 178.

Computation of Time

"51. 4. That the Charterers shall pay for the use and hire of the said Vessel at the rate of ....
52. .... United States Currency per ton on vessel's total deadweight carrying capacity, including bunkers and
53. stores, on .... summer freeboard, per Calendar Month, commencing on and from the day of her delivery, as aforesaid, and at
54. and after the same rate for any part of a month; hire to continue until the hour of the day of her re-delivery . . . "

Local or elapsed time

Because delivery often takes place in a different time zone from redelivery, the question arises whether the period of hire is to be calculated by reference solely to local dates and times at the delivery and redelivery ports, or alternatively by reference to the time that has elapsed between Greenwich Mean Time upon delivery and upon redelivery.

In *The Arctic Skou* [1985] 2 Lloyd's Rep. 478, the question had to be decided under a New York Produce form charter in which the references in the printed form to payment of hire "per Calendar Month" and "part of a month" in Line 54 were deleted and substituted by references to payment of hire "per day" and "part of a day". Leggatt, J., held that payment of hire had to be made by reference to elapsed times and not to local times. He said at page 480: "It seems to me that, upon any sensible commercial approach when one is concerned with a time charter, the principal question must be for how long the vessel has been on hire; and that must be the period for which any charterer would expect to have to pay and any owner would expect to be reimbursed. The ingenuity of lawyers enables an argument to be mounted such as would attribute to the parties an intention that the calculation of time should instead be calculated by reference to the local times prevailing. It seems to me that, on looking at a time charter such as this, one would need to find clear language pointing to or affirming that intention before one could safely attribute it to the parties."

The judge considered the various references to time in the charter, including particularly the reference in Line 54 to hire continuing "until the hour of the day of her redelivery", but took the view that this did not refer to the time which would show on a clock at the place of redelivery; it only pointed to the actual time of redelivery. He accordingly concluded that there was nothing in the charter which compelled him to conclude that hire was to be calculated by reference to local times, but on the contrary, the language used, particularly the references to "day" instead of "calendar month", made appropriate the calculation of the actual period that had elapsed, in computing the period of hire.

As the judgment in *The Arctic Skou* was based at least in part on the material changes which the parties had made to the printed form, the decision leaves open the question whether calculations should also be made by reference to elapsed time when the form is unamended. As was pointed out in previous editions of this work, the reference in printed Line 53 to hire being payable "per Calendar Month" does not suggest an intention to insist upon the exact number of elapsed days and hours since this is itself (by contrast with "per 30 days" in the Baltime form) a varying period. But it seems likely that in future cases the courts will adopt the initial premise of Leggatt, J.'s judgment, namely that in the computation of hire under a time charter there is a presumption in favour of elapsed time and that this will prevail unless the words of the charter show a clear intention that local time is preferred.

American Law

The American cases are divided on the question of whether the computation of time under the charter is to be made by reference to local dates and times at the places of delivery and redelivery or by elapsed time.

In *The Fernglen*, 1971 AMC 213 (Arb. at N.Y. 1970), the panel stated that "the accepted method of computing the duration of a charter is the difference in local times" at the port of delivery and at the port of redelivery. "If the Charterer intended to use Greenwich Mean Time as a method of doing this, he should have specifically stated it in the Charter Party." 1971 AMC at 215.

See also *The Bordatxoa*, S.M.A. No. 891 (Arb. at N.Y. 1974), holding that "If the contract does not so specify we believe that under the N.Y. Produce Exchange form the hour of delivery and redelivery should be measured by the local clock"; *The Toxotis*, S.M.A. No. 855 (Arb. at N.Y. 1974); *The Haverton*, S.M.A. No. 743 (Arb. at N.Y. 1973); *The Thunderhead*, S.M.A. No. 617 (Arb. at N.Y. 1971); *The Argo Sky*, S.M.A. No. 627 (Arb. at N.Y. 1971).

This view was rejected, however, in *The North Hills*, 1973 AMC 2318 (Arb. at N.Y. 1972). There the panel held that the fact that the vessel was delivered on the U.S. Pacific Coast and redelivered in Thailand did not entitle the owner to recover hire for an additional 14 hours because of the difference in time zones. According to the panel:

> Let us assume that two vessels were delivered simultaneously to the same Charterer in the same West Coast port, for a voyage across the Pacific with option to be used as a warehouse in the port of delivery. If both vessels were delivered at the same Pacific Standard Time and one vessel only went across the Pacific, the Charterer would have to pay 14 hours more hire for the vessel redelivered in the Far East, had local time been applied at both ends, which would be irrational.
>
> Accordingly, this panel unanimously finds in favor of the Charterer and disallows the claim of the Owner. (1973 AMC at 2320.)

In *The Atlantic Glory*, S.M.A. No. 76 (Arb. at N.Y. 1962), the majority of the panel held that it would be inequitable to use local time since charterer had the right to deduct hire for time the vessel was not at its disposal and the vessel was not at charterer's disposal during the 14–hour time differential between the U.S.—East coast and Japan, the place of redelivery. The majority concluded that "a New York Produce Exchange form of time charter . . . is based on a 'calendar month', is an expression of lapsed time and accordingly should be adjusted for hire payment purposes to the lapsed period of Time Charter and not the local clock". See also *The Doros*, S.M.A. No. 616 (Arb. at N.Y. 1971), where the panel rejected the "local time" approach.

In *Steamship Co. Gorm* v. *United States Shipping Bd. Emergency Fleet Corp.* (*The Knud II*), 285 F. 142 (2d Cir. 1922), the charter contained an express provision for payment of hire for fractional parts of a month, as follows:

> That the said charterers shall pay as hire . . . pro rata for any fractional part of a month (the days to be taken as fractions of a month of 30 days) . . . .

The court held that the quoted provision of the charter provided a workable method of calculating hire for fractional parts of a month, including those periods when the vessel was off-hire. According to the court:

> The theory of a time charter party is that the vessel is maintained by the owner in the service of the charterer, and the charterer pays the owner for the time of such service; if there is any interruption

in such service, then the hire ceases, and the question then becomes: How long was the vessel in the charterer's service; that is, how long was she on hire? This clause provides a method of calculation for any fractional part of the month, and that is applicable to cessation of hire in the middle of the term, as well as to a period of overlap. (285 F. at 144.)

Redelivery

[Clause 4 continued]

"54. . . . hire to continue until the hour of the day of her re-delivery in like good order and condition, ordinary
55. wear and tear excepted, to the Owners (unless lost) at ....
56. .... unless otherwise mutually agreed. Charterers are to give Owners not less than .... days
57. notice of vessels expected date of re-delivery, and probable port."

Redelivery at end of charter period

This is considered under Lines 13 and 14 of the New York Produce form at pages 88 to 96 above.

Hire to continue until . . . re-delivery

For the relevance of these words from Line 54 in cases where the ship is redelivered after the end of the charter period see page 89 above.

Re-delivery in like good order

The charterers will be liable in damages if as a result of a breach of any of their obligations under the charter they redeliver the ship in a worse condition than when delivered, ordinary wear and tear excepted.

The charterers may even be liable where the condition on redelivery has not been caused by a breach of any of their obligations under the charter, but this is doubtful. The doubt stems mainly from the difficulty of fitting a strict or absolute obligation to redeliver the ship in like good order alongside the owners' obligations to maintain the ship in an efficient state throughout the charter period (see page 165 above) and to insure her (see page 441 below).

Scrutton, L.J., in *Limerick* v. *Stott* (1921) 7 Ll.L.Rep. 69 remarked on this difficulty and reserved his view as to whether the obligation to redeliver in like good order could apply at all "to damage not caused in any way by the charterers".

Under the maintenance clause the owners will be obliged to make good much of the damage which occurs during the charter and they will only recover the cost of repairs from the charterers when they can show that the damage was caused by matters for which the charterers are responsible. There are, nevertheless, categories of damage which the owners may not be obliged to repair under the maintenance clause, such as damage caused shortly before the end of the charter and damage which does not affect the efficiency of the ship in the trade in which she is employed.

It seems illogical that the charterers should only have to bear the cost of repairs effected during the currency of the charter if the damage was caused by them, but should have to bear the cost of all residual damage at the end of the charter, whether caused by them or not. Yet this would be the position if the charterers' redelivery obligation were to be construed strictly.

Furthermore the terms as to insurance which require the owners to insure the ship against marine and war risks would have little effect unless they protected the charterers from claims for damage by insured perils not in any way caused by them.

It is suggested therefore that the clauses should be construed so as to restrict the charterers' obligation to redeliver in like good order to damage caused by some breach of their other obligations under the charter or to damage for which they are responsible under the employment and indemnity clause (see page 196 below).

However, Acton, J., adopted a stricter view of the charterers' obligation in the following case. It is a somewhat unsatisfactory case, not only because the umpire's findings of fact were inadequate, but also because it makes no reference to whether the owners were under obligation to insure the ship, as would normally be the position under the Baltime form.

The *Pencarrow* was chartered on the Baltime form for a Baltic round voyage from the United Kingdom. She carried coal out and iron ore back. During the loading and discharging of the ore, damage was caused to the holds. The owners did not prove any negligence by the charterers, but claimed from them for failing to redeliver their ship "in the same good order as when delivered to the charterers (fair wear and tear excepted)". The umpire found that none of this damage was "fair wear and tear" and that the charterers must pay for its repair. Before the High Court, the charterers argued that if, in using the ship in permitted trades and without negligence, damage was caused, such damage could only be "fair wear and tear". Acton, J., rejected this argument and found for the owners. He said:

> "I think that there may be things done to that which is hired or lent, as the case may be, without any negligence, and such as may possibly have been in the contemplation of the parties as things which might perhaps be done by a tenant or a hirer without any actual breach of the contract of letting or hiring, which may still not be within the words 'fair wear and tear'."

Chellew Navigation v. *Appelquist* (1933) 45 Ll.L.Rep. 190.

Redelivery of damaged ship

The charterers may make a valid redelivery of a damaged ship at the end of the charter period, even if that damage has been caused by a breach of their obligations under the charter. They may thus bring to an end their obligation to pay hire. The owners cannot refuse the redelivery and are left to a claim for damages.

The *Wye Crag* was to be redelivered at the end of her time charter "in same good order as when delivered". The charterers were responsible for damage to her bottom and the owners refused to accept redelivery from them until the necessary repairs had been completed. McCardie, J., held that good redelivery could be made and the obligation to pay hire thereby terminated despite the condition of the ship, in respect of which damages were claimable.

Wye Shipping v. *Compagnie du Chemin de Fer Paris-Orleans* (1922) 10 Ll.L.Rep. 85.

The Court of Appeal has decided similarly in the case of a demise chartered ship. Although there were words in the particular charter which might have been thought likely to produce the contrary result, the relevant damage was, in that case, so exceptionally severe that to carry out the repairs would have been futile.

The *Puerto Buitrago* was demise chartered for 17 months. The ship was to be redelivered "in the same good order and condition as on delivery" and it was agreed that "Charterer before redelivery, shall make all such repairs and do all such work . . . at its expense and time". It was, nevertheless, held by the Court of Appeal that after the end of the charter period the charterers might make a good redelivery of the ship in badly damaged condition, subject to the owners' claim for damages. The damage was such that the necessary repairs would have greatly exceeded her value when repaired.

The Puerto Buitrago [1976] 1 Lloyd's Rep. 250.

(For consideration of this case in the context of early redelivery, see page 94 above, and also *The Odenfeld* [1978] 2 Lloyd's Rep. 357 and *The Alaskan Trader* [1983] 2 Lloyd's Rep. 645.)

Ordinary wear and tear

In deciding whether damage is or is not "ordinary wear and tear", the nature of a particular trade for which the ship is chartered is a relevant factor.

The *Empress of Britain* was chartered for troop carrying during the First World War. Clause 5 of the time charter provided: "The basis of payment is to be the cost of replacing the ship in the same state and condition (fair wear and tear and depreciation excepted) as when taken up, . . . reimbursement of any expenses, other than those ordinarily incurred in running the ship, paid by the owners, and a rate of hire sufficient to yield a fair shipping trade profit after allowing for running and establishment expenses and depreciation of ship and engines."

After the war the ship was repaired and refitted as a liner and a dispute arose as to the Crown's liability for part of the cost of that work which was referred to arbitration. The arbitrator disallowed the expenses claimed on the ground that the damage was "ordinarily incurred" while in service as a troop carrier. The House of Lords agreed.

Lord Buckmaster said: "When once it be accepted that the expenses which the respondents seek to recover from the Crown are expenses which naturally fall under the head of wear and tear, and if you consider that phrase in relation to the purpose for which the vessel was used, there only remains the consideration whether Clause 5 is to be interpreted by the consideration of that purpose or no. I find it difficult to see how the charter-party of a vessel which is expressly stated to be hired for the purpose of conveying troops and for similar objects can have that fact excluded from the consideration of what are the expenses which are to be incurred in the course of the running. I entirely agree with the award made by the learned arbitrator."

Canadian Pacific Railway v. *Board of Trade* (1925) 22 Ll.L.Rep. 1.

Redelivery at a place other than that agreed

The charterers must redeliver the ship at the port or place named in Lines 55 and 56 of the New York Produce form or Clause 7 of the Baltime form. If in breach of this obligation the charterers make redelivery elsewhere the owners may claim damages, which will usually be based on the net profit that they would have made from a notional voyage ordered by the charterers to bring the ship to the named port or place, less the net profit earned by alternative employment during the period of that notional voyage: see *The Bunga Kenanga* [1981] 1 Lloyd's Rep. 518, and *The Rijn* [1981] 2 Lloyd's Rep. 267. In the latter case, Mustill, J., said, at page 270, that the owner "has a contractual right to have the ship kept in employment at the charter rate of hire until the service is completed. This does not happen until the ship reaches the redelivery range, and the voyage to that range forms part of the chartered service. In a case such as the present, therefore, the tender is not only in the wrong place but also at the wrong time; and full compensation for the breach requires the charterer to restore to the owner the hire which he would have earned if the voyage had in fact been performed." In that case redelivery was to be at a range of Far East ports and Mustill, J., held that for the purpose of assessing damages the notional final voyage should be that which would reduce those damages to the minimum, namely a voyage in ballast to the nearest safe port in the redelivery range.

American Law

Redelivery in like good order

The Jaramar, 1969 AMC 354 (Arb. at N.Y. 1969), concerned the charterer's responsibility under the New York Produce charter form to redeliver the vessel "in like good order and condition . . . ". A joint survey held on delivery established that "all cargo compartments were swept clean". On redelivery, however, a survey showed that the holds were unswept. The owner therefore ordered the holds cleaned, and commenced an arbitration proceeding to recover the cost of and an allowance for the time required for the cleaning. The charterer did not contest its liability for the cleaning costs. The panel held that the owner also was entitled to hire until the vessel was cleaned and in like good order and condition as upon delivery.

Where the necessity for fumigation arises out of the ship's service under the charter, the charterer is bound to bear the cost and the loss of time. See *Dampskibs* v. *Munson Line S.S. Co.*, 20 F.2d 345 (2d Cir. 1927); *The Muggenburg*, S.M.A. No. 898 (Arb. at N.Y. 1974), holding the charterer liable for fumigation expenses and delay attributable to the inherent vice of grain cargo; *The Ellen Klautschke*, S.M.A. No. 361 (Arb. at N.Y. 1965), holding that where the charterer redelivered after trading in tropical ports without fumigating the vessel and the New Orleans Board of Trade found live infestation on board, the owner was entitled to hire until the fumigation was completed plus the expense of the fumigation.

Where the charterer retendered the vessel to the owner with unrepaired structural damages, it was held that the owner could not refuse to accept redelivery "unless the damages [were] such as to make the vessel unseaworthy and thereby deprive the Owner of the immediate use of his ship". *The Chris*, S.M.A. No. 199 (Arb. at N.Y. 1958).

The charterer's duty to redeliver the vessel in "like good order and condition" does not encompass damage to the vessel resulting from mutually excepted causes such as those listed in Clause 16 of the New York Produce form. See, e.g., *The Lysland*, S.M.A. No. 419 (Arb. at N.Y. 1969), denying the owner's claim for hull damage caused by negligent navigation; and *The Napier*, S.M.A. No. 525 (Arb. at N.Y. 1970), holding that the charterer was not liable for damage resulting from an explosion caused by crew negligence.

The owner need not immediately carry out repairs after redelivery in order to have standing to recover damages from the charterer under Clause 4. In *The Prometheus*, S.M.A. No. 1154 (Arb. at N.Y. 1977), the charterer was held liable for the established cost of deferred repairs where the ship was not redelivered in like good order and condition as required by Clause 4. If the damages are not repaired, the method usually used to compute the owner's loss is to determine the diminution of the vessel's value, that is, to compare her value in sound condition with her value in damaged condition. *The Arizona*, S.M.A. No. 1259 (Arb. at N.Y. 1978).

In *The Theofilos J. Vatis*, S.M.A. No. 1994 (Arb. at N.Y. 1984), a hard film of cement had coated the vessel's cargo holds after having carried warm bulk cement. The charterer was held to have failed to redeliver in "like good order and condition, ordinary wear and tear excepted." The panel ruled, however, that the cleaning and repairing had left the holds in a better condition than required under the charter. The panel thus awarded owner the cost of cleaning and repairing the holds, less an amount representing the increase in value.

Ordinary wear and tear excepted

"Ordinary wear and tear" was defined in *Moran Towing Co.* v. *Gammino Constr. Co.*, 363 F.2d 108, 1966 AMC 2263, 2271–72 (5th Cir. 1966), in the following manner:

Wear and tear means normal depreciation. . . . No doubt what is "normal" must be responsive to practices in the service for which the vessel is intended . . . The effects of negligence are not wear and tear and they do not become wear and tear merely because they may be anticipated.

In *The Managua*, S.M.A. No. 352 (Arb. at N.Y. 1966), the panel stated:

It is well known, as confirmed by the testimony of two marine surveyors, that scratches, nicks, gouges, dents, bendings and shearings of the metal parts of a ship's holds, hatches and decks that are inherent in the usual method of discharge of most bulk cargoes by grab buckets, bulldozers, payloaders or other mechanical equipment, but which, when not major, do not affect the strength or function of the structural members of a ship's holds, hatches, bulkheads and decks, . . . are considered "normal wear and tear".

A similar approach was taken in *Neubros Corp.* v. *Northwestern Nat. Ins. Co.*, 359 F.Supp. 310, 320 (E.D.N.Y. 1972), holding that liability for damage to the vessel would be imposed on the charterer unless he could show that the damage resulted despite the exercise of due care on his part.

Similarly, in *Hudson Valley Light Weight Aggregate Corp.* v. *Windsor Bldg. & Supply Co.*, 446 F.2d 750 (2d Cir. 1971), a barge operating under a demise charter sustained damages while carrying a cargo of heavy aggregate. The court held that the owner makes out a *prima facie* case of negligence against the charterer when it shows that the barge was delivered in good condition and returned in damaged condition. The charterer must then come forward with proof that the accident occurred without any negligence on its part, and that it exercised due care in the handling of the barge. See also *B.H. Inc.* v. *Anthony M. Meyerskin Inc.* 149 F.Supp. 219 (E.D.N.Y. 1957); *The G.G. Post*, 64 F.Supp. 191, 195 (W.D.N.Y. 1945); *Wilson Shipping Corp. Ltd.* v. *Tamarack Corp.*, S.M.A. No. 645 (Arb. at N.Y. 1971); *The Elna II*, S.M.A. No. 576 (Arb. at N.Y. 1957); *The Theokeetor*, S.M.A. No. 604 (Arb. at N.Y.); *The North Marchioness*, S.M.A. No. 77 (Arb. at N.Y. 1962); *The Stavros Commantaros*, 1961 AMC 370 (Arb. at N.Y. 1961).

The phrase "ordinary wear and tear excepted" has been held not to apply to the cleanliness of the vessel. *The Argo Sky*, S.M.A. No. 627 (Arb. at N.Y. 1971).

Redelivery at a place other than that agreed

The charterer must redeliver the vessel at the specific place or within the range stated in the charter. See *The Trafalgar*, 1938 AMC 463 (Arb. at N.Y. 1938), holding that redelivery in Limerick, Ireland, was a violation of the charterer's duty to redeliver at a safe port in the United Kingdom. According to the panel, Irish Free State ports were not part of the United Kingdom. See also *The Severoles*, 1935 AMC 1135 (Arb. at N.Y. 1935) and *The Gerdt Oldendorff*, S.M.A. No. 1981 (Arb. at N.Y. 1984).

A redelivery at any place other than that stated in the charter would give the owner the right to recover damages caused by the charterer's breach. The damages would consist of the owner's lost profits during a hypothetical voyage to the required place of redelivery. The owner, of course, remains under a duty to mitigate damages. If alternative employment is found during the period the hypothetical voyage would require, the owner's damages would be reduced to the extent of its earnings under the alternative employment.

In *The New York Getty*, S.M.A. No. 2200 (Arb. at N.Y. 1986), although the charter provided for redelivery at a U.S. Gulf port, redelivery was accepted by owner when the vessel entered a drydock for repairs at Jacksonville. Charterer sought a refund of hire it had paid in advance on the assumption that the vessel would redeliver at a U.S. Gulf port. The panel held that charterer was entitled to a refund:

> When a charterer is prepared to redeliver at the place stipulated in the charter but the owner elects to take delivery at a place short of the stipulated place, charterer is not required to pay additional hire or for additional fuel beyond the place where the actual redelivery occurs, absent a special agreement to the contrary.

See discussion above at page 103.

Dunnage

In *The Milly Gregos*, S.M.A. No. 2190 (Arb. at N.Y. 1986), charterer redelivered the vessel with substantial quantities of dunnage on board after the discharge of its last cargo. Owner claimed for hire and expenses incurred in removing the dunnage. The charter contained a clause which permitted the charterer to redeliver the vessel with unclean holds and pay a lump sum in lieu of hold cleaning. The panel ruled, however, that this clause did not encompass the cost of removing substantial quantities of dunnage. The quantity left on board was on the order of 250/300 tons of dunnage and the panel ruled that this was an unreasonable amount to be left on board. It would seem to follow from the panel's decision that very minor quantities of dunnage left on board would have been covered by the lump sum provision for hold cleaning. The panel awarded owner damages, including loss of hire for the time required to clean the holds as well as fuel consumed, and other disposal expenses.

Payment of Hire and Withdrawal

"58 5. Payment of said hire to be made in New York in cash in United States Currency, semi-monthly in advance, and for the last half month or
59. part of same the approximate amount of hire, and should same not cover the actual time, hire is to be paid for the balance day by day, as it becomes
60. due, if so required by Owners, unless bank guarantee or deposit is made by the Charterers, otherwise failing the punctual and regular payment of the
61. hire, or bank guarantee, or on any breach of this Charter Party, the Owners shall be at liberty to withdraw the vessel from the service of the Char-
62. terers, without prejudice to any claim they (the Owners) may otherwise have on the Charterers."

General

The standard forms of time charter recognise the importance to the owners of the regular receipt of hire by the inclusion of a provision such as that in Lines 60 to 62 of the New York Produce form, which allows the owners to terminate the charter altogether should the charterers fail to pay the hire due on or before each appropriate date.

In *Tankexpress* v. *Compagnie Financière Belge des Pétroles* (1948) 82 Ll.L.Rep. 43, Lord Wright said: "The importance of this advance payment to be made by the charterers, is that it is the substance of the consideration given to the shipowner for the use and service of the ship and crew which the shipowner agrees to give. He is entitled to have the periodical payment as stipulated in advance of his performance so long as the charterparty continues. Hence the stringency of his right to cancel."

Were it not for this withdrawal clause the owners would not usually have such a right, for at common law the mere lateness of a payment of hire would entitle the owners to damages but would not necessarily allow them to withdraw: only if in all the circumstances the conduct of the charterers showed unwillingness or inability to pay, or if otherwise the failure to make timely payment amounted to a repudiation of the charter could the owners bring the charter to an end (see page 218 below). In effect the withdrawal clause confers on the owners a contractual option to end the charter in the circumstances described. Whether it confers more than a contractual option and entitles the owners to treat a failure to pay hire punctually as a breach of condition (which may affect the question of damages), is a matter on which there is conflicting authority: see page 218 below. But whatever may be the legal effect of the exercise of the right of withdrawal, the owners need show no more, in order to exercise that right, than that the hire due has not been paid on or before the appropriate date; they need not concern themselves with the reasons for the charterers' failure to pay on time, see page 205 below.

Cash

"Cash" in this context includes types of payment which have become in commercial usage the equivalent of cash, being irrevocable and giving to the owners the unconditional and immediate use of the hire. It includes inter bank transfers and banker's drafts and also "banker's payment slips" as used in *The Georgios C.* [1971] 1 Lloyd's Rep. 7. It probably also includes "payment orders" under the London Currency Settlement Scheme: see *The Laconia* [1977] 1 Lloyd's Rep. 315.

In *The Brimnes* [1972] 2 Lloyd's Rep. 465, at page 476, Brandon, J., said regarding the meaning of the words "payment . . . in cash": "In my view these words must be interpreted against the background of modern commercial practice. So interpreted it seems to me that they cannot mean only payment in dollar bills or other legal tender of the U.S. They must, as the shipowners contend, have a wider meaning, comprehending any commercially-recognised method of transferring funds, the result of which is to give the transferee the unconditional right to the immediate use of the funds transferred."

Edmund Davies, L.J., in the Court of Appeal [1974] 2 Lloyd's Rep. 241, at page 248, specifically agreed with that definition. (See also the judgment of Lawton, L.J., in *The Laconia* [1976] 1 Lloyd's Rep. 395, at page 402.)

The owners' right to the immediate use of the funds transferred must be "unconditional".

The *Chikuma* was chartered on the New York Produce form, hire being payable to her owners' bank in Genoa. A monthly payment of hire was paid to that bank on the due date; but the paying bank, which was also situated in Genoa, included in its telex transfer a "value date" four days ahead. The effect of this stipulation in Italian banking practice was that the owners could have withdrawn the funds from their bank at once but could have then been obliged to pay interest on the funds from then until the "value date". The owners withdrew their ship under Clause 5.

The House of Lords, reversing the Court of Appeal and restoring the decision of Robert Goff, J., held that the owners were entitled to withdraw; the payment made did not amount to "cash" because the liability to pay interest on the funds transferred prevented the owners from having an "unconditional" right to their immediate use. Lord Bridge referred to the statement of Brandon, J., in *The Brimnes*, above, and added: "The underlying concept is surely this, that when payment is made to a bank otherwise than literally in cash, i.e., in dollar bills or other legal tender (which no one expects), there is no 'payment in cash' within the meaning of clause 5 unless what the creditor receives is the equivalent of cash, or as good as cash . . . The book entry made by the owners' bank on Jan. 22 in the owners' account was clearly not the equivalent of cash . . . In substance it was the equivalent of an overdraft facility which the bank was bound to make available."

The Chikuma [1981] 1 Lloyd's Rep. 371.

Banker's drafts and payment orders

Where the charterers' bank delivers to the owners' bank a banker's draft or equivalent document, payment under the charter is complete at the time of such delivery: see *The Brimnes* [1974] 2 Lloyd's Rep. 241. This is so despite the fact that there will be a period of internal processing before the bank will actually credit the owners' account. Lord Salmon pointed out in *The Laconia* [1977] 1 Lloyd's Rep. 315 that a certain amount of processing would be needed before a credit was raised in an owner's account even where the charterers paid in cash.

The position is probably the same when the charterers' bank delivers to the owners' bank a "payment order" under the London Currency Settlement Scheme. This is so even though the processing work may mean that the owners' account will not be credited until up to about 24 hours after receipt of the "payment order" by their bank. This question arose in *The Laconia*, but the House of Lords disposed of that case on other grounds. There the hire was to be paid "to owners . . . into their account with First National City

Bank of New York, 34, Moorgate, London, E.C.2 to the credit of O.F.C. Account No. 705586". Of the three members of the House of Lords who expressed tentative opinions on the point two considered that payment was effective upon delivery of the "payment order" to the owners' bank. This accorded with the decision on this point of the Court of Appeal. Lord Salmon expressed the view that, "there is no real difference between a payment in dollar bills and a payment by payment orders which in the banking world are generally regarded and accepted as cash". Lord Russell said: "I would as at present advised incline to the view that, a payment order being as between the banks the equivalent of cash—meaning I take it irrevocable and 'good'—it should suffice for punctual payment that such cash equivalent be tendered in due time to the nominated bank to be credited to the named account: this was the method of payment laid down: you cannot pay 'into' an account, whether you are tendering cash or its equivalent." Lord Fraser expressed the contrary view, that payment should be made in sufficient time to enable the owners' account to be credited by the due date.

It is suggested that it is in the interest of reasonable commercial certainty that the view of the majority in the House of Lords should be followed. See also the judgments of Lord Denning, M.R., and Lawton, L.J., in the Court of Appeal in *The Laconia*, and the judgment of Lloyd, J., in *The Afovos* [1980] 2 Lloyd's Rep. 469.

Telex transfers

It was pointed out by Megaw, L.J., in *The Brimnes* [1974] 2 Lloyd's Rep. 241, at page 257, that "there is no useful analogy between, on the one hand, a payment made by delivery of cash or a cheque (where a cheque is a permissible method of payment) and, on the other hand, telex instructions to pay . . . The receipt of a cheque is not the receipt of mere instructions. It is the receipt of an instrument—a chose in action—which has an inherent value, because the holder of it obtains, by virtue of his holding of the document, a legal right to a sum of money, which right he can enforce, if necessary by action. The receipt of a telex containing instructions to transfer funds from one account into another account confers on the holder of the telex no such right. It is instructions to pay, not a payment."

The House of Lords in *The Afovos* [1983] 1 Lloyd's Rep. 335, declined to decide at what stage payment was to be regarded as made when payment was effected by means of a telex transfer. Lord Diplock merely observed (at page 342) that it was likely to depend in most cases upon the proof of the practice of bankers current at the time in question, rather than upon any determination of the question as a matter of law.

In *The Brimnes*, where the charterers' bank had its own account with the payee bank named in the charter and instructed that bank to transfer the relevant amount from its own account to the account of the owners, it was held by the Court of Appeal that payment as required by the charter—"in cash in United States currency to Morgan Guaranty Trust Co. of New York, . . . for the credit of the account for" the owners—was not made at the time of the telex instructing Morgan Guaranty to transfer from the one account to the other but only when, during their processing of that telex, Morgan Guaranty took an effective decision to credit the owners' account. (See also *The Zographia M* [1976] 2 Lloyd's Rep. 382.)

In *The Afovos* [1980] 2 Lloyd's Rep. 469, Lloyd, J., said, at first instance: "I would hold that when payment is made by telex transfer from one bank to another, for the account of a customer, the payment is complete when the telex is received and tested by the receiving bank; so that if the owners were to make an enquiry at their bank they would be told, 'Yes, the money has arrived for your account'. It is unnecessary that the funds should have been credited to the owners' account. Still less is it necessary that the owners should have been in a position to transfer the funds out of the account. It is enough that the funds should have been received by the bank *for* the owners' account." In that case the charter provided that hire was to be paid "in London, to the First National Bank of Chicago . . . for the credit of (the owners') account". Evidence was given as to the procedure followed by the bank on receipt of an incoming telex payment, but it does not appear from the judgment whether the completion of the testing of the incoming telex was coincident with a decision to credit the payee's account or whether it preceded such a decision.

Where the owners' bank has an account with the charterers' bank payment under the charter will not be complete until the owners' bank has received notice that its account with the charterers' bank has been credited in this way.

The hire for the *Effy* was payable "to Messrs. A. M. Nomikos, U.S. dollar account No. 7450 held by Messrs. Williams Deacon's Bank Ltd., 22 St. Mary Axe, London E.C.3". In accordance with their usual practice the charterers paid a particular instalment of hire by instructing an Israeli bank to transfer the necessary funds and to ensure these reached the owners' bank by the due day which was a Sunday. This bank in turn instructed a New York bank in similar terms. The New York bank, acting in accordance with the practice in New York, waited until the Monday, and they then credited the account of Williams Deacon's Bank with them for the account of the owners. Their cabled advice of this credit did not reach Williams Deacon's Bank until early on the Tuesday morning. Mocatta, J., held that the hire had not been paid before the cable arrived at Williams Deacon's Bank. It was not until after the receipt of the cable that the owners could have obtained confirmation from their bank that the credit had been set up in New York and without that confirmation no drawing upon the hire could have been made by the owners. Neither payment nor tender had been effected before receipt of that cable.

The Effy [1972] 1 Lloyd's Rep. 18.

Variation of method of payment, agreed by owners

For a discussion of the situation where a particular method of payment has been approved by the owners and use of this method leads to payment being late, see page 206 below.

Payment of less than amount due

The right of the owners to withdraw arises not only when no hire is paid or when hire is paid late. It also arises when a timely payment has been made, but for less than the amount due, and the outstanding balance is not paid by or on the due date. See *The Agios Giorgis* [1976] 2 Lloyd's Rep. 192 and *The Mihalios Xilas*, below; in both cases it was conceded by counsel for the charterers that a timely but insufficient payment gave rise to the right to withdraw.

The *Mihalios Xilas* was chartered on the Baltime form. Additional Clause 39 provided for the payment of hire monthly and for "the last month's hire to be estimated and paid in advance, less bunker cost and Owners' disbursements and other items of Owners' liability up to such time as vessel is expected to be re-delivered . . . ". Hire for the ninth month was due on 22 March. On 21 March the charterers paid considerably less than a full month's hire and their agents explained to the owners that the shortfall was because the charterers were deducting in respect of certain advances and estimated bunkers and disbursements on redelivery, showing that they regarded this hire payment as the last under the charter. In arbitration the umpire found that the charterers' estimate that the ship would be redelivered at the end of the ninth month was not reasonable, also that the amount deducted was in any event unreasonable and excessive.

It was accepted before Kerr, J., that in these circumstances the owners were entitled to withdraw. The judge said: "In the result there was accordingly an underpayment by the charterers of the ninth month's hire, and it was not disputed that on the facts found this constituted a 'default of payment' for the purposes of the second paragraph of cl. 6 containing the right to withdraw the vessel."

(The question for decision by the courts, which eventually reached the House of Lords, was whether the owners had subsequently waived their right to withdraw; as to which see page 214 below.)

The Mihalios Xilas [1976] 2 Lloyd's Rep. 697, [1978] 2 Lloyd's Rep. 397 and [1979] 2 Lloyd's Rep. 303. (See also *The Lutetian* [1982] 2 Lloyd's Rep. 140, at page 154.)

Payment of hire when use of ship being withheld

If a periodic payment of hire falls due at a time when the use of the ship is being withheld, it seems that the charterers will still be bound to pay the hire due, subject only to deduction of (*a*) any amounts for which the charter specifically provides, including off-hire, and (*b*) any claim for wrongful withholding of the use of the ship in respect of a period wholly before the date on which the hire is due.

In *Tankexpress* v. *Compagnie Financière Belge des Pétroles* (1946) 79 Ll.L.Rep. 451, Atkinson, J., held that the charterers were not in breach of charter in failing to make a particular payment of hire because on the due date the master was, on the owners' orders, wrongfully refusing to obey their instructions to load the ship. Although the House of Lords decided the case on other grounds (1948) 82 Ll.L.Rep. 43, both Lord Porter and Lord du Parcq made comments, *obiter*, suggesting that Atkinson, J., was in error and that the obligation to pay hire continued (unless of course the conduct of the owners amounted to a repudiation of the whole contract and the charterers decided to accept it and treat the contract as discharged). Lord Porter said that, although he did not think it necessary to reach a conclusion on the point, " . . . I doubt whether there is any half-way house between acceptance of the repudiation and continuance of the charter with the consequent obligation to continue to pay hire . . . ". Lord du Parcq said " . . . I have not been persuaded that a charterer who has agreed to pay a month's hire in advance is absolved from making the payment if, although the owners have not sought to repudiate the contract, the ship is not in fact at the disposal of the charterer for some days immediately before and after the first day of the month of hire".

See also *The Charalambos N. Pateras* [1971] 2 Lloyd's Rep. 42, and the principle stated by MacKinnon, L.J., in *Halcyon Steamship* v. *Continental Grain* (1943) 75 Ll.L.Rep. 80, at page 84, set out at page 200 below.

Payment of hire when ship off-hire on due date

In *The Lutetian* [1982] 2 Lloyd's Rep. 140, Bingham, J., held that under the New York Produce form the charterers were not obliged to pay an instalment of hire on the due date if the ship was off-hire at that time, as Clause 15 provided that when time was lost from the listed causes "the payment of hire shall cease". He accepted the contention that in such circumstances the charterers' obligation to make payment of the next monthly instalment of hire in advance was suspended until immediately before the vessel was again at the service of the charterers. This decision seems difficult to reconcile with the general principle set out at the start of this chapter, and may produce serious uncertainty in practice. It is suggested that it be treated with caution pending consideration by higher courts.

Deductions from hire permitted by the terms of the charter

The charterers may deduct from payments of hire those amounts specifically permitted by the terms of the charter. Thus advances for ship's disbursements under Lines 65 and 66 of the New York Produce form "shall be deducted from the hire"; see the judgment of Donaldson, J., in *Seven Seas* v. *Atlantic* [1975] 2 Lloyd's Rep. 188. The same is provided in Lines 99 to 101 of that form in respect of time lost, fuel consumed and expenses incurred as a result of a reduction in speed caused by a defect in or breakdown of the ship's hull, machinery or equipment. It is not stated so clearly that a deduction is permitted in respect of off-hire claims under Lines 97 to 99 of Clause 15 of the New York Produce form, where the relevant words are "the payment of hire shall cease for the time thereby lost". But in *The Lutetian* [1982] 2 Lloyd's Rep. 140, 149, both counsel and the court accepted that it was permissible for hire paid in respect of a past period of off-hire to be deducted from the next monthly hire payment. It was also decided by the Court of Appeal in *The Nanfri*, below, that off-hire under the Baltime Clause 11 (A) ("no hire to be paid in respect of any time lost thereby . . . Any hire paid in advance to be adjusted accordingly") could be deducted from a subsequent hire payment. No deduction is, however, permitted in respect of an anticipated period of off-hire: see *The Lutetian* above. The cost of fuel used for domestic consumption under Lines 133 and 134 of the New York Produce form may also be deducted from hire; as to which see the judgment of Donaldson, J., in *Seven Seas* v. *Atlantic* [1975] 2 Lloyd's Rep. 188.

Permitted deductions may be made from a subsequent hire payment even though the amount of the deduction has not previously been determined by arbitrators or agreed with the owners. An argument by owners to the contrary was rejected by Kerr, J., and the Court of Appeal in *The Nanfri*, below. Lord Denning, M.R., said: "There is no doubt that the charterer can make the deduction, but the question is when? Have they to be agreed or established before he can make the deduction? There is no authority that I know to that effect. It seems to me that he is entitled to quantify his loss by a reasonable assessment made in good faith—and deduct the sum so quantified from the hire." See also *The Kostas Melas* [1981] 1 Lloyd's Rep. 18 at page 25.

In November 1974 the *Nanfri*, *Benfri*, and *Lorfri* were fixed to the same charterers by three separate but virtually identical Baltime charters for about six years. To the usual Baltime off-hire Clause 11 (A) and 11 (B), was added, as 11 (C), part of the New York Produce form off-hire clause reading "If upon the voyage the speed is reduced by defect in . . . machinery . . . the time so lost and the cost of any extra fuel consumed in consequence thereof . . . to be deducted from hire". In July and September 1977 the charterers made deductions from hire payments under each of the charters. They also gave notice that under Clause 11 (C) they intended to deduct $47,122 from the hire due for the *Nanfri* on 1 October 1977, in respect of an alleged reduction in her speed following an engine breakdown on a voyage in 1975. The owners protested and gave notice of arbitration in respect of some of the deductions that had been made and on the question whether the charterers had the right unilaterally to deduct from hire sums not previously agreed as valid.

The case developed and reached the House of Lords on different issues, which are considered at page 268 below. The House of Lords did not find it necessary to comment on the following points, but in the Court of Appeal:

(a) all members of the court were unanimous in their view that valid claims under Clause 11(A) and (C) could be deducted from subsequent hire payments;

(b) Lord Denning, M.R., and Goff, L.J. (with Cumming-Bruce, L.J., dissenting) said that the charterers could also deduct from hire their claim for damages when the owners had in breach of charter deprived them for a period of the use of the ship either in whole or in part;

(c) as to the amounts that the charterers might deduct in respect of (a) and (b) above, Lord Denning, M.R., held these to be "sums quantified by a reasonable assessment made in good faith", but Goff, L.J.'s judgment proceeded on a different basis, namely that in deciding to make a deduction the charterers act at their peril.

The Nanfri [1978] 1 Lloyd's Rep. 581, [1978] 2 Lloyd's Rep. 132 (C.A.) and [1979] 1 Lloyd's Rep. 201 (H.L.).

Deductions from hire of claims for damages: equitable set off

General

The balance of authority is now in favour of the view that the charterers may deduct from hire a claim for damages in respect of a period during which the owners have in breach of charter deprived the charterers of the use of the ship in whole or in part. Claims which can be so set off were described by Lord Denning, M.R., in *The Nanfri* [1978] 2 Lloyd's Rep. 132, at page 140, as those which "arise out of the same transaction or are closely connected with it", and "which go directly to impeach the plaintiff's demands, that is, so closely connected with his demands that it would be manifestly unjust to allow him to enforce them without taking into account the cross-claim". It is not yet clear exactly which types of claim fall within this concept, although a breach of the charter speed warranty has been held to do so (*The Chrysovalandou Dyo* [1981] 1 Lloyd's Rep. 159) as has a failure by the owners to load a full cargo (*The Teno* [1977] 2 Lloyd's Rep. 289), whereas claims such as those in respect of damage to cargo may not be deducted (*The Nanfri* [1978] 2 Lloyd's Rep. 132, at page 141). This problem is considered more fully in the paragraphs which follow.

Deprivation of the use of the ship

The law on this subject is still not fully developed. Until a case that turns on this concept reaches the House of Lords it seems best to approach the subject on an historical basis.

In *Naxos Shipping* v. *Thegra Shipping (The Corfu Island)* (1973), an unreported case, Ackner, J., held that charterers were entitled to deduct from hire a claim in respect of the alleged breach of a speed warranty. In *Seven Seas* v. *Atlantic Shipping* [1975] 2 Lloyd's Rep. 188, Donaldson, J., held that there was no general right of set off in respect of claims for damages, there being no reason to treat hire differently from freight, against which no such right to set off is allowed (see *The Brede* [1973] 2 Lloyd's Rep. 333, *The Aries* [1977] 1 Lloyd's Rep. 334 and *The Dominique* [1989] 1 Lloyd's Rep. 431). He did, however, have to reconcile with this view the following remarks made by MacKinnon, L.J., in *Halcyon Steamship* v. *Continental Grain* (1943) 75 Ll.L.Rep. 80, at page 84: "It was pointed out in a recent case in this Court that under such a time charter the charterers can only be relieved from the continuous payment of the agreed hire in two events: firstly, if the cesser of hire clause applies to the facts, and, secondly, if they can set off or counter-claim hire for a certain time as the whole or part of their claim for damages caused to them by a breach on the part of the shipowner of his duties under the charter-party." (The recent case to which MacKinnon, L.J., was referring was probably *Sea &*

Land Securities v. *William Dickinson* (1942) 72 Ll.L.Rep. 159.) Donaldson, J., emphasised the words referring to hire "for a certain time" in the quoted passage, and said that the exception seemed to be limited to a case in which a specific period of time is wholly lost.

Parker, J., faced with these decisions, held in *The Teno* [1977] 2 Lloyd's Rep. 289 that there was a right to set off against hire under a charter on the Baltime form a claim for damages in respect of a period when the use of the ship was wholly or partially withheld. In that case Parker, J., was dealing with a defence raised by the charterers to a claim by the owners for hire, arising out of the failure of the ship to load a full cargo. He left undecided the question whether the right of set off extended to other claims, such as claims for damage to cargo. In support of his decision he relied on statements in *Sea & Land Securities* v. *William Dickinson* (1941) 71 Ll.L.Rep. 166 and (1942) 72 Ll.L.Rep. 159 (C.A.), *Halcyon Steamship* v. *Continental Grain* (1943) 75 Ll.L.Rep. 80 and *The Charalambos N. Pateras* [1971] 2 Lloyd's Rep. 42 and said: "The foregoing cases show a continuous recognition since 1941 of a right to set off against a claim for time charter hire damages for breach of contract where, at any rate, the breach consists in wrongful withdrawal of the vessel for a certain time."

Parker, J., then considered the nature of the equitable right of set off and concluded that it should cover not only total but also partial withdrawal of the use of the ship. Referring to *Hanak* v. *Green* [1958] 2 Q.B. 9, he continued: "From that judgment I conclude that where the cross claim not only arises out of the same contract as the claim but is so directly connected with it that it would be manifestly unjust to allow the claimant to recover without taking into account the cross claim there is a right of set off in equity of an unliquidated claim. These conditions are clearly satisfied where an owner claims hire in respect of a period in which he has not provided his ship at all. They are in my judgment equally satisfied when, as here, he claims hire in respect of a period when, in breach of contract, he has provided less than full use of the vessel. It may be that they are not satisfied where the cross claim is of an entirely different nature e.g. for damage to cargo but this does not arise for decision now."

In *The Nanfri* [1978] 1 Lloyd's Rep. 581 (see page 199 above) Kerr, J., was asked by counsel to state the law as it had been generally understood by commercial lawyers before the recent series of cases ending with *The Teno*. He said that it had generally been thought that there was no right to set off any cross claim against voyage charter freight or against time charter hire, particularly as the express provisions in most time charters that certain specified items could be deducted from hire were taken to be exhaustive. He continued: "If a claim or cross-claim did not fall within them [the expressly permitted deductions], then the general view was that hire was payable continuously and in full; it could only be raised by way of a separate cross-claim in debt or damages. The continuity and security of payments of hire, subject to the expressly permitted deductions, were considered the essential safeguards of the owners under time charters, in the same way as in relation to freight under voyage charters. However, while I feel confident that this was generally held view, I am in no way impugning the conclusion reached in *The Teno*, particulary since the decision of the House of Lords in *Gilbert-Ash (Northern) Ltd.* v. *Modern Engineering (Bristol) Ltd.* [1974] A.C. 689."

When *The Nanfri* came before the Court of Appeal ([1978] 2 Lloyd's Rep. 132) Lord Denning, M.R., and Goff, L.J., held that the judgment of Parker, J., in *The Teno* was correct and that the charterers could deduct where the owners had wrongfully deprived them of the use of the ship in whole or in part. Cumming-Bruce, L.J., delivered a dissenting judgment on this point. Lord Denning, M.R., said that "when the shipowner is guilty of a breach of contract which deprives the time charterer of part of the consideration for which the hire has been paid in advance, the charterer can deduct an equivalent amount of the hire falling due for the next month . . . In my opinion therefore in a time charter, if the shipowner wrongly and in breach of contract deprives the charterer for a time of the use of the vessel, the charterer can deduct a sum equivalent to the hire for the time so lost". This case was decided in the House of Lords on other grounds and without any guidance on this topic.

In *The Chrysovalandou Dyo* [1981] 1 Lloyd's Rep. 159, Mocatta, J., allowed a deduction from hire for a failure to comply with the speed warranty in the charter on the basis of the right of equitable set off. See also the judgment of Robert Goff, J., in *The Kostas Melas* [1981] 1 Lloyd's Rep.18.

Hobhouse, J., in *The Leon* [1985] 2 Lloyd's Rep. 470, having cited the previous authorities, said, at page 475: "In fields of commercial law certainty of contractual rights and remedies is of the greatest importance. The right to be paid time charter hire and the right to withhold payment are particularly clear examples where such certainty of the law must exist. The Court of Appeal has formulated a simple rule which represents the relevant application of the underlying principle. If the formulation is to be redrawn a better case would have to be made out than has been made before me and it is not appropriate for a Court of first instance to undertake that task . . . In the present context there is a series of precedents and we must accept their guidance".

Other claims of the charterers

In his judgment in *The Nanfri* (above) Lord Denning, M.R., said that the right to set off was confined "to cases when the shipowner has wrongly deprived the charterer of the use of the vessel or has prejudiced him in the use of it". He continued: "I would not extend it to other breaches or default of the shipowner, such as damage to cargo arising from the negligence of the crew." Goff, L.J., agreed with the exclusion of claims for damage to cargo. In an unreported judgment from 1979, *The Lok Manya*, Mustill, J., followed this authority in denying the right to set off a cargo damage claim, and in so doing treated the cost of dumping the damaged cargo at sea and the three days used in that operation as an integral part of the cargo damage claim: in the Court of Appeal in 1980, Lord Denning, M.R., *obiter*, cast doubt on the consequent denial of the right to set off the three days' wasted hire.

In *The Aliakmon Progress* [1978] 2 Lloyd's Rep. 499 (see page 429 below) the ship had been damaged by contact with a quay allegedly caused by negligence of her crew; the necessary repairs caused her to lose an anticipated cargo and she had to wait 39 days for another. Lord Denning, M.R., said: "I doubt whether any such claims would be admissible as equitable set off. Equitable set off, as we indicated in those cases [*The Nanfri*, above], is only available where the charterers have been deprived of the use of the ship by the fault of the owner. Here the charterers had the use of the ship, but could not get a cargo." (In any event, the charterers' claim was held invalid by the Court of Appeal because the owners could rely on a defence under the U.S. Carriage of Goods by Sea Act: see page 426 below.)

Hobhouse, J., in *The Leon* [1985] 2 Lloyd's Rep. 470, rejected a claim that a right to equitable set off arose from breaches in respect of (*a*) a failure to keep accurate logs, (*b*) the master being a party to the creation of false documentation by bunker suppliers and (*c*) a breach of duty by the owners as bailee of the charterers' bunkers. He said of these breaches, at page 474: "They do not relate to the use of the vessel. There is no suggestion that in the present case the charterers ever directly or indirectly lost even a minute of the ship's time as a result of any of these breaches nor is there any suggestion that at any time by reason of any of the breaches the whole reach of the vessel's holds, etc., were not at charterers' disposal or that the master did not prosecute the voyages with despatch or comply with the order of the charterers as regards the vessel's employment."

The amount that the charterers may deduct

Assuming that the charterers have the right to make a deduction, either because the charter expressly allows this (see page 199 above) or because of an equitable right to set off (see page 200 above), the question arises how much they may deduct. Do the charterers calculate the amount of a deduction at their peril, so that the owners may withdraw their ship if for any reason the charterers deduct a larger amount than that which is eventually held to be correct? Kerr, J., in *The Nanfri* [1978] 1 Lloyd's Rep. 581 formally adopted a view more favourable to the charterers, namely that they are not in default if in respect of a permitted deduction they withhold "any sum which they claim *bona fide* and assess on a reasonable basis". In the Court of Appeal [1978] 2 Lloyd's Rep. 132 this approach was followed by Lord Denning, M.R., who said: "If the charterer quantifies his loss by a reasonable assessment made in good faith—and deducts the sum quantified—then he is not in default. The shipowner cannot withdraw his vessel on account of non-payment of hire nor hold him guilty at that point of any breach of contract. If it subsequently turns out that he has deducted too much, the shipowner can of course recover the balance. But that is all." But the judgment of Goff, L.J., proceeded on the harsher view, namely that in deciding how much to deduct the charterers act at their peril. (Neither Cumming-Bruce, L.J., nor the House of Lords gave any guidance on this point.) In *The Chrysovalandou Dyo* [1981] 1 Lloyd's Rep. 159, Mocatta, J., faced with a deduction assessed reasonably and made in good faith but subsequently found to be excessive, was obliged to choose between these conflicting views and chose that of Lord Denning, M.R., "which seems to me to be in accord with what commercial considerations demand". See also the judgment of Robert Goff, J., in *The Kostas Melas* [1981] 1 Lloyd's Rep. 18 to the same effect.

Although the weight of authority to date is thus for the view that the charterers are not in breach if they deduct on the basis of a reasonable assessment made in good faith, the law on the subject cannot yet be seen as finally settled.

Bona fide belief in right to deduct not sufficient

If there is no right of deduction, either under the terms of the charter or on the basis of equitable set off (see above), the fact that the charterers bona fide and reasonably believe that they have a right of deduction will not prevent the owners from exercising their right of withdrawal for non-payment or under-payment of hire: see *The Lutetian* [1982] 2 Lloyd's Rep. 140, at page 154.

But if the owners so conduct themselves as to mislead the charterers into believing that there is no objection to the charterers' calculations, the owners may be estopped from relying upon the incorrectness of the deduction; see *The Lutetian* above, at pages 157 and 158.

Semi-monthly

These words, in Line 58 of the New York Produce form, are often altered by the parties to "monthly". A month in this context means a calendar month. Monthly hire will be due on the same numbered day in each calendar month. In *Freeman* v. *Reed* (1863) 4 B. & S. 174, Cockburn, C.J., said: "the calendar month . . . is complete when, starting from the given day in the first month, you come to the corresponding day in the succeeding month whatever be the length of either." If a month does not have a corresponding day, hire will be due on its last day. For a more recent review of this subject see *Dodds* v. *Walker* [1980] 1 W.L.R. 1061, where a majority of the Court of Appeal followed the "corresponding day" rule and held that four calendar months from 30 September expired on 30 January, despite the fact that the period then began at the end of one month but finished before the end of the fourth. Their decision was affirmed by the House of Lords, [1981] 1 W.L.R. 1027.

The Baltime form avoids this difficulty of long and short months by providing in Lines 49 and 50 that hire be paid "every 30 days". For this calculation months can be disregarded.

In advance

Hire is to be paid "in advance". Thus each periodic payment must be made by the charterers on or before but not later than the due day. Lord Wright said in *Tankexpress* v. *Campagnie Financière Belge des Pétroles* (1948) 82 Ll.L. Rep. 43, at page 53: "The importance of this advance payment to be made by the charterer is that it is the substance of the consideration given to the shipowner for the use and service of the ship and crew which the shipowner agrees to give. He is entitled to have the periodical payment as stipulated in advance of his performance so long as the charter-party continues."

In the absence of express agreement or settled practice, the charterers have until midnight on the due day in which to effect each periodic payment, regardless of the hour at which the obligation to pay hire had commenced at the beginning of the charter period: *The Afovos* [1982] 1 Lloyd's Rep. 562, [1983] 1 Lloyd's Rep. 335 (H.L.)

The obligation to pay hire in advance applies equally to the first as to subsequent instalments. Branson, J., so held in *Kawasaki* v. *Bantham Steamship* (1938) 60 Ll.L.Rep. 70. Thus under the New York Produce form the charterers must pay either before the expiry of the Clause 5 notice period or before they use the ship pursuant to that clause. Problems may arise if, contrary to the view expressed at page 228 below, the hire period can begin upon delivery of the ship in a place directed by the charterers and without reference to Clause 5: in order to prevent the charterers being faced with unexpected delivery and immediate withdrawal of the ship under Line 61 it would be necessary for the court either to hold that the first hire instalment need not be paid in advance (following the unsatisfactory judgment of Roche, J., in *Budd* v. *Johnson, Englehart* (1920) 2 Ll.L. Rep. 27) or to imply a term that the owners should give reasonable notice of when they would deliver (a proposal made in *The Zographia M* [1976] 2 Lloyd's Rep. 382).

Payment due on a non-banking day

If the due day for a particular payment falls on a Sunday or some other non-banking day the charterers must make their payment on an earlier banking day: see the judgment of Ackner, J., in *The Zographia M* [1976] 2 Lloyd's Rep. 382. Similarly, in *The Laconia*

[1977] 1 Lloyd's Rep. 315, at page 323, Lord Salmon made the following (*obiter*) remarks: "Punctual payment cannot be made on the day after it falls due, but I cannot see any reason in the present case why it could not be made before that day. If the hire is to be paid to the owners' bank semi-monthly in advance and an instalment happens to fall due on a Sunday when the banks are closed, then as the banks are also closed on Saturday, payment, in my view, should be tendered on the previous Friday. This will be payment in advance. If it is not tendered until the Monday it will not be made in advance of the period for which it is tendered."

Absolute obligation

The obligation to pay on or before the due date is an "absolute" one. Lord Porter in *Tankexpress* v. *Compagnie Financière Belge des Pétroles* (1948) 82 Ll.L.Rep. 43, said at page 51: "Apart from some special circumstances excusing performance, it is enough to constitute default that payment has not in fact been made: neither deliberate non-performance nor negligence in performing the contract is required."

Hire for last half month

Baltime form

If the charter does not expressly provide to the contrary, hire payable in advance for a month or half a month will be payable in full even where it is clear that the ship will be redelivered before the end of the month or half month: *Tonnelier* v. *Smith* (1897) 2 Com. Cas. 258. After redelivery, the amount overpaid is to be calculated and repaid by the owners: *Stewart* v. *Van Ommeren* [1918] 2 K.B. 560. This general rule in *Tonnelier* v. *Smith* applies to the Baltime form.

New York Produce form

The New York Produce form provides to the contrary in Lines 58 to 60: "for the last half month or part of same the approximate amount of hire, and should same not cover the actual time, hire is to be paid for the balance day by day, as it becomes due, if so required by Owners, unless bank guarantee or deposit is made by the Charterers . . . " Thus less than the full semi-monthly hire may be paid in advance where redelivery will be made before the end of that period. The charterers are obliged to pay in advance only an amount calculated in accordance with their estimate as to the probable date of redelivery. But the charterers must pay hire for the whole period up to that estimated date; thus Mocatta, J., held the charterers in breach in *The Chrysovalandou Dyo* [1981] 1 Lloyd's Rep. 159, when they paid hire for a period which ended three days before their own estimate of the redelivery date. Moreover, the charterers' estimate must be made on objectively reasonable grounds; it is not sufficient that it should have been made *bona fide*: see *The Mihalios Xilas* [1978] 2 Lloyd's Rep. 397 and [1979] 2 Lloyd's Rep. 303, where the relevant clause read: "the last month's hire to be estimated and paid in advance, less bunker costs . . . up to such time as vessel is expected to be redelivered . . . ". Although the words of Lines 59 and 60 of the New York Produce form are somewhat different from those in *The Mihalios Xilas* it is anticipated that they would be construed in the same way so far as this point is concerned.

Where the words of the charter permit deductions of specified items from the last hire payments, the amount of such deductions must also be made on objectively reasonable grounds: *The Mihalios Xilas*, above.

Repudiation

Repeated late payment of hire instalments does not necessarily amount to a repudiation of the charter by the charterers entitling the owners, without relying on the express right of withdrawal, to terminate the contract by withdrawing the ship: see *The Brimnes* [1972] 2 Lloyd's Rep. 465, and [1974] 2 Lloyd's Rep. 241 (C.A.). For further comments see under "Withdrawal and the right to damages" at page 217 below.

The right to withdraw

If the charterers fail to make punctual payment of an instalment of hire, that is to say payment on or before the due date, the owners are entitled by the withdrawal clause to withdraw the ship from their service and thus bring the charter to an end.

Lateness of payment arising from previously approved method

The owners may not, however, withdraw where the lateness of the payment has arisen from the use by the charterers of a particular method of making payment which has, with the owners' approval, been used for the previous instalments in substitution for strict compliance with the requirements of the charter—unless and until reasonable notice has been given to the charterers that strict compliance will in future be required. While such a particular accepted method continues in force the charterers are obliged only to set the process in motion in reasonable time to ensure timely payment in the ordinary course.

The *Petrofina* was time chartered by her Norwegian owners to Belgian charterers for seven years from 1937. By Clause 11, the hire was to be paid "In cash, monthly, in advance, in London" and her owners were entitled to withdraw her "In default of such payment". In practice the charterers invariably posted a cheque for the relevant amount from Brussels to Hambro's Bank in London, at the same time advising the owners in Oslo and their brokers in Paris that they were doing so. The cheques were posted two days before the day the hire was due to allow for the ordinary course of post. It was found as a fact that this had become the "accepted method between the parties". These cheques always reached the bank on time until a payment in late September 1939 was delayed in the post by the outbreak of war. On the day after the due day this payment had not been received and the owners withdrew their ship. It was held by the House of Lords that they were not entitled to do so.

The method of payment adopted by the charterers with the approval of the owners had become an agreed working arrangement between them and the owners could not suddenly and without notice insist instead on strict adherence to the terms of the contract. Lord Uthwatt said: "So long as the arrangement stood, it represented an agreed method of working out the obligation as to payment imposed by the charterparty, as distinct from an agreement to vary its terms. So long as it stood, the shipowners could not demand, nor the charterers insist on making, payment otherwise than in accordance with the terms of the arrangement."

Tankexpress v. *Compagnie Financiére Belge des Pétroles* (1948) 82 Ll.L.Rep. 43.

The House of Lords accepted in the above case that the owners could put an end to such a working arrangement by proper notice to the charterers. This would re-establish their right to withdraw in the event of default by the charterers in their obligation to pay hire exactly as required by the charterparty. Lord Wright said: "Hence, while the shipowners, the appellants, were entitled to insist for the future months of the charter on what might be regarded as a more correct fulfilment of the terms of Clause 11, they could only do so on giving reasonable notice of their intention and could not cancel until the notice had operated." (See also *The Effy* [1972] 1 Lloyd's Rep. 18.)

The mere fact that on previous occasions payments of hire have been made late and yet accepted without protest is unlikely to prevent the owners from withdrawing in the face of another failure by the charterers to pay on time; for the charterers to be able to rely on the above decision of the House of Lords they must show that their lateness has arisen from the operation of a previously approved *method or route* for payment: see *The Scaptrade* [1981] 2 Lloyd's Rep. 425 and [1983] 1 Lloyd's Rep. 146 (C.A.) at page 150.

Owners estopped from withdrawing by previous representation

It is, however, possible for conduct by the owners, in the face of late payments of hire, to amount to a clear representation to the charterers that the right to withdraw will not be exercised in respect of late payment of subsequent instalments. If the owners then unexpectedly purport to exercise that right in respect of such lateness, they will be prevented from doing so if the court is willing in all the circumstances to invoke the principle of equitable estoppel.

Giving the judgment of the Court of Appeal in *The Scaptrade* [1983] 1 Lloyd's Rep. 146, Robert Goff, L.J., said that in order to rely upon the principle of equitable estoppel, the charterers had first to establish that the owners had represented unequivocally that they would not enforce their strict legal right to withdraw, and secondly, that it would be inequitable to allow the owners to enforce their right, having regard to the dealings which had taken place between the parties. The former requirement might, however, be fulfilled if a reasonable man in the shoes of the charterers would have inferred from the owners' conduct that they were making such a representation; and as to the latter requirement, it either had to be shown, or be capable of being inferred, that the charterers had actually been influenced by the owners' representation. In the case in question, it was held that it was not possible to infer from the owners' acceptance of a number of late payments, or from a claim for interest on one late payment, a sufficient representation to give rise to an equitable estoppel. Further, the charterers had not relied upon the owners' conduct.

Withdrawal must be final

"Withdraw" means finally withdraw. The owners do not have the right to withhold temporarily the services of their ship. Nor do they have such right from any other source save where it is expressly granted by the contract, as for example by the lien clause, Clause 18. In a case on the Baltime form, *International Bulk Carriers* v. *Evlogia Shipping (The Mihalios Xilas)* [1978] 2 Lloyd's Rep. 186, Donaldson, J., said: "Temporary withdrawal of a vessel for non-payment of hire is a right which could only exist if specially conferred upon the owners by the terms of the time charter. No such right is conferred by this charter-party."

The *Agios Giorgis* was time chartered on the New York Produce form for the period of a trip from Korea to Charleston and Norfolk. At about the time she reached Charleston a monthly payment of hire became due and from this the charterers made a deduction, subsequently found to be excessive, in respect of a breach of the speed warranty. The owners objected to any such deduction and therefore instructed the master to prevent discharge of the cargo for Norfolk (none of which belonged to the charterers) when he arrived there. This he did until the owners had persuaded the charterers to pay the monies deducted and discharge was prevented for nearly two days. The charterers claimed successfully that the owners were in breach of the obligation in Clause 8 to prosecute the voyage with the utmost despatch and render customary assistance.

Mocatta, J., held as follows:

(1) the charterers had failed to make "punctual and regular payment of the hire", as they were not entitled to make any deduction from hire in respect of their claim and in any event they had deducted too much (see pages 197 to 200 above);
(2) this gave the owners the right to withdraw their ship finally from the charterers under Clause 5, but the owners had no right to make a temporary withdrawal or suspension of their ship's services either under that clause or otherwise, unless Clause 18 (the lien clause) applied;
(3) Clause 18 did not apply because the cargo over which it was said a lien had been exercised did not belong to the charterers.

The Agios Giorgis [1976] 2 Lloyd's Rep. 192.

(But see *The Aegnoussiotis* [1977] 1 Lloyd's Rep. 268, *International Bulk Carriers* v. *Evlogia Shipping (The Mihalios Xilas)* [1978] 2 Lloyd's Rep. 186, and *The Cebu* [1983] 1 Lloyd's Rep. 302; and also page 397, below, on the effect of the lien clause.)

Late payment by charterers: effect on the right to withdraw

The right to withdraw is not lost merely because the charterers tender the overdue hire before the owners have given notice. If the charterers fail to pay in time they are in default and their tender of hire thereafter cannot alter that position. A decision of the Court of Appeal to the contrary on a charter on the Baltime form (*The Georgios C.* [1971] 1 Lloyd's Rep. 7) was expressly overruled by the House of Lords in *The Laconia* [1977] 1 Lloyd's Rep. 315, where the charter under consideration was on the New York Produce form.

Baltime form; "In default of payment"

It should be noted that the words in Lines 51 to 54 of the Baltime form differ somewhat from those in the New York Produce form. They provide for the right of withdrawal "In default of payment". In *The Georgios C.* [1971] 1 Lloyd's Rep. 7, the Court of Appeal held that these words meant "in default of payment and so long as default continues", so that a late payment or tender of hire by the charterers would extinguish the right of withdrawal if this right had not been exercised by the owners prior to that payment or tender. This construction, and the decision it led to, were overruled by the decision of the House of Lords in a case concerning the New York Produce form, *The Laconia*, above.

Lord Wilberforce there emphasised that the words "in default of payment" had to be related to the obligation in Line 50 of the Baltime form to pay hire instalments "in advance", saying: "The Court of Appeal have in effect construed the words 'in default of payment ' not as meaning 'in default of payment in advance', but as meaning 'in default of payment whether in advance or later, so long as the vessel has not been withdrawn.' This is a reconstruction not a construction of the clause". This decision of the House of Lords brought the effect of the relevant words in the Baltime form into line with the effect of the corresponding words in the New York Produce form, "failing the punctual and regular payment of the hire".

Notice of withdrawal

The notice of withdrawal must be given to the charterers. Notice given to the master is not effective as against the charterers. In *The Georgios C.* [1971] 1 Lloyd's Rep. 7, Lord Denning, M.R., said of the owners: "They only gave notice to their own master. That was, I think, insufficient. In order to exercise a right to withdraw a ship, the shipowners must give notice to the charterers. The withdrawal only operates from the time notice is received by the charterers."

The owners must indicate clearly that they are exercising their right of withdrawal. An equivocal statement which may or may not mean that they treat the contract as at an end is not sufficient. Donaldson, J., said in *The Aegnoussiotis* [1977] 1 Lloyd's Rep. 268: "No particular form of words or notice is required, but the charterers must be informed that the owner is treating the non-payment of hire as having terminated the charter-party". The effectiveness of such a clear indication to the charterers of the owners' decision to withdraw will not be prejudiced merely because thereafter the ship continues, for example, to load cargo or carry cargo to destination: see the judgment of Robert Goff, J., in *The Tropwind* (*No. 2*) [1981] 1 Lloyd's Rep. 45, at page 52, which is considered correct on this point despite *obiter* comments of Lord Denning, M.R., to the contrary, [1982] 1 Lloyd's Rep. 232. (As to notices under anti-technicality clauses see page 210 below.)

Equitable relief from forfeiture

The owners' right to withdraw may operate very harshly against the charterers, who may lose a valuable charter and suffer heavy losses in consequence of a small error on their part or that of their bankers. This led some judges, following certain observations by Lord Simon in *The Laconia* [1977] 1 Lloyd's Rep. 315, to consider invoking the equitable power to give relief against forfeiture, a power developed to mitigate the harsh effect of forfeiture clauses in leases of land. However, it was held by the House of Lords in *The Scaptrade* [1983] 2 Lloyd's Rep. 253, affirming the decision of the Court of Appeal, that there was no jurisdiction to grant equitable relief in cases of withdrawal under time charters.

Lord Diplock, with whom the other Lords agreed, pointed out that a time charter, not being a charter by demise, transferred to the charterers no interest in or right to possession of the ship. It was a contract for services to be rendered to the charterers by the shipowners through the use of their ship and crew. The courts had always declined to grant a decree for specific performance of a contract for services. To grant an injunction restraining shipowners from exercising their right of withdrawal, as would be necessary to give the "relief from forfeiture" requested, was effectively the same as ordering specific performance of the charter contract. Consequently it would amount to the grant of a decree for specific performance of a contract for services. This was sufficient reason in itself to reject the suggestion that the equitable principle of relief from forfeiture could be extended to prevent owners from exercising their strict contractual rights under the withdrawal clause in a time charter. Lord Diplock expressly confined the decision to time charters that are not by demise, adding that: "Identical considerations would not be applicable to bareboat charters and it would in my view be unwise for your Lordships to express any views about them."

Robert Goff, L.J., in the Court of Appeal (at page 153 of [1983] 1 Lloyd's Rep. 146) dealt with the question of hardship in these terms: "The possibility that shipowners may snatch at the opportunity to withdraw ships from the service of time charterers for non-payment of hire must be very well known in the world of shipping; it must also be very well known that anti-technicality clauses are available which are effective to prevent any such occurrence. If a prospective time charterer wishes to have any such clause included in the charter, he can bargain for it. If he finds it necessary or desirable to agree to a charter which contains no such clause, he can warn the relevant section of his office, and his bank, of the importance of securing timeous payment."

Anti-technicality clauses

An anti-technicality clause is a clause designed to modify the rigour of the withdrawal clause. In dry cargo time charters, it usually provides for a 48 hour or 72 hour notice to be given by the owners to the charterers, after default has occurred, before withdrawal. There is no printed provision of this kind in the New York Produce or Baltime forms, but the parties frequently add an anti-technicality clause in typescript. The tanker charter forms usually include a printed provision like that in Clause 3(f) of the S.T.B. form: "In default of punctual and regular payment as herein specified, the Owner will notify . . . at . . . whereupon the Charterer shall make payment of the amount due within ten (10) days of receipt of notification from the Owner, failing which the Owner will have the right to withdraw the Vessel . . . "

A valid notice under such an anti-technicality clause cannot be given until after midnight on the due day, which is when the charterers become in default. This was decided by the House of Lords in *The Afovos*, below. See also *The Lutetian* [1982] 2 Lloyd's Rep. 140.

The wording of the notice to the charterers under such an anti-technicality clause must be absolute in terms; it must make it clear that the owners are giving an ultimatum that unless the hire is paid within 48 hours (or other period specified in the particular clause) they will withdraw their ship: see the judgment of Lord Denning, M.R., in *The Rio Sun* [1981] 2 Lloyd's Rep. 489, and *The Afovos*, below.

The charter for the *Afovos* was on the New York Produce form with an added anti-technicality clause (Clause 31) which provided: "When hire is due and not received the Owners, before exercising the option of withdrawing the vessel from the Charter-Party, will give Charterers forty-eight hours notice, Saturdays, Sundays and Holidays excluded and will not withdraw the vessel if the hire is paid within these forty-eight hours." Hire was due on 14 June. The charterers' bank in Italy intended to remit the funds in good time by telex transfer to the owners' bank in London. Due to an un-notified change of telex number by the owners' bank and a failure by the charterers' bank to check the answerback, the telex transfer did not reach the owners' bank. At 16 40 hours on 14 June the owners' agents telexed the charterers: "Owners have instructed us that in case we do not receive the hire which is due today, to give charterers notice as per cl. 31 of the charterparty for withdrawal of the vessel from their service." It was held by the Court of Appeal that:

(1) there was no default in payment of hire by the charterers until after midnight on the due date;
(2) on a true construction of Clause 31, the 48 hour notice could not be given until after the last moment for payment;
(3) in any event, the notice was not a good notice because it was conditional in terms.

The decision of the Court of Appeal was affirmed by the House of Lords.
The Afovos [1982] 1 Lloyd's Rep. 562 (C.A.) and [1983] 1 Lloyd's Rep. 335 (H.L.).

For a case in which it was argued by the owners (eventually without success) that the charterers had waived the need for such notice from the owners before withdrawal, see *The Rio Sun* [1981] 2 Lloyd's Rep. 489 and [1982] 1 Lloyd's Rep. 404.

Waiver of the right to withdraw

Having become entitled to withdraw their ship, the owners may lose that right if by their conduct they waive the failure of the charterers to pay the hire on time. For waiver see the general comments at pages 59 to 60 above. In this context the doctrine of waiver can best be expressed in terms of election: when the charterers have defaulted on the timely payment of an instalment of hire the owners have a choice whether to exercise their right to withdraw or, alternatively, to refrain from doing so and allow the charter to continue; if the owners act in such a way as to indicate to the charterers a choice that the charter shall continue then they will be held to have elected accordingly and thus to have waived their right to withdraw. In the words of Lord Scarman in *The Mihalios Xilas* [1979] 2 Lloyd's Rep. 303, at page 314: "When a man, faced with two alternative and mutually exclusive courses of action, chooses one and has communicated his choice to the person concerned in such a way as to lead him to believe that he has made his choice, he has completed his election". And "The consequence of the election, if established, is the abandonment, i.e., the waiver, of a right"—in this context, the right to withdraw. Examples of cases in which it has been argued that the right to withdraw has been waived are set out below.

Acceptance of a late payment

The owners may accept a late tender of the hire as if it had been paid punctually. If they are found to have done so they will be held to have waived their right to withdraw. In *The Brimnes* [1974] 2 Lloyd's Rep. 241, Cairns, L.J., said: "I consider . . . that if a month's hire in advance is tendered late, but before withdrawal, and is accepted without qualification, it must be taken to be accepted as hire for the month, which must amount to an election not to enforce the right of withdrawal, so constituting a waiver of that right".

Whether the owners have accepted a late tender in this way is matter of fact, and the court will examine all the relevant circumstances to see whether they have done so.

Acceptance, and thus a waiver of the right to withdraw, may be found from the owners or their bank retaining tendered funds for an unreasonable time without giving a notice of withdrawal. But acceptance will not be found merely from the fact that the owners' bank receives funds from the charterers and commences internal processing of them.

The *Laconia* was chartered on the New York Produce form, hire being payable semi-monthly in advance into the owners' account with the London branch of First National City Bank. A periodic payment fell due on a Sunday, but it was only at about 1500 hours on the Monday following that the charterers' bank delivered to the owners' bank a "payment order" for the appropriate amount. Shortly thereafter the bank began processing this document, which between banks is the equivalent of cash but which does not usually produce a credit in the customer's account for about 24 hours. Meanwhile, the owners' bank telephoned the owners' London agents, as they had previously been requested to do when the hire was received, and were told to refuse and return it, which they did by a parallel payment order next morning. The owners gave the charterers notice at 1855 hours on Monday evening that they were withdrawing the ship.

The House of Lords held that the owners were entitled to withdraw and had done so effectively. The late tender of hire could only be relevant if the owners were held to have accepted it and thus waived their right to withdraw, and the receipt of the payment order by their bank and the processing work that was begun upon it did not amount to any such waiver.

Lord Salmon said: "I doubt whether even if the processing of the payment order had been completed and the owners' account had been credited with the full amount of the payment order before that amount was returned to the Midland Bank on the following day, a finding of waiver could have been justified . . . . Certainly it was not within the banker's express or implied authority to make commercial decisions on behalf of their customers by accepting or rejecting late payments of hire without taking instructions. They did take instructions and were told to reject the payment. They did so and returned it to the charterers on the following day which on any view must have been within a reasonable time. If the bank had kept the payment for an unreasonable time, the charterers might well have been led to believe that the owners had accepted payment. This would have amounted to a waiver of their right to withdraw the vessel. But nothing of the kind happened in the present case."

The Laconia [1977] 1 Lloyd's Rep. 315 (H.L.).

Once the owners have given a valid notice of withdrawal, their subsequent retention of the hire will not of itself be taken as an affirmation of the contract waiving the withdrawal or their right to make it. In *The Mihalios Xilas* [1979] 2 Lloyd's Rep. 303, below, Lord Scarman said: "Owners were bound within a reasonable time after default to give notice of withdrawal. If they did not do so, they would be held to have waived the default. They gave notice on the afternoon of Mar. 26. Unless the retention of the hire at that time is to be treated as an election to continue the charter, the notice was valid, being given (as the umpire found) within a reasonable time. In my judgment, the retention of advance hire, unaccompanied by any other indications of an election, is not the unequivocal act required by law, and does not, of itself, amount to an election against withdrawal."

In appropriate circumstances the retention of hire after a valid withdrawal could give rise to a fresh contract on the same terms as the original charter. Brandon, J., considered this possibility in *The Brimnes* [1972] 2 Lloyd's Rep. 465, although he found that, as the owners' agents and solicitors had made it clear that the hire was being retained not as hire but as security for cross claims, no common intention to enter into a new contract could be inferred.

Acceptance of a timely but insufficient payment

If the charterers make a timely but insufficient payment of hire, the mere acceptance of that payment is unlikely to amount to a waiver by the owners of their right to withdraw if the deficiency has not been made good on or before the due date. The owners will normally be entitled to hold the insufficient payment and to wait and see whether the charterers pay the balance in time. In *The Mihalios Xilas*, below, the House of Lords rejected an argument that the owners had waived their right because, although receiving notice two days before the due date that an insufficient payment was to be made, they did not instruct their bankers to reject the underpayment, which was actually received the next day. Lord Scarman said: "Since there was no default until Mar. 22 [the due date], this is a submission of 'advance waiver'. It is, I suppose, a theoretical possibility, but cases will be rare. I agree with Mr. Justice Kerr that, where there is insufficient payment made prior to the last date for payment, it is not possible . . . for an owner to know whether he is entitled to withdraw the ship until the expiry of the last date for payment." The position might, of course, be different if by their words or positive conduct the owners led the charterers to believe that they had elected to accept the insufficient payment as payment in full or to forgo their right to withdraw.

Where the charterers have made a timely but insufficient payment the owners are entitled to a reasonable time in which to investigate the correctness of the charterers' deductions before deciding to withdraw: see page 214 below.

Delay in exercising the right to withdraw

The owners have a reasonable time in which to give notice that they are exercising their right to withdraw: unreasonable delay may amount to waiver of that right. They will usually be expected to react quickly: Lord Wilberforce said in *The Laconia* [1977] 1 Lloyd's Rep. 315: "The owners must within a reasonable time after the default give notice of withdrawal to the charterers. What is a reasonable time—essentially a matter for arbitrators to find—depends on the circumstances. In some, indeed many cases, it will be a short time—viz. the shortest time reasonably necessary to enable the shipowner to hear of the default and issue instructions". See also *The Mihalios Xilas* [1979] 2 Lloyd's Rep. 303 at pages 312 and 316; and *The Antaios* (*No. 2*) [1983] 2 Lloyd's Rep. 473, [1984] 2 Lloyd's Rep. 235 (H.L.).

The owners will not be held to have delayed unreasonably if, believing there to have been a default, they take time to make enquiries of their bank to ensure that the money has definitely not been received.

Hire for the *Balder London* was payable to a New York bank to the account of a London bank for the owners' account. The tenth monthly payment was due on Thursday, 17 April. Because of a change in personnel in the charterers' office no steps were taken to arrange for this payment. The owners, who were in Oslo, telephoned the London bank after midday on Friday, 18 April and were told that no payment had been made from New York. They asked that a check should be made with the New York bank and that they should be telephoned back. On the morning of Monday, 21 April, the owners again telephoned the London bank, from whom they had heard nothing, discovered that payment had still not been received there and asked again for a check with New York. On that afternoon the owners heard from London that the New York bank had confirmed that the money had not been received by them; they gave notice of withdrawal shortly thereafter. Mocatta, J., held that, although the owners might have pressed their bankers harder on Friday, 18 April, their conduct could not be regarded as unreasonable and thus their withdrawal was effective: the owners had satisfied the first sentence of the extract from Lord Wilberforce's judgment quoted above, and the third sentence "is stated too rigidly, though it may well be applicable in many cases".

The Balder London [1980] 2 Lloyd's Rep. 489.

Moreover, it may be reasonable in the circumstances of a particular case for the owners to take time to consider their position or to take legal advice before deciding to withdraw. Commenting on the above observation of Lord Wilberforce, Lloyd, J., said in *The Scaptrade* [1981] 2 Lloyd's Rep. 425, at page 429: "But what is the shortest time reasonably necessary will still depend on all the circumstances of the case. In some cases it will be reasonable for owners to take time to consider their position, as withdrawal under a time charter is a serious step not lightly to be undertaken. In other cases it may be reasonable for owners to seek legal advice. It seems to me inconceivable that Lord Wilberforce was intending to exclude such matters from consideration when he referred to "the shortest time reasonably necessary to hear of the default and give instructions."

The *Scaptrade* was chartered on the Shelltime 3 form, hire being payable in New York. A hire payment was due on Sunday, 8 July, but was not made. The employee of the owners concerned with hire payments waited for confirmation from the bank that the payment had been made, but made no enquiries until Thursday, 12 July, when a telex enquiry was sent to the sole brokers. The employee then referred to her superior and after a further telex enquiry and consultation with lawyers, the ship was withdrawn the same day (12 July). Lloyd, J. relying upon the decision of the

Court of Appeal in *Tyrer* v. *Hessler* (1902) 7 Com. Cas. 166, held that the withdrawal had been made within a reasonable time.

The Scaptrade [1981] 2 Lloyd's Rep. 425.

Even though the period of delay before notice of withdrawal is given may not be unreasonable, the withdrawal will be invalid if the owners have affirmed the charter in the meantime. If the owners, between the date the hire is due and the date of withdrawal, and with knowledge of the default, lead the charterers to believe by word or conduct that they have elected to continue with the charter, the subsequent withdrawal will be wrongful. Contrast the decision of the Court of Appeal in *Tyrer* v. *Hessler* (1902) 7 Com. Cas. 166 (delay of seven days, during which master telegraphed for cargo to be ready at the next port, held not to be an unreasonable time within which to withdraw) with *Nova Scotia* v. *Sutherland* (1899) 5 Com. Cas. 106 (act of master in loading cargo after due date and before notice of withdrawal two days later, held to amount to waiver of the right to withdraw); and see the observations on *Tyrer* v. *Hessler* in *The Scaptrade*, above, and by Staughton, J., in *The Antaios* (*No. 2*) [1983] 2 Lloyd's Rep. 473 at page 475. See also page 211 above and on the question of waiver generally, page 59 above.

Moreover, when hire is paid in time but in an insufficient amount, the owners are entitled to a reasonable time in which to investigate the correctness of the charterers' deductions before deciding to withdraw.

The *Mihalios Xilas* was chartered on the Baltime form. Additional Clause 39 provided for the payment of hire monthly and for "the last month's hire to be estimated and paid in advance, less bunker cost and Owners' disbursements and other items of Owners' liability up to such time as vessel is expected to be re-delivered . . . ". Hire for the ninth month was due on 22 March. On 21 March the charterers paid considerably less than a full month's hire and their agents explained to the owners that the shortfall was because the charterers were deducting in respect of certain advances and estimated bunkers and disbursements on redelivery, showing that they regarded this hire payment as the last under the charter. The owners, on the afternoon of 22 March, a Friday, asked the charterers for vouchers supporting the deduction for advances and disputed the charterers' estimate of the redelivery date and the amount of the deduction for bunkers and disbursements on redelivery. They followed this with another request on Monday, 25 March, but no further details were supplied and the owners withdrew their ship shortly after noon on Tuesday, 26 March.

In arbitration the umpire found (*a*) that the charterers' estimate that the ship would be redelivered at the end of the ninth month was not reasonable, (*b*) that the amount deducted was in any event unreasonable, and (*c*) that the owners' decision to withdraw had been made within a reasonable time.

The House of Lords held that the owners had made a valid withdrawal. They rejected an argument that the owners had, by their delay, waived their right to withdraw. Lord Diplock said: "Waiver requires knowledge and I agree with the umpire that the owners were entitled to a reasonable time to make enquiries of the charterers and of the master of the vessel (as they did) with a view to ascertaining whether [the charterers' estimates were based on reasonable grounds] before electing whether to withdraw or not. That being so, his finding that from Mar. 21 to noon on Mar. 26 was a reasonable time to do so is one of fact which cannot be disturbed."

The Mihalios Xilas [1979] 2 Lloyd's Rep. 303 (H.L.).

Effect of withdrawal

Upon a valid withdrawal by the owners the charter comes to an end. But the owners may continue to be liable to the owners of cargo under bills of lading issued while the charter was in being and binding on them (as to which see pages 261 to 273 below).

Where, after withdrawal from the charter, the owners perform further services at the request of the charterers, they may become entitled to remuneration for those services under a new contract. Robert Goff, J., in *The Tropwind* (*No. 2*) [1981] 1 Lloyd's

Rep. 45, discussed the nature of an owner's right to such remuneration. He said, at page 53: "the first question to be asked is whether the services so rendered by the shipowners were rendered at the request (express or implied) of the charterers, in which event the charterers will ordinarily be liable to pay a reasonable remuneration for the services rendered, a liability which can probably be categorised as contractual. If, however, there was no such request, then there can be no contractual liability on the charterers; and their liability (if any) to pay remuneration for the services so rendered can only derive from the principles of the law of restitution." In that case the charterers were found by the judge to have made a request that the ship continue to load and then carry the cargo to destination; having complied with this request, the owners were entitled to be remunerated at the current market rate.

The Court of Appeal, [1982] 1 Lloyd's Rep. 232, reversed the judge's decision that the ship had been validly withdrawn and therefore the question of remuneration after withdrawal did not arise for them to decide. But Lord Denning, M.R., expressed the view that if there was cargo on board at the time of the notice of withdrawal and the shipowner carried it to destination, he did so by way of fulfilling the original charter or bill of lading and not in response to any new request by the charterer. So he could not recover the market rate either on a quantum meruit or otherwise. Dunn, L.J., expressed no view on this point other than to say that he would not necessarily agree with the views of Lord Denning if the point arose for decision.

The charterers are entitled to repayment of hire they have paid in respect of the period after the withdrawal of the ship: *Wehner* v. *Dene Steam Shipping* [1905] 2 K.B. 92, and *The Mihalios Xilas* [1979] 2 Lloyd's Rep. 303.

Or on any breach of this Charter Party

If these words from the withdrawal clause of the New York Produce form are given their literal meaning—allowing withdrawal for any breach of any term of the charter however slight—the potential effect is so draconian that arbitrators and judges have been obliged to consider carefully whether any adequate justification can be found for some more restrictive interpretation. As Purchas, L.J., said in *The Athos* [1983] 1 Lloyd's Rep. 127, at page 143, the courts are presented with a stark choice: "Should the clause be allowed to stand unmitigated in its effect or should the Court rewrite the clause so that its effect would be reasonably acceptable in the Court's view to commercial men?"

While there is no authoritative decision of the courts on the proper construction of these words, and there are conflicting decisions and *dicta* at first instance and in the Court of Appeal, the view has been firmly expressed in the House of Lords in *The Antaios* (*No. 2*) [1984] 2 Lloyd's Rep. 235, at pages 241 and 243, that the words are not to be read literally but are to be restricted, by commercial commonsense, to a repudiatory breach—that is to say a breach of such seriousness as to entitle the owners to treat the charter as discharged by the charterers' conduct (see page 55 above).

In *The Tropwind* (*No. 1*), below, Kerr, J., held that the words might cover an unjustified refusal to make a payment which had become due and would cover orders to an unsafe port or orders to load a dangerous or excluded cargo, but would not cover a breach which consisted merely in failing to make a timely payment of items other than the charter hire itself.

The *Tropwind* was chartered on the New York Produce form for nine to 12 months for worldwide trading within Institute Warranty limits. The charterers could breach these limits subject to paying the appropriate additional insurance premium. The limits were breached and additional premium became payable. The owners withdrew the ship alleging that the charterers had failed to remit the additional premium "in due time". They argued that although the charter did not provide a time within which the additional premium should be paid it became payable within a reasonable time, that in the circumstances such time was 14 days, and that as no such payment had been made they could withdraw the ship on that breach of the charter.

Kerr, J., held that the phrase "or on any breach of this Charter Party" did not cover late payments other than of the hire, saying: "It might be applicable to an unjustified *refusal* to make some other payment, as opposed to cases of mere delay, and it would certainly be applicable to other kinds of breaches, such as ordering the vessel to an unsafe port, loading dangerous cargoes or cargoes expressly excluded from the charter as provided by another clause in the present case. But in my view any businessmen reading this clause, while of course realising that any delay in paying the hire gives rise to the right of withdrawal, would be astonished to be told that any delay in making some other payment which might become due is also covered by these general words. If this had been the intention, then the requirement of punctual payment could easily have been widened so as to include all sums which might become due, as well as the payment of hire". He also rejected the owners' contention as to the time for payment of the additional premium and held that while the owners were correct in contending that the payment had to be made within a reasonable time, 14 days was in the circumstances of the case too short a period.

The Tropwind (No. 1) [1977] 1 Lloyd's Rep. 397.

Neill, J., at first instance in *The Athos*, below, found himself unable to follow the decision of Kerr, J., despite the fact that it had been referred to with apparent approval by Lord Simon in *The Laconia* [1977] 1 Lloyd's Rep. 315. However, the Court of Appeal, while affirming Neill, J.'s decision, disagreed by a majority with his interpretation of "any other breach" and endorsed the interpretation adopted by Kerr, J., in *The Tropwind (No. 1)* above.

The New York Produce form charter for the *Athos* included an additional clause reading as follows: "35. War Risk Insurance is always to be maintained and the orders of Owners' War Risk Underwriters are always to be followed. Charterers to reimburse Owners for . . . extra War Risk Insurance following receipt of invoices and supporting vouchers on payment of next hire". Hire, payable monthly in advance, was due on the 25th of each month.

In February 1980 the charterers ordered the ship to Iran, which at that time was a dangerous area. The owners were consequently obliged to pay additional premium to their War Risks Association. This premium was calculated on the ship's insured value which had been maintained at the same level for several years despite a large drop in her market value. Moreover the percentage applied to this insured value to produce the premium payable was considerably increased by the owners' decision to include optional cover from the Association in respect of the risk of the ship being "trapped" in Iran. Upon hearing of the additional premium payable the charterers objected both to the insured value and to the percentage applied to it. At the end of March, after some exchanges on these issues, the owners sent the charterers the Association's debit note for the premium and requested payment not later than the date of the next hire payment. On 18 April the charterers paid the monthly hire due on 25 April but did not pay the requested premium. When the owners protested the charterers suggested arbitration. By a letter which reached the charterers on 22 May the owners set out in full their case for recovery of the premium and enclosed credit notes from the Association allowing them certain percentage discounts against that premium. Meanwhile the charterers had on 20 May paid the monthly hire due on Sunday, 25 May. The owners, having made enquiries of their bank after 26 May, a holiday, and established that no payment in respect of the premium had been received, withdrew their ship on 29 May.

Neil, J., held as follows:

1. The extent of the insurance cover was a matter for the owners' discretion, to be exercised according to the standard of the prudent owner; in this case the owners had been entitled to maintain the insured value of their ship despite the fall in her market value and to elect for the inclusion of the "trapping" cover.

2. The charterers were obliged to pay under Clause 35 only the net premium after deduction of the percentage discounts allowed to the owners by the Association. Therefore the obligation to pay under that clause did not arise until the letter of 22 May reached the charterers, for until the credit notes enclosed therewith were received there had not been full "receipt of invoices and supporting vouchers". There was no waiver by the charterers of the benefit of the discounts nor of their right to receive invoices and supporting vouchers.

3. A failure to make timely payment of an amount due under Clause 35 was a "breach of this Charter Party" under Clause 5 entitling the owners to withdraw their ship.

4. But, as the charterers had already paid that month's hire before 22 May, their payment of premium under Clause 35 "on payment of next hire" could be made with their payment of the hire due on 25 June. Thus the owners had not been entitled to withdraw their ship on 29 May.

5. Had the owners, contrary to his decision above, been entitled to withdraw their ship under Clause 5, they would not have waived this right by delaying withdrawal until 29 May while enquiries were made of the bank.

The Court of Appeal affirmed Neill, J.'s decision on points 2 and 4 above, but a majority (Kerr, L.J. and Stephenson, L.J., Purchas, L.J., dissenting) expressed the opinion, *obiter*, that Neill, J.'s literal interpretation of Clause 5 under point 3 above was incorrect and that the more restrictive interpretation adopted by Kerr, J., in *The Tropwind (No. 1)*, above, was to be preferred.

The Athos [1981] 2 Lloyd's Rep. 74 and [1983] 1 Lloyd's Rep. 127 (C.A.).

The *obiter* view of the majority of the Court of Appeal in *The Athos* was that the intention of Clause 5 was, as Kerr, L.J., said at page 137: "to single out the payment of hire by the due date as a crucial obligation in relation to payments, and to draw a distinction between payments—other than hire—on the one hand, and breaches of a different nature on the other hand". But that view left open the possibility that in regard to breaches other than those involving payment, even trivial breaches might entitle an owner to withdraw under Clause 5. That possibility can now, it is thought, be discounted, following *The Antaios*, below, in which the House of Lords expressed the firm view that the words referred only to repudiatory breaches.

In *The Antaios* (*No. 2*) [1984] 2 Lloyd's Rep. 235 (which was concerned with the grounds upon which leave might be given to appeal against an arbitrator's award), Lord Diplock in the House of Lords summarised, at page 238, the arbitrators' reasons for their award as being that "breach" in the phrase "or on any breach of this Charter Party" means "a repudiatory breach—that is to say: a fundamental breach of an innominate term or breach of a term expressly stated to be a condition, such as would entitle the shipowners to elect to treat the contract as wrongfully repudiated by the charterers". The arbitrators rejected the owners' construction—that the words should be given their literal meaning—on the ground that it was "wholly unreasonable, totally uncommercial and in total contradiction to the whole purpose of the N.Y.P.E. time charter form". Lord Diplock and Lord Roskill, with whom the other members of the House of Lords agreed, both stated that the arbitrators were "obviously right in their decision on the 'repudiatory breach' point".

Withdrawal and the right to damages

There is conflicting authority as to the nature of the withdrawal clause which affects the question of the damages to which the owners may be entitled on withdrawal. If at the time of a valid withdrawal there is hire outstanding, the owners clearly have the right to claim the unpaid hire together with any other amounts due from the charterers at the time of withdrawal. But the question arises whether the owners may claim in addition damages for any loss they suffer because the market rate of hire is lower than the charter rate.

Failure to pay hire amounting to a repudiation

It is clear that the owners may claim such damages where they can show that the charterers repudiated the contract.

Conduct may amount to repudiation where it shows an intention no longer to be bound by the contract or an inability to perform such that the threatened non-performance would have the effect of depriving the owners of substantially the whole benefit of the charter: see *per* Lord Diplock in *The Afovos* [1983] 1 Lloyd's Rep. 335, at page 341.

But failure to pay an instalment of hire on the due date is unlikely to amount to a repudiation, and if due merely to a mistake could hardly do so: see the comments of Lord Denning, M.R., in *The Georgios C.* [1971] 1 Lloyd's Rep. 7, at page 14 and in *The Tropwind* (*No. 2*) [1982] 1 Lloyd's Rep. 232, at page 237; see also those of Lord Diplock in *The Afovos*, above, at page 341. Even repeated lateness of payment is unlikely to do so: *Decro-Wall* v. *Marketing* [1971] 1 W.L.R. 361, and *The Brimnes* [1972] 2 Lloyd's Rep. 465 and [1974] 2 Lloyd's Rep. 241 (C.A.). Where, however, the conduct of the charterers is such that it is reasonable to infer unwillingness or inability on their part to pay there may well be repudiation. In *Leslie Shipping* v. *Welstead* [1921] 3 K.B. 420 the charterers had dishonoured a bill they had given for one month's hire and the next had not been paid at all. It was held by Greer, J., that the owners were entitled to treat the charter as ended and to claim damages as well.

Failure to pay hire not amounting to a repudiation

Where, as will ordinarily be the case, a failure to pay hire by the due date does not amount to a repudiation of the charter, damages for the loss of the charter might, nevertheless, be recoverable if the provisions as to payment of hire and withdrawal amounted to an essential term or "condition" of the contract (see page 55 above).

Brandon, J., in *The Brimnes* [1972] 2 Lloyd's Rep. 465, considered an argument that the relevant provisions of the New York Produce form amounted to an essential term and said at page 482: " . . . I have reached the conclusion that there is nothing in Clause 5 which shows clearly that the parties intended the obligation to pay hire punctually to be an essential term of the contract, as distinct from being a term for breach of which an express right to withdraw was given." The Court of Appeal [1974] 2 Lloyd's Rep. 241, affirmed Brandon, J.'s decision on this point (see particularly the remarks of Edmund Davies, L.J., at page 252). Similar views were expressed at first instance and in the Court of Appeal in *The Georgios C.* [1971] 1 Lloyd's Rep. 7, at pages 11 and 13. See also *Leslie Shipping* v. *Welstead* [1921] 3 K.B. 420.

A contrary view was expressed by Lord Diplock in *United Scientific* v. *Burnley Council* [1978] A.C. 904, where he said at page 924: "In commercial contracts for the sale of goods *prima facie* a stipulated time of delivery is of the essence, but *prima facie* a stipulated time of payment is not . . . : in a charterparty a stipulated time of payment of hire is of the essence." Again, in *The Afovos* [1983] 1 Lloyd's Rep. 335, at page 341, speaking specifically of Clause 5 of the New York Produce form, Lord Diplock observed that the second part of the clause "goes on to provide expressly what the rights of the owners are to be in the event of any such breach by the charterers of their primary obligation to make punctual payment of an instalment. The owners are to be at liberty to withdraw the vessel from the service of the charterers; in other words they are entitled to treat the breach when it occurs as a breach of condition and so giving them the right to elect to treat it as putting an end to all their own primary obligations under the charter-party then remaining unperformed." Lord Roskill, in *Bunge* v. *Tradax* [1981] 2 Lloyd's Rep. 1 at page 12, also referred to time charter withdrawal clauses as conditions.

In a claim under a computer leasing agreement it was held by the Court of Appeal in *Lombard North Central* v. *Butterworth* [1987] Q.B. 527 that a clause providing that punctual payment of the hire should be "of the essence" of the lease, was a condition, breach of which entitled the lessor to recover from the lessee all the future instalments of hire, subject only to deduction of the resale value of the repossessed computer. The correctness of this decision has been questioned: see Treitel [1987] LMCLQ 143. But in any event the wording of the withdrawal clauses in the New York Produce form and Baltime form can be distinguished from the wording of the clauses in the *Lombard North Central* case, in that in the latter there was an express reference to time being "of the essence". This might not be a material distinction where there are interdependent obligations (see *Bunge* v. *Tradax*, above), but it is suggested that the obligation to pay hire by the due date does not fall into this category.

The question remains whether the statements of Lord Diplock and Lord Roskill, above, are to be taken to mean that the payment of hire and withdrawal clause constitutes a condition in the fullest sense of that term. It would have the result that on a falling market, the owners, having withdrawn because of some slight delay in the payment of hire, could go on to recover damages for the loss of the charter—a surprising result even though that is, apparently, the position under American law (see page 226 below). However, none of these three observations was directed to the issue of damages after withdrawal. Moreover two were *obiter* and, although the third—Lord Diplock's comments in *The Afovos*—formed part of his reasoning in that case, it has been pointed out that he could have reached the same conclusion for a more straightforward reason (see Reynolds [1984] LMCLQ 189). It may in any event be that all that was meant was that by adding an option to withdraw to the payment of hire obligation, the parties themselves gave to that obligation one characteristic of a true condition or essential term, namely that breach entitles the innocent party to treat the contract as discharged.

It is submitted, in conclusion, that it is not necessary to treat the ordinary payment of hire and withdrawal clause in a time charter as a condition in the strict sense, so as to entitle the owners to recover damages for loss of the charter upon any breach, however slight, when what is to happen in the event of late payment of hire is expressly provided for by the clause. It is considered that damages for loss of the charter should be recoverable only in cases where the failure to pay hire by the due date can be shown to be repudiatory. But uncertainty remains until the House of Lords has shed more light on this important question.

Injunction

For the circumstances in which the court may grant injunctions where owners withdraw or threaten to withdraw their ship, see page 54 above.

American Law

Cash

Strictly speaking, "cash" in the United States is either actual currency or Federal Reserve funds. There is a widespread commercial practice, however, of accepting ordinary checks, payment orders or telex transfers as the equivalent of "cash". This is so even though the owner's bank may require a day or more for the check or transfer to clear and give the owner unrestricted use of the funds. Such practice was called into question in *The Penta*, S.M.A. No. 1603 (Arb. at N.Y. 1981), where the panel unanimously ruled that the charterer's tender of charter hire by ordinary check which cleared after the due date was in breach of its obligation to make payment in "cash". According to the panel:

> The words "in cash" must mean the one making the payment has the obligation to see to it the recipient has the use of the funds without a qualification attached thereto. [Charterer] should have accomplished this by a wire transfer, or if they chose to pay by check, a check could have been tendered either in federal funds or sufficiently in advance as to allow time for the check to clear.

While this case did not involve a withdrawal of a vessel, it is no doubt correct in defining "cash" and indicates that certain commercial arbitrators in New York agree with the strict English rule of what is required to make a timely hire payment.

Payment of less than full hire/deductions

The problem of what deductions are permitted from hire payments is a vexatious one. Under the New York Produce form, the charterer has no right to withhold hire except as expressly provided in the charter for off-hire or advances. Thus, in *The Uranus*, 1977 AMC 586 (Arb. at N.Y. 1977), the panel was unanimous in its decision that the charterer was in breach of the charter by withholding hire against its claim for alleged cargo damage. According to the panel:

> The Panel agrees the Charterer was in breach of the hire payment provisions of the charter party by withholding hire due against his pending cargo claim. Under the N.Y. Produce Exchange form hire is payable in full without deduction excepting those deductions permitted by Clauses 5 and 15 and other express provisions as are described in the charter. Charterer's remedy for pursuing a cargo claim not recognized by Owner is to proceed to arbitration. (1977 AMC at 590).

A similar result was obtained in *The Katina*, S.M.A. No. 1310 (Arb. at N.Y. 1979), where a panel upheld a withdrawal when charterer made unauthorized and excessive deductions from hire. Similarly, in *The Myriam*, 1952 AMC 1625 (Arb. at N.Y. 1952), it was held that deductions for off-hire and related claims were excessive and that the owner was entitled to withdraw the vessel for non-payment of hire. In *The Brookhurst*, S.M.A. No. 87 (Arb. at N.Y. 1960), it was held that the charterer was not entitled to deduct amounts from the last charter hire payment for an alleged speed deficiency and disbursements, and that under Clause 5 of the New York Produce form, the owner was justified in withdrawing the vessel as a result of the charterer's failure to pay hire when and as due under the charter.

In *The Aetolia*, S.M.A. No. 1993 (Arb. at N.Y. 1984), the panel held that there is no cessation of hire clause in the New York Produce form which permits charterer to deduct hire for time used to secure cargo in slack holds. According to the panel, this operation formed part of the charterer's obligations to load, stow, and trim the cargo. In addition, the panel held that claims for cargo damage or loss did not give charterer a right to withhold hire.

It has been argued that a charterer may not withhold hire for disputed off-hire claims. On the other hand, the off-hire clause (Clause 15) itself appears to contemplate that hire simply has not been earned and is not payable to the extent of any actual breakdown or speed deficiency. Hence, a charterer can argue persuasively that if off-hire has accrued, he is entitled to deduct it, whether or not the owner consents. Of course, the *caveat* is that the charterer must be sure of his ground. Thus, if he withholds more from hire than is later established as correct, he has to that extent failed to pay hire and a withdrawal would be proper. At the same time, an owner who withdraws by reason of disputed off-hire deductions should similarly be sure of his ground, since if the deductions are later found to be correct the withdrawal may be held wrongful. The severe risks attaching to a mistake in this area suggest that where there is a good faith dispute the parties should consider an escrow arrangement followed by a prompt submission of the dispute to arbitration.

Equally vexing is the question of whether a charterer can deduct anticipated off-hire. For example, if a vessel is scheduled to go into dry dock in the succeeding month, must the charterer pay a full month's hire? The case of *The Noto*, 1979 AMC 116 (Arb. at N.Y. 1976) suggests not, but the authorities are divided and a charterer risks a withdrawal if full hire is not paid "in advance".

The posting of security for hire can itself lead to difficulties. In *The Mare Felice*, 1974 AMC 2150 (Arb. at N.Y. 1971), the charterer had paid the owner U.S. $50,000 as security together with the second hire payment, which was to be applied against the last hire payment. The charterer failed to make the third hire payment on the due date, and the owner withdrew the vessel. The charterer's primary defense was that the owner was not justified in terminating the charter since the overdue hire payment could be taken from the security deposit. The panel held that the withdrawal was proper, since the charter specifically gave the owner the right to withdraw the vessel if hire payments were late. As to the security deposit, the majority stated:

> The majority considers the security deposit to be only drawn upon so that the funds therefrom may exhaust themselves simultaneously with the redelivery of the vessel and thus the number of days' hire which the security deposit represented was to be applied to the last number of days of hire accordingly. (1974 AMC at 2152.)

The near sanctity of owner's right to hire is demonstrated by the arbitration award in *The Dagny Skou*, S.M.A. No. 2416 (Arb. at N.Y. 1987). The vessel was operating under a five-year time charter. During the course of the charter, the charterer, which was an Argentine company, was served with an order of attachment issued by the Argentine court on the application of creditors of owner. Pursuant to the court order, charterer paid funds into the registry of the court and, thereafter, deducted the amount deposited with the court from hire. The panel held that the deduction from hire was improper.

In *The Thekos*, S.M.A. No. 2253 (Arb. at N.Y. 1986), the panel held that post-redelivery speed or performance claims, and claims for attorneys' fees, were not permitted deductions under Clause 5 or 15.

In *The Ocean Advance*, S.M.A. No. 1677 (arb. at N.Y. 1982), the panel stated that though charterer had the right, under the New York Produce form, to sublet the vessel, there was no provision permitting charterer to withhold hire from owner based upon the non-payment of sub-freights by a sub-charterer to charterer.

"In advance"

There are numerous cases holding that the owner is entitled to withdraw the vessel from the charterer's service if hire is not paid when it is due under Clause 5 of the New York Produce form. See, e.g., *The Admiralty Flyer*, S.M.A. No. 349 (Arb. at N.Y. 1967), holding that the owner was entitled to withdraw the vessel from the service of the charterer when it defaulted in the payment of hire as provided in Clause 5. In *The Egle*, S.M.A. No. 815 (Arb. at N.Y. 1973), the panel upheld the owner's withdrawal of the vessel about five months before the redelivery date on the basis of Clause 5. The owner withdrew the vessel nine days after the 38th hire payment was due and after giving notice of its intention of doing so if the payment was not made immediately.

The first question to be determined is when each installment falls due. For example, if hire commences at 5 a.m. on Monday, 1 March, the next installment would of course be due on 15 March. It seems widely accepted in New York that hire due on 15 March could be paid at any time during business hours that day, even though the semi-monthly period had commenced at 5 a.m. See *The Penta*, S.M.A. No. 1603 (Arb. at N.Y. 1981). There is, however, *dictum* to the contrary. See *The Vermont I*, S.M.A. No. 747 (Arb. at N.Y. 1970).

Even more troublesome are hire payments falling due on a Saturday, Sunday, or holiday. Under the English rule, payment must be made on the preceding business day. However, in a New York arbitration, *The Maria G. Culucundis*, 1954 AMC 325 (Arb. at N.Y. 1952), a contrary rule was adopted. There an installment of hire fell due on 23 December, a Saturday. The charterer did not tender a check for the hire until 2 p.m. Tuesday, 26 December. The owner withdrew the vessel, but in a subsequent arbitration of the charterer's claim for damages, the withdrawal was held wrongful. This result is consistent with the New York General Construction Law, §25 (McKinney Supp. 1974), which provides that any payment falling due on a Saturday, Sunday or holiday may be made on the following business day.

Modification by course of conduct

Both the time-of-payment and the method-of-payment provisions can be modified by the owner's course of conduct. Thus, in *The Spyros Lemos*, 1967 AMC 2357 (Arb. at N.Y. 1967), the charterer's method of making cable remittances resulted in the crediting of the owner's account one or two days after the due date. However, the owner failed to object to this practice until he served a notice of withdrawal following a late receipt of payment. The withdrawal was held wrongful. A similar result was reached in *The Pandora*, 1973 AMC 1561 (Arb. at N.Y. 1972), where failure to protest late payments was held to deprive an owner of the right to withdraw the vessel without a prior warning. So in *The Essi Gina*, S.M.A. No. 534 (Arb. at N.Y. 1970), the prior record of payments showed that, over a period of seven years under the charter, owner had on 18 different occasions accepted payments made from one to five days late without protest. On this record, the panel held that the owner was not justified in withdrawing the vessel for the late payment. According to the panel:

> The Arbitrators gave careful consideration to the language of Clause 5 of the Charter, which states " . . . otherwise failing the punctual and regular payment of the hire, or bank guarantee, or on any breach of this Charter Party, the Owners shall be at liberty to withdraw the vessel from the service of the Charterers . . . ". That language is clear and without ambiguity. It refers to "punctual and regular payment". It says nothing about punctual and regular receipt, and the Arbitrators are satis-

fied that the history of seven years of payment of charter hire by the Charterers without question or protest by the Owners established a pattern of punctuality and regularity on the part of Charterers that could not be so suddenly set aside by the Owners in one single instance that was not even an exceptional instance.

In *The Proton*, S.M.A. No. 160 (Arb. at N.Y. 1966), it was held that the owner was not entitled to withdraw the vessel because by "word and correspondence [it had] established a modus operandi" which allowed late payment. This principle was upheld in *Cochin Refineries* v. *Triton Shipping*, 1978 AMC 444 (Arb. at N.Y. 1978), where the panel ruled that since evidence established that the shipowner had long acquiesced in delayed payments, it was not justified in withdrawing the vessels from an affreightment contract for failure to pay freight. See also *The Robertina*, S.M.A. No. 1151 (Arb. at N.Y. 1977).

These cases do suggest, however (as does the strong dissent in *Cochin Refineries*, above) that even if late payments are not at first protested, an owner may restore his right to punctual payment by giving express notice of his intent to strictly enforce the withdrawal clause in the future. Moreover, there are cases in which withdrawal was permitted on grounds of late payment, even though the owner did not protest previous late payments. See *The Vermont I*, S.M.A. No. 747 (Arb. at N.Y. 1970); *The Orient Lakes*, S.M.A. No. 181 (Arb. at N.Y. 1964). Hence, a charterer who habitually makes late payments which are accepted without protest may be lulled into a false sense of security.

Whether a warning is required

It is often put to a legal advisor by an owner whether a warning is required before an actual notice of withdrawal is sent. In England, no such principle appears to apply. New York arbitrators, however, have traditionally followed a more liberal approach in deciding withdrawal cases. Hence, a warning is prudent, even if it prompts the charterer into making payment and curing the default. In *The Noto*, above, a distinguished panel of arbitrators suggested that because withdrawal was such a drastic remedy a warning must first be given.

The relative liberality of New York arbitrators, however, should not be understood to mean withdrawal will not be upheld. In *The Athenian Horizon*, S.M.A. No. 1197 (Arb. at N.Y. 1977), a withdrawal was upheld for a delay in payment of a few days, even though the charterer had remitted the hire and only the close of banking hours precluded owner's receipt of it by the deadline given. In the words of the panel:

Charterers had an absolute obligation to pay hire in advance, failing which gave rise to the contractual right of the owners to withdraw.

See also *The Admiralty Flyer*, S.M.A. No. 349 (Arb. at N.Y. 1967). In *The Egle*, S.M.A. No. 815 (Arb. at N.Y. 1973), the panel upheld the owner's withdrawal of the vessel about five months before the redelivery date on the basis of the withdrawal clause in the New York Produce form. The owner withdrew the vessel nine days after the 38th hire payment was due, and after giving notice of its intention of doing so if the payment was not made immediately.

Notice of withdrawal

As under English law, an owner who wishes to treat a charterer's default in payment as grounds for termination of the charter must promptly communicate this to the charterer.

No special wording is required; the customary message is to the effect that "as a result of your failure to pay hire when due owners are hereby withdrawing the vessel from your further service without prejudice to their claims for damages".

Acceptance of late payment of hire

The American cases have not wrestled with the distinctions cited in the English decisions. In *The U.S.* 219 (*No.* 11), 21 F. Supp.466 (E.D. Pa. 1937), the court held that the acceptance of late hire extinguished the right of withdrawal. This appears correct in principle, since acceptance of a payment for the future use of the ship is inconsistent with a withdrawal. Moreover, in *The San Juan Venturer*, 1974 AMC 1053 (Arb. at N.Y. 1974), a majority of the arbitrators held that a right of cancellation was waived where a late payment of freight was remitted and accepted prior to the withdrawal notice, even though the freight was in payment of the past services of the vessel.

Late tender of payment

Whether an owner is entitled to withdraw after rejecting a late tender of payment remains in doubt. In an early court case, *Luckenbach* v. *Pierson*, 229 F. 130 (2d Cir. 1915), the Court of Appeals for the Second Circuit did uphold a withdrawal made after a tender of hire had been rejected. However, a panel of arbitrators in New York subsequently held that an unaccepted tender will preclude a valid withdrawal if the charterer is not given a notice of withdrawal prior to the tender. *The Noto*, 1979 AMC 116 (Arb. at N.Y. 1976).

Withdrawal with cargo on board

If the vessel is performing a voyage at the time of the default, the notice of withdrawal cannot in a true sense be effective until the voyage is completed and all of the cargo is discharged. *Luckenbach* v. *Pierson*, above; *Diana Compania Maritima S.A.* v. *Subfreights of the Admiralty Flyer*, 280 F. Supp. 607, 1968 AMC 2093 (S.D.N.Y. 1968). See also *Antria* v. *Triton*, 1980 AMC 681 (E.D.Pa. 1978), where the court ruled that an owner who withdrew a loaded vessel and carried the cargo to its destination had an "equitable" claim to the bill of lading freights only if the vessel was withdrawn before the freights became due. The presence of cargo on board, however, should not preclude a valid withdrawal, whether one takes the view that a withdrawal is not effective until completion of the cargo voyage, or is effective immediately with the owner assuming the time charterer's obligations to the cargo interests. Cf. *The Noto, supra*. See *The Athenian Horizon*, S.M.A. No. 1197 (Arb. at N.Y. 1977), discussed above at page 223.

Bank error

The rule in New York insofar as bank errors are concerned is not as strict as the English law. In *The Pandora* (*No. 2*), S.M.A. No. 755–A (1973), a payment of hire was remitted by a bank employed by the charterer, through an intermediary bank, to the bank designated by the owner. Because of an error by the intermediary bank, the payment was not received by the owner's bank. When the owner notified the charterer of the non-receipt of the hire and the withdrawal of the vessel, the charterer made inquiries of its bank.

However, a further five or six-day delay ensued before the source of the error was discovered and the late payment transmitted. In upholding the withdrawal, the panel noted that the charterer had an opportunity to correct the default in payment after having been advised thereof by the owner. Accordingly, it was the charterer's failure to correct the default promptly which led the panel, somewhat reluctantly, to sustain the right of withdrawal.

A fascinating footnote to *The Pandora* case is the ensuing litigation against the banks. The charterer sued both its local bank, Continental Illinois, and its correspondent through whom payment to the owner was to be effected, Swiss Bank Corp. In *Evra Corp.* v. *Swiss Bank Corp.*, 522 F. Supp. 820 (N.D.I11. 1981), rev'd 673 F.2d 951 (7th Cir. 1982), the court found that the failure to consummate the crucial hire payment came about when telex payment instructions sent by Continental Illnois to Swiss Bank Corp. in Geneva were ignored by the latter either because the telex was lost or the Swiss Bank Corp's machine had run out of paper (Continental Illnois' telex machine had received an "answerback" confirming the electronic receipt of the message). It was held (*a*) that under applicable Illnois law Swiss Bank Corp. owed a duty of care to charterer, (*b*) that Swiss Bank Corp. was negligent in failing to log incoming telexes and insuring that its machine had paper and (*c*) the charterer's damages exceeding $2,000,000 in lost profits on the cancelled charter were foreseeable and recoverable from Swiss Bank Corp. On appeal, however, the decision was reversed, the appellate court relying on the principle established in *Hadley* v. *Baxendale* in holding that the damages were too remote and consequential to be recoverable.

Another New York case on this point is *The Essi Gina*, S.M.A. No. 534 (Arb. at N.Y. 1970). There, a check was mailed to the bank designated by the owner, but two days after the due date the bank advised that the check had not been received. The next day the vessel was withdrawn and tender of a substitute check for the hire was rejected. A few days later the bank discovered the missing check, although there was no mention in the award as to when the check had arrived at the bank. The arbitrators held that the error was solely the bank's, that the charterer was blameless, and that the withdrawal was wrongful.

Similarly, in *The Meltemi*, S.M.A. No. 491 (Arb. at N.Y. 1970), the charter specified "punctual" payment of hire. The owner withdrew the vessel because at the close of business on the anniversary date, payment had not been received by its bank in New York. However, payment had been authorized by a Canadian bank on the morning of the due date, but was delayed because of a breakdown of the telex machine and arrived the next morning. On these facts, the majority of the panel held that owner was not entitled to withdraw the vessel, and that payment of hire was made in accordance with both accepted practice and the express terms of the charter.

It is submitted that these decisions can be read as permitting the charterer to correct any delay in payment occasioned by a bank error as long as (*a*) the charterer itself is not contributorily responsible for the delay, and (*b*) the charterer promptly corrects the default in payment as soon as it learns of it. It is also submitted that these decisions are in keeping with the traditional concepts of equity in New York arbitrations which tend to avoid a harsh result for a party who has acted diligently and in good faith.

No case in New York seems to have dealt expressly with the issue of delays due to bank errors on the basis of the principles of agency. It would seem that if a bank is designated by the owner for the payment of hire, the bank is the owner's agent and any error by the bank in crediting the owner's account must be imputed to the owner. In *The Erie*,

S.M.A. No. 497 (Arb. at N.Y. 1970), it was held that owner had no right to withdraw where a check for payment due on 19 May was mailed on that date and received by the owner's bank the next morning. Payment was not credited to the owner until 21 May, but it was held that this was the result of the owner's failure to properly advise its bank of an assignment.

By the same token, the bank through which the charterer remits the hire is the charterer's agent or sub-agent. Accordingly, errors by the charterer's bank or an intermediate bank should be imputed to the charterer. Although *The Pandora* (*No. 2*) and *Essi Gina* decisions indicate that an innocent and diligent charterer may receive favorable treatment in New York, the severe risks involved warrant the establishment of a kind of "fail-safe" mechanism to insure the timely receipt of the hire by the owner's bank.

"Or on any breach of this Charter Party"

Clause 5, read literally, would permit withdrawal for any breach by the charterer. However, the principle of *ejusdem generis* should apply, and this would permit withdrawal only in cases of breaches of like seriousness to the failure to pay hire. In *The Arietta Venizelos*, 1973 AMC 1012 (Arb. at N.Y. 1972), a withdrawal was held valid where the charterer nominated a port which was known to be unsafe because of threats of guerrilla attacks on tankers. The decision was under the Texacotime form, but provides a helpful analogy here.

Effect of withdrawal

There may be an important distinction between American and English law relating to the consequences of a withdrawal. The English approach is probably to treat the right of withdrawal as an "option" to cancel, exercisable upon the happening of an event, i.e., late payment of hire (see page 219 above). Under this view, the owner may withdraw but may not recover damages for repudiation, unless the charterer's conduct with regard to the payment itself amounts to a repudiation even without a withdrawal clause. Hence, as a practical matter, withdrawal will only be made in a rising charter market.

The American view, however, is that mere late payment of hire entitles the owner to treat the charter as repudiated. The "withdrawal" clause is thus construed as the equivalent of a "time is of the essence" provision, any breach of which is sufficient to be treated as grounds for termination. Hence, in New York the charterer would risk being held liable for damages if the owner were to withdraw in a falling market after a late payment.

Damages in the event of wrongful withdrawal or cancellation

The proper measure of damages for a wrongful withdrawal or cancellation of charter is the difference between the original charter rate and the prevailing market rate for equivalent business at the time of the breach. *Orion Shipping & Trading* v. *Eastern States Petroleum Corp.*, 312 F.2d 299 (2d Cir. 1963) cert. denied 373 U.S. 949 (1963). The purpose of this approach is to put the non-breaching party in the same position he would be in had the breaching party performed its obligations under the charter. The market rate is usually determined by reference to other charters for comparable vessels in the same or comparable trade fixed on or about the date of the breach, see *United Transp. Co.* v. *Berwind-White Coal Mining Co.*, 13 F.2d 282 (2d Cir. 1926); *Liberty Navigation and*

T. Co. v. *Kinoshita & Co. Ltd.*, 285 F.2d 343 (2d Cir. 1960); *McNear* v. *Leblond*, 123 F. 384 (9th cir. 1903).

In *The Moshill*, S.M.A. No. 2069 (Arb. at N.Y. 1985), to determine owner's damages for charterer's nonperformance of a time charter, the panel adopted the approach of comparing the amount of hire which would have been earned or was payable over the remaining term of the charter, with actual earnings from or the cost of substitute voyages performed from the time of the default to the expiration of the minimum term of the contract.

There will be occasions when there is no prevailing market for equivalent business at the time of the breach. This may be attributable to the nature of the trade the vessel is engaged in or simply fluctuations in market conditions. In this situation, the court or arbitrators should nonetheless determine a market rate based on the available information.

In cases arising under time or voyage charters, the injured party will have an obligation to take reasonable steps to mitigate damages. *Aaby* v. *States Marine Corp.*, 107 F. Supp. 484 (S.D.N.Y. 1951). The duty to mitigate, however, may not arise where there has been a breach of a long term contract of affreightment. Compare *Orion Shipping & Trading* v. *Eastern States Petroleum Corp.*, S.M.A. No. 573 (Arb. at N.Y. 1962), with *McAllister Bros. Inc.* v. *A & S Transp. Co.*, S.M.A. No. 1989 (Arb. at N.Y. 1984) and *Alumina Tansp. Corp.* v. *Occidental Chemical Co.*, S.M.A. No. 2136 (Arb. at N.Y. 1985).

See generally *Arbitration between Guinomar and Martin Marietta Aluminium Inc.*, S.M.A. No. 2534 (Arb. at N.Y. 1988).

Right to deny charterer use of vessel

In *The Dominique*, S.M.A. No. 2535 (Arb. at N.Y. 1989), because charterer was late in making a payment of hire, owner withheld the use of the vessel until the payment was received. The arbitrators ruled that while owner had the right to withdraw the vessel by reason of the late payment, it had no right to temporarily deny the vessel's use to charterer. The panel observed that in so holding, the decision was in accord with *The Aghios Giorgis* [1976] 2 Lloyd's Rep. 192 and *The Helindas*, S.M.A. No. 1589 (Arb. at N.Y.).

From when Time is to Count

[Clause 5 continued]

"62. . . . Time to count from 7 a.m. on the working day

63. following that on which written notice of readiness has been given to Charterers or their Agents before 4 p.m., but if required by Charterers, they

64. to have the privilege of using vessel at once, such time used to count as hire.

65. Cash for vessel's ordinary disbursements at any port may be advanced as required by the Captain, by the Charterers or their Agents, subject

66. to $2\frac{1}{2}\%$ commission and such advances shall be deducted from the hire. The Charterers, however, shall in no way be responsible for the application

67. of such advances.

68. 6. That the cargo or cargoes be laden and/or discharged in any dock or at any wharf or place that Charterers or their Agents may

69. direct, provided the vessel can safely lie always afloat at any time of tide, except at such places where it is customary for similar size vessels to safely

70. lie aground.

71. 7. That the whole reach of the Vessel's Hold, Decks, and usual places of loading (not more than she can reasonably stow and carry), also

72. accommodations for Supercargo, if carried, shall be at the Charterers' disposal, reserving only proper and sufficient space for Ship's officers, crew,

73. tackle, apparel, furniture, provisions, stores and fuel. Charterers have the privilege of passengers as far as accommodations allow, Charterers

74. paying Owners .... per day per passenger for accommodations and meals. However, it is agreed that in case any fines or extra expenses are

75. incurred in the consequence of the carriage of passengers, Charterers are to bear such risk and expense."

Commencement of hire

There is a reference to Lines 62 to 64 of Clause 5 of the New York Produce form in Lines 18 to 21, which provide that the ship is to be placed at the charterers' disposal "in such dock or at such wharf or place . . . as the Charterers may direct" and continue, "If such dock, wharf or place be not available time to count as provided for in clause No. 5 . . . ".

It has been argued that if the dock, wharf or place selected by the charterers is available, then hire is payable from the time the ship reaches it and thus becomes at the disposal of the charterers, and that Clause 5 is only relevant to determine from when hire is payable if that dock, wharf or place is not available. While the point has yet to be decided, it is suggested that the better construction of the relevant passages is that Clause 5 is the exclusive provision relating to the commencement of hire, Line 21 being intended to reinforce rather than contradict this view by stating that Clause 5 is to be applied even if, on the arrival of the ship, the dock, wharf, or place is not immediately available. Clause 5 ties in with the words of the cancelling Clause 14. The latter clause depends upon the giving of the Clause 5 notice of readiness: it would clearly work far less satisfactorily if hire could commence otherwise than in accordance with these notice provisions in Clause 5.

This interpretation is consistent with the view expressed by Branson, J. (*obiter*) on the working of Clause 5 in *Kawasaki* v. *Bantham Steamship* (1938) 60 Ll.L.Rep. 70. He said at page 77: "I fail to follow the force of the argument which suggests that upon the true construction of the last paragraph of Clause 5 of the charter-party the period does not commence until 7 o'clock in the morning after the notice of readiness has been given. It seems to me that the words 'but if required by charterers, loading to commence at once, such time used to count as hire', is an alternative provided by the charter to the giving of notice. The business of it is this, that when the ship arrives, the ship can put upon the charterers the obligation to take delivery by giving this notice. They give the notice at 4 p.m., and then, whether the charterers take delivery or not, at 7 a.m. on the next working day the period begins to run; but, on the other hand, the charterers may be very anxious to get possession of the ship, and then there is the alternative that they can come and ask for it, and if they come and ask for it, it is to be handed over at once and loading is to commence at once. But then, of course, with the commencement of loading commences the period of the charter and the obligation to pay chartered hire."

On this view, delivery for the purpose of the commencement of hire takes place when the charterers accept the ship and start to use her or, alternatively, on the expiry of the notice period, whichever is the earlier.

Once use of the ship has been made by the charterers at their request, Line 64 will operate to start the charter period running, whether the charterers use the ship continuously or only intermittently from then on. Thus, once time has started, all time counts, just as it would have done after the notice period had expired, despite the ambiguity in the phrase "such time used". In a laytime case under a voyage charter, Donaldson, J., has held "unless used" to allow only the time actually used by charterers to count towards the laytime used (*The Helle Skou* [1976] 2 Lloyd's Rep. 205), but the essentially different character of hire should produce a different result so far as Line 64 is concerned.

It is suggested that Clause 5 does not require notice to be given on a working day and that the word "that" in Line 63 refers back to "day" rather than to "working day".

For potential conflicts between Lines 62 to 64 and Line 94 ("That if required by Charterers, time not to commence before . . . "), see page 287 below.

Advances

Line 66 allows the charterers to deduct the advances mentioned in Line 65 from hire. For comments on permitted deductions from hire, see pages 199 to 203 above.

Safely lie always afloat

For comments on the safety of berths selected by the charterers, see pages 153 and 154 above.

American Law

From when time is to count

Under Clause 5 of the New York Produce form, hire commences at 7 a.m. on the working day after notice of readiness has been given to the charterer, provided notice is given before 4 p.m. See, e.g., *The Hopeville*, 1968 AMC 2650 (Arb. at N.Y. 1968). Under Line 21, hire commences as provided in Clause 5, even if the berth is not available. If the dock or wharf is immediately available when notice of readiness is given, however, hire will nevertheless not commence until the next working day. See *The Alexandros Koryzis*, S.M.A. No. 271 (Arb. at N.Y. 1968). The charterer may choose to use the vessel sooner than the next working day after notice has been given. If he does so, the charterer is, of course, obliged to pay hire for the time used. Contrary to the English view that hire runs continuously once the charterer begins loading cargo or otherwise using the vessel, the American rule is that the charterer must pay hire only for the hours of actual use. See *The Antonis*, S.M.A. No. 273 (Arb. at N.Y. 1959).

Utmost Despatch

"76. 8. That the Captain shall prosecute his voyages with the utmost despatch, and shall render all customary assistance with ship's crew and
77. boats."

Prosecution of voyage

There may be a failure to prosecute a voyage with the utmost despatch where the master puts into, or delays at, a port of refuge unnecessarily (*Istros* (*Owners*) v. *Dahlstrom* (1930) 38 Ll.L.Rep. 84, page 467 below); or where the master wrongfully refuses to put into a port to which he has been ordered by the charterers (*The Charalambos N. Pateras* [1972] 1 Lloyd's Rep. 1, page 470 below) or wrongfully prevents the loading or discharge of cargo (*The Agios Giorgis* [1976] 2 Lloyd's Rep. 192, page 208 above).

Engineers

Although the words refer specifically to the Captain, they cover also any failure by the engineers to prosecute the voyage with the utmost despatch: *The Apollonius* [1978] 1 Lloyd's Rep. 53.

Subject to exceptions clauses

The obligation may, however, be qualified by the exceptions in the charter.

The *Keifuku Maru* was time chartered for six months. Clause 9 of the charter provided: "The Captain shall prosecute his voyages with the utmost dispatch . . . ", and Clause 14: "Throughout this charter losses or damages, whether in respect of goods carried or to be carried, or in other respects arising or occasioned by the following causes, shall be absolutely excepted, viz: . . . negligence, default, or error in judgment of the pilot, master or crew . . . in the management or navigation of the steamer."

The umpire's findings of fact indicated that there had been delays due to insufficient consumption of coal on passage although there was no lack of coal. Bailhache, J., considered this amounted to a finding of negligence on the part of the master. He held that there was a breach of Clause 9 and that the owners were not protected by Clause 14 because that clause could not be construed so as to "wipe out" the obligation in Clause 9.

The Court of Appeal asked the umpire for further findings, which, when given, were that the loss of speed was due to "general slackness" but not to negligence. A majority of the Court of Appeal held that these findings made it unnecessary to consider Clause 14; but Scrutton, L.J., took the view that Clause 14 overrode Clause 9, because there were still matters to which Clause 9 might apply even if Clause 14 was given full effect.

A majority of the House of Lords agreed with the Court of Appeal that the umpire's findings determined the matter in favour of the charterers. On the relationship between Clauses 9 and 14 three members of the court expressed opinions agreeing with Scrutton, L.J., that Clause 14 would override Clause 9 in the event of negligence. Viscount Cave, L.C., on the other hand, considered that Bailhache, J., was right in taking the opposite view.

Suzuki v. *Beynon* (1926) 24 Ll.L.Rep. 49 (H.L.), affirming 20 Ll.L.Rep. 179 (C.A.) and 18 Ll.L.Rep. 415.

(See also the judgment of Wright, J., in *Istros* (*Owners*) v. *Dahlstrom* (1930) 38 Ll.L.Rep. 84, and page 467 below.)

It is thought therefore that against a claim for breach of the obligation to prosecute a voyage with the utmost despatch under Line 76 of the New York Produce form the owners may be able to rely on defences available under the United States Carriage of Goods by Sea Act, incorporated by Clause 24. In particular the defence of "neglect or default . . . in the navigation or in the management of the ship" is available under Section 4(2) (*a*) of that Act. The relevant provisions of the Act are, by Section 2, applicable only "in relation to the loading, handling, stowage, carriage, custody, care, and discharge" of cargo. But it was held in *Adamastos* v. *Anglo-Saxon Petroleum* [1958] 1 Lloyd's Rep. 73 that the losses of charterers under a consecutive voyage charter as a result of the ship failing to perform as many voyages as she should were within the words of Section 2. Presumably the same would be true of similar losses caused by the master's failure to prosecute a voyage under a time charter with the utmost despatch, so that the defences given by the Act might be available in some cases even where the charterers' losses arose otherwise than from physical loss of or damage to the cargo.

The obligation may also be modified by the general exceptions in Lines 103 to 106 of the New York Produce form. For comments on these exceptions see page 348 below. For the incorporation of the United States Act see page 425 below. For the effect of Clause 13 of the Baltime form on the obligation to prosecute voyages with the utmost despatch see page 467 below.

Customary assistance

This means the "assistance" or services that the master and crew would normally give or perform when the ship is not under charter. Whether any particular service is "customary" is a matter of fact. Among other relevant factors will be the flag of the ship, the articles signed by the crew and the trade in which the ship is engaged.

In relation to the cleaning of rust from the holds on a ballast passage before the loading of grain and after the carriage of muriate of potash, phosphate rock and manganese ore, a London umpire made the following findings of fact which are recorded in the judgment of Donaldson, J., in *Splosna Plovba* v. *Agrelak Steamship* [1975] 1 Lloyd's Rep. 139:

> 28. The removal of soft non-adhering rust is the duty of the crew, and can be performed, albeit with difficulty in ships of the size of the *Bela Krajina*, always given time and calm weather . . .
>
> 29. The removal of hard adhering rust is a major operation which cannot be done by the crew during the course of a ballast voyage. It necessitates the erection of staging, and mechanical de-rusting equipment . . . It cannot be done efficiently and completely by the crew on a vessel of the size of the *Bela Krajina* . . .
>
> 32. Cleaning of holds does not include chipping steel. It does include removal of large loose rust patches in accessible locations. Customary assistance does not extend to scaling operations requiring the use of sophisticated tools loke pneumatic chipping hammers, high pressure water jets or sandblasting equipment.

American Law

Utmost despatch

The purpose of Clause 8 is to impose a duty on the master to carry out voyages ordered by the charterer without interruption and as quickly as circumstances and safety will permit.

In *Lowber* v. *Bangs*, 69 U.S. 728 (1865), the charter provided "ship to proceed from Melbourne to Calcutta with all possible despatch." The court held that "We cannot give any other construction to [this] language . . . than that she was to proceed direct from one place to the other, and that to this extent, *at least*, time was intended to be made of the essence of the contract." Moreover, the court found that this provision went to the "entire root of the contract", and that the charterer was released from the contract because the vessel diverted to Manila en route to Calcutta, and consequently arrived at the latter port more than three months later than she would have had she not made the diversion.

The master's duty to prosecute the voyage with the utmost despatch, however, must be balanced against his paramount duty to provide for the safety of the vessel, her crew and cargo. If the master acts in good faith and with a reasonable exercise of judgment in the particular circumstances in concluding that the voyage must be delayed for the safety of the vessel, crew or cargo, such delays would not constitute a violation of the charter. There are circumstances, moreover, which will justify a deviation from or temporary discontinuance of the voyage.

In *The Styria*, 101 F. 728 (2d Cir. 1900), mod. on other grounds, 186 U.S. 1 (1902), the vessel loaded a cargo of sulphur at Sicily for shipment to New York. Before departing from Sicily, the master learned that the war between Spain and the United States had broken out. Because sulphur was a contraband article, the master had the cargo unloaded and put in a warehouse in Sicily. He gave the consignees written notice of his actions, and advised that "on finding risky my passage to New York, with the actual sulphur cargo, for facts of war" he was discharging the cargo. (186 U.S. at 10.) The court held that the master's actions were fully justified in the circumstances, in that "his conduct . . . had due regard to the interest of all concerned in the ship and in the cargo . . .." (186 U.S. at 20.) See also discussion below at page 495.

In *The Robertina*, S.M.A. No. 1151 (Arb. at N.Y. 1977), the owner ordered the master to detain the vessel at Cristobal because the charterer was delinquent in paying a hire installment. The owner could not exercise a lien on the cargo, as it was being shipped under prepaid bills of lading. Moreover, the owner could not effect a withdrawal for late payment of hire because it had tolerated numerous late payments in the past. The detention of the vessel was found by the arbitrators to be merely a pressure tactic designed to force the charterer to pay hire at a time and place when the owner could not enforce a lien on the cargo. In these circumstances, the arbitrators found that the owner was in violation of its duty under Clause 8 to prosecute the voyage with the utmost despatch.

In *The Medita*, S.M.A. No. 1150 (Arb. at N.Y. 1977), the arbitrators held that the master did not violate his duty to prosecute the voyage with the utmost despatch when he deviated from his course to avoid heavy weather.

The master may delay the voyage when he reasonably believes the vessel is in jeopardy, if, for example, a dangerous cargo is on board and he wishes to seek expert assistance in assuring the safe stowage of the cargo. In *The Fernglen*, 1971 AMC 213 (Arb. at N.Y. 1970), the panel held that the master was justified in keeping the vessel at anchor for eight days while he brought in experts to counsel him on the proper stowage of a cargo of scrap which included steel turnings.

In *The Continental Trader*, S.M.A. No. 1503 (Arb. at N.Y. 1980), the vessel encountered delays at Bandar Shapour following completion of discharge due to political unrest and strikes in the port which affected the port authorities, tugs and pilots. The master refused to sail without official clearance from the port authorities or a pilot. Eventually, when the vessel had nearly exhausted her supply of fresh water and fuel the vessel did leave without the assistance of a pilot, but only after port clearance was granted and tugs came alongside. The panel unanimously denied the charterer's claim that the master failed to prosecute the voyage with the utmost despatch. As stated by the panel:

> . . . The Panel falls back on the ancient rule of the Sea that the master of a ship is the final judge in matters affecting the safety of his ship . . . The master acted within his rights, indeed his unavoidable duty, to act with prudent restraint and caution when there was no pilot, no tug and no official clearance, until he was forced to compromise such forbearance to prevent disablement or greater harm to the vessel by proceeding under less than ideal conditions without pilot.

Customary assistance

In *The Andros City*, S.M.A. No. 1156 (Arb. at N.Y. 1977), the owner claimed reimbursement of a sum paid to the crew for sweeping and washing cargo holds at the request of the charterer. The charter contained a typewritten addition to the New York Produce form which provided for the payment by the charterer to the crew of a lumpsum for overtime. The issue raised in the case was whether the customary assistance provision of Clause 8 entitled the charterer to require that the crew perform ordinary cleaning and hold washing and, if so, whether the monthly lumpsum overtime payment the charterer was required to make was the measure of remuneration for this work.

The panel held that the cleaning and washing of cargo holds is not a part of the usual and customary work of the ship's crew. In so holding, the arbitrators noted that the collective bargaining agreement for the vessel treated hold cleaning as an activity for which the crew members involved were entitled to special remuneration. The panel stated that the overtime provision related to the crew's performance of its usual duties in docking and undocking and keeping the vessel available for the charterer's use. The panel noted, however:

> The interpretation of Clause 8 lies at the core of this dispute and it, therefore, must be examined carefully. To do so it is necessary to isolate the first and second parts of the clause. The first part, requiring "That the Captain shall prosecute his voyages with the utmost despatch, and shall render all customary assistance with ship's crew and boats" is in essence an acknowledgement of the vessel's obligation to exercise all possible effort to perform as efficiently and expeditiously as possible. It cannot and should not be read out of context or interpreted in a vacuum so as to shift responsibilities which are specifically provided for in other portions of this clause and others. The latter part of Clause 8 allocates the expense of loading, stowing, trimming and discharging cargo to the Charterer, and in this respect the Panel considers the hold cleaning function, subsequent to delivery and where it is not related to hold maintenance or the vessel's seaworthiness, is for Charterer's account.
>
> The "customary assistance" of Clause 8 may, under appropriate circumstances, be read as to require the master and crew to sweep and wash holds of cargo residue during ballast voyages or to

perform other work for Charterer which they would normally do for Owner, but the essential thrust of this obligation is to protect the Charterer from the possibility of an unreasonable refusal of Owner to cooperate rather than to allow Charterer the unlimited right to order the use of ship's labor for its own use at the expense of the Owner.

Employment Clause

[Clause 8 continued]

"77. . . . The Captain (although appointed by the Owners), shall be under the orders and directions of the Charterers as regards employment and
78. agency;"

Obedience to charterers' orders

It is not up to the master to question unduly the orders of the charterers as to the employment of the ship. It was said by Roche, J., in *Portsmouth Steamship* v. *Liverpool & Glasgow Salvage Association* (1929) 34 Ll.L.Rep. 459, that the master was entitled to follow these orders "within the limits of obviously grave danger". It is suggested that one situation in which the master is not only entitled but may also be obliged to refuse the orders of the charterers is where these endanger the safety or seaworthiness of his ship. It should also be noted that not every order is an order "as regards employment"—see the comments below.

Although the master is obliged to employ his ship in accordance with the orders of the charterers, he is not necessarily obliged to obey their orders immediately.

The *Anastasia* was time chartered for a trip on the New York Produce form. She was ordered to load jute at Chalna and the master was told by the charterers' agents there that, although this cargo was for Europe, he should tell the local authority that he was carrying it to Singapore, to which port the bills of lading would be made out. Shortly after the ship sailed from Chalna, the charterers cabled the master with orders to return to Chalna to load more jute. The master exchanged cables with the charterers for some time and eventually obeyed their order only after establishing that despite the fact that he had now entered in his log the true destination of the ship, the charterers still wished him to return to Chalna. Donaldson, J., held that the master was justified in delaying his obedience to the charterers' orders. Having described the responsibility of the master's job, he said: "It seems to me that against that background it must be the duty of the master to act reasonably upon receipt of orders. Some orders are of their nature such that they would, if the master were to act reasonably, require immediate compliance. Others would require a great deal of thought and consideration before a reasonable master would comply with them."
Midwest Shipping v. *Henry* [1971] 1 Lloyd's Rep. 375.

Nor is the master bound to obey orders which the charterers are not entitled to give under the terms of the charter. In *The Sussex Oak* (1950) 83 Ll.L.Rep. 297, a case concerning orders to an unsafe port, Devlin, J., said, at page 307: "I cannot think that the clause in a time charter-party which puts the master under the orders of the charterers as regards employment is to be construed as compelling him to obey orders which the charterers have no power to give." (For the facts of this case, see page 139 above.)

Thus the master is not obliged to obey orders of the charterers to deliver cargo to a person not entitled to receive it: see *The Sagona* [1984] 1 Lloyd's Rep. 194, per Staughton, J., at page 205. But if the order is complied with and the owners suffer loss as a result, they will normally be entitled to recover their loss from the charterers by way of indemnity: see *The Stork* [1955] 1 Lloyd's Rep. 349, below. Further, as Hobhouse, J., pointed out in *The Kanchenjunga* [1987] 2 Lloyd's Rep. 509, at page 515: "Generally speaking a person is entitled to act in the faith that the other party to a contract is carrying out his part of it properly. Even if the breach of contract is clear it is vital to the proper conduct of business that the relevant party should be able if he considers the breach a minor one to proceed without sacrificing his right to be indemnified. But this does not mean that a master can enter ports that are obviously unsafe and then charge the charterers with the damage done. It is also the rule that an aggrieved party must act reasonably and try to minimize his damage."

Although the master is under the orders and directions of the charterers, the owners remain liable for negligence of the master, subject to any exceptions in the charter. In *Raynes* v. *Ballantyne* (1898) 14 T.L.R. 399, a ship which was under time charter caused damage to the charterers' own pier as a result of the master's negligence. It was held by the House of Lords that (apart from the exceptions clause in the charter) the owners were liable. Lord Herschell said: "The captain was appointed by the owners, but was to be under the directions of the charterers. The effect of that contract was to place the vessel at the complete disposal of the charterers within the limits specified in the charter, and subject to the same limits the master was bound to obey the orders of the charterer, although no doubt he was still the servant of the shipowner. Consequently, apart from the clause [the exceptions clause], the owner would be responsible for any negligence of the master, although the owner had no voice to control the master, who was carrying out the charterer's instructions."

The master of the *Aquacharm* was ordered by charterers under a New York Produce form charter to load to the draft permitted for a transit of the Panama Canal. He negligently loaded to a greater draft. Lloyd, J., held that the owners would have been liable for consequent losses had it not been for an effective defence incorporated into the charter by Clause 24 (as to which defence see page 430 below). His judgment was affirmed by the Court of Appeal.

The Aquacharm [1980] 2 Lloyd's Rep. 237, and [1982] 1 Lloyd's Rep. 7 (C.A.).

But the obligation on the master to obey the charterers' orders is not absolute, being only to exercise reasonable skill and care. See *The Aquacharm*, above.

Implied indemnity

In the New York Produce form (unlike the Baltime form) there is no express indemnity given to the owners. But an indemnity will normally be implied against liability incurred by the owners as a consequence of complying with the charterers' orders or directions.

The *Strathlorne* was time charterered, the charter providing that the captain (although appointed by the owners) should be under the orders and directions of the charterers as regards employment, agency or other arrangements. The charter also contained an express indemnity clause. The ship was sub-chartered for a voyage with rice from Rangoon to Swatow and bills of lading were tendered to and signed by the master. At Swatow the charterers' agents directed the master that they would be responsible for delivery of the cargo and they caused it to be delivered without production of the bills of lading. The bills of lading had not been taken up from the bank which held them and were never paid for. In the event, the owners were held liable to the bank for the value of the rice misdelivered. It was held by Roche, J., and the Court of Appeal that, irrespective of the express indemnity provision (the scope of which was doubtful), an indemnity in favour of the owners was to be implied at common law against the liability they incurred as a result of the master complying with the charterers' orders.

The Court of Appeal, in affirming the judgment of Roche, J., applied the principle laid down by Tindal, C.J., in *Toplis* v. *Grane* and quoted in *Dugdale* v. *Lovering* (1875) L.R. 10 C.P. 196:

"... when an act has been done by the plaintiff under the express directions of the defendant which occasions an injury to the rights of third persons, yet if such an act is not apparently illegal in itself, but is done honestly and *bona fide* in compliance with the defendant's directions, he shall be bound to indemnify the plaintiff against the consequences thereof."

Strathlorne Steamship v. *Andrew Weir* (1934) 49 Ll.L.Rep. 306 and (1934) 50 Ll.L.Rep. 185.

Accordingly, in such circumstances the owners will be entitled to an indemnity, unless the act of the master in complying with the charterers' orders or directions is manifestly wrongful or "manifestly tortious". To disqualify a claim for indemnity an act must always involve "an element of turpitude and does not extend to the case where the actor has carelessly failed to make enquiries which would have revealed the true nature of the act, or where he has culpably but not recklessly drawn the wrong inference from such enquiries as he has made". *Per* Mustill, L.J., in *The Nogar Marin* [1988] 1 Lloyd's Rep. 412 at page 417.

The *Sagona* was time chartered on the Beepeetime 2 form, Clause 20 of which provided that the master was to be under the orders and directions of the charterers as regards employment, and incorporated an indemnity in favour of the owners against liabilities arising from signing bills of lading in accordance with the directions of the charterers or their agents. The charterers ordered the ship to deliver a cargo of gasoil at Nordenham to Mabanaft. Following the common (although not universal) practice in the carriage of oil cargoes at that time (1978), the master did not insist upon the production of a bill of lading or a letter of indemnity before delivering the cargo. Mabanaft were not in fact entitled to the cargo, the ship was arrested and the owners suffered losses in consequence which they sought to recover from the charterers by way of indemnity. It was held by Staughton, J., applying *Strathlorne* v. *Weir* above, that the owners' losses had been caused by compliance with the charterers' orders in the light of the practice which was then common, the master's action in delivering the cargo without a bill of lading was not manifestly illegal nor was there anything which should have excited the master's suspicion; accordingly the owners were entitled to recover their losses under an implied indemnity.

The Sagona [1984] 1 Lloyd's Rep. 194.

(See also *The Nogar Marin* [1988] 1 Lloyd's Rep. 412.)

The implied indemnity, as with the express indemnity in the Baltime form, should cover not only liabilities that the owners may incur, but also other loss or damage they may suffer, as for example damage suffered by their ship at an unsafe port to which she has sailed in compliance with the charterers' orders (see page 155 above), or the reasonable costs of defending legal proceedings (see *The Caroline P* [1984] 2 Lloyd's Rep. 466, 476).

See also for implied indemnities in connection with bills of lading, page 262 below.

Express indemnity

Under some time charters, as in the case of *Strathlorne Steamship* v. *Andrew Weir* above and in the case of the Baltime charter (Lines 71 to 73), an express right is given to the owners to be indemnified by the charterers against consequences or liabilities arising out of the master complying with the charterers' orders (see page 469, and for an example of a recovery under an express indemnity clause see *Portsmouth Steamship* v. *Liverpool & Glasgow Salvage Association* (1929) 34 Ll.L.Rep. 459, the facts of which are summarised at page 241).

Indemnity arising from the signing of bills of lading

If the master is required by the charterers to sign or permit to be signed bills of lading which impose on the owners greater liability than that which they have assumed under the charter, the owners will usually be entitled to be indemnified by the charterers in respect of their additional liability. See pages 262 to 264 below.

Indemnity not dependent on charterers' fault

The indemnity in favour of the owners against the consequences of complying with the charterers' orders operates quite independently of any fault on the part of the charterers. In *The Athanasia Comninos* [1981] COM LR 132, see page 240 below, Mustill, J., rejecting an argument by charterers that Article IV, Rule 3, of the Hague Rules protected them from liability under the implied indemnity in the New York Produce form, said: "they would need to use much clearer language than this to introduce the idea of fault into the shipowner's implied indemnity, where it has never been before."

Employment

"Employment" has, in this context, been held by the House of Lords to mean "employment of the ship", not employment of persons, and to include orders to proceed to certain ports for loading and discharge of cargo (see page 155 above), but to exclude orders as to how those instructions are to be executed in terms of navigation, which always remains the responsibility of the master.

The *Ramon de Larrinaga* was on requisition to the Crown on the terms of the T.99A time charter, including a clause virtually identical to the employment and indemnity clause of the Baltime form. In October 1939 she was ordered to proceed on a voyage from Newport to St. Nazaire and then to Cardiff for a joint survey prior to redelivery. After discharge at St. Nazaire she was ordered by the sea transport officer there to proceed at once to Quiberon Bay, despite adverse weather, and join a convoy for Cardiff. She set out but subsequently grounded and was damaged. One basis on which the owners claimed indemnity from the Crown was that the damage to the ship had been caused by the master's compliance with charterers' orders.

This argument was rejected by the House of Lords because, although the orders to St. Nazaire and then to Cardiff were orders by the charterers as regards employment, the orders of the sea transport officer as to how and when the ship should navigate to Cardiff were not, and, in any event, the damage was not caused by the charterers' orders, although it occurred while they were being carried out.

Lord Wright said, at page 173: "These sailing orders [of the sea transport officer] which the Judge found were given were, in my opinion, merely dealing with matters of navigation in regard to carrying out the orders [of the charterers] to proceed to Cardiff. It was the duty of the master to exercise his judgment in such matters of navigation."

Larrinaga Steamship v. *The Crown* (1944) 78 Ll.L.Rep. 167.

(See also *Weir* v. *Union Steamship* [1900] A.C. 525 and *Stag Line* v. *Ellerman & Papayanni Lines* (1949) 82 Ll.L.Rep. 826.)

That matters of navigation and ship management remain always the responsibility of the owners and their servant, the master, is underlined by the words of Lines 170 and 171 in the New York Produce form. So while it was held by Staughton, J., in *The Erechthion* [1987] 2 Lloyd's Rep. 180, below, that the orders of a harbour master to proceed to an anchorage to lighten were orders as to employment, the advice of the pilot as to precisely where the ship should anchor was a matter of navigation.

The *Erechthion*, while under time charter on the New York Produce form, was ordered by the charterers to discharge at Port Harcourt. Since her draft was too deep, she was ordered by the harbour master to proceed to an anchorage in the river to lighten, where she grounded. It was common ground that there was to be implied in the charter an obligation to indemnify the owners against the consequences of complying with the charterers' order to go to Port Harcourt. It was held by Staughton, J., that the charterers' order was to be regarded as an order to go to such discharging place there as the harbour authority should designate. He held that the harbour master's order was an order as to employment and remitted to the arbitrators the question whether the grounding was proximately caused by this order, rather than by the advice of the pilot as to where within the anchorage the ship should anchor, which was a matter of navigation only.

The Erechthion [1987] 2 Lloyd's Rep. 180.

(See also *The Isabelle* [1982] 2 Lloyd's Rep. 81 and *The Mediolanum* [1984] 1 Lloyd's Rep. 136, and pages 154 and 155 above where these cases are discussed.)

An order by the charterers that the ship is to proceed to or remain at a certain port is an order "as regards employment". Thus, in *Temple Steamship* v. *V/O Sovfracht* (1945) 79 Ll.L.Rep. 1, see page 105 above, the obedience of the master to the wrongful orders of the charterers to delay at Murmansk and thereafter proceed to Garston did not amount to a waiver and did not prejudice the claim of his owners against the charterers under that charter (an amended Baltime form), since the master was under the orders of the charterers as to employment. See also *Larrinaga Steamship* v. *The Crown* (1944) 78 Ll.L.Rep. 167, above, and *The Eugenia* [1963] 2 Lloyd's Rep. 381.

Similarly, an order to load a particular cargo has been held an order "as regards employment". If the order to load that cargo causes loss to the owners, then the right to indemnity from the charterers arises.

The *Ann Stathatos* was time chartered on a wartime version of the Baltime form which included, as in Clause 9 of the present form, the statement that the master was to be "under the orders of the charterer as regards employment" and an express indemnity against the consequences of his obeying such orders. The charterers ordered the ship to load a cargo of coal, which gave off methane gas. Repairs to water tanks in the 'tween decks were being undertaken, pending sailing of the ship's convoy, when a series of explosions damaged the ship. The arbitrators found that the direct cause of the explosions was a combination of the explosive atmosphere and a spark produced by the repairs. The owners claimed that the charterers should indemnify them for the damage to the ship.

Devlin, J., held that an order to load a particular cargo was an order as to the employment of the ship and so was within the scope of the indemnity provision, but, on the facts found by the arbitrators, the loading was not the direct cause of the loss and so no right to an indemnity arose.

Royal Greek Government v. *Minister of Transport* (1949) 83 Ll.L.Rep. 228.

The *Athanasia Comninos* and the *Georges Chr. Lemos* were chartered to the same charterers on the New York Produce form. Both were ordered by the charterers to load coal in Sydney, Nova Scotia for Birkenhead. Shortly after sailing each ship was damaged by an explosion caused by ignition of a mixture of air and methane gas, which had been emitted from the coal after loading. The owners sought to recover from the charterers in respect of these damages. It was conceded by the charterers that their order to load the coal fell within the scope of the indemnity implied from Clause 8, even if the owners failed (as they did at the trial) to prove that the coal loaded had properties making it unusually dangerous as compared with other coal cargoes. But the charterers claimed that there had been faults by each of the owners and/or their crews which broke the chain of causation between their orders to load the coal and the explosions. Mustill, J., found no such fault with regard to the *Georges Chr. Lemos*, but that the ignition of the gas and air mixture on the *Athanasia Comninos* had been caused by a crew member lighting a match for a cigarette in the forecastle. Accordingly he held the charterers liable to the owners of the former ship, but not to the owners of the latter. (With regard to the former ship, the judge rejected a defence put forward by the charterers on the basis of Article IV, Rule 3 of the Hague Rules; as to which see page 128 above and page 431 below.)

Mustill, J., said: "It seems to me perfectly possible to have a loss which is caused by the shipment of a cargo having certain properties, even if the properties of the cargo in question are no different from those of other cargoes of the same description. In the present case, if one asks the question (eliminating the possibility of fault on the part of the shipowner) 'Why was there an explosion?', the answer is—'Because there was methane in the hold.' And if one goes on to ask 'Why was there methane in the hold?', the answer is—'Because the Time Charterers called on the vessel to load coal.' This answer is in my opinion sufficient to found an indemnity, without proof that the coal was in any way unusual."

The Athanasia Comninos [1981] COM LR 132.

Causation

For the owners to succeed under the indemnity, they must prove an unbroken chain of causation between the instructions of the charterers and the loss suffered: *Royal Greek Government* v. *Minister of Transport* (*The Ann Stathatos*), and *The Athanasia Comninos*, above. Donaldson, J., said in *The White Rose*, below: "A loss may well arise in the course of compliance with the time charterers' orders, but this fact does not, without more, establish that it was caused by and is in law a consequence of such compliance and, in the absence of proof of such causation, there is no right to indemnity." See also *The Erechthion* [1987] 2 Lloyd's Rep. 180. In *The Aquacharm* [1982] 1 Lloyd's Rep. 7 (the facts of which are set out at page 303 below), Griffiths, L.J., said: "the owners have failed to show that the transhipment expenses were incurred as a direct consequence of complying with the charterers' orders . . . The burden is on the owners claiming the indemnity to establish that the charterers' orders caused the loss—this they have failed to do and they are not therefore entitled to be indemnified against the expenses of the transhipment." (See also "Ordinary expenses and navigational risks", below.)

The *White Rose*, on charter on the Baltime form, was ordered to load grain at Duluth. In accordance with their obligations under Clause 4, the charterers appointed as loading stevedores a firm of average competence by local standards. One of their men, having left his station for his own purposes, fell through an unfenced part of a 'tween deck hatch. He sued the owners for damages for his injuries in the Minnesota courts and the owners became obliged to spend money on legal fees and to contribute towards the settlement of his claim. The owners claimed to be indemnified by the charterers under Clause 9. Their claim was rejected by Donaldson, J., because the accident, and thus the owners' loss, had been caused by the lack of fencing (for which the charterers were not responsible) and the negligence of the injured man himself, and not by either their compliance with the charterers' orders to load grain at Duluth or the selection by the charterers of incompetent stevedores.

The White Rose [1969] 2 Lloyd's Rep. 52.

The *Hillcroft* was chartered to lighten the *West Hesseltine* aground off the Cape Verde Islands. The charter obliged the captain to "follow the instructions of the charterers" who were to "indemnify the owners from any consequences, or liabilities that may arise" therefrom. The charterers ordered the transfer of barrels of palm oil which leaked, despite careful handling, and damaged the *Hillcroft*'s holds. The ship was also damaged by the transfer of large mahogany logs. Roche, J., held that the charterers were liable to indemnify the owners in both these cases, but not for further damage following the escape of oil from her forepeak tank, for although this had also been loaded on the charterers' instructions, the effective cause of its escape was the subsequent breaking of a pipe connected to that tank.

Portsmouth Steamship Co. Ltd. v. *Liverpool & Glasgow Salvage Association* (1929) 34 Ll.L.Rep. 459.

(See also the judgment of Lord Porter in *Larrinaga Steamship* v. *The Crown* (1944) 78 Ll.L.Rep. 167, at page 176.)

Ordinary expenses and navigational risks

Moreover, the owners are not entitled to recover from the charterers under their indemnity the ordinary expenses and losses of trading, despite the fact that in a broad sense these are incurred as a result of their obedience to the orders of the charterers. This was expressed by Lloyd, J., in *The Aquacharm* [1980] 2 Lloyd's Rep. 237 in the following words: "It is of course well settled that owners can recover under an implied indemnity for the direct consequences of complying with the charterers' orders. But it is not every loss arising in the course of the voyage that can be recovered. For example, the owners cannot recover heavy weather damage merely because, had the charterers ordered the vessel on a different voyage, the heavy weather would not have been encountered. The connection is too remote. Similarly, the owners cannot recover the expenses incurred in the course of ordinary navigation, for example, the cost of ballasting, even though in one sense the cost of ballasting is incurred as a consequence of complying with the charterers' orders: see *Weir and Others* v. *Union Steamship Co. Ltd.* [1900] A.C. 525. The same considerations apply in the present case. The costs of transhipment were an ordinary expense incurred in the course of navigation."

Agents

The provision in Lines 77 and 78 of the New York Produce form gives the charterers the right (and presumably the duty) to appoint the agents to handle the business of the ship in each port.

Lord Wright in *Larrinaga Steamship* v. *The Crown* (1944) 78 Ll.L.Rep. 167, said, at page 172: "The shipowner is entitled in the ordinary course to decide to what firm or person in each port the ship in the course of the charter-party is to be consigned as agent. The selection is here left to the charterers."

Reference should also be made to Line 39 of the New York Produce form, which requires the charterers to "provide and pay for . . . Agencies . . . ". Comments on the responsibility of the charterers for the choice of suitable agents and the extent of their liability for the agents' acts or omissions appear at page 175 above.

American Law

Employment clause

It is a basic element of a time charter that the master and crew are employed by the owner, and remain his employees throughout the term of the charter. At the same time, the master must carry out the instructions and orders of the charterer. The charterer's right to give orders to the master, however, is by no means unlimited or absolute. For example, the master may justifiably refuse to carry out orders from the charterer to enter an unsafe berth. Nor does the master act under the orders of the charterers insofar as the navigation or management of the ship is concerned. In addition, where circumstances dictate the necessity to deviate from the voyage, the master may do so. See, e.g., *The Medita*, S.M.A. No. 1150 (Arb. at N.Y. 1977). In that case, in addition to holding that the master was justified in taking refuge at a port because of heavy weather, the arbitrators held that he was entitled to demand that the charterer supply additional bunkers to ensure that the vessel could safely cross the North Atlantic in the bad weather conditions expected in the month of December. See discussion at page 233 above.

If the charter incorporates the U.S. Carriage of Goods by Sea Act, deviation from the charterer's orders is expressly permitted by Section 4(4):

> Any deviation in saving or attempting to save life or property at sea, or any reasonable deviation shall not be deemed to be an infringement or breach of this chapter or of the contract of carriage, and the carrier shall not be liable for any loss or damage resulting therefrom: *Provided, however*, that if the deviation is for the purpose of loading or unloading cargo or passengers, it shall, *prima facie*, be regarded as unreasonable. (46 U.S.C. §1304(4)).

A master's protest of the charterer's instructions prior to a casualty may protect the owner, even if there is negligence on the part of the master. See *MacKenzie McAllister* v. *United States*, 1942 AMC 1215 (E.D.N.Y. 1942). In some situations, however, the master's negligence may result in liability resting with the owner, even if the charterer's directions were imprudent. For example, a master's acceptance of a port he knows is not safe has been held to be intervening negligence which relieves the charterer from liability for breach of its warranty of safe port. *American President Lines Ltd.* v. *United States*, 208 F.Supp. 573, 1968 AMC 830 (N.D. Cal. 1961). Moreover, if a master accepts a port nominated by a charterer with knowledge of local conditions, it has been held that the charterer will not be liable on its warranty of safe port, since the warranty was not relied upon by the master. See *Tweedie Trading Co.* v. *New York & Boston Dyewood Co.*, 127 F.2d 278 (2d Cir. 1903), *cert.* denied 193 U.S. 669 (1903); *Pan Cargo Shipping Corp.* v. *United States*, 234 F.Supp. 623, 1965 AMC 2649 (S.D.N.Y. 1964), aff'd 323 F.2d 525, 1967 AMC 850 (2d Cir. 1967), *cert.* denied 386 U.S. 836 (1967).

In *The Aetolia*, S.M.A. No. 2157 (Arb. at N.Y. 1985), the panel held that the master was justified in insisting that the cargo in slack holds be secured before the vessel sailed. According to the panel, the master's request to secure both its slack holds was prudent and consistent with the vessel's stability requirements. The vessel was held to be on-hire for the time lost while the holds were secured. The panel further held that the master was justified in following the advice of a local agent at Buenos Aires not to load his vessel to a draft in excess of the maximum prevalent safe draft of 32 feet, even though there was evidence that certain other owners had exceeded the published draft. Charterer, therefore, did not have a claim for damages for shutout cargo.

Indemnity rights between owner and charterer

The owner has a right of indemnity from the charterer for liabilities incurred in carrying out its orders. The basic rule was stated by the court in *Nissho-Iwai Co. Ltd.* v. *M/T Stolt Lion*, 617 F.2d 907, 913 (2d Cir. 1980) that "a right to indemnification between a vessel owner and charterer exists when one is held liable for a fault for which the other is primarily liable".

Issues involving rights of indemnity most frequently arise in the context of cargo claims brought against both the owner and charterer. See discussion below, at pages 255 to 260.

Loading, Stowing, Trimming and Discharging Cargo

[Clause 8 continued]

"78. . . . and Charterers are to load, stow, and trim the cargo at their expense under the supervision of the Captain,"

Transfer of responsibility to the charterers

In the absence of express provision, the obligation to load, stow, trim and discharge the cargo is at common law on the owners: see *The Filikos* [1983] 1 Lloyd's Rep. 9. Line 78 of the New York Produce form has the effect of shifting from the owners to the charterers the primary responsibility for loading, stowing and trimming the cargo: see *Court Line* v. *Canadian Transport* (1940) 67 Ll.L.Rep. 161, and page 247 below.

Discharge

Where, as is frequently the case, the words "and discharge" are added after the word "trim" in Line 78 of the New York Produce form it is clear that the primary responsibility for discharge is also put on to the charterers.

The position is less clear if the words "and discharge" are not added. It is submitted, however, that if it is usual in the trade (as it almost invariably will be under modern time charter arrangements) for the charterers, or those for whom they are responsible, to provide and pay for stevedores at ports of discharge, the position will be the same as if the words "and discharge" had been added to Clause 8.

Under Clause 2 of the New York Produce form the charterers are to "provide and pay for . . . all other usual expenses except those before stated". It is considered that stevedoring expenses at ports of discharge will fall within "other usual expenses" where such expenses are usually borne by charterers. Further, it was said by Greer, J., in *Brys & Gylsen* v. *Drysdale* (1920) 4 Ll.L.Rep. 24, a case relating to responsibility for stowage under a voyage charter, that: "where a Charter-party uses the words 'provide and pay' or 'employ and pay' ['a stevedore'], I think the effect of such a clause is to transfer the duty and obligation, which would otherwise rest on the shipowner, to the Charterer . . ."

Discharge during the course of the voyage

The charterers' obligations in regard to discharge usually apply only to discharge at the designated discharging place. If discharge is necessary during the course of the voyage, then *prima facie* the cost of such discharge falls not upon the charterers but upon the owners. The position will be different if the discharge is necessitated by the charterers' breach or can be shown to be a necessary consequence of the charterers' orders; in the former case the owners would be entitled to recover the expenses of discharge as damages and in the latter by way of indemnity under the employment clause (see page 239 above).

The *Aquacharm* was time chartered for a trip on the New York Produce form, Clause 8 being amended to include "and discharge". Having been ordered to load to maximum draft for a passage through the Panama Canal, the master negligently failed to take into account that in passing through a freshwater lake which forms part of the Canal, the ship's forward draft would increase. The ship was consequently refused entry to the Canal and part of the cargo had to be discharged, carried through the Canal on another ship and then reloaded. It was held by the Court of Appeal that the costs of discharging were not recoverable under Clause 8, which was applicable only to discharging at the port of discharge, and that the claim for an indemnity failed because of the master's negligence.
The Aquacharm [1982] 1 Lloyd's Rep. 7.

The *Pythia* was time chartered for a trip to the Shatt-al-Arab on the New York Produce form, Clause 8 being amended to include "and discharge". Part of the cargo had to be lightened at an anchorage at the mouth of the River Shatt, the remaining cargo being due for discharge at Khorramshahr, about 60 or 70 miles up river. After lightening at the anchorage, the ship was in collision and had to return to the anchorage to discharge the Khorramshahr cargo. It was held that the costs of discharging the Khorramshahr cargo at the anchorage (which the charterers had not designated as a new discharging place) were not the liability of the charterers under Clause 8.
The Pythia [1982] 2 Lloyd's Rep. 160.
(See also *The Hellas in Eternity*, LMLN 221–23, April 1988.)

In *The Pythia*, above, Robert Goff, J., said at page 164: "If the time charterers order the ship to load cargo at one port for carriage to another, it is the owners' obligation to comply with those orders and therefore to carry the cargo in the chartered ship to the designated discharging port. If the ship encounters an impediment on the way, the owners may be excused responsibility for the consequences by reason of an exception clause in the charter, though if they can overcome that impediment by reasonable measures and they do not take such measures they cannot say that the consequent delay has been caused by the excepted peril. If those reasonable measures involve expense they must incur it."

Effect of Carriage of Goods by Sea Act

The division of responsibility for cargo operations by Clause 8 is not, under English law, affected by the incorporation of the U.S. Carriage of Goods by Sea Act into the charter by Clause 24. This is so despite the obligation placed upon the carrier, in this context the owners (see *The Khian Zephyr* [1982] 1 Lloyd's Rep. 73), by Section 3(2) of that Act properly and carefully to load, stow and discharge the goods carried. The parties are free to divide the various cargo operations between themselves as they think fit, the Act providing for the manner in which the operations are to be carried out. Devlin, J., considering the equivalent provision in Article III, Rule 2 of the Schedule to the Carriage of Goods by Sea Act 1924, said in *Pyrene* v. *Scindia Navigation* [1954] 1 Lloyd's Rep. 321: "The phrase 'shall properly and carefully load' may mean that the carrier shall load and that he shall do it properly and carefully: or that he shall do whatever loading he does properly and carefully. The former interpretation perhaps fits the language more closely, but the latter may be more consistent with the object of the Rules. Their object . . . is to define not the scope of the contract service but the terms on which that service is to be performed. The extent to which the carrier has to undertake the loading of the vessel may depend not only upon different systems of law but upon the custom and practice of the port and the nature of the cargo. It is difficult to believe that the Rules were intended to impose a universal rigidity in this respect, or to deny freedom of contract to the carrier. The carrier is practically bound to play some part in the loading and discharging, so that both operations are naturally included in those covered by the contract of carriage. But I see no reason why the Rules should not leave the parties free to determine by their own contract the part which each has to play. On this view the whole contract of carriage is subject to the Rules, but the extent to which the loading and discharging are brought within the carrier's obligations is left to the parties themselves to decide."

This interpretation was approved by the House of Lords in *Renton* v. *Palmyra* [1956] 2 Lloyd's Rep. 379.

It follows from this interpretation of the Hague Rules that the incorporation of Section 3(2) of the U.S. Carriage of Goods by Sea Act does not under English law import into the charter an obligation on the owners, as carriers, to carry out or be responsible for the loading, stowing, or discharging of the cargo, when under other provisions of the charter the responsibility for undertaking these operations is put on the charterers.

(For general comments on the effect of the incorporation of the U.S. Carriage of Goods by Sea Act into the charter see page 425.)

Baltime form

Clause 4 of the Baltime form provides by Lines 34 and 35 that the charterers are to "arrange and pay for" loading, trimming, stowing and unloading. It is submitted that these words, likewise, are sufficient to transfer to the charterers the responsibility for these operations, whether the Hague Rules are incorporated into the charter or not. See page 459 below and *The Filikos* [1981] 2 Lloyd's Rep. 555, [1983] 1 Lloyd's Rep. 9 (C.A.).

Under the supervision of the Captain

The master has the right to supervise the cargo operations, particularly from a ship safety point of view, irrespective of the words "under the supervision of the Captain". But, leaving aside considerations of safety, he has no duty to the charterers to supervise: see the comments of Steyn, J., in the voyage charter case of *The Panaghia Tinnou* [1986] 2 Lloyd's Rep. 586, at page 591.

These words only qualify the primary responsibility that the New York Produce form places on the charterers for the loading and stowing of the cargo:

(a) if loss or damage is attributable to want of care in matters particularly within the province of the master, such as, for example, the stability of the ship; or
(b) if the master actually supervises the cargo operations and loss or damage is attributable to that supervision.

The *Ovington Court* was time chartered under the New York Produce form for a voyage to the North Pacific and return to the United Kingdom or Continent. During the currency of the charter the owners became liable to compensate receivers of a cargo of wheat for damage caused by improper stowage. The charterers resisted the owners' claim for indemnity, contending that stowage was the responsibility of the Captain. The House of Lords held that the improper stowage was the charterers' responsibility and that the owners were entitled to an indemnity.

Having rejected the contention that the words "under the supervision of the Captain" threw the responsibility for stowage on to the Captain, Lord Atkin went on, at page 166:

> "The supervision of the stowage by the captain is in any case a matter of course; he has in any event to protect his ship from being made unseaworthy; and in other respects no doubt he has the right to interfere if he considers that the proposed stowage is likely to impose a liability upon his owners. If it could be proved by the charterers that the bad stowage was caused only by the captain's orders, and that their own proposed stowage would have caused no damage, no doubt that might enable them to escape liability. But the reservation of the right of the captain to supervise, a right which in my opinion would have existed even if not expressly reserved, has no effect whatever in relieving that charterers of their primary duty to stow safely; any more than

the stipulation that a builder in a building contract should build under the supervision of the architect relieves the builder from duly performing the terms of his contract."

Lord Wright also said, at page 168:

" . . . under Clause 8 of this charterparty the charterers are to load, stow, and trim the cargo at their expense. I think these words necessarily import that the charterers take into their hands the business of loading and stowing the cargo. It must follow that they not only relieve the ship of the duty of loading and stowing, but as between themselves and the shipowners relieve them [the shipowners] of liability for bad stowage, except as qualified by the words 'under the supervision of the captain' . . . These words expressly give the master a right which I think he must in any case have, to supervise the operations of the charterers in loading and stowing . . . But I think this right is expressly stipulated not only for the sake of accuracy, but specifically as a limitation of the charterers' rights to control the stowage. It follows that to the extent that the master exercises supervision and limits the charterers' control of the stowage the charterers' liability will be limited in a corresponding degree."

Court Line v. *Canadian Transport* (1940) 67 Ll.L.Rep. 161.

If the ship is damaged by the negligence of the stevedores in these operations, the damage will be recoverable by the owners from the charterers under this clause, subject to any defence that the damage was in fact attributable to the master's supervision.

"and responsibility" of the Captain

Where it is intended by the parties that responsibility for the operations set out in Line 78 shall be upon the owners, it is usual for the words "and responsibility" to be inserted after "supervision". The addition of these words has been held to effect a *prima facie* transfer from the charterers back to the owners of liability for the entire operation of loading, stowing, trimming and (where the charter is suitably amended) discharging of the cargo, unless it can be shown that the charterers have intervened and in so doing have caused the relevant loss or damage. This *prima facie* transfer of liability to the owners covers not only loss or damage to the cargo but also damage caused to the ship. It is not confined to the mechanical process of handling the ship's gear and cargo, but extends also to the strategic planning of cargo operations.

In each of the three cases which follow, the charter was on the New York Produce form, with Line 78 amended to include "discharge" and with "and responsibility" inserted after "supervision". Each charter also incorporated an additional clause providing, with insignificant variations, that: "The Master shall supervise the stowage of the cargo thoroughly and let one of his officers control all loading, handling, (stowage) and discharge of the cargo . . .."

The *Shinjitsu Maru No. 5* was time chartered by disponent owners for a trip from New Zealand to West Africa. She was ordered to load palletised cargo in New Zealand and it was planned to construct boxing in the holds (which were not of a suitable shape for pallets) and also, after five tiers of pallets had been loaded, to build above them a wooden floor upon which forklift trucks could be used to load the rest of the cargo. Loading of the pallets began before the boxing was complete and the stow was insufficiently firm. Moreover, the shippers refused to allow forklifts to operate on the planned wooden floor, for fear of damage to the cargo already in stow, and the floor was not therefore constructed. The master was unhappy with the resulting stow. He protested to the stevedores, but was ignored. A surveyor appointed by the stevedores advised the master that the stow would be safe with additional lashing, but in fact the ship was, as the arbitrators found, unseaworthy on sailing by reason of the instability of the stow. Shortly after sailing the cargo shifted and the ship had to put back to re-stow the cargo, with consequent loss of time and expenses. Arbitrators held that the master was negligent, but apportioned liability as to 60 per cent. to the owners and as to 40 per cent. to the charterers. It was held by Neill, L.J. (as he had then become), sitting at first instance, that:

(1) the addition of the words "and responsibility" *prima facie* transferred liability for bad stowage to the owners; they could escape this liability only by proving that the relevant loss had been caused by some intervention or interference by the charterers (the converse situation to that prevailing under the unamended clause);
(2) there was no evidence of interference by the charterers themselves and, although it was admitted that the charterers were responsible for the actions of the shippers, there was no interference by the shippers sufficient to found an estoppel or sufficiently causative of the loss to give rise to any liability on the charterers;
(3) the stevedores and the surveyor appointed by them were not to be regarded as agents of the charterers;
(4) the dominant and the effective cause of the loss was the negligence of the master, having regard to his responsibility for stowage under this charter and his overall responsibility for the seaworthiness of the ship;
(5) the Law Reform (Contributory Negligence) Act 1945 did not apply and no apportionment of fault could be made. (The Court of Appeal in *Forsikringsaktieselskapet Vesta* v. *Butcher* [1988] 1 Lloyd's Rep. 19, disagreed with Neill, L.J.'s reasoning on the question of the application of the 1945 Act, although it does not necessarily follow that they would have disagreed with the decision in this particular case; see page 250 below.)

A.B. Marintrans v. *Comet Shipping (The Shinjitsu Maru No. 5)* [1985] 1 Lloyd's Rep. 568.

The *Argonaut* was time chartered for a trip and loaded granite blocks for discharge at two ports. At both discharging ports the ship's tank tops were damaged as a result of unsafe methods of working adopted by the stevedores and (at the first port only) the inadequacy of the forklift trucks employed. Arbitrators held that the master was not to blame for the damage caused at the first port, because that was mainly attributable to matters outside "the master's province" (inadequacy of stevedore's gear brought on board) and he had not failed to seek adequately to control the stevedoring operations. But they held that, with the experience of damage at the first port, he should have insisted on better precautions being taken at the second port and so was responsible for the damage suffered there.

Leggatt J., followed Neill, L.J.'s decision as to the effect of the additional words "and responsibility" in *The Shinjitsu Maru No. 5*. He held that Clause 8 as amended placed the primary duty on the owners and, in the absence of actual intervention by the charterers, the owners were responsible for all cargo operations whether or not "within the master's province". The charterers were therefore not liable for the damage to the tank tops at either port.

The Argonaut [1985] 2 Lloyd's Rep. 216.

In the third case, *The Alexandros P* [1986] 1 Lloyd's Rep. 421, in which the New York Produce form charter was similarly amended, Steyn, J., followed the decisions in *The Shinjitsu Maru No. 5* and in *The Argonaut*. This case also related to stevedore damage to the ship and Steyn, J., emphasised that the *prima facie* transfer of liability from the charterers to the owners covered all the operations referred to in Clause 8 and covered negligence of the stevedores in planning those operations as much as in the mechanical carrying out of the operations themselves.

Estoppel

Circumstances might conceivably arise in which it could not be said that intervention by the charterers or those for whom they were responsible actually caused the relevant loss or damage, but in which the conduct of the charterers or their representatives (for example a supercargo or a surveyor appointed by them) might be held to estop them from asserting that the master was at fault. Neill, L.J., considered such an argument in *The Shinjitsu Maru No. 5*, above, but rejected it as there was no finding of fact by the arbitrators which would have supported such a conclusion. But in *Ismail* v. *Polish Ocean Lines (The Ciechocinek)* [1976] 1 Lloyd's Rep. 489, a voyage charter case, the Court of Appeal held that a shipper was estopped from asserting that the stowage of cargo was deficient, when the charterers' appointed representative had attended the loading, had given assurances as to the packing of the cargo and had issued instructions as to the stowage.

Law Reform (Contributory Negligence) Act 1945

The Law Reform (Contributory Negligence) Act 1945 provides for the apportionment of liability for negligence where damage is suffered by the claimant as a result partly of his own fault. In *The Shinjitsu Maru No. 5*, above, Neill, L.J., concluded in broad terms that the Act did not apply to a claim in contract. In analysing that conclusion in *Forsikringsaktieselskapet Vesta* v. *Butcher* [1986] 2 Lloyd's Rep. 179 and [1988] 1 Lloyd's Rep. 19 (C.A.)—a case relating to breach of the professional duty of care owed by reinsurance brokers to their clients—Hobhouse, J., with whom the Court of Appeal agreed, pointed out that contract cases in which the question of contributory negligence might arise could be divided into three categories:

(1) where the defendant's liability arises from some contractual provision which does not depend on negligence on the part of the defendant;
(2) where the defendant's liability arises from a contractual obligation which is expressed in terms of taking care (or its equivalent) but does not correspond to a common law duty to take care which would exist in the given case independently of contract;
(3) where the defendant's liability in contract is the same as his liability in the tort of negligence independently of the existence of any contract.

Insofar as Neill, L.J., in the *The Shinjitsu Maru No. 5* excluded the operation of the 1945 Act from cases within category (3), Hobhouse, J., and the Court of Appeal in *Vesta* v. *Butcher* held that he was wrong, that in such cases (including the case before them) the 1945 Act did apply and that an apportionment of damages could be made. In so holding, they considered themselves bound by the decision of the Court of Appeal in *Sayers* v. *Harlow U.D.C.* [1958] 1 W.L.R. 623 (personal injury to a contractual visitor to premises).

Hobhouse, J., expressed the view at page 197 of the first instance report that *The Shinjitsu Maru No. 5* was probably a category (1) case, but at most a category (2) case, and that in regard to category (1) cases "one would not expect there to be much dispute that the Act does not apply". It was not necessary to decide whether the 1945 Act applied to category (2) cases, but the Court of Appeal expressed agreement with the construction of the 1945 Act adopted by Pritchard, J., in the New Zealand case *Rowe* v. *Turner Hopkins & Partners* [1980] 2 N.Z.L.R. 550, to the effect that the power to apportion arises only where the defendant is liable in tort and the concurrent liability in contract is immaterial.

In *Quinn* v. *Burch* [1966] 2 Q.B. 370, Paull, J., had held that the Act did not apply to a case which might be categorised as either a category (1) or a category (2) case. By contrast, Brabin, J., at first instance in *De Meza* v. *Apple* [1974] 1 Lloyd's Rep. 508, had decided that the Act did apply to a category (2) situation; but the Court of Appeal in that case ([1975] 1 Lloyd's Rep. 498) declined to express a view on the issue.

For circumstances in which the 1945 Act might apply in certain unsafe port cases see page 149 above.

The Inter-Club New York Produce Exchange Agreement

The absence of clear guidance in the New York Produce form on how liability for cargo claims was to be divided between owners and charterers led the major Protection and

Indemnity Associations (who insure the cargo liabilities of both owners and time-charterers) to draw up an agreement to facilitate the settlement of claims between those Associations who are parties to the Agreement.

Owners and charterers are not bound to follow the Agreement merely because they are members of the Associations, but the Associations do undertake to recommend their members to consent to their disuptes being resolved in accordance with its terms. Sometimes the Agreement is expressly incorporated into a New York Produce form charter. Where this is done, the effect is "to make the terms of an agreement between clubs applicable directly between charterer and owner": *The Ion* [1980] 2 Lloyd's Rep. 245, at page 248. See also *The Strathnewton* [1983] 1 Lloyd's Rep. 219, and page 253 below.

In its current form, which now incorporates a two-year time limit for notification of claims, the Agreement reads as follows:

INTER-CLUB NEW YORK PRODUCE EXCHANGE AGREEMENT

(As amended May 1984)

Preamble

Memorandum of Agreement (hereinafter referred to as "the Agreement") as to the apportionment of liability for cargo claims arising under the New York Produce Exchange Charter between Assuranceforeningen Gard, Assuranceforeningen Skuld, The Britannia Steam Ship Insurance Association Limited, The Liverpool and London Steamship Protection and Indemnity Association Limited, The London Steam-Ship Owners' Mutual Insurance Association Limited, Newcastle Protection and Indemnity Association, The North of England Protecting & Indemnity Association Limited, The Standard Steamship Owners' Protection and Indemnity Association Limited, The Standard Steamship Owners' Protection and Indemnity Association (Bermuda) Limited, The Steamship Mutual Underwriting Association Limited, The Sunderland Steamship Protecting & Indemnity Association, Sveriges Angfartygs Assurans Forening, The United Kingdom Mutual Steamship Assurance Association (Bermuda) Limited and The West of England Ship Owners Mutual Protection and Indemnity Association (Luxembourg) (hereinafter together referred to as "the parties").

(1) Application and interpretation of the Agreement

Subject to the undermentioned conditions the formula as set forth in Clause 2 shall apply in respect of Charters on the New York Produce Exchange form entered into after the 1st. June 1984.

(i) It shall be a condition precedent to settlement under the Agreement that the cargo claim, including any legal costs incurred thereon, shall have been properly settled or compromised and the cargo carried under a bill or bills of lading incorporating the Hague or Hague-Visby Rules or containing terms no less favourable. Ex gratia settlements made for business or other reasons where there is no legal liability to pay the claim shall be borne in full by the party by whom the payment is made and for the purpose of this Agreement no regard shall be had to such payments.

(ii) (a) For the Agreement to apply, the cargo responsibility clauses in the New York Produce Exchange Charter must not be materially amended. A material amendment is one which makes the liability for cargo claims, as between Owners and Charterers, clear. In particular the addition of the words "and discharge" in Clause 8 shall not be deemed to be a material amendment.

(b) However the addition of the words "and responsibility" with reference to the words "under the supervision" in Clause 8 together with the addition of the words "cargo claims" in the second sentence of Clause 26 shall render the Agreement inoperative. The addition of these two amendments, or the addition only of the words "cargo claims" in Clause 26, without any other material provision in the Charter shall mean that Owners shall bear all cargo claims subject to Charterers' contribution under the Berth Standard of Average Clause/Charterers' Contribution Clause (1971), if applicable.

(c) If the only material amendment is the addition of the words "and responsibility" with reference to the words "under the supervision" in Clause 8, it is agreed by the parties hereto that it shall mean that the apportionment of cargo claims as set out in Clause 2 shall be varied in the following manner:—

Claims for loss of or damage to cargo due to unseaworthiness and claims for condensation damage resulting solely from improper ventilation	100% Owners
Claims for damage (including slackage/ullage) due to bad stowage or handling, and claims for condensation damage resulting otherwise than from improper ventilation	50% Owners 50% Charterers
Except as provided in the second paragraph of Clause (2), short delivery claims (including pilferage) and claims for overcarriage	50% Owners 50% Charterers

(iii) The Agreement shall apply regardless of the place of Arbitration or the legal forum and whether or not the Charter contains a Clause Paramount incorporating therein the Hague or Hague-Visby Rules and/or the Berth Standard of Average Clause (otherwise known as the General Standard of Claim Clause/Charterers' Contribution Clause (1971).

(iv) Any claims pursued under this Agreement by or on behalf of either Charterers or Owners should be notified to the other party in writing as soon as possible but in any event within two years from the date of discharge or the date when the goods should have been discharged, failing which any recovery shall be deemed to be waived and time barred. Such notification should record bill of lading details and the nature and amount of the claim.

(v) Where the Charter contains the Berth Standard of Average Clause/Charterers' Contribution Clause (1971), such clause is to be applied after liability has been apportioned in accordance with Clause (2) or Clause (1)(ii)(c) as the case may be and Charterers' contribution under such clause shall be per cargo voyage and not per bill of lading or parcel of cargo notwithstanding anything to the contrary contained therein.

(vi) Where Sub-Charters are involved the Agreement, unless the parties hereto otherwise agree in any specific case, shall be applied in stages starting with the party who first settles the cargo claims. For example in the case of a single sub-charter, if the cargo claims are settled by the Sub-Charterers, the said claims shall first be apportioned between the Sub-Charterers and the Charterers in accordance with the Agreement, the Charterers being treated for the purpose as if they were the "Owners", the balance falling to Charterers' account thereafter being apportioned between the Charterers and Owners in accordance with the Agreement.

(vii) The Agreement is not binding on Members but in all cases the parties will recommend without qualification its acceptance to Members.

(2) Apportionment of cargo claims

In all cases where the Agreement applies cargo claims shall be apportioned as hereunder:—

Claims for loss of or damage to cargo due to unseaworthiness	100% Owners
Claims for damage (including slackage/ullage) due to bad stowage or handling	100% Charterers
Except as provided in the succeeding paragraphs of this clause, short delivery claims (including pilferage), claims for overcarriage, and claims for condensation damage	50% Owners 50% Charterers

As regards short delivery and overcarriage claims, where there is clear and irrefutable evidence that the shortage or overcarriage, as the case may be, was due to act, neglect or default on the part of Owners' or Charterers' servants or agents, then the party whose servants or agents were at fault shall bear the claim in full. Thus if there is corroborated eyewitness evidence that the shortage was due to pilferage by a stevedore, the claim will fall 100% to the account of Charterers, but if by a crewmember, then 100% to Owners, subject in the latter case to Charterers' contribution under the Berth Standard of Average Clause/Charterers' Contribution Clause (1971).

Claims for condensation damage shall be apportioned as provided in the first paragraph of this clause, except where there is clear evidence that the damage was due solely to bad stowage in which event such claims shall fall 100% to Charterers' account but where there is clear evidence that the damage resulted solely from improper ventilation, such claims shall be borne 100% by Owners.

(3) Extension of agreement

It shall be open to the parties to apply in whole or in part the Agreement if they so desire notwithstanding that it is not strictly applicable by reason of any of the matters set forth in Clause 1.

(4) Duration

The Agreement shall continue in force until varied or terminated. Any variation to be effective must be approved in writing by all the parties but it is open to any Association to withdraw from the Agreement on giving to all the other parties not less than three months' written notice thereof, such withdrawal to take effect at the expiration of that period. After the expiry of such notice the Agreement shall nevertheless continue as between all the parties, other than the party giving such notice who shall remain bound by and be entitled to the benefit of this Agreement in respect of all cargo claims arising out of charters commenced prior to the expiration of such notice.

For example if the Standard Association gave written notice of withdrawal from the Agreement on the 1st. of January 1985, it would be bound to apply the Agreement in respect of cargo claims arising out of charters commenced at any time on or before the 31st. March 1985.

(5) Operation

Nothing herein contained shall affect any settlement already concluded between the parties to this Agreement.

Incorporation of Inter-Club Agreement and Carriage of Goods by Sea Act

The one-year time limit on cargo claims by charterers against owners, to which a charter on the New York Produce form is normally subject as a result of the incorporation of the United States Carriage of Goods by Sea Act (see *The Agios Lazaros* [1976] 2 Lloyd's Rep. 47), does not apply under a charter into which the parties have expressly incorporated the original (1970) version of the Inter-Club Agreement: *The Strathnewton* [1983] 1 Lloyd's Rep. 219 (C.A.). In that case Kerr, L.J., said, at page 225, that the Agreement "cuts right across any allocation of functions and responsibilities based on the Hague Rules . . . " and "provides a more or less mechanical apportionment of financial laibility which is wholly independent of these standards of obligation". See also *The Benlawers* [1989] 2 Lloyd's Rep. 51. But the current (1984) version of the Inter-Club Agreement, above, requires notification of claims within two years of the date of discharge, or the date when the goods should have been discharged, failing which any recovery is deemed to be waived and time barred (see Clause (1)(iv) of the Agreement.)

Berth Standard of Average Clause

This clause, which is referred to in the Inter-Club New York Produce Exchange Agreement and which is often incorporated in time charters for liner trading, reads as follows:

In the event of the vessel loading on the berth and/or loading general cargo the Charterers shall bear a sum equal to . . . per gross ton of the vessel's maximum register in respect of claims arising on any cargo voyage from improper handling during loading and discharging, improper stowage, short delivery (whether from pilferage or any other cause whatsoever) or over-carriage for which there may be as between Owners and Charterers responsibility on the part of the Owners and also in respect of any reconditioning expenses incurred in order to avoid or mitigate any such claims. If the Owners shall pay any such claims in the first instance they shall be indemnified by the Charterers to the foregoing extent.

For cases in which the Berth Standard of Average Clause was considered see *Clan Line* v. *Ove Skou* [1969] 2 Lloyd's Rep. 155 and *The Filikos* [1981] 2 Lloyd's Rep. 555, [1983] 1 Lloyd's Rep. 9 (C.A.).

Charterers to have benefit of owners' P. &. I. cover

For a decision on the frequently added clause providing for the charterers to have the benefit of the owners' protection and indemnity cover, see *Court Line* v. *Canadian Transport* (1940) 67 Ll.L.Rep. 161.

American Law

The leading American case on the respective obligations of owner and charterer for the loading and stowage of the cargo is *Nichimen Company* v. *The Farland*, 462 F.2d 319 (2d Cir. 1972). In that case, the cargo interests sued both A/S Vigra, the vessel owner, and Seaboard Shipping Co. Ltd., the time charterer, for damage to a cargo of steel. The court held that the cargo interests were entitled to recover, and it was then left to determine whether Vigra, as the owner, or Seaboard, as charterer, was ultimately liable for the loss. The court first noted the long recognized principle that "absent any special provision or circumstance, the duty to load, stow and discharge cargo—and the consequences for failing to do so properly—fall upon the ship and her owners". (462 F.2d at 330.) The court then went on to find that Clause 8 of the New York Produce form shifts responsibility for stowage to the charterer:

> . . . Under Clause 8, the safety of the stowage, insofar as cargo damage is concerned, generally is the primary responsibility of the charterer. (462 F.2d at 332.)

The court further noted, however, that there are instances in which an owner may be liable for cargo damage, even where the master was not involved in the loading or stowage. Thus, if cargo damage was caused by the owner's failure to exercise due diligence to make the vessel seaworthy or maintain her in a "thoroughly efficient state" during the voyage, the owner would be liable:

> If cargo damage were to occur because of some defect in the vessel which the Captain had failed to discover and correct, primary liability would rest with the owner; the cause of the damage would not be within the scope of the responsibilities which Clause 8 was intended to shift from the owner to the charterer . . . Likewise, if some inherent vice of the vessel would make otherwise proper stowage hazardous and the Captain and owner failed to reveal this to the charterer or his stevedore, we doubt whether Clause 8 would relieve the owner of primary liability for cargo damage. (Id.)

The decision in *The Farland* is in line with the earlier Supreme Court case of *The Nidarholm*, 282 U.S. 681 (1931). There a cargo of lumber was shipped on deck under a time charter with provisions similar to those of Clause 8. Immediately after loading the vessel developed a five-degree list. This was followed by the collapse of the "cribs" upon which the deck cargo had been stowed, and a quantity of cargo went over the side and was lost. The court held that the list, which contributed to the collapse of the deck stow, was a fault attributable to the owner as part of its responsibility to maintain the vessel's seaworthiness in the sense of her stability and trim. However, the court also found fault on the part of charterer insofar as the cribs, which were a function of stowage, should have been able to withstand the stress of a five-degree list. Hence, damages were divided evenly.

In an early decision, the District Court in New York held in *The Santona*, 152 Fed. 516 (S.D.N.Y. 1970):

> The ship is the Owners' ship and the Master and crew his servants for all details of navigation and care of the vessel; but for all matters relating to the receipt and delivery of the cargo, and those earnings of the vessel which flow into the pockets of the Charterers, the Master and crew are the servants of the Charterers. There is, in fact (to borrow a simile from another branch of the law), an estate carved out of the ship and handed over for a specified term to the Charterer, and that estate consists of the capacity of the vessel for carrying freight and earning freight moneys, and the use of the vessel, Master and crew, for the advancement of the Charterers' gains.

In *Nissho-Iwai Co. Ltd.* v. *M/T Stolt Lion*, 617 F.2d 907, 1980 AMC 868 (2d Cir.

1980), rev'g 1979 AMC 2415 (S.D.N.Y. 1979), the court reiterated the rule it enunciated in *The Farland*, stating that the responsibility for discharge of cargo remained with the owner in the absence of any "Clause 8" charterparty provision or any action or custom of the parties which would serve to shift the burden onto the charterer.

The Farland was also followed in *Seguros Banvenez S.A.* v. *S/S Oliver Drescher*, 761 F.2d 855, 1985 AMC 2168 (2d Cir. 1985). See also *Nitram Inc.* v. *Cretan Life*, 599 F.2d 1359, 1366 (5th Cir. 1979). See generally *Thyssen Inc.* v. *S.S. Fortune Star*, 777 F.2d 57, 1986 AMC 1318 (2d Cir. 1985) stating in *dictum* that a charterer responsible under a Clause 8 type charter provision for a deviation because of the on deck stowage of cargo could not be held liable for punitive damages.

Under the supervision of the Captain

Perhaps the most difficult problem under Clause 8 concerns the role of the master. The English view, that the master's active participation in loading and stowage may render the owner *ipso facto* liable, generally has not been followed in New York. Rather, the approach is to consider not whether the master acted, but in what capacity he acted. Thus, it is said that the master "wears two hats" or performs a dual agency. To the extent he is carrying out the owner's responsibility to furnish a vessel that is seaworthy in the traditional sense (i.e., watertight, stable, in proper trim and structurally sound) he acts as the owner's agent. However, to the extent he is carrying out the charterer's responsibility properly to load, stow and discharge (which also represents "seaworthiness" in the modern sense, *vis-à-vis* cargo interests) he acts as the charterer's agent. Thus, both the master and crew become the charterer's "borrowed servants" when the charterer uses them to discharge the responsibilities assumed by the charterer under Clause 8. The principle was enunciated in *The Farland* as follows:

> . . . we think the Owner's liability for cargo damage due to improper stowage is limited to instances in which the Captain intervenes in the stowage process to protect the vessel's safety and ability to withstand the perils of the sea; to the extent that he acts merely to protect the cargo, the charterer is responsible. (462 F.2d at 333.)

See also *The Agios Panteleimon*, S.M.A. No. 1477 (Arb. at N.Y. 1980), where the panel concluded that the master was responsible for the proper stowage of the cargo and the safe and proper navigation of the vessel which included proper draft planning. It was the responsibility of the owner and the master to take into account the fact that the ship had a sag when making plans as a navigator to implement load and trim parameters. In *The Drosia*, S.M.A. No. 1303 (Arb. at N.Y. 1979), the panel ruled that time lost in off-loading fuel and water when the master negligently allowed the vessel to be loaded over her load line was for the owner's account and charterer was entitled to off-hire. But in *The Robertina*, S.M.A. No. 1151 (Arb. at N.Y. 1977), the panel held that while the captain may be the servant of the owner with respect to vessel safety and stability, he is the servant of the charterer with respect to the utilization of the vessel's available capactiy, and the risk of being unable to load a particular quantity of cargo because of improper stowage or trimming must be borne by the charterer.

In *Spence* v. *Mariehamns R/S*, 766 F.2d 1504, 1986 AMC 685 (11th Cir. 1985), the court held that "under the supervision of the captain" did not impose a duty on the vessel owner to supervise stevedoring operations in loading or discharging cargo. In that case, the vessel owner was excused from liability for injuries suffered by a longshoreman during the unloading of cargo.

In *The Aetolia*, S.M.A. No. 2157 (Arb. at N.Y. 1985), the panel held that the owner was not liable for the cost of securing cargo which resulted from the master's failure to prepare a pre-plan for the stowage of the cargo in a way which would not have required the cargo's securing. According to the panel, this fell within the charterer's duty to load, stow, and trim the cargo.

The panel also ruled that expenses incurred in the securing of the cargo for purposes of trim are for the charterer's account under Clause 8. See also *The Unibulk Fir*, S.M.A. No. 1505 (Arb. at N.Y. 1980); *The North Emperor*, S.M.A. No. 1284 (Arb. at N.Y. 1978); and *The Dorothea Boulton*, S.M.A. No. 1211 (Arb. at N.Y. 1978).

See also *Int'l Produce Inc.* v. *The Frances Salman*, 1975 AMC 1521, 1523–24, 1544 (S.D.N.Y. 1975); *A/S Brovanor* v. *Central Gulf S.S. Corp.*, 323 F.Supp. 1029, 1032 (S.D.N.Y. 1970); *Isbrandtsen Co.* v. *George S. Boutwell*, 1958 AMC 351 (S.D.N.Y. 1957); *Socomet* v. *Sliedrecht*, 1975 AMC 314 (S.D.N.Y. 1975); *The Mesologi*, 1971 AMC 2498 (Arb. at N.Y. 1971); *Interstate Steel Corp.* v. *S.S. Coastal Gem*, 371 F.Supp. 112 (S.D.N.Y. 1970); *Yeramex International* v. *Tendo*, 595 F.2d 943, 1979 AMC 1282 (4th Cir. 1979), rev'g 1977 AMC 1807 (E.D. Va. 1977); *Board of Commissioners of the Port of New Orleans* v. *M/V Space King*, 1978 AMC 856 (E.D. Va. 1978).

Still another difficulty arises when the words "and responsibility of the Captain" are added at the end of Clause 8, as is frequently done. Do these words shift liability for improper stowage back to the owner, as may be the case in England? Probably not. In *Coca-Cola Co.* v. *The Norholt*, 333 F.Supp. 946, 1972 AMC 388 (S.D.N.Y. 1971), the owner of a cargo of tea commenced an action against the vessel owner and the time charterer. The cargo owner reached a settlement agreement with both parties, who then had a trial to determine which should bear the loss. The court held that the cargo damage was caused in part by an unseaworthy condition, and in part by improper stowage. As to the latter cause, the charterer attempted to shift liability to the owner by contending that under Clause 8 of the charter, the owner had assumed responsibility for the stowage. The printed charter form had been amended, so that Clause 8 included the following language:

> Charterers are to load, *discharge*, stow and trim the cargo at their own expense under the supervision of the Captain *and responsibility of the Captain.*

The trial judge found that notwithstanding the amendments to Clause 8, "in reading the charter agreement as a whole, and as supplemented by the various acts of the parties, I must conclude that the charterer took great pains to reserve to itself virtually every facet of the stowage". The charterer had prepared a preliminary cargo stowage plan, and had made the alternate decision, over the master's protest, to stow the tea in the No. 1 hold, immediately above a cargo of noxious cresylic acid. The decision appears to be correct, since the words "and responsibility" may be read as merely emphasizing or enlarging the master's basic obligation to protect both the vessel and her cargo. If a shift of responsibility to the *owner* is intended, with the potentially drastic consequences attendant, clearer language should be employed. For example, an addition at the end of Clause 8, reading "provided, however, that any act or omission by the Master or crew in assisting in the loading, stowage or discharge of the cargo shall be the responsibility of the owner", should certainly suffice to achieve this objective.

In *The Holland*, S.M.A. No. 2114 (Arb. at N.Y. 1985), the charter had been amended to include a typewritten clause which stated: "if on deck, at charterer's risk and responsibility and at Master's discretion." The vessel loaded a cargo of rolled liner board paper which was stowed in the holds and on deck. The vessel was unstable, however, because too much cargo was loaded on deck. As a result of the vessel's unstable condition, she developed a serious list which resulted in the loss of deck cargo overboard and the wetting of cargo in the holds. The panel ruled that owner bore sole responsibility for the cargo damage. The panel stated that insofar as the seaworthiness and safety of the vessel were concerned, the master was responsible on behalf of the owner to assure himself that the vessel was stable. Because the cargo damage was attributable to the master's failure to make proper stability calculations, owner was responsible for the damage. According to the panel, the amendment to the charter relating to the loading of deck cargo did not shift liability to charterer.

A further issue which arises under Clause 8 concerns the extent of the charterer's liability for improper stowage. In the vast majority of cases, of course, the loss is limited to cargo. There are instances, however, where improper stowage can damage the ship herself or some third party. That the charterer's liability might extend beyond cargo cases was noted in *The Farland* but was not an issue there. However, the issue was squarely met in *Fernandez* v. *Chios Shipping*, 71 Civ. 2786 (S.D.N.Y. 1976), aff'd 542 F.2d 145 (2d Cir. 1976), where the court permitted a shipowner to recover indemnity from a time charterer with respect to a claim by a longshoreman injured during unloading operations. The court's decision was based on the time charterer's responsibility under Clause 8. The court stated:

> It is possible to read . . . *Nichimen* . . . to stand for the narrow proposition that, in cases of cargo damage, the ship owner is entitled to indemnity from the time charterer only upon a showing that either the direct or statutorily imputed negligence or other fault of the charterer caused the damage . . . However, such a restricted reading seems unjustified.
>
> What seems more likely is that, as between the ship owner and the charterer, Clause 8 of the time charter agreement shifts responsibility for loading, stowage, trimming, and discharge of cargo to the charterer, and the charterer must indemnify the ship owner for cargo damage which results from any improper performance of any of the stipulated cargo operations. In this view, the duty to perform the cargo operations carried with it an absolute obligation to indemnify the owner for any such damage, irrespective of any "fault" on the part of the charterer, and irrespective of the relationship, under agency law, between the charterer and the party which it employs to carry out its duties under the time charter agreement.
>
> The court is persuaded that the latter is the correct view . . . As between the shipowner and the charterer, it seems both a reasonable and fair construction of this clause [Clause 8] to require indemnity from the charterer for cargo damage, as discussed above. Since the charterer is "primarily responsible" for stowage and discharge, and since the ship captain's supervisory role is reduced to that of vetoing any plan which would imperil the seaworthiness of the ship, it would seem unfair to later predicate the indemnity *only* upon a direct showing of negligence by the charterer (who would, presumably hire a reputable stevedore to do the loading or discharge), or to allow the charterer to argue that it should not be held liable for the negligence of the stevedore, because the stevedore might be technically an independent contractor under the laws of . . . agency.
>
> * * *
>
> It seems clear to this court that, as construed by the Court of Appeals in *Nichimen*, Clause 8 shifts primary responsibility for the active control of cargo operations to the charterer . . . Moreover, where, as in this case, the finding of unseaworthiness against the shipowner is, in fact, predicated upon unsafe conditions created by stevedore and shipper rather than upon any conditions created by the shipowner, there seems to be no basis in equity for denying indemnity from the charterer, when the ship's captain retained such limited responsibility for cargo operations under the charter agreement.

The holding in *Fernandez* was expressly followed by the Ninth Circuit in *Turner* v. *Japan Lines Ltd.*, 651 F.2d 1300, 1981 AMC 2223 (9th Cir. 1981).

In *Haluapo* v. *Akashi Kaiun, K.K.S.A.M. Inc.*, 748 F.2d 1363, 1985 AMC 1107 (9th Cir. 1984), the Ninth Circuit explained its decision in *Turner* extensively in order to distinguish it from the instant case. In *Haluapo*, the vessel was bareboat chartered, then time chartered, then voyage chartered. The plaintiff was a longshoreman who was injured while discharging cargo. The injury was caused by a defective winch on board the vessel. The only party over whom plaintiff could obtain jurisdiction was the time charterer. The court dismissed that action on the grounds that the time charterer had no involvement in the operation of the vessel or the loading of the cargo, nor did it have knowledge of any defects on board the ship nor the ability to control the actions of the crew. The court distinguished *Turner*, finding that in *Turner* the time charterer had actually hired the stevedore. Moreover, according to the court, unlike the situation in *Turner*, the time charterer had no right or ability to control the actions of the crew members. It is questionable whether the latter statement of the court is a valid distinction. It appears that the court reached this conclusion based on uncontradicted affidavits submitted by the time charterer. In *Turner*, the court had found that the master of the vessel was an agent of the time charterer for certain purposes relating to the loading and discharge of cargo.

Similarly, in *The Mount Athos*, S.M.A. No. 1570 (Arb. at N.Y. 1981), the vessel's shell plating was punctured during the loading of a cargo of steel scrap as the result of stevedore negligence. The panel held that the damage was the responsibility of the charterer. According to the panel, the fact that the master was personally involved in the loading operation did not operate to shift liability for the damage away from the charterer.

In contrast, the court in *Desormeaux* v. *Oceans International Corp.*, 1979 AMC 1962 (W.D. La. 1979), held that under Clause 8 a time charterer is liable neither to an injured longshoreman for damages nor to the shipowner for indemnification in the absence of any evidence that the charterer exercised the kind of supervision and control over loading operations which would give rise to liability on the part of the charterer as an independent contractor. In holding thus, the court rejected *Fernandez* in favor of the Fifth Circuit interpretation of Clause 8 as stated in *D/S Ove Skou* v. *Herbert*, 365 F.2d 341, 1966 AMC 2223 (5th Cir. 1966), *cert.* denied 400 U.S. 902 (1970). In *Ove Skou*, the court denied the owner's claim for indemnity from the charterer, reasoning that:

> The typical clause specifying that the Captain shall be under the orders of the Charterers "as regards employment and agency" and that "charterers are to load, stow, and trim the cargo" does not give to Time Charterer any operational control over these activities. Rather, these charter party provisions are essentially a specification of the party—owner or charterer—upon whom the ultimate financial cost rests for any one or more of the activities.
>
> Although the charterer is to secure and pay for such port authorities as pilotage, towage, port charges, including arrangements for loading and discharging of cargo, such activities if conducted by the ship or its crew do not become those for which the time chaterer has an operational responsibility . . . In the absence of circumstances which would give rise to a liability for action taken by an independent contractor—none of which are present here—Time Charterer had no responsibility to shipowner or to third persons including longshoremen for acts of omission or commission by the stevedores.

See also *Bourgeois* v. *Bergen Juno*, 1979 AMC 1396 (E.D. La. 1978); *Warnock* v. *Daiichi Chuo Kisen Kaisha*, 1983 AMC 1463 (E.D. Ore. 1981); *Shaw* v. *South African Marine Corp.*, 1983 AMC 1578 (E.D. Va. 1982); *Roby* v. *Hyundai Merchant Marine*, 700 F. Supp. 316, 1989 AMC 1126 (E.D. La. 1988).

In *Hayes* v. *Wilh. Wilhelmsen Enterprises Ltd.*, 818 F.2d 1557, 1988 AMC 259 (11th Cir. 1987), the court dismissed a personal injury claim asserted against the time charterer of the vessel. Plaintiff was a longshoreman who was injured when he slipped on hydraulic fluid which had leaked from the hydraulically-operated cargo doors of the vessel. The court noted that while Clause 8 of the New York Produce form shifts responsibility for cargo operations to the time charterer, maintenance of the vessel's cargo doors was not within the scope of the responsibility assumed by the time charterer under Clause 8. According to the court, the condition on the deck affected the seaworthiness of the vessel and remained the responsibility of owner. Owner was liable for the negligence of the master and crew in failing to clean up or warn of the fluid. In so holding, the court appears to have relied upon the Second Circuit's decision in *Fernandez* v. *Chios Shipping*. The court's decision includes the concurring opinion of Senior District Judge Eaton which contains an extensive review of the case law and questions the wisdom of relying upon *Fernandez* except in cases involving indemnity claims between a shipowner and time charterer.

Interclub Agreement

In *The Trade Yonder*, S.M.A. 2435 (Arb. at N.Y. 1987), the charter incorporated the February 1970 Interclub Agreement. The panel denied most of charterer's claims for indemnity with respect to the settlement of cargo claims for shortage, physical damage and staining. The panel held that, because the charter was not amended to add the word "responsibility" to Clause 8 of the charter, under the Interclub Agreement, liability remained with charterer. However, the arbitrators apportioned liability as between owner and charterer 50/50 with respect to shortage claims on the basis of the Interclub Agreement.

Owner and charterer had been sued by the cargo receivers for condensation damage, shortages, and handling damage. Prior to trial, the cases were settled by owner, who then demanded contributions from charterer in accordance with the Interclub Agreement. Charterer declined owner's demand, and the matter was submitted to arbitration. In holding charterer liable to pay for 50 per cent. of the condensation damage, the panel applied paragraph 2 of the Interclub Agreement, quoted above at page 251. The panel found that the condensation damage at issue was not caused solely by bad stowage, nor was it the result merely of improper ventilation. Although the panel stated that it appeared that insufficient ventilation was the major cause of the condensation and that one might conclude that there was a greater degree of owner's faults, under the Interclub Agreement, there is to be an equal sharing of the damages unless there is "clear evidence" that one party was "solely" at fault. Having found that the condensation damage was not solely the fault of either improper ventilation or bad stowage, the arbitrators ruled that they were bound to apply the equal division of damages provided for in the Interclub Agreement.

Signing of Bills of Lading

[Clause 8 continued]

"78. . . . the Captain, who is to sign Bills of Lading for
79. cargo as presented, in conformity with Mate's or Tally Clerk's receipts."

As presented

The master of a ship chartered on the New York Produce form must normally sign bills of lading "as presented" to him by the charterers or their agents.

The *Ellen* was chartered to carry coke from Cardiff to Bilbao, the charter providing that the master was to sign bills of lading as presented. There was a threat of increased import duties on shipments of coke arriving after 30 June and the owners were apprehensive that these extra duties might be deducted from the balance of freight which was payable on delivery. The master refused to sign bills of lading in the ordinary form and insisted on inserting the words "vessel not liable for duties on cargo by non arrival before the 1st July". The charterers refused to accept such bills and eventually the ship sailed without bills of lading being signed. In the event, the apprehension about the imposition of increased duties proved unfounded. It was held that the master was in breach in refusing to sign bills of lading in the ordinary form and Bramwell, L.J., said, at page 124: "the captain was bound to sign a bill of lading. That means a bill of lading in the ordinary form, and not a bill of lading different from the ordinary forms, unless there is some special cause for his doing it, and there was none such here." However, since the charterers could not establish any damage resulting from the master's refusal to sign the bills, nominal damages only were awarded.
Jones v. *Hough* (1879) 5 Ex.D. 115.
(See also *Hansen* v. *Harrold* [1894] 1 Q.B. 612, *The Anwar Al Sabar* [1980] 2 Lloyd's Rep. 261 and *The Garbis* [1982] 2 Lloyd's Rep. 283.)

But there are circumstances in which the master of a ship under time charter may refuse to sign bills of lading. These circumstances, and the consequences of the master signing bills of lading which he might be entitled to refuse to sign, have not yet been comprehensively defined by the courts.

Jones v. *Hough* and the other authorities cited above were all cases relating to voyage charters. Time charterers have even wider powers to determine the form and contents of the bills of lading they may call on the master to sign. This was made clear by Lord Wilberforce in *The Nanfri* [1979] 1 Lloyd's Rep. 201 (and see pages 268 and 403), a case in which owners of ships chartered on the Baltime form instructed their masters to refuse to sign bills of lading marked "freight prepaid" and to insist that all bills would be claused so as to incorporate the terms of the time charters. He said, at page 206:

"It is important in this connection to have in mind that the present charters are time charters, the nature and purpose of which is to enable the charterers to use the vessels during the period of the charters for trading in whatever manner they think fit. The issue of bills of lading in a particular form may be vital for the charterers' trade, and indeed in relation to this trade, which involves c.i.f. or c. & f. contracts, the issue of freight pre-paid bills of lading is essential if the trade is to be maintained. Furthermore, Clause 9, as is usual in time charters, contains an indemnity clause against all consequences or liabilities arising from the master signing bills of lading. This underlines the power of the charterers, in the course of exploiting the vessel, to decide what bills of lading are appropriate for their trade and to instruct the masters to issue such bills, the owners being protected by the indemnity clause."

Bills imposing on owners greater liabilities than imposed by charter

It follows that the master of a ship under time charter will generally have no right to object if bills of lading are presented to him for signature which, by their terms, expose the owners to greater liabilities than those assumed by them under the terms of the time charter. But the owners will normally be entitled to recover from the charterers by way of indemnity (express or implied) any extra liability they incur.

Breach of contract

The earlier authorities on inconsistency between charter terms and bill of lading terms concern voyage charters. There is much support in them for the view that it is a breach of the contract for the charterers to require the master to sign a bill imposing on his owners a greater liability than they have agreed to accept under the charter, for example because the bill does not include an exception against a particular peril which is excepted under the charter.

The owners of the *Invermore* entered into a charter under which they were excepted from liability for negligence of the master. The charter further provided that the master was "to sign clean bills of lading for his cargo . . . without prejudice to this charter". The charterers presented and the master signed bills of lading which although purporting to incorporate the conditions of the charter, did not effectively incorporate the negligence clause. Ship and cargo were lost owing to the negligence of the master and the owners incurred liability to the bill of lading holders which they would not have incurred had the bills been subject to the negligence clause. It was held by the Court of Appeal and the House of Lords that the owners were entitled to recover from the charterers the amount they had been obliged to pay the bill of lading holders.
Kruger v. *Moel Tryvan* [1907] 1 K.B. 809 (C.A.) and [1907] A.C. 272 (H.L.).

In the Court of Appeal and the House of Lords the reason most relied upon for allowing the owners to recover was that the charterers were in breach in presenting such a bill and the owners were entitled to damages as a result. Similar views are evident in subsequent voyage charter cases, including the House of Lords case of *Elder, Dempster* v. *Dunn* (1909) 15 Com. Cas. 49 (bills with incorrect marks) and the Court of Appeal decision in *Dawson Line* v. *Adler* (1931) 41 Ll.L.Rep. 75 (bill showing less than actual weight of cargo, upon which freight was payable).

Implied indemnity

The other ground frequently relied on in the above cases, on its own or in the alternative, was that the inconsistency between charter and bill gave rise to an implied right of indemnity. Bingham, J., in *The C. Joyce* [1986] 2 Lloyd's Rep. 285, expressed the view—which was endorsed by the Court of Appeal in *The Nogar Marin* [1988] 1 Lloyd's Rep. 412, 420—that crucial to both grounds of decision in the House of Lords cases above "was the finding of disparity between the bills which the charterers were under the charter-party entitled to present and the bills which they did present". Bingham, J., continued: "From this finding the conclusion naturally follows, and it matters little whether the owners claim damages for breach of contract, of which an indemnity will be the measure, or an indemnity arising from the loss they have suffered from complying with the charterers' request to do something which they were not obliged to do under the charter-party."

These comments may be appropriate to voyage charter cases, but it is submitted that they are not necessarily appropriate in the case of time charters. It cannot be a breach of contract, under the usual forms of time charter requiring the master to sign bills of lading as presented, for the charterers to present for signature a bill which is more onerous in its terms than the charter. Nor can the presentation of such a bill for signature be said to oblige the owners "to do something which they were not obliged to do under the charter-party". It would be quite contrary to the purpose of normal time charters which is (within the limits of the express terms of the charters) "to enable the charterers to use the vessels during the period of the charters for trading in whatever manner they think fit": *The Nanfri* [1979] 1 Lloyd's Rep. 201, *per* Lord Wilberforce at page 206. It would furthermore be contrary to good sense. Consider the position under a time charter which does not incorporate the Hague Rules or any national legislation giving effect to them; most bills of lading issued under the charter will differ from it in that they will incorporate the Hague Rules by express reference or because they are compulsorily made subject to the Rules by the domestic legislation of the country of shipment or the country of intended destination. It cannot be correct to look at this in terms of breach or in terms of the presentation of non-contractual or improper bills of lading (see *The Paros* [1987] 2 Lloyd's Rep. 269, at page 273). It is submitted that under a time charter in the usual form, an indemnity should in such circumstances be implied either as a matter of construction or as a matter of business efficacy: see *The Nogar Marin* [1987] 1 Lloyd's Rep. 456, at page 460, *per* Staughton, J.

That this is the position under a New York Produce form charter was accepted by the parties in *The Caroline P* [1984] 2 Lloyd's Rep. 466 (see page 264 below), although Neill, J., did not rule out the possibility that the case could have been put on the basis of breach (see page 475 of the report.) It was common ground between the parties that since the bills of lading imposed more onerous obligations on the owners than those stipulated in the charter, the owners were entitled to the benefit of an implied indemnity. (Contrast the voyage charter case of *The C. Joyce* [1986] 2 Lloyd's Rep. 285, where it was held that the owners were not entitled to an indemnity under a heavily amended Gencon charter.)

In *Kruger* v. *Moel Tryvan* [1907] A.C. 272, Lord Loreburn, L.C., explained the implied indemnity in these words: "the shipowners undertook to carry a cargo on the footing that they were not to be liable for the master's negligent navigation, and the charterers have made them so liable by the bills of lading. Hence arises a duty to give adequate indemnity".

Express indemnity

Where the time charter contains an express indemnity (see the Baltime form, Lines 71 to 74), the effect will, in general, be the same as in the case where an indemnity is implied.

The time charter of the *Port Victor* contained exceptions against the negligence of master and crew. It also provided that the master should "sign bills of lading at any rate of freight the charterers or their agents may choose, without prejudice to the stipulations of this charterparty, and the charterers hereby agree to indemnify the owners from any consequences that may arise from the captain following the charterers' instructions and signing bills of lading". Bills of lading which contained no exception from negligence were presented and signed by the master and in consequence the owners were unable to recover general average contributions from cargo following a collision caused by the negligence of the master. It was held by the Court of Appeal that the owners were entitled to an indemnity from the charterers in respect of the loss suffered through not being able to recover general average contributions.

Milburn v. *Jamaica Fruit* [1900] 2 Q.B. 540.

(See also *The Nanfri* [1979] 1 Lloyd's Rep. 201.)

It may be in certain circumstances that an implied indemnity is wider in its scope than the express indemnity (see *Strathlorne Steamship* v. *Andrew Weir* (1934) 50 Ll.L.Rep. 185, and page 237 above).

Time when claim for indemnity arises

For limitation purposes, it is important to know when time starts to run on a claim for indemnity. If the claim is under an implied general indemnity, such as an implied indemnity in favour of owners under a time charter, time starts to run only upon the ascertainment of the liability by court judgment or otherwise. If the claim is under an express indemnity, it will depend upon whether the indemnity is to be construed as an indemnity against liability (in which case time will run from the time the liability is incurred) or as a general indemnity).

The *Caroline P.* was chartered on the New York Produce form, Clause 8 being amended to make the charterers responsible for discharge as well as loading and stowage. Bills of lading were presented, and signed on behalf of the master, which made the owners responsible for these operations to their endorsees. The owners were held liable in proceedings before the Iraqi courts, at the suit of the endorsees, for loss and damage to cargo caused in these operations. The question arose whether, on a claim by the owners against the charterers for an indemnity, time ran from the discharge of the cargo, when the liability was first incurred, or from the date of the first judgment of the Iraqi court, when the liability was first ascertained. It was common ground between the parties that in the circumstances some indemnity in favour of the owners was to be implied under the charter. It was held by Neill, J., that the indemnity to be implied was against the consequences of the master signing the bills of lading and that such an indemnity, being a general indemnity, did not become enforceable until the liability had been ascertained by the first judgment of the Iraqi court.

The Caroline P. [1984] 2 Lloyd's Rep. 446.

(For the express indemnity under Clause 9 of the Baltime form see pages 469 and 470 below.)

Extraordinary terms or terms "manifestly inconsistent" with charter

It has been said that the master is not obliged to sign bills of lading which contain extraordinary terms or terms which are "manifestly inconsistent" with the charter. In *Kruger* v. *Moel Tryvan* [1907] A.C. 272, Lord Halsbury said, at page 282: "When it is said that the master must sign any bill of lading submitted to him, I cannot agree. If the bill of lading tendered is manifestly inconsistent with the charterparty, I think it would be his duty to refuse . . . ". Lord Dunedin, in *Tillmanns* v. *Knutsford* [1908] A.C. 406, at page 410, spoke of stipulations of an "extraordinary character" in the following passage:

"Had the bill of lading contained stipulations of such an extraordinary character that the master might have refused to sign, then that defence would have been equally open upon the question of whether the signature of the charterers bound the owners."

(See page 270 above; and see also *The Berkshire* [1974] 1 Lloyd's Rep. 185, 188, *The Vikfrost* [1980] 1 Lloyd's Rep. 560, 567 and *The Garbis* [1982] 2 Lloyd's Rep. 283, 287.)

The fact that the terms of the bill of lading differ from the terms of the charter is in itself of no consequence; it is only if the bill of lading terms are extraordinary or are "manifestly inconsistent" with the charter in the sense that they are prohibited by the charter or contrary to its whole tenor, that the master may refuse to sign.

It is implicit in the passage cited above from *Tillmanns* v. *Knutsford* and also from the judgment of Browne, L.J., in *The Vikfrost* (see page 268 below) that if the master would have been entitled to refuse to sign a bill of lading because of its "manifest inconsistency" with the charter, then neither the charterers nor their agents would have the power to sign such a bill of lading on the master's behalf. However, they might in certain circumstances be regarded as having ostensible authority (see pages 39 above and 273 below).

Bill for destination outside charter limits

The master has the right, and probably the duty also, to refuse to sign a bill of lading which names a port of discharge outside the charter trading limits. MacKinnon, L.J., said in *Halcyon Steamship* v. *Continental Grain* (1943) 75 Ll.L.Rep. 80: "The limits of trading . . . are Institute Warranty limits, not north of Holland. If the charterers shipped a cargo in America and then tendered bills of lading to the captain under which he was to deliver to Copenhagen or Danzig, of course he would rightly refuse to sign . . . ".

Bill not incorporating clause required by charter

The master will probably be entitled to refuse to sign bills of lading presented to him for signature which do not incorporate terms which the time charter expressly provides are to be incorporated in bills of lading issued under it; for example, if clauses required by Clause 24 of the New York Produce form are not included in bills issued under a charter on that form.

But the master may not refuse to sign bills of lading because they do not incorporate other terms of the time charter, such as the lien clause, or the terms of the time charter generally. In *The Nanfri* [1979] 1 Lloyd's Rep. 201, Lord Wilberforce said, at page 206: "It must be clear that the owners cannot require bills of lading to be claused so as to incorporate the terms of the time charter: such a requirement would be contrary to the whole commercial purpose of the charterers". (And see further below under "Freight prepaid" bills.)

Bill misrepresenting the condition of the cargo

The master has the right, and the duty, not to sign bills which acknowledge the receipt in apparent good order and condition of cargo which is in fact damaged (or not received).

It follows from the master's duty to inspect the cargo and to ensure that the bills of lading reflect its apparent condition upon shipment that normally there will be no implied indemnity in favour of the owners if the charterers present clean bills for damaged cargo and these are signed by the master or the owners' agents.

The *Nogar Marin* was chartered for a voyage on the Gencon form. On completion of loading a cargo of iron rods in coils, a clean mate's receipt was tendered by or on behalf of the charterers which was signed by the master. In fact some of the coils were rusty and the master, who had inspected the cargo before loading, was negligent in signing without adding a reference to the rust. Subsequently the ship's agents, on the strength of the clean mate's receipt, signed clean bills of lading on the master's behalf. The owners consequently incurred liability to the receivers of the cargo under the bills of lading. On a claim by the owners for an indemnity from the charterers it was held by the Court of Appeal, affirming the decision of Staughton, J., and the arbitrators, that the claim failed, because:

(1) the charterers were not in breach of any implied term of the charter; no term was to be implied that the charterers or their agents must tender a mate's receipt or bills of lading

accurately describing the condition of the cargo, since responsibility for properly inspecting the cargo and recording its apparent condition in these documents remains with the master;

(2) in any event, even if the charterers had been in breach of some implied obligation, the master's negligent failure to check the condition of the cargo properly, to qualify the mate's receipt and to require the bills of lading to be claused, was sufficient to break any chain of causation; and

(3) no indemnity was to be implied in favour of the owners; the master's duty to verify the condition of the cargo before signing bills of lading was so well known in the trade that the charterers' tender to him of clean bills could not be understood as an implied request that they be signed clean in exchange for an indemnity against consequent claims.

The Nogar Marin [1988] 1 Lloyd's Rep. 412.

Under the New York Produce form the bills must include exceptions from apparent good order and condition which have been noted on the mate's receipts. It is suggested, however, that the master cannot be required to sign clean bills for damaged cargo because the damage has not been noted on the mate's receipts; his general duty, affecting as it does the interest of innocent endorsees of the bills, should be overriding. In *The Almak* [1985] 1 Lloyd's Rep. 557, a case concerning a misdated bill, Mustill, J., said at page 561: "The obligation to sign bills of lading as presented could not of course ever require the master to sign bills which stated a falsehold."

Loss of right to indemnity

If the master, knowing the cargo to be damaged, signs a clean bill of lading at the request of the charterers, the owners will probably lose any right that they might otherwise have to be indemnified by the charterers in respect of liability thereby incurred to endorsees under the bill of lading: see the *Brown, Jenkinson* case, below. And this may be so even in the absence of a deliberate decision to issue clean bills of lading for damaged cargo, if the master is negligent in checking its condition on shipment. For his negligence may then be held to be the proximate cause of the owners' loss: see *The Nogar Marin*, above. But the master may be justified in signing clean bills if there is a genuine dispute as to the condition of the cargo or if the only apparent defects are trivial.

Agents for the owners of the *Titania* signed clean bills of lading acknowledging shipment in apparent good order and condition of cargo which was in fact shipped in patently defective barrels. The clean bills of lading were issued against letters of indemnity from the shippers. Having paid claims by the consignees of the cargo, the owners sought to recover under a letter of indemnity. It was held by the Court of Appeal that the letter of indemnity was unenforceable against the shippers since the owners, through their agents, were a party with the shippers to a fraud. The bill of lading, containing a false representation, had been issued with knowledge that those into whose hands the bill might come (whether receivers or bankers) would rely upon the representation.

(The court recognised that the issue of clean bills against letters of indemnity might be proper in certain limited circumstances, as where there was a *bona fide* dispute as to the condition or packing of the cargo or where the defects were trivial.)

Brown, Jenkinson v. *Percy Dalton* [1957] 2 Lloyd's Rep. 1.

Bill bearing incorrect date

In *The Almak* [1985] 1 Lloyd's Rep. 557, Mustill, J., expressed the firm view that a master would not be bound to sign a bill of lading bearing an incorrect date. He continued at page 561: "He would always be entitled to refuse if he noticed the discrepancy. If he did notice it and nevertheless chose to sign, it might be that the shipowner would lose his right of indemnity, on the grounds that:—(i) the decision to sign incorrect bills with knowledge of the true facts broke the causal connection between the request to sign and the subsequent loss, or (ii) the act of signing was 'manifestly unlawful in itself', so as to take the case outside the charterer's implied right of 'indemnity at common law." See also *The Nogar Marin*, above.

Bill misstating quantity or nature of cargo shipped

The fact that the master is required to sign bills of lading "as presented" does not mean that he is bound to sign a bill in whatever terms the charterers demand in these respects. There is an implied requirement that the bills should relate to goods actually shipped and that they should not contain a description of the goods which is known to be incorrect: see *The Boukadoura*, below; see also *The Almak* and *The Nogar Marin*, above.

The *Boukadoura* was voyage chartered on the STB Voy form. Clause 20(*a*) of the charter (which is in similar terms to Clause 20(a) of the STB Time form) provided that "Bills of lading shall be signed by the Master as presented . . . and the Charterer shall indemnify the Owner against all consequences . . . which may arise from . . . an irregularity in papers supplied by the Charterer or its Agents". The charterers presented bills for a certain quantity of oil which the master maintained (correctly as it turned out) was greater than the quantity actually shipped. The master wished to qualify his signature to the bill, but the charterers refused to accept this and the ship was delayed while the cargo was re-measured. It was held by Evans, J., that the master was entitled to refuse to sign an unqualified bill, that the inaccuracy in the bill as to quantity loaded was an "irregularity" within the meaning of Clause 20(*a*) and that the owners could recover from the charterers the losses incurred as a result of the delay.

The Boukadoura [1989] 1 Lloyd's Rep. 393.

Bill wrongly stating cargo to be under deck

The master has a duty not to sign bills which state that cargo has been loaded under deck when he knows this to be untrue.

Bill containing demise clause

It was argued in *The Berkshire* [1974] 1 Lloyd's Rep. 185, that a demise clause in a bill of lading was an "extraordinary clause" (see page 264 above), that the charterers could not lawfully tender a bill of lading containing such a clause to the master for signature and, therefore, could not bind the owners by signing such a bill of lading themselves. Brandon, J., said: "I must confess that I do not understand this argument. All the demise clause does is to spell out in unequivocal terms that the bill of lading is intended to be a shipowners' bill of lading. The charter-party entitles the charterers to present to the master for signature by him on the shipowners' behalf, or to sign themselves on the same behalf, bills of lading of that kind. How then can it be said that the demise clause is . . . an extraordinary clause? In my view, so far from being an extraordinary clause, it is an entirely usual and ordinary one."

In *The Vikfrost* (see below) it was held that agents of sub-time charterers of a ship had implied authority to issue bills of lading containing a demise clause, where the head time charter gave the head charterers an option to sub-let and permitted the issue of bills of lading with a demise clause in similar form. See also *The Jalamohan* [1988] 1 Lloyd's Rep. 443.

"Freight prepaid" bills

The master may not refuse to sign "freight prepaid" bills of lading, nor require a lien clause in the charter to be incorporated into the bills, in order to render effective the owners' rights of lien on freights or sub-freights for amounts due under the charter.

The *Nanfri* and two other ships were fixed to the same charterers under similar charters on the Baltime form. The charterers made certain deductions from hire which the owners contended the charterers were not entitled to make. Despite the owners' protest and a reference of the dispute to arbitration the charterers made a further deduction. The owners thereupon instructed the masters of all three ships (a) to withdraw all authority to issue or sign bills of lading on their behalf, (b) to refuse to sign "freight prepaid" bills of lading presented to them and (c) to insist that all bills of lading be endorsed with a clause incorporating the terms of the time charter, including the lien clause. The charterers were using the ships in the Great Lakes grain trade and in that trade it was usual for bills to be marked "freight prepaid", without reference to the terms of any time charter. The owners argued, however, that they were entitled to instruct their masters to refuse to sign any bill of lading which might prejudice the owners' right under Clause 18 of the Baltime form to lien "all cargoes and sub-freights belonging to the Time-Charterers and any Bill of Lading freight for all claims under this Charter".

It was held by the House of Lords, affirming the Court of Appeal and (on this point) Kerr, J., that under the employment clause in the charter (Clause 9) the charterers could require the masters to sign "freight prepaid" bills without any mention of the terms of the time charters; the owners might be denied rights of lien but were protected by their rights of indemnity.

The Nanfri [1979] 1 Lloyd's Rep. 201.

(And see also pages 199 and 403.)

Bill containing foreign jurisdiction clause

The fact that the charter contains a jurisdiction clause requiring disputes under the charter to be referred to arbitration in one country will not entitle the master to refuse to sign bills of lading containing a jurisdiction clause requiring disputes to be referred to arbitration in, or to the courts of, a different country. Such bills will not be "manifestly inconsistent" with the charter and the charterers or their agents will normally have implied authority to issue bills containing such a clause.

The *Vikfrost* was let under a head time charter which provided that disputes under the charter were to be decided in Oslo by arbitration in accordance with Norwegian law. The ship was then sub-let under a sub-charter which contained a London arbitration clause. Agents of the sub-charterers issued and signed, on the master's behalf, bills of lading which provided that the bills should be governed by English law and that disputes under them should be referred to the High Court in England to the exclusion of the jurisdiction of the courts of any other country. It was held by the Court of Appeal that the sub-charterers' agents had power to issue and sign such bills of lading. Browne, L.J., said, at page 568: " . . . there is no inconsistency between the jurisdiction clause in the charter-party and the jurisdiction clause in the bill of lading. The charter-party provided for disputes between the owners and the charterers under the charter to be referred to arbitration in Oslo. This is not inconsistent with the provisions of the bill of lading that disputes under a different contract between different parties—the owners and the bill of lading holders—are to be decided by the High Court here."

The Vikfrost [1980] 1 Lloyd's Rep. 560.

(For a fuller report of this case see page 272 below. See also *The Paros* [1987] 2 Lloyd's Rep. 269.)

Without prejudice to the charter-party

Some time charters stipulate that bills of lading are to be signed "without prejudice to the charter-party". These words do not affect the obligation of the master to sign bills of lading presented to him by the charterers; they mean only that the contract between the owners and the charterers contained in the charter remains unaffected by the signature of bills of lading in (possibly) different terms. See *Hansen* v. *Harrold* [1894] 1 Q.B. 612, *Turner* v. *Haji Goolam* [1904] A.C. 826 and *The Nanfri* [1979] 1 Lloyd's Rep. 201, 206.

Bills signed by the master personally

The master has, under common law, an ordinary or general authority to sign bills of lading on behalf of the owners. The owners will be bound by a bill of lading issued within the general authority of the master even if, in any particular case, the owners have limited the master's general authority, unless the bill of lading holder knew of the limitation.

The time charter for the *Boston City* contained the unusual provision that "In signing bills of lading it is expressly agreed that the captain shall only do so as agent for the charterers". The master signed bills of lading which expressly incorporated all the conditions of the charter, but the endorsees of the bills of lading did not see the charter and were unaware of the provision in question. It was held by the Court of Appeal that the bill of lading contracts were with the owners. Lopes, L.J., said:

> "The holders of the bill of lading, in the absence of [very clear and very explicit words], would naturally believe and imagine that the master when he signed the bill of lading was exercising the ordinary authority which attaches to him in his capacity of master."

Manchester Trust v. *Furness, Withy* [1895] 2 Q.B. 539.

Thus where bills of lading are signed by the master the bill of lading contracts will usually, although not invariably, be between the holders of the bill of lading and the owners. Sheen, J., in *The Venezuela* [1980] 1 Lloyd's Rep. 393 (see page 273 below) said:

" . . . when the charter-party does not amount to a demise of the ship and when possession of the ship is not given up to the charterer, then it is probable that the contract contained in a bill of lading signed by the master is made with the shipowner and not with the charterer. (See *Wehner* v. *Dene Steam Shipping Company* [1905] 2 K.B. 92 and *Tillmanns* v. *Knutsford, supra*.) But that is not an invariable rule and 'it always falls to be decided on the facts and documents of the particular case' (per Mr. Justice Roche in *Wilston Steamship Company Ltd.* v. *Andrew Weir & Co.* (1925) 22 Ll.L.Rep. 521; (1925) 31 Com. Cas. 111, at pages 522 and 114)."

Contracts which are made with the owners are not entered into by the master and owners as agents for the time charterers, although they are entered into for the time charterers' benefit. It follows that it is the owners rather than the time charterers who are entitled to collect the bill of lading freight under such contracts, although they will be bound to account for it to the charterers, after deduction of any hire outstanding under the charter: for further comment on this question see page 399.

It is possible for the master's signature to bind the charterers; but only if the wording of the bill of lading and the surrounding circumstances make it quite clear that the master, in signing, was not exercising his general authority to bind the owners but was doing so only as agent for the charterers.

The *Lindenhall* was time chartered by her owners to Edward Perry & Co. by a charter which included an employment and indemnity clause similar to that in the Baltime form. Bills of lading for the carriage of oil from the U.S.A. to Japan were made out on a form headed "Edward Perry & Co.'s Steamship Line" and referred to a freight contract between the shippers, the Standard Oil

Co., and the charterers, which described the cargo and stated the freight to be paid. These bills of lading were signed by the master. Walton, J., held that, despite this signature, the shippers' contract of carriage was in the circumstances with the charterers rather than the owners of the ship.

Samuel v. *West Hartlepool Steam Navigation* (1906) 11 Com. Cas. 115.

(See also for a case concerning the bills of a well-known liner company, signed by the master of a chartered-in ship: *Elder, Dempster* v. *Paterson, Zochonis*, summarised below.)

Owners as bailees on terms of bills of lading

The fact that the master may be held to have signed the bill of lading as agent for the charterers will not necessarily mean that the bill of lading terms will be inapplicable as between the owners and the cargo owners.

The *Grelwen*, owned by Griffiths Lewis, was chartered in by the Elder, Dempster Line to supplement their own ships on the West African trade. Bills of lading were issued for palm oil bearing the names "African Steamship Company and the British and African Steam Navigation Company. Managers, Elder Dempster & Company" and were signed by the master "P. Bedford, Agent". The casks of palm oil were crushed by bags of palm kernels stowed over them. The bills protected the carrier against liability for bad stowage, but not against liability for unseaworthiness. The owners of the goods (Paterson, Zochonis) sued the owners, the time charterers and the two companies they managed. Rowlatt, J., held, (1922) 12 Ll.L.Rep. 69, that the contract was not with the owners but with the African Steamship Company and this part of his decision was not challenged on appeal.

The House of Lords held, reversing Rowlatt, J., and the Court of Appeal, that the damage to the goods was attributable to bad stowage rather than unseaworthiness and that both the African Steamship Company and the owners of the ship were entitled to rely upon the exceptions in the bill of lading. The owners were so entitled despite not being parties to the contract.

Elder, Dempster v. *Paterson, Zochonis* [1924] A.C. 522.

The correctness of the decision that the owners were entitled to rely upon the exceptions in a bill of lading to which they were not a party has been much discussed. It was held by the House of Lords in *Midland Silicones* v. *Scruttons* [1961] 2 Lloyd's Rep. 365 that the decision could only now be supported on the grounds that, the master having signed the bill of lading, it must be inferred that the owners received the goods as bailees on the terms of the bill. See *Morris* v. *Martin* [1965] 2 Lloyd's Rep. 63, *The Eurymedon* [1974] 1 Lloyd's Rep. 534, *Gadsen* v. *Australian Coastal Shipping* (1977) 31 F.L.R. 157 (Aust.) and *The Kapetan Markos N.L. (No. 2)* [1987] 2 Lloyd's Rep. 321.

Bills signed by the charterers or their agents

Authority to sign

The stipulation in Lines 78 and 79 of the New York Produce form that the captain is "to sign Bills of Lading for cargo as presented" coupled with the provision in Line 77 that he is to be under the orders and directions of the charterers as regards employment and agency, generally gives the charterers or their agents authority to sign bills of lading as agents for the master. Brandon, J., in *The Berkshire* [1974] 1 Lloyd's Rep. 185, at page 188, said: "The effect of such a clause [Clause 8 of the New York Produce form] in a charter-party is well settled. In the first place, the clause entitles the charterers to present to the master for signature by him on behalf of the shipowners bills of lading which contain or evidence contracts between the shippers of goods and the shipowners, provided always that such bills of lading do not contain extraordinary terms or terms manifestly inconsistent with the charter-party; and the master is obliged, on presentation to him of such bills of lading, to sign them on the shipowners' behalf. In the second place, the charterers may, instead of presenting such bills of lading to the master for signature by him on behalf of the shipowners, sign them themselves on the same behalf. In either case, whether the master signs on the directions of the charterers, or the charterers short-circuit the matter and sign themselves, the signature binds the shipowners as principals to the contract contained in or evidenced by the bills of lading. Authority for the propositions set out above is to be found in *Tillmanns & Co.* v. *S.S. Knutsford*, [1908] 2 K.B. 385; [1908] A.C. 406. See also, as regards terms manifestly inconsistent with the charter-party, *Kruger & Co. Ltd.* v. *Moel Tryvan Ship Co. Ltd.* [1907] A.C. 272, at pp. 278-8."

In *The Berkshire* the master had in fact given express authority to the charterers' agents to sign the bills of lading. Where there is such actual authority from the owners or the master, either by a special charter clause to that effect or by agreement after the charter is signed, then there is no doubt that the charterers or their agents may bind the owners. But in the passage set out above, Brandon, J., was not relying on the express authority given by the master and it appears that the authority will normally be implied from the usual terms of a time charter.

The *Knutsford* was time chartered to Watts, Watts & Co. of London. Cargo for Vladivostock was loaded, during the currency of the charter, at Middlesbrough and London. Three bills of lading were signed by the master personally, dated 12 October. A fourth bill (presumably for the London cargo) dated 26 October was signed by Watts, Watts & Co. "For the Captain and Owners". The charter provided that the captain was to be "under the orders and direction of the charterers as regards employment, agency, or other arrangements" and that the charterers were to "indemnify the owners from all consequences or liabilities that may arise from the captain signing bills of lading by the order of charterers or of their agents".

The owners argued that they were not bound by the bill signed by the charterers, but it was held by Channell, J., the Court of Appeal (Vaughan Williams, L.J., doubting) and unanimously by the House of Lords that the owners were as much bound by the bill signed by the charterers as they were by those signed by the master personally. Kennedy, L.J., said in the Court of Appeal [1908] 2 K.B. 385, at page 406:

> "It does not lie in the mouth of the [owners] to deny the authority of the signature as one made on behalf of the owners and captain, because they have themselves by the contract agreed that the captain shall act as the charterers shall direct, and therefore a signature which the charterers have made as on behalf of the owners and captain must, I think, be treated, when they are sued by the shippers who put their goods on board, as a signature which they cannot repudiate, because they gave the charterers, in the express terms of their contract, the right of directing the signature to the document to be made, and must be taken impliedly to have given, both as against the captain and against themselves, an authority to the charterers to sign on behalf of either or both of them."

Tillmanns & Co. v. *S.S. Knutsford* [1908] A.C. 406.

Although there is some suggestion in the above case that the master may have tacitly approved the signature of the bill of lading on his behalf (see the speech of Lord Loreburn, L.C., [1908] A.C. at page 408), nevertheless the clear reason for the decision is that authority was to be implied from the terms of the charter.

Authority for sub-charterers or their agents to sign bills of lading on behalf of the master may also be implied from a head time charter in similar terms, particularly where the charter contains an option to sub-let: *The Vikfrost* [1980] 1 Lloyd's Rep. 560, see page 268 above and page 272 below.

Baltime form

Under Clause 9 of the Baltime form, there is no provision that the master is to sign bills of lading as presented, but it is stipulated that the master is to be under the orders of the charterers as regards employment and agency and that the charterers are to indemnify the owners against the consequences of the master or agents signing bills of lading. It is considered therefore that, on the authority of *Tillmanns* v. *Knutsford* above, the position is the same under the Baltime form as it is under the New York Produce form.

Tanker charters

In some tanker time charters the position regarding the signature of bills of lading is spelt out specifically. Thus Clause 20 (a) of the STB form provides:

"Bills of Lading shall be signed by the Master as presented . . . However, at Charterer's option, the Charterer or its Agents may sign Bills of Lading on behalf of the Master . . . "

Bills binding on the owners

Bills of lading signed by the charterers or their agents "for the master" will usually be regarded as binding the owners.

The *Wilston* was employed under a time charter which provided that bills of lading might be signed by the master on the orders of the charterers. Bills of lading were issued headed "Joint Service to River Plate. Andrew Weir & Co. Agents: Turner Morrison & Co. Ltd . . . ". Turner Morrison, who were the agents of the time charterers, Andrew Weir, signed the bills of lading. Andrew Weir paid claims under the bills of lading and sought an indemnity from the owners. The owners resisted on the ground that they and not the time charterers were the party to the bills of lading. There were references in the body of the bills of lading to "The Company" which might have referred to the time charterers, but there were also references to "master, owners or agents of the vessel". Roche, J., held that the bills of lading evidenced contracts with the owners and not with Andrew Weir, because they had been signed "for the master".

Wilston v. *Andrew Weir* (1925) 22 Ll.L.Rep. 521.

But, although the manner in which the charterers or their agents sign is an important factor in determining whether a bill of lading is binding upon the owners or the charterers, it is not necessarily decisive. It is necessary in each case to consider all the contractual terms as well as the surrounding circumstances.

The *Vikfrost* was time chartered by the owners to Salen on terms that bills of lading issued for voyages under the charter might be signed by the charterers' agents on the master's behalf and might contain the demise clause in the Salen bill of lading or a similar demise clause. The Salen demise clause provided that if the ship was not owned by or chartered by demise to the company or line issuing the bill of lading, the bill should take effect as a contract with the owner or demise charterer as principal. The charter also contained an employment and indemnity clause and the master was to sign bills of lading as presented.

Under an option to sub-let, Salen sub-chartered to Lauritzen. Sub-agents of Lauritzen signed bills of lading on Lauritzen's headed bill of lading form on behalf of the master. These bills contained a demise clause in terms similar to the Salen demise clause.

It was held by Mocatta, J., and the Court of Appeal that the sub-charterer's agents had implied authority to sign bills of lading so as to bind the owners. The head charter imposed no restrictions on clauses to be inserted in bills of lading and gave liberty to include a demise clause. It expressly authorised sub-letting and the owners must have contemplated that sub-charterers would be entitled, under a sub-charter, to require the master to sign bills of lading or to sign bills on his behalf.

The Vikfrost [1980] 1 Lloyd's Rep. 560.

(On the inclusion of an English jurisdiction clause in the bills of lading see page 268 above.)

Charterers may have ostensible authority to bind the owners

The practice of owners whose ships are time chartered to leave it to the charterers or their agents to prepare and sign bills of lading "for the master" is now widespread. It may now be that even in the absence of express provision, owners who time charter their ships and put them on the charterers' berths without taking positive steps to indicate the contrary will be taken to have held out the charterers and their agents as having authority to make bill of lading contracts on their behalf. The charterers and their agents would thus have ostensible authority to bind the owners irrespective of any actual authority.

The *Nea Tyhi* was chartered for a trip on the New York Produce form. An additional clause gave the owners an express indemnity from the charterers in respect of liabilities arising from the charterers or their agents, including the master, signing bills of lading.

The ship loaded on deck a consignment of plywood which there suffered damage by rainwater. The bills of lading were issued by the charterers' agents and signed by them for the master; they contained the typewritten words "shipped under deck". The owners contended that they had no liability to the receivers of the plywood under these bills as the charterers' agents had no authority to issue or sign them in that form.

Sheen, J., held that, although the charterers' agents had no actual authority to issue and sign "under deck" bills for cargo on deck, they did have ostensible authority and accordingly the owners were bound by the bills.

The Nea Tyhi [1982] 1 Lloyd's Rep. 606.

The case above illustrates one problem that may arise from the charterers or their agents signing bills rather than presenting them to the master for his signature, namely that they may sign bills which the master could or even should have refused to sign. To take another example, they may sign a bill for a port outside the trading limits in the charter. No doubt this will be beyond any actual authority (express or implied) which they may have from the owners. But if, as may well be the case, they have ostensible authority through being held out by the owners as empowered generally to sign bills for them, the bill of lading will bind the owners to a shipper or holder of the bill of lading who has no notice of the lack of actual authority.

Bills binding on the charterers

The terms of the bill of lading signed by the charterers or their agents "on behalf of the master" may indicate so clearly that the charterers are the carriers under the contract of carriage evidenced by the bill that the charterers will be bound by the bill despite the manner in which it is signed.

The owners of the *Samjohn Governor* fixed her on the Baltime form to charterers who in turn sub-time chartered her to a company who ran a regular liner service from Japan to South America. The sub-charterers' agents in Japan issued a bill of lading on the sub-charterers' usual liner form, the back of which was headed with the initials of the sub-charterers and another company with whom they operated a joint service, and contained an identity of carrier clause referring to whichever was the operator as "the carrier": there was no demise clause or other indication in it that the ship was on time charter. Under the printed words "signed by or on behalf of the Master", the agents had signed in ink; below their signature was printed first a horizontal line, then the initials of the sub-charterers and then the name of the agents, "general agents and as agents for the Master". In the Admiralty Court Sheen, J., held that the sub-charterers and not the owners were the party to the bill. He said that if there had been nothing in the bill other than the agents' signature to indicate who was the contracting party he would have accepted that this was the owner, on the authority of *Tillmanns & Co.* v. *S.S. Knutsford*, above; but the contents of the bill clearly indicated that it was the sub-charterers alone who were contracting as carrier and it was they who were bound by the bill.

Sheen, J., said: "If those goods had been carried in a ship owned by [the sub-charterers], the shipment would have been made in precisely the same manner as in this case . . . It seems to me that if [the sub-charterers] did not wish to contract as 'the carrier', then the bill of lading issued by [them] should at least have made it clear with which company the shipper was entering into the contract of carriage."

The Venezuela [1980] 1 Lloyd's Rep. 393.

The charterers or their agents may also sign bills of lading without purporting to sign "for the master". Depending upon the wording of the bill of lading and the surrounding circumstances, it may well then be held that the contracts of carriage are with the charterers rather than with the owners. This is particularly likely where the charterers are themselves the owners or operators of ships providing a regular service and have chartered in the ship in question to supplement that service.

A collision occurred between the *Ruggiero di Flores* and the *Okehampton* and the question arose in subsequent proceedings whether or not MacAndrews as sub-time charterers of the *Ruggiero di Flores* would have been entitled to the bill of lading freight for cargo on that ship. The cargo of fruit had been loaded at Spanish ports and had been in the possession of MacAndrews who ran a regular service from those ports with their own ships, the *Ruggiero di Flores* having been chartered in to supplement the service. MacAndrews signed the bills of lading in their own name, giving two copies to the shippers and sending one to their own representative in Hamburg who was to take delivery from the ship and then hand the cargo over against presentation of the bills by the endorsees.

It was held by the Court of Appeal that the bills of lading evidenced contracts of carriage with MacAndrews and not with the owners. Hamilton, L.J., said:

"I think it is not unimportant to recollect that the ship is an Italian ship, that she is loading in Spanish ports, and that she is loading from a firm which carries on a well-known business in those Spanish ports—circumstances which enhance the probability that the carrying contractor would be the well-known firm and not the unknown owners of a foreign steamer."

The Okehampton [1913] P. 173.

American Law

Mate's receipts

A mate's receipt, which is usually issued by the chief mate after the cargo has been loaded, serves to acknowledge receipt of the goods on board, thus shifting responsibility for their care and custody to the carrier. See *Continental Grain Co.* v. *American Commercial Barge Line Co.*, 332 F.2d 26 (7th Cir. 1964); *E.T. Barwick Mills Inc.* v. *Hellenic Lines Ltd.*, 331 F.Supp. 161 (S.D. Ga. 1971), aff'd 472 F.2d 1406 (5th Cir. 1973).

Bills of lading

A bill of lading may serve multiple functions with respect to the carriage of goods by sea, including (1) document of title, (2) receipt for the goods, and (3) contract of carriage. Where cargo is owned by the charterer, the charter operates as the contract of affreightment and the bill of lading will serve only as a document of title and a receipt. *The Fri*, 154 F. 333 (2d Cir. 1907). Where the cargo owner is a third party, however, the bill operates as evidence of the contract of carriage.

Signing of bills of lading

Under the general maritime law, the master has a general authority to issue and sign bills of lading on behalf of the owner. This basic principle was stated by the Supreme Court in *The Schooner Freeman*, 59 U.S. 182 (1856):

> We are of the opinion that, under our admiralty law, contracts of affreightment, entered into with the master, in good faith, and within the scope of his apparent authority as master, bind the vessel to the merchandise for the performance of such contracts . . . .

The master's authority to sign bills of lading derives from his right to bind the owner in matters relating to the employment and business of the ship. *Pope* v. *Nickerson*, F.Cas. No. 11,273 (C.C.D. Mass. 1844). See generally, *The Flash*, F.Cas. No. 4,857 (S.D.N.Y. 1847); *The Aurora*, 14 U.S. (Wheat. 1) 96 (1816); *Bulkley* v. *Naumkeag Steam Cotton Co.*, 65 U.S. 386 (1860); *Instituto Cubano de Est. Del Azucar* v. *T/V Golden West*, 246 F.2d 802, 1957 AMC 1481 (2d Cir. 1957); *Gans S.S. Line* v. *Wilhelmsen*, 275 F. 254, 262 (2d Cir. 1921), *cert.* denied *sub-nom. Barber & Co.* v. *Wilhelmsen*, 257 U.S. 655 (1921).

Absent unusual express instructions, the master's authority is not unlimited. He is, for example, not authorized to bind the owner to a fraud by wilfully signing false bills of lading. *The Schooner Freeman*, above; *Pope* v. *Nickerson*, above. As the court noted in *The Schooner Freeman*, above, the party taking a bill of lading issued and signed by a ship's master "assumes the risk, not only of the genuineness of the signature, and of the fact that the signer was master of the vessel, but also of the apparent authority of the master to issue the bill of lading". As in the case of any party acting on the basis of another's apparent authority, the party receiving a bill of lading from the master is under a duty to ascertain the facts upon which his authority depends. See *Yeramex Int'l* v. *S.S. Tendo*, 595 F.2d 943, 944, 1979 AMC 1282, 1283 (4th Cir. 1979).

Bills signed by the master personally

Bills of lading signed by the master on behalf of the owner will, of course, evidence a contract between the latter and the holder of the bill. As stated in *Aljassim* v. *S.S. South Star*, 323 F.Supp. 918, 922, 1971 AMC 1703, 1707 (S.D.N.Y. 1971):

> The contract evidenced by the bill of lading issued by the master of the ship chartered but not demised is the contract of the ship, the charterer who caused their issue, and that of the owner whose master as authorized agent issued them.

See also *Gans S.S. Line* v. *Wilhelmsen*, 275 F. 254, 262–63 (2d Cir. 1921), *cert.* denied *sub-nom. Barber & Co.* v. *Wilhelmsen*, 257 U.S. 655 (1921).

Bills signed by charterer or his agents

The shipowner is not personally liable on bills of lading issued by a charterer and not signed by the master where the owner's name does not appear thereon. See *United Nations Children's Fund* v. *S.S. Nordstern*, 251 F.Supp. 833 (S.D.N.Y. 1965); *Tube Products of India* v. *S.S. Rio Grande*, 334 F.Supp. 1039, 1971 AMC 1629 (S.D.N.Y 1971). Even a bill of lading signed by the charterer "for the master" is a charterer's bill of lading on which the owner will not be personally liable, *unless* the master or owner actually authorized the signature by the charterer, or clothed the charterer with the apparent authority to bind the owner to the bill of lading as a contracting party. *Yeramex Int'l* v. *S.S. Tendo*, above; see *Demsey & Associates* v. *S.S. Sea Star*, 461 F.2d 1009 (2d Cir. 1972); *Ross Industries Inc.* v. *M/V Gretke Oldendorff*, 483 F.Supp. 195, 1980 AMC 1397 (E.D. Tex. 1980).

The New York Produce form expressly grants the charterer the right to issue bills of lading and requires that the master sign them "as presented". Under American law, in signing bills presented by the charterer the master may do so strictly as agent for the charterer, rather than as agent of the owner as was traditionally the case under the general maritime law. Thus, the master's signature on the charterer's bill of lading cannot only bind the charterer, but in certain circumstances may be binding solely on the charterer.

In *Yeramex Int'l* v. *S.S. Tendo*, above, it was held that the owner was not liable *in personam* as a contracting party where the charterer had no actual authority to bind the owner to the bill of lading and no apparent authority existed to bind the owner because neither the handling of the cargo nor the terms of the bill of lading could reasonably have misled the shipper or other third parties to believe that the owner was a party to the charterer's bill of lading which was issued "for the master".

The court based its ruling on the concept discussed above at page 256 of the master "wearing two hats" in performance of his duties under the charter. As the court stated:

> . . . the terms of the vessels' time charters grant the masters dual authority to act separately as agents for the owner and as agents for the charterer in matters involving the separate responsibilities for ship, as assumed by the owner, and for cargo, as assumed by the charterer. (595 F.2d at 944.)

Similarly in *Mahroos* v. *Tatiana L*, 1988 AMC 757 (S.D.N.Y. 1986), it was held that the vessel owner was not a carrier subject to *in personam* liability under the bill of lading issued by charterer where the charterer issued bills that were entirely inconsistent with the mate's receipts for the goods. Whereas the mate's receipts indicated that much of the cargo was damaged prior to loading, the bills of lading did not note that the cargo was damaged prior to loading and stated that the cargo was "loaded clean on board". Although the charter included a special clause which specifically stated that charterer was authorized to issue bills of lading on owner's behalf, that clause restricted this authority to bills issued "according to the mate's receipts". The court held that charterer was without authority to sign the bills on behalf of owner in the manner they did and that owner, therefore, was not a carrier suable under COGSA.

In *S. A. Cockerill* v. *M. V. Kyung Ju*, 1983 AMC 1517 (M.D. Fla. 1982), the court held that a head charter which authorizes the charterer to issue bills of lading on behalf of the owner does not also extend such authorization to a sub-charterer absent specific language to that effect.

While the owner may be bound contractually only by bills of lading actually signed by the master or his authorized agent, the vessel may be liable *in rem* for cargo damage even if the bill was issued by the charterer. In *British West Indies Produce Inc.* v. *S.S. Atlantic Clipper*, 353 F.Supp. 548, 1973 AMC 163 (S.D.N.Y. 1973), the vessel loaded a cargo of yams which were damaged during a voyage from the West Indies to New York. Bills of lading were issued by the charterer, and were *not* signed by the master. The court held the vessel liable *in rem* for the cargo damage, saying:

> That the vessel was operated under a charter to Atlantic Lines, Ltd. does not affect the liability of the vessel; and neither is it of consequence that the master did not sign the bills of lading. Once the S.S. Atlantic Clipper sailed with the consignee's cargo on board, it constituted ratification of the bills of lading. (1973 AMC at 170.)

The vessel, however, was held entitled to full indemnity, including attorneys' fees, from the charterer, who had controlled the loading and stowage of the cargo.

The vessel is liable *in rem* once the cargo is on aboard with knowledge of the master. It is at this moment that the unity of ship and cargo comes into existence. Moreover, the vessel may be liable *in rem* even if the master does not know the terms of the charterer's bill of lading, as he is presumed to have knowledge of its terms. *The G.A. Tomlinson*, 293 F. 51, 52 (W.D.N.Y. 1923).

In *Insurance Company of North America* v. *S.S. American Argosy*, 732 F.2d 299, 1984 AMC 1547 (2d Cir. 1984), the court ruled that a ship could not be held liable *in rem* under a bill of lading issued by an NVOCC without the authorization of the ship's owner or charterer. The court noted that the owner had issued its own bill of lading for the voyage and that the cargo damage occurred during on-carriage by a different carrier after the defendant vessel had delivered the cargo in good condition.

Charterer's liability as carrier/demise clause

It has long been held in the United States that a charterer who books cargo and who issues his own bill of lading will also be liable as a "carrier" under the U.S. Carriage of Goods by Sea Act (COGSA). *The Quarrington Court*, 36 F.Supp. 278 (S.D.N.Y. 1940), aff'd 122 F.2d 266 (2d Cir. 1941); *Glynwed Steels Ltd.* v. *Great Lakes and European Lines Inc.*, 1979 AMC 1290 (N.D. I11. 1978).

In *Centennial Insurance Co.* v. *Constellation Enterprise*, 1987 AMC 1155 (S.D.N.Y. 1986), the court dismissed a cargo damage claim against the vessel owner on the grounds that the owner was not a "carrier" under the bill of lading. The bill of lading was printed on a form prepared by charterer which expressly provided that the contracting carrier under the bills was the charterer. Although the bill stated that charterer acted as agent "for the master" in issuing it, there was no evidence that the charterer had authority to bind the owner of the vessel as a carrier.

What of an "intermediate" time charterer, however, who does not book cargo or issue its own bill of lading form? In *Thyssen Steel Corp.* v. *The Adonis*, 364 F.Supp. 1332, 1974 AMC 389 (S.D.N.Y. 1973), the vessel was time chartered by Adonis to Teseo, and Teseo entered into a sub-voyage charter with Atlantic. Thyssen brought an action against Teseo for cargo damage. It was held that since Teseo had not issued bills of lading for the cargo, it was not liable for the loss. The court stated:

> Under COGSA, only a carrier who has entered into a contract of carriage with the shipper has a duty to properly and carefully load, handle, stow, carry, keep, care for, and discharge the goods carried . . . The bills of lading . . . were issued by agents of Atlantic on its own form. No evidence was presented at trial to show that Teseo authorized Atlantic or its agents to sign or issue the bills of lading on Teseo's behalf. Though the Voyage Charter authorized the master to sign bills of lading, the record indicates that the master did not sign the bills of lading and no evidence was presented to show that he authorized Atlantic or its agents to sign on his behalf. Accordingly, as Teseo did not enter into a contract of carriage with Thyssen, Teseo is not a carrier under COGSA . . . (1974 AMC at 393.)

The court also rejected the contention that the cargo owner could recover from Teseo as a third-party beneficiary of the charter between Adonis and Teseo, which provided that Teseo was responsible for the loading and stowage. According to the court, there was no evidence that Clause 8 of the time charter between Adonis and Teseo "was inserted for the benefit of the shipping public, including Thyssen". (*Id.*)

Thyssen was followed by the court in *Yasuda Fire and Marine Ins. Co. Ltd.* v. *M/V Indian City*, 1981 AMC 1451 (M.D. Fla. 1980).

In *Glynwed Steels Ltd.* v. *Great Lakes and European Lines Inc.*, above, the court also rejected a third party beneficiary claim of the shipper, declaring that this theory of liability conflicts with the clear intent of COGSA. The court held that since the charterer, and not the owner, was the carrier, and since the Act provides that the carrier is the party bound to exercise due diligence to make the ship seaworthy, COGSA precluded the application of any third party beneficiary theory treating the shipper as the beneficiary of the owner's warranty of seaworthiness to the charterer.

See also *United Nations Children's Fund* v. *The Nordstern*, 251 F.Supp. 833 (S.D.N.Y. 1965); *The Muskegon*, 10 F.2d 817 (S.D.N.Y. 1924); *The Blandon*, 287 F. 722 (S.D.N.Y. 1922); *The Poznan*, 276 F. 418 (S.D.N.Y. 1921).

Ratification of bills of lading

In certain circumstances, bills of lading may become valid even though they are not signed by the master or his authorized agent. In *The Blandon*, 287 F. 722, 723–24 (S.D.N.Y. 1922), the court held that the master will be deemed to have ratified bills of lading issued by the charterer once he sets sail with cargo on board. As the court stated, once the vessel breaks ground " . . . the bill of lading, though signed by the charterer only, is the measure of the ship's duty and the cargo's privilege".

See also *The G. A. Tomlinson*, 293 F. 51 (W.D.N.Y. 1923); *The Muskegon*, above; *United Nations Children's Fund* v. *S.S. Nordstern*, above; *Tube Products of India* v. *S.S. Rio Grande*, 334 F.Supp. 1039, 1041 (S.D.N.Y. 1971); *Cavcar Company* v. *M. V. Suzdal*, 723 F.2d 1096, 1984 AMC 609 (3d Cir. 1983).

Owner's liability in tort

In some cases, cargo owners have succeeded in establishing liability on the part of the owner for claims sounding in tort where the owner was not a party to the contract of carriage. In *The Poznan*, 276 F. 418 (S.D.N.Y. 1921), the court held that while the owner was not liable under bills of lading signed by the charterer, it was liable in tort when it ordered the vessel to deviate and thereby interfered with the charterer's performance of its contract. See also *Sunil Industries* v. *The Ogden Fraser*, 1981 AMC 2670 (S.D.N.Y. 1981).

Where the owner is not a party to the contract of carriage for the cargo, it will not be entitled to the benefit of exceptions from or limitations of liability which may be available thereunder. In *Toho Bussan Kaisha Ltd.* v. *American President Lines*, 265 F.2d 418, 1959 AMC 1114 (2d Cir. 1959), it was held that the one-year time bar applicable under Section 3(6) of COGSA operates only as to claims arising out of the contract of carriage. Similarly, in *Sunil Industries* v. *The Ogden Fraser*, above, the court held that the one-year COGSA limitation period did not apply with respect to a claim against the owner since it was not a party to the contract of carriage for the goods.

As presented

The master is under a duty to the charterer to sign bills of lading "as presented" to him. As the court observed in *Field Line (Cardiff) Ltd.* v. *South Atlantic S.S. Line*, 201 F. 301, 304 (5th Cir. 1912), "the provision in the charter party that the master shall sign bills of lading is not a mere authority for him to do so, but an agreement that he shall do so, for a breach of which the owner is liable". See also *The Misphah*, F.Cas. No. 9648 (D.Del. 1878) (a voyage charter case).

Bills imposing on owner greater liabilities than imposed by charter

The master is required to sign bills as presented by the charterer, even if they conflict with the charter or expose the owner to liabilities other than those imposed by the charter. In this situation, however, the owner will have a right of indemnity against the charterer for any losses sustained, whether or not the charter expressly provides that bills of lading shall be without prejudice to the charter. See, e.g., *Field Line (Cardiff) Ltd.* v. *South Atlantic S.S. Line*, above; *Kennedy* v. *Weston & Co.*, 136 F. 166 (5th Cir. 1905).

This is not to say, however, that the charterer has the absolute right to require the master to sign any bills of lading it might present. For example, the master is not obliged to sign bills of lading for cargo which has not in fact been loaded, or which name a discharge port outside the allowed trading limits. See *The Alonzo*, F.Cas. No. 257 (D.Me. 1869); *The Loch Rannoch*, 192 F. 219 (D.Me. 1911), aff'd 208 F. 884 (1st Cir. 1913). The master may also refuse to sign a "clean" bill of lading when he knows that the goods were not in good order and condition when received. *Kennedy* v. *Weston & Co.*, above. Moreover, the master may decline to sign a bill of lading if it purports to bind third persons he knows are not parties to the contract of affreightment. See *Ramsay Scarlett & Co. Inc.* v. *S.S. Koh Eun*, 462 F.Supp. 277, 286–87 (E.D. Va. 1978). The master also has no authority to sign blank bills of lading. *The Joseph Grant*, Fed.Cas. No. 7538 (D. Wis. 1857).

Bills signed "without prejudice" to the charter

Where the charter provides that bills of lading shall be signed "without prejudice to this charter", the rights and liabilities of the owner and charterer as between themselves will not be affected by the bill. The rule was recognized by the Supreme Court in *Crossman* v. *Burrill*, 179 U.S. 100, 109 (1900), where the court stated:

> . . . The provision of the charter party which requires "the bills of lading to be signed as presented, without prejudice to this charter", while it obliges the master to sign bills of lading upon request of the charterers, does not mean that the bills of lading, or the consignee holding them, shall be subject to all the provisions of the charter, but only that the obligations of the charterers to the ship and her owners are not to be affected by the bill of lading so signed.

See also *Field Line (Cardiff) Ltd.* v. *South Atlantic S.S. Line*, above. There, the master protested against the contents of bills of lading presented for his signature, but signed them on demand of the charterer. The bills covered a shipment of lumber and timber, and provided:

> General average payable according to York-Antwerp rules, 1890, excepting that jettison of deck cargo (and freight thereon) for the common safety should be allowable as general average.

This provision was in direct conflict with the charter, which provided that "no jettison of deck cargo shall be made good as general average". On the voyage, it was necessary to jettison the lumber and timber. When the general average was stated, the owner was compelled to incur the cost of the jettisoned lumber, but, because the bills of lading for all the other cargo shipped on the voyage were in conformity with the charter, the owner could not look to the other cargo interests for contribution. The court held that, in these circumstances, the owner had a valid cause of action against the charterer for indemnity since the charterer had caused the master to issue bills of lading which conflicted with the charter and which subjected the owner to a loss.

Express restrictions on issuance of bills of lading

The owner and charterer are, of course, free to impose restrictions on the issuance of bills of lading if they wish. For example, in *The Scan Venture*, S.M.A. No. 1627 (Arb. at N.Y. 1982), the charter was on the New York Produce form, but contained an additional clause which stated in part:

> Bills of lading to be signed without prejudice to the charter party and in accordance with mate's and/or tally clerk's receipts. In the event charterers wish issuance of liner bills of lading, then authority at each time to be requested from owners.

The arbitrators ruled unanimously that this clause placed a restriction on the charterer's right to require the master to sign liner bills of lading, and that liner bills issued by the charterer without the owner's advance approval were improper.

Shipper's right to demand bill of lading

Under the general maritime law, the shipper of cargo is entitled to demand the issuance of a bill of lading for goods loaded on board the vessel, for which purpose the bill will serve as a receipt. See, e.g., *The Delaware*, 81 U.S. 579 (1872); *Watt* v. *Cargo of Lumber*, 161 F. 104 (2d Cir. 1908); *Akt. Brunsgaard* v. *Standard Oil of N.J.*, 283 F. 106 (2d Cir. 1922); *The Alonzo*, F.Cas. No. 257 (D.Me. 1869).

In the case of shipments to or from ports of the United States in foreign trade under bills of lading governed by COGSA, the shipper's right to demand the issuance of a bill is governed by Section 3(3).

The Harter Act contains a similar provision in Section 4, and provides for a fine not exceeding $2,000 against an owner who refuses to issue on demand a bill of lading demanded in accordance with the Act. Other United States legislation which governs bills of lading includes the Pomerene Act, 49 U.S.C. §§81–124, which governs only bills issued by common carriers engaged in transporting goods between places in the United States or from United States ports to foreign countries.

Master's right to demand production of bill of lading before delivery of cargo

The master is entitled to require the production of original bills of lading prior to the commencement of discharge. In *The Bless River*, S.M.A. No. 1889 (Arb. at N.Y. 1983), owner was excused from responsibility for a delay in the commencement of discharge and the cost of guaranteed stevedore labor where charterer failed to provide the master with either original bills of lading or an indemnity agreement.

Identity of carrier clause

Many bills of lading contain "identity of carrier" clauses which provide as follows:

> The contract evidenced by this bill of lading is between the merchant and the owner of the vessel named herein (or substitute) and it is therefore agreed that said shipowner only shall be liable for any damage or loss due to any breach or non-performance of any obligation arising out of the contract of carriage, whether or not relating to the vessel's seaworthiness . . . It is further understood and agreed that as the line, company or agent who has executed this bill of lading for and on behalf of the master is not a principal in the transaction, said line, company or agent shall not be under any liability arising out of the contract of carriage, nor is carrier nor bailee of the goods.

Such "demise" clauses are void as a matter of law when used by a charterer to attempt to shift its potential liability for cargo loss to the shipowner. *Epstein* v. *United States*, 86 F. Supp. 740 (S.D.N.Y. 1949); *Blanchard Lumber Co.* v. *S.S. Anthony II*, 259 F. Supp. 857, 865–66, 1967 AMC 103, 120–21 (S.D.N.Y. 1966). The courts have held that such clauses are invalid as a matter of public policy since they represent an effort by the time charterer who normally drafts bills of lading to transfer its liability to the owner.

While a charterer cannot rely on a demise clause to shift liability to the owner, it has been held that the cargo interest may rely on the clause. In *Recovery Services International* v. *S/S Tatiana L*, 1988 AMC 788 (S.D.N.Y. 1986), the court held that since the shipper was not responsible for the inclusion of the identity of carrier clause in the bill of lading, it was entitled to rely on it for purposes of imposing liability on the shipowner.

Baltime form

See discussion below at page 472.

Log

"80. 9. That if the Charterers shall have reason to be dissatisfied with the conduct of the Captain, Officers, or Engineers, the Owners shall on
81. receiving particulars of the complaint, investigate the same, and, if necessary, make a change in the appointments.
82. 10. That the Charterers shall have permission to appoint a Supercargo, who shall accompany the vessel and see that voyages are prosecuted
83. with the utmost despatch. He is to be furnished with free accommodation, and same fare as provided for Captain's table, Charterers paying at the
84. rate of $1.00 per day. Owners to victual Pilots and Customs Officers, and also, when authorized by Charterers or their Agents, to victual Tally
85. Clerks, Stevedore's Forman, etc., Charterers paying at the current rate per meal, for all such victualling.
86. 11. That the Charterers shall furnish the Captain from time to time with all requisite instructions and sailing directions, in writing, and the
87. Captain shall keep a full and correct Log of the voyage or voyages, which are to be patent to the Charterers or their Agents, and furnish the Char-
88. terers, their Agents or Supercargo, when required, with a true copy of daily Logs, showing the course of the vesel and distance run and the con-
89. sumption of fuel.
90. 12. That the Captain shall use diligence in caring for the ventilation of the cargo."

American Law

Charterer's voyage instructions

In *The Andros Mentor*, S.M.A. No. 2125 (Arb. at N.Y. 1985), the vessel was chartered for a trip from Vancouver to the Philippine Islands. Charterer presented the master with voyage orders to follow the instructions of a weather routing service. The master declined to follow these instructions, however, and instead took a more southerly route by recommended service retained by owner. Although the route recommended by owner's company added about 688 miles to the length of the voyage, the master decided to follow it because, based on prior experience in trans-pacific crossings, he believed the more southerly route would be safer and more economical. Charterer later deducted hire for the additional time required to complete the voyage.

The panel's decision illustrates the interplay between Clauses 11 and 24 of the New York Produce form. The panel stated that whereas Clause 11 confers a duty upon charterer to provide the master with written instructions and sailing directions, it also implies a duty upon the master to follow them. Because under a time charter the risk of delay due to bad weather rests with charterer, Clause 11 permits charterer to use a weather routing service of its choice and for its own account. At the same time, the responsibility for safe navigation remains with the master:

The Master is not under an absolute obligation to follow the advice of any routing service; he is the sole judge when it comes to deciding upon the best and safest course to take from point of origin to destination, having in mind the best interests of both Owner and Charterer and the safety of his vessel, cargo and crew.

The panel found that the master's announcement at the outset of the voyage that he would not follow the routing proposed by charterer's routing service was a technical breach of Clause 11. Based upon all the evidence, however, the panel concluded that the master was justified in following the course recommended by owner's routing service.

The panel stated that the phrase "sailing directions" in Clause 11 "only entitles a charterer to give general instructions" rather than specific routing orders. Examples given by the panel were "via Panama Canal" or "via Cape Town", but stopping short of any interference with the navigation of the vessel.

Preservation of a Master's right to exercise his judgment and prerogatives in matters of navigation at sea are of paramount importance, and only in matters where the evidence shows such judgment to be severely flawed or negligent will he be subject to criticism or claim.

The panel further ruled that charterer may *not* order the vessel to violate Institute Warranty Limits without the owner's assent.

Log of the voyage

For a number of reasons, it is important that the master maintain a full and accurate logbook which, at the charterer's request, is available to it. Correct log entries are particularly important to the charterer with respect to speed or performance claims. These claims depend in large measure on weather conditions encountered by the vessel and a reliable logbook will often be the only acceptable evidence of weather encountered on the voyage.

The Largo, S.M.A. No. 1230 (Arb. at N.Y. 1978) illustrates the problems which may arise when the logbook is found to be unreliable. The vessel was chartered by the disponent owner to the charterer for a time charter trip. The charterer made a speed claim, which the disponent owner defended on the grounds that the logbook indicated unfavorable winds, seas and fog. The panel found, however, that the log was not sufficiently complete to assist it in evaluating the vessel's performance. The disponent owner argued that it had no control over the employees of the registered owner and was not responsible for the deficiencies in the logbook. The panel rejected this argument, however, and stated:

The defense of Owner that as Disponent Owner it had no control over the employees of the Owner and logbooks is without merit. The Charter Party clearly stipulates in Clause 11 that the Master shall maintain a full and correct log of the voyages, and furnish Charterer *when required* (emphasis added) with a true copy of the logs. It was incumbent upon Disponent Owner, in its relationship as primary Charterer of the vessel to request, obtain and see to it that accurate logs were submitted to Owner.

The United Bounty, S.M.A. No. 2040 (Arb. at N.Y. 1984) provides another illustration of the importance of maintaining an accurate logbook. The case involved charterer's claim for a speed deficiency and owner's counterclaim for credit for the value of bunkers underconsumed. The charterer's claim was based upon an analysis of the voyage prepared by a weather routing service. The ship's logs and the routing service's voyage analysis did not differ insofar as distance travelled and time used were concerned. There were major differences, however, between the two as to the reported weather conditions. The panel noted that, ordinarily, arbitrators would accept the reports of the ship because the master and officers "are deemed to be the best judges on the spot of actual conditions". There is a heavy burden on charterer to prove that the logs are not reliable. The panel carefully scrutinized the logs and found that there was a clear pattern of reporting adverse currents and winds consistently for almost the entire time at sea. The panel stated that it determined that "weather patterns reported by the ship were often at direct odds in terms of wind direction to a degree that is most unusual". Based upon its review, the panel concluded that the logs were not reliable and based its decision instead on the weather routing service's voyage analysis.

There are statutory requirements under American law for keeping a logbook and making entries therein on United States flag vessels. 46 U.S.C. §§ 11301–11303. Among other things, it is required that logbook entries shall be made as soon as possible after the occurrence and be signed. Violation of the statutes gives rise to a civil penalty.

Continuation of Charter

91. 13. That the Charterers shall have the option of continuing this charter for a further period of ....
92. ....
93. on giving written notice thereof to the Owners or their Agents..............days previous to the expiration of the first-named term, or any declared option."

Exercise of the option to continue

In order to exercise an option such as that given to them by Clause 13 of the New York Produce form, the charterers must give a clearly worded notice to the owners. See *The Trado* [1982] 1 Lloyd's Rep. 157, where Parker, J., said: "Those who have options in their favour must, if they wish to exercise them, exercise them in words which are not really capable of doubt."

Once the charterers have given notice that they exercise their option, their decision cannot be revoked; the same is true of notice by the charterers that they do not exercise the option: *The Trado*, above.

Effect upon optional allowance in Line 14

Where the basic period of the charter in Line 14 (see page 88 above) includes an express allowance of so many days more or less at the charterers' option and the charterers exercise an option given them under Clause 13 to continue the charter for another similar period, the allowance in Line 14 is to be disregarded in calculating the maximum total charter period.

The *Aspa Maria* was chartered for a period of "six months 30 days more or less at charterers' option". By Clause 13 the charterers were given "the option of continuing this charter for a futher period of further six months 30 days . . . at charterers' option declarable at the end of fourth month". The charterers exercised the option under Clause 13 and the question arose whether the resulting total maximum charter period was 12 months and 30 days or 12 months and 60 days. The Court of Appeal held that the former was correct. The first 30-day provision was merely an express margin of tolerance to the basic six months period which should be ignored once the charterers exercised their option under Clause 13.

Gulf Shipping Lines v. *Compania Naviera Alanje* [1976] 2 Lloyd's Rep. 643.

American Law

Continuation of charter

Under Clause 13, the parties may provide that the charterer shall have the option of extending the charter for whatever further period is agreed. Great care must be exercised in specifying the additional period allowed, as well as when notice must be given. See *The Cielo Rosso*, 1980 AMC 2088 (Arb. at N.Y. 1980), for an example of the difficulties that may arise where care is not exercised in drafting provisions relating to continuation of the charter.

The *Santa Katerina*, 1974 AMC 1383 (Arb. at N.Y. 1974), involved the application of an addendum modelled on Clause 13 of the New York Produce form which permitted the charterer to extend the charter for a further period of "three (3) consecutive calendar months, three weeks more or less, at Charterers' option on giving written notice thereof to the Owners....". Owner contended that the charterer was not permitted to undertake a voyage at the end of the extended period which would have required redelivery after 25 August, the date the fixed three-month extension was to expire. The arbitrators decided the charterer was entitled to "not only the fixed period of three months, but the three weeks more or less flexible period". Since the vessel was redelivered within the three-week period, there was no overlap.

In *The Jagat Padmini*, S.M.A. No. 1097 (Arb. at N.Y. 1977), the vessel was chartered "for about minimum 6 months, Charterers' option 15 days more or less—Charterers' option additional 6 months to be declared within 4 months of delivery". The panel held that the charterer was entitled to keep the vessel for exactly 12 months and 15 days. Although the redelivery clause contained the word "about ", it was held that the leeway intended was "15 days, more or less".

It has been held that if the charter period is extended by the addition of time the vessel is off-hire, the time in which the charterer may exercise an option to continue the charter for a further period is also extended. *The Tropigas Far East*, S.M.A. No. 1594 (Arb. at N.Y. 1981). The charter was for an initial period of three years, and gave the charterer an option to extend for further periods of one year provided that the option was exercised at least six months in advance of the charter termination date. During the initial three-year term, the vessel went off-hire and it was agreed by the owner and charterer that the expiration date 15 October 1979, would be extended to 24 October. Subsequently, the charterer twice exercised its option to extend, in each case giving notice before 15 April, or six months before the original 15 October deadline. Charterer later elected to exercise its option to extend a third time, but gave notice on 22 April. The owner contended that the charterer's exercise of the option was untimely. The arbitrators ruled for charterer, holding that since the termination date of the original hire period and each extension thereof had been changed to 24 October from 15 October, the option declaration deadline was similarly extended.

Cancelling Clause

"94. 14. That if required by Charterers, time not to commence before .... and should vessel
95. not have given written notice of readiness on or before .... but not later than 4 p.m. Charterers or
96. their Agents to have the option of cancelling this Charter at any time not later than the day of vessel's readiness."

General

Speaking of the cancelling clause in *The Democritos* [1976] 2 Lloyd's Rep. 149, Lord Denning, M.R., said at page 152: "Its effect is that, although there may have been no breach by the owners nevertheless the charterers are, for their own protection, entitled to cancel if the vessel is not delivered in a proper condition by the cancelling date".

The cancelling clause gives to the charterers an automatic right to cancel the charter in certain described circumstances; unlike the withdrawal clause its operation does not depend upon breach of contract by the owners. Fault or lack of it on the part of the owners is not relevant: see *Smith* v. *Dart* (1884) 14 Q.B.D. 105, at page 110, and *The Madeleine* [1967] 2 Lloyd's Rep. 224, at page 239, quoted below. Likewise it is considered that the requirement of readiness and fittedness is absolute for the purposes of the cancelling clause: see page 114 above.

Thus the right of the charterers to cancel under this clause must be distinguished from the charterers' right to treat the contract as discharged because of breach by the owners. For consideration of the circumstances in which this separate right may arise, see pages 65 to 68 above.

Use by charterers before date stated

Conflicts may arise between Line 94 and the provisions of Lines 62 to 64, discussed at page 228 above. First, the notice period provision in Lines 62 and 63 may, if Line 94 is ignored, cause hire to be payable for a time earlier than that stipulated in Line 94. It is suggested that in this situation Line 94 will prevail and that hire will not commence until the agreed time is reached. Second, the charterers may start to use the ship before expiry of the notice period, thus activating the provision in Line 64 for immediate counting of hire. It is suggested that in this event the counting of hire should not be suspended until the time stipulated in Line 94. The charterers have, by electing to use the ship at once, opted not to rely on Line 94, as otherwise they could have done. (The position may be different under a voyage charter: see *Pteroti* v. *National Coal Board* [1958] 1 Lloyd's Rep. 245.)

Requirement of readiness

Under the New York Produce form the charterers are given the option to cancel if the ship shall not have given notice of readiness by the stated date; and the owners' notice of readiness must be valid as well as timely. It will not be valid if the ship is not ready and complying with the requirements of Lines 21 to 24. For comments on the requirement of readiness and when it is satisfied see pages 114 to 120 above.

Similarly under the Baltime form the charterers have the option of cancelling under Clause 22 if the ship is not delivered by the due date in the condition required by Clause 1, namely, "in every way fitted for ordinary cargo service".

The *Madeleine* was chartered under the Baltime form for a period of three months. The cancelling date, as extended by agreement, was 10 May. On 6 May the ship's de-ratting exemption certificate expired. On 9 May the ship completed discharge of her inward cargo. But after inspecting her the port health authorities refused to issue a new de-ratting exemption certificate. They ordered fumigation, with a view to issuing thereafter a de-ratting certificate. In the absence of a valid de-ratting exemption certificate the ship could not trade as the charter provided. Fumigation could not be completed before 12 May. At 8 a.m. on 10 May the charterers advised the owners that they cancelled the charter and they gave a further notice of cancellation at 8.48 p.m. the same day. The certificate was issued on 12 May and the owners claimed that the charterers' cancellation was wrongful. It was held by Roskill, J., that the ship had to be delivered in the condition required by Clause 1 ("in every way fitted for ordinary cargo service", which meant in a seaworthy condition) and that since the ship was not delivered in a seaworthy condition by 6 p.m. on 10 May the charterers were entitled to cancel.

The Madeleine [1967] 2 Lloyd's Rep. 224.

Of the cancelling clause Roskill, J., said, at page 239 of the above report: "It is important to emphasise that that which the charterers are claiming to exercise is an express contractual right given by Clause 22. Their right to cancel does not in any way depend upon any breach of the charter-party by the owners. Entitlement to cancel depends not on any breach by the owners but upon whether the owners have timeously complied with their obligations under Clause 1."

Notice of readiness

The owners' notice of readiness under the New York Produce form must be in writing as required by Line 95 and the ship must be at the place referred to in Line 18 where she is to be put at the disposal of the charterers. To be valid a notice must be accurate in all material respects.

Minor infringements

But, as the cancelling option is in the nature of a forfeiture provision, the courts will hesitate to allow it to operate where the failure to be ready is technical or of little real significance and relates to a deficiency in gear or equipment that does not affect the safety of ship or cargo. In *Noemijulia Steamship* v. *Minister of Food* (1950) 83 Ll.L.Rep. 500, Delvin, J., said: "I find it hard to believe that if, for example, a winch, which would not be needed for some days after the loading began, required an hour or two's overhaul, the cancellation of the charter would be justified . . . . It must always be remembered that this is a forfeiture clause and so not to be applied lightly. It would be a misfortune, I think, if defects of no real significance in the adventure were to be used as a means of throwing up a charter at the last moment." Delvin, J., was there discussing the cancelling clause in a voyage charter, but there is no reason why his remarks should not apply equally to time charters. Indeed, Roskill, J., assumed them to be equally applicable to the cancelling clause in the Baltime form in his judgment in *The Madeleine* [1967] 2 Lloyd's Rep. 224, at page 237.

See also *The Arianna* [1987] 2 Lloyd's Rep. 376 at page 116 above, and the extract from the judgment of Greer, J., in *New York and Cuba Mail Steamship* v. *Eriksen and Christensen* (1922) 27 Com. Cas. 330, concerning minor deficiencies not affecting the safety of ship or cargo, quoted at page 117 above.

But in voyage charter cases concerning the condition of the the ship's holds to receive cargo, the requirement of readiness is applied strictly: see page 114 above. In *The Tres Flores* [1972] 2 Lloyd's Rep. 384 and [1973] 2 Lloyd's Rep. 247, differing views were expressed by Mocatta, J., at first instance and Roskill, L.J., in the Court of Appeal on the question whether this strict approach which was applied in laytime cases was equally applicable when considering the operation of the cancelling clause.

Mocatta, J., said at page 394 of the report at first instance:

"... there may well be a distinction to be drawn between cases concerned with the starting of laytime and cases concerned with cancelling clauses. In the latter type of case the consequence of holding a ship not to have made her cancelling date may be extremely serious in as much as the charterer will then be able to terminate the charter-party. In the laytime cases the worst that can happen would be that the decision taken as to the validity of the notice of readiness may affect the amount of demurrage due or the amount of despatch money to be paid."

In the Court of Appeal Roskill, L.J., said, at page 252:

"If it be said that the maintenance of an absolute rule of this kind (subject only to question of *de minimis*) may work hardship on shipowners or lead to unjust results, the answer is that the parties are always free to modify the common-law rule. In the present case that rule might have been modified by a 'time lost waiting for berth' provision. But in this class of case, where not only questions of laytime and demurrage arise, but also the right of a charterer to cancel because a ship is not ready by a stated date, it is of crucial importance that the basic principle must be able to be simply applied to the given facts of a particular case.... One has only to take this example. If [counsel's] contention be right what would be the position where there was only a short interval of time between the geographical arrival of the vessel and the cancelling date and notice of readiness was given in the expectation that a particular defect making the ship unfit to load might be remedied within a matter of hours, but this prediction was falsified in the event? What is the position of the parties to be if that defect has not in the event been remedied before the cancelling date? Is the notice of readiness, *prima facie* good on [counsel's] argument, suddenly to become retrospectively bad because of an unexpected turn of events? The complications of such a situation are endless. The sure way of avoiding such complications is to have a rule which can be applied with absolute certainty."

There may be no reason to differentiate between readiness for laytime purposes and readiness for cancelling purposes where the deficiency in question relates to the condition of holds to receive the proffered cargo. But, as Devlin, J., pointed out in the *Noemijulia Steamship* case, above, the cancelling clause is in the nature of a forfeiture clause and so not to be applied lightly. It is suggested that if the deficiency in question does not affect the safety of the ship or of the cargo immediately to be loaded, account should be taken of such matters as the length of the charter period and the scope of the trading and cargo options. "Readiness" should be interpreted in a business sense: see *The Arianna* [1987] 2 Lloyd's Rep. 376 and page 116 above.

The burden is upon the charterers to establish the lack of readiness upon which they rely: see the judgments of the Court of Appeal in *Noemijulia Steamship* v. *Minister of Food* (1950) 84 Ll.L.Rep. 354.

Misdescription

It is suggested that the ship need only, in the context of the cancelling clause, be ready in accordance with the requirements of Lines 21 to 24 of the New York Produce form. The fact that when notice of readiness is given the ship does not comply with some aspect of her description in Lines 3 to 11 does not of itself give the charterers the right to cancel. For example, the right to cancel should not arise under this clause merely because the ship is not then capable of the speed described in Lines 9 and 10, provided that her speed is not so reduced as to prevent her being "in every way fitted for the service" under Line 22. The charterers do of course have other remedies independent of the cancelling clause, as to which see page 61 above.

Premature notice of readiness

By analogy with voyage charter cases on notices of readiness to commence laytime, it seems that if at the time a notice is given the ship is not ready the notice is ineffective and does not become effective upon the ship becoming ready subsequently, unless the charterers expressly or impliedly agree that a fresh notice need not be given. See the judgment of Donaldson, J., in *Christensen* v. *Hindustan Steel* [1971] 1 Lloyd's Rep. 395, at page 399, distinguishing the case of *The Massalia* [1960] 2 Lloyd's Rep. 352, (where Diplock, J., held that a fresh notice was not necessary), as being a case dependent on its own special facts. See also *The Tres Flores* [1973] 2 Lloyd's Rep. 247, *The Helle Skou* [1976] 2 Lloyd's Rep. 205 and *The Demosthenes V (No. 1)* [1982] 1 Lloyd's Rep. 275. For a case on the effect of accepting a notice of readiness where subsequently the ship is found not to have been ready see *The Shackleford* [1978] 1 Lloyd's Rep. 191 and [1978] 2 Lloyd's Rep. 154.

No absolute obligation on owners to deliver by the cancelling date

No absolute obligation is undertaken by the owners that the ship shall arrive by the cancelling date. As was said by A.L. Smith, J., in *Smith* v. *Dart* (1884) 14 Q.B.D. 105, at page 110: "The shipowner does not contract to get there by a certain date, but says: 'If I do not get there you may cancel'."

In the absence of express provision, the owners' obligation is only to exercise reasonable diligence from the conclusion of the charter to deliver the ship in a fit condition by the cancelling date. This obligation will be implied.

The *Democritos* was chartered on 8 November 1969, on the New York Produce form "for about a trip via port or ports via the Pacific, duration about 4 to 6 months". The ship was to be delivered at Durban and the cancelling date was 20 December. The ship had been drydocked for special survey in September, and she had then loaded cargo for Bombay. In the course of discharge at Bombay it was discovered that No. 2 'tween deck had collapsed. The ship left Bombay on 4 December and arrived at Durban on 16 December. The damage to the 'tween deck was such that it could not be repaired before the cancelling date but on 18 December the charterers accepted the ship with the damage unrepaired. The charterers subsequently claimed that there was an absolute obligation to deliver the ship in a condition conforming with the charterparty by the cancelling date. It was held by the Court of Appeal that there was no such absolute obligation: the only obligation on the owners was to exercise reasonable diligence to deliver the ship in a fit condition by the cancelling date and there was no finding that the owners had failed in this respect.

The Democritos [1976] 2 Lloyd's Rep. 149.

It seems from observations on the cancelling clause in a voyage charter in *The Heron II* [1966] 1 Lloyd's Rep. 595 (C.A.) and [1967] 2 Lloyd's Rep. 457 (H.L.), that if there is a breach of the owners' obligation of reasonable diligence which results in a delayed tender of delivery, the owners will be liable for loss suffered by the charterers in consequence, even though the ship is tendered for delivery before the cancelling date. Diplock, L.J., said, at page 610 of the Court of Appeal report: "The fixing of a cancellation date in a charter-party merely gives warning to the shipowner that non-arrival by the cancelling date may go to the root of the contract so as to entitle the shippers to rescind. It does not relieve the shipowner of his primary obligation to proceed with all convenient speed to the loading-port or of his secondary obligation in the event of non-performance of that primary obligation, to make reparation in money to the shippers for any loss sustained by them as a result of such non-performance." See also the remarks of Lord Upjohn at page 486 of the House of Lords report.

No right (or obligation) to cancel before cancelling date

The charterers are not entitled to cancel under this clause before the cancelling date, even though it may seem inevitable that the ship will arrive after the cancelling date. Roskill, J., in *The Madeleine* [1967] 2 Lloyd's Rep. 224, said with reference to the cancelling provisions in the Baltime form, the first sentence of Clause 22: " . . . if there were what I will call an anticipatory right to cancel under the clause, it could only arise by necessary implication into Clause 22. For my part, I have great difficulty in seeing how, where there is an express right given to cancel if the vessel is not delivered by May 10 [the cancelling date], an implied right can concurrently exist to cancel at some earlier point of time, namely, when it becomes inevitable that the stated cancelling date will not be able to be attained by the ship."

This statement was approved by a majority of the Court of Appeal in *The Mihalis Angelos* [1970] 2 Lloyd's Rep. 43, in holding that in the case of a voyage charter the right to cancel did not arise before the cancelling date.

Conversely, the owners cannot require the charterers to declare in advance of their presentation of the ship whether or not they will exercise their option to cancel, even after the cancelling date has passed: *Moel Tryvan* v. *Weir* [1910] 2 K.B. 844. The same is true where, although the ship is at the place of delivery, she is not ready. In *The Democritos* [1975] 1 Lloyd's Rep. 386, at page 397, Kerr, J., said: "It is clear from the facts found that [the repair of 'tween deck damage] could not have been done by the cancelling date of Dec. 20. The charterers, on the other hand, were not obliged to do anything until the vessel was tendered to them in readiness under the charter. Once Dec. 20 had passed they could cancel if they wished; alternatively they could continue to do nothing and wait until the vessel was tendered. Under cl. 14 they then retained their option to cancel until the vessel was tendered in readiness after Dec. 20."

The fact that the charterers may not exercise their option to cancel under this clause before the cancelling date does not affect any rights the charterers may have at common law, or the time at which such rights may be exercised. Thus the charterers may have at common law and separately from their option under this clause a right to treat the charter as discharged and such a right may arise and may be exercised before the cancelling date. Roskill, J., said in *The Madeleine* [1967] 2 Lloyd's Rep. 224, at page 244: " . . . the fact that there is no contractual right to cancel in advance does not prevent a charterer seeking to claim the right to rescind in advance of the cancelling date.... Where the charterer seeks to say that the contract has been frustrated or that there has been an anticipatory breach which entitles him to rescind then he has such rights as are given to him at common law." See also the part of Scrutton, L.J.'s unreported judgment from *Bank Line* v. *Capel* [1919] A.C. 435, which is set out in the judgment of Roskill, J., at [1967] 2 Lloyd's Rep. page 243.

Exercise of the option to cancel

Lines 94 to 96 of the New York Produce form give the charterers the option to cancel if the owners have not given written notice of readiness by, at the latest, 4 p.m. on the stated day. The time 4 p.m. corresponds with Line 63. It seems that placing the ship at the disposal of the charterers in the place selected for delivery, under Lines 18 to 21, is not sufficient: if there is no written notice by the due time, the charterers may cancel.

Cancelling option and other rights

The exercise by the charterers of their right to cancel does not deprive them of the right to claim damages if the owners were in breach of any of their obligations under the charter and the charterers suffered loss as a result.

In a voyage charter case, *Nelson & Sons* v. *Dundee East Coast Shipping*, 1907 S.C. 927 it was held that charterers were entitled to damages even though they had exercised the right to cancel. Lord M'Laren said, at page 934: " . . . it was submitted by the [charterers] that no damages were due, in respect of that the insertion of the clause giving an option to cancel came in place of the common law obligation to provide a ship or pay compensation. I do not think the clause was inserted for any such purpose."

Similarly, an election by the charterers not to exercise their right of cancellation will not necessarily deprive them of the usual remedies for breach of contract: see *The Democritos* [1975] 1 Lloyd's Rep. 386, at page 397 and pages 121 and 290 above. See generally on the question of waiver page 59 above.

American Law

Cancelling date

A late tender of the vessel gives the charterer an option to cancel, which he may or may not choose to exercise. Unless there is modifying language in the charter, the charterer's right to cancel for late delivery is absolute and may be exercised regardless of the cause of the delay. See *Karran* v. *Peabody*, 145 F. 166 (2d Cir. 1906).

The owner, on the other hand, is under an absolute duty to tender the vessel, and must offer to make delivery even if the cancelling date has expired. See *The Progreso*, 50 F. 835 (3d Cir. 1892); *The Samuel W. Hall*, 49 F. 281 (S.D.N.Y. 1892); *The Orient Point*, S.M.A. No. 246 (Arb. at N.Y. 1961).

In general, a late tender by the owner will give the charterer an option to cancel, but will not create a right to recover damages from the owner. See *Sanday* v. *United States Shipping Board Emergency Fleet Corp.*, 6 F. 2d 384 (2d Cir. 1925), *cert.* denied 269 U.S. 556 (1925); *The Michael L*, S.M.A. No. 1301 (Arb. at N.Y. 1979).

In *Sanday*, the charter was for a voyage from Galveston to Rio de Janeiro, and gave the charterer the right to cancel if the vessel nominated to perform was not ready to load at Galveston on or before 15 November 1920. The vessel was at Norfolk on 11 November, and, it being obvious she could not make Galveston by the cancelling date, the charterer rejected the tender and made arrangements for another vessel. The vessel arrived in Galveston three days late, and was apparently tendered at that time. The charterer meanwhile commenced an action against the vessel owner for damages it claimed arose from the late tender, on the theory that the charter bound the owner to tender a ship on or before the cancellation date. The court dismissed the action, holding that the very purpose of a cancelling clause was to preclude an action for damages resulting from a late tender, and stating:

> When no delivery date is named in a charter, the promise of the owner is to tender with reasonable dispatch, and for a breach of that promise of course the charterer may sue. If he does, he undertakes to show that the owner has not used reasonable dispatch in tendering the ship. We entirely agree that his promise is not affected by the presence of a cancellation clause, and so it appears to have been held in *Nelson & Sons* v. *Dundee East Coast Shipping Co. Limited*, 44 Scottish Law Reporter, 661 (1907, Court of Session).
>
> But that is quite different from saying that the cancellation date *ipso facto* establishes a promise of the owner to tender the ship on or before the cancellation day or at any other definite time. It seems to us very clear that the language is expressly chosen to avoid such a result, and that, although the owner accepts the hazard of tendering the ship after the cancellation date only to have her refused . . . he does not undertake anything else beyond reasonable dispatch. Such an undertaking must be expressed in a promise to tender by the cancellation date, and that the charterer's option to cancel does not in any sense imply. (6 F.2d at 385)

A right to recover damages exists if the owner has materially misrepresented the vessel's position, or her readiness for delivery, in the charter. See *Davison* v. *Von Lingen*, 113 U.S. 40, 49–50 (1885); *The Michael L*, above. In addition, if the owner breaches his duty to proceed with "reasonable dispatch" in making delivery of the vessel, the charterer may have a right to damages. Such a right could arise where, for example, owner makes an unreasonable intermediate voyage, or carries out repairs. See *The Gilia*, 1972 AMC 1738 (Arb. at N.Y. 1972); *The Caribbean Wave*, S.M.A. No. 278 (Arb. at N.Y.

1961); *The Noto*, 1979 AMC 116 (Arb. at N.Y. 1976). *The Federal Fraser*, S.M.A. No. 1804 (Arb. at N.Y. 1983).

Condition on delivery

See discussion above at page 76.

Off-hire Clause

"97. 15. That in the event of the loss of time from deficiency of men or stores, fire, breakdown or damages to hull, machinery or equipment,
98. grounding, detention by average accidents to ship or cargo, drydocking for the purpose of examination or painting bottom, or by any other cause
99. preventing the full working of the vessel, the payment of hire shall cease for the time thereby lost; and if upon the voyage the speed be reduced by
100. defect in or breakdown of any part of her hull, machinery or equipment, the time so lost, and the cost of any extra fuel consumed in consequence
101. thereof, and all extra expenses shall be deducted from the hire."

General principle

The off-hire clause operates as an exception to the charterers' primary obligation to pay hire continuously throughout the charter period. Commenting on Clause 15 of the New York Produce form, Kerr, J., said in *The Mareva A.S.* [1977] 1 Lloyd's Rep. 368, at page 381: "It is settled law that *prima facie* hire is payable continuously and that it is for the charterers to bring themselves clearly within an off-hire clause if they contend that hire ceases. This clause undoubtedly presents difficulties of construction and may well contain some tautology, e.g. in the reference to damage to hull, machinery or equipment followed by 'average accidents to ship'. But I think that the object is clear. The owners provide the ship and the crew to work her. So long as these are fully efficient and able to render to the charterers the service then required, hire is payable continuously. But if the ship is for any reason not in full working order to render the service then required from her, and the charterers suffer loss of time in consequence, then hire is not payable for the time so lost."

Thus the burden is on the charterers to show that the off-hire clause operates in the relevant circumstances. Bucknill, L.J., said in *Royal Greek Government* v. *Minister of Transport* (1948) 82 Ll.L.Rep. 196, at page 199: "the cardinal rule . . . in interpreting such a charter-party as this, is that the charterer will pay hire for the use of the ship unless he can bring himself within the exceptions. I think he must bring himself clearly within the exceptions. If there is a doubt as to what the words mean, then I think those words must be read in favour of the owners because the charterer is attempting to cut down the owners' right to hire."

Not dependent on breach

The off-hire clause operates entirely independently of any breach of contract by the owners. If the charterers successfully invoke the clause their consequent rights will be spelt out by the words of the clause itself and any entitlement to damages depends on the separate principles of common law relating to breach of contract. In the words of Staughton, J., in *The Ioanna* [1985] 2 Lloyd's Rep. 164, at page 167: "Off-hire events are not necessarily a breach of contract at all. So one should not be too surprised if one finds that [the off-hire clause] leads to a different answer than would ensue in the case of a claim for damages for breach of contract."

Loss of time

The happening of one of the listed incidents, such as a breakdown of machinery, does not result in an automatic interruption of hire. It must be shown also that time was lost to the charterers in consequence.

Thus, a breakdown of the propulsion machinery will not usually put the ship off-hire if it happens and is cured during a period of loading or discharging cargo. Regard must be had to the particular work that is required of the ship at the relevant time and only if that is affected does the possibility of off-hire arise. It follows that a ship may be off-hire by reason of a breakdown of propulsion machinery while she is, or is required to be, at sea but on hire again immediately that machinery is no longer relevant to the particular service the charterers next require.

The time charter of the *Westfalia* included an off-hire clause which provided: "In the event of loss of time from deficiency of men or stores, break-down of machinery, want of repairs, or damage, whereby the working of the vessel is stopped for more than forty-eight consecutive working hours, the payment of hire shall cease until she be again in an efficient state to resume her service." While carrying cargo from Africa to Harburg, her high-pressure engine broke down and she was obliged to put into Las Palmas. Repairs could not be effected there and she had to be towed to Harburg, although some assistance was given by the ship's low pressure engine. On arrival at Harburg the cargo was discharged, with the ship's steam winches and cargo machinery working efficiently. The House of Lords held that the ship was off-hire during the tow from Las Palmas to Harburg, for although the cargo was moved to destination in the ship, she was not fully efficient during the tow because she could not proceed without the aid of the tug. Once discharge began, however, the ship came on hire again as she was efficient for what was then required of her. Lord Halsbury said: "It appears to me, therefore, that at that period there was a right in the shipowner to demand payment of the hire, because at that time his vessel was efficiently working; the working of the vessel was proceeding as efficiently as it could with reference to the particular employment demanded of her at the time."
Hogarth v. *Miller* [1891] A.C. 48.

Thus the fact that a ship proceeds on a voyage in an unseaworthy condition does not necessarily mean that she will be off-hire until the unseaworthiness is remedied. The charterers must still demonstrate that one of the events referred to in the off-hire clause operated and that it caused loss of time: see *The Hermosa* [1980] 1 Lloyd's Rep. 638 (ship with defective hatch covers proceeding on a ballast voyage).

"Net loss of time" and "period" off-hire clauses

In *Hogarth* v. *Miller*, above, the ship came on hire again as soon as she was capable of performing the service then required by the charterers. This was in accordance with the wording of the off-hire clause in that charter. The New York Produce form off-hire clause is differently worded, providing that "the payment of hire shall cease for the time thereby lost", without reference to the time at which efficiency is resumed. The intention seems to be that what is to be allowed to the charterers is the net overall time lost to them consequent upon the happening of the specified event. Under off-hire clauses such as that in *Hogarth* v. *Miller* the intention is clearly different. The wording is directed in such clauses towards establishing a clear-cut "period" of off-hire: for example, in *Tynedale* v. *Anglo-Soviet* (1936) 41 Com. Cas. 206 (page 299 below) the wording of the clause was "hire to cease from commencement of such loss of time until steamer is again in efficient state to resume service" and Lord Roche stated: "The ascertainment of the net loss is something foreign to the clause as drawn." The off-hire period starts with one event and ends with another.

Robert Goff, J., in *The Pythia* [1982] 2 Lloyd's Rep. 160 held that, by contrast with such "period" clauses, the New York Produce form clause was a "net loss of time" clause. This view had already been accepted by both counsel at first instance in *The H.R. Macmillan* [1973] 1 Lloyd's Rep. 27 and was adopted, *obiter*, by Lord Denning, M.R., in the Court of Appeal ([1974] 1 Lloyd's Rep. 311, at page 314). Lord Denning there pointed out that in accordance with this interpretation of the clause, the breakdown of one of a ship's cranes would produce no cesser of hire at all if the remaining cranes were able to do and did do the work required so that no time was lost. In this respect the wording of the Baltime form ("any time lost thereby") is similar to the New York Produce form.

Both the New York Produce and Baltime forms of off-hire clause are, therefore, "net loss" clauses and should be applied as such. But, on the authorities as they now stand, this is subject to the exception that the assessment of the lost time should take no account of any period after the ship is again fully efficient. In the Baltime form this is spelt out specifically. In the case of the New York Produce form, this is the construction placed on the clause in *The Marika M* [1981] 2 Lloyd's Rep. 622 and *The Pythia* [1982] 2 Lloyd's Rep. 160, see below.

In *The Bridgestone Maru No. 3* [1985] 2 Lloyd's Rep. 62, it was held by Hirst, J., that the off-hire clause in the Shelltime 3 form of tanker time charter was a "period" clause and not a "net loss of time" clause.

From when full hire again becomes payable

Under a "period" off-hire clause it is clear that hire becomes payable again as soon as the ship becomes once more fully efficient.

A time charter of the *Carisbrook* provided that "In the event of loss of time from . . . damage preventing the working of the vessel for more than twenty-four running hours, the payment of hire shall cease until she be again in an efficient state to resume her service". The ship went aground and had to discharge her cargo. She was then repaired. The question arose whether hire was payable from the completion of repairs on 18 October or only from the completion of reloading on 30 October. It was held that after completing repairs the ship was again in an efficient state and hire became payable. Bailhache, J., said: "It is quite true that there was time lost by the accident until 8.30 a.m. on October 30, and if the clause had said that hire should not be payable during 'all time lost in consequence of an accident' [charterers' counsel's] contention would, I think, have been right. But that is not the language used."

Smailes v. *Evans* [1917] 2 K.B. 54.

Under a "net loss of time" clause the charterers should logically be entitled, as was indicated by Bailhache, J., in the above case, to deduct any time lost in consequence of the event which put the ship off-hire, even after the ship again becomes fully efficient; for example, where a ship has had to put back the charterers should be entitled to deduct any time lost by the ship in regaining the position she was in when the event occurred.

But the decisions in *Vogemann* v. *Zanzibar* and *The Marika M*, below, do not support such a conclusion, at least so far as Clause 15 of the New York Produce form is concerned. The facts of the former case were as follows:

The off-hire clause in the time charter of the *Zanzibar* provided: "That in the event of loss of time from deficiency of men or stores, breakdown, or damage of machinery or damage to rudder or propeller, grounding, but not in river, detention by average accidents to ship or cargo, or by other cause preventing the full working of the vessel (loading and/or discharging cargo), the payment of hire shall cease for the time exceeding twenty-four hours thereby lost". The *Zanzibar* was en route from Hamburg to the United States when an average accident obliged her to put back to Queenstown for repairs. She was admittedly off-hire from the time of the accident until she sailed from Queenstown. The charterer argued that she remained off-hire until she once again reached the spot where the accident had happened, "time" having been "lost" up to that point.

Phillimore J., said (6 Com. Cas. page 253) that the question whether hire was payable by the charterer during the time occupied by the ship in regaining the spot where the accident occurred turned on the meaning of "detention by average accidents to ship or cargo". He went on: "I think that the safest way of construing that clause [the off-hire clause] is to regard it as one of exception or defeasance. By the clause certain days are deducted from those for which hire is to be paid, and it was, I think, the duty of the charterer to insert in the clause everything which he wished to have deducted. There is no provision in terms covering the time in question in this case, but the words I have read are relied on by the plaintiff in support of his contention. In my opinion the word 'detention' does not apply here. 'Detention' is not quite such a strong word as, for example, 'delay'. A vessel is detained when she is sent back to a port for repairs, and so long as she is kept there for the purpose of being repaired. But I do not think that a vessel can be said to be detained when, the repairs having been finished, she has made a fresh start and is once more proceeding on her voyage."

The judge added an observation that it would be very difficult to calculate the exact time at which the ship had recovered the lost ground.

The Court of Appeal affirmed this decision. Collins, M.R., said he considered Phillimore, J., was right, but then added: "When the accident ceased to prevent the full working of the vessel, the hire became again payable. This is the natural construction of the clause, and any other construction would involve intricate calculations as to the time which had been lost."

Stirling, J., and Cozens-Hardy, L.J., also agreed, the former saying: "In order to prevent the hire running there must be an accident preventing the full working of the vessel; therefore when she had been repaired, and was once more in full working order, she was no longer 'detained' within the meaning of the clause in question."

Vogemann v. *Zanzibar* (1902) 7 Com. Cas. 254.

The decision in *Vogemann* v. *Zanzibar* is authority for the narrow proposition that where time is lost from "detention by average accidents" hire ceases only for the period of the detention. It seems also to be authority for the wider proposition that the clause in question (which is in all relevant respects identical to the clause in the New York Produce form) should not be construed so as to allow the deduction of time lost after the ship again becomes fully efficient.

Certainly Lord Roche in *Tynedale* v. *Anglo-Soviet* (see below) considered that the case laid down the wider principle, although he did not refer to the difference in wording of the off-hire clauses in the two cases. He said that in *Vogemann* v. *Zanzibar*, " . . . the shipowner had the advantage of the construction which I regard as the true construction, inasmuch as the charterer was made to pay for time when the ship, after being inefficient and after having been repaired and become efficient again, was spending time in getting back to that position on the voyage which she left to proceed to the port of refuge—that is to say, the shipowner got paid although time was lost owing to the breakdown, inasmuch as when the events which led up to and constituted a bar to the claim for hire ceased, hire began to run again". ((1936) 41 Com. Cas. 206, at page 220.)

Parker, J., in *The Marika M*, below, also considered that the decision of the Court of Appeal in *Vogemann* v. *Zanzibar* was authority for the wider principle and was binding on him.

The *Marika M*, which was chartered on the New York Produce form, was due to berth at Bahrain on 18 July and would have done so had she not grounded on 17 July. She refloated on 27 July and then had to wait for a berth until 6 August. The charterers contended that the period of off-hire continued beyond 27 July (when she was again fully efficient) until 6 August since this period was

also time lost as a result of the grounding. The owners denied that the ship was off-hire after she refloated and was again in full working order. In upholding the arbitrator's award in favour of the owners, Parker, J., emphasised the difficulty of assessing any consequential loss of time and the fact that the interpretation contended for by the owners appeared to have been accepted for many years.
The *Marika M* [1981] 2 Lloyd's Rep. 622.
(See also the judgment of Robert Goff, J., in *The Pythia* [1982] 2 Lloyd's Rep. 160.)

It seems therefore that under English law—unlike the position under American law (see page 311 below)—full hire becomes payable under Clause 15 of the New York Produce form as soon as the ship again becomes efficient. It also seems that hire will not restart under this exception until the ship is fully efficient, so that after, say, a total breakdown, the resumption of partial efficiency will not be sufficient to bring the exception into effect (see Partial inefficiency, below) and the net loss calculation will continue until full efficiency is achieved. Full efficiency has to be judged against the service which the charterers require at the particular time: see *Hogarth* v. *Miller* [1891] A.C. 48.

In the Baltime form the position is clarified by additional words. Clause 11(A) is clearly a "net loss of time" clause because of the use of the words "no hire to be paid in respect of any time lost thereby", but the additional words "during the period in which the Vessel is unable to perform the service immediately required" make it clear that full hire again becomes payable after the resumption of (full) efficiency.

Partial inefficiency

Under clauses which provide that the hire is to cease until the ship is again in an efficient state to resume her service ("period" clauses), partial inefficiency has the same effect as total inefficiency. In either case the ship is put completely off-hire and no allowance is made for the partial working of the ship.

The *Horden* was chartered under an earlier version of the Baltime form. The off-hire clause provided that: "In the event of loss of time caused by dry-docking or by other necessary measures to maintain the efficiency of steamer or by . . . damage to hull or other accident preventing the working of the steamer and lasting more than 24 consecutive hours, hire to cease from commencement of such loss of time until steamer is again in efficient state to resume service . . . ". As a result of the shifting of the ship's deckload of timber on a voyage from Archangel to Liverpool, her foremast was badly damaged. This did not affect the remainder of the voyage to Liverpool but at Liverpool she could only discharge her aft part by her own means. She could not discharge from the forward part because of the broken mast, and floating derricks had to be employed. The charterers contended that the ship was off-hire for the whole period of discharge because she was inefficient throughout. The owners argued that as long as the ship could discharge, however slowly, she was efficient and hire continued. It was held by the Court of Appeal that the full working of the ship was prevented by the partial inefficiency of the ship's discharging gear and that the ship was off-hire for the whole period of discharge. Lord Roche said: "The mast being damaged did not prevent or hinder her steaming, but it did hinder or prevent her discharging in the sense in which prevention was construed in the House of Lords in *Hogarth* v. *Miller*—as preventing discharge or the working of the ship happening in accordance with the contract."
Tynedale v. *Anglo-Soviet* (1936) 41 Com. Cas. 206.

In *Hogarth* v. *Miller* no allowance was made for the assistance given during the tow by the ship's own low pressure engine.

But under the off-hire clause in the New York Produce form, which is a "net loss of time" clause, hire should be deductible in the case of partial inefficiency only if and to the extent that time is actually lost by reason of the partial inefficiency. Speaking of the off-hire clause of the New York Produce form in *The H.R. Macmillan* [1974] 1 Lloyd's Rep.

311, Lord Denning, M.R., said: "Taking that clause by itself, it would mean that, if one crane broke down, there would have to be an inquiry as to the time lost thereby. That would be a most difficult inquiry to undertake. For instance, if one broke down and the other two cranes were able to do, and did do, all the work that was required, there would be no 'time lost thereby'; and there would be no cessation of hire. But if there was work for three cranes, and there was some loss of time owing to the one crane breaking down, there would have to be an assessment of the amount of time lost. In that event, as the Judge pointed out, the question would have to be asked: 'How much earlier would the vessel have been away from her port of loading or discharge if three . . . cranes, instead of two, had been available throughout?' The Judge called that a 'net loss of time' clause."

Event occurring before beginning of charter period

If time is lost during the charter period as a result of one of the named causes, it does not matter that the incident causing that loss occurred before the beginning of the charter period. Thus, if during the charter period the ship drydocks in order to repair damage caused by grounding before that period began, the ship will be off-hire: *The Essex Envoy* (1929) 35 Com. Cas. 61; and see *The Apollonius* [1978] 1 Lloyd's Rep. 53. The same is true of a reduction in speed under Lines 99 to 101 of the New York Produce form; deduction from hire may be made in respect of time lost by a defect in the ship's hull that existed at the time of delivery under the charter: see *The Ioanna* [1985] 2 Lloyd's Rep. 164, at page 310 below.

Deficiency of men

The expression "deficiency of men" does not apply to the situation in which there is on board a full complement of officers and men able to work but some or all of them refuse to do so.

In December, 1943, the officers and crew of the *Ilissos* refused for over six days to sail from Newcastle, New South Wales, except in a convoy. The Court of Appeal held that, as there was no numerical insufficiency, the expression "deficiency of men" did not apply.

Royal Greek Government v. *Minister of Transport* (1948) 82 Ll.L.Rep. 196.

Even if there is a numerical deficiency of men, the ship will not be off-hire if the numerical deficiency does not affect the efficiency of the ship and thus does not prevent the full working of the vessel: see *The Good Helmsman* [1981] 1 Lloyd's Rep. 377, at page 422. All the causes listed in Lines 97 and 98 of the New York Produce form, including "deficiency of men", are subject to the opening words of Line 99, "preventing the full working of the vessel"; see *The Mareva A.S.* [1977] 1 Lloyd's Rep. 368 and page 301 below.

Illness

There was discussion in the *Royal Greek Government* case as to whether there would be a "deficiency of men" where there was on board a full complement of officers and men but a (large) number of them were incapable of work through illness or injury. Sellers, J., at first instance (81 Ll.L.Rep. at page 359) expressed the view that the answer would be "yes" but this was doubted by Bucknill, L.J., in the Court of Appeal (82 Ll.L.Rep., at page 199).

For there to be a deficiency of men, there must be a deficiency of officers and crew. "Men" does not include gunners to man the guns to protect a merchant ship against enemy submarines: *Radcliffe* v. *Compagnie Général Transatlantique* (1918) 24 Com. Cas. 40.

Breakdown

Where loss of time results from machinery defects and the condition of the machinery becomes progressively worse, a "breakdown" occurs when it becomes reasonably necessary to make for a port of refuge for repairs: *Giertsen* v. *Turnbull*, 1908 S.C. 1101.

Detention by average accidents to ship or cargo

Detention

Detention by average accidents means more than mere delay as a result of average accidents. There must, in the words of Kerr, J., in the case which follows, be "some physical or geographical constraint upon the vessel's movements in relation to her service under the charter".

A ship which was chartered on the New York Produce form carried grain from the U.S. Gulf to Algiers. The cargo was wet damaged owing to leakage through defective hatch covers. Because of the damage, discharge at Algiers took 15 days longer than it otherwise would have done; but at all times the ship was fully capable of performing every service required of her and, in particular, fully capable of discharging cargo from all her holds. It was held that the ship was not "detained" by an average accident to her cargo and was not, therefore, off-hire.

The Mareva A.S [1977] 1 Lloyd's Rep. 368.

(See also *Vogemann* v. *Zanzibar* (1901) 6 Com. Cas. 253, and 7 Com. Cas. 254.)

Average accidents

An "average accident" means an accident which causes damage; it does not mean a general average accident: *The Mareva A.S.* [1977] 1 Lloyd's Rep. 368.

Or by any other cause preventing the full working of the vessel

Preventing the full working of the vessel

The words "preventing the full working of the vessel" qualify not only "any other cause" but also all the preceding specifically enumerated causes in Lines 97 and 98 of the New York Produce form, "deficiency of men" and so on. Kerr, J., said in *The Mareva A.S.* [1977] 1 Lloyd's Rep. 368, at page 382: "The word 'other' in the phrase 'or by any other cause preventing the full working of the vessel' in my view shows that the various events referred to in the foregoing provisions were also only intended to take effect if the full working of the vessel . . . was thereby prevented and time was lost in consequence."

Kerr, J., held in that case that the *Mareva A.S.* was not off-hire following the average accident to her cargo as this did not prevent the full working of the ship. Even though the cargo was wet damaged owing to leakage through defective hatch covers, it was held that the ship was not off-hire during the time taken to discharge the damaged cargo: for the service then required—the discharge of cargo—the ship was fully efficient Kerr. J., said in the same passage, at page 382: "if, for instance, the cargo is damaged as the result of an accident, but the vessel's ability to work fully is not thereby prevented or impaired, because the vessel in herself remains fully efficient in all respects, then I do not think that the charterers bring themselves within the clause."

The meaning of "full working of the vessel" has been considered in subsequent cases concerning "any other cause" and is dealt with in the paragraphs which follow.

Any other cause

As is the case with the other causes listed in Lines 97 and 98 of the New York Produce form, hire will cease when time is lost by "any other cause"only if that cause prevents the full working of the vessel. In *The Aquacharm* (below) Lord Denning, M.R.., said; "We are to inquire first whether the 'full working of the vessel' has been prevented. Only if it has, do we consider the 'cause' ". Thus in *Court Line* v. *Dant & Russell* (below) Branson, J., expressed the view that a ship trapped by an obstruction in a river was not off-hire when the ship herself remained fully efficient.

The *Errington Court* was time chartered on the New York Produce form in March 1937. In the course of the charter she was ordered to Wu-hu, 750 miles up the Yangtze River. After her arrival there war broke out between Japan and China and the Chinese sank ships in the river to form a boom to prevent Japanese ships coming up it. The *Errington Court* was trapped in consequence. Branson, J., held that the charter was frustrated, but he considered, *obiter*, the alternative argument that the ship was off-hire. He said at page 352:

> "The charterers rely on Clause 15 for this. The argument depends upon the delay caused by the boom coming within the words 'any other cause preventing the full working of the vessel'. In my opinion, it does not. I do not rely on the case of *Hogarth* v. *Miller* for this conclusion but upon the words of this charterparty which are materially different from those which the Court had to construe in that case. The words are not apt to cover a case where the ship is in every way sound and well found, but is prevented from continuing her voyage by such a cause as this."

Court Line v. *Dant & Russell* (1939) 44 Com. Cas. 345.

(See also *The Wenjiang* [1981] 2 Lloyd's Rep. 308 and [1982] 1 Lloyd's Rep. 128 (C.A.), where the Court of Appeal refused leave to appeal from an arbitrator's decision that a ship detained by a local war in the River Shatt remained on hire under the Shelltime 3 form.)

In *Court Line* v. *Dant & Russell*, above, the ship herself remained fully efficient, restrained from performing the service required by the charterers only by something entirely external to herself, the boom across the river. In a series of recent cases the courts have been faced with more difficult situations in which the restraint comes, directly or indirectly, from something upon or relating to the ship. The question then arises whether the ship is to be regarded as fully efficient. Moreover, while it may still be possible in some such cases to treat the ship as fully efficient and the restraint as external to the ship, thus matching both aspects of the situation in *Court Line* v. *Dant & Russell*, in other cases the restraint can hardly be regarded as external. It must then be decided whether it is indeed essential to the owners' case that the restraint be external or whether, on the contrary, all that matters is the first aspect, namely that the ship herself be fully efficient to perform the services required. The issue may be affected by the question whether "any other cause" is limited not merely by "preventing the full working of the vessel" but also, by the *ejusdem generis* rule or some more general rule of construction, to causes similar to those listed in Lines 97 and 98 (none of which is wholly extraneous to the ship). The *ejusdem generis* rule is discussed separately at page 305 below. In many of the cases which follow the application of the rule had been excluded by the addition of the word "whatsoever" after the words "any other cause".

In *The Aquacharm*, below, Lloyd. J., expressed the correct test as being "whether the vessel is fully efficient in herself, that is to say, whether she is fully capable of performing the service immediately required of her. If she is, then she is not off-hire, even though she is prevented from performing that service by some external cause . . . "

The *Aquacharm* was time chartered for a trip on the New York Produce form. Having been ordered to load to maximum draft for a passage through the Panama Canal, the master negligently failed to take into account that in passing through a fresh water lake which forms part of the Canal the ship's forward draft would increase. The ship was consequently refused entry to the Canal; after considerable delay part of the cargo had to be discharged, carried through the Canal on another ship and then reloaded. It was argued by the charterers that the ship was off-hire because she was prevented by her draft from performing the service immediately required. Lloyd, J., held that the ship was fit "in herself" to perform the service immediately required and was therefore not off-hire. This decision was upheld by the Court of Appeal.

The Aquacharm [1980] 2 Lloyd's Rep. 237, and [1982] 1 Lloyd's Rep. 7 (C.A.).

In *The Aquacharm* it was the excess quantity of cargo on board, resulting in the excessive draft, which prevented the ship performing the service required, namely, transiting the Canal. There was no deficiency in the ship herself, her machinery, equipment or crew. In the words of Lord Denning, M.R.: "The vessel is still working fully, but she is delayed by the need to unload part of the cargo." In the case which follows, however, it was a matter affecting the crew which led to the ship being prevented from performing the service required.

The *Apollo* was chartered on the New York Produce form. While she was discharging at Naples two of her crew members were taken to hospital with suspected typhus. She then sailed to Lower Buchanan to load. On arrival off that port she was met by health officials who, upon being told of what had happened at Naples, inspected the crew and the ship. Although no evidence of typhus was found, the officials disinfected parts of the ship before granting free pratique. The delay in obtaining free pratique because of the inspection and disinfection caused nearly 30 hours loss of time to the charterers. They claimed they were entitled to put the ship off-hire under Clause 15, which had been amended by the addition of the word "whatsoever" after "or by any other cause". Mocatta, J., held that: (a) the application of the *ejusdem generis* rule was excluded by the word "whatsoever"; (b) the meaning of the phrase "any other cause whatsoever" was limited by the general context of the charter and the words "preventing the full working of the vessel"; and (c) the action of the health officials—more than a "mere formality" in the circumstances—did prevent the full working of the vessel; and so the ship was off hire during the time lost.

The Apollo [1978] 1 Lloyd's Rep. 200.

(Compare a delay caused by immigration authorities to an efficient ship short of only one deserting crew member, *The Good Helmsman* [1981] 1 Lloyd's Rep. 377, at page 422.)

In *The Aquacharm* [1982] 1 Lloyd's Rep. at page 11, Griffiths, L.J., commented on this decision in *The Apollo*: "A ship suspected of carrying typhus is prevented from working fully until it is cleared, for no responsible person would use it in such a condition. The incapacity of the ship to work in such a case is directly attributable to the suspected condition of the ship itself, and in my view is clearly distinguishable from the present case."

Lloyd, J., extended the scope of the relevant words in *The Mastro Giorgis* [1983] 2 Lloyd's Rep. 66 by upholding an award of arbitrators that a ship was off-hire under Clause 15 of the New York Produce form (again amended by the addition of "whatsoever" after "any other cause") when the ship was prevented from sailing by an arrest at the suit of receivers of a cargo of grain which had been damaged in the course of the voyage. Lloyd, J., held that where the word "whatsoever" was added, *any* cause might suffice to put the ship off hire, whether physical or legal, if it prevented the full working of the vessel for the service immediately required. But in deciding whether a cause prevented the full working of the ship a distinction still had to be drawn between causes which were totally extraneous and causes which were attributable to the condition of the ship herself. He said, at page 69: "one must have regard not only to the physical condition of the vessel, but also, in the words of the arbitrators, to her qualities and characteristics, to which I would also add, her history and ownership . . . The arrest was, in my view, directly attributable to the history, if not the condition, of this particular vessel."

The second stage in Lloyd, J.'s reasoning was challenged by Webster J. in *The Roachbank* [1987] 2 Lloyd's Rep. 498, on the ground that where the clause was amended by the addition of the word "whatsoever" it was probably unnecessary to consider the nature of the cause at all: the essential question was simply whether the full working of the vessel was prevented. He did not consider it necessary to draw a distinction between totally extraneous and other causes unless Clause 15 was in unamended form (in which case the causes might exclude those that were wholly extraneous to the ship by operation of the *ejusdem generis* rule, see below).

The *Roachbank* was chartered on the New York Produce form, Clause 15 being amended by the addition of the word "whatsoever" after "any other cause". In the South China Sea the ship sighted a boat in distress and took on board from it a large number of Vietnamese refugees. When the ship arrived at Kaohsiung the authorities refused to allow the refugees to land and required the ship to lie outside the port. The charterers claimed that the ship was off hire for the time so lost. On appeal from arbitrators, Webster, J., declined to disturb the finding of the majority of the arbitrators that neither the presence of the refugees on board nor their number prevented the *Roachbank* from performing the service immediately required of her, which was to enter Kaohsiung and load cargo. Hence the full working of the vessel was not prevented and the ship remained on hire.

The Roachbank [1987] 2 Lloyd's Rep. 498.

A similar conclusion in relation to actions taken against the ship by outside agencies (in this case the International Transport Workers Federation or ITF), was reached in *The Manhattan Prince*, below, under a Shelltime 3 charter in which the equivalent wording is " . . . any other cause preventing the efficient working of the vessel . . . ".

The *Manhattan Prince* was chartered on the Shelltime 3 form, the off-hire clause (Clause 21) being unamended. In response to an earlier threat of boycott by the ITF, the owners had undertaken to employ crew complying with ITF's terms. Subsequently the owners employed a replacement crew not paid at ITF rates and as a result of ITF action the ship was boycotted at Oxelsund and suffered delay. It was held that the ship was not off hire. Legatt, J., considered that both *The Apollo* and *The Mastro Giorgis* were decided on the ground that the addition of "whatsoever" to the New York Produce form of hire clause excluded the *ejusdem generis* rule. But he held that the phrase "efficient working" in the context of Clause 21 of the Shelltime 3 charter meant "efficient physical working" and that although the ship was prevented from working in the way the charterers would have wished by the action of the ITF, she was fully operational.

The Manhattan Prince [1985] 1 Lloyd's Rep. 140.

In another case under an unamended Shelltime 3 off-hire clause, *The Bridgestone Maru No. 3* [1985] 2 Lloyd's Rep. 62, it was held that a ship was off hire during a period of delay at an Italian port caused by the failure of a booster pump to comply with regulations of the Registro Italiano Navale (RINA). Hirst, J., said, at page 83: "To adapt the words of Lord Justice Griffiths in *The Aquacharm*, the incapacity of the ship to discharge was attributable to the suspected condition of the ship itself, and as a result the crew could not use the relevant part of the machinery, namely, the pump."

The approach suggested by Webster, J., in *The Roachbank*, above—to determine first whether the "full working of the vessel" is prevented and only then, if necessary, to consider the question of causation—accords with that of Lord Denning in *The Aquacharm*, quoted above at page 302, and seems correct. But it affords only limited guidance in answering the question when, in any given circumstances, the "full working" of the ship is to be regarded as prevented. The authorities as to the test to be applied seem correctly summarised by Lloyd, J., in *The Aquacharm*, above: "whether the vessel is fully efficient in herself, that is to say, whether she is fully capable of performing the service immediately required of her". But is "efficiency" restricted to actual physical efficiency as Legatt, J., considered in *The Manhattan Prince* [1985] 1 Lloyd's Rep. 140, in the context of the unamended off-hire clause in the Shelltime 3 charter; or does it extend to the ship's documentary and legal status; or even to matters related to the qualities and characteristics of the ship, as well as to her history and ownership, as Lloyd, J., considered in *The Mastro Giorgis*, above? The Court of Appeal refused leave to appeal in *The Roachbank* [1988] 2 Lloyd's Rep. 337, so there is no further guidance to be had from that case.

It is therefore difficult to deduce from the authorities as they stand a unified approach to the question of "efficiency", but it is suggested that the decisions are consistent with a conclusion that the prevention of "full working of the vessel" in the context of Clause 15 of the New York Produce form or "efficient working of the vessel" in the context of Clause 21 of the Shelltime 3 extend beyond the actual physical condition of the ship to her documentary or legal status.

If the full or efficient working of the ship in that sense is prevented, it is then necessary to consider whether, as Webster, J., said in *The Roachbank*, above, the prevention results from any of the named causes or from "any other cause", giving the latter words (if not amended by the addition of "whatsoever") a meaning which excludes causes which are wholly external to the ship. It seems that the concept of the wholly external cause, although perhaps of less significance than once suggested, remains relevant in this context.

Any other cause and the ejusdem generis rule

The weight of judicial opinion appears to be in favour of the view that the scope of the words "any other cause" should be restricted in accordance with the *ejusdem generis* rule, or at least that their meaning is limited by their context in the off-hire clause and in the charterparty. If, however, the word "whatsoever" is inserted in the off-hire clause after "any other cause", the *ejusdem generis* rule is excluded.

The *ejusdem generis* rule is a rule of construction to limit the literal wide meaning of general words which follow particular words or phrases. It seems to have grown out of a concern that parties drawing up a document may, while their minds are concerned with the particulars about which they are contracting, use general words which when read literally have a wider meaning than was intended. The true intention of the parties may, of course, be clear from the words and phrases they have used in this or other parts of their contract and this makes it difficult to draw from the cases clear guidelines as to when the rule will be invoked and when not.

In some cases it has been assumed that where general words follow a list of particular items, an attempt should automatically be made to apply the rule. The question then becomes not whether the rule should be applied at all but whether it can be applied where, for example, no *genus* can be formulated to cover all the particular items. But Devlin, J., pointed out in *Chandris* v. *Isbrandtsen-Moller* [1951] 1 K.B. 240, that in the absence of any indication in the text of the charter that the general words were to have a limited meaning, they should be allowed their ordinary, fuller meaning. He relied on the Court of Appeal decision in *Anderson* v. *Anderson* [1895] 1 Q.B. 749, where Lord Esher, M.R., said: " . . . *prima facie* general words are to be taken in their larger sense, unless you can find that in the particular case the true construction of the instrument requires you to conclude that they are intended to be used in a sense limited to things *ejusdem generis* with those which have been specifically mentioned before."

Rigby, L.J., added that the mere fact that general words followed specific words was certainly not enough to show an intention that the *ejusdem generis* rule was to be applied. It is suggested that this approach is correct.

There has been no decision on whether the rule should be applied to these general words in similar contexts to that in which they appear in the New York Produce form. It was assumed in *Adelaide Steamship* v. *The Crown* (*No. 2*) (1923) 17 Ll.L.Rep. 324, that an attempt should be made to do so, but the point was not decided. In *The Apollo* [1978] 1 Lloyd's Rep. 200, Mocatta, J., held that the application of the *ejusdem generis* rule was excluded by the addition of the word "whatsoever" after "any other cause", but his judgment suggests that he would otherwise have sought to apply the rule. Lloyd, J., in *The Mastro Giorgis* [1983] 2 Lloyd's Rep. 66, came to a similar conclusion, although in that case the point was conceded by counsel for the owners. Legatt, J., in *The Manhattan Prince* [1985] 1 Lloyd's Rep. 140 considered that the reasoning in *The Mastro Giorgis* was based on the exclusion of the *ejusdem generis* rule. In the case before him, he said: "One may take account of the *ejusdem generis* principle in the sense that the causes of loss of time which are specified may indeed throw light upon the proper meaning to be ascribed to the phrase 'efficient working of the vessel'."

Lloyd, J., in *The Aquacharm* [1980] 2 Lloyd's Rep. 237, expressed the view that it did not matter whether the rule applied, but added (page 239): "[Counsel] on behalf of the charterers, accepted that there must be some limitation of the full width of the words, if only because the words must be construed in their context or 'matrix'. But that is only another way of saying the same thing. The *ejusdem generis* rule is, as it seems to me, only an illustration of the more general rule that all contractual provisions are to be construed in the context, whether linguistic or circumstantial, in which they are found."

In *The Roachbank* [1987] 2 Lloyd's Rep. 498, at page 507, on the other hand, Webster, J., considered that the *ejusdem generis* rule should probably be applied. He said: "Where the off-hire clause is unamended and does not contain the word 'whatsoever', then the *ejusdem generis* rule could, and probably should, be applied. . . . and, although it is not necessary for me to decide the point, it would come as no surprise to me if it were to be decided that a cause wholly extraneous to the vessel was not a cause within the meaning of the words 'any other cause' in that clause." In this way the concept of the extraneous or external cause may be revived where "whatsoever" has not been added, although of less importance than once believed in the interpretation of the "full working of the vessel"; see page 305 above.

But an attempt to apply the rule strictly might nevertheless fail for want of a *genus* covering the causes previously enumerated; see the comments of Mocatta, J., in *The Apollo* above, on an argument by counsel that the words should be restricted to causes internal to the ship and her crew to the exclusion of external interference or delays. It is therefore suggested that the true view as to the construction of the general words is most accurately expressed by Lloyd, J., in *The Aquacharm*, quoted above.

The words of the Baltime form ("or other accident") have been held not subject to the *ejusdem generis* rule: see page 474 below.

Cause must be fortuitous

The words "any other cause" must also be restricted to causes which are fortuitous rather than the natural result of the use that the charterers make of the ship.

During the service of the *Rijn* under the New York Produce form her hull became fouled by marine growth during a protracted period of waiting for and then loading cargo. With regard to the time lost in consequence the charterers claimed that the ship was off-hire because the fouling was "any other cause preventing the full working of the vessel", and that a deduction from hire should be made under the second part of Clause 15, Lines 99 to 101, because speed had been reduced "by defect in . . . her hull". Mustill, J., rejected both these claims. He said: "The draftsman cannot possibly have intended that hire should cease in every circumstance where the full working of the vessel is prevented. This reading would be commercial nonsense, and would make the second half of the clause redundant. In my judgment, only those causes qualify for consideration which are fortuitous, and are not the natural result of the ship complying with the charterers' orders. These requirements would be complied with, in the case of fouling by marine growth, in the exceptional situation where the growth was of a wholly extraordinary and unpredictable nature: see *Cosmos Bulk Transport Incorporated* v. *China National Foreign Trade Transportation Corporation* [1978] 1 Lloyd's Rep. 53 [*The Apollonius*], a decision on a rather different form of words, where there was a very special finding of fact by the arbitrator. But in the great majority of cases, the accretion of growth is simply a natural consequence of the ship remaining in service, with nothing fortuitous about it . . . I have formed the same opinion as regards the claim under the second part of the clause. I am bound to say that I find it hard to visualise the accumulation of marine growth during the contract service as a 'defect' in the hull. But even if it were, the defect arose as a natural consequence of the way in which the charterers chose to employ the ship. I do not consider that the loss of time thus caused should be deducted from the amount of time for which hire is payable".

The Rijn [1981] 2 Lloyd's Rep. 267.

(But for a case where a ship was delivered with her bottom fouled, see *The Ioanna* [1985] 2 Lloyd's Rep. 164 and page 310 below.)

Incident caused by charterers' breach

If an event falling within the wording of the off-hire clause has been caused by some breach of the express or implied terms of the charter by the charterers, the courts may deal with it in one of two ways. They may either declare the ship to be off-hire but allow the owners to claim hire back from the charterers as damages or they may hold that the ship remains on hire. Usually it will make little difference which course is followed, but in certain circumstances it may be important.

Although it may be argued that the off-hire clause makes no mention of fault and should be allowed to operate automatically provided only that the events which occur are within its wording (see page 295 above), there is some authority supporting the opposite view that the charterers are not entitled to rely on the clause if the events which cause it to operate result from their breach of contract. It seems to have been assumed by the Court of Appeal in *Board of Trade* v. *Temperley* (1927) 27 Ll.L.Rep. 230 that if the charterers' breach of an express or implied term of the contract had caused the loss of time they could not have relied on the clause (see particularly the judgment of Scrutton, L.J., at page 232), but no breach was established. See also a similar assumption in *Fraser* v. *Bee* (1900) 17 T.L.R. 101. In the case which follows there is clear support for the somewhat narrower proposition that the charterers may not rely on the clause when the loss of time relates to something which under the charter it is their duty to supply, although the decision could have been reached on construction alone.

Delay was caused to the *Megna* by faulty bunker coal, supplied by the charterers, heating dangerously. The off-hire clause provided:

> "That in the event of loss of time from . . . breakdown of machinery or damage to hull preventing the working of the steamer for more than 24 consecutive hours, the hire shall cease until she be again in an efficient state to resume her service; or if breakdown or damage occurs at sea, not resulting from the cargo, necessitating putting back, hire shall cease until steamer is again in the same position . . . ".

It was held that both parts of the clause were limited to breakdown of machinery or damage to hull, and as neither had happened the clause did not operate. Greer, J., also said that the hire should not cease where the loss of time had been caused by "anything for which the charterer is responsible", in this case their bunkers.
Nourse v. *Elder Dempster* (1922) 13 Ll.L.Rep. 197.

In *Lensen* v. *Anglo-Soviet* (1935) 52 Ll.L.Rep. 141, the Court of Appeal held that a ship remained on hire under the Baltime form during repairs to her hull caused by a breach by the charterers of their obligation to order her to a safe berth. The leading judgment, of Greer, L.J., is based in part upon the charterers being unable to rely on the off-hire clause while employing the ship outside the limits agreed in the charter and partly on the indemnity clause, but also refers to the right of the owners to recover hire as damages "if technically the vessel was off-hire". Although the decision must be regarded as authoritative so far as concerns delay resulting from orders of the charterers covered by an express or implied indemnity, particularly where the orders are for trading outside the charter limits (including orders to unsafe ports or berths), it probably does not support any wider proposition. The reference by Greer, L.J., to the possibility of the ship being "technically" off-hire introduces a further reason for caution. Nevertheless, the combined effect of the cases cited above may be that the off-hire clause does not operate where the event which would otherwise cause it to operate flows from a breach by the charterers.

Payment of hire shall cease

In *The Lutetian* [1982] 2 Lloyd's Rep. 140, Bingham, J., held that under the New York Produce form the charterers were not obliged to pay an instalment of hire on the due date if the ship was off-hire at that time, as Clause 15 provided that when time was lost from the listed causes "the payment of hire shall cease". He accepted the contention that in such circumstances the charterers' obligation to make payment of the next monthly instalment of hire in advance was suspended until immediately before the ship was again at the service of the charterers. This decision seems difficult to reconcile with the general principle set out at page 194 above, and may produce serious uncertainty in practice. It is suggested that it be treated with caution pending consideration by higher courts.

Bunkers and other obligations during off-hire periods

The mere fact that hire is not payable by operation of the off-hire clause does not curtail the other obligations of the charterers during the relevant period. Thus, unless express provision has been made to the contrary, the charterers remain responsible for providing and paying for bunkers while the ship is off-hire. See, for example, *Arild* v. *Hovrani* [1923] 2 K.B. 141. In the New York Produce form express provision is made by Clause 20 to relieve the charterers from payment for bunkers consumed, but this clause does not cover other obligations and if relief in respect of these is required appropriate words must be inserted. There is no such express provision in the Baltime form (see *Arild* v. *Hovrani*, above), nor in the Shelltime 3 (see *The Ioanna* [1985] 2 Lloyd's Rep. 164). It is, therefore, common to amend Clause 4 of the Baltime form by the addition of the words "whilst on hire" at the very beginning of the clause: see page 176 above.

Effect on other remedies of owners and charterers

Claims by charterers

The off-hire clause does not destroy or cut down any right the charterers may have to claim damages from the owners even in respect of matters specifically mentioned in the clause. If the charterers can prove that they have suffered damages in excess of or in addition to the loss of use of the ship as a result of a breach of charter by the owners then they may recover these damages. In *The Democritos* [1975] 1 Lloyd's Rep. 386, Kerr, J., said at page 401: "since this point appears rarely to have arisen in practice, it is right to repeat that it was common ground that if a period of off-hire results from a breach of the charter on the part of the owners, then the charterers would in law be entitled to damages quite apart from not being liable for hire, or being able to recoup any hire paid in respect of this period, if they can establish that they have thereby suffered additional loss". So if, for example, serious delay were caused by a breakdown of ship's gear due to a breach of the owners' obligations of fittedness or seaworthiness on delivery or of maintenance in an efficient state thereafter, and the delay were to deprive the charterers of a profitable voyage, the charterers would not be restricted to a claim for repayment of hire under the off-hire clause. If the loss of profit exceeded the hire lost, the owners would be entitled, subject to any questions of remoteness, to claim the loss of profit by way of damages, giving credit for any hire recovered under the off-hire clause. (See *The H.R. Macmillan* [1973] 1 Lloyd's Rep. 27 concerning delay caused by breakdowns of the ship's specially fitted gantry cranes; see also *Sea & Land Securities* v. *Dickinson* (1942) 72 Ll.L.Rep. 159, and, by analogy, *Leslie Shipping* v. *Welstead* [1921] 3 K.B. 420, where it was held by Greer, J., that an owner's right to damages was not cut down by the withdrawal clause in the charter.)

Claims by owners

Equally, if the off-hire clause is operated as a result of some breach of contract by the charterers, the owners may claim from the charterers the hire they have lost as all or part of their damages for that breach.

The Dodecanese was time chartered on the Baltime form for employment "in lawful trades for the conveyance of lawful merchandise". The charterers loaded her with ammunition and other explosives for the British forces in Egypt, although they knew that this was prohibited by the Egyptian authorities. The ship was blacklisted by the authorities in consequence and when, subsequently, the ship suffered a machinery breakdown, the authorities delayed her repairs so that they took 30 days instead of four days. The charterers put the ship off hire for the whole 30 days under the off-hire clause, but it was held by Pilcher, J., that the owners were entitled to recover, as damages and for breach of the charterers' obligation to ship only "lawful merchandise", the hire for the 26 days which they had lost under the off hire clause.

Leolga v. *Glynn* [1953] 2 Lloyd's Rep. 47. (See also *Lensen* v. *Anglo-Soviet* (1935) 52 Ll.L.Rep. 141).

Off-hire deductions and withdrawal

For the circumstances in which charterers may make deductions from the hire in respect of off-hire periods and for the assessment of such deductions, see under "Payment of hire and withdrawal" at pages 199 to 203 above.

Reduction in speed under Lines 99 to 101 of the New York Produce form

Lines 99 to 101 of the New York Produce form make additional provision for a deduction from hire covering time lost, extra fuel consumed and all extra expenses arising from reduction of the ship's speed on a voyage by reason of "defect in or breakdown of any part of her hull, machinery or equipment".

Bottom fouling

In *The Rijn* [1981] 2 Lloyd's Rep. 267, see page 307 above, Mustill, J., held that loss of speed resulting from the accumulation of marine growth on the ship's hull during the course of the charter did not constitute a "defect" for the purpose of Line 100, particularly as it arose as the natural consequence of the way in which the charterers chose to employ the ship. In *The Ioanna* [1985] 2 Lloyd's Rep. 164, below, on the other hand, Staughton, J., held that a reduction in speed during the charter service due to the ship's bottom having been fouled prior to delivery did constitute a "defect" in hull within the meaning of Line 100. See also *The Apollonious* [1978] 1 Lloyd's Rep. 53.

Saving in fuel

If as a result of a reduction in speed there is a reduction in the consumption of one of the types of fuel used, the saving may be set off against the cost of any extra consumption of another type of fuel used; but in a claim under the off-hire clause the owners will be entitled to no overall credit if the saving on one fuel exceeds the extra cost of another. Only if the claim can be put as a claim in damages will the owners be entitled to an overall credit in such circumstances.

The trip time charter of the *Ioanna* described the ship as having her "hull, machinery and equipment in a thoroughly efficient state and appearance" and the off-hire clause contained a provision that " . . . if upon the voyage the speed be reduced by defect in or breakdown of any part of her hull, machinery or equipment, the time so lost and the cost of any extra fuel consumed in consequence thereof, and all extra expenses are to be for Owners' account and may be deducted from the hire". The ship was delivered with her bottom fouled and thus not in a "thoroughly efficient state". In consequence she failed to maintain her warranted speed. Her diesel oil consumption was increased, but her fuel oil consumption was reduced. On the charterers' claim to recover for the loss of time and the cost of excess diesel oil consumption, it was held by Staughton, J. that:

(1) if the charterers had to put their claim as a claim in damages for breach, the owners would be entitled to set off any overall saving in fuel consumption against the damages for loss of time;
(2) but the charterers could put their claim under the off hire clause because a ship whose speed was reduced by her hull being foul on delivery could properly be described as having her speed reduced by "defect in . . . her hull";
(3) the reference to "any extra fuel consumed" did not refer only to fuel oil, but meant the net cost of extra fuel oil and diesel oil taken together;
(4) if the saving on fuel oil exceeded the extra cost of diesel oil the charterers could claim nothing, but would not have to give credit for the net saving.

The Ioanna [1985] 2 Lloyd's Rep. 164.

(But see *The Rijn*, above, in relation to bottom fouling developing during the course of the charter.)

American Law

General principle

The rule adopted by the American courts is that if one of the causes listed in the off-hire clause results in a loss of time to the charterer, it automatically suspends the obligation to pay hire, without regard to fault. The rule was best summarized in the leading case of *Clyde Commercial S.S. Co.* v. *West India S.S. Co.*, 169 F. 275 (2d Cir. 1909), *cert.* denied 214 U.S. 523, where the court stated:

> [A]rticle 15 must be understood to state absolute categories in which the parties intended the hire to be suspended whether the Owner was at fault or not . . . .(169 F. at 278.)

Loss of time

The off-hire clause reflects the fact that what the charterer has bargained for in return for his hire payments is the right to use the vessel. In *The Yaye Maru*, 274 F. 195 (4th Cir. 1921), *cert.* denied 257 U.S. 638, a time chartered vessel was at anchor at Baltimore waiting for an embargo on her intended cargo of coal to be lifted, when another vessel collided with her. The *Yaye Maru* was damaged and repairs were required. Meanwhile, the embargo on coal continued until after the repairs had been completed. In the ensuing litigation, the owner contended that since the charterer would not have used the vessel for any purpose other than to wait at anchor during the repair period, the vessel was not off-hire. The court rejected this argument, however, and held that it was not important whether the charterer *would* actually have used the ship while she was under repair. Rather, since it *could* not have used her, he was entitled to off-hire. As stated by the court:

> Surely, the right to off-hire, otherwise existing, was not lost by nonuser. The injury impaired the power to use, by destroying to a degree the "thoroughly efficient state" in which the vessel was agreed to be kept, and when that happened, and for such time as it continued, the charterer became entitled to off-hire, whatever permissible use he was then making of the vessel, or whether he was using her at all. He could not be held for hire when the power to use was taken away. (274 F. at 197–98.)

A breakdown of the vessel's engines, hull, or machinery which does not impair the charterer's actual use of the vessel does not put her off-hire. If the breakdown occurs while the vessel is loading or unloading cargo, and it does not interfere with these activities, the charterer remains bound to pay hire.

Resumption of hire

American courts and arbitrators would probably follow the rule that the charterer should be allowed the net overall time lost to it as the result of any of the causes enumerated in the off-hire clause. In *The Chris*, S.M.A. No. 199 (Arb. at N.Y. 1958), the panel held that the "universally followed" interpretation of Clause 15 is that where the vessel has been forced to deviate from the voyage for repairs, the off-hire period extends beyond the time the vessel is physically fit to proceed again, and includes the time required to return to the position at which hire was suspended. In *The Grace V*, S.M.A. No. 1760 (Arb. at N.Y. 1982), off-hire was calculated not from the moment stowaways were discovered, but from the point of diversion of the vessel back to the loadport until the vessel regained a point equidistant to the initial diversion point. See also *The Chrysanthi G.L.*, S.M.A. No. 1417 (Arb. at N.Y. 1980).

The New York Produce off-hire clause is different from that at issue in *Dunlop S.S. Co.* v. *Tweedie Trading Co.,* 162 F. 490, 493 (S.D.N.Y. 1908), aff'd 178 F. 673 (2d Cir. 1910). There, the off-hire clause provided that in the event of a breakdown, payment of hire was to cease until the vessel was "again in an efficient state to resume her service". The court held that the charterer was relieved of its obligation to pay hire only until the vessel was restored to a seaworthy condition. On the authority of that case, therefore, it appears a court would hold that where the charter provides for cessation of hire payments until the vessel is again in an efficient state to resume her service, hire would recommence immediately after the breakdown was repaired, even if the vessel had to deviate for the repairs. Under the New York Produce form, however, the result would probably be quite different, and it is believed that the charterer would be awarded an allowance for off-hire reflecting the net amount of time lost. *The Chris*, above; Cf. *National Transp. Corp.* v. *Texaco*, 1976 AMC 1549 (Arb. at N.Y. 1976).

Deficiency of men

Incapacity

Under the American cases a vessel will go off-hire due to the incapacity of a full complement of officers and crew to work. In *Clyde Commercial S.S. Co.*, above, the vessel was first delayed at Colon because the second and third engineers had developed a fever and could not attend to their duties. The court held that this delay was caused by a deficiency of men, and, accordingly, the vessel was off-hire for the time lost.

Similarly, in *The Robertina*, S.M.A. No. 1151 (Arb. at N.Y. 1977), the vessel was held to be "deficient in men" when the chief engineer was hospitalized. The panel held that the ship was off-hire until a replacement engineer arrived on board.

A "deficiency of men" may also be constructive, as distinguished from an actual deficiency. In *Tweedie Trading Co.* v. *George D. Emery Co.*, 154 F. 472 (2d Cir. 1907), the vessel was held at quarantine in New York Harbor for about two days. The members of the crew who were actually sick were physically removed from the vessel. Substitute crewmen were engaged, but were not permitted aboard until an inspection had been completed. It was held that

> . . . from her arrival at quarantine until the new men were put aboard a deficiency of men prevented the working of the vessel within the meaning of [the off-hire] clause. (*Id.* at 473.)

Thus, while the owner had a full crew complement ready to work, there was a constructive deficiency of men resulting from their inability to work because of the quarantine. See also *Gow* v. *Gans S.S. Line*, 174 F. 215 (2d Cir. 1909), and *Noyes* v. *Munson S.S. Line*, 173 F. 814 (S.D.N.Y. 1909), holding that there was a constructive deficiency of men when the vessel was quarantined; *The Canadia*, 241 F. 233 (3d Cir. 1917), where there was held to be a deficiency of men because the crew was drunk and unruly; *Northern S.S. Co.* v. *Earn Line S.S. Co.*, 175 F. 529 (2d Cir. 1910), where there was a deficiency of men due to sickness.

There was also a deficiency of men in *The Alcazar*, S.M.A. No. 1512 (Arb. at N.Y., 1981). The vessel was detained by the Coast Guard at Pensacola, Florida because there were eight Polish officers on board. Pensacola is considered by the United States to be a sensitive naval defense area and access is restricted under the U.S./U.S.S.R. Maritime

Agreement. The panel held that the eight Polish officers were "deficient" because they were prohibited by law from entering the port of Pensacola, and that this condition was the cause of the delay so that the ship was off-hire.

A similar situation arose in *The Family Anthony*, S.M.A. No. 1820 (Arb. at N.Y. 1983). The vessel was to carry arms and ammunition from a number of United States ports to Saudi Arabia. The vessel's crew, however, included six Russian engineers who were barred from entry to two of the loadports. Unlike *The Alcazar*, in which the barred crew members rejoined the vessel after she departed the loadport, the Russians were not allowed to rejoin the ship until after the cargoes had been discharged. The reason for this was that a portion of the cargo was highly security sensitive, a fact of which charterers had not advised owner. The panel thus held that owner was entitled to recover the cost of transporting the Russians from the United States to Moscow and, subsequently, the cost of returning them to Dubai where they rejoined the ship.

In recent years, a number of so-called "flag of convenience" vessels have been delayed as a result of strikes or boycotts organized by the International Transport Workers Federation ("ITF"). In the usual case, the delay occurs because shore workers will honor a picket line or boycott announced by the ITF when a vessel calls at a port to load or discharge. It seems clear that such delays do not give rise to any off-hire unless the crew members of the vessel are themselves withholding their labor. Rather, the boycott must be considered as equivalent to, say, a strike of longshoremen. Since it is the charterer who chooses the trading pattern, it is the charterer who takes the risk of strikes which preclude or delay the vessel's operation. The fact that the chartered vessel is singled out for union retaliation as a "flag of convenience" vessel should not alter the position. The solution, of course, is for the charterer to require, by a special clause, that the owner will meet the requirements of the ITF. If by such a clause the owner warrants that he will conform to the requirements of the ITF, and he fails to do so, he is in breach of the charter and consequently should be liable for resulting delays.

The owner cannot refuse to enter a port nominated by the charterer because he anticipates ITF problems unless the charter is drafted to exclude trade to ITF areas.

In *The United Faith*, S.M.A. No. 1409 (Arb. at N.Y., 1980), a sole arbitrator was presented with the question of whether the owner could refuse to load the sub-charterer's cargo for discharge at a port within the Antwerp/Hamburg range because it anticipated an ITF boycott there. Both the head-charter and the sub-charter contained a typewritten clause which provided that the vessel would be off-hire for any time lost by reason of a boycott or blacklisting, provided such delays were not caused by actions of the ITF. The clause also stated that the vessel did not have an ITF certificate. The arbitrator held that the owner could not refuse to perform the voyage. The arbitrator stated that "the proper and most acceptable means of limiting a vessel's obligations to trade to ITF areas is to specifically exclude the troublesome areas from the trading limits of the charter-party": since this had not been done in the charter at issue, the owner was obliged to perform the voyage.

Unwillingness to work

In *United States* v. *The Marilena P.*, 433 F.2d 164, 1969 AMC 1155 (4th Cir. 1969), Clause 17 of the charter contained the following language:—

> In the event of loss of time from deficiency of men including but not limited to strikes . . . the payment of hire shall cease from the time thereby lost . . . .

Crew members went on strike to protest a voyage to a war zone. The court held that there was a deficiency of men under Clause 17, and that the vessel was off-hire until an adequate complement of men and officers went back to work. It is to be noted, however, that the New York Produce form does not contain an off-hire provision for crew strikes, and it is questionable whether a strike such as occurred in *The Marilena P.* would be deemed a "deficiency of men" under that form. See *Edison S.S. Corp.* v. *Eastern Minerals*, 167 F. Supp. 601 (D. Mass. 1958).

In *The Thunderbird*, S.M.A. No. 54 (Arb. at N.Y. 1964), charterer ordered the vessel to proceed to Camden despite its knowledge that there was a possibility of labor trouble. She berthed 35 minutes after shore laborers went on strike. The charterer ordered the vessel to shift to Wilmington, but she was unable to move of her own power because her engineers were committed to observe the picket line. Tug assistance was also unavailable, and, consequently, the vessel remained at Camden until the strike ended. The charterer contended that the engineers' refusal to man the engine room constituted a "deficiency of men" within the meaning of Clause 15, and that the vessel was off-hire for the time lost due to the strike. The panel held for the owner, however, and found that since the charterer ordered the vessel to Camden with knowledge of possible labor difficulties, it could not "equitably claim that payment of hire for the time so lost should be excused".

In *Montauk Oil Transportation Corp.* v. *Sonat Marine Inc.*, 1989 AMC 1147 (2d Cir. 1989), the chartered barge experienced delays due to a strike in New York harbor. The charter did not contain any provision allocating the risk of delay due to strikes. The court held that in the absence of an allocation of risk by the express terms of the contract, it would follow the time-honored maritime doctrine which places the burden on charterer for strike delays. Accordingly, the barge was held to be off-hire for time lost because of the strike. Because the court found that part of the delay was caused by owner's fault, the court made an equitable apportionment of the time lost.

Detention by average accidents to ship or cargo

In the leading case of *Barker* v. *Moore & McCormack Co.*, 40 F.2d 410, 1930 AMC 779 (2d Cir. 1930), the court held that an "average accident" occurs when there is an unexpected functional impairment of the vessel which prevents her full use. In that case, it was held that heavy weather, which resulted in a substantial increase in the vessel's fuel consumption and made a diversion to pick up additional bunkers necessary, was not an "average accident". As stated by Judge Chase:

> Whatever else may be thought, it surely is true that an accident of some kind is necessary to call into play the off-hire clause on account of "average accidents". It may be urged with some plausibility that bad weather in winter on the North Atlantic is an accident in the sense that whether or not it may be encountered on any voyage is somewhat a matter of chance. Yet, in a sea notorious for its severe weather at that time of year, the parties to this charter may well be said to have chosen words ill-suited to express their idea if by "average accidents" it was intended to cast upon the libelant whatever loss in time might be occasioned by rough, though not disabling, weather on the voyage. This would be directly in conflict with the general purpose of a charter on time rather than on a voyage basis. Accident is one of those hard-worked words too well known to make definition very needful, and having too many shades of meaning to make attempted definition, apart from its particular setting, a reliable guide. The plain purpose of this charter was to give the respondent the benefit of a fast voyage and let it assume the risk of a slow one, provided always nothing happened to prevent the ship doing all it was designed to do in the face of whatever conditions were met. If the expression is construed *ejusdem generis*, it would have to mean something that prevented "the

full working of the vessel". And we think it should be so construed. Not something preventing ground-gaining accomplishment, but some unexpected functional impairment making impossible the full use of the ship, with all the power and means of locomotion with adequate crew and equipment, to overcome the forces of nature and make time against the wind and waves. When taken in this sense, it is obvious that there was no accident of any kind. The ship at all times did all that could have been expected of it under the adverse conditions. (40 F.2d at 411–12.)

Average accidents to "cargo" will also result in the vessel going off-hire under the New York Produce clause. This provision is frequently deleted, however, with the result that time lost due to accidents which affect only the cargo, and do not affect the operation of the vessel, will be for the charterer's account.

In *The Andros Oceania*, S.M.A. No. 2012 (Arb. at N.Y. 1984), the collapse of the deck-stow of a cargo of logs was found to be an average accident. Because the accident resulted from charterer's failure to properly load and secure cargo, however, the panel rejected charterer's claim for return of hire.

Dry-docking

The vessel is off-hire while she is in dry dock for the purposes stated in Line 98. *Munson S.S. Line* v. *Miramar S.S. Co.*, 166 F. 722 (2d Cir. 1908), mod. on other grounds 167 F. 960 (2d Cir. 1909), *cert.* denied 214 U.S. 526 (1909); *Falls of Keltie S.S. Co.* v. *United States & Australasia S.S. Co.*, 108 F. 416 (S.D.N.Y. 1901). Delays encountered while waiting for a dry dock to become available will *not* result in the vessel going off-hire. *Albis Co.* v. *Munson*, 139 F. 234 (2d Cir. 1905). In *Noyes* v. *Munson S.S. Line*, 173 F. 814 (S.D.N.Y. 1909), however, the owner was held liable for time lost while awaiting dry-docking. There, the charter had only two days to run when the vessel was required to be dry-docked in accordance with the charter terms. The owner declined to dry-dock her at that time, but immediately after the vessel was redelivered, put her into dry dock for repairs. On these facts, the charterer was held entitled to a return of hire for two days.

Fire

Only the loss of time directly attributable to fire is allowed as off-hire. In *The Canadia*, 241 F. 233 (3d Cir. 1917), hire was held to have been suspended from the moment the vessel caught fire at the pier on 8 October until the fire was extinguished and she was again in a fit condition to begin discharging on 15 October. Owing to delays at the berth, however, it was not until 4 December that the discharging operation was actually completed, and the vessel was declared unfit to carry cargo. Because they had had the full use of the ship from 15 October through 4 December, however, the charterer was held responsible for hire during that period.

Breakdown or damages to hull, machinery or equipment

Off-hire will not be allowed unless there is an actual loss of time resulting from one of these enumerated causes. The principle is illustrated by *Steamship Knutsford Co.* v. *Barber & Co.*, 261 F. 866 (2d Cir. 1919), *cert.* denied 252 U.S. 586 (1920). There, the court held that the vessel was not off-hire following a fire while the cargo was removed for inspection:

We think that the time necessary to examine and restow the sugar was not "loss of time" within the meaning of article 16, but that the charterer was using the ship at that time for a purpose which, though it necessarily delayed her, was still his own, and was not due to any damage to the ship. (261 F. at 868.)

By the same token, the court recognized that time lost for inspection of damage to the holds and repairs did constitute a "loss of time" under the off-hire clause. (*Id.*)

There must be a "complete breakdown" of the engines to put the vessel off-hire. *Amer. Asiatic Co.* v. *Robert Dollar Co.*, 282 F. 743, 746 (9th Cir. 1922), *cert.* denied 261 U.S. 615 (1922).

The fact that the vessel's winches were not of sufficient power for the charterer's purposes was held not to be a breakdown of machinery under the off-hire clause (although the court went on to hold that because of this deficiency, the vessel was not "in every way fitted for the service"). *Munson S.S. Line* v. *Miramar S.S. Co.*, above.

In *Lake Steam Shipping Co.* v. *Bacon*, 129 F. 819 (S.D.N.Y. 1904), aff'd on opinion below, 145 F. 1022 (2d Cir. 1906), the vessel stranded, and after being refloated, was forced to deviate for repairs. She eventually reached the intended discharge port, and there unloaded her cargo. It was held that the charterer was not liable for hire from the time of the stranding until she reached the discharge port.

In *Temple Steamship Co.* v. *Mercator Marine Corp.*, 1959 AMC 641 (Arb. at N.Y. 1958), the vessel's compasses froze as a result of contact by an electro-magnet against her bulkheads during the loading of a cargo of scrap metal. The vessel was delayed while a gyro compass was installed and the charterer was held entitled to a deduction from hire for the delay.

In *The Anoula A*, S.M.A. No. 307 (Arb. at N.Y. 1967), the panel held that heavy weather damages were a "breakdown or damages to hull" under Clause 15, and that the vessel was off-hire during the time repairs were effected.

Any other cause

American cases follow the *ejusdem generis* principle of construction in interpreting this provision. In *Edison S.S. Corp.* v. *Eastern Minerals*, 167 F. Supp. 601, 605 (D. Mass. 1958), the court held that the crew's refusal to operate the ship's winches in sympathy with picketing by members of a labor union which was trying to organize the charterer's employees was not a cause which put the vessel off-hire. As stated by Judge Wyzanski:

> The grounds for non-payment were clearly specified in paragraph 15 of the time charter. No reference was made to strikes or picket lines. The type of excuses listed were of an entirely different nature. And, although there was added to the listed grounds specified, a general phrase "loss of time . . . by any other cause preventing the full working of the vessel", that clause must be interpreted in the light of the familiar *ejusdem generis* canon of construction. However widely it may be stretched, the clause does not cover a loss of time attributable to labor activities directed solely at conditions in the charterer's enterprise. *Inclusio unius exclusio alterius.*

Accord *The Sea Ranger*, S.M.A. No. 1240 (Arb. at N.Y. 1978); *The London Confidence*, S.M.A. No. 1257 (Arb. at N.Y. 1978); *The Binship*, S.M.A. No. 1416 (Arb. at N.Y. 1980).

In *The Andros Island*, S.M.A. No. 1548 (Arb. at N.Y. 1980), however, the arbitrators adopted a broader test for determining whether the vessel was off-hire. As a result of the outbreak of hostilities between Greece and Turkey over Cyprus and the invasion of Cyprus by Turkish troops, the master of a Greek-flag vessel refused the charterer's order to berth and load cargo for discharge in Romania. Since the voyage would have required that the vessel cross through Turkish territorial waters, the owner instructed the master to refuse to load the cargo. The arbitrators ruled that the owner's actions were not justified. The panel found, however, that the vessel was not off-hire by reason of any of the specific clauses in the charter. Rather, according to the panel: " . . . even though a situation of off-hire in the conventional conception did not exist at any time, charterers were nevertheless effectively deprived of the services of the vessel and her crew, for which they had contracted with owners." Accordingly, the charterer was held entitled to a refund of hire for the time lost.

In *The Hira II*, S.M.A. No. 2246 (Arb. at N.Y. 1986), a dispute arose between the owner and charterer as a result of the master's refusal to berth the vessel. The master contended that the vessel was overdraft for entry into port. The majority of the panel ruled that the master's refusal to berth the vessel did not put the vessel off-hire. The arbitrators noted that the vessel remained ready and capable of following charterer's orders, but the master was not obligated to berth in an overdraft condition. The alternatives available to charterer included lightening the cargo and claiming damages; deviating to another port and claiming damages; or demanding that the master be replaced. The arbitrators further observed that if charterer sustained its burden of proving that the master acted unreasonably in the circumstances, charterer would be entitled to recover its provable damages. A mere claim of right to recover damages, however, did not justify charterer's refusal to pay hire. According to the panel: "revenue, be it in the form of freight or timecharter hire is the very essence of the shipping trade and therefore any attempt to disrupt, delay or default in an obligation to pay, must be narrowly viewed within the parameters of the exact terms, which the parties agree to."

Arrest

When the vessel is placed under arrest, does she go off-hire? That question has arisen in a number of cases, and it appears that the answer is that if the arrest results from acts for which the owner is responsible, the vessel will be off-hire; if, on the other hand, the acts of the charterer or those for whom it is responsible cause the arrest, the vessel remains on-hire.

In *The Wismar*, S.M.A. No. 1454 (Arb. at N.Y. 1980), the ship was arrested by a sub-charterer who claimed that the owner had tortiously interfered with its rights under the sub-charter by refusing to load its cargo. The charterer under the head charter was not a party to the action in which the vessel was arrested, and it declared the vessel off-hire from the time of the arrest until the owner took steps to free her. The arbitrators held that the charterer's action was justified. Since the arrest removed the vessel from its service and the arrest did not result from its actions, the charterer was not required to pay hire for the period of the vessel's non-availability.

The Mesis, S.M.A. No. 2167 (Arb. at N.Y. 1985), concerned charterer's claim for a refund of hire for the period the vessel was detained at Oran by the Algerian authorities pending owner's posting of security against oil pollution charges filed against the vessel. The vessel had carried a cargo of sugar from New Orleans to Oran, Algeria. Cargo operations went smoothly, but on the day before the vessel was to complete discharging and depart, a harbor official boarded the vessel and accused the master of having caused an oil spill. The next day, the vessel was formally charged with polluting the harbor and a demand was made for a guaranty for 100,000 dinars pending a court investigation. The vessel was delayed at Oran for five days during which owner attempted to satisfy the Government's demand for security. Acceptable security was finally proffered and, after a short hearing, the vessel was found guilty of the pollution charge. The assessed fine was paid and, a week after the oil spill, the vessel was permitted to leave Oran. Charterers sought reimbursement for the hire paid during that period. Owner contended that the decision of the Algerian court lacked any credence. The panel found, however, that it lacked authority to review the matter and held that the parties were bound by the judgment of the Algerian court. In addition, the panel concluded that the matter of providing security for the fine was a direct result of the pollution incident and that the time lost was not for charterer's account.

In *The Sea Ranger*, S.M.A. No. 1240 (Arb. at N.Y. 1978), the charterer was held liable for hire during the period the vessel was under arrest. The arrest was caused by cargo receivers in Bahrain whose claims were ultimately dismissed by the court. The panel noted that there was no doubt that a charterer remains liable for hire during those periods that the vessel is under arrest or otherwise legally detained by reason of its own misconduct. That was not the situation in *The Sea Ranger*, however, since the charterer was held by the court in Bahrain to be blameless. The issue raised, therefore, was whether the charterer was bound to pay hire while the use of the vessel was lost by reason of a wrongful arrest by a third party cargo receiver.

The panel held that the vessel did not go off-hire during the period of the arrest and explained its reasons as follows:

> Generally speaking, the time charterer remains fully liable for the payment of hire unless this responsibility is terminated or interrupted by the fault of the shipowner or an express provision of the charter party. There is no charter party provision that we are aware of that suspends charterer's obligation to pay hire because of a third party attachment of the vessel, based upon a cargo related activity or other responsibility of charterer, regardless of the merit or righteousness of the third party claim. While it is true that charterer has been deprived of the use of a vessel for which it is being asked to pay, the contrary result would perhaps be more inequitable. Should an owner be forced to suspend its right to collect hire when his vessel is under arrest because of an unfounded claim arising out of a charterer related activity? Unless the charter party specifically says otherwise, the answer is obviously no.

The panel also found that arrest and detention did not fit under the "any other cause" provision in Clause 15 since, applying the doctrine of *ejusdem generis*, they were not causes of the same kind as those specifically enumerated in Clause 15.

The Sea Ranger was distinguished in *The Orient Horizon*, S.M.A. No. 1709 (Arb. at N.Y. 1982). The panel held that the vessel was off-hire during the period of arrest and made the following comments regarding *The Sea Ranger* case:

> The Panel's decision there was predicated on the fact that Charterer's loss of use of the vessel was the result of an arrest related to its activity even though the underlying claim for that arrest was unfounded. In this case the arrest was clearly associated with an Owner related activity even though the facts reveal little semblance of Owner's fault. However small Owner's fault may have been, if any, certainly Charterer had no involvement in the circumstances giving rise to the vessel's arrest. Therefore, it would be improper and inequitable to require Charterer to continue to pay hire for the period of arrest during which it was deprived of the vessel's use and for which it bore no responsibility or blame.

See also *The Athenian Horizon*, S.M.A. No. 1197 (Arb. at N.Y. 1977), where the charterer was held liable to pay hire for time lost while the vessel was under arrest in connection with the charterer's unsuccessful action against the owner for a wrongful withdrawal.

In *The Mercandian Supplier II*, S.M.A. No. 2509 (Arb. at N.Y. 1988), a sole arbitrator decided the vexing question of whether owner or charterer bears responsibility for delays caused by the arrest of the vessel by the United States Customs Service following the discovery of about 10,500 lbs. of marijuana in a container. The container was loaded in Jamaica and a container seal supplied by charterer was intact upon the vessel's arrival at Miami. The marijuana was discovered during an inspection of the container which took place during the discharging operation. The Customs authorities levied a fine of

$1,380,800, which required a 10% bond for the release of the vessel. Neither owner nor charterer came forward with the bond and the vessel was delayed. Charterer declared the vessel off-hire during the period of the delay and withheld hire. The sole arbitrator ruled that owner was entitled to hire for the entire period. The arbitrator found that the facts that the container was stuffed and loaded by the shipper and charterer and that the marijuana was smuggled aboard by the shipper established that, as between owner and charterer, the latter bore responsibility for the lost time.

And if upon the voyage the speed be reduced

In the absence of this provision, reduced speed would not be considered an off-hire event, although the charterer may have a right to damages. See *Steamship Knutsford Co.* v. *Barber & Co.*, 261 F. 866, 870 (2d Cir. 1919), *cert.* denied 252 U.S. 586 (1920).

Other obligations of charterer

American courts have followed the English view that operation of the off-hire clause does not suspend the charterer's other duties under the charter. See *Northern S.S. Co.* v. *Earn Line*, 175 F. 529 (2d Cir. 1910); *Norwegian Shipping & Trade Mission* v. *Nitrate Corp. of Chile Ltd.*, 1942 AMC 1523 (Arb. at N.Y. 1942).

Effect on other remedies of owner and charterer

The off-hire clause ordinarily provides the sole measure of the charterer's damages for time lost due to the specified contingencies. *Aaby* v. *States Marine Corp.*, 80 F. Supp. 329 (S.D.N.Y. 1948), aff'd 181 F.2d 383 (2d Cir. 1950), *cert.* denied 340 U.S. 829 (1950).

In *Aaby*, the vessel was under charter for one year, and broke down almost immediately after delivery. Two and one-half days were required for repairs. The court held that the charterer was not entitled to treat the charter as having been cancelled, since the breakdown did not frustrate the commercial purpose of the charter. According to the court, the charterer's remedy for loss of time was provided by the off-hire clause, which excused them from paying hire for the repair period.

The principle was stated quite plainly by Judge Hough in *The Ask*, 156 F. 678, 681 (S.D.N.Y. 1907):

> The Ask broke down and repaired temporary repairs . . . For such contingencies the charter party provides a stipulated measure of damages—i.e., loss of charter hire—and no other measure is permissible . . . .

The off-hire clause is obviously limited in scope, however, and while it may operate to relieve the charterer of its obligation to pay hire in certain contingencies, it does not provide any means for reimbursing it for consequential damages it may suffer as the result, for example, of an engine breakdown. Moreover, it does not apply to breaches of any other warranties under the charter as the result of which damages may be incurred. Thus, the clause should not be understood as limiting the charterer's right of recovery for consequential damages resulting from the breakdown. This was recognized in the District Court opinion in *Aaby*. According to the court:

> It is perfectly clear, however, that the breakdown, in the present case, falls squarely within the language of Clause 15, and would ordinarily be dealt with under that clause. It was purely a minor breakdown which . . . occasioned a total time loss of less than two days and a half. For this time

loss the respondent is concededly entitled to be relieved from the payment of hire. *It also has a right of action for any special damages it may have sustained as a result of the breach of warranty.* (80 F. Supp. at 333.) (Emphasis added.)

In *The Polyxeni*, S.M.A. No. 1961 (Arb. at N.Y. 1984), owner cited *The Seafaith*, 1955 AMC 2062, 2063 (Arb. at N.Y. 1954), for the proposition that charterer's recovery was limited only to hire and that other consequential damages were not recoverable because they are not included in the off-hire clause. The panel chose not to agree with *The Seafaith*, and cited the First Edition of *Time Charters* to support its conclusion that consequential damages may be recoverable.

In *The Captain John*, 1973 AMC 2005 (Arb. at N.Y. 1973), the vessel was forced to put into Lisbon for extensive repairs en route to Hamburg with a cargo of molasses. The cargo was discharged and carried to destination on another vessel. In addition, the charterer hired substitute vessels to fulfill other contracts while the *Captain John* underwent repairs. The panel held that the vessel was off-hire while repairs were carried out. Under the charter, the charterer was entitled to tack on the amount of time the vessel was off-hire. Notwithstanding this right, however, the majority held that the charterer could recover the cost of chartering the substitute vessels, less the cost it would have incurred for hire and fuel if the *Captain John* had been operating, and less any savings from extending the time period.

In *The Tordenskjold*, S.M.A. No. 1091 (Arb. at N.Y. 1977), the panel held that in addition to off-hire, the charterer was entitled to such other provable damages as may have been sustained during the off-hire period. In that case, the vessel was off-hire while the owners replaced flanges to conform with Coast Guard regulations for the carriage of propylene. The panel found, however, that the charterer had failed to prove any damages. See also *Fort Morgan S.S. Co.* v. *Baltimore & Jamaica Trad. Co.*, 284 F. 1, 4 (4th Cir. 1922), holding that the off-hire clause "has no relation to damages . . . resulting from the negligence of the navigating officers in stranding the vessel . . . "; *The Ask*, 156 F. 678, 681 (S.D.N.Y. 1907), where the court remarked with respect to a perishable cargo, that "it could hardly be contended that the ship might conceal her known defects, load her cargo, and then remain in port making repairs, with no greater liability than temporary loss of charter hire . . . ".

A more restrictive approach has been adopted in some cases. See, e.g., *Cia. Estrella Blanca Ltda.* v. *The Nictric*, 247 F. Supp. 161 (D.Ore, 1965), aff'd *per curiam* 368 F.2d 575 (9th Cir. 1966), holding that the time charterer's exclusive remedy against the owner was under the off-hire clause, even though the deficiency in the vessel's cargo gear which interrupted loading reduced the amount of demurrage the time charterer could recover under the sub-voyage charter.

In *The Largo*, S.M.A. No. 1230 (Arb. at N.Y. 1978), the charterer contended that the vessel was off-hire while awaiting a berth where the vessel arrived some hours after the master's last ETA and the berth which had been reserved was assigned to another vessel. The panel denied the claim, concluding that the delay claimed was consequential in nature, and that the charterer had no recourse under the charter. The panel indicated, however, that its decision was influenced in part by the fact that it had awarded the charterer a speed claim allowance for the voyage which resulted in the late arrival.

In *The Stolt Capricorn*, S.M.A. No. 2359 (Arb. at N.Y. 1987), the charter was held to have been commercially frustrated because of extensive delays at a discharge port while the vessel was under arrest. The vessel was placed off-hire for all of the time lost until the charter was deemed terminated by virtue of the frustration. Charterer sought to recover lost profits which would have been earned under a subcharter had the vessel not been detained. While the panel found that it was true that the charterer would have earned profits under the subcharter, it concluded that "since charterers were made whole for the time lost under the time charter through the return of hire, it would be a 'double-dip' to also grant them the lost profits for a voyage which the vessel, under the prevailing conditions, could not have completed within the available time frame".

In *The Universe Explorer*, 1985 AMC 1014 (Arb. at N.Y. 1984), arbitrators held that charterer's sole remedy for the loss of time the vessel was detained from entering a berth in Nigeria because of its prior contacts with South Africa was to place the vessel off-hire. Although charterer had to pay additional freight to charter a substitute vessel, the panel denied its claim for damages. The panel adhered to the position that the off-hire clause provides the sole measure of charterer's damages for time lost due to the specified contingencies in the off-hire clause. In addition, the panel found that under the mutual exceptions clause, no damages could be recovered by either party for losses due to "restraint of princes, rulers or people".

Clauses giving charterer option to cancel

It is not uncommon to find that the charter contains a typewritten clause which gives the charterer an option to cancel the contract should the vessel be off-hire for a specified period of time. Such clauses have been enforced by New York arbitration panels. See, e.g., *The M/V Argo Leader*, S.M.A. No. 2065 (Arb. at N.Y. 1985) (option to cancel should vessel be off-hire for an aggregate of 36 days or longer within any 12-month period due to mechanical breakdown); *The M/V Theodora*, S.M.A. No. 2333 (Arb. at N.Y. 1985) (option to cancel should the vessel be off-hire for a continuous period of more than 30 consecutive days).

Frustration of Charter

"102. 16. That should the Vessel be lost, money paid in advance and not earned (reckoning from the date of loss or being last heard of) shall be
103. returned to the Charterers at once."

Loss of the ship

The loss of a ship under time charter will have different consequences depending upon the circumstances in which it occurs and upon its causes. A loss may be attributable to a breach of charter by one of the parties; for example a loss may be caused by unseaworthiness for which the owners are liable under the terms of the charter (see pages 64 and 114 above and page 428 below), or to a breach by the charterers of their safe port obligations (see page 136 above). In such circumstances the party in breach will be liable to the other party in damages, but unless there is a substitution clause in the charter (see page 325 below) providing effectively for substitution after loss, the parties will be excused from further performance by reason of the loss of the ship upon which performance depended.

A loss, and the events giving rise to it, may be completely provided for under the charter so that the contract determines the rights of the parties upon the happening of the loss (see page 330 below). If, however, there is incomplete provision in the charter, and if the loss was not due to the default of either party, the parties may be discharged from the obligation of further performance under the doctrine of frustration. Lines 102 and 103 of the New York Produce form are incomplete provisions, so that in appropriate cases the doctrine of frustration will apply to discharge the parties automatically, and the term as to repayment of hire may be modified by the Law Reform (Frustrated Contracts) Act 1943, see page 337 below.

It is also convenient to deal here with the other circumstances, apart from loss of the ship, in which the parties to a time charter may be discharged automatically under the doctrine of frustration. Clause 16 of the New York Produce form and Clause 16 of the Baltime form both provide for a cessation of hire if the ship is lost. There are other circumstances in which the time charter will be terminated automatically without the agreement or election of the parties.

The doctrine of frustration

Where an event occurs without default of either party, whether it be the total loss or commercial destruction of the ship under time charter, or requisition or detention of the ship for an inordinate period of time, or whether it be that performance of the time charter becomes illegal or impossible because of the destruction or discontinuance of something essential to its performance, the contract will be terminated by operation of law if the effect of the event is such as to destroy the identity of the charter service or to make it, as a matter of business, a totally different thing, which the contract is not wide enough to encompass. As it was put by Lord Radcliffe in *Davis Contractors* v. *Fareham U.D.C.* [1956] A.C. 696, at page 729: "frustration occurs whenever the law recognizes that without default of either party a contractual obligation has become incapable of being performed because the circumstances in which performance is called for would render it a thing radically different from that which was undertaken by the contract. *Non haec in foedera veni*. It was not this that I promised to do."

The doctrine was re-stated by Lord Simon in *National Carriers* v. *Panalpina* [1981] A.C. 675, at page 700, in the following terms: "Frustration of a contract takes place when there supervenes an event (without default of either party and for which the contract makes no sufficient provision) which so significantly changes the nature (not merely the expense or onerousness) of the outstanding contractual rights and/or obligations from what the parties could reasonably have contemplated at the time of its execution that it would be unjust to hold them to the literal sense of its stipulations in the new circumstances; in such case the law declares both parties to be discharged from further performance." For consideration of the meaning of a "supervening event" see the judgment of Hobhouse, J., in *The Super Servant Two* [1989] 1 Lloyd's Rep. 148 and page 335 below.

Lord Roskill in the *Panalpina* case emphasised that the effect of frustration is to discharge the parties automatically: "Its operation does not depend on the action or inaction of the parties" (see page 712 of the above report). Thus the fact that the parties may have treated the contract as continuing after a frustrating event will not prevent the operation of the doctrine.

The *Singaporean* was time chartered in 1916 for a period of 10 months, the ship to be placed at the charterers' disposal in March 1917. Prior to delivery she was requisitioned. The owners thought the period of requisition would be short and asked the charterers to confirm that they would still take the ship after her release. The charterers did so, but the ship remained under requisition until March 1919.

It was held by the Privy Council that the charter was frustrated by the requisitioning of the ship and that the parties were thereupon discharged irrespective of the subsequent correspondence between them. There was no new contract and the fact that the parties considered the charter to be still in being was irrelevant.

Hirji Mulji v. *Cheong Yue S.S. Co.* [1926] A.C. 497.
(See also *B.P. Exploration* v. *Hunt* [1981] 1 W.L.R. 232, 241.)

Similarly the fact that the charterers may, after a frustrating event, be willing to pay hire or continue to pay hire for the ship will not prevent the owners from relying on the doctrine: see *Bank Line* v. *Capel* [1919] A.C. 435, below.

Question of fact and law

Where there is an appeal to the courts from an arbitration award which decides that a contract has or has not been frustrated, it is important to know which part of the award the courts will treat as dealing with a question of fact and which part as dealing with a question of law, because the courts will review the arbitrators' decisions on questions of law but will generally refrain from interfering with their decisions on questions of fact. In recent years the courts have sought to draw the distinction in frustration cases.

In *Universal Cargo Carriers* v. *Citati* [1957] 1 Lloyd's Rep. 174, at page 192, Devlin, J., said that "while the application of the doctrine of frustration is a matter of law, the assessment of a period of delay sufficient to constitute frustration is a question of fact". On the other hand, Kerr, J., in *The Angelia* [1972] 2 Lloyd's Rep. 154 found this statement difficult to reconcile with the view expressed in *Davis Contractors* v. *Fareham U.D.C.* [1956] A.C. 696 by Lord Radcliffe, at page 727, that "the description of the circumstances that justify the application of the rule and, consequently, the decision whether in a particular case those circumstances exist are . . . necessarily questions of law". Furthermore he did not consider that Devlin, J.'s statement accorded with the decisions of the Court of Appeal in *In re Comptoir Commercial Anversois and Power* [1920] 1 K.B. 868 and of the House of Lords in *Tsakiroglou* v. *Noblee Thorl* [1961] 1 Lloyd's Rep. 329.

In *The Nema* (see below), Templeman, L.J., in the Court of Appeal did not consider there was a conflict between Devlin, J.'s statement in the *Citati* case and Lord Radcliffe's view in *Davis Contractors* v. *Fareham U.D.C.* The former case, he said, "was dealing with the narrow question of how much delay in a relevant case is sufficient to constitute frustration and not with the question whether delay was a circumstance which could result in frustration". Lord Roskill in the House of Lords in *The Nema* doubted whether *The Angelia* was rightly decided and said: "*Tsakiroglou & Co. Ltd.* v. *Noblee Thorl G.m.b.H.* [1962] A.C. 93 decided that, while in the ultimate analysis whether a contract was frustrated was a question of law, yet as Lord Radcliffe said at page 124 in relation to that case ' . . . the conclusion is almost completely determined by what is ascertained as to the mercantile usage and the understanding of mercantile men' . . . when it is shown on the face of a reasoned award that the appointed tribunal has applied the right legal test, the Court should in my view only interfere if on the facts found as applied to that right legal test, no reasonable person could have reached that conclusion. It ought not to interfere merely because the Court thinks that upon those facts and applying that test, it would not or might not itself have reached the same conclusion, for to do that would be for the Court to usurp what is the sole function of the tribunal of fact."

It seems therefore that the question is one of mixed fact and law (see *National Carriers* v. *Panalpina* [1981] A.C. 675, at page 688). The question whether delay or delay of the type experienced in the particular case is capable of frustrating the contract is a matter of law, but the question whether the delay is of sufficient length to cause frustration is a matter of fact. Consequently, where the courts are satisfied that the arbitrators have understood and applied the legal test of frustration they will be slow to alter their decision on the question whether the facts do or do not satisfy that test. In *The Nema*, below, Lord Roskill said: "For the future I think that in those cases which are otherwise suitable for appeal [as to which see page 369 below] the Court should only interfere with the conclusion on issues such as those which arise in cases of frustration expressed by arbitrators in reasoned awards, either if they are shown to have gone wrong in law and not to have applied the right legal test, or if, whilst purporting to apply the right legal test, they have reached a conclusion which no reasonable person could, on the facts which they have found, have reached."

The *Nema* was chartered for 6/7 consecutive voyages to carry titanium slag from Sorel on the St. Lawrence to Calais or Hartlepool, between April and December 1979. Clause 5 excluded time lost through strikes from laytime and Clause 27 gave the owners the option to cancel if shipment was prevented by "general strike". After the first voyage there was a strike at the titanium plant in Sorel and when the *Nema* arrived there on 20 June 1979, she was unable to load. Addenda to the charter were then entered into under which the second voyage was postponed on certain terms and the owners agreed to lift seven further cargoes in 1980. However, the strike, which was not a general strike, continued and in September 1979, with no prospect of the strike ending, the question whether the charter was frustrated was referred to arbitration.

The arbitrator treated the voyages for the 1979 season as divisible from the agreement for the voyages for the 1980 season and held that by 26 September 1979 the contract for the 1979 season was frustrated. On appeal to the Commercial Court, Robert Goff, J., held that the charter constituted one indivisible contract extending over two seasons, but that even if the 1979 season could be regarded as a separate contract, the strike did not affect it so radically as to frustrate the 1979 contract.

The Court of Appeal, whose decision was affirmed by the House of Lords, restored the arbitrator's decision, agreeing with him that the charter was divisible into separate seasons for the 1979 and 1980 voyages. It was held further that unless the arbitrator misdirected himself on a point of law or unless his decision was one that no reasonable arbitrator could reach, the arbitrator's conclusion on the question of frustration should be accepted.

The Nema [1980] 2 Lloyd's Rep. 83 and 339 (C.A.) and [1981] 2 Lloyd's Rep. 239 (H.L.).

(For cases on divisible and indivisible contracts, see *Larrinaga* v. *Soc. Franco-Américaine des Phosphates* (1923) 14 Ll.L.Rep. 457 (contract of affreightment) and *Dominion Coal* v. *Roberts* (1920) 4 Ll.L.Rep. 434 (time charter).)

Frustration by loss of the chartered ship

A time charter will be frustrated not only by the actual total loss of the chartered ship, but also if she is so badly damaged that she has effectively been destroyed as a commercial vessel. See *Blane Steamships* v. *Minister of Transport* [1951] 2 Lloyd's Rep. 155, a demise charter case.

Substitution clause

Where the loss of the chartered ship results in frustration of the charter, any clause permitting the substitution of another ship will be of no effect. If it is intended to allow substitution after loss, therefore, particularly clear words must be used to prevent the contract being frustrated by the loss.

The seven-year time charter for the *World Sky* incorporated a clause giving her owners the right to substitute for her a larger ship. During the charter service she ran aground and became a total loss. McNair, J., held that as the time charter had been frustrated by the total loss of the *World Sky* her owners no longer had a right (nor a duty) to make a substitution.

Niarchos v. *Shell Tankers* [1961] 2 Lloyd's Rep. 496.

(See also *The Badagry* [1985] 1 Lloyd's Rep. 395 and page 62 above.)

Frustration by delay

For delay of whatever kind to frustrate a contract its effect must be radical, as is suggested by the following passage from the judgment of Goddard, J., in *Tatem* v. *Gamboa* (1938) 61 Ll.L.Rep. 149, at page 156: "if the foundation of the contract goes, either by the destruction of the subject-matter or by reason of such long interruption or delay that the performance is really in effect that of a different contract, you can if you wish (and no doubt parties often do) provide for what in that event is to happen; but if you do not, then the performance of the contact is regarded as frustrated." (But note the support of Lord Denning, M.R., for a "slightly more liberal approach" in *The Nema* [1980] 2 Lloyd's Rep. 339, at page 346.)

Delay in commencement of charter

The prospect of delay in the commencement of a contract may be held sufficient to frustrate that contract if the anticipated delay would make performance of the contract a radically different obligation from that originally contracted for.

The *Quito* was chartered in February 1915 for a period of 12 months with cancelling date 30 April. The ship was not delivered by 30 April but the charterers did not cancel and on 11 May the ship was requisitioned. During May and June the owners tried to obtain the ship's release, but failed. In August 1915 the owners agreed to sell the ship conditionally on obtaining her release from the

Government. A release was agreed only on terms that the owners provided a substitute. The ship was released in September and sold. The charterers claimed damages for non-delivery. It was held by a majority of the House of Lords that the postponement of the commencement date of the charter for what was thought an indefinite period which would probably be lengthy frustrated the contract. Lord Sumner said at page 460: " . . . I am of opinion that the requisitioning of the *Quito* destroyed the identity of the chartered service and made the charter as a matter of business a totally different thing. It hung up the performance for a time, which was wholly indefinite and probably long. The return of the ship depended on considerations beyond the ken or control of either party."

Bank Line v. *Capel* [1919] A.C. 435.

(For consideration of another aspect of this case, see page 330 below.)

In the earlier case of *Jackson* v. *Union Marine Insurance* (1874) L.R. 10 C.P. 125 the Court of Exchequer Chamber held that the charterers of a ship for a voyage from Newport to San Francisco with rails were not obliged to load the ship, which would have presented in early January but grounded and needed repairs taking until the end of August. Caution should be exercised in applying the reasoning to modern conditions. But it is interesting in showing an earlier approach to this problem. The charterers were released from their obligation to load not because the charter had become frustrated but because a condition precedent to their obligation had not been fulfilled, namely that the ship would be at Newport in time to carry out the voyage intended. Baron Bramwell said: " . . . the shipowner undertook to use all possible dispatch to arrive at the port of loading, and also agreed that the ship should arrive there 'at such a time that in a commercial sense the commercial speculation entered into by the shipowner and charterers should not be at an end, but in existence.' That latter agreement is also a condition precedent. Not arriving at such a time puts an end to the contract; though, as it arises from an excepted peril, it gives no cause of action."

Although it does not follow from this reasoning that the charterers could not have required the shipowner to tender for loading however late (a point which did not arise in the case), modern reasoning would probably treat both parties as discharged from their obligations by frustration of their contract.

Prolongation of charter for trip or voyage

Delay during the performance of a charter contract—for example the prolongation of a voyage as a result of breakdown of the ship or the closure of a canal—may be sufficient to cause frustration. The courts have, however, been reluctant to hold the instances of delay that have come before them sufficient to have this effect. This follows the House of Lords decision in *Davis Contractors* v. *Fareham U.D.C.* [1956] A.C. 696, summarised below. But it may be noted that the leading shipping cases relate to non-perishable cargoes and to situations in which the result of the delay has been no more than extra expense for the owners or the charterers, in voyage or time charters respectively.

Building contractors agreed with a local authority to build 78 houses on a certain site within eight months for £92,425. For various reasons, including in particular a lack of skilled labour and adverse weather, the building took 22 months and the eventual cost to the contractors was £115,233. They claimed that as a result of the long delay the contract had become frustrated and that they were entitled to be paid, instead of its fixed price, on a *quantum meruit* basis. The House of Lords held that despite the delay and consequent extra expense to the contractors the contract had not been frustrated and they were entitled only to the fixed price.

Lord Reid said, at page 724: "It may be that delay could be of a character so different from anything contemplated that the contract was at an end, but in this case, in my opinion, the most that could be said is that the delay was greater in degree than was to be expected. It was not caused by

any new and unforseeable factor or event: the job proved to be more onerous but it never became a job of a different kind from that contemplated in the contract".
Davis Contractors v. *Fareham U.D.C.* [1956] A.C. 696.

The *Eugenia* was time chartered on the Baltime form for a trip from Genoa to India via the Black Sea. Before the terms of the charter were fixed the parties, who were aware of the danger of the Suez Canal being closed, discussed special terms to deal with that situation. In the end no such terms were agreed, but the charter did include the usual printed War Clause 21. The ship loaded a cargo of iron and steel goods in the Black Sea and then proceeded to Port Said. When she arrived there the Egyptian anti-aircraft guns were already firing and the zone was, as the court held, "dangerous" within the meaning of the War Clause. The owners' agent called upon the charterers' agent on 30 October 1956, to take action under the War Clause to ensure that the ship should not enter Port Said or the Suez Canal. No action was taken and the charterers' agent in Port Said made arrangements for the ship to enter the Canal which she did on 31 October 1956. On the evening of the same day the Egyptians blocked the Canal and the *Eugenia* was trapped until January 1957 when the northern passage out of the Canal was cleared. The southern end was not cleared until April 1957. It was held by the Court of Appeal that:

1. The charterers were in breach of the War Clause in allowing the ship to enter the Canal.
2. The fact that the ship was trapped was the charterers' own fault and they could not rely on the detention in the Canal as a ground of frustration.
3. The fact that the ship would, if not trapped, have had to proceed around the Cape to India did not frustrate the charter because the cargo was not perishable and the prolongation (138 days from delivery to redelivery against 108 days) was not so great that it made the voyage around the Cape radically different: the only real difference was that it was considerably more expenseive and this was not a ground for regarding the contract as frustrated.

Ocean Tramp Tankers v. *Sovfracht (The Eugenia)* [1963] 2 Lloyd's Rep. 381.

The *Captain George K.* was voyage chartered to carry sulphur in bulk from Mexico to Kandla and Bombay at a time when the Suez Canal was open and there was no reason to anticipate its closure. However, when she reached the northern end of the Canal her master was advised it had been closed by the war which had recently started in that area. Her owners thereupon sent her back through the Mediterranean and around the Cape to her destination. She eventually sailed a distance of 18,400 miles against the 9,700 that she would have sailed had the Canal remained open. Her owners claimed extra expenses of $67,969 on the basis that the original charter had been frustrated. Mocatta, J., rejected this claim, but only because he felt bound by the Court of Appeal decision in *The Eugenia*, above, without which he "would have concluded that the voyage performed was fundamentally different in kind from that clearly contemplated by the charter".
The Captain George K. [1970] 2 Lloyd's Rep. 21.

The *Dunolly* was time chartered for one Baltic round (a voyage from the U.K. to Baltic ports and back to the U.K.). She was delivered in early July 1914, sailed to the Baltic and was loading in Finland when, at the beginning of August, war broke out. She was prevented from leaving Finland by orders of the Russian authorities. The Court of Appeal held the charter frustrated, as the charterers were deprived for an indefinite period of the agreed use of the ship.
Scottish Navigation v. *Souter* [1917] 1 K.B. 222.

Only contractual route becomes impossible

It seems probable that had the only permitted route under the charter in *The Eugenia* (above) been through the Suez Canal then the charter would have been held frustrated.

The judge at first instance, Megaw, J., dealt with this possibility in the following words: "If, by the express or implied terms of a charter-party, the parties have agreed that a particular route, and that route only, is to be followed, then, if the vessel is, in the commercial sense, prevented from using that route, it may not be necessary for the court to consider whether any other route was commercially practicable. The contractual obligation can be performed only by a particular route which the parties have defined and agreed." ([1963] 2 Lloyd's Rep. 155, at page 174.)

The Court of Appeal in *The Eugenia* overruled the decision of Pearson, J., in *The Massalia* [1960] 1 Lloyd's Rep. 594 that the provision "Captain also to telegraph to 'Maritsider Genoa' on passing Suez Canal" created an obligation to follow the Suez route on a charter voyage from India to Italy. But nothing was said by the court to prevent the frustration of a charter which did make it clear that one route only was to be followed when that route became impossible.

In practice the point may not often be important in the case of time charters, as even when their duration is fixed by reference to the time that a particular voyage will take it is unusual to stipulate the route to be followed.

Interruptions to the service during the charter period

This is the most usual type of delay so far as concerns time charters for a certain number of years or months as opposed to time charters for a trip.

A time charter may be held to be frustrated if performance of it is sufficiently interrupted by the ship being, for example, requisitioned or physically trapped.

The authorities show that for the charter to be frustrated the interruption must be of very substantial duration, particularly in relation to the unexpired balance of the charter period at the time of the alleged frustration. If at that time it is likely that any substantial period of the charter will remain after the interruption has ceased then the courts will be unlikely to hold that the contract has been frustrated. No doubt, however, circumstances could occur in which the courts would so hold: for example where a ship was chartered for a special and urgent trade, or where, although in the distant future the charter service could be resumed for a time before the end of the period, no service at all could be rendered for a disproportionate part of the total charter period. See *The Wenjiang* (*No. 2*) [1983] 1 Lloyd's Rep. 400, 408 and *National Carriers* v. *Panalpina* [1981] A.C. 675, 697, 707.

Moreover it should be noted that where arbitrators, having applied the correct legal test of frustration, decide that the facts of the particular case before them do satisfy that test, the courts will be reluctant to interfere with that decision, even where they might themselves have come to a different decision; see *The Nema* [1981] 2 Lloyd's Rep. 239 and pages 324 and 325 above, also *The Wenjiang* [1982] 1 Lloyd's Rep. 128. This may be significant as it is the view of at least one London arbitrator that "a slightly more liberal approach" should be taken in this area, a view adopted by Lord Denning, M.R., in *The Nema* [1980] 2 Lloyd's Rep. 339, at page 346.

The tanker *F.A. Tamplin* was time chartered for five years from December 1912. In December 1914 the ship was requisitioned for a short period and then before her return was requisitioned a second time in February 1915. She then had structural alterations made to her to fit her as a troop carrier. The owners contended that the charter was frustrated by the requisition and the alterations made to the ship. At the time the case was heard by the House of Lords, 19 months of the charter remained unexpired. It was held by a majority of three to two that the charter was not frustrated: although the period of the requisition was indefinite, there was a sufficient chance that the ship might be available for further service under the charter before its expiry. Earl Loreburn said, at page 405:

> "There may be many months during which this ship will be available for commercial purposes before the five years have expired. It might be a valuable right for the charterer during those months to have the use of the ship at the stipulated freight. Why should he be deprived of it?"

Tamplin Steamship v. *Anglo-Mexican Petroleum* [1916] 2 A.C. 397.
(See also the summary of *Bank Line* v. *Capel* [1919] A.C. 435, at page 325 above.)

(This case should be treated with caution: it was the owners who argued that the charter was frustrated; the charterers, who hoped to obtain the compensation which the Admiralty were paying at a rate in excess of the charter hire, were content for the charter to continue despite the fact that they would not receive the contracted services during requisition. It is conceivable that if the Admiralty compensation had been lower than the hire and the charterers had refused to continue with the charter the decision of the House of Lords might have been different: see the comments of Lord Dunedin in *Metropolitan Water Board* v. *Dick, Kerr* [1918] A.C. 119, at page 129.)

The *Errington Court* was chartered on the New York Produce form in March 1937. Redelivery was to be in Australia between 15 December 1937 and the end of January 1938. She loaded cargo at Portland, Oregon in July, 1937 and on 7 August arrived at Wu-hu, 750 miles up the Yangtze River. The Japan/China War broke out on 13 August and the Chinese sank ships in the river to form a boom to prevent the Japanese coming up it. The evidence was that at the time the ship became trapped (on 3 September when she had completed discharge of her cargo) it was expected that she would be prevented from sailing down river indefinitely. In holding that the charter was frustrated, Branson, J., said: "It was urged, on behalf of the owners, that the doctrine of frustration cannot apply to a time charter unless the ship is physically removed from the control of both parties. I cannot see why the adventure in question before me was any the less frustrated than was the adventure in the *Bank Line* case. All power in the ship's officers to continue the adventure was taken away, in the one case by requisition, and, in the other, by the construction of the boom."

Court Line v. *Dant & Russell* (1939) 44 Com. Cas. 345.

The *Silveroak* was time chartered for 30 months on the New York Produce form. Seventeen months after the commencement of the charter the ship was requisitioned by the British Government under prerogative powers (giving the Crown the right to possession only so long as required for Defence of the Realm). It was estimated at the time of requisition that the requisition might last three to four months, as in fact it did, so the ship was returned with about 10 months of the charter still to run. It was held by Diplock, J., that the charter was not frustrated.

Port Line v. *Ben Line* [1958] 1 Lloyd's Rep. 290.

The *Breconian* was chartered for about 15 months and was delivered in December 1914. She was requisitioned by the British authorities in October 1915, when the charter had $4\frac{1}{2}$ months to run. Her owners claimed that the charter was thereby frustrated and this was accepted by the Court of Appeal (without calling on the owners' counsel to argue).

Heilgers v. *Cambrian Steam Navigation* (1917) 34 T.L.R. 72.

(See also *Pacific Phosphate* v. *Empire Transport* (1920) 36 T.L.R. 750, at page 330 below; and *The Evia* (*No. 2*), summarised at page 333 below.)

Events contemplated or provided for by the parties

The fact that the event may have been contemplated by the parties or even anticipated at the time the contract was entered into does not prevent the operation of the doctrine of frustration, unless the parties made express provision for it and that express provision is widely enough drawn to cover fully the different circumstances which have arisen.

Events contemplated

The *Molton* was chartered to an agent of the Republican Government of Spain for a period of 30 days from 1 July 1937. It was expressly provided that the purpose of the charter was to evacuate refugees from North Spain to France. The ship carried out one voyage and then was seized by a Nationalist ship on 14 July. She was held until 7 September. It was held by Goddard, J., that, even on the assumption that the parties had at the time of the charter contemplated that the ship would or might be seized, the charter was frustrated. It was a charter for a very short period at a very high rate of freight for a specific purpose within geographical limits and the seizure destroyed the foundation of the contract.

Tatem v. *Gamboa* (1938) 61 Ll.L.Rep. 149.

In *Ocean Tramp Tankers* v. *Sovfracht (The Eugenia)*, above, the parties considered making a provision for the event which in fact occurred (the closure of the Suez Canal) but could not agree on the terms, so they decided to "leave it to the lawyers to sort out" if the eventuality should arise. Lord Denning, M.R., stated that the doctrine was not for this reason excluded.

Events provided for

Where express provision is made in the charter for the event which occurs the question is whether it is a complete provision. In *Bank Line* v. *Capel* [1919] A.C. 435, see page 325 above, the charter contained an express provision that the charterers were to have the option of cancelling if the ship should "be commandeered by Government during this charter" and the ship was in fact commandeered (or requisitioned). It was held that this did not prevent the frustration of the charter. Lord Finlay said, at page 443, that the clause giving the option, " . . . merely means that in case of the vessel being commandeered, the charterers might cancel at once without having to show that the detention was likely to last so long as to put an end to the contract within the meaning of the authorities".

Viscount Haldane said, at page 445: "What is clear is that where people enter into a contract which is dependent for the possibility of its performance on the continued availability of the subject-matter, and that availability comes to an unforeseen end by reason of circumstances over which its owner had no control, the owner is not bound unless it is quite plain that he has contracted to be so."

Likewise, when the allegation is of frustration as a result of delay or of interruption in performance, any provisions in the charter must be examined in their context to see whether on a true construction they are sufficiently wide to cope with the new situation. If they are not—and in practice few will be sufficiently wide to cope with a situation which is so radical as to cause frustration—then they will not prevent frustration. In *Fibrosa* v. *Fairbairn* [1943] A.C. 32 Viscount Simon said, at page 40: "The principle is that where supervening events, not due to the default of either party, render the performance of a contract indefinitely impossible, and there is no undertaking to be bound in any event, frustration ensues, even though the parties may have expressly provided for the case of a limited interruption."

The defendants agreed in August 1913 to supply the plaintiffs with 12 ships of a certain type for each of the years 1914 to 1918 to carry each month a cargo of phosphate from Ocean Island/Nauru to Europe. The contract provided that in the event of a war involving Great Britain endangering shipping either party could opt to suspend the contract until the end of the war with the period of suspension being added to the end of the contract period. The defendants claimed to suspend the contract in August 1914. In June 1919 all their owned ships then being under requisition, they alleged that the whole contract had been frustrated. Rowlatt, J., accepted that the contract had been frustrated, although it was not restricted to the supply of their own ships and despite the war clause mentioned above. The report of his judgment reads in part:

" . . . it was true that war of some kind was contemplated, but it was necessary to inquire not only whether such a war as that which happened was contemplated, but whether the consequences of war which had followed were in the minds of the parties. Looking at the facts he thought that the parties had contemplated a state of affairs in which there would be some risk, but they never contemplated such a war as actually happened or its consequences. The whole shipping industry had been dislocated; the Government had taken control and shipowners were *de facto* not free."

Pacific Phosphate v. *Empire Transport* (1920) 36 T.L.R. 750.

(See also *Tamplin* v. *Anglo-Mexican* [1916] 2 A.C. 397 (exception of "restraints of princes"); *The Penelope* [1928] P. 180; *The Nema* [1980] 2 Lloyd's Rep. 339 and page 324 above (strikes clauses); and *Capel* v. *Soulidi* [1916] 2 K.B. 365 (in which the charter provided for cancellation without any option if the ship was commandeered).)

Assessment of extent of interruption

Time at which assessment to be made

The length and effect of the interruption must be assessed at the time and without the benefit of hindsight. In *Anglo-Northern* v. *Jones* [1917] 2 K.B. 78 the rule was stated by Bailhache, J., at page 85, in the following terms: "the parties must have the right to claim that the charterparty is determined by frustration as soon as the event upon which the claim is based happens. The question will then be what estimate would a reasonable man of business take of the probable length of the withdrawal of the vessel from service . . . and it will be immaterial whether his anticipation is justified or falsified by the event."

So in *Court Line* v. *Dant & Russell* (1939) 44 Com. Cas. 345, and page 329 above, the probable length of delay was judged entirely on the evidence of expectations as at the beginning of September 1937. It was held to be immaterial that in the event the Chinese boom was breached by the Japanese on 9 December and that the ship sailed down river on 17 December, leaving sufficient time for her to reach Australia and redeliver within the period stipulated. At the time the ship was trapped by the boom in early September the evidence was that the ship was likely to be blocked indefinitely, and it mattered not that this was subsequently proved wrong. Branson, J., said: "The Court must, as the parties have to when the event arises which is alleged to cause frustration, estimate as best it can the probable duration of that event. The probabilities as to the length of the deprivation, and not the certainty arrived at after the event, is material." What actually happened is relevant only as an aid to determining the reasonable probabilities at the time the decision was called for: see *Denny, Mott & Dickson* v. *James B. Fraser & Co.* [1944] A.C. 265, 277, 278, and *National Carriers* v. *Panalpina* [1981] A.C. 675, 707.

In *The Nema* [1980] 2 Lloyd's Rep. 339, see above, Templeman, L.J., at page 349, dismissed as irrelevant the fact that the strike unexpectedly ended only nine days after the arbitrator had decided that it had frustrated the charter.

Strikes

Since strikes are by their nature of uncertain duration and may terminate at any time they will not usually be held to frustrate a charter: see the judgment of Sellers, L.J., in *Reardon Smith* v. *Ministry of Agriculture* [1961] 1 Lloyd's Rep. 385, at page 404. Nevertheless, there is nothing in principle to prevent a strike having this effect in appropriate circumstances, and the following case was cited by Sellers, L.J., in the above case without disapproval.

The *Penelope* was chartered under a consecutive voyage charter of 12 months from a date to be fixed between 20 May and 20 June 1926, to carry coal from South Wales to Italy. On 1 May the general coal strike began and no coal could be exported for six months—until November 1926 as a result of the strike and thereafter until towards the end of December as a result of Government embargo. It was held that in early September, after the ship had carried out two substitute voyages by agreement, the charter was frustrated, performance of the contract according to its true intent having been prevented.

The Penelope [1928] P. 180.

In *The Nema* [1981] 2 Lloyd's Rep. 239 neither the Court of Appeal nor the House of Lords were prepared to disturb the decision of an arbitrator that a strike that after three months still showed no prospects of ending frustrated a consecutive voyage charter, which had then only a further three months to run (see page 324 above for a fuller account of the facts of the case). Lord Roskill said, at page 255: "I am quite unable to say that the conclusion which [the arbitrator] reached was one which he was not, on the facts which he found, fully entitled to reach. It was not suggested that a strike could never bring about frustration of an adventure. But it was pointed out that most attempts to invoke strikes as a cause of frustration have in the past failed. *The Penelope* [1928] P. 180 is almost the only example of success, and in that case the underlying reasoning of the judgment is far from easy to follow, even though the decision may well be correct . . . I see no reason in principle why a strike should not be capable of causing frustration of an adventure by delay. It cannot be right to divide causes of delay into classes and then say that one class can and another class cannot bring about frustration of an adventure. It is not the nature of the cause of delay which matters so much as the effect of that cause upon the performance of the obligations which the parties have assumed one towards the other."

War

For the reasons expressed by Lord Roskill in *The Nema*, above, it has been doubted whether any presumption about the effect of war still exists.

The presumption was said to be that a state of war will last indefinitely and consequently that delay caused by a war and likely to last throughout it will be of such inordinate duration as to cause the frustration of commercial contracts. In the case of *Geipel* v. *Smith* (1872) L.R. 7 Q.B. 404, which concerned the prevention of a voyage by the French blockade of Hamburg, Lush, J., said at page 414: "a state of war must be presumed to be likely to continue so long, and so to disturb the commerce of merchants, as to defeat and destroy the object of a commercial adventure like this." These words have often been approved since, for example by Lord Atkinson in *Horlock* v. *Beal* [1916] 1 A.C. 486, at page 501. Lord Wright in *Denny, Mott and Dickson* v. *James B. Fraser* [1944] A.C. 265, at page 278, also referred to them with approval, although he explained:

"It is true that Lush, J., was there referring to a single definite adventure, not to a continuous trading, but the real principle which applies in cases of commercial responsibility is that business men must not be left in indefinite suspense. If there is a reasonable probability from the nature of the interruption that it will be of indefinite duration, they ought to be free to turn their assets, their plant and equipment and their business operations into activities which are open to them, and to be free from commitments which are struck with sterility for an uncertain future period."

But Lord Sumner in *Akties. Nord-Osterso Rederiet* v. *E. A. Casper, Edgar & Co.* (1923) 14 Ll.L.Rep. 203, at page 206, emphasised that whether the mere outbreak of war (apart from cases of illegality) would cause frustration would depend upon its effects on the charter. Wars vary greatly in their intensity and geographic scope; some may be expected to have a devastating effect on a particular charter while others might affect it slightly or not at all. Moreover, any presumption that a state of war will last indefinitely can be rebutted in a particular case and in any event does not necessarily mean that the state of war will continue indefinitely to affect performance of the contract.

Mustill, J., in *The Chrysalis* [1983] 1 Lloyd's Rep. 503, having reviewed the authorities, concluded that the position was as follows: "(1) Except in the case of supervening illegality, arising from the fact that the contract involves a party in trading with someone who has become an enemy, a declaration of war does not prevent the performance of a contract; it is the acts done in furtherance of the war which may or may not prevent performance, depending on the individual circumstances of the case. (2) If there is any presumption at all, it relates to the duration of the state of war, not to the effects which the war may have on the performance of the contract. The war itself and its effects on the contract are by no means necessarily coterminous. (3) Any presumption as to the indefinite duration of the war is capable of being rebutted."

In cases arising out of the war between Iraq and Iran which began in 1980, the courts were called upon to review the decisions of arbitrators as to the date upon which particular charters were frustrated by the effects of the war. Different arbitrators came to different conclusions as to the date of frustration on substantially the same sets of facts, but it was established by the decisions of the House of Lords in *The Nema* [1981] 2 Lloyd's Rep. 239 and *The Evia* (*No. 2*) [1982] 2 Lloyd's Rep. 307, that it was not permissible for the courts on an appeal in any particular case to pay attention to the decisions of other arbitrators with a view to achieving uniformity. The courts could interfere with the decisions of arbitrators only if it was shown that they had misdirected themselves in law or that the decision was one which no reasonable arbitrators could properly have reached.

The *Evia* was chartered on the Baltime form for 18 months, two months more or less, and subject to the option was due to be re-delivered on 20 May 1981. On 22 September 1980 she was at Basrah when war broke out between Iraq and Iran and hostilities in the area of the Shatt-al-Arab prevented her sailing. On 1 October some of her crew were repatriated leaving only a skeleton crew on board. Initially it was generally thought that the hostilities would be of short duration, but by 4 October it became clear that each of the combatants was heavily committed and that the Shatt-al-Arab had become a theatre of major operations. The Court of Appeal upheld the decision of the Umpire that the charter was frustrated on 4 October. The House of Lords agreed.

The Evia (No. 2) [1981] 2 Lloyd's Rep. 613, [1982] 1 Lloyd's Rep. 334 (C.A.) and [1982] 2 Lloyd's Rep. 307 (H.L.).

In *The Wenjiang* (*No. 2*) [1983] 1 Lloyd's Rep. 400, on the other hand, an arbitrator decided on similar facts that a twelve-month time charter, due to expire in March or April 1981, was frustrated on 24 November 1980. Bingham, J., found no grounds for interfering with the arbitrator's decision, although the Court of Appeal in giving leave to appeal ([1982] 1 Lloyd's Rep. 128) had suggested that, on a full hearing, a date early in October might prove more appropriate. Mustill, J., in *The Chrysalis* [1983] 1 Lloyd's Rep. 503, likewise refused to disturb a finding by a legal arbitrator that a time charter for a trip was frustrated, in similar circumstances, by 24 November 1980.

Where a delay appears at first to be likely to be of short duration the contract will be frustrated as soon as it appears that the delay will, after all, be inordinately lengthy. Lord Sumner in *Bank Line* v. *Capel* [1919] A.C. 435, said, at page 455: " . . . when the causes of frustration have operated so long or under such circumstances as to raise a presumption of inordinate delay, the time has arrived at which the fate of the contract falls to be decided."

Financial loss

It does not necessarily follow from the fact that circumstances have occurred which impose a heavier financial burden than expected on one party to the contract that the contract will be frustrated. Financial loss would have to be extraordinary to produce that result: see the decision of the House of Lords in *Davis* v. *Fareham U.D.C.* [1956] A.C. 696. In that case Lord Radcliffe said, at page 729: " . . . it is not hardship or inconvenience or material loss itself which calls the principle of frustration into play. There must be as well such a change in the significance of the obligation that the thing undertaken would, if performed, be a different thing from that contracted for."

Similarly, Lord Denning, M.R., said in *The Eugenia* [1963] 2 Lloyd's Rep. 381, at page 390: "The fact that it has become more onerous or more expensive for one party than he thought is not sufficient to bring about a frustration. It must be more than merely more onerous or more expensive. It must be positively unjust to hold the parties bound."

Again, Lord Sumner said in *Larrinaga* v. *Société Franco-Américaine des Phosphates* (1923) 14 Ll.L.Rep. 457, at page 464: "All the uncertainties of a commercial contract can ultimately be expressed, though not very accurately, in terms of money, and rarely, if ever, is it a ground for inferring frustration of an adventure, that the contract has turned out to be a loss or even a commercial disaster for somebody."

Thus, for example, the losses caused to a party to a charter by an unexpectedly large upsurge in the price of bunkers or by the periodic fluctuations of the freight market will not cause the charter to be frustrated. Commenting on such a suggestion in *Occidental* v. *Skibs A/S Avanti* [1976] 1 Lloyd's Rep. 293, at page 325, Kerr, J., said: "The fact that these ships were chartered during a boom period when rates were high, which was then followed by a period of depression during the currency of the charters, is a normal phenomenon of the fluctuations to which the tanker market is ordinarily subject from time to time. This resulted in losses to the charterers, though not in itself in profits to the owners since the rates of hire were fixed for the currency of the charters. If, instead of falling, the market had moved even higher, as it did in 1973, then the charterers would have been able to earn corresponding profits, but any suggestion of frustration would have been equally groundless."

Effect of fault

Breach of contract

A party to the charter will not be able to rely upon the doctrine of frustration if an event which makes further performance impossible has been caused by his breach of the charter. Strictly speaking this is not a situation of frustration at all but rather a case of discharge of the contract by breach, and the damages against the party in breach may include losses flowing from the event that might otherwise have been regarded as the basis of the frustration of the contract.

In *Monarch Steamship* v. *Karlshamns Oljefabriker* [1949] A.C. 196, Lord Wright and Lord Porter took the view that breach by the owners of the seaworthiness obligation prevented their reliance upon frustration against a claim by the owners of cargo. Donovan, L.J., said in *The Eugenia* [1963] 2 Lloyd's Rep. 381, that it was common ground that the charterers could not rely on the trapping of the ship in the Suez Canal as frustrating the charter if they were in breach of the War Clause in sending her in. In the same case Lord Denning, M.R., said simply: "They were in breach of the War Clause in entering it. They cannot rely on a self-induced frustration . . . ".

However, what would have been a breach of contract preventing reliance upon the doctrine of frustration may not have this effect if it is covered by a suitably worded exceptions clause in the charter. For example, if the chartered ship sinks because of negligent navigation by the owners' servants, the owners will nevertheless be able to plead frustration if the contract protects them from liability arising from this particular cause. In the case on page 337 below, *Constantine* v. *Imperial Smelting*, Lord Wright lent support to this view by saying: "Exceptions, however, may be important . . . as excluding fault if the frustrating event was induced by what, apart from the exception, would be an actionable breach of contract." The view also seems to be in line with general principle. In the leading case of *Jackson* v. *Union Marine* (1874) L.R. 10 C.P. 125, Baron Bramwell said: "Now, what is the effect of the exception of perils of the seas, and of delay being caused thereby? . . . I think this: they excuse the shipowner, but give him no right." See also the judgment of Hobhouse, J., in *The Super Servant Two* [1989] 1 Lloyd's Rep. 148, at page 156.

Deliberate act or election

Moreover, if the event relied upon as being an event frustrating the charter is brought about by the deliberate act or choice of one of the parties, not in itself a breach of contract, he will not be allowed to rely upon the doctrine of frustration in his defence.

The *St. Cuthbert*, a steam trawler, was chartered in 1928 for 12 months with a provision that the charter should thereafter continue from year to year unless terminated by three months' notice on either side. It was expressly agreed that the ship should be used in the fishing industry only. In 1932 it was agreed that the charter should be renewed at a reduced rate of hire, and when this new agreement was entered into it was known to both parties that legislation had been passed prohibiting the use of otter trawls without a licence. The *St. Cuthbert* was fitted with and could only use such a trawl. The charterers operated four other trawlers fitted with otter trawls and applied for licences for the five ships. Only three licences were granted and the charterers did not include the *St. Cuthbert* among the three ships they nominated for them. The charterers contended that the charter was frustrated on the ground that it had become illegal to operate the ship for the only purpose permitted by the charter (in the fishing industry) and that they were therefore relieved from further performance. It was held by the Privy Council that the frustration was "self induced" and that the charterers could not rely on their own election not to nominate the *St. Cuthbert* for a licence in order to excuse themselves from liability under the charter.

Maritime National Fish v. *Ocean Trawlers* (1935) 51 Ll.L.Rep. 299.

Delivering the judgment of the Privy Council, Lord Wright said: "What matters is that they could have got a licence for the *St. Cuthbert* if they had so minded. If the case be figured as one in which the *St. Cuthbert* was removed from the category of privileged trawlers, it was by the appellants' hand that she was so removed, because it was their hand that guided the hand of the Minister in placing the licences where he did and thereby excluding the *St. Cuthbert*. The essence of 'frustration' is that it should not be due to the act or election of the party."

The owners of the self-propelled barge *Super Servant Two* undertook to carry a drilling rig from Japan to Rotterdam. The contract allowed them to use either the *Super Servant Two* or her sister barge the *Super Servant One*. They formed the intention to use the former barge but before the time arrived to start her approach voyage she sank while transporting another rig and became a total loss. As her sister barge was already scheduled for other work they claimed that the loss of the *Super Servant Two* had frustrated the contract. At the trial of certain preliminary issues Hobhouse, J., held that the owners could not rely upon frustration if, as was pleaded against them, the barge had sunk because of negligant supervision of discharging operations by their servants; that doctrine depended upon the occurrence of a "supervening event" and the loss of the barge could not be so described if, as pleaded, it was an event "within the reasonable control of one of the parties". Moreover, the owners could have chosen to carry out the contract with their other barge; it was not the loss of the *Super Servant Two* which prevented their performance but their own decision not to use the *Super Servant One*. Thus the owners' failure was "self-induced".

Hobhouse, J., said: "Where the promisor has alternative modes of performing the contract and one becomes impossible, that does not make it impossible for him to perform the contract. If the impossibility only comes about because the promisor makes some choice or election, then it is that choice or election which causes the alleged impossibility, not any antecedent event."

The Super Servant Two [1989] 1 Lloyd's Rep. 148.

Negligence

The same may also be true if the event relied upon has been caused by a negligent act, not in itself a breach of contract. Hobhouse, J., in *The Super Servant Two*, above, held that the owners of the barge could not rely upon her loss to frustrate a contract of carriage yet to commence where the events surrounding the loss were within their control; a failure to exercise proper skill in such circumstances prevented reliance upon the loss (which could not be considered as a "supervening event") although the failure was not in breach of contract or of any other relevant duty of care.

But in *Constantine* v. *Imperial Smelting*, below, both Lord Wright and Viscount Simon doubted whether mere negligence could amount to "default" and lead to it being held that frustration had been self-induced. Viscount Simon said: " . . . I do not think that the ambit of 'default' as an element disabling the plea of frustration to prevail has as yet been precisely and finally determined. 'Self induced' frustration, as illustrated by the two decided cases . . . involves deliberate choice, and those cases amount to saying that a man cannot ask to be excused by reason of frustration if he has purposely so acted as to bring it about. 'Default' is a much wider term and in many commercial cases dealing with frustration is treated as equivalent to negligence. Yet in cases of frustration of another class, arising in connection with a contract for personal performance, it has not I think been laid down that, if the personal incapacity is due to want of care, the plea fails." ([1942] A.C. 154, at page 166.) Lord Wright added (at page 195) that, "mere negligence seems never to have been suggested as sufficient to constitute 'fault' in this connection". See also *The Evia* (*No. 2*) [1982] 1 Lloyd's Rep. 334. Hobhouse, J., in *The Super Servant Two*, above, referred to these comments and said, at page 156: "I consider that they are not good law if they are taken to suggest that events within the reasonable control of one of the parties can frustrate a contract". Whether they can so easily be rejected remains to be decided by higher courts: see McKendrick [1989] LMCLQ 3.

Burden of proof

The burden of proving that frustration was self induced is upon the party arguing that the doctrine of frustration should not be applied. Thus if the owners establish that *prima facie* the charter is frustrated the burden is on the charterers to prove that this situation was induced by the owners.

The *Kingswood* while under voyage charter suffered a serious explosion in her auxiliary boiler which caused such extensive damage that the time needed for repairs was (as the parties agreed) so great as to frustrate the commercial object of the voyage. The charterers contended, however, that the owners were not excused from liability for failing to load a cargo unless they established that the explosion occurred without their fault. The matter was referred to arbitration and the arbitrator was unable to say, on the evidence, what the cause of the explosion was: he could neither exclude the possibility that negligence of the owners' servants was involved nor the possibility that the explosion occurred without their negligence. The question thus became whether the burden was upon the charterers to prove default on the part of the owners or, alternatively, upon the owners to prove absence of such default. It was held by the House of Lords that the burden of proof lay on the charterers who were alleging that the charter was not frustrated.

Constantine v. *Imperial Smelting* [1942] A.C. 154.

Obligations following frustration

Common law position

At common law frustration immediately brings a contract and the obligations of the parties to it to an end. Rights which existed at the time of frustration continue and those which did not then exist can never arise. Thus contractual payments which are not yet due never have to be made. Conversely, advance payments already due remain due in full, and if already paid may be retained: see, for example, *Lloyd Royal* v. *Stathatos* (1917) 34 T.L.R. 70, where the Court of Appeal rejected the charterers' claim for the return of hire paid in advance; it was said that the charterers could recover only under some provision of the charter and as the charter had been frustrated all its provisions had gone. Since 1943 this rule as to advance payments has been modified to the extent that an advance payment may be refunded if the whole consideration for it has failed (*Fibrosa* v. *Fairbairn* [1943] A.C. 32), but the consideration must have wholly failed and this will often not be the case.

Modification of common law by Frustrated Contracts Act 1943

This situation was modified by the Law Reform (Frustrated Contracts) Act 1943. The Act does not deal with the question whether a contract is or is not frustrated: it deals only with the subsequent position of the parties to a contract which has, on the principles discussed above, been held to have been frustrated. The Act applies to time charters. It does not apply either to voyage charters or to bills of lading, which remain subject to the old common law rules. It is therefore important to decide into which category, time or voyage, a frustrated charter falls.

The charter for the *Eugenia* was on the Baltime form. Its duration was expressed as being, "for a trip out to India via Black Sea from . . . Genoa . . . ". The charterers were to pay hire every month. The trading limits were, "Genoa via Black Sea thence India". Megaw, J., held this to be a time charter, and this the Court of Appeal approved although overruling his judgment that the contract had been frustrated (as to which see page 327 above).

Ocean Tramp Tankers v. *Sovfracht* (*The Eugenia*) [1963] 2 Lloyd's Rep. 155 and 381.

(See also *Temple Steamship* v. *Sovfracht* (1945) 79 Ll.L.Rep. 1, and *The Democritos* [1976] 2 Lloyd's Rep. 149.)

The Act applies only to contracts which are "governed by English law", that is to say contracts whose proper law is English law. Section 1(2) and (3) and Section 2(3) of the Act were considered generally in the case of *B.P. Exploration Co.* v. *Hunt* [1979] 1 W.L.R. 783 and [1981] 1 W.L.R. 232, (C.A.).

The effect of the Act on the rights of the parties to a frustrated time charter may be summarised as follows:

1. Sums paid before the time of frustration are to be repaid and sums payable before that time cease to be payable: but the court is given a discretion to allow such sums to be retained in whole or in part by the party to whom they were paid or payable where he has expended money in or for the performance of the contract. See Section 1(2).

Thus a semi-monthly payment of hire in advance will be repayable upon the frustration of the charter at any time during that half month (see, for an example, *The Eugenia* [1963] 2 Lloyd's Rep. 155, at page 177); but the court could be expected to use its discretion to allow the owners to retain the running costs expended by them in performing the charter during that half month prior to the time of frustration. Additionally or in the alternative, the owners might seek a payment under Section 1(3). See point 3 below as to earlier periodic payments.

2. Where one party receives a valuable benefit, before the time of frustration, from something done by the other party in or for the performance of the contract, then the court is given a discretion to require a suitable payment to be made by him to that other party. In assessing the just sum to be paid (if any) the court must take into account:—(a) any expenses incurred by the benefited party including any sums paid or payable under Section 1(2); and (b) the effect in relation to the benefit, of the circumstances giving rise to frustration. See Section 1(3).

This sub-section gives the court an alternative to its discretion to order retention under Section 1(2), above, where an advance payment of hire has been paid or become payable. Section 1(2) is restricted to incurred expenses (presumably running expenses) whereas Section 1(3) would permit the court to order, in a suitable case, a payment equivalent to the full amount of the hire for the appropriate number of days.

3. Where the court decides that part of the frustrated contract can properly be "severed" from the rest of the contract, for example because that part was wholly performed before the time of frustration, that part shall be treated as if it had not been frustrated at all. See Section 2(4).

Thus when a time charter which provides for monthly payments of hire is frustrated by an event occurring during, say, its seventh month, the court may and presumably will "sever" and therefore leave undisturbed each of the payments of hire made in respect of the previous six months. (No suggestion was raised in *The Eugenia* [1963] 2 Lloyd's Rep. 155, that the Act should be applied to any semi-monthly hire payment earlier than the one made for the period in which the alleged frustration occurred. Also the owners were held entitled to recover the cost of bunkers on board on delivery in accordance with Clause 5 of the Baltime form.)

Exclusion of effects of Frustrated Contracts Act

Section 2(3) of the Act provides that: "Where any contract to which this Act applies contains any provision which, upon the true construction of the contract, is intended to have effect in the event of circumstances arising which operate, or would but for the said provision operate, to frustrate the contract, or is intended to have effect whether such circumstances arise or not, the court shall give effect to the said provision and shall only give effect to the foregoing section of this Act to such extent, if any, as appears to the court to be consistent with the said provision."

It is suggested that the stipulations in Lines 102 and 103 of the New York Produce form and Lines 119 to 122 of the Baltime form as to the manner in which hire is to be dealt with if the ship is lost are stipulations to which Section 2(3) of the Act applies.

Charterers' property

When a time charter has been frustrated the charterers are entitled to bunkers and other stores then on board for which they have paid in accordance with the charter. Megaw, J., said in *The Eugenia* [1963] 2 Lloyd's Rep. 155, at page 177: "These stores were, in the circumstances, the property of the charterers, since they had paid, or have to pay, for them, and they are no longer liable to be used by the owners for the charterers' purposes." (The charterers were held liable to pay, however, the price of bunkers, galley fuel and water which were on board at the time of delivery, in accordance with Baltime Clause 5; see point 3 above.)

American Law

Money paid in advance and not earned

The mutual exceptions clause is preceded by the following language:—

That should the Vessel be lost, money paid in advance and not earned (reckoning from the date of loss or being last heard of) shall be returned to the Charterers at once.

The quoted language should, as a matter of draftsmanship, appear in a clause separate and apart from the mutual exceptions language that follows it, since the latter provision has no application to it. The charterer's right to a refund of prepaid hire in the event the vessel is lost, or in the event the vessel goes off-hire under Clause 15, is an independent right, just as the owner's duty to make repayment is an independent duty, performance of which is not in the usual case rendered impossible by any of the mutually excepted perils. See *Clyde Commercial S.S. Co.* v. *West India S.S. Co.*, 169 F. 275 (2d Cir. 1909), *cert.* denied 214 U.S. 523 (1909), where the court found that the charterer was obligated to pay hire despite a delay caused by restraint of princes.

Frustration of charter

Under American law, either the owner or charterer may be relieved of his obligations under a charter if an unforeseen occurrence renders performance of the charter impossible or "commercially impracticable". There are strict criteria, however, which must be met in order for the doctrine of frustration to apply.

The leading American case on frustration of charters is *Transatlantic Financing Corp.* v. *United States*, 363 F.2d 312, 1966 AMC 1717 (D.C. Cir. 1966). There, the chartered owner of the *Christos* sought to recover from the voyage charterer additional costs incurred in transporting cargo from the United States to Iran as a result of the closing of the Suez Canal. The owner contended that the charter provided that the voyage was to be performed by the "usual and customary" route from Texas to Iran via the Suez Canal, and that the closing of Suez rendered performance of the charter impossible. The owner did deliver the cargo by going around the Cape of Good Hope and sought to recover the additional costs incurred in doing so.

In considering the owner's claim of impossibility, the court stated the factors which must be considered in determining whether a frustration has occurred in the following manner:—

The doctrine ultimately represents the ever-shifting line, drawn by courts hopefully responsive to commercial practices and mores, at which the community's interest in having contracts enforced according to their terms is outweighed by the commercial senselessness of requiring performance. When the issued is raised, the court is asked to construct a condition of performance, based on the changed circumstances, a process which involves at least three reasonably definable steps. First, a contingency—something unexpected—must have occurred. Second, the risk of the unexpected occurrence must not have been allocated either by agreement or by custom. Finally, occurrence of the contingency must have rendered performance commercially impracticable. Unless the court finds these three requirements satisfied, the plea of impossibility must fail. (363 F.2d at 315–316.)

After reviewing the facts of the case in the context of these three criteria, the court concluded that the first two requirements were in fact met. The closing of the Suez Canal was found to have been unexpected, and the risk of this contingency had not been allocated between the parties. The court went on to conclude, however, that while the closing of the Suez Canal increased the cost of completing the voyage, the additional cost was not so extreme as to have made performance of the charter commercially impracticable and, consequently, there was no frustration.

Event must be unforeseen

The first of the requisite elements of a claim of frustration is that the event giving rise to it must be unexpected. As the Court of Appeals for the Second Circuit held: "Discharge under this doctrine has been limited to instances where a virtually cataclysmic, wholly unforeseeable event renders the contract valueless to one party." *United States* v. *Gen. Douglas MacArthur Sr. Vil. Inc.*, 508 F.2d 377, 381 (2d Cir. 1974). See also *United States* v. *Buffalo Coal Mining Co.*, 345 F.2d 517, 518 (9th Cir. 1965), where the court held that:

> . . . [T]he parties should be bound unless their contractual purpose was frustrated by a completely unforeseeable cause. And the test of foreseeability should be an objective one, not a subjective inquiry into the state of mind of the parties.

The concept of foreseeability is illlustrated by *The Poznan*, 276 F. 418, 425 (S.D.N.Y. 1921). An action was commenced against the vessel owner for breach of a contract to deliver cargo at Havana. He defended on the ground that for a period of six weeks in October and November while the vessel lay at anchor at Havana, there was no berth or lightering vessel available due to port congestion, and that the contract was frustrated by impossibility of performance. The court rejected the defense, finding that when the charter was entered into in September it was known that the port was congested. Thus, according to the court, the delays encountered in October and November could not be deemed to have been unforeseeable:

> The case is clearly not one of frustration . . . It is perhaps needless to repeat that these are but instances of the general rule that subsequent events, making the performance of a contract impossible, may be so unforeseen and so completely disapppoint the expectation of the parties as to absolve the promisor from performance . . . Yet any promisor recognizes that his performance is subject to some risks, which may prevent fulfillment, and such risks he must be understood as accepting when he makes the promise . . . To excuse performance altogether and leave the promisee without remedy for his loss, courts have always found it necessary, though with various degrees of strictness, that the intervening event which prevents performance shall be so improbable as to be outside any contingency, which, had the parties been faced with it, they would have agreed that the promisor should undertake . . . *Prima facie* he is bound, however impossible it may be for him to perform . . . (276 F. at 425).

In *The Kronprinzessin Cecilie*, 244 U.S. 12, 22 (1917), the U.S. Supreme Court held that the owner of a German vessel bound for England with a cargo of gold was entitled to turn back to New York when war broke out between Germany and England. The court held that performance of the contract was excused because "it cannot be believed that the contractee would have demanded or the contractor would have assumed" the risk of capture created by the outbreak of the war.

However, in *Mádeirense Do Brasil S/A* v. *Stulman-Emrick Lumber Co.*, 147 F.2d 399 (2d Cir. 1945), by an agreement entered into in October 1940, a seller of lumber was obligated to contract with an ocean carrier for the transportation of the lumber from Brazil for delivery to the buyer at New York. The seller defended against the buyer's claim for non-performance on the ground that a shortage of ships made it impossible to carry out the contract. The court rejected this defense, stating:

> [Seller] further seeks to excuse its failure to perform by claiming that it could not deliver the goods as required, because no ships were available. Although this claim is not disputed by [buyer], the factual issue need not be decided, for even had there been no ships available, [seller] was not, under the circumstances of this case, excused from performance. For [seller's] letters indicate clearly that at the time of the making of the second contract it was aware of the fact that boats were at a premium. Indeed, it pressed for the second contract largely because it expected that additional shipment to facilitate its procuring a ship. There was no startling change in conditions. The war in Europe had been underway for more than a year, and Pearl Harbor was still in the future. Further, neither the United States nor any of the South American countries entered the war for a year or more after making the contract. Hence, the lack of ships in January 1941, was a foreseeable risk which [seller] took upon itself; and it cannot under such circumstances plead the defense of force majeure . . . (147 F.2d at 403).

Glidden Co. v. *Hellenic Lines Ltd.*, 275 F.2d 253 (2d Cir. 1960), presents a final example of the "foreseeability" test. The case arose out of the closing of the Suez Canal, which the owner claimed frustrated a chartered voyage from India to the U.S. Because the charter gave the owner an option to sail via Suez, the Cape of Good Hope, or the Panama Canal, the court concluded that the parties had contemplated the possibility that the voyage might have to be performed by a route other than through the Suez Canal, and that the voyage was not frustrated.

Allocation of risk

The second requirement for frustration is that there be no allocation of the risk as between the owner or the charterer, either by the express language of the charter or by custom. This principle is closely linked to the foreseeability element of the defense, since if there is a contractual allocation of the risk, it obviously cannot be said to be "unexpected".

Performance commercially impracticable

The greatest difficulty in frustration cases inevitably arises from the requirement that performance must have been rendered impossible, or, as the court stated in *Transatlantic*, "commercially impracticable". In *Cameron-Hawn Realty Co.* v. *City of Albany*, 207 N.Y. 377, 381, 101 N.E. 162, 163 (1913), in what is recognized as a classic statement of the law of impossibility, the court stated:

> It is a well-settled rule of law that a party must fulfill his contractual obligations . . . (If) what is agreed to be done is possible and lawful, the obligation of performance must be met. Difficulty or improbability of accomplishing the stipulated undertaking will not avail the obligator. It must be shown that the thing cannot by any means be effected. Nothing short of this will excuse non-performance.

While the "commercially impracticable" standard is less stringent than that of impossiblity, it nonetheless places a very heavy burden of proof on the party claiming a frustration. Thus, performance of a charter will not be deemed "commercially impracticable" because it has become more difficult or more expensive. In *American Trading & Production Corp.* v. *Shell International Marine Ltd.*, 453 F.2d 939 (2d Cir. 1972), a vessel on a voyage from Texas to India was in the mid-Atlantic Ocean when the Suez Canal was closed at the outbreak of war in the Middle East. The owner sent the vessel around the Cape of Good Hope to complete the voyage, and commenced an action against the charterer for the extra expenses incurred, on the theory that the chartered voyage was frustrated, and that the shipment was delivered on a *quantum meruit* basis. The court adopted the three tests set down in *Transatlantic*, and found that the first two were satisfied. The court went on to conclude, however, that the chartered voyage was not made commercially impracticable by the closing of the Suez Canal. While the added cost of the voyage around the Cape was about 33 per cent. of the original freight, the court held that to justify a claim of frustration, the extra cost must be "extreme and unreasonable", and that the costs incurred by the owner did not meet this test.

A similar result was reached in *The Paros*, S.M.A. No. 1025 (Arb. at N.Y. 1976), where the charterer was held to have wrongfully cancelled the charter in anticipation of long delays at the loading port. In rejecting the defense of frustration, the panel stated:

> We do not consider an anticipated loading delay of three months to create an "excessive and unreasonable" cost. Knowledgeable owners and charterers recognize that this is an unhappy but not unusual occurrence in many areas of the world.

The Mermaid I, S.M.A. No. 1836 (Arb. at N.Y. 1983), concerned a voyage charter but provides a useful analogy. The case involved a vessel which was involved in a collision immediately after she had been accepted by the charterer. The collision occurred while the ship was waiting at an anchorage for a loading berth to become available. The panel unanimously ruled that such a collision was not an "unexpected contingency", and thus the first element necessary to establish frustration had not been met. The second criteria was also held not to have been met in that "the risk of delay that occurred was allocated in the contract by the terms and conditions governing the running of laytime". Furthermore, the panel held that the third element was not proven "because charterer did have cargo to load in numerous other vessels which should have been provided to 'Mermaid I' despite some extra cost or inconvenience the adjusted schedules might have caused the charterer".

Default of third parties preventing performance

An issue that has arisen with some frequency, particularly under voyage charters, is whether the charterer can be excused from performance of the charter because of contractual difficulties with either the shipper or the receiver. The general rule appears to be that problems extrinsic to the charter will not excuse performance. For example, in *Krulewitch* v. *National Importing & Trading Co. Inc.*, 186 N.Y.S. 838 (App. Div. 1921), National contracted to sell Krulewitch a shipment of Tapioca flour. The contract provided that the goods would be shipped "from Java Feb/Mch". Because of an embargo on shipments to New York imposed by the governmental authorities of Java that resulted in a suspension of direct transportation to New York, National claimed it was excused from performance. The court rejected this defense, finding that, notwithstanding the embargo, the goods could have been shipped to New York via intermediary ports, albeit at greater expense. Moreover, the court held that National's difficulties in arranging transportation for the cargo could not excuse performance of its contract with Krulewitch:

> The availability of transportation facilities was a matter extrinsic to the contract; it did not concern the plaintiff; he agreed to pay for the goods at the dock in New York, how they were to be brought there was no part of his concern . . . (186 N.Y.S. at 840).

In *Bardons & Oliver Inc.* v. *Amtorg Trading Corp.*, 123 N.Y.S. 2d 633 (Sup. Ct. 1948), aff'd without opinion 275 App. Div. 748, 88 N.Y.S. 2d 272 (1st Dep't 1949), aff'd 301 N.Y. 622, 93 N.E. 2d 915 (1950), A agreed to sell certain machines to B, who intended to export them from the United States to the Soviet Union. When B was unable to obtain an export license from the United States Government, it contended that its contract with A was frustrated. In rejecting B's defense, the court stated:

> The agreement does not mention that its validity or performance shall be dependent upon defendant procuring an export license. It definitely sets forth the obligations of the parties under it and is clear and unambiguous. Neither party assumed any obligation in this contract with respect to the shipment out of the country. Under the contract in concern, delivery was to be "F.O.B. cars, Cleveland, Ohio . . . ". Thus all that the seller undertook to do was to place the goods on board railroad cars in his country suitably marked and with bills of lading properly executed. Transshipment was a matter which concerned defendant alone. Certainly if defendant wished to make performance dependent upon its obtaining an export license, it could readily have made this a condition and inserted such a provision in the contract. It did not do so and this claim cannot, in my opinion, now be successfully advanced . . . (123 N.Y.S. 2d at 634).

The Erisort, S.M.A. No. 1022 (Arb. at N.Y. 1976), also illustrates this point. There the voyage charterer was held liable for its failure to provide a cargo of scrap as required by the charter. The panel rejected the charterer's alternative defenses that it was unable to perform because it had not received an export permit for the cargo from the Government of Guatemala, and because the supplier had failed to perform its contract with the charterer. Similarly, in *Econolines Inc. and Mohammed Al-Haddad, et al.*, 1980 AMC 424 (Arb. at N.Y. 1979), where the buyers of certain asphalt cargoes repudiated the purchase contract, charterer's claim of frustration of charter was denied.

For a contrary view, see *Tradax International S.A.* v. *Government of Pakistan*, 1973 AMC 1609 (Arb. at N.Y. 1973).

Effect of fault

The frustrating event must not have been brought about by one of the parties to the contract. In *Gemini Shipping* v. *Seas Shipping*, S.M.A. No. 1253 (Arb. at N.Y. 1978), it was held that the charterer could not invoke *force majeure* or frustration defenses when the Government of Thailand refused to permit the export of zinc ore contemplated by the shipping contract because the charterer contributed to the suspension of exports by failing to comply with its concession agreement to construct a zinc smelter in Thailand.

Changes in law

There are a number of cases in which frustration has been claimed because of subsequent changes in the law that affected performance of the charter. In this regard, it is most important to distinguish between changes in American law governing performance of the contract from similar changes in foreign law. The reason for this is that while prohibitions imposed by domestic law will excuse performance on grounds of frustration, the rule is the reverse where foreign law is involved. Thus, the general rule under American law is that impossibility due to foreign law does not excuse non-performance of contractual obligations. *J. Zeevi & Sons Ltd.* v. *Grindlays Bank (Uganda) Ltd.*, 37 N.Y. 2d 220, 371 N.Y.S. 2d 892 (1975), *cert.* denied 423 U.S. 806; *Central Hanover Bank & Trust Co.* v. *Siemens & Halske Akt.*, 15 F.Supp. 927 (S.D.N.Y. 1936), aff'd on opinion below 84 F.2d 993 (2d Cir. 1936); *Gonzalez* v. *Industrial Bank*, 12 N.Y. 2d 33, 234 N.Y.S. 2d 210 (1962).

The point is illustrated by *Tweedie Trading Co.* v. *James P. McDonald Co.*, 114 F. 985 (S.D.N.Y. 1902). Tweedie and McDonald entered into a contract by which Tweedie agreed to make four trips with its steamer to transport laborers from Barbados to Colon. After the second trip, the colonial government of Barbados promulgated a decree forbidding the future embarkation of any laborers, and consequently, McDonald was unable to provide any workers for the third and fourth voyages. Tweedie commenced an action for freights lost on the last two voyages, and the court held in its favor. According to the court:

The contract was valid in its inception, both at the place of making and the place of performance, and was capable of being performed until an event intervened which was not in the contemplation of the parties when the contract was made. It seems to be settled that an impossibility of performance, arising from natural causes, in a case of this kind, cannot be recognized as a defense, but that one arising from a governmental act which would render performance illegal would be an excuse. It is contended here by the Tweedie Company, however, that the excuse cannot prevail, because, though performance was prevented by the law, such law, being foreign, was merely a fact, and the case should for that reason fall within the general rule. On the other hand, it is urged by the McDonald Company that the law of the place of performance governed the contract, and, as such law made fulfillment impossible, the contract was dissolved. The question really is, do the legal acts of the agents of a foreign government, which prevent the full performance of a contract of this character, control the rights of the parties? Contracting parties are subject to the contingencies of changes in their own law, and liable to have the execution of their contracts prevented thereby; but it is on the ground of illegality, not of impossibility. Prevention by the law of a foreign country is not usually deemed an excuse, when the act which was contemplated by the contract was valid in view of the law of the place where it was made, . . . and *a fortiori* when it was also then valid at the place of performance. It was intended that this contract should be performed. The law of the place of performance, in the absence of evidence of a contrary intention, ordinarily governs the incidents of a performance . . . .

See also *Krulewitch* v. *National Importing & Trading Co. Inc.*, above, where the court held that a foreign embargo furnished no excuse for the failure to perform a contract; *P. N. Gray & Co.* v. *Cavalliotis*, 276 F. 565 (E.D.N.Y. 1921), aff'd without opinion 293 F. 1018 (2d Cir. 1923), holding that "foreign embargoes are ordinarily not an excuse for nonperformance"; *Richards & Co.* v. *Wreschner*, 156 N.Y.S. 1054, 1057 (Sup. Ct. 1915), holding "it is well settled that impossibility due to a foreign war is no excuse"; *Glynn* v. *United Steel Works Corp.*, 160 Misc. 405, 289 N.Y.S. 1037 (Sup. Ct. 1935), holding that a German moratorium could not prohibit payment of German notes payable in New York; *Sokoloff* v. *National City Bank*, 139 N.Y. 158, 145 N.E. 917 (1924), holding that a Russian decree confiscating accounts in a New York bank's Petrograd branch did not excuse the bank's obligation to repay the plaintiff's deposit.

There are cases, however, in which the parties have been excused from their obligations under the charter because the act of a foreign state has made performance impossible. *Texas Co.* v. *Hogarth Shipping Co.*, 256 U.S. 619 (1921), is a leading case. There, a British vessel on voyage charter was requisitioned by the British Government for war service. The Supreme Court held that this act of state excused the owner from performing:

Here the ship, although still in existence and entirely seaworthy, was rendered unavailable for the performance of the charterparty by the requisition . . . In other words, compliance with the charterparty was made impossible by an act of state, the charterer was prevented from having the service of the ship and the owner from earning the stipulated freight . . . These, we think, must be regarded as entered into on an implied condition that, if before the time for the voyage the ship was rendered unavailable by such a supervening act as the requisition, the contract should be at an end and the parties absolved from liability under it. (256 U.S. at 629–31.)

Embargo

Notwithstanding the general rule that the acts of foreign governments ordinarily do not provide grounds for finding a frustration, commercial arbitrators have in some cases held that an embargo imposed by a foreign government does excuse non-performance. In *The Caliopi Carras*, S.M.A. No. 1111 (Arb. at N.Y. 1977), the panel found the contract frustrated when the Libyan oil embargo precluded shipments to the United States, as had been contracted for. Similarly, in *The Gota River*, S.M.A. No. 1241 (Arb. at N.Y. 1978), the seizure of the charterer's crude supply by the Ecuadorian Government was held to frustrate a contract for shipment from Ecuador.

However, if the embargo or other government interference does not make performance impossible or commercially impracticable, there will be no finding of frustration. For example, in *The Corona*, S.M.A. No. 961 (Arb. at N.Y. 1975), the Arab oil embargo prevented shipment to the Netherlands, but charterer had a wide range of discharge port options and frustration was denied. Similarly, in *Retla Steamship* v. *Canpotex*, 1977 AMC 1594 (Arb. at N.Y. 1977), the charterer alleged that it could not discharge phosphate at Singapore because of severe congestion in shore facilities following a collapse of the market for phosphate in Southeast Asia and the refusal of the Indonesian Government to allow imports of fertilizer. It was held that these conditions did not make discharge at the agreed transhipment port of Singapore so difficult as to amount to frustration.

The same result obtained in *The Tore Knudsen*, S.M.A. No. 1108 (Arb. at N.Y. 1977), where the Turkish government banned the export of petroleum products, but charterer had the option to load at other ports, and in *The Thomas A & Thomas Q*, 1979 AMC 202 (Arb. at N.Y. 1978), where a Libyan embargo did not affect the charterer's option to load at other North African ports.

See also *The Golden Gate*, S.M.A. No. 2188 (Arb. at N.Y. 1986), where the panel declined to hold that the charter was frustrated by the closing of trade waters between Costa Rica and Guatemala since charterer had the option of trading in other locales.

Effect of total loss—substitution clause

In an English decision, *Niarchos (London) Ltd.* v. *Shell Tankers Ltd.* [1961] 2 Lloyd's Rep. 496, it was held that the loss of a vessel terminated the charter and therefore extinguished owner's option to substitute. The decision was followed in a New York arbitration, *The Mary Ellen Conway*, 1973 AMC 772 (Arb. at N.Y. 1973). However, a subsequent New York arbitration panel, in *The Giovanna Lolli-ghetti*, 1974 AMC 2161 (Arb. at N.Y. 1974), declined to follow the reasoning of the *Niarchos* case. There, the vessel was lost before delivery to the time charterer. The charterer refused to accept a substitute nominated by the owner, and the owner claimed an anticipatory breach of the charter. A majority of the panel accepted the owner's argument that "if options are enforceable only if mandatory, they are no longer options", and held that the time charter was not frustrated by the loss and that the owner was entitled to exercise its privilege to substitute.

Similarly, in *The Grand Zenith*, 1979 AMC 2179 (Arb. at N.Y. 1979), even though the vessel was lost during the charter period, the arbitrators held that the owner retained an option under the charter to substitute another vessel. Since the owner wished to exercise the option, the loss of the named ship did not constitute a frustration of the charter. The panel's award concerning damages issues in *The Grand Zenith* is reported at S.M.A. No. 2186 (Arb. at N.Y. 1986).

Constructive total loss

In *Asphalt Intl.* v. *Enterprise*, 514 F.Supp. 1111 (S.D.N.Y. 1981), aff'd 667 F.2d 261 (2d Cir. 1982), the court considered the issue of whether damage to a vessel exceeding her repaired value frustrated the charter. The vessel was operating under a long term time charter when she was damaged in a collision. Prior to the collision the vessel had a fair market value of $750,000, and the estimated repair costs were a minimum of $1,500,000. Since her insured value was some $2,500,000 she was not a constructive total loss for insurance purposes. The owner concluded, however, that the vessel was not worth repairing and scrapped her. Charterer then sued for breach of charter, contending that the owner had a duty to repair the vessel or, alternatively, provide a substitute vessel. The court held that repair costs well in excess of the vessel's sound market value represented an excessive and unreasonable burden on the owner not contemplated by the charter, and that performance was excused on the grounds of "commercial impracticability". The court also held that the owner was under no duty to provide a substitute vessel.

Exceptions

[Clause 16 continued]

"103. . . . The act of God, enemies, fire, restraint of Princes, Rulers and People, and all dangers and accidents of the Seas,

104. Rivers, Machinery, Boilers and Steam Navigation, and errors of Navigation throughout this Charter Party, always mutually excepted."

General

These Lines constitute the main exceptions clause in the New York Produce form. The protection they afford is, however, quite restricted. In particular they do not include an exception of negligence. The owners are given wider protection by the United States Carriage of Goods by Sea Act, incorporated into the charter by Clause 24. Such protection as is given by these Lines is extended to the charterers as well as to the owners.

Not restricted to loss of ship

Lines 103 and 104 are of general application and are not restricted in their application to the loss of the ship by their proximity to the first sentence of Clause 16. Mocatta, J., rejected an argument that they were so restricted in *The Oliva* [1972] 1 Lloyd's Rep. 458.

United States Carriage of Goods by Sea Act

If Clause 24 is unamended so that the United States Carriage of Goods by Sea Act is incorporated into the charter, the exceptions in Clause 16 are relevant only insofar as (a) the relevant liability does not arise in relation to the "loading, handling, stowage, carriage, custody, care, and discharge of" the goods nor in relation to other contractual activities performed by the owners under the charter (see page 430 below), or (b) they extend the exceptions listed to the charterers as well as to the owners. In almost all cases the exceptions under Section 4(2) of the United State Carriage of Goods by Sea Act, where they are applicable, are more extensive than those under Clause 16. Furthermore Section 4(2)(*a*) provides an exception in respect of neglect or default in the navigation or in the management of the ship, whereas Clause 16 contains no such exception of negligence but only an exception against errors of navigation, which has been held not to exclude negligent navigation: see below.

It follows that where, as is sometimes the case, the Clause Paramount and thus the United States Carriage of Goods by Sea Act are deleted from Clause 24, the exceptions remaining are very limited. On the other hand, the voyage by voyage obligation of due diligence to make the ship seaworthy, described at page 428 below, will not arise.

Act of God

Cockburn, L.J. said in *Nugent* v. *Smith* (1876) 1 C.P.D. 423, at page 437: "all that can be required of the carrier is that he shall do all that is reasonably and practically possible to insure the safety of the goods. If he uses all the known means to which prudent and experienced carriers ordinarily have recourse, he does all that can be reasonably required of him; and if, under such circumstances, he is overpowered by storm or other natural agency, he is within the rule which gives immunity from the effects of such *vis major* as the act of God."

Apart from extraordinary conditions of wind or sea, lightning or frost (*Siordet* v. *Hall* (1828) 4 Bing. 607) may amount to "act of God". This exception also appears in the United States Act, Section 4(2)(*d*).

Enemies

This probably covers the actions of enemies of the state whose flag the ship flies and of enemies of the states in which the charterers or owners, if companies, are registered. It certainly includes enemies of those states of which the parties, if individuals, are nationals: *Russell* v. *Niemann* (1864) 34 L.J.C.P. 10.

Section 4(2)(*f*) of the United States Act contains the exception "Act of public enemies".

The exception will afford no protection if what occurs is caused by negligence.

Fire

Again this exception can only be relied upon if the fire is not caused by negligence.

While under time charter the *Thrasyvoulos* was carrying a quantity of spirit. During unloading, a plank was dropped into the hold as a result of negligence on the part of the charterers' stevedores; this caused a spark from which a fire followed and the ship was destroyed. The time charter provided: "loss or damage from fire . . . always mutually excepted." It was held by the Court of Appeal that the charterers could not rely on the exception: the fire was caused by their servants' negligence and in the absence of clear words the exception did not cover negligence.

Polemis v. *Furness Withy* (1921) 8 Ll.L.Rep. 263 and 351.

If Clause 24 of the New York Produce form is unamended so that the United States Act is incorporated, the exception in respect of fire will be widened by virtue of Section 4(2)(*b*) to "Fire, unless caused by the actual fault or privity of the carrier." But the protection under Section 4(2)(*b*) will be lost if the owners have failed to exercise due diligence to make the ship seaworthy before and at the beginning of the voyage and the unseaworthiness causes the fire: *Maxine Footwear* v. *Canadian Government* [1959] 2 Lloyd's Rep. 105.

Where the ship is a British ship, the owners and charterers will also have the protection of Section 502 of the Merchant Shipping Act 1894, as amended by the Merchant Shipping (Liability of Shipowners and Others) Act 1958. This provides that the owner or charterer of a British ship:

" . . . shall not be liable to make good to any extent whatever any loss or damage happening without his actual fault or privity in the following cases; namely,—(i) Where any goods, merchandise, or other things whatsoever taken in or put on board his ship are lost or damaged by reason of fire on board the ship . . . "

This statutory protection will not be lost by unseaworthiness, even if unseaworthiness caused the fire, provided there is not fault or privity on the part of the owners or charterers, as the case may be.

Damage "by reason of fire" in Section 502(*i*) includes damage by smoke and damage from water used to extinguish the fire: *The Diamond* [1906] P. 282. "Fire" does not include heating unless there has been actual combustion: *Tempus Shipping* v. *Dreyfus* [1930] 1 K.B. 699.

Restraint of Princes, Rulers and People

These words cover forcible interference by a government or state preventing or impeding the performance of the charter, such as the imposition of restrictions on trade, action taken pursuant to Customs or quarantine regulations, action to protect the government's own proprietary interests in the cargo or action taken for political reasons.

The words will also cover a *risk* of forcible interference when the restraint is actually in being and will affect the performance of the charter if an alternative course of action is not adopted. The test is whether a reasonable man would consider performance likely to be affected by the restraint. See *Watts* v. *Mitsui* [1917] A.C. 227; *Phosphate Mining* v. *Rankin* (1915) 21 Com. Cas. 248; and *Nobel's Explosives* v. *Jenkins* [1896] 2 Q.B. 326.

Actual physical force is not a necessary ingredient. In *Rickards* v. *Forestal* [1942] A.C. 50 Lord Wright said, at page 81: "there may be a restraint, though the physical force of the state concerned is not immediately present. It is enough, I think, that there is an order of the state, addressed to a subject of that state, acting with compelling force on him, decisively exacting his obedience and requiring him to do the act which effectively restrains the goods." (See also *Miller* v. *Law Accident Insurance* [1903] 1 K.B. 712 and *The Bamburi* [1982] 1 Lloyd's Rep. 312.)

Nor does the fact that the ship is outside the jurisdiction of the state exercising the restraint prevent reliance on the exception, if the owner (and probably also the charterers as operators of the ship) are within the state and subject to its jurisdiction.

The Swedish owners of the *Zamora* chartered her to British charterers for a period of six months in 1916, the trading limits including "United Kingdom, Continent (Dunkirk, Sicily limits)". The ship carried out one voyage from the U.K. to Italy but the owners refused to allow the charterers to send her on a second voyage. The charter include an exception against restraint of princes and the owners maintained that, under Swedish Emergency Regulations, they were not permitted to trade the ship outside Swedish waters. Bailhache, J., held that although the ship was not within the jurisdiction of the Swedish courts, the owners themselves were and that they were protected by the exception.

Furness, Withy v. *Banco* [1917] 2 K.B. 873.

But the exception will not apply:

(a) to actions by any body of persons who do not constitute the ruling power, or the executive of the ruling power, of the country: *Nesbitt* v. *Lushington* (1792) 4 T.R. 783. Thus it would not apply to actions of rebels or guerrillas:

(b) to arrest or detention under ordinary judicial process: *Finlay* v. *Liverpool* (1870) 23 L.T. 251. In *The Anita* [1970] 2 Lloyd's Rep. 365, Mocatta, J., held that where a ship was confiscated by state officials the interposing of a decision by an extraordinary military tribunal did not prevent the confiscation being a restraint of people (the judge was reversed on other grounds at [1971] 1 Lloyd's Rep. 487). Under Section 4(2)(*g*) of the United States Act, however, the exception of restraint of princes, rulers, or people, is expressly extended to include "seizure under legal process":

(c) to a restraint arising from a state of affairs which existed at the time the charter was entered into, where the law applicable was known to the party seeking to rely on the exception: see *Ciampa* v. *British India* [1915] 2 K.B. 774 (fumigation under decree of ship from plague port); *Induna* v. *British Phosphate Commissioners* (1949) 82 Ll.L.Rep. 430 (ban on night working unknown to both parties to charter); and *Reardon Smith* v. *Ministry of Agriculture* [1959] 2 Lloyd's Rep. 229, [1961] 1 Lloyd's Rep. 385 (strikes).

(d) to a restraint resulting from negligence.

Section 4(2)(*g*) of the United States Act gives the wider exception of "Arrest or restraint of princes, rulers, or people, or seizure under legal process".

Dangers and accidents of the Seas, Rivers

This covers perils peculiar to seas or rivers or to the navigation of a ship at sea or in rivers which cannot be avoided by the exercise of reasonable care. Thus damage cause by an exceptionally severe gale is within the exception where there has been no negligence. But the entry of seawater may be within the exception although the weather is not severe. Thus the exception covers its entry following the striking, without negligence, of an iceberg or a sunken rock or another ship being negligently navigated or as a result of rats gnawing through a lead pipe: *The Xantho* (1887) 12 App. Cas. 503, and *Hamilton, Fraser* v. *Pandorf* (1887) 12 App. Cas. 518.

The exception also covers damage resulting from action necessarily and reasonably taken to counter dangers and accidents of the seas or rivers, such as the closing of ventilators to prevent the entry of seawater during a storm: *Canada Rice Mills* v. *Union Marine* [1941] A.C. 55.

But the exception relates to dangers and accidents of the seas rather than on the seas, so fire or lighting, for example, are not within it: see *Hamilton, Fraser* v. *Pandorf*, above. In *Canada Rice Mills* v. *Union Marine*, above, Lord Wright said: "Rain is not a peril of the sea, but at most a peril on the sea."

Section 4(2)(*c*) of the United States Act excludes "Perils, dangers, and accidents of the sea or other navigable waters".

Machinery, Boilers and Steam Navigation

Lord Coleridge, C.J., said in *Mercantile Steamship* v. *Tyser* (1881) 7 Q.B.D. 73, of "risks of steam navigation": "These risks, I think, must mean physical risks . . . incident to vessels propelled by steam machinery. The breakdown of an engine, the disabling of a screw, and things of that kind . . . though they happened in calm water and fair weather . . . "

The exception will, however, afford no protection if what occurs is caused by negligence.

Errors of Navigation

The effect of this exception is limited by the rule of construction that words of exception do not cover negligence unless they show a clear intention to do so. As there may be errors of navigation which do not amount to negligence, the words afford no protection against negligent navigation: see *The Satya Kailash* [1984] 1 Lloyd's Rep. 588, in which the Court of Appeal affirmed the decision of Staughton, J., on this point ([1982] 2 Lloyd's Rep. 465) and approved the decision of Bingham, J., to the same effect in *The Emmanuel C* [1983] 1 Lloyd's Rep. 310.

As to the wider protection given by Section 4(2)(*a*) of the United States Act, see below where the text of that provision is set out.

Always mutually excepted

These words make the exceptions available to the charterers as well as the owners. And if an exception, such as fire, is not apt to protect the owners from liability in the event of negligence, then since the exceptions are mutual it will not protect the charterers in the event of their negligence or that of their servants: see *Polemis* v. *Furness Withy* (1921) 8 Ll.L.Rep. 263 and 351, cited above under "Fire", and *Fagan* v. *Green* [1926] 1 K.B. 102, at page 108.

Exceptions under the United States Carriage of Goods by Sea Act

Section 4(2)

The full list of exceptions provided by Section 4(2) of the United States Carriage of Goods by Sea Act and incorporated into the charter by Clause 24 (as to which see pages 424 to 432 below) is as follows:

(a) Act, neglect, or default of the master, mariner, pilot, or the servants of the carrier in the navigation or in the management of the ship;
(b) Fire, unless caused by the actual fault or privity of the carrier; [see above]
(c) Perils, dangers, and accidents of the sea or other navigable waters; [see above]
(d) Act of God; [see above]
(e) Act of war;
(f) Act of public enemies; [see above]
(g) Arrest or restraint of princes, rulers, or people, or seizure under legal process; [see above]
(h) Quarantine restrictions;
(i) Act or omission of the shipper or owner of the goods, his agent or representative;
(j) Strikes or lockouts or stoppage or restraint of labor from whatever cause, whether partial or general: *Provided*, That nothing herein contained shall be construed to relieve a carrier from responsibility for the carrier's own acts;
(k) Riots and civil commotions;
(l) Saving or attempting to save life or property at sea;
(m) Wastage in bulk or weight or any other loss or damage arising from inherent defect, quality, or vice of the goods;
(n) Insufficiency of packing;
(o) Insufficiency or inadequacy of marks;

(p) Latent defects not discoverable by due diligence; and
(q) Any other cause arising without the actual fault and privity of the carrier and without the fault or neglect of the agents or servants of the carrier, but the burden of proof shall be on the person claiming the benefit of this exception to show that neither the actual fault or privity of the carrier nor the fault or neglect of the agents or servants of the carrier contributed to the loss or damage.

Section 4(3)

Section 4(3) of the United States Carriage of Goods by Sea Act provides as follows: "The shipper shall not be responsible for loss or damage sustained by the carrier or the ship arising or resulting from any cause without the act, fault, or neglect of the shipper, his agents, or his servants."

An attempt by charterers to use this provision as a defence to a claim by owners under the implied indemnity arising from Clause 8 of the New York Produce form (see page 237 above) was rejected by Mustill, J., in *The Athanasia Comninos* [1981] COM LR 132 (see page 240 above and page 431 below). Mustill, J., cast doubt on whether this provision had any meaning at all in the context of a time charter.

Charter exceptions and the first sentence in Lines 102 and 103

The exceptions contained in the second sentence of Clause 16 in Lines 103 to 104 do not operate to prevent the repayment of hire in the circumstances set out in the first sentence in Lines 102 and 103. An argument to this effect was rejected by Mocatta, J., in *The Oliva* [1972] 1 Lloyd's Rep. 458, who said at page 462 that the words of exception in the second sentence "have no application to the [owners'] obligation in the first sentence to repay unearned hire".

Principles traditionally applied to the construction of exemption clauses

Exceptions clauses have traditionally been strictly construed. They afford no protection if, upon careful examination, their words do not cover the relevant breach of contract, and any ambiguity will be resolved against the party seeking to rely upon them. They are construed *contra proferentem*. Thus a clause in a sale contract excluding any "warranty expressed or implied" was held by the House of Lords not to exclude liability for breach of a condition: *Wallis* v. *Pratt & Haynes* [1911] A.C. 394.

Moreover, a clause the words of which cover the relevant acts or events may still not protect the party seeking to rely upon it if this is held to be inconsistent with the main purpose of the contract. Thus the House of Lords In *Glynn* v. *Margetson* [1893] A.C. 351 refused to allow an owner who had failed to carry a consignment of oranges direct to destination to rely upon a voyage liberty clause,in his bill of lading despite the fact that the words of this clause did permit the shipowner to act as he had. Lord Herschell said, at page 355: "My Lords, the main object and intent, as I have said, of this charterparty is the carriage of oranges from Malaga to Liverpool. That is the matter with which the shipper is concerned; and it seems to me that it would be to defeat what is the manifest object and intention of such a contract to hold that it was entered into with a power to the shipowner to proceed anywhere that he pleased, to trade in any manner that he pleased, and to arrive at the port at which the oranges were to be delivered when he pleased."

Lord Halsbury also said, at page 357: "Looking at the whole of the instrument, and seeing what one must regard, for a reason which I will give in a moment, as its main purpose, one must reject words, indeed whole provisions, if they are inconsistent with what one assumes to be the main purpose of the contract."

Similarly, owners who delivered goods without production of the bill of lading to a person who was not entitled to receive them were held by the Privy Council not protected by a clause terminating their responsibility after discharge from the ship: *Sze Hai Tong Bank* v. *Rambler Cycle* [1959] 2 Lloyd's Rep. 114. Giving the judgment of the Judicial Committee, Lord Denning said that the clause "must at least be modified so as not to permit the shipping company deliberately to disregard its obligations as to delivery".

These principles may in appropriate circumstances be applied so as to prevent the party in breach from relying on the exceptions in Lines 103 and 104 of the New York Produce form or the exceptions brought into that charter by the incorporation of the Harter Act and the United States Carriage of Goods by Sea Act.

Recent modification of these principles

It should, however, be noted that in recent cases there has been a clear lessening of judicial antipathy to exception clauses in contracts between parties of approximately equal bargaining power. This may lead to such clauses being construed less strictly than in the past. Of particular significance may be the following comments of Lord Diplock in *Photo Production* v. *Securicor* [1980] 1 Lloyd's Rep. 545, at page 554: "My Lords, the reports are full of cases in which what would appear to be very strained constructions have been placed upon exclusion clauses, mainly in what today would be called consumer contracts and contracts of adhesion. As Lord Wilberforce has pointed out, any need for this kind of judicial distortion of the English language has been banished by Parliament's having made these kinds of contracts subject to the Unfair Contract Terms Act, 1977. In commercial contracts negotiated between business-men capable of looking after their own interests and of deciding how risks inherent in the performance of various kinds of contract can be most economically borne (generally by insurance), it is, in my view, wrong to place a strained construction upon words in an exclusion clause which are clear and fairly susceptible of one meaning only . . . "

Most charter contracts are clearly of the type in Lord Diplock's contemplation in the above passage. Therefore the relevance of traditionally leading authorities concerned with the rights of shipowners against innocent bill of lading holders, such as *Glynn* v. *Margetson* above, is likely to decline in future, at least so far as concerns the strictness with which exceptions clauses in charters should be construed against the owners or charterers seeking to rely upon them as against the other party to the charter contract.

"Fundamental breach"

It was thought at one time that a party could not rely upon an exceptions clause in his contract if he had committed a "fundamental" breach of that contract, which might be either (a) one or more breaches of contract which were so serious as to go to the root of the contract and amount to a repudiation of it or (b) any breach of a term which was so important that it was considered a fundamental term of the contract.

Sometimes this was explained merely as a rule (albeit a strong rule) of construction. In the words of Pearson, L.J., in *U.G.S. Finance* v. *National Mortgage Bank of Greece* [1964] 1 Lloyd's Rep. 446, at page 453: " . . . there is a rule of construction that normally an exception or exclusion clause or similar provision in a contract should be construed as not applying to a situation created by a fundamental breach of the contract." But in other cases it seemed that the supposed rule was elevated from a guide to construction to a special rule of law positively preventing reliance upon exception clauses in the face of a fundamental breach. In *Suisse Atlantique Société d'Armement Maritime* v. *N.V. Rotterdamsche Kolen Centrale* [1966] 1 Lloyd's Rep. 529, the House of Lords held that no such rule of law existed and that the earlier cases were to be explained as based on strict construction of the clauses in question. However a further theory, connected with the doctrine of deviation, was subsequently developed to the effect that when the contract was discharged by breach it came to an end, with the result that exemption clauses contained in it were displaced. This approach was adopted by the Court of Appeal in *Harbutt's Plasticine* v. *Wayne Tank and Pump* [1970] 1 Lloyd's Rep. 15, where defective equipment caused a fire which destroyed the factory into which it had been installed. The Court held that the negligent contractors could not rely on a clause limiting their liability despite the clause being worded sufficiently widely to apply to what had happened.

In *Photo Production* v. *Securicor* [1980] 1 Lloyd's Rep. 545 the House of Lords expressly overruled the *Harbutt's Plasticine* decision and made it clear that the effectiveness of an exceptions clause depended upon the proper construction of that clause in relation to the whole contract and to the breach that had occurred. Subsequently the House of Lords in *George Mitchell* v. *Finney Lock Seeds* [1983] A.C. 803 removed any lingering doubt as to whether the doctrine of fundamental breach, although rejected as a rule of law in the *Securicor* case, might survive as a rule of construction. It seems that the doctrine in all its manifestations is now dead. The courts will continue to construe exceptions clauses *contra proferentem* and require that the words used clearly cover what has happened, but there is no longer any special doctrine to be applied to them.

It may be noted that the doctrine of fundamental breach was developed to deal with cases in which individual consumers were threatened by wide and carefully drafted exceptions clauses in the standard form contracts of large companies. Lord Reid pointed out in the *Suisse Atlantique* case that the same policy considerations do not necessarily apply to contracts between parties with more equal bargaining power (such as shipowners and charterers), and meanwhile legislation specifically in favour of consumers, such as the Unfair Contract Terms Act 1977, is making it less necessary for the courts to develop general principles in their defence. In *Photo Production* v. *Securicor*, above, Lord Scarman said, at page 555: "I applaud the refusal of the trial judge, Mr. Justice MacKenna, to allow the sophisticated refinements into which, before the enactment of the Unfair Contract Terms Act, 1977, the Courts were driven in order to do justice to the consumer to govern his judgement in a commercial dispute between parties well able to look after themselves. In such a situation what the parties agreed (expressly or impliedly) is what matters; and the duty of the Courts is to construe their contract according to its tenor." (See also Lord Wilberforce at page 549 and Lord Diplock at page 554.)

(The Unfair Contract Terms Act 1977 ordinarily applies neither to charters of ships nor to contracts for the carriage of goods by ships. Accordingly it is not dealt with here as such.)

American Law

Mutual exceptions clause

The purpose of the mutual exceptions clause is to protect either owner or charterer from liability to the other for damages resulting from any of the specified excepted causes. The leading American case in which the clause was applied was *Clyde Commercial S.S. Co.* v. *West India S.S. Co.*, 169 F. 275 (2d Cir. 1909), *cert.* denied 214 U.S. 523 (1909). There the court explained the function of the clause in the following manner:

> By mutual we understand that the parties intended the exceptions to protect each from liability to the other whenever performance of any covenant was prevented or delayed by any exception. If the owner were prevented from maintaining the vessel in an efficient state or from giving the whole space contracted for or from prosecuting the voyage with dispatch or from properly ventilating the cargo or cleaning the ship's bottom by any of these exceptions, he would not be responsible to the charterer. On the other hand, if the charterer were so prevented from furnishing coals, paying port charges or furnishing pilots or from paying hire on the date fixed, it would be relieved from liability therefor to the owner, and, in the case of charter hire, the owner could not withdraw the steamer as provided in article 6. (169 F. at 277.)

See also *The Marine Sulphur Queen*, 460 F.2d 89, 1972 AMC 1122 (2d Cir. 1972), *cert.* denied 409 U.S. 982 (1972); *The Toledo*, 122 F.2d 255 (2d Cir. 1941), *cert.* denied 314 U.S. 689 (1941); *The African Glen*, 1969 AMC 1465, 1467 (A.S.B.C.A. 1969); *Gans Line* v. *Wilhelmsen (The Themis)*, 275 F. 254 (2d Cir. 1921), *cert.* denied 257 U.S. 655 (1921).

The mutual exceptions clause does not excuse either party from performing their many independent obligations under the charter, unless that performance is actually prevented by one of the excepted causes. While the clause most often works to the benefit of the shipowner, his warranty of seaworthiness is not modified by it. Any loss caused by an unseaworthy condition, or the failure to exercise due diligence if the charter is so modified, will not be excused by Clause 16. *The Caledonia*, 157 U.S. 124 (1895); *The Marine Sulphur Queen*, above. The owner must also bear in mind that this clause will, in the usual case, be strictly construed against him on the theory that it has been inserted in the charter for his own benefit. See *Compania de Navegacion La Flecha* v. *Brauer*, 168 U.S. 104, 118 (1897).

It is settled that the mutual exceptions clause does not affect the rights and obligations of either party under the off-hire provisions of Clause 15. Thus, even if the vessel suffers a breakdown as the result of a cause which is also listed in the mutual exceptions clause, the charterer will be excused from his duty to pay hire, or will be entitled to recover prepaid hire for that period. The rule was stated in *Clyde Commercial S.S. Co.* v. *West India S.S. Co.*, above, as follows:

> . . . [A]rticle 15 must be understood to state absolute categories in which the parties intended the hire to be suspended whether the Owner was at fault or not, and therefore . . . article 17 ["general exceptions" clause] does not apply to them at all. (169 F. at 278.)

In that case, the vessel was first delayed at Panama as the result of a deficiency of men which was held to relieve the charterer from his obligation to pay hire for the time lost. The vessel proceeded on her voyage, but was delayed because of a quarantine order applying to vessels coming from Panama. This latter delay, the court held, was attributable to a restraint of princes, which was mutually excepted under Clause 16. The charterer therefore was not excused from paying hire for that period.

Act of God

To fall within the scope of this exception, an event must be "due to natural causes, without human intervention". *Gans S.S. Line* v. *Wilhelmsen*, above. Therefore, when an attempt to widen the Panama Canal triggered a slide which blocked it, the event was held not to be an act of God which would excuse a failure by the charterer to redeliver a vessel to its owner on time. *Id.*

Furthermore, the event must be so overwhelming and unanticipated as to "fairly preclude charging a carrier with responsibility for damage occasioned by its failure to guard against it in protection of property committed to its custody". *Compania de Vapores Insco S.A.* v. *Missouri Pacific R. Co.*, 232 F.2d 657, 660 (5th Cir. 1956), *cert.* denied 352 U.S. 880 (1956). See also *New Rotterdam Insurance Co.* v. *S.S. Loppersum*, 215 F. Supp. 563, 567 (S.D.N.Y. 1963).

An act of God is no excuse, if negligence contributed to the damage caused by the event. *Sidney Blumenthal & Co.* v. *Atlantic Coast Line R. Co.*, 139 F.2d 288 (2d Cir. 1943), *cert.* denied 321 U.S. 795 (1944). It also does not obviate the duty of a carrier to use reasonable diligence to save the shipper's property and protect it from further loss. *McNeil Higgins Co.* v. *Old Dominion S.S. Co.*, 235 F. 854, 857 (7th Cir. 1916).

Fire

In *The Buckeye State*, 39 F. Supp. 344, 347 (W.D.N.Y. 1941), "fire" was defined as follows:

> "Fire" is caused by ignition or combustion, and it includes the idea of a visible heat or light.

Thus, it has been held that heat and smoke alone, without combustion or flames, are not "fire". *Western Woolen Mill Co.* v. *Northern Assurance Co. of London*, 139 F. 637, 639 (8th Cir. 1905), *cert.* denied 199 U.S. 608; *Cargo Carriers* v. *Brown S.S. Co.*, 95 F.Supp. 288, 290 (W.D.N.Y. 1950). Like the English cases, decisions of American courts hold that fire damages will include those resulting from smoke and water or other materials used to extinguish the fire. See, e.g., *American Tobacco Co.* v. *Goulandris*, 173 F.Supp. 140, 177–78 (S.D.N.Y. 1959), aff'd 281 F.2d 179, 1962 AMC 2655 (2d Cir. 1960). In that case, the court found that some of the damage to the cargo of tobacco occurred prior to the actual fire, due to spontaneous heat resulting from inherent vice of the cargo. The court held that this damage "prior to the actual fire is all part and parcel of the one continuous and uninterrupted process", and excused the owner from any liability.

In addition to the widened exception for fire damages provided under the U.S. Carriage of Goods by Sea Act, discussed below at pages 433 and 434, the Limitation of Liability Act includes a provision, known as the "Fire Statute", which also provides the owner with a broader defense than that given by the general exceptions clause. The Fire Statute provides as follows:—

> No owner of any vessel shall be liable to answer for or make good to any person any loss or damages, which may happen to any merchandise whatsoever, which shall be shipped, taken in, or put on board any such vessel, by reason or by means of any fire happening to or on board the vessel, unless such fire is caused by the design or neglect of such owner. (46 U.S.C. §182.)

The last words of the statute, excusing the owner from liability unless the fire is caused by his "design or neglect", have been held to have essentially the same meaning as the "actual fault and privity" requirement of COGSA. *In The Matter of The Complaint of Ta*

Chi Navigation (Panama) Corp. (The Eurypylus), 677 F.2d 225 (2d Cir. 1982); *Asbestos Corp. Ltd.* v. *Compagnie de Navigation Fraissinet (The Marquette)*, 480 F.2d 669, 672, 1973 AMC 1683, 1686, (2d Cir. 1973). Under both statutes, the owner will not be liable for damage caused by the fire unless he is personally at fault. *Walker* v. *Transp. Co.*, 70 U.S. 150 (1866); *The Marquette*, above, 1973 AMC at 1687n.7. Thus, a fire resulting from the negligence of the master or other officers and crew will not be attributed to the owner. *Consumers Import Co.* v. *Kabushiki Kaisha Kawasaki Zosenjo*, 320 U.S. 249, 1943 AMC 1209 (1943); *Earle & Stoddart Inc.* v. *Ellerman's Wilson Line*, 287 U.S. 420, 1933 AMC 1 (1932); *American Tobacco Co.* v. *The Katingo Hadjipatera*, 81 F.Supp. 438, 446 (S.D.N.Y. 1948), mod. on other grounds 194 F.2d 449 (2d Cir. 1951). In the case of a corporate vessel owner, the negligence must be that of a managing officer or agent.

To invoke the Fire Statute or COGSA, the shipowner must prove that the cargo loss complained of was caused by fire. The burden of proof is then on the cargo owner to establish that the fire was caused or its extinguishment was prevented by the shipowner's negligence or an act within his actual fault or privity. *The Eurypylus*, above. It is important to note that this involves a different allocation of burdens of proof as between the carrier and cargo than generally applies in a non-fire case. Whereas in a non-fire case the burden is on the carrier to show that he exercised due diligence to make the vessel seaworthy, the fire exemptions shift that burden of proof to the cargo owner. *The Eurypylus*, above; *The Marquette*, above. Thus, the burden is on the cargo owner to prove that the fire was caused by negligence of the shipowner or the shipowner's failure to exercise due diligence to correct an unseaworthy condition which either caused the fire or prevented its extinguishment. But see *Sunkist Growers Inc.* v. *Adelaide Shipping Lines Ltd.*, 603 F.2d 1327 (9th Cir. 1979), *cert.* denied 449 U.S. 1012 (1980), holding contrary to *The Eurypylus* and *The Marquette*, that the burden of proof is on the carrier to show that it exercised due diligence to provide a seaworthy vessel in order to avail itself of the Fire Statute or Section 4(2)(*b*) of COGSA.

Where the cause of the fire is undetermined, the owner will be excused from liability under the Fire Statute, since the burden of proof is on the cargo owners to prove that the owner's negligence caused the loss. *In re Caldas*, 350 F. Supp. 566, 1973 AMC 1243 (E.D. Pa. 1972), aff'd without opinion *sub nom. In re Anderson, Clayton & Co.*, 485 F.2d 678 (3d Cir. 1973). This same result would be reached in an action where COGSA is applicable. See *The Marquette*, above.

Restraint of Princes, Rulers and People

A restraint of princes involves the exercise of sovereign power in a manner which prevents performance of the charter. As stated in *Baker Castor Oil Co.* v. *Insurance Co. of North America*, 60 F.Supp. 32, 1945 AMC 168 (S.D.N.Y. 1944), aff'd 157 F.2d 3, 1946 AMC 1115 (2d Cir. 1946), *cert.* denied 329 U.S. 800 (1947):

> Restraint of princes means the operation of the sovereign power by the exercise of vis major, in its sovereign capacity . . . .

This defense comprises non-performance caused by an actual stopping of a vessel by a blockade in time of war, *Olivera* v. *Union Insurance Co.*, 16 U.S. 183, 4 L.Ed. 365 (1818), as well as a delay in delivery based on a well-founded apprehension of capture by the cruisers of a belligerent, *The Styria*, 101 F. 728 (2d Cir. 1900), mod. on other grounds, 186 U.S. 1 (1902). See also *The George J. Goulandris*, 36 F.Supp. 827, 1941

AMC 1804 (D.Me 1941). The defense extends to a non-war time, official quarantine of a vessel, *Clyde Commercial S.S. Co.* v. *West India S.S. Co.*, above, but does not extend to detention of a vessel by a government official acting beyond the scope of his authority. See *Northern Pacific R. Co.* v. *American Trading Co.*, 195 U.S. 439 (1904).

There must be official government action to have a "restraint of princes". In *The Andros Island*, S.M.A. No. 1548 (Arb. at N.Y. 1980), for example, the owner contended that certain instructions issued by the Greek Ministry of Merchant Shipping to Greek vessels following the outbreak of hostilities between Greece and Turkey over Cyprus fell under the general exceptions clause. The arbitrators found, however, that the instructions were not government orders, but were instead only warnings and precautionary recommendations which did not require any obedience by the owner. The owner was held not to be entitled to the protection of the general exceptions clause.

In *The Otelia*, 1980 AMC 424 (Arb. at N.Y. 1979), a sole arbitrator held that the threatened refusal of a minor department of the Government of Iraq to permit the vessel to enter the discharge port in Iraq was not a restraint of princes since it was not shown that the actions of the department represented an official action of the Government. At the same time, it was clearly recognized by the arbitrator that official government action to prohibit the vessel's entry would constitute a restraint of princes.

The detention of a vessel by reason of a court order issued in the course of regular legal proceedings has been held not to be a restraint of princes. *The Gabriele Wesch*, 1981 AMC 1324 (Arb. at N.Y. 1981).

In *The Universe Explorer*, 1985 AMC 1014 (Arb. at N.Y. 1984), the vessel was not permitted by the Government to load a cargo of oil in Nigeria from 18 September 1979 until 8 October 1979 because she had previously taken on stores by helicopter off Cape Town, South Africa. The Government acted pursuant to a Nigerian regulation which prohibited ships from entering Nigerian waters if they had called at a port in South Africa within six weeks preceding arrival in Nigeria. The panel ruled that the vessel was off-hire during the entire period in question under a clause in the charter which provided that hire would cease in the event of loss of time due to the interference of authorities. In addition to its claim that the vessel was off-hire, charterer claimed damages. The panel held, however, that the restraint of princes provision in the general exceptions clause prevented any recovery of damages.

Dangers and accidents of the Seas, Rivers

The peril of the sea defense is broader in scope than "act of God", and may include losses other than those caused by entirely natural forces. See *The Majestic*, 166 U.S. 375 (1897).

"Peril of the Sea" was perhaps most dramatically described in *The Rosalia*, 264 F. 285, 288 (2d Cir. 1920), as "something so catastrophic as to triumph over those safeguards by which skillful and vigilant seamen usually bring ship and cargo to port in safety". See also *Duche* v. *Thomas and John Brocklebank*, 40 F.2d 418, 1930 AMC 717 (2d Cir. 1930); *The Warren Adams*, 74 F. 413, 415 (2d Cir. 1896), *cert.* denied 163 U.S. 679; *The Giulia*, 218 F. 744, 746 (2d Cir. 1914). The cases since *The Rosalia* have widened the exception somewhat, and as noted in *The Philippine Bear*, 1960 AMC 670, 677 (A.S.B.C.A. 1959), "more recently less emphasis has been given to the extraordinary or catastrophic features of 'perils of the sea' ". Thus, in *Davison Chemical Co.* v. *Eastern Transp. Co.*, 30 F.2d 862, 1929 AMC 161 (4th Cir. 1929), it was held that cargo damage was caused by a peril of the sea, albeit the storm, though violent, was not unusual for that time of year. As Judge Parker noted:

> Storms of the greatest intensity are to be anticipated in certain waters at certain seasons; and, if that fact removed them from the classification of perils of the sea, that term might as well be stricken from bills of lading. (30 F. 2d at 864.)

Machinery

As used in Clause 16, "machinery" refers to the whole of the vessel's machinery.

In *The Toledo*, 30 F. Supp. 93 (E.D.N.Y. 1939), aff'd 122 F. 255 (2d Cir. 1941), *cert.* denied 314 U.S. 689, a fracture of a crankshaft web was held to be an "accident of machinery". The court gave full effect to the mutual exceptions clause, and held that the charterer was not entitled to recover losses it suffered when the vessel's breakdown made it necessary to ship cargo on other vessels. The fracture was caused by a latent defect which the court found was not discoverable by the exercise of due diligence. The defect was such, however, that it made the vessel unseaworthy both at the time of the making of the charter and on delivery to the charterer. The court held that the owner was nonetheless entitled to the benefit of the exceptions clause from accidents of machinery occurring after the making of the charter.

Errors of navigation

The effect of this exception is to excuse the owner from liability for any damages sustained by the charterer as the result of errors in navigation on the part of the vessel's officers. The exception will apply, however, only if there is no finding that a breach of the owner's warranty of seaworthiness caused or contributed to the error in navigation or the damages claimed. *The Binship*, S.M.A. No. 1416 (Arb. at N.Y. 1980).

Exceptions under the Carriage of Goods by Sea Act

The Carriage of Goods by Sea Act contains exceptions from liability which benefit both the owner and the shipper of the cargo. The owner is entitled to the benefit of all the provisions of Section 4(2), which states:

> (2) Neither the carrier nor the ship shall be responsible for loss or damage arising or resulting from—
>
> (a) Act, neglect, or default of the master, mariner, pilot, or the servants of the carrier in the navigation or in the management of the ship;
> (b) Fire, unless caused by the actual fault or privity of the carrier;
> (c) Perils, dangers, and accidents of the sea or other navigable waters;
> (d) Act of God;
> (e) Act of war;
> (f) Act of public enemies;
> (g) Arrest or restraint of princes, rulers, or people, or seizure under legal process;
> (h) Quarantine restrictions;
> (i) Act or omission of the shipper or owner of the goods, his agent or representative;
> (j) Strikes or lockouts or stoppage or restraint of labor from whatever cause, whether partial or general: *Provided*, That nothing herein contained shall be construed to relieve a carrier from responsibility for the carrier's own acts;
> (k) Riots and civil commotions;
> (l) Saving or attempting to save life or property at sea;
> (m) Wastage in bulk or weight or any other loss or damage arising from inherent defect, quality, or vice of the goods;

(n) Insufficiency of packing;
(o) Insufficiency or inadequacy of marks;
(p) Latent defects not discoverable by due diligence; and
(q) Any other cause arising without the actual fault and privity of the carrier and without the fault or neglect of the agents or servants of the carrier, but the burden of proof shall be on the person claiming the benefit of this exception to show that neither the actual fault or privity of the carrier nor the fault or neglect of the agents or servants of the carrier contributed to the loss or damage.

The incorporation in the charter of COGSA or the Harter Act does not destroy or weaken the exceptions set out in Clause 16. *The Toledo*, 30 F.Supp. 93, 96 (E.D.N.Y. 1939), aff'd 122 F.2d 255 (2d Cir. 1941), *cert.* denied 314 U.S. 689. Thus, the owner may have the benefit of the defenses available under COGSA or the Harter Act in addition to those which may be raised under the exceptions clause. See also *The Westmoreland*, 86 F. 2d 96, 1936 AMC 1680 (2d Cir. 1936).

The Carriage of Goods by Sea Act also contains provisions which may affect the shipper's liability. Section 4(3) states:

> The shipper shall not be responsible for loss or damages sustained by the carrier or the ship arising or resulting from any cause without the act, fault, or neglect of the shipper, his agent, or his servants.

Where the charterer is not the shipper of the goods, it is doubtful that it would be entitled to the benefit of these provisions, particularly if it is a "carrier" of the shipment under COGSA.

Rules of Construction

See discussion above at pages 28 to 29.

Liberties

[Clause 16 continued]

"105. The vessel shall have the liberty to sail with or without pilots, to tow and to be towed, to assist vessels in distress, and to deviate for the

106. purpose of saving life and property."

Deviations

It is not considered that the concept of deviation in its strict sense is applicable to period time charters, although it may apply in the case of certain trip charters (see page 95 above). The liberties considered under this heading appear therefore to be relevant mainly to the obligations under Clause 8 of the New York Produce form to proceed with the utmost despatch and to comply with the charterers' orders as to employment (see pages 231 and 236 above).

The United States Carriage of Goods by Sea Act, incorporated by Clause 24 of the New York Produce form, modifies the latter part of Lines 105 and 106. Its provisions, which supplement those of the charter (see pages 424 to 432 below), include Section 4(4), which reads:

> Any deviation in saving or attempting to save life or property at sea, or any reasonable deviation shall not be deemed to be an infringement or breach of this chapter or of the contract of carriage, and the carrier shall not be liable for any loss or damage resulting therefrom: *Provided, however*, That if the deviation is for the purpose of loading or unloading cargo or passengers it shall, *prima facie*, be regarded as unreasonable.

It will be seen that "any reasonable deviation" is included (see *Stag Line* v. *Foscolo, Mango* (1931) 41 Ll.L.Rep. 165, and *The Daffodil B* [1983] 1 Lloyd's Rep. 498) and to this extent the incorporation of the section extends the liberties given by Lines 105 and 106. However, the words of the proviso to the section (which do not appear in the British Act) should be noted.

Arbitration

"107. 17. That should any dispute arise between Owners and the Charterers, the matter in dispute shall be referred to three persons at New York,

108. one to be appointed by each of the parties hereto, and the third by the two so chosen; their decision or that of any two of them, shall be final, and for

109. the purpose of enforcing any award, this agreement may be made a rule of the Court. The Arbitrators shall be commercial men."

The scope of this chapter

It is not intended that this chapter should attempt to cover all aspects of the English law on arbitration or even to explore fully those aspects which have been selected for comment. Instead an outline treatment is offered, with special attention being given to the phrases used in Clause 17 of the New York Produce form and their interaction with the Arbitration Acts. American law is covered in more detail: see page 372 below. For a full treatment of the English law on the subject see *Mustill & Boyd* on *Commercial Arbitration*.

Place of arbitration

Where the parties want any disputes they may have to be settled by arbitration in London, the namc of that city is typed in place of New York in Line 107 of the New York Produce form. Line 174 of the printed form of the Baltime charter provides for disputes to be referred to arbitration in London or such other place as may be agreed.

The choice of law to be applied by the arbitrators

Arbitrators must apply to the dispute before them whatever law is the governing or proper law of the charter.

Where the parties have indicated expressly the law they prefer, that law will be the proper law.

In the absence of an expressed choice, other indications of the parties' intentions will be sought. If the language which they have used shows a common intention as to the law they wish to be applied then this will be honoured by the tribunal. See the speech of Lord Diplock in *Amin Rasheed* v. *Kuwait Insurance* [1983] 2 Lloyd's Rep. 365 at page 368.

Where the intentions of the parties have neither been expressed nor implied, the proper law will be the national law or the system of law with which the charter has the closest and most real connection.

Tunisian charterers made a "tonnage contract" in Paris with French owners on an English form of tanker voyage charter for the carriage of oil between two ports in Tunisia (whose civil law is based on the French Code Napoleon). Freight was payable in Paris in French francs. The ships to be nominated were to be owned, controlled or chartererd by the owners. The owned ships flew the French flag and it was found as a fact by the arbitrators that both parties contemplated that these owned ships would be used "at least primarily" to perform the contract.

Clause 13 provided: "This Contract shall be governed by the laws of the Flag of the Vessel carrying the goods, except in cases of average or general average, when same to be settled according to the York-Antwerp Rules, 1950."

Clause 18 provided: "Any dispute arising during execution of this Charter-Party shall be settled in London."

The House of Lords held that the proper law of the contract was French law. The majority came to this decision on the basis that Clause 13, read in the light of the contemplation of the parties that the owners' French flag ships would "at least primarily" be used, showed a choice of French law. Further it was unanimously agreed that if Clause 13 did not show such a choice, nevertheless French law was the proper law of the contract because it was the system of law with which the transaction had its closest and most real connection.

Compagnie Tunisienne v. *Compagnie d'Armement Maritime* [1970] 2 Lloyd's Rep. 99.

The selection of London as the place of arbitration will usually be taken to indicate that the parties' wish is that English law should be applied as the proper law of the charter. But this will not invariably be so, for contrary indications may prove more powerful, as they did in the *Compagnie Tunisienne* case, above. Lord Wilberforce there said, at page 114: "An arbitration clause must be treated as an indication, to be considered together with the rest of the contract and relevant surrounding facts. Always it will be a strong indication; often, especially when there are parties of different nationality or a variety of transactions which may arise under the contract, it will be the only clear indication. But in some cases it must give way where other indications are clear." See also *The Parouth* [1982] 2 Lloyd's Rep. 351 (C.A.) and generally on the choice of law *Dicey & Morris on the Conflict of Laws*, 11th edition, at page 1161.

Whether or not English law is the proper law of the contract, if London is chosen by the parties as the place of arbitration, the procedure to be followed will almost certainly be governed by English law: see *James Miller & Partners* v. *Whitworth Street Estates* [1970] A.C. 583 and *Naviera Amazonica Peruana* v. *Compania Internacional de Seguros del Peru* [1988] 1 Lloyd's Rep. 116.

Incorporation of the time limit in Section 3(6) of the United States Carriage of Goods by Sea Act

It was held by the Court of Appeal in the voyage charter case of *The Agios Lazaros* [1976] 2 Lloyd's Rep. 47, that by incorporating the Hague Rules the parties had brought into the charter all the Rules including the time limit provision in Article III, Rule 6. The same court has held that this time limit applies to arbitration proceedings as well as to court proceedings: *The Merak* [1964] 2 Lloyd's Rep. 527.

The equivalent in the United States Carriage of Goods by Sea Act of Article III, Rule 6 of the Hague Rules is Section 3(6). This is incorporated into the New York Produce form by Clause 24.

The result is that "the carrier and the ship" will be "discharged from all liability in respect of loss or damage unless suit is brought within one year after delivery of the goods or the date when the goods should have been delivered". This clearly covers suits by the charterers against the owners. It does not, however, cover suits by the owners against the charterers; this is so even where the charterers are the carrier under the relevant bill(s) of lading, because, although Section 1(*a*) of the United States Act defines "carrier" as including "the charterer who enters into a contract of carriage with a shipper", in the context of the time charter the word "carrier" must refer to the owners and not to the charterers. See *The Khian Zephyr* [1982] 1 Lloyd's Rep. 73.

The application of this provision in the United States Act is restricted to claims for loss or damage to, or of, or connected with the goods carried or to be carried: see *The Standard Ardour* [1988] 2 Lloyd's Rep. 159, and page 431 below. For the effect on the time limit of incorporating the Inter-Club Agreement see page 253 above.

When "suit is brought" in arbitration

Section 3(6) of the United States Act bars claims unless "suit is brought" within one year. In arbitration "suit is brought" when one party serves upon the other a notice in writing requiring that other to appoint an arbitrator or agree to the appointment of an arbitrator: *The Agios Lazaros* [1976] 2 Lloyd's Rep. 47 and see below.

Extension of time for commencing arbitration under Section 27 of the Arbitration Act 1950

The court has power under Section 27 of the Arbitration Act 1950 to extend the time within which arbitration is to be commenced where the court "is of opinion that in the circumstances of the case undue hardship would otherwise be caused". This power exists whether or not the time has already expired. But if the time has expired the applicant must act expeditiously: see *The Eurotrader* [1987] 1 Lloyd's Rep. 418.

The power under Section 27 may be exercised by the court in respect of a time limit which is brought into the charter by the incorporation of the Hague Rules or legislation, such as the United States Act, giving effect to the Rules: see the decision of the Court of Appeal in *The Virgo* [1978] 2 Lloyd's Rep. 167.

As to what will be "undue hardship" in the opinion of the courts, see *The Pegasus* [1967] 1 Lloyd's Rep. 302; *The Simonburn* (*No. 2*) [1973] 2 Lloyd's Rep. 145; *The Bratislava* [1977] 2 Lloyd's Rep. 269; *The Aspen Trader* [1981] 1 Lloyd's Rep. 273 and *The Eurotrader*, above.

Appointment of arbitrator

Where an arbitration agreement provides that an arbitrator is to be appointed by each party, the arbitrator is properly appointed by one of the parties (1) asking an arbitrator if he is willing to accept appointment as arbitrator in the dispute; (2) obtaining his consent and appointing him as arbitrator; and (3) notifying the appointment to the other party to the dispute (*Tradax Export* v. *Volkswagenwerk* [1970] 1 Lloyd's Rep. 62).

Commencement of arbitration

Section 34(3)(*a*) of the Limitation Act 1980, re-enacting with insignificant amendments, Section 27(3) of the Limitation Act 1939, provides that: " . . . an arbitration shall be treated as being commenced . . . when one party to the arbitration serves on the other party or parties a notice requiring him or them to appoint an arbitrator or to agree to the appointment of an arbitrator."

This provision applies also, by analogy, to the one year time limit provision in Article III, Rule 6 of the Hague Rules: see *The Agios Lazaros* [1976] 2 Lloyd's Rep. 47. See also

Sections 29(2), 33 and 44(3) of the Arbitration Act 1950 and *The Rimon* [1981] 2 Lloyd's Rep. 640.

The notice to the other party may be served personally or by letter, cable or telex, but it must reach the other party before the expiry of the time limit. Parker, J., said in *The Pendrecht* [1980] 2 Lloyd's Rep. 56, at page 65: "The provisions appear to me to indicate an intention to put a party as nearly as may be in the position as if he were bringing a High Court action. There being no formal act which he can take, which will of itself stop time running, he must get his notice either to the opposite party or to a place at or from which it may in due course be expected to reach the other party."

Arbitration Acts

If the charter provides that arbitration is to be in London, the procedure in the arbitration will almost certainly be governed by English law (see above). Such arbitrations are governed by the Arbitration Acts 1950, 1975 and 1979 as amended by the Administration of Justice Acts 1981, 1982 and 1985. Relevant parts of the three Arbitration Acts, as so amended, are set out in Appendix C.

Reference to "three persons"

Under Section 9 of the Arbitration Act 1950, an arbitration agreement providing for a reference to three arbitrators had effect as if it provided for the appointment of an umpire instead of a third arbitrator. However, Section 6(2) of the Arbitration Act 1979 gives full effect to a reference to three arbitrators and substitutes the following section for Section 9 of the 1950 Act:

> Unless the contrary intention is expressed in the arbitration agreement, in any case where there is a reference to three arbitrators, the award of any two of the arbitrators shall be binding.

In practice, parties frequently agree between themselves that unless the two arbitrators first appointed disagree, a third arbitrator shall not be appointed until the case reaches the stage of a formal hearing.

Number of arbitrators not specified

If the arbitration agreement does not specify the number of arbitrators who are to decide the dispute, the reference will be deemed to be to a single arbitrator (1950 Act, Section 6).

Commercial men

Lawyers practising in commercial matters are not "commercial men" within Line 109 of the New York Produce form. But a full-time professional arbitrator is.

The arbitration clause in a voyage charter for the *North Duchess* provided: "The Arbitrators shall be commercial men." One party appointed a full-time professional arbitrator who, although originally qualified as a lawyer, no longer practiced as such. It was held by Donaldson, J., that his engagement as a full-time professional arbitrator in commercial and maritime disputes put him within the class of commercial men. But it was said, *obiter*, that practising lawyers, although practising in the commercial field, would not be so regarded.

Pando v. *Filmo* [1975] 1 Lloyd's Rep. 560.

An umpire appointed by the arbitrators must also be a "commercial" man; if he is not then the defective appointment is not cured by the appearance before the umpire of arbitrators or counsel for the parties: *Rahcassi* v. *Blue Star* [1967] 2 Lloyd's Rep. 261.

Stay of suit pending arbitration

If one of the parties to an arbitration agreement institutes proceedings before the court, the other party may apply to the court to stay those proceedings pending arbitration. Where neither of the parties to the arbitration agreement nor the place of arbitration is outside the U.K. (a "domestic arbitration agreement") the court has a discretion to grant a stay under Section 4(1) of the Arbitration Act 1950.

But where the arbitration agreement is not a "domestic arbitration agreement", the court must grant a stay of the proceedings under Section 1 of the Arbitration Act 1975:

> . . . unless satisfied that the arbitration agreement is null and void, inoperative or incapable of being performed or that there is not in fact any dispute between the parties with regard to the matter agreed to be referred . . .

(See *Nova (Jersey) Knit* v. *Kammgarn Spinnerei* [1977] 1 Lloyd's Rep. 463, *The Rena K* [1978] 1 Lloyd's Rep. 545 and *The Cleon* [1983] 1 Lloyd's Rep. 586.)

Failure of party to appoint arbitrator

Section 7 of the Arbitration Act 1950 provides that where the reference is to two arbitrators, one to be appointed by each party, and one of the parties fails to appoint an arbitrator after having been called upon to do so, the party who has already appointed an arbitrator may appoint that arbitrator as sole arbitrator in the dispute. But the party failing to make an appointment must first be given seven clear days' notice before that step is taken. See The *Bengal Pride* [1986] 1 Lloyd's Rep. 167.

Where the reference is to three arbitrators, one to be appointed by each party, and one party refuses to do so or does not do so within a reasonable time (or within the time specified in the agreement, if any), the other party may, after notice, apply to the court to appoint an arbitrator. (Section 10(3) of the Arbitration Act 1950, added by the Administration of Justice Act 1985.)

Powers of arbitrators in conduct of arbitration

The parties to the arbitration may decide between themselves on the course which the arbitration is to take; for example, they may decide whether there is to be an exchange of pleadings, whether there is to be mutual discovery of documents between the parties, whether there is to be an oral hearing or whether the arbitrators are to be asked to decide the dispute on the basis of written submissions alone. If the parties cannot agree on such matters, the arbitrators may be asked to give directions. All these matters are within the power of arbitrators, both at common law and by statute. See *Bremer Vulkan* v. *South India* [1981] 1 Lloyd's Rep. 253; see also *The Jhansi Ki Rani* [1980] 2 Lloyd's Rep. 569, for a case on arbitrators' powers regarding adjournment of the hearing.

Section 12(1) of the Arbitration Act 1950 provides that in the absence of a contrary intention the parties to the reference shall "do all . . . things which during the proceedings on the reference the arbitrator or umpire may require".

Arbitrators may not, however, make orders for security for costs (*In re Unione Stearinerie Lanza and Wiener* [1917] 2 K.B. 558) nor dismiss a case for want of prosecution (*Bremer Vulkan* v. *South India*, above). Nor, it seems, may they strike out a claim or a defence for a failure to comply with their orders, although they may in such circumstances proceed straight to a hearing after an appropriate warning to the party in default: *Crawford* v. *A. E. A. Prowting* [1973] Q.B. 1. Further, arbitrators have no power to order concurrent hearings of two arbitrations unless the parties so agree: *The Eastern Saga* [1984] 2 Lloyd's Rep. 373.

Powers of the court

Appointment of arbitrators

Where the reference is to a single arbitrator and the parties cannot agree on an appointment, either party may apply to the court to appoint the sole arbitrator (1950 Act, Section 10(1) (*a*)).

The court may also, on application being made to it, make appointments where a third arbitrator or umpire refuses to act, is incapable of acting or dies (1950 Act, Section 10(1) (*d*)), where the parties or the arbitrators fail to appoint a third arbitrator or umpire (1950 Act, Section 10(1) (*c*)), where an arbitrator or umpire is to be appointed by a person who is neither a party to the arbitration nor an existing arbitrator and that person fails to make the appointment (1950 Act, Section 10(2)) and where in a reference to three arbitrators one party refuses to appoint an arbitrator or fails to do so within the time specified (1950 Act, Section 10(3).)

Under the Arbitration Act 1950 it was necessary for arbitrators to appoint an umpire immediately following their own appointment (1950 Act, Section 8) although their failure to do so did not deprive them of jurisdiction if the two arbitrators agreed on an award: see *The Dalny* [1979] 2 Lloyd's Rep. 439. But under Section 6(1) of the 1979 Act, amending Section 8(1) of the 1950 Act, the requirement now is that the umpire may be appointed at any time, subject to the proviso that the arbitrators must appoint an umpire forthwith if they cannot agree.

Conduct of the arbitration

Under Section 12(6) of the Arbitration Act 1950 the court has powers to control arbitrations by making orders in respect of security for costs, discovery of documents, the giving of evidence, the preservation and inspection of property and injunctions.

These powers of the court do not prejudice any powers the arbitrators may have to make orders in respect of these matters, but normally the powers of the arbitrators are much more restricted than those of the court: see above.

Under Section 5(1) and (2) of the Arbitration Act 1979, if any party fails to comply with the order of an arbitrator, the arbitrators or any of the parties may apply to the court to extend the arbitrators' powers to enable them to strike out pleadings and to proceed with the arbitration in the absence of one of the parties.

Great difficulties have been caused by arbitrations in which no steps have been taken for a long time, as the court does not have power to strike out the claim in an arbitration on the grounds of delay in the same way as it would have if the case were before the court: see above.

The obligation to proceed with the arbitration is mutual; it does not rest on the claimant alone. The House of Lords so held in *Bremer Vulkan* v. *South India* [1981] 1 Lloyd's Rep. 253, although the decision has been much criticised: see the cases cited below. Hence, as the law now stands, the respondent in an arbitration which has proceeded further than the formal appointment of arbitrators will not be released from his agreement to arbitrate merely because of delay on the part of the claimant; but there may be cases where the circumstances and the length of the delay are such that the court will infer an intention to abandon the arbitration agreement or an estoppel: see *The Splendid Sun* [1981] 2 Lloyd's Rep. 29 (C.A.); *The Hannah Blumenthal* [1983] 1 Lloyd's Rep. 103 (H.L.); *The Leonidas D* [1985] 2 Lloyd's Rep. 18 (C.A.) and *The Antclizo* [1988] 2 Lloyd's Rep. 93 (H.L.).

Appeal to the court under 1979 Act

Under Section 1 of the 1979 Act there is a right of appeal to the High Court on any question of law arising out of an arbitration award, provided:

(a) the award is a reasoned award; or, if it is not a reasoned award, such an award was requested before the award was made or there was a special reason why reasons were not requested (Section 1(6); and see *Hayn Roman* v. *Cominter* [1982] 1 Lloyd's Rep. 295); and
(b) the court considers that the determination of the question of law could "substantially affect the rights of one or more of the parties" and grants leave to appeal (Section 1(3)(*b*) and (4); and see *The Nema* [1981] 2 Lloyd's Rep. 239, below).

For an award to be a "reasoned award" under (a) above it is not necessary that it should be in any particular form; indeed it is not expected that such an award will be as formal as the "special cases" stated by arbitrators for the opinion of the court under the 1950 Act. Donaldson, L.J., said in *Bremer* v. *Westzucker* [1981] 2 Lloyd's Rep. 130, at page 132: "All that is necessary is that the arbitrators should set out what, on their view of the evidence, did or did not happen and should explain succinctly why, in the light of what happened, they have reached their decision and what that decision is. That is all that is meant by a 'reasoned award' . . . The point which I am seeking to make is that a reasoned award, in accordance with the 1979 Act, is wholly different from an award in the form of a special case. It is not technical, it is not difficult to draw and above all it is something which can and should be produced promptly and quickly at the conclusion of the hearing."

As to (b) above, the House of Lords in *The Nema* [1981] 2 Lloyd's Rep. 239 laid down the following guidelines for judges as to the exercise of their discretion on an application for leave to appeal from an arbitration award:

(i) Where the question of law involved in the case is the construction of a "one-off" clause (as opposed to a regularly used or "standard" clause) leave to appeal should not be given unless the arbitrator has quite obviously made a mistake. Lord Diplock said, at page 247: "Where, as in the instant case, a question of law involved is the construction of a 'one-off' clause the application of which to the particular facts of the case is an issue in the arbitration, leave should not normally be given unless it is apparent to the Judge upon a mere perusal of the reasoned award itself without the benefit of adversarial argument, that the meaning ascribed to the clause by the arbitrator is obviously wrong. But if on such perusal it appears to the Judge that it is possible that argument might persuade him, despite first impression to the contrary, that the arbitrator might be right, he should not grant leave; the parties should be left to accept, for better or worse, the decision of the tribunal that they had chosen to decide the matter in the first instance."

(ii) Where the clause to be construed is a "standard" clause, a rather less stringent test is appropriate, particularly where a decision upon its meaning by the courts would result in greater certainty in the commercial law. But, in the words of Lord Diplock at page 248: "leave should not be given even in such a case, unless the Judge considered that a strong *prima facie* case had been made out that the arbitrator had been wrong in his construction; and where the events to which the standard clause fell to be applied in the particular arbitration were themselves 'one-off' events, stricter criteria should be applied on the same lines as those that I have suggested as appropriate to 'one-off' clauses" (see under (i) above).

(iii) Where the question for decision is whether certain events have caused a contract to be frustrated (or whether a party is discharged from his contractual obligations by a breach of a condition by the other party) leave to appeal should generally be granted only where the arbitrator had clearly misdirected himself in law or where the decision was clearly such that no reasonable arbitrator could have reached it—particularly where the events being considered are "one-off" events. But where the events being considered are "events of a general character that affect similar transactions between many other persons engaged in the same kind of commercial activity, the closing of the Suez Canal, the United States soya bean embargo, the war between Iraq and Iran . . . ", Lord Roskill suggested, at page 248, that the judge might be correct to grant leave to appeal provided he thought that the decision reached by the arbitrator was wrong.

While these guidelines laid down by the House of Lords have provided a framework for the lower courts, it has been pointed out in the Court of Appeal (*The Rio Sun* [1981] 2 Lloyd's Rep. 489) that they are guidelines only and that, in the words of Lord Denning, M.R.: "The only fetter strictly imposed by the [1979 Act] is that leave is not to be given *unless* it is a point of law which substantially affects the rights of the parties" (that is to say, the rights of the parties to the arbitration rather than those of other persons in the general commercial community, to whose interests the House of Lords appears to have directed its attention in *The Nema*, above). For further consideration of the guidelines laid down in *The Nema*, see the judgment of Parker, J., in *The Kerman* [1982] 1 Lloyd's Rep. 62 and the House of Lords decision in *The Antaios* (*No. 2*) [1984] 2 Lloyd's Rep. 235.

The court, in granting leave to appeal, may impose conditions on the party applying for leave (Section 1(4); and see *Mondial* v. *Gill & Duffus* [1980] 2 Lloyd's Rep. 376).

An appeal against an award may also be brought with the consent of all other parties to the reference and, in this case, the leave of the court is not required (Section 1(3) (*a*)).

On determining an appeal, the court may confirm, vary, or set aside the award; or it may remit the award to the arbitrator with its opinion on the question of law (Section 1(2)).

The parties to a maritime arbitration may, by agreement, exclude the right of appeal to the court, but, with one exception, only by an agreement entered into *after* the commencement of the arbitration (Section 4(1)(*c*)(*i*)). The exception is in the case of a contract which is expressed to be governed by foreign law and to which at least one of the parties is foreign (Sections 4(1)(*c*)(ii) and 3(6)). In such a case, an exclusion agreement entered into before the commencement of any arbitration will be valid (Section 3(1)).

Appeal to Court of Appeal

An appeal to the Court of Appeal against a decision of the High Court on an appeal from arbitrators may only be made by leave of the High Court or Court of Appeal and if it is certified by the High Court that the question of law is one of general public importance or that for some other special reason it should be considered by the Court of Appeal (Section 1(7)).

For guidelines on the grant of leave where there are conflicting decisions or conflicting dicta of judges at first instance, see *The Antaios* (*No. 2*) [1984] 2 Lloyd's Rep. 235 and *The Roachbank* [1988] 2 Lloyd's Rep. 337.

Unless the High Court gives leave, the Court of Appeal has no jurisdiction to hear an appeal from a decision of the High Court to grant or refuse leave to appeal against an award of arbitrators: see Section 1(6A), *Aden Refinery* v. *Ugland Management* [1986] 2 Lloyd's Rep. 336 and *The Antaios* (*No. 2*), above.

Powers of arbitrators to award interest

An arbitrator may award interest at such rate as he thinks fit on any sum he awards, up to the date of the award, and on any sum which is the subject of the arbitration and which is paid before the award is made, up to the date of payment (1950 Act, Section 19A, added by the Administration of Justice Act 1982.) But he may not award interest by way of general damages on sums paid before the commencement of the arbitration, even though paid late: *President of India* v. *La Pintada Cia. Navegacion* [1984] 2 Lloyd's Rep. 9 (H.L.), overruling *Tehno-Impex* v. *Gebr. van Weelde* [1981] 1 Lloyd's Rep. 587 (C.A.). In respect of sums paid before the commencement of the arbitration, he may only award interest where (a) the claim for interest can properly be advanced as a claim for debt under a specific provision in the contract, or (b) the claim for interest can be advanced as a claim for special damage under the second part of the rule in *Hadley* v. *Baxendale* (1854) 9 Ex. 341: see the *La Pintada* case above, and *The Lips* [1987] 2 Lloyd's Rep. 311.

Interim awards

Arbitrators have power to make interim awards under Section 14 of the Arbitration Act 1950. Thus they may make an interim award for time charter hire due but unpaid, if they are satisfied that the amount is properly due and that the charterers have no valid grounds for withholding payment, even though there may be other matters in dispute between the parties which have been referred to the arbitrators for decision: *The Kostas Melas* [1981] 1 Lloyd's Rep. 18.

American Law

Agreement to arbitrate

Maritime arbitration is strictly a creature of agreement between the parties to specify a method of resolving disputes which arise between them. The place of the arbitration and the composition of the panel are matters to be decided by the parties, although it is customary to choose either New York or London as the place for the arbitration and to specify that the arbitration shall be conducted by a panel of three persons. Clause 17 of the New York Produce form, like other standard time charter forms, constitutes such an agreement, and binds the owner and charterer to submit any disputes between them to arbitration by a panel of three persons in New York.

Choice of law

The selection of New York as the place of arbitration, absent some express choice of law provision, will generally mean that American law governs the merits. This will be the general maritime law of the United States as expressed in the judicial decisions of the Federal courts sitting as Admiralty courts. Of course, English precedents and state law (particularly New York law) will be considered in the absence of a Federal case precedent. However, state statutes (such as the Uniform Commercial Code) are not applicable to maritime contracts of their own force and should only be followed when there is no established principle under the general maritime law on the point at issue.

Consolidated arbitration

It has not yet been settled whether the District Court has power to order consolidation of separate arbitrations which involve common issues of law and fact. There is nothing in the Federal Arbitration Act itself which confers this power. Rather, it is a judicially created doctrine. The purposes of consolidation were summarized by Judge Haight:

> [T]he consolidated arbitration is a pragmatic procedural tool of the equity court, fashioned to deal with multi-party and multi-contract cases where to permit several arbitrations would bring about a clear and present danger of conflicting findings and resulting injustice.

In re Transportacion Maritima Mexicana S.A., 636 F. Supp. 474, 476 (S.D.N.Y. 1983).

The classic example of a situation where consolidation is useful to all concerned is where the vessel has been subchartered and an occurrence gives rise to claims under all the charters in the chain. As a general rule, the parties themselves may always consolidate separate proceedings by agreement. There is a split of opinion in the Circuit Courts of Appeal whether the District Court may order consolidation absent unanimous consent among the parties.

The Second Circuit upheld the power of a District Court to consolidate, stating:

> . . . we think the liberal purposes of the Federal Arbitration Act clearly require that this act be interpreted so as to permit and even to encourage the consolidation of arbitration proceedings in proper cases. . . .

Compania Espanola de Petroleos S.A. v. *Nereus Shipping S.A.*, 527 F.2d 966, 975, 1975 AMC 2421, 2434 (2d Cir. 1975), *cert. denied*, 426 U.S. 936 (1976).

The First Circuit reached the same conclusion, relying upon both the Federal Arbitration Act and Massachusetts state law. *New England Energy Inc.* v. *Keystone Shipping Co.*, 855 F.2d 1 (1st Cir. 1988).

The Ninth Circuit declined to follow the holding of *Compania Espanola* in *Weyerhaeuser Co.* v. *Western Seas Shipping Co.*, 743 F.2d 635, 1985 AMC 30 (9th Cir.), *cert. denied*, 469 U.S. 1061 (1984). In *Weyerhaeuser*, the court stated that the District Court's authority under the Arbitration Act was only to determine whether a written arbitration agreement exists, and if it does, to enforce it in accordance with its terms. The court thus held that consolidation could not be ordered absent the consent of the parties.

The same approach was taken by the Fifth Circuit in holding that, absent agreement between the parties, the District Court cannot compel consolidation. *Del E. Webb Const.* v. *Richardson Hospital Auth.*, 823 F.2d 145 (5th Cir. 1987).

Further muddying the waters was a decision of the District Court for Southern District of New York in *Ore & Chemical Corp.* v. *Stinnes Interoil Inc.*, 606 F. Supp. 1510 (S.D.N.Y. 1985). In *Ore & Chemical*, the court agreed with the rationale of *Weyerhaeuser*, *above*, and held that a court does not have the power to compel consolidated arbitration absent a provision for such consolidation in the arbitration agreements. Regarding the decision in *Compania Espanola*, *above*, the court opined that if the "Second Circuit were to reconsider the issue, it would overrule" *Compania Espanola*. 606 F. Supp. at 1512. It is doubtful, however, that the District Court was correct in this prediction. In other cases, the District Court in New York has adhered to the Second Circuit decision in *Compania Espanola*. See *Elmarina Inc.* v. *Comexas N.V.*, 679 F. Supp. 388, 1988 AMC 2674 (S.D.N.Y. 1988); *Sociedad Anonima* v. *Cia de Petroleos de Chile*, 634 F. Supp. 805 (S.D.N.Y. 1986) and cases discussed therein.

An alternative to consolidation was utilized in *The Kostas Melas*, 1988 AMC 68 (S.D.N.Y. 1983). Disputes arose between owner and charterer which were subject to arbitration before a panel constituted in accordance with the Rules of the Society of Maritime Arbitrators. A further dispute arose out of the same voyage between charterer and the supplier of a grain cargo under a grain supply agreement. The grain supply agreement called for arbitration before the Grain Arbitration Panel of the American Arbitration Association. The court rejected charterer's motion for a consolidated arbitration, but granted an order directing that the arbitration proceedings be conducted jointly. In its order, the court outlined a procedure to be followed by the prospective arbitration panels in conducting the hearings.

Statutory recognition of arbitration

The Federal Arbitration Act, 9 U.S.C. §§1–14, 201–208 is applicable to arbitration agreements in any maritime contract. This statute provides for the compelling of arbitration, for the staying of judicial proceedings pending arbitration, for the entering of judgments on awards and generally for the ultimate supervision of the arbitral process by the Federal courts. The New York State courts have concurrent jurisdiction to oversee arbitrations (New York Civil Practice Law and Rules. §7501), although in the event of any conflict, the Federal law governs. The vast majority of maritime arbitration cases, however, are initiated in the Federal courts.

Written agreement to arbitrate

The Act expressly provides that "a written provision" in a charterparty providing for arbitration shall be valid. 9 U.S.C. §2. While an oral charterparty is a valid, enforceable agreement, an oral agreement to arbitrate disputes is not enforceable under the Arbitration Act. The charter need not have been signed by the parties, however, and a telex or other writing confirming the fixture is a sufficient writing to make the agreement to arbitrate enforceable under the Arbitration Act. See *A/S Custodia* v. *Lessin Int'l Inc.*, 503 F.2d 318, 320 (2d Cir. 1974); *Ocean Industries Inc.* v. *Soros Assoc. Int'l Inc.*, 328 F.Supp. 944 (S.D.N.Y. 1971).

Bills of lading frequently incorporate by reference the terms and conditions of a charter, including the arbitration clause. Where this occurs, there is an arbitration agreement between the carrier and the bill of lading holder. The owner, for example, would be entitled to demand arbitration of any cargo claims brought under the bill of lading. See, e.g., *Son Shipping Co.* v. *DeFosse & Tanghe*, 199 F.2d 687 (2d Cir. 1952); *Lowry & Co.* v. *S.S. Le Moyne d'Iberville*, 253 F.Supp. 396, 1966 AMC 2195 (S.D.N.Y. 1966); *Midland Tar Distillers Inc.* v. *M.T. Lotos*, 362 F.Supp. 1311, 1973 AMC 1924 (S.D.N.Y. 1973); *Amoco Overseas Co.* v. *S.T. Avenger*, 387 F.Supp. 589, 1975 AMC 782 (S.D.N.Y. 1975).

The bill of lading will effectively incorporate an arbitration clause when it clearly refers to the charter and the bill of lading holder has either actual or constructive notice of the incorporation. *Midland Tar Distillers Inc.* v. *M.T. Lotos*, above. If the bill of lading contains a space where reference can be made to a charter and that space is left blank, ordinarily there would be no incorporation of the charter or the arbitration clause. *Southwestern Sugar & Molasses Corp.* v. *Eliza Jane Nicholson*, 126 F.Supp. 666, 1955 AMC 746 (S.D.N.Y. 1954); *Tropical Gas Co.* v. *M.T. Mundogas Caribe*, 388 F.Supp. 647, 1975 AMC 987 (D.P.R. 1974); *Cia. Platamon de Navegacion S.A.* v. *Empresa Colombiana de Petroleos*, 478 F.Supp. 66, 1980 AMC 538 (S.D.N.Y. 1979); *United States Barite Corp.* v. *M.V. Haris*, 1982 AMC 925 (S.D.N.Y. 1982). If the bill of lading is ambiguous, perhaps by making reference to a "charter" which is not further identified, the court may look to extrinsic evidence to determine the intent of the parties. In the example just given, if the charter negotiations indicate that the parties intended that bills of lading incorporate the charter and the consignee has actual or constructive notice of this intent, the arbitration clause of the charter should be deemed to have been effectively incorporated.

An arbitration clause inserted in bills of lading by the owner or charterer without the agreement of the shipper of the cargo was held to be invalid in *Pacific Lumber & Shipping Co. Inc.* v. *Star Shipping A/S*, 464 F.Supp. 1314, 1979 AMC 2137 (W.D. Wash. 1979). The court held in that case that the bills of lading were invalid contracts of adhesion because a London arbitration clause was never negotiated or discussed with the shippers.

Staying suits pending arbitration

The party having a claim may choose to assert it in a lawsuit rather than initiate arbitration. In such a case, the other party is nevertheless entitled to arbitration and may, under Section 3 of the Arbitration Act, obtain a stay of the lawsuit pending arbitration of the dispute. In addition, the claimant in a lawsuit may himself obtain a stay of his own action pending arbitration.

In considering a Section 3 motion for a stay pending arbitration, the only issues for the court to consider concern the making and performance of the agreement to arbitrate. If the court finds that the dispute is subject to arbitration, it has no discretion to refuse to grant a stay under Section 3. In *Seguros Banvenez S.A.* v. *S/S Oliver Drescher*, 761 F.2d 855, 1985 AMC 2168 (2d Cir. 1985), the charter between owner and charterer provided for London arbitration of any disputes. Cargo sued the owner and charterer for the loss of five cranes. The District Court ruled in favor of cargo. Owner and charterer filed cross claims for indemnity or contribution. Citing considerations of judicial economy, the court declined to grant owner's motion for a stay under Section 3. The Court of Appeals reversed, holding that the District Court had no discretion to decline to grant the stay. The Court of Appeals further vacated the District Court's decision in favor of owner granting it indemnification by charterer for the cargo loss.

The practice of one or both parties initially utilizing the judicial process has not infrequently given rise to the issue of whether arbitration has been waived. It seems clear that the claimant does not automatically lose his right to arbitration merely by commencing suit, although he should expressly reserve the right to arbitration in the complaint. Likewise, the filing of an answer to the complaint, even one containing an affirmative defense or counterclaim which is arbitrable, or the filing of a third party complaint, will not amount to waiver, although again it would be imprudent not to expressly reserve the right to demand arbitration in the answer or third party complaint. The test of waiver is whether the other party would be prejudiced by permitting the case to go to arbitration, and is usually determined by the length of the delay in making the demand or by the extent of pre-trial discovery that has been conducted. See *Carcich* v. *Rederi A/B Nordie*, 389 F.2d 692, 1968 AMC 299 (2d Cir. 1968); *Demsey & Assoc.* v. *S.S. Sea Star*, 461 F.2d 1009, 1972 AMC 1440 (2d Cir. 1972).

The issue of waiver arose in *Seguros Banvenez S.A.* v. *S/S Oliver Drescher*, above. The court held that a finding of prejudice was necessary to support a ruling that a party had waived its right to demand arbitration. The court noted that the party had pleaded its right to demand arbitration at the outset of the case when it filed an answer to the complaint and its cross-claim and participated in discovery and a trial only because the District Court had refused to grant its motion for a stay of the action pending London arbitration. According to the Court of Appeals, "waiver may not be inferred on the basis of conduct relating to non-arbitrable issues". (1985 AMC at 2178.)

Compelling arbitration

If a demand for arbitration has gone unanswered, or has been rejected by the other party, the claimant may, under Section 4 of the Arbitration Act, file a petition to compel arbitration and, under Section 5, demand that the court appoint an arbitrator on behalf of the defaulting party. Similarly, if the two arbitrators appointed by the parties are unable to agree on a third arbitrator, Section 5 permits the court to fill the vacancy on motion of either party. Where the existence of an agreement to arbitrate is denied, the court, under Section 4, can order a summary trial of the issue. See *Interocean Shipping Co.* v. *National Shipping & Trading Corp.*, 462 F.2d 673 (2d Cir. 1972); *Interocean Shipping Co.* v. *National Shipping & Trading Corp.*, 523 F.2d 527 (2d Cir. 1975), *cert.* denied 423 U.S. 1054 (1976); *A/S Custodia* v. *Lessin Int'l Inc.*, 503 F.2d 318 (2d Cir. 1974). In *Interbras Cayman Co.* v. *Orient Victory Shipping Co. S.A.*, 663 F.2d 4, 1982 AMC 737 (2d Cir. 1981) (*per curiam*), the court held that where a party resisting arbitration submits evidence sufficient to raise a genuine issue of fact as to whether it is a party to an arbitration agreement, a summary trial is required.

When a petition to compel arbitration is filed under Section 4, the only issues to be decided by the court are whether there is an arbitration agreement and, if so, whether and why one party has failed, refused or neglected to arbitrate. *Conticommodity Services Inc.* v. *Philipp & Lion*, 613 F.2d 1222 (2d Cir. 1980); *Hanskar Shipping Co.* v. *Iron Ore Co. of Canada*, 1980 AMC 1249 (S.D.N.Y. 1980). Issues relating to the merits of the underlying claim are left for decision by the arbitrators. As the court put it in *Conticommodity Services*, above:

> [A] court under Section 4 is limited to determining whether a party refused to arbitrate, not whether it rightfully refused. (613 F.2d at 1227.)

Thus, for example, questions concerning the timeliness of an arbitration demand are to be decided by the arbitrators. *Conticommodity Services*, above, 613 F.2d at 1226.

See also *Gov't of India* v. *Cargill*, 867 F.2d 130 (2d Cir. 1989); *Son Shipping Co.* v. *De Fosse & Tanghe*, 199 F.2d 687, 1952 AMC 1931 (2d Cir. 1952), holding that the question of whether a claim for cargo damage was time-barred was for the arbitrators to decide when the claim was subject to arbitration; *Trafalgar Shipping Co.* v. *Int'l Milling Co.*, 401 F.2d 568, 1969 AMC 1006 (2d Cir. 1968), holding that issues of laches and timeliness of suit are solely for the arbitrator; *World Brilliance Corp.* v. *Bethlehem Steel Co.*, 342 F.2d 362, 364, 1965 AMC 881, 882 (2d Cir. 1965), holding that the issue of whether the right to arbitrate has been lost by laches or waiver is for the arbitrators.

In very narrow circumstances, the court will decide whether a demand for arbitration is so untimely that, under the doctrine of laches, it will be barred. See *Conticommodity Services Inc.* v. *Philipp & Lion* above, 613 F.2d at 1226. This will be limited to questions of delay that relate to the issues the court is required to decide under Section 4, namely, the making of an arbitration agreement and the failure, refusal or neglect to arbitrate. For example, if a party shows that its ability to present proof in relation to the demand for arbitration has been prejudiced by the delay of the other in making the demand, it would be within the court's power to determine whether the dilatory party should be permitted to use the Arbitration Act to compel an arbitration. In *Polar Shipping Ltd.* v. *Oriental Shipping Corp.*, 680 F.2d 627, 1982 AMC 2330 (9th Cir. 1982), the charter was on the Shelldemise form and contained a clause providing either party with the right to elect London arbitration provided such election was made within 21 days of the receipt of written notice of a dispute. Because arbitration was not demanded within the prescribed time period, the court held that the right to arbitration was lost.

It is within the court's power, however, to decide whether the arbitration agreement covers the particular dispute concerning which arbitration is sought. *John Wiley & Sons Inc.* v. *Livingston*, 376 U.S. 543, 546–47 (1964).

Appointment of arbitrators or umpire

In certain circumstances which are enumerated in Section 5 of the Arbitration Act, the court has the power to appoint an arbitrator. Where the arbitration agreement itself provides for a method of appointing arbitrators, under Section 5 the court is obliged to follow the contract. The same is true if a vacancy arises in the arbitration panel due to death or other reasons. Where the agreement does not provide a method for the appointment of arbitrators, the court is to appoint a single arbitrator. See *Ore & Chem. Corp.* v. *Stinnes Interoil Inc.*, 611 F. Supp. 237, 240–41 (S.D.N.Y. 1985).

A particularly difficult issue arises in the case of the death of a party appointed arbitrator during the course of the arbitration. In *Marine Products Export Corp.* v. *M/T Globe Galaxy*, 1987 AMC 2310 (S.D.N.Y. 1987), appeal dismissed for lack of jurisdiction, 1987 AMC 2314 (2d Cir. 1987), a dispute arose under a charter which provided for arbitration by "arbitrators experienced in the shipping business" with each side to appoint one arbitrator. The clause further stated "the two thus chosen, if they cannot agree, shall nominate a third arbitrator who shall be an admiralty lawyer". When disputes arose, both sides duly appointed their arbitrator and a chairman was appointed to serve as umpire. During the course of the arbitration, one of the party appointed arbitrators died. The party who had appointed the deceased made a motion to the District Court under Section 5 for an order directing the parties to appoint new arbitrators and to commence the arbitration again from the beginning. According to the court, as provided in Section 5 of the Arbitration Act, there was a "lapse" in "filling the vacancy" on the panel due to the parties' disagreement as to what should happen following the death of the party appointed arbitrator. The court stated:

> Parties cannot be compelled to arbitrate commercial disputes unless they have agreed in a binding contract to do so. By the same token, they cannot be compelled to arbitrate in a manner contrary to their express agreement.

The problem which arose in the *Globe Galaxy*, above, can be avoided by incorporating in the charterparty or any written submission agreement the rules of the Society of Maritime Arbitrators which include a provision for the appointment of a replacement arbitrator in the event of a vacancy.

Pre-arbitration discovery

The court will generally decline to grant pre-trial discovery when the parties have agreed to arbitrate the dispute. In certain exceptional circumstances, however, the courts have allowed pre-trial discovery to proceed even though the dispute was to be arbitrated. In *Koch Fuel* v. *South Star*, 1988 AMC 1226 (E.D.N.Y. 1987), charterer contended that the vessel owner had converted part of the cargo of fuel oil. Charterer's claim was subject to London arbitration under the charter. Because the vessel was about to leave port and it was believed that crew members having knowledge of facts related to the alleged conversion would be unavailable to act as witnesses in the London arbitration, the court granted the charterer's application for leave to take depositions in conjunction with its action to arrest the vessel for security in aid of the London arbitration. The court found that the circumstances relating to the likely unavailability of witnesses were exceptional enough to permit its intervention to order depositions.

Disputes subject to arbitration

The language used in the New York Produce form, "any dispute . . . between owners and charterers", has been broadly construed. *In re Canadian Gulf Line*, 1938 AMC 1123, 98 F.2d 711 (2d Cir. 1938); *Caribbean Steamship Co. S.A.* v. *Sonmez Denizcilik ve Ticaret A.S.*, 598 F.2d 1264, 1979 AMC 1270 (2d Cir. 1979). The clause, of course, covers any disputes between the owner and charterer concerning their respective rights and obligations under the charter. In addition to contractual disputes, it has been held to cover disputes arising by operation of law.

In *Boyle* v. *Rederij Shipmair VI*, 1979 AMC 2844 (E.D.Pa. 1979), a longshoreman brought an action against the owner for personal injuries he sustained while he was assisting in loading cargo. The owner impleaded the charterer, who, in turn, moved for a stay pending arbitration of the indemnity claims asserted against him by the owner. The owner opposed the motion for arbitration on the grounds that its claims against the charterer for indemnity and/or contribution arose not out of the charter but by reason of duties and obligations imposed by operation of law. The court held that the claims were subject to arbitration, and stated:

> . . . [T]he broad language of the arbitration clause covers the present dispute between the vessel owner and the charterer. Since the provision expressly applies to any dispute, the arbitration clause is not limited to purely contractual disputes but also covers those arising out of operation of law. (1979 AMC at 2845–46.)

In *Caribbean Steamship Co. S.A.* v. *Sonmez Denizcilik ve Ticaret A.S.*, above, the court held on the "unusual set of circumstances" presented that the owner was required to arbitrate with charterer a subrogated cargo claim it obtained by assignment from the insurer of its parent company. The facts were that the owner chartered the vessel to Caribbean, and the vessel loaded cargo which was owned by Caribbean's parent company, Reynolds. In the course of the voyage, the vessel sank and there was a total loss of cargo. Reynolds did not have an arbitration agreement with the owner, and the court held that it could not "pierce its own subsidiary's corporate veil" and demand arbitration with the owner under the charter with Caribbean. Reynold's subrogated insurer, however, assigned the cargo claim to Caribbean. Under the terms of the assignment, any recovery made by Caribbean was to be for the account of its assignor, the insurer. Having obtained this "assignment", Caribbean then demanded arbitration with the owner, and the court held that it was entitled to do so.

The court stated that the charterer could not force the owner to arbitrate Reynold's cargo claim. As the court observed:

> One cannot make an arbitrable claim out of a non-arbitrable one by assigning it to a person having a broad "any dispute" arbitration contract with the party against whom the claim lies, at least in the absence of evidence showing that the parties to the arbitration contract intended such a result. (1979 AMC at 1273.)

The court, however, went on to find that there was a "dispute" between the owner and charterer which was subject to arbitration. According to the court, by accepting the assignment from the insurer, the charterer caused what was "in effect, a claim for indemnity to be somewhat accelerated." While the charterer had not been held liable to Reynolds for the cargo loss, the court concluded that in the circumstances, its claim against the owner was sufficiently akin to a true indemnity claim that it was entitled to arbitrate it with the owner, subject, of course, to whatever defenses the owner might have.

Caribbean Steamship Co. was certainly an "unusual case" and, for this reason, it may be of limited significance as a precedent. If nothing else, however, it plainly demonstrates the strong policy followed by the court in resolving doubts in favor of arbitration.

Abandonment of arbitration

The failure to prosecute an arbitration can result in an award dismissing the claim on the grounds of abandonment. In *The Marathon*, S.M.A. No. 2425 (Arb. at N.Y. 1987), the arbitrators granted an award dismissing an arbitration with prejudice against the party who initiated it because of its failure to prosecute the claim over a period of 13 years. While the delay involved in *The Marathon* was extraordinary, the principle established by the decision is sound and certainly applicable to delays in prosecution of shorter time periods depending upon the facts of each case. Claims were also dismissed for lack of prosecution in *The Agios Nikolaos III*, S.M.A. No. 2540 (Arb. at N.Y. 1988) and *The Archangelos III*, S.M.A. No. 2541 (Arb. at N.Y. 1988).

Power to award interest, fees and costs

It has been held that arbitrators have inherent power to award interest and may, in their discretion, set the rate of interest at an amount which exceeds statutory limits for interest on judgments. *Finagrain Compagnie Commerciale Agricole et Financiere S.A.* v. *Federal Commerce & Navigation* (1974) *Ltd.*, 80 Civ. 0839 (S.D.N.Y., 3 September 1980) (slip opinion). In that case, the court held that an award of interest at the rate of 17 per cent. was within the power of the arbitrators.

In *In re Telfair Shipping Co.* v. *Institute Rio*, 1978 AMC 1120 (S.D.N.Y. 1978), the court confirmed an award allowing interest at the rate of $8\frac{1}{2}$ per cent. In *Oceania Shipping Corp.* v. *Thos. P. Gonzalez Corp.*, 442 F.Supp. 997 (S.D.N.Y. 1977), an award of 8 per cent. interest was upheld.

Arbitrators have power to order the parties to bear the costs of the proceeding, and may direct whatever apportionment of the costs they consider fair in the circumstances of the case. In *Oceania Shipping Corp.* v. *Thos. P. Gonzalez Corp.*, above, the court upheld an award where costs were apportioned 75 per cent. to one party and 25 per cent. to the other.

Unless the arbitration clause so provides, however, it appears that arbitrators do not have power to award attorneys' fees. In *Transvenezuelian Shipping Co. S.A.* v. *Czarnikow-Rionda Co. Inc.*, 1982 AMC 1458 (S.D.N.Y. 1982) the court held that the arbitrators exceeded their powers in awarding attorneys' fees where the arbitration clause of the charter did not expressly grant this power. *Accord*, *Sammi Line Co. Ltd.* v. *Altamar Navegacion S.A.* (*The Maria Sitinas*) 1985 AMC 1790 (S.D.N.Y. 1985). See also *Federal Commerce & Navigation Co. Ltd.* v. *Associated Metals & Minerals Corp.*, 1979 AMC 1733. 1734 (S.D.N.Y. 1978), where the court held that the Arbitration Act "contains no authorization for an award of fees".

In some cases, arbitrators have held that the fact that both parties claimed an allowance for attorneys' fees constituted an agreement between the parties that the panel had power to award such fees even in the absence of any empowering language in the charter. See, e.g., *The Manila Enterprise*, S.M.A. No. 2060 (Arb. at N.Y. 1983); *The Liberian Statesman*, S.M.A. No. 2092 (Arb. at N.Y. 1985). While it is doubtful that this approach is correct as a matter of law, it demonstrates the importance of clarifying either in the arbitration clause itself or in a submission agreement whether the parties intend that the arbitrators have power to award attorneys' fees and costs.

Punitive damages

In recent decisions, the courts and certain New York arbitrators have recognized the power of arbitrators to award punitive damages in appropriate cases where the arbitration is subject to the Federal Arbitration Act. There is nothing in the Arbitration Act itself which expressly empowers arbitrators to award punitive damages. Rather, the courts which have so held have relied upon the arbitration agreement at issue in the particular case before them, finding the contract broad enough to include punitive damage claims. Thus, in *Willis* v. *Shearson/American Express Inc.*, 569 F. Supp. 821 (N.D.N.C. 1983), the court held that a broad arbitration clause in a securities contract encompassed claims for punitive damages and stated: "Hence, the parties by their contract have authorized any arbitrator who may hear this matter to award punitive damages." 569 F. Supp. at 829.

Willis was followed in *Willoughby Roofing & Supply Co. Inc.* v. *Kajima Int'l Inc.*, 598 F.Supp. 353 (N.D. Ala. 1984), *aff'd per curiam* 776 F.2d 269 (11th Cir. 1985) where the court again emphasized its finding that the right arose from the arbitration agreement.

Punitive damages have been awarded under the general maritime law in cases involving maritime torts and for breach of contract where the conduct constituting the breach was also a tort. See generally *Thyssen Inc.* v. *Fortune Star*, 777 F.2d 57, 1986 AMC 1318 (2d Cir. 1985); *Protectus Alpha Navigation Co. Ltd.* v. *North Pacific Grain Growers Inc.*, 767 F.2d 1379, 1986 AMC 56 (9th Cir. 1985); *Muratore* v. *Scotia Prince*, 663 F.Supp. 484, 1988 AMC 859 (D. Me. 1987). In addition, there are United States statutes which might apply in an arbitration which provide for awards of punitive or exemplary damages.

The parties to an arbitration agreement may certainly limit the power of the arbitrators to award punitive damages. However, where there is a broad arbitration agreement such as the one in the printed New York Produce form, there is no reason to suppose that the scope of relief available to a claimant is any less broad than the governing law itself.

In *The Octonia Sun*, 1988 AMC 832 (Arb. at N.Y. 1988), a sole arbitrator awarded the claimant punitive damages where he found that the owner's conversion of cargo was "part and parcel of an ongoing practice of diverting cargo to ship's bunkers. Such conduct cannot and should not be considered acceptable practice and, in fact, should be vigorously condemned".

In *The Ellis Pontos*, S.M.A. No. 2116 (Arb. at N.Y. 1985), the panel declined to award punitive damages but appears to have assumed that it had power to award them. Similarly, in *The Kapetan Antonis*, 1989 AMC 551 (Arb. at N.Y. 1988), the arbitrators stated that they had power to award punitive damages, but declined to exercise it.

If the arbitration agreement is governed by New York State law, arbitrators are not permitted to award punitive damages. *Garrity* v. *Lyle Stuart Inc.*, 40 N.Y.2d 354, 386 N.Y.S.2d 831 (1976); *Publishers Ass'n of New York City* v. *Newspaper & Mail Deliverers' Union*, 280 A.D. 500, 114 N.Y.S. 2d 401 (1st Dep't. 1952).

Security in aid of award

One of the more important features of American maritime arbitration is contained in Section 8 of the Arbitration Act, which permits a claimant to obtain security for his claim by arresting or attaching the vessel or other property of the defendant, notwithstanding that the claim is subject to arbitration. Arrest or attachment of the defendant's property gives the court jurisdiction to order arbitration, and to retain jurisdiction over the parties to enter a decree on the arbitration award. In the usual Section 8 case, the action is commenced by "process of maritime attachment" or an arrest of the vessel, cargo or freight. It has been held, however, that non-maritime attachment remedies may also be used to initiate a Section 8 action. See *Murray Oil Products Co.* v. *Mitsui & Co.*, 146 F.2d 381 (2d Cir. 1944). Thus, Section 8 permits attachment for the dual purpose of providing the aggrieved party with security for his claim and giving the court jurisdiction over the defendant to order him to proceed to arbitration. See *The Anaconda* v. *American Sugar Refining Co.*, 322 U.S. 42 (1944); *Schoenamsgruber* v. *Hamburg American Line*, 294

U.S. 454 (1935); *The Belize*, 25 F.Supp. 663 (S.D.N.Y. 1938), appeal dismissed 101 F.2d 1005 (2d Cir. 1939). In the latter case, the court summarized the purpose of Section 8 in the following way:

> The purpose of section 8 is to give an aggrieved party in a maritime controversy the benefit of jurisdiction *in rem* or by foreign attachment and at the same time to save his right to an arbitration. . . . Under this section, libel and seizure of a vessel or other property may be the initial step in a proceeding to enforce an agreement for arbitration . . . . A person who commences suit in admiralty "by libel and seizure of the vessel or other property of the other party according to the usual course of admiralty proceedings" does not repudiate the arbitration clause and is not foreclosed from later demanding an arbitration. The statute is explicitly to that effect. (25 F.Supp. at 665).

An action may be commenced by attachment or arrest under Section 8 even if the arbitration clause provides for arbitration in London or some other foreign jurisdiction. See *Andros Compania Maritima* v. *Andre & Cie. S.A.*, 430 F.Supp. 88, 1977 AMC 668 (S.D.N.Y. 1977); *Atlas Chartering Services Inc.* v. *World Trade Group Inc.*, 453 F.Supp. 861, 1978 AMC 2033 (S.D.N.Y. 1978); *Paramount Carriers Corp.* v. *Cook Industries Inc.*, 465 F.Supp. 599, 1979 AMC 875 (S.D.N.Y. 1979).

It is of the utmost importance in this context that the attachment or arrest be effected under Section 8. In *McCreary Tire & Rubber Co.* v. *CEAT S.p.A.*, 501 F.2d 1032 (3d Cir. 1974), *Metropolitan World Tankers Corp.* v. *P.N. Pertambangan Minjakdangas Dumi National*, 1976 AMC 421 (S.D.N.Y. 1976), and *Sanko Steamship Co. Ltd.* v. *Newfoundland Refining Co. Ltd.*, 1976 AMC 417 (S.D.N.Y. 1976), aff'd on opinion below, 1976 AMC 417 (2d Cir. 1976), pre-arbitration attachments obtained pursuant to state law were vacated. In the first two cases, the attachments were vacated on the ground that to let them stand would be contrary to the Convention on the Recognition and Enforcement of Foreign Arbitral Awards, discussed below. In *Sanko*, the attachment was dismissed on grounds of *forum non conveniens*.

As a matter of good practice, in an arrest action, the complaint should name not only the property which is the subject of the *in rem* proceeding, but also the owner of the property. It has been held under Section 8, however, that the court may compel the shipowner to arbitrate even where the complaint named only the vessel *in rem* as a defendant. *E.A.S.T. Inc.* v. *Alaia*, 1988 AMC 1396 (E.D.La. 1987). See also *Industrial y Frutera Colombiana S.A.* v. *The Brisk*, 195 F.2d. 1015, 1952 AMC 738 (5th Cir. 1952).

Confirmation of the award

Section 9 of the Arbitration Act provides for the confirmation of an arbitration award. The award may be confirmed under the Act, however, only if the arbitration agreement expressly provides that a judgment of the court may be entered upon the award. In the New York Produce form, this requirement is fulfilled by the words "may be made a rule of the Court". The failure to include these or words of equivalent import in the arbitration agreement could create unnecessary difficulties in enforcing the award, since it has been held that the absence of such a provision precludes the courts from entering a judgment on the award. *Varley* v. *Tarrytown Associates Inc.*, 477 F.2d 208 (2d Cir. 1973); *Splosna Plovba of Piran* v. *Agrelak S.S. Corp.*, 381 F.Supp. 1368 (S.D.N.Y. 1974). In some cases the court has found that the parties intended that the arbitration agreement should allow the entry of a judgment on the arbitration award, even without explicit language to that effect. See *I/S Stavborg* v. *National Metal Converters Inc.*, 500 F.2d 424 (2d Cir. 1974).

It is possible to obtain judicial enforcement of the award without resorting to Section 9 of the Arbitration Act. The usual procedure would be to commence an action and seek summary judgment based on the award.

Only a final award can be confirmed. *E. B. Michaels* v. *Mariforum Shipping S.A.*, 624 F.2d 411, 1980 AMC 1901 (2d Cir. 1980). Thus, an interim award dealing, for example, with only the issue of the liability where damages questions have been reserved cannot be confirmed.

A partial final award or an interim award, however, that finally and definitively disposes of an independent claim may be confirmed even if other separate claims remain before the panel. *Eurolines Shipping Co. S.A.* v. *Metal Transp. Corp.*, 491 F.Supp. 590, 1980 AMC 2445 (S.D.N.Y. 1980). An award which is valid only in part may be confirmed in part, so long as the valid portion concerns claims that are separable from the invalid section. This exception to the general rule that in order to be "final" the award must resolve all the issues submitted to arbitration was explained by the court in *Puerto Rico Maritime Shipping Authority* v. *Star Lines Ltd.*, 454 F.Supp. 368 (S.D.N.Y. 1978), as follows:

> [I]f an award is valid in part and invalid in part, and the valid portion concerns claims that are "separate" from and "non-dependent" on claims covered by the invalid portion, the valid portion of the award is confirmable, notwithstanding the absence of an award that finally disposes of all the claims that were submitted to arbitration.

Partial final awards to shipowners for withheld freight were confirmed in *Unimarine S.A.* v. *Interessentslskapet Wind Endeavor*, 1984 AMC 405 (S.D.N.Y. 1981) and *Marabueno Compania Naviera S.A.* v. *Cayman Caribbean Carriers*, 1984 AMC 1849 (S.D.N.Y. 1984). Similarly, in *Southern Seas Navigation Ltd.* v. *Petroleos Mexicanos*, 606 F.Supp. 692, 1985 AMC 2190 (S.D.N.Y. 1985), an interim ruling setting an upper limit on charterer's claim and requiring that charterer reduce the amount stated in a Notice of Claim of Lien which charterer had filed on owner's Liberian registry to such limit was an award which could be confirmed by a court.

However, where a court refuses to confirm a partial final award, such refusal is not a final decision which is subject to an immediate appeal. *Liberian Vertex Transports Inc.* v *Associated Bulk Carriers Ltd.*, 738 F.2d 85, 1984 AMC 2841 (2d Cir. 1984).

An application to confirm an award must be brought within one year after the award is made. 9 U.S.C. §9. However, where both parties to an arbitration are foreign, even if the award is rendered in the United States, it will be subject to the Convention on the Recognition and Enforcement of Foreign Arbitral Awards, 9 U.S.C. §201, *et seq.* Thus, where an award is issued between two foreign parties, the award may be confirmed within three years pursuant to 9 U.S.C. §207 instead of the one-year limit stated in 9 U.S.C. §9. *Bergeson* v. *Joseph Muller Corp.*, 710 F.2d 928, 1983 AMC 1960 (2d Cir. 1938).

Once the panel has issued a final award, it becomes *functus oficio* and no longer has any power to reconsider its decision. *Ottley* v. *Schwartzberg*, 819 F.2d 373, 376 (2d Cir. 1987); *Proodos Marine Carriers Co.* v. *Overseas Shipping & Logistics*, 578 F.Supp. 207, 211 (S.D.N.Y. 1984). The court is authorized under the Arbitration Act, however, to correct obvious mathematical errors, 9 U.S.C. §11. In addition, where the court finds that the panel has rendered an indefinite, incomplete or ambiguous award, the court may remand the case to the arbitrators for clarification. See discussion below, at page 390. As we shall also discuss below, the power of the court to overturn a final arbitration award is quite deliberately circumscribed by the Arbitration Act.

Vacating the award

"Final Award"

Section 10 of the Arbitration Act specifies a number of grounds upon which an arbitration award may be vacated. Just as only a final award may be confirmed under Section 9 of the Act, only a "final award" properly can be the subject of a motion to vacate under Section 10.

In *E. B. Michaels* v. *Mariforum Shipping S.A.*, 624 F.2d 411, 1980 AMC 1901 (2d Cir. 1980), the charterer moved under Section 10 for an order vacating a "Decision & Interim Award" which dealt with issues of liability only and left certain claims for later decision. The court held that the motion was premature because the decision of the arbitrators was not "final". According to the court:

> In order to be "final", an arbitration award must be intended by the arbitrators to be their complete determination of all claims submitted to them . . .
>
> Generally, in order for a claim to be completely determined, the arbitrators must have decided not only the issue of liability of a party on the claim, but also the issue of damages.

See also *Mobil Oil Indonesia Inc.* v. *Asamera Oil (Indonesia) Ltd.*, 43 N.Y. 2d 275, 281–82, 401 N.Y.S. 2d 186, 187–88 (1977); *Finagrain Compagnie Commerciale Agricole et Financiere S.A.* v. *Federal Commerce & Navigation* (1974) *Ltd.*, 80 Civ. 0839 (S.D.N.Y., 3 September 1980) (slip opinion); *Golden Eagle Liberia Ltd.* v. *Amoco Transport Company*, 1979 AMC 698 (N.Y. County, Special Term, Part I, 1979).

The District Court does not have power under the Arbitration Act to review interlocutory rulings by arbitrators or to supervise the arbitration proceedings. *Compania Panemena Maritima San Gerassimo S.A.* v. *J. E. Hurley Lumber Co.*, 244 F.2d 286, 1957 AMC 1759 (2d Cir. 1957). Thus, rulings by the arbitrators on such matters as discovery, the issuance of subpoenas, objections to evidence and the limitless miscellany of procedural and substantive matters that arise in the course of an arbitration are not subject to review by the District Court except to the extent such rulings might provide grounds for attacking the final award: *see generally Complaint of Koala Shipping & Trading Inc.*, 587 F.Supp. 140 (S.D.N.Y. 1984). Even challenges to the qualifications or partiality of the arbitrators cannot be entertained by the District Court until a final award is rendered. *E. B. Michaels* v. *Mariforum Shipping S.A.*, above, 624 F.2d at 414n.4. See also *Florasynth Inc.* v. *Pickholz*, 750 F.2d 171, 174 (2d Cir. 1984).

As the court stated in *Commonwealth Oil Refining Co. Inc.* v. *S.S. Grand Commonwealth*, 1978 AMC 975, 976 (M.D. Fla. 1978):

> Once the District Court determines that the matter in dispute should be settled by arbitration, then it should not interfere with the work of the arbitrators during the course of their proceedings. To intervene would place this court in a position of reviewing the acts of the arbitrators in "midstream". This would open up a Pandora's Box for delaying tactics. The plaintiff will have ample opportunity for review of its grievances at the proper time. Any award by the arbitrators is subject to review by this Court in accordance with law.

"Time Limits"

Under 9 U.S.C. §12, a motion to vacate, modify or correct an award must be served within three months after the award is filed or delivered.

In *Florasynth Inc.* v. *Pickholz*, 750 F.2d 171 (2d Cir. 1984), the court held that the failure to move to vacate the award within three months precludes a party from later seeking that relief in opposing a motion to confirm the award. A motion to confirm filed within the three months' period prior to the filing of a motion to vacate imposes an obligation on the other party to move to vacate the award if he intends to do so. *Id.*; *The Hartbridge*, 57 F.2d 672 (2d Cir. 1932), *cert. denied* sub nom. *Munson S.S. Line* v. *North England S.S. Co.*, 288 U.S. 601 (1933).

"*Grounds of Attack*"

Section 10 of the Arbitration Act specifies the grounds upon which an arbitration award may be vacated, and it has been held that, with one exception, these are the *only* grounds upon which an award can be challenged. *Bell Aerospace Co. Division of Textron Inc.* v. *Local 516*, 500 F.2d 921 (2d Cir. 1974). There is a Federal policy which strongly favors arbitration, and it is for this reason that Congress has limited the opportunities for successful attacks on awards emerging from that process. Indeed, it has been noted that arbitration awards are presumed to be valid, and the burden of persuasion on the party moving to vacate is a very heavy one.

The grounds for challenging an award include the following:

> 10. (*a*) Where the award was procured by corruption, fraud or undue means.

As the plain language of this section indicates, it was designed to allow for the vacating of awards obtained by bribery, blackmail, duress and other forms of corruption.

In *Bonar* v. *Dean Witter Reynolds Inc.*, 835 F.2d 1378, 1383 (11th Cir. 1988), the court set forth a three-part test to determine whether an award should be vacated under Section 10(*a*):

1. The movant must establish the fraud by clear and convincing evidence.
2. The fraud must not have been discoverable upon the exercise of due diligence prior to or during the arbitration.
3. The person seeking to vacate the award must demonstrate that the fraud materially related to an issue in the arbitration.

Bonar is in accord with *Foster* v. *C.F. Turley Jr.*, 808 F.2d 38 (10th Cir. 1986); *Karpinnen* v. *Karl Kiefer Machine Co.*, 187 F.2d 32 (2d Cir. 1951); *Mobil Oil Indonesia Inc.* v. *Asamera Oil (Indonesia) Ltd.*, 487 F. Supp. 63 (S.D.N.Y. 1980); and *Newspaper Guild of New York* v. *New York Post Corp.*, No. 32 Civ. 7226 (DNE) (S.D.N.Y. 14 July 1983) (available on LEXIS, Genfed library, Dist. file).

It has been argued that "undue means" has a broader context, and should apply where the conduct of one of the parties in the arbitration, while not "corrupt" in nature, nonetheless has been prejudicial to the other. In *Drayer* v *Krasner*, 572 F.2d 348 (2d Cir. 1978), a disgruntled former employee of a securities concern brought an action for damages allegedly caused by the wrongful termination of his employment. The employee had been fired as the result of his alleged negligence in connection with a securities fraud. He was indicted for his involvement in the alleged fraud, but was acquitted although others who were involved were convicted. During the course of the arbitration, the securities company offered the indictment and a court decision affirming the conviction of the other participants in the fraud in evidence. While the arbitrators declined to accept these materials in evidence, apparently some or all of the arbitrators read them. The arbitration award went against the employee, who moved to vacate it on the grounds that he had been prejudiced by the arbitrators' reading of the indictment and the court decision.

The court denied the motion to vacate, and held that the open offer by the other party of prejudicial evidence did not fall within the meaning of "undue means". The court purposely confined its holding to the particular facts before it, however, and did not rule out the possibility that the acceptance in evidence of highly prejudicial evidence resulting in an adverse award might be deemed "undue means" under Section 10(*a*).

In another case involving an attack on an arbitration award under Section 10(*a*), *Catz American Co.* v. *Pearl Grange Fruit Exchange Inc.*, 292 F.Supp. 549 (S.D.N.Y. 1968), the court rejected the contention that the submission in evidence of a related court decision involving the petitioner's refusal to arbitrate, wherein the court stated that its defenses were "insubstantial" and a "sham", was "undue means".

See also *National Bulk Carriers Inc.* v. *Princess Management Co. Ltd.*, 597 F.2d 819, 825 (2d Cir. 1979), where the court held that the introduction of evidence concerning a settlement offer did not cause prejudice that would justify vacating the award.

10. (*b*) Where there was evident partiality or corruption in the arbitrators, or either of them.

It is not sufficient under this section that there is an "appearance of bias" on the part of one or more of the arbitrators to render the award open to attack. Rather, there must be proof of actual bias. In *International Produce Inc.* v. *A/S Rosshavet*, 638 F.2d 548, 1981 AMC 472 (2d Cir. 1981), *cert.* denied 69 L.Ed. 2d 389 (1981), there was a dispute between the owner and charterer of the *Ross Isle* arising out of a grounding. Each side appointed an arbitrator, and the two so chosen selected Hammond Cederholm as third arbitrator and chairman. The owners were represented in the arbitration by firm A; the charterers by firm B. Cederholm had no financial interest in either the owner or the charterer. He was, however, directly involved in another dispute in which the parties were different, but law firms A and B were again involved on opposite sides. Cederholm was involved in the second case for a customer of the brokerage company he was employed by and which was represented by firm A. His role in the dispute was such that he was called to testify on direct examination by firm A, and was subjected to cross-examination by lawyers from firm B.

The *Ross Isle* award was favorable to the clients of firm A, and the clients of firm B moved to vacate it, claiming that Cederholm's relationship with firm A in the second case created an appearance or presumption of partiality. The District Court agreed, and vacated the award.

The Court of Appeal reversed, and held that the mere appearance of bias is not sufficient to overturn an award. Rather, the act requires proof of actual bias.

The burden of proving "actual bias" is a heavy one. Indeed, as the court observed in *Merit Ins. Co.* v. *Leatherby Ins. Co.*, 714 F.2d 673, 681 (7th Cir. 1983), "of course actual bias might be present yet impossible to prove". It will be the very rare case where an ostensibly neutral arbitrator will admit that he is biased in favor of one of the parties. In recognizing the difficulties of proving bias, the court in *Merit Ins. Co.* concluded that "evident partiality" within the meaning of Section 10(*b*) could be shown "if circumstances are such that a man of average probity might reasonably be suspected of partiality . . . ". The court cautioned, however, that "the circumstances must be powerfully suggestive of bias . . . ".

A similar approach was taken in *Morelite Const. Corp.* v. *New York City District Council Carpenters Benefit Funds*, 748 F.2d 79, 84 (2d Cir. 1984), where the court stated that "evident partiality" will be found "where a reasonable person would have to conclude that an arbitrator was partial to one party to the arbitration".

In *Morelite*, the court vacated an arbitration award where the arbitrator was the son of the Vice President of one of the parties. The court found that the father–son relationship alone was sufficient to demonstrate "evident partiality". Without inquiring into how close the father and son were or how divergent their views were on the issues giving rise to the arbitration, the court nonetheless concluded:

> And without knowing more, we are bound by our strong feeling that sons are more often loyal to their fathers, partial to their fathers, and biased on behalf of their fathers. We cannot in good conscience allow the entering of an award grounded in what we perceive to be such unfairness. (748 F.2d at 84.)

See also *Standard Tankers (Bahamas) Co. Ltd.* v. *M/T Akti*, 438 F. Supp. 153, 1978 AMC 181 (E.D.N.C. 1977), holding that "to constitute evident partiality, some overt misconduct or demonstration or partiality is required".

An award was vacated in *Commonwealth Coatings Corp.* v. *Continental Casualty Co.*, 393 U.S. 145 (1968), on the basis of a finding that there was "evident partiality" on the part of the arbitrator. There, the arbitrator had earned some $12,000 in fees for consulting services rendered to the prevailing party over a period of about four years, and had even provided services on the dispute he was arbitrating. These facts were not disclosed to the losing party, and the court held that his failure to disclose required that the award be vacated. It appears from the decision that an arbitrator who "has a substantial interest in a firm which has done more than trivial business with a party" to the arbitration has an obligation to disclose that fact or risk a challenge on grounds of evident partiality when the award is issued.

So in *Miseroachi & Co. S.p.A.* v. *Peavey Int'l Inc.*, 78 Civ. 1571 (S.D.N.Y., 15 September 1978), an award was vacated where the arbitrator's company received commissions totalling $41,073.33 from one of the parties. The court stated that:

> . . . an arbitrator's receipt of income in amounts like those involved here from one of the parties to the arbitration is a matter which (1) must be disclosed and (2) is disqualifying upon objection unless waived or otherwise rendered immaterial.

See also *Transmarine Seaways Corp.* v. *Marc Rich & Co. A.G.*, 480 F.Supp. 352, 1979 AMC 1496 (S.D.N.Y. 1978), aff'd without opinion, 614 F.2d 1291, 1979 AMC 2906 (2d Cir. 1980), *cert.* denied 445 U.S. 930 (1980), where the court rejected a motion to vacate an award which complained that one of the arbitrators was employed by a company which, in turn, acted as agent for another company which had asserted unrelated claims against the party. The court held that the arbitrator's own relationship with the party did not require vacation of the award.

> 10. (*c*) Where the arbitrators were guilty of misconduct in refusing to postpone the hearing, upon sufficient cause shown, or in refusing to hear evidence pertinent and material to the controversy; or of any other misbehavior by which the rights of any party have been prejudiced.

It is fundamental that the arbitrators must conduct the proceedings in a manner which provides both parties with a fair and full opportunity to be heard and submit evidence on all issues before them. *Standard Tankers (Bahamas) Co. Ltd.* v. *M/T Akti*, 438 F.Supp. 153, 1978 AMC 181 (E.D.N.C. 1977). Section 10 (*c*) of the Arbitration Act provides that an award may be vacated if one of the parties is prejudiced by the manner in which the arbitration is conducted.

In *Totem Marine Tug & Barge Inc.* v. *North American Towing Inc.*, 607 F.2d 649, 1980

AMC 1961 (5th Cir. 1979), the award was vacated because of the arbitrators' *ex parte* communication with counsel for one of the parties which was prejudicial to the other party. The arbitrators had decided to award damages to the owner for a wrongful cancellation by the charterer, and measured the quantum of damages in part on the owner's loss of hire. After the close of the hearings and without advising the charterer's counsel, the arbitrators contacted the attorney representing the owner by telephone to ascertain the vessel's earnings. The reason for the call was that while all of the arbitrators had notes concerning the damages, each had a different figure written down. The number supplied by the owner's counsel differed from all of the numbers the arbitrators had noted, but it was accepted by the panel and incorporated in the award. The court found that the damages issue was clearly subject to dispute, and that the panel's *ex parte* communication with the owner's counsel constituted misbehavior sufficiently prejudicial to warrant vacation of the award under Section 10 (*c*).

The award was also vacated in *Cofinco Inc.* v. *Bakrie & Bros. N.V.*, 395 F.Supp. 613 (S.D.N.Y. 1975). That case involved disputes under contracts for the sale of green coffee which were arbitrated under the Rules of the Green Coffee Association. Under those rules, the case initially came before a three-man panel whose rulings were subject to appeal to a five-member panel. At the initial hearing, the claimant submitted only a partial record of evidence concerning its claim, and the respondent raised a threshold defense that the claim was time barred. The respondent submitted no evidence concerning the merits of the claim. The three-man panel adjourned the portion of the arbitration concerning the merits of the claim in order to first decided the time bar issue, which it later resolved in respondent's favor. The claimant then took an appeal to the five-man panel, which reversed on the time bar question. Moreover, based on the only incomplete evidence offered by the claimant in support of its claim, the five-man panel entered an award on the merits which was in favor of the claimant. The respondent moved to vacate the award, and contended that it had been deprived of its opportunity to defend the claim on the merits. The court held in favor of the respondent and vacated the award. According to the court, the five-man panel fell afoul of 9 U.S.C. §10 (*c*) "in refusing to hear evidence pertinent and material to the controversy" and was guilty, therefore, of misconduct. The court stated that:

> It makes no difference that the appellate panel may have acted only in neglectful disregard rather than by explicitly "refusing" to hear the evidence. The fundamental right to be heard was grossly and totally blocked. (395 F.Supp. at 615.)

See also *Chevron Transport Corp.* v. *Astro Vencedor Compania Naviera S.A.*, 300 F.Supp. 179, 1969 AMC 1582 (S.D.N.Y. 1969), where an award was vacated because of the failure of the arbitrators to make ship's logbooks in the possession of one of the parties available to the other: *Katz* v. *Uvegi*, 18 Misc. 2d 576, 583, 187 N.Y.S. 2d 511, 518 (Sup. Ct. 1959), aff'd 11 A.D. 2d 773, 205 N.Y.S. 2d 972 (App. Div. 1960), holding that:

> Arbitrators cannot conduct *ex parte* hearings or receive evidence except in the presence of each other and of the parties, unless otherwise stipulated.

In *Standard Tankers (Bahamas) Co. Ltd.* v. *M/V Akti*, above, the owner contended that the panel's refusal to allow it a second opportunity to cross-examine a key witness was a procedural error which deprived it of a fair hearing. The court denied the owner's motion to vacate the award and stated that "to amount to a procedural error which mandates vacation of the award, the actions of the panel must deprive the defendant of a fair hearing when viewed as a whole". (1978 A.M.C. at 185.)

See, generally, *The Konkar Pioneer*, 668 F.Supp. 267, 271–72 (S.D.N.Y. 1987).

10. (*d*) Where the arbitrators exceeded their powers, or so imperfectly executed them that a mutual, final, and definite award upon the subject matter submitted was not made.

The vague standards provided for in Section 10 (*d*) have been given a degree of plain meaning in the case decisions interpreting them.

"*Where the Arbitrators Exceeded Their Powers . . .*"

An award may be vacated if the arbitrators decide a claim that has not been submitted to them. This section of the Act, however, has been strictly interpreted, and any doubts about the scope of the submission agreement will be resolved in favor of coverage. As the court stated in *Andros Compania Maritima S.A.* v. *Marc Rich & Co. A.G.*, 579 F. 2d 691, 703 (2d Cir. 1978):

> We have consistently accorded the narrowest of readings to the Arbitration Act's authorization to vacate awards '[W]here the arbitrators exceeded their powers,' 9 U.S.C. §10 (*d*), especially where that language has been invoked in the context of arbitrators' alleged failure to correctly decide a question which all concede to have been properly submitted in the first instance.

As stated at the beginning of this section, arbitration is a creature of agreement between the parties. And, as the court stated in *Western Electric Co. Inc.* v. *Communication Workers of America, AFL-CIO*, 450 F.Supp. 876, 881 (S.D.N.Y. 1978) aff'd without opinion 591 F.2d 1333 (2d Cir. 1978).

> The powers of an arbitrator are defined by the agreement of the parties: the question they submit both establishes and limits the arbitrator's jurisdiction. It is the reviewing court's duty to determine whether the arbitrator has acted within that jurisdiction.

Where an arbitration is held pursuant to a submission agreement, that agreement will specify the claims to be decided by the panel and will then set the bounds of the proceedings. However, if the charter contains an arbitration clause, that is sufficient it itself to bind the parties to arbitrate any disputes covered by the clause. In this situation, the power of the arbitrators will be determined by the statement of claims submitted to them for decision.

In *Totem Marine Tug & Barge Inc.* v. *North American Towing Inc.*, 607 F.2d 649, 1980 AMC 1961 (5th Cir. 1979), the arbitrators ruled that Totem wrongfully terminated the charter. North American had claimed damages of $45,000 by reason of Totem's failure to redeliver the vessel at the agreed port. The claim covered the cost of returning the vessel. In its claim, North American did not seek to recover damages for charter hire due for the balance of the charter period. The panel nonetheless awarded North American damages which included the balance of hire due under the charter. Totem then moved to vacate the award on the grounds that the arbitrators exceeded their powers in rendering an award on a matter not submitted to them.

The court agreed with Totem that the arbitrators exceeded their powers by awarding damages for unpaid charter hire to North American. The court noted that the statement of claim submitted by North American made no reference to the claim for unpaid hire, and that the case had been argued and briefed by the parties without reference to that claim. Moreover, the court rejected the contention that the damage claim was "naturally intertwined in the general scope of the breach of contract claim".

The arbitrators also were held to have exceeded their powers in *The Matter of Cephalonian Shipping Co. S.A.*, 1979 AMC 1451 (S.D.N.Y. 1979). There, the District Court vacated an interim award because the arbitrators addressed the issue of failure to mitigate damages when all damages issues had been reserved by the parties for later submission following the panel's ruling on specified issues relating to the validity and performance of a settlement agreement.

The arbitrators are entitled to go beyond a specific issue, however, if in deciding that issue it is necessary to resolve other questions of law or fact. In *Federal Commerce & Navigation Co.* v. *Kanemastu-Gosho Ltd.*, 457 F.2d 387, 1972 AMC 946 (2d Cir. 1972), there was a master charter providing for 10 voyages. The first two voyages were not performed and a dispute arose. The parties were in disagreement on whether the arbitrators should decide just the dispute concerning the failure to perform the first two voyages, or whether they should deal with the validity of the master charter. It was finally agreed that they should submit for decision the question of whether the master charter had been voided by reason of various actions taken by the owner. The arbitrator nonetheless ruled on both the continuing validity of the master charter and the effect of the cancellation of the first two voyages. The owner then moved to vacate the award on the ground that the arbitrator had exceeded his powers.

The court upheld the award. It found that to decide the question submitted concerning the continuing validity of the master charter, the arbitrator had to deal also with the circumstances which led to the cancellation of the first two voyages. The court reasoned that the owner was on notice that the arbitrators would have to decide this subordinate issue in order to resolve the main question. According to the court, "an arbitrator is entitled to pass on every question of law or fact necessary to the disposition of the issue submitted to him". (457 F.2d at 389.)

The court further observed that it would be inappropriate to circumscribe the powers of the arbitrators so as to require that they treat the narrow issue submitted as an all or nothing proposition precluding consideration of anything else. To do so, the court observed, "would deny the power of the arbitrators to compromise the dispute in a manner which to them seemed appropriate and fair, as their knowledge of commercial practices qualified them to be". (457 F.2d at 390.)

As the court stated in *The Matter of Cephalonian Shipping Co. S.A.*, above:

> [A]s long as the award reflects a decision on issues either actually or necessarily before the arbitrator or as long as the award reflects a compromise on those issues, the award is entitled to affirmance.

In *The Machitis*, 1978 AMC 1120 (S.D.N.Y. 1978), the court held that the arbitrators did not exceed their powers in interpreting a *force majeure* clause, notwithstanding the contention that the clause was so clear on its face that no interpretation was required.

In *The Evryalos*, 1980 AMC 296 (S.D.N.Y. 1979), the court upheld the award even though the arbitrators did not answer the question submitted in the specific terms in which it was phrased.

In *The Konkar Pioneer*, 668 F. Supp. 267 (S.D.N.Y. 1987), the court held that arbitrators had authority to order a charterer to deposit the withheld charter hire which was in dispute in an interest-bearing jointly-held escrow account. According to the court, while there was no submission agreement which explicitly gave the panel authority to establish an escrow account, the arbitrators had implicit authority to order the deposit of funds in escrow.

In *Sun Ship Inc.* v. *Matson Navigation Co.*, 785 F.2d 59 (3d Cir. 1986), the court rejected as frivolous the argument that arbitrators exceeded their powers in awarding prejudgment interest at the prime rate rather than at the statutory rate prescribed by Pennsylvania law.

In *Gov't of India* v. *Cargill Inc.*, 867 F.2d 130 (2d Cir. 1989), the court held that arbitrators did not exceed their powers in exercising the discretion to extend the time for the issuance of the award.

" . . . [A] mutual, final and definite award"

An award may be vacated if it is not "final" and "definite" in deciding the issues submitted. In *Cofinco Inc.* v. *Bakrie & Bros. N.V.*, 395 F.Supp. 613, 616 (S.D.N.Y. 1975), for example, the award was vacated because the arbitrators failed to make a definite award of a sum certain. Without specifying amounts the arbitrators had simply awarded the claimant various "accrued expenses" and interest "at the average prime rate". As the court stated:

> The goal of the proceeding was, and remains, a sum certain. (395 F.Supp. at 616).

However, the courts have generally preferred to exercise their power to remand the case to the arbitrators to provide them with an opportunity to clarify the award. In *Americas Ins. Co.* v. *Seagull Compania Naviera S.A.*, 774 F.2d 64, 67 (2d Cir. 1985), the court stated that an ambiguous award should be remanded to the arbitrators to enable the court to know what it is being asked to enforce. An award was also remanded in *Olympia & York Florida Equity Corp.* v. *Gould*, 776 F.2d 42 (2d Cir. 1985) for the same reason. But see *Ottley* v. *Schwartzberg*, 819 F.2d 373 (2d Cir. 1987), holding that it was improper to remand to the arbitrators for the purpose of having the panel monitor compliance with their award.

Manifest disregard of the law

It has become an accepted principle that in addition to the grounds set out in Sections 10 (*a*)–(*d*), an award may be vacated if it was made in "manifest disregard of the law" or was "irrational". There are many cases in which the courts have so stated. See, e.g., *Wilko* v. *Swan*, 346 U.S. 427, 436–37 (1953), where the Supreme Court implied that awards rendered in "manifest disregard" of applicable law are subject to review; *Andros Compania Maritima S.A.* v. *Marc Rich & Co. A.G.*, 579 F.2d 691, 704 (2d Cir. 1978); *Sobel* v. *Hertz, Warner & Co.*, 469 F.2d 1211, 1214 (2d Cir. 1972); *San Martine Compania de Nav. S.A.* v. *Saquenay Term. Ltd.*, 293 F.2d 796 (9th Cir. 1961).

The principle was summarized in *Brotherhood of Railroad Trainmen* v. *Central of Georgia Co.*, 415 F.2d 403, 411–12 (5th Cir. 1969), as follows:

> In the arbitration context, an award "without foundation in reason or fact" is equated with an award that exceeds the authority or jurisdiction of the arbitrating body . . . The requirement that the result of arbitration have "foundation in reason or fact" means that the award must, in some logical way, be derived from the wording or purpose of the contract.

The Court of Appeals for the Second Circuit brought a welcome measure of clarity to this issue in *Merrill Lynch Pierce Fenner & Smith Inc.* v. *Bobker*, 808 F.2d 930 (2d Cir. 1986). The District Court had vacated a securities arbitration award on the ground that the arbitrators had acted in "manifest disregard" of the securities laws. In reversing the District Court, the Court of Appeals stated:

> Although the bounds of this ground have never been defined, it clearly means more than error or misunderstanding with respect to the law . . . The error must have been obvious and capable of

being readily and instantly perceived by the average person qualified to serve as an arbitrator. Moreover, the term "disregard" implies that the arbitrator appreciates the existence of a clearly governing legal principle but decides to ignore or pay no attention to it. (808 F.2d at 933.)

The court was clearly motivated by its oft expressed policy of deferring to arbitration as a favored method of resolving disputes. Under this standard, the scope of judicial review is extremely circumscribed and the proponent of a manifest disregard argument will bear the very heavy burden of showing that the arbitrators ignored governing law which was "well defined, explicit and clearly applicable". 808 F.2d at 934. The same rule was later applied by the court in *Gov't of India* v. *Cargill Inc.*, 867 F.2d 130 (2d Cir. 1989).

The required elements of a successful challenge on this ground have been set out in a number of decisions. Thus, in *The Machitis*, 1978 AMC 1120 (S.D.N.Y. 1978), the court stated:

The Court believes the real question to be whether the arbitrator's construction of the contract failed to meet the test of fundamental rationality . . . So long as the result is not irrational, arbitrators are free to fashion the law to fit the facts . . . The reviewing Court is bound by the arbitrators' interpretation of the contract . . . and will not set it aside for errors of fact or law or a misinterpretation of a contract where the arbitrators have not gone beyond the scope of the submission. (1978 AMC at 1123.)

In *I/S Stavborg* v. *National Metal Converters Inc.*, 500 F.2d 424 (2d Cir. 1974), the court found that the award was based on a "clearly erroneous interpretation of the contract" but that this interpretation was not "irrational" and therefore not a basis for upsetting the award. According to the court,

Whatever arbitrators' mistakes of law may be corrected, simple misinterpretations of contracts do not appear one of them. (500 F.2d at 432.)

It does seem to be established, however, that arbitrators are obliged to attempt to apply the law which governs the particular dispute before them. In *Sobel* v. *Hertz, Warner & Co.*, 469 F.2d 1211, 1214 (2d Cir. 1972), the court stated that "if the arbitrators simply ignore the applicable law, the literal application of a 'manifest disregard' standard should presumably compel vacation of the award".

It is equally correct, however, that the arbitrators' ruling will not be disturbed if there is "even a barely colorable justification for the outcome reached . . . ". *Andros Compania Maritima S.A.* v. *Marc Rich & Co. A.G.*, above.

In *Finagrain Compagnie Commerciale Agricole et Financiere S.A.* v. *Federal Commerce & Navigation* (1974) *Ltd.*, 80 Civ. 0839 (S.D.N.Y., 3 September 1980) (slip opinion), the District Court came close to vacating an award on grounds of manifest disregard of the law. The case arose out of a demurrage dispute which, after arbitrators had been appointed, was settled. The charterer later reinstated the claim, and the owner contended that the settlement barred the claim. The panel held that in settling the dispute, the charterer had waived its right to demand arbitration; the panel further held, however, that because of certain changed circumstances, the "waiver ceased to be effective" and that the charterer was entitled to assert the claim. The owner moved to vacate the award. The District Court stated that:

[W]ere the Court convinced that, under the factual circumstances, the Panel correctly had characterized Finagrain's settlement letter as a binding waiver, then the majority's further conclusion that upon Federal's later offer of compromise . . . the waiver "ceased to be effective" might well merit a vacation of the award for "manifest disregard of the law" . . . For if there was a valid, binding waiver, it could not thus be rescinded.

The court went on to conclude, however, that the arbitrators did not mean what they said when they referred to a "waiver", and that instead of a valid irrevocable waiver, there was "a discontinuance of arbitration without prejudice, or perhaps a conditional waiver of arbitration".

See, generally, *Sun Oil Co.* v. *Western Sea Transport Ltd.*, 1978 AMC 1372 (S.D.N.Y. 1978), holding that the panel's failure to follow another arbitration award was not a manifest disregard of the law; *The Machitis*, 1978 AMC 1120 (S.D.N.Y. 1978), where the court declined to disturb the panel's interpretation of a general exceptions clause; *Anthony Shipping Co. Ltd.* v. *Hugo Neu Corp.*, 482 F.Supp. 965, 1980 AMC 1477 (S.D.N.Y. 1980), holding that the dismissal of a claim by the arbitrators on grounds of laches was not in manifest disregard of the law.

An award cannot be vacated merely because the arbitrators have not stated the reasons for their decision. In *United Steelworkers of America* v. *Enterprise Wheel & Car Corp.*, 363 U.S. 593, 598 (1960) the Supreme Court reaffirmed the principle that "arbitrators have no obligation to the Court to give their reason for an award".

Violation of public policy

A variation on the judicially-created doctrine of manifest disregard of the law was fashioned in *In re Sea Dragon Inc.*, 574 F.Supp. 367, 1984 AMC 699 (S.D.N.Y. 1983). The District Court vacated an award on the ground that it was against the public policy of the United States. The award directed the charterer to pay freight to the owner, which payment had been enjoined by a Netherlands court sequestration order obtained by a creditor of charterer. The court found that the effect of the award was to direct the charterer to violate the Dutch decree. Such a result would have placed charterer in an untenable position and, more importantly, was contrary to the doctrine of comity. Because the award compelled a violation of Dutch law, it was found to be contrary to American public policy.

Convention on the Recognition and Enforcement of Foreign Arbitral Awards

If the arbitration agreement provides for arbitration in London or some other foreign jurisdiction, it may nonetheless be enforced in New York or elsewhere in the United States under Sections 201–208 of the Arbitration Act. These sections implement the United Nations Convention on the Recognition and Enforcement of Foreign Arbitral Awards, and include provisions by which the aggrieved party may compel the other to proceed to arbitration in the foreign jurisdiction or enforce an award rendered abroad. In addition to the United States, most of the major maritime nations, including the United Kingdom, are parties to the Convention.

With respect to motions to compel arbitration under the Convention, it has been held that "the Convention contemplates a very limited inquiry by courts". *Sedco* v. *Petroleos Mexicanos*, 767 F.2d 1140, 1986 AMC 706 (5th Cir. 1985). In *Ledee* v. *Ceramiche Ragno*, 684 F.2d 184, 185–86 (1st Cir. 1982), the court outlined four questions to be answered in deciding whether a motion to compel arbitration under the Convention should be granted:

1. Is there an agreement in writing to arbitrate the dispute; in other words, is the arbitration agreement broad or narrow;
2. Does the agreement provide for arbitration in the territory of a convention signatory;
3. Does the agreement to arbitrate arise out of a commercial legal relationship;
4. Is a party to the agreement not an American citizen?

The Convention requires that District Courts compel arbitration if these criteria are met.

Foreign arbitration awards governed by the Convention can be enforced in the District Courts of the United States. To advance the objectives of the Convention, under 9 U.S.C. §208 a summary procedure in the form of a motion can be utilized to obtain confirmation. Thus, a number of awards have been confirmed upon motions supported by affidavits. See, e.g., *Imperial Ethiopian Gov't* v. *Baruch-Foster Corp.*, 535 F.2d 334, 335 n.2 (5th Cir. 1976).

Under Section 207, an action to enforce an arbitral award falling under the Convention must be made within three years after the award was issued. In order to bring an enforcement action in the United States, however, the respondent must be subject to *in personam* jurisdiction in the court in which the action is brought in the United States. In *Transatlantic Bulk Shipping Ltd.* v. *Saudi Chartering S.A.*, 1985 AMC 2432 (S.D.N.Y. 1985), the court declined a petition for confirmation of a London arbitration award because the respondent was not subject to personal jurisdiction in New York.

The Convention also applies to commercial arbitration awards rendered in the United States. *Bergeson* v. *Joseph Muller Corp.*, 710 F.2d 928 (2d Cir. 1983). There, the court noted that the fact that the award might also have been enforced under the Arbitration Act was of no significance. According to the court, "there is no reason to assume that Congress did not intend to provide overlapping coverage between the Convention and the Federal Arbitration Act". 710 F.2d at 934. The point was of considerable importance to the party seeking to enforce the award because, while the one-year limitation on actions to enforce awards under the Arbitration Act had run, the three-year period provided for in the Convention had not.

Only the limited grounds set out in Article V are available under the Convention to oppose confirmation of an award which falls under the Convention. The defense that the arbitrators exceeded their powers is available under Article V(1) (*c*). This section is similar in scope to Section 10 (*d*) of the Arbitration Act, discussed above. This defense is to be construed narrowly, but allows a party "to attack an award predicated upon arbitration of a subject-matter not within the agreement to submit to arbitration". *Parsons & Whittemore Overseas Co. Inc.* v. *Société Generale de L'Industrie du Papier*, 508 F.2d 969, 976 (2d Cir. 1974).

In *Waterside Ocean Navigation* v. *Int'l. Nav. Ltd.*, 737 F.2d 150, 1985 AMC 349 (2d Cir. 1984), the party opposing confirmation of London arbitration awards relied upon the public policy defense set out in Article V(2). It was argued that the awards on damages were based on perjured testimony and that confirmation would be contrary to the public policy against fraud. The court rejected this argument. While agreeing that in order to maintain the integrity of the judicial system "it is important that a litigant not be encouraged to 'blow hot and cold' in a series of proceedings" (737 F.2d at 152) the court stated that it would be contrary to the purposes of the Convention were the court to inquire into the record to determine the significance of alleged inconsistencies in the evidence reviewed by the arbitrators. The court suggested that the forum in which the alleged inconsistent testimony was given should be looked to for whatever remedies were available to rectify any injury arising therefrom. The court adhered to its prior ruling in *Fotochrome Inc.* v. *Copal Co.*, 517 F.2d 512 (2d Cir. 1975) that "the public policy defense should be construed narrowly . . . [and] should apply only where enforcement would violate our 'most basic notions of morality and justice' ". 737 F.2d at 152. See also *Parsons & Whittemore Overseas Co. Inc.* v. *Société Generale de L'Industrie du Papier*, above; *Fertilizer Corp. of India* v. *IDI Mgt. Inc.*, 530 F.Supp. 542 (S.D. Ohio 1982).

The judicially-created ground of "manifest disregard of the law" discussed above for seeking to vacate an arbitration award under the Arbitration Act is not available under the Convention. *Brandeis Intsel Ltd.* v. *Calabrian Chemicals Corp.*, 656 F. Supp. 160, 165 (S.D.N.Y. 1987). The court further ruled in that case that "manifest disregard" of law was not the equivalent of contravening public policy within the meaning of Article V of the Convention. The issue was discussed, but not decided in *Parsons & Whittemore Overseas Co. Inc.* v. *Société Generale de L'Industrie du Papier*, above.

Under Article VI of the Convention, the court asked to enforce the award may, in its discretion, adjourn decision on the enforcement of the award if an application to have the award set aside or suspended has been made to the court or other competent authority in the country where the award was made.

There is an important provision in Article VI which gives the court the power to order the other party to give suitable security to the party seeking to enforce the award. The District Court relied upon Article VI in adjourning enforcement proceedings in *Spier* v. *Calzaturificio Tecnica S.p.A.*, 663 F.Supp. 871 (S.D.N.Y. 1987) pending resolution of a challenge to the award before the Italian court. The court observed that adjourning the enforcement action was preferable to the possible alternative course of granting a judgment on the award, only to find out later that the award was set aside by the court of the country where it was issued. 663 F.Supp. at 875.

See also *Fertilizer Corp. of India* v. *IDI Management Inc.*, 517 F.Supp. 948, 962 (S.D. Ohio 1981), reconsideration denied 530 F.Supp. 542 (S.D. Ohio 1982), where the court adjourned its decision on enforcement of an award rendered in India until the Indian courts decided with finality whether the award was valid. The court directed that security be posted under Article VI pending the outcome of the Indian proceedings.

American courts will allow actions under Section 8 to obtain security in aid of an arbitration agreement which is enforceable under the Convention even though the Convention itself does not expressly authorize attachments or arrests. In *Paramount Carriers Corp.* v. *Cook Industries Inc.*, 465 F.Supp. 599, 1979 AMC 875 (S.D.N.Y. 1979), the court upheld a maritime attachment under Section 8 in connection with a demurrage dispute which was subject to arbitration under the Convention. The issue was raised but not decided in *Polar Shipping Ltd.* v. *Oriental Shipping Corp.*, 680 F.2d 627, 1982 AMC 2330 (9th Cir. 1982).

Post-award, pre-judgment interest can be awarded by the District Court in enforcing awards covered by the Convention. *Waterside Ocean Nav.* v. *Int'l Nav. Ltd., above*, 737 F.2d at 153–155.

Binding effect of arbitration award on third parties

In certain situations, an arbitration award may be binding on third parties who did not participate in the arbitration. In *SCAC Transport (USA) Inc.* v. *S.S. Danaos*, 845 F.2d 1157 (2d Cir. 1988), the court held that a stevedore was bound by the results of an arbitration between the owner and charterer after the stevedore had been properly vouched into the proceeding. The underlying claim was for damage to a truck which occurred while it was being loaded aboard the vessel. Owner settled with cargo interests and demanded arbitration with charterer to seek indemnity. The charter provided for London arbitration. The charterer then tendered defense of the London arbitration to the stevedore, but the stevedore declined to accept it. The arbitration then proceeded and an award was entered in favor of owner and against the charterer. The charterer then sued the stevedore for indemnity in New York and prevailed. The court held that, because of its declination of the tender of defense, the stevedore was bound by the finding of the London arbitrators that its negligence caused the accident. The court noted that, in a case of this type, arbitration provided an effective and efficient remedy for all concerned, and held that "absent a particularized showing of prejudice, a stevedore may be vouched into arbitration under a charter party by a charterer where the stevedore is the charterer's indemnitor". (845 F.2d at 1158).

Time to commence proceedings

See page 434 below.

Liens

"110. 18. That the Owners shall have a lien upon all cargoes, and all sub-freights for any amounts due under this Charter, including General Aver-
111. age contributions, and the Charterers to have a lien on the Ship for all monies paid in advance and not earned, and any overpaid hire or excess
112. deposit to be returned at once. Charterers will not suffer, nor permit to be continued, any lien or encumbrance incurred by them or their agents, which
113. might have priority over the title and interest of the owners in the vessel."

Important distinction between English and American law

English and American law differ significantly as to the nature of the liens given by this clause. Under American law (as to which see page 406 below) Clause 18 will generally create maritime liens enforceable by an action *in rem*. Under English law the liens are contractual only (see below) and no maritime liens are created.

The nature of the owners' lien upon cargoes

In English law liens may be maritime liens in admiralty or may be granted by the common law, by equity, by statute or by contract. The lien of owners over cargoes, given by Line 110 of the New York Produce form or Line 126 of the Baltime form is a contractual lien only. It has no independent root in admiralty, common law, equity or statute. Consequently it creates a right only as between the parties to the contract in which it is contained. So it does not give the owners any right, as against bill of lading holders other than the time charterers, to lien their cargo.

The *Bombay* was time chartered for six months with an option to sublet and was sub-chartered for a round voyage. The head charter provided that bills of lading were to be signed at any rate of freight the charterers or their agents might direct without prejudice to the charter. The charter further provided that the owners were to have a lien "upon all cargoes for freight or charter money due under this charter." Bills of lading were issued to the sub-charterers and the owners sought to exercise a lien on the sub-charterers' cargo for time charter hire. It was held by the Privy Council that the owners had no right of lien on the sub-charterers' cargo. Lord Lindley said: "as regards . . . giving a lien upon all cargoes for freight or charter money due under that charter. This is a stipulation binding on the time charterer, and gives the shipowner a more extensive lien than he would have for freight payable in advance. But this clause does not override or limit the power of the captain to issue bills of lading at different rates of freight, or entitle the shipowners to a lien on the goods of persons who have come under no contract with them conferring a lien for the freight payable under the time charter. A right to seize one person's goods for another person's debt must be clearly and distinctly conferred before a Court of justice can be expected to recognise it."

Turner v. *Haji Goolam* [1904] A.C. 826.

In such a case, if the owners, owed monies by the charterers, exercise their lien by refusing to release the cargo from their ship, they will have a good defence to a claim by the charterers for breach of Clause 8 of the New York Produce form ("That the Captain shall prosecute his voyages with the utmost despatch") and hire will continue to be payable for the period of delay. See *The Chrysovalandou Dyo* above and page 398 below.

Possessory

The lien given to owners by Line 110 of the New York Produce form or Line 126 of the Baltime form is a possessory lien, the owners' right being to retain possession of cargo until monies owed to them by the charterers have been paid. In *Hammonds* v. *Barclay* (1802) 2 East 227, Grose, J., said: "A lien is a right in one man to retain that which is in his possession belonging to another, till certain demands of him the person in possession are satisfied." This accurately describes the nature of the owners' lien upon cargo, which is in their possession by being on their ship.

Over which cargoes the lien may be exercised

As stated above, the owners' lien gives them no right as against cargo owners other than the time charterers themselves where that lien has not been incorporated into the relevant bill of lading. But the question arises whether the owners may nevertheless detain cargo in such circumstance *as between themselves and the time charterers.*

Baltime form

It is clear from Line 126 of the Baltime form that the owners are given a right to lien only those cargoes which belong to the charterers: "The Owners to have a lien upon all cargoes and sub-freights belonging to the Time-Charterers." See *The Mihalios Xilas* [1978] 2 Lloyd's Rep. 186.

New York Produce form

By contrast with the words in Line 126 of the Baltime form, the words in Line 110 of the New York Produce form do not expressly limit the cargoes that may be liened to those owned by the charterers. This raises the question whether the owners may, *as against the charterers*, detain on board their ship cargo not owned by the charterers, despite the fact that, in the absence of a bill of lading provision incorporating the charter lien clause, they have no right of lien as against the cargo owners. There are conflicting decisions on this point.

Mocatta, J., in *The Agios Giorgis* [1976] 2 Lloyd's Rep. 192 (see page 208 above) held that the owners were not, even as against the charterers, justified in detaining cargo under Line 110 of the charter where the charterers had failed to pay hire and the cargo detained belonged to other parties. But a contrary conclusion was reached shortly thereafter by Donaldson, J., in *The Aegnoussiotis* [1977] 1 Lloyd's Rep. 268.

In both the above cases payments of time charter hire were overdue and the owners instructed their masters not to discharge the cargo until the hire was paid. The cargoes in both cases belonged to parties other than the charterers. In *The Agios Giorgis*, Mocatta, J., took the view that even assuming the right to lien was governed by the proper law of the charter (as opposed to the law of the place where the supposed lien was exercised) English law required for the valid exercise of a contractual lien that the owner of the cargo held should be a party to the contract. Since that was not the case the owners had no right of lien to justify their refusal to discharge the cargo.

In *The Aegnoussiotis*, Donaldson, J., was aware of the decision of Mocatta, J., but took a different view. He said: "In my judgment, cl. 18 is to be construed as meaning what it says, namely, that the time charterers agree that the owners shall have a lien upon all cargoes. In so far as such cargoes are owned by third parties, the time charterers accept an obligation to procure the creation of a contractual lien in favour of the owners. If they do not do so and the owners assert a lien over such cargo, the third parties have a cause of action against the owners. But the time charterers themselves are in a different position. They cannot assert and take advantage of their own breach of contract. As against them, the purported exercise of the lien is valid."

Lloyd, J., in *The Cebu* [1983] 1 Lloyd's Rep. 302, at page 306, expressed a preference for the view of Donaldson, J., in *The Aegnoussiotis*, on the ground that it was more in accord with the law as stated in *Paul* v. *Birch* (1743) 2 Atk. 621. Certainly the approach of Donaldson, J., gives practical effect to the stipulation that the owners shall have a lien on all cargoes. It also appears to be more consistent with assumptions made by the Court of Appeal in *Tonnelier and Bolckow, Vaughan* v. *Smith* (1897) 2 Com. Cas. 258, but the law on this point is not yet fully developed.

If the decision of Donaldson, J., in *The Aegnoussiotis* is correct, the detention of cargo not belonging to the charterers may in certain circumstances be valid as against the charterers but wrongful as against the bill of lading holders. This raises the question whether the owners would have any right to an indemnity from the charterers in respect of liability incurred to the bill of lading holders for wrongful detention of their cargo. If, in the somewhat unlikely event that the cargo were detained by the master and the owners without knowledge of the ownership of the cargo or of the terms of bills of lading issued by the charterers, it would seem that a right of indemnity should arise. If, on the other hand, the cargo were wrongfully detained with knowledge of the ownership of the cargo and of the terms of the bills of lading, there should be no right of indemnity in respect of any liability to the bill of lading holders. Such action would be manifestly wrong: see, by way of analogy, *Strathlorne Steamship* v. *Weir* (1934) 50 Ll.L.Rep. 185, page 237 above, and for comments generally on the employment and indemnity clause pages 236 to 242.

Where the bills of lading incorporate (expressly or by reference) the charter lien clause the problem discussed above does not arise; the owners then have a contractual right to lien the cargo, whether or not it is owned by the charterers, and this they may exercise. See the judgment of Mocatta, J., in *The Chrysovalandou Dyo* [1981] 1 Lloyd's Rep. 159, at page 165.

Where the lien on cargoes may be exercised

If the owners do have the right to lien cargo, they cannot usually exercise this right by halting the laden ship en route to the port of discharge. In *The Mihalios Xilas* [1978] above, the owners halted the ship at a bunkering port on the voyage. Donaldson, J., said: "I do not think that a shipowner can usually be said to be exercising a lien on cargo simply by refusing to carry it further . . . It may be possible to exercise a lien by refusing to complete the carrying voyage, but I think that this can only be done when, owing to special circumstances, it is impossible to exercise a lien at the port of destination and any further carriage will lead to loss of possession of the cargo following arrival at that port."

It seems, however, that it will usually be sufficient for the ship to have anchored off the declared port of discharge. Mocatta, J., so held in *The Chrysovalandou Dyo* [1981] 1 Lloyd's Rep. 159. He rejected an argument by the charterers that, on the basis of the above judgment of Donaldson, J., the owners could not exercise their lien "unless the vessel was at a discharging spot, whether wharf of buoy", saying: "To require this might involve unnecessary expense and in certain cases cause congestion in the port."

The nature of the owners' lien upon sub-freights

This lien is similar to the owners' lien upon cargoes, discussed above, in that it is contractual only. It differs, however, in that it operates not as a right to retain possession of something already in the owners' possession but as a right to intercept that which is moving from a third party to the charterers. Indeed this makes it doubtful whether it can properly be described as a "lien" at all, see page 401 below.

The meaning of "sub-freights"

Sub-freights include any renumeration earned by the charterers from the employment of the ship, whether by way of voyage freight or time charter hire. Lloyd, J., so held in *The Cebu* [1983] 1 Lloyd's Rep. 302, following *Inman Steamship* v. *Bischoff*, below. He also held that in the context of the New York Produce form they include all sub-freights, including sub-sub-freight and sub-timecharter hire, whether due to the charterers direct or not: see page 402 below. They may also include any monies which could be regarded as monies derived from the employment of the ship by the time charterers.

The *City of Paris* was time chartered for a monthly hire, the owners having effected an insurance "on freight outstanding". A claim under the policy proceeded on the footing, which was acccepted by the House of Lords, that "freight" included time charter hire. Lord Blackburn said, quoting Lord Tenterden in *Flint* v. *Flemying* 1 B. & Ad. 48: " 'Freight as used in the policy of insurance, imports the benefit derived from the employment of the ship'; so that description covers the monthly hire of the ship for time."

Inman Steamship v. *Bischoff* (1882) 7 App. Cas. 670.

(See also *Seven Seas* v. *Atlantic Shipping* [1975] 2 Lloyd's Rep. 188 and the judgments of the Court of Appeal in *The Nanfri* [1978] 2 Lloyd's Rep. 132, in which divergent views were expressed on whether "hire" was to be treated as "freight", but in the context of the application of the rule as to deductions from freight.)

Sub-freights payable to the owners

If the owners are parties to the bill of lading contract they will not have to rely upon rights of lien, for they, rather than the charterers, will be entitled to receive the freight, although they will be bound to account for it to the charterers. Rights of lien will only be relevant where the charterers are contractually entitled to receive the sub-freights in the first instance. As Greer, J., said in *Molthes Rederi* v. *Ellerman's Wilson Line* (1926) 26 Ll.L.Rep. 259, at page 262: "It seems a misuse of words to say that a shipowner has a lien on the debt due to him under the contract made with him by a bill of lading. The lien clause in the charter-party is needed to give the owner a lien in those cases where the sub-freight is due to the charterer and not to the owner . . . "

Where a ship is under time charter, bill of lading freight will normally, in practice, be paid to the charterers' agents, even though the cargo is shipped under bill of lading contracts to which the owners are a party. If the owners notify the charterers' agents of their claim to the bill of lading freight before the agents receive the freight the agents may be obliged to collect it for the owners rather than for the charterers. The same is probably true where notice is given by the owners after freight has been received by the agents: this was decided in *Wehner* v. *Dene* [1905] 2 K.B. 92, but was expressly left open in the subsequent case of *Molthes Rederi* v. *Ellerman's Wilson Line* (1926) 26 Ll.L.Rep. 259: see further below.

The owners are bound to account to the time charterers for any bill of lading freight received by them after they have deducted the amount due to them under the time charter. The owners may deduct only those sums that are due to them at the time the bill of lading freight was paid to the agents.

The *Ferndene* was on time charter and was sub-time chartered for a trip. Bills of lading were issued under the sub-timecharter and were signed by the master. The sub-timecharterers appointed agents to collect the bill of lading freight. On 15 December these agents received the freight from the consignees. On 16 December the owners gave notice to the agents of their claim for the freight collected. At that time there remained unpaid a part of the semi-monthly hire due under the head time charter on 9 December. On 23 December a further semi-monthly hire payment became due to the owners. The question arose whether it was the sub-timecharterers or the owners who were entitled to the bill of lading freight. Channell, J., held:

1. Since the bill of lading contract was with the owners, they were entitled to the bill of lading freight.
2. The agents appointed by the sub-time charterers were to be regarded, in the absence of evidence to the contrary, as agents for the owners as well as for these charterers.
3. Accordingly, the owners were entitled to the freight received by the agents on 15 December but were bound to account for it to the sub-time charterers, deducting only the amount due to the owners at the date of receipt.
4. Accordingly, the owners were not entitled to deduct the amount of hire which only became due on 23 December.

Channell, J., said: "Now, although the owner has the right to demand the bill of lading freight from the holder of the bill of lading because the contract is the owner's contract, yet the owner has also, of course, contracted by the charterparty that for the use of his ship he will be satisfied with a different sum, which will also in the great majority of cases be less than the total amount of the bills of lading freights; and, therefore, if the owner were himself to demand and receive the bills of lading freight, as he might do if he chose, he would still have to account to the charterer or the sub-charterer, as the case might be, for the surplus remaining in his hands after deducting the amount due for hire of the ship under the charterparty."

Wehner v. *Dene* [1905] 2 K.B. 92.

Before the bill of lading freights are paid, the owners may call upon the agents appointed by the charterers to collect the freight to do so on their behalf instead. The agents may then be obliged to collect the freight as the owners' agents and pay it to them. The agents will not be entitled to deduct from the freight so collected disbursements incurred by them in their capacity as agents for the charterers.

The *Sproit* was time chartered on the Baltime form and sub-chartered for a voyage. Agents were appointed at the port of discharge by the time charterers to attend to discharge and collect freight. Before any freight was paid representatives of the owners required these agents to collect the freight as agents for the owners, because a considerable amount of hire was overdue under the time charter. The agents agreed, but subsequently refused to hand over the freight collected on the ground that disbursements incurred by them already exceeded the amount in hand. It was held by Greer, J., that although the agents were agents for the time charterers, the owners were entitled to call upon them to collect the freight on their behalf when they (the owners) were parties to the bill of lading contracts. It was held further that the agents were not entitled to deduct from the freight disbursements incurred by them in their capacity as agents for the time charterers. The judge expressly refrained from expressing an opinion as to whether (as had been decided in *Wehner* v. *Dene*, above) the agents in such circumstances would be bound to account to the owners for freight received before the owners gave notice of their claim: he found difficulty in reconciling the decision of Channell, J., in *Wehner* v. *Dene*, above, with the decision of the Court of Appeal in *Tagart, Beaton* v. *Fisher*, below.

Molthes Rederi v. *Ellerman's Wilson Line* (1926) 26 Ll.L.Rep. 259.

Sub-freights payable to the charterers

The lien given to the owners by Line 110 of the New York Produce form extends also to situations in which the charterers are entitled to receive the bill of lading freight or where the sub-freights are payable to the charterers under sub-charters. But this lien differs from the lien that the owners have over cargoes; the latter is a possessory lien capable of being exercised by the owners by holding on to cargo that is already in their possession, whereas the former depends not on the retention of existing possession but on the interception of the sub-freights before they can be paid over to the charterers. See the judgments of Robert Goff, J., in *The Lancaster* [1980] 2 Lloyd's Rep. 497, and of Mocatta, J., in *The Vestland* [1980] 2 Lloyd's Rep. 171. Lord Russell in *The Nanfri* [1979] 1 Lloyd's Rep. 201, at page 210, said of the owners' lien on sub-freights: "The lien operates as an equitable charge upon what is due from the shipper to the charterer, and in order to be effective requires an ability to intercept the sub-freight (by notice of claim) before it is paid by shipper to charterer." See also *The Attika Hope* [1988] 1 Lloyd's Rep. 439, below.

The right of the owners to intercept sub-freights due to the charterers will be lost once the freight is paid to the agents appointed by the charterers to collect it. Greer J., said in *Molthes Rederi* v. *Ellerman's Wilson Line* (1926) 26 Ll.L.Rep. 259, above, that where sub-freights were due to the charterers: " . . . the owner could only become entitled to the sub-freight by virtue of the lien clause, and it would be too late to exercise his lien after the debt had been paid to and received by the charterer personally or through his agent."

This was the effect of a decision of the Court of Appeal in the case of *Tagart, Beaton* v. *Fisher* [1903] 1 K.B. 391 which is summarised below, although the case does not satisfactorily explain why the sub-freights were due to the charterers rather than to the owners. It was suggested by Greer, J., in the *Molthes Rederi* case, above, that it was because the freight was not paid under the bill of lading contract, the bill of lading having been issued to the charterers and having taken effect as a receipt only. It was inferred by Greer, J., that the freight was paid under a sub-charter.

The *Askehall* was chartered under a time charter which provided that the owners should have a lien upon all cargoes and sub-freights for any amount due under the charter. Freight was paid by the consignees to agents appointed by the time charterers to collect the freight on their behalf. After the consignees had paid the freight, but before the agents had parted with it, the owners purported to exercise a lien on the freight in the hands of the agents. It was held by the Court of Appeal that payment to the time charterers' agents was payment to the time charterers themselves and the owners' right of lien was lost.

Tagart, Beaton v. *Fisher* [1903] 1 K.B. 391.

Freights payable to sub-charterers

The right of the owners under Line 110 of the New York Produce form to intercept sub-freights extends to sub-freights due to sub-charterers—and not therefore payable to the time charterers direct—if, under the terms of the sub-charter, the time charterers have similar rights of lien to those given to the owners under the head charter.

The *Cebu* was time chartered on the New York Produce form, then sub-time chartered by the head charterers to Lamsco and then again was sub-time chartered by Lamsco to Itex. Both the sub-charters were also on the New York Produce form. The owners claimed that there was hire due to them under the head charter and the case proceeded on the assumption that an equivalent amount of hire was due to the head charterers from Lamsco. The owners sent notices to Itex and later to Lamsco purporting to exercise their lien under Clause 18 of the head charter. It was held by Lloyd, J., that:

(1) "sub-freights" in the context of Clause 18 of the New York Produce form included not only sub-time charter hire but also sub-sub-time charter hire; and
(2) the owners' lien which was in the nature of an equitable assignment, attached not only to hire due to the head charterers, but also to hire due to the sub-time charterers, Lamsco; the head charterers, by virtue of the Clause 18 lien in the sub-time charter, were themselves entitled, as assignees, to intercept the sub-sub-time charter hire due from Itex to Lamsco and they had validly assigned this right to the owners by Clause 18 in the head time charter.

The Cebu [1983] 1 Lloyd's Rep. 302.

Lloyd, J., in the above case indicated that the same result would not have followed had the charters been on the Baltime form, because in that form the lien was limited to all cargoes and sub-freights "belonging to the Time-Charterers".

Priority of claims

Where the charterers assign sub-freights to a third party, the question whether the owners' lien for sub-freights or the claim of the third party assignee has priority will be determined by priority of notice in accordance with the rule in *Dearle* v. *Hall* (1828) 3 Russ. 1.

The *Attika Hope* was time-chartered on the New York Produce form on 16 November 1983. On 15 December the time charterers entered into a voyage charter. At around the same date the time charterers assigned the voyage charter freight to a third party and notice of that assignment was given to the sub-charterers. On 13 January the owners notified the sub-charterers that they were exercising their lien under Clause 18 of the time charter. The sub-freight was payable on 15 January, being 20 days after release of bills of lading. On 17 January the assignees demanded payment of the freight to them under the assignment. It was held by Steyn, J., that the third party assignee had priority, the notice of assignment having been given before the owners' notice of 13 January. The sub-charterers, having been persuaded subsequently to pay the sub-freight to the owners, were liable to pay the freight again to the assignees.

The Attika Hope [1988] 1 Lloyd's Rep. 439.

When owners' lien registrable as a charge

If the time charterers are a company incorporated in England or Wales, the owners' lien on sub-freights will be void against any liquidator or creditor of the time charterers unless the particulars of the lien are registered as a charge under Sections 395 or 410 of the Companies Act 1985 within 21 days of the charge being created: *The Ugland Trailer* [1985] 2 Lloyd's Rep. 372, and *The Annangel Glory* [1988] 1 Lloyd's Rep. 45. Non-registration may also have the same result in the case of time charterers who are overseas companies having a place of business here (see Section 409 of the 1985 Act) and time charterers incorporated or having places of business in countries with legislation similar to the Companies Act 1985.

It was held in the above cases that it was the time charter itself, as the instrument creating the charge, which was registrable under Section 395 of the 1985 Act (formerly Section 95 of the Companies Act 1948) at the time the charter was entered into. In *The*

Ugland Trailer the impracticability of the registration of time charters under Section 395 was strongly emphasised, but Nourse, J., felt compelled to ignore the commercial considerations having regard to what he regarded as the clear wording of the statute. Saville, J., took the same view in *The Annangel Glory*. Granted that Clause 18 of both the New York Produce form and Baltime form of time charters constitute agreements to assign future sub-freights by way of charge, it is still difficult to see how an equitable assignment becomes effective until there are amounts actually due from the time charterers to the owners under the charter. If the relevant date for registration of particulars of the lien were the date upon which amounts became due to the owners under the charter (when the time charter would also become registerable as the instrument evidencing the creation of the charge), many of the commercial objections advanced in *The Ugland Trailer* would be met.

Freight pre-paid bills of lading

Despite the fact that a freight pre-paid bill may prejudice the owners' right under Clause 18 of the Baltime charter to lien "all cargoes and sub-freights belonging to the Time-Charterers and any Bill of Lading freight", the master cannot refuse to sign such bills if they are required by the charterers. See *The Nanfri* [1979] 1 Lloyd's Rep, 201, particularly Lord Wilberforce, at page 206: "This clause [18], just as much as cl. 9, must be read in the context of the whole contract, and must be related to the commercial situation which exists under time charters. The lien clause must be read as giving the owners a lien upon such freights or sub-freights as, in the event, come to be payable, and which in fact are payable, under any sub-charter or bill of lading, but it cannot be read as interfering with the time charterers' primary right to use the ship and to direct the master as to its use." The same principle should apply under the New York Produce form. For further comments see page 268 above. See also *The Shillito* (1897) 3 Com. Cas. 44.

For any amounts due under this Charter

The lien can only be exercised in respect of hire already accrued due at the time the sub-freights are liened. Disbursements made by the owners which by the terms of the charter are the responsibility of the charterers are "amounts due under this Charter".

The *Lindenhall* was employed under a time charter which provided that the owner should have a lien upon all cargoes and all sub-freights for any amounts due under the charter. Hire was payable in advance. The ship was ordered to load cargo in the U.S. for Japan. The charterers issued bills of lading (to which the owners were not a party) under which part of the freight was payable on delivery. In the course of the voyage the charterers became insolvent and the owners had to pay for fuel and incur other disbursements which were the charterers' responsibility under the terms of the charter. At the port of discharge, the master collected (in one sum) the balance of freight and then sought to set off the cost of fuel and disbursements incurred on the voyage as well as an amount of charter hire which became due after the balance of bill of lading freight had been paid. Walton, J., held that:

(1) As the bill of lading contract was with the charterers and not the owners, the master received the freight by virtue only of the right of lien under the charter.
(2) The owners' lien covered the cost of fuel and other disbursements incurred on the voyage since these were the responsibility of the charterers and thus "amounts due under this charter".
(3) The lien could be exercised in respect of any advance hire which had accrued due at the

time the balance of the bill of lading freight was paid. It could not be exercised in respect of hire which did not accrue due until after that time.

(4) The owners were obliged to account to the charterers for the excess of the freight they had collected over the amounts in respect of which they had a valid lien under (2) and (3) above: but they were entitled to set-off in this account the hire that had accrued due after the bill of lading freight was collected and also their claim for damages for the failure of the charterers to carry out the charter.

Samuel v. *West Hartlepool* (1906) 11 Com. Cas. 115 and (1907) 12 Com. Cas. 203.

Charterers' lien on the ship

By Line 111 of the New York Produce form the charterers are reciprocally given "a lien on the Ship for all monies paid in advance and not earned". Clause 18 of the Baltime form confers an identical right.

Although the lien given to the charterers cannot be a true possessory lien, for a time charterer unlike a demise charterer does not obtain and so cannot retain possession of the ship, it seems that it confers a similar right, namely to prevent the owners at the end of the charter period from resuming control of the use of the ship for their own purposes. Rigby, L.J., giving the majority judgment of the Court of Appeal in *Tonnelier and Bolckow, Vaughan* v. *Smith* (1897) 2 Com. Cas. 258, said that the provision, "that the charterer was to have a lien on the ship for all moneys paid in advance and not earned, makes it plain, if it were otherwise doubtful, that the payments in advance were to be provisional only and not final, and would entitle the charterer to postpone delivery of the ship until the unearned payments were repaid." These remarks were questioned by Lord Sumner in *French Marine* v. *Compagnie Napolitaine* [1921] 2 A.C. 494. He said, at page 516: "The difficulty of reading this lien as meaning that the charterer can refuse redelivery of the ship and yet not be under a continuing liability for further hire is obvious, and lien on the ship in the strict sense he had none . . . I reserve any opinion as to the meaning and effect of this so-called lien." But, after careful consideration of these comments of Lord Sumner, Robert Goff, J., in *The Lancaster* [1980] 2 Lloyd's Rep. 497 followed and developed the view of Rigby, L.J., by holding that the charterers could at the end of the charter period redeliver the ship, subject to their lien, and then restrain the owners from resuming control over the use of the ship "presumably by injunction". It will be noted that the approach of Robert Goff, J., parts from the words used by Rigby, L.J. ("to postpone [re-]delivery") in order to meet the difficulty pointed out by Lord Sumner that if in order to exercise their lien the charterers did postpone redelivery they would continue to be liable to pay hire.

But this lien given to the charterers does not give them any further right over the ship or over the insurance monies payable upon her loss. In *The Lancaster*, above, it was argued by the charterers that it was an equitable lien upon the ship, that following the loss of the ship it attached to the hull insurance proceeds, and that it ranked ahead of the rights of certain banks to whom those proceeds had been assigned pursuant to mortgages. Robert Goff, J., rejected each of these three assertions. So far as the first was concerned, he restricted the operation of the lien to that described in the preceding paragraph and, drawing support from the judgment of Roskill, L.J., in *The Panglobal Friendship* [1978] 1 Lloyd's Rep. 368, rejected the suggestion that the lien gave any property interest in the ship.

Any lien or encumbrance

The effect of Lines 112 and 113 of the New York Produce form is that if the charterers through their fault or that of their agents cause the ship to be arrested in respect of any "lien or encumbrance" which might give to a third party a right having priority over the owners' interest in the ship, the charterers must put up security to obtain her release. Liens which have this effect would include common law maritime liens—such as those attaching to claims for salvage and collision damage—which the claimant may enforce by an admiralty action *in rem*, that is to say against the ship herself, even after a subsequent sale of the ship to an innocent purchaser. It seems that they also include the statutory liens (more properly, the "statutory rights of action *in rem*") which English law gives to claimants for those maritime claims which are listed in the Supreme Court Act 1981, including claims in respect of, for example, loss of life or personal injury, loss of or damage to goods carried, pilotage, general average, and "any claim arising out of any agreement relating to the carriage of goods in a ship or to the use or hire of a ship". The statutory liens, unlike maritime liens, are effective only where at the time the action is brought the ship remains in the ownership of the person who is liable for that claim *in personam* (see *The Monica S.* [1967] 2 Lloyd's Rep. 113); but subject to that restriction they do, upon commencement of the action *in rem*, make the claimant a secured creditor, having a charge over the ship which may give him a priority over the owner's "title and interest" in his ship. (For an authoritative survey of the history and effect of maritime and statutory liens, see the speech of Lord Diplock in *The Halcyon Isle* [1980] 2 Lloyd's Rep. 325.)

The *Vestland* was chartered on the Linertime form, which includes a provision (the second sentence of Clause 20) worded exactly as Lines 112 and 113 of the New York Produce form. Cargo claims arose under bills of lading by which the owners were bound, but based on orders of the charterers to discharge cargo at a port other than that named in the bill of lading and on their agents' failure to care for the cargo thereafter. The ship was arrested in Canada in respect of these claims, pursuant to Admiralty procedures similar to those provided for in English law in respect of statutory liens under the Administration of Justice Act 1956 (now the Supreme Court Act 1981). The charterers were unwilling and unable to provide adequate security to release the ship and the owners likewise refused to do so. Eventually, 10 days after the arrest, the charterers said that unless the owners forthwith arranged for the release of the ship the charterers would treat their conduct as a repudiation of the charter. The owners maintained their refusal and, next day, the charterers entered their own caveat against the release of the ship and claimed damages from the owners. Subsequently the owners alleged that the charterers' failure to provide security and their entry of the caveat was a repudiation by them.

In consequent proceedings in London, arbitrators stated as a question of law for the Commercial Court whether the owners had wrongfully repudiated the charter. Mocatta, J., held that they had not done so. He held that the second sentence of Clause 20 operated: the ship had been "encumbered" by the statutory action *in rem* in Canada, which was a "lien" which could prevail over the owners' interest in the ship and which had been "incurred" by the charterers or their agents. Consequently the owners had been entitled to insist that the necessary security be provided by the charterers.

The Vestland [1980] 2 Lloyd's Rep. 171.

American Law

The maritime lien

The possession of a maritime lien either (a) in the case of the owner, on the vessel's cargo or freight, or (b) in the case of the charterer or cargo owner, on the vessel herself, confers a right to proceed *in rem* against the property. It is the very essence of a maritime lien that it confers a right in the property itself, be it the vessel, her cargo or her freight. For this reason, maritime liens play an important role in the chartering of vessels, as the ownership of a lien provides both the owner and charterer with a form of security by creating rights in the maritime property engaged in the venture.

Perhaps the classic description of the maritime lien was stated in *The Young Mechanic*. 30 F.Cas. 873, 876 (No. 18, 180) (C.C.D. Me. 1855), where the court characterized it as fundamentally,

> A right which enables a creditor to institute a suit, to take a thing from any one who may possess it, and subject it, by a sale, to the payment of his debt; which so inheres in the thing as to accompany it into whosoever hands it may pass by a sale; which is not divested by a forfeiture or mortgage, or other incumbrance created by the debtor . . . or in contradistinction to a mere personal right or privilege. Though tacitly created by the law, and to be executed only by the aid of a court of justice, and resulting in a judicial sale, it is as really a property in the thing as the right of a pledgee or the lien of a bailee for work . . . For it has been settled so long, that we know not its beginning, that a suit in the admiralty to enforce and execute a lien, is not an action against any particular person to compel him to do or forbear any thing; but a claim against all mankind; a suit *in rem*, asserting the claim of the libellant to the thing, as against all the world. It is a real action to enforce a real right.

Maritime liens may arise by operation of the general maritime law or by contract. The liens expressly provided for in Clause 18 of the New York Produce form are, of course, contractual in nature. In either case, under American law, the lien can be enforced only by an action *in rem* against the property involved. Under English law the position is significantly different. See page 396 above.

Executory contracts

A maritime lien for breach of charter does not arise if the contract is merely executory. *The Schooner Freeman* v. *Buckingham*, 59 U.S. 182 (1856): *The Saturnus*, 250 F. 407, 408 (2d Cir. 1918), *cert.* denied 247 U.S. 521 (1918); The *Valmar*, 38 F. Supp. 618, 1941 AMC 872 (E.D. Pa. 1941); *Bunn* v. *Global Marine Inc.*, 428 F. 2d 40, 1970 AMC 1539 (5th Cir. 1970); *European-American Banking Corp.* v. *M/S Rosaria*, 486 F. Supp. 245, 255 (S.D. Miss. 1978). There is, unfortunately, a division of authority as to when, in the case of time charters, the charter is no longer executory. It has been held that the charter remains executory until the vessel is actually delivered to the charterer. In *Rainbow Line Inc.* v. *The Tequila*, 480 F. 2d 1024, 1027n.6, 1973 AMC 1431, 1435n.6 (2d Cir. 1973), the court stated:

> Delivery of the vessel commences the performance of a time charter and removes it from executory status.

So also in *The Oceano*, 148 F. 131, 133 (S.D.N.Y. 1906), the court stated:

> As soon as the performance of a charter party is commenced a lien exists on the vessel in favor of the shipper or charterer, and a suit in rem may be maintained for any liability of the master or owner arising therefrom . . . .

In *E.A.S.T. Inc.* v. *Alaia*, 1988 AMC 1396 (E.D.La. 1987), the District Court followed *The Tequila* in holding that a maritime lien may arise for a breach of a time charter once the vessel was placed at the charterer's disposal. See also *The Director*, 26 F. 708, 710 (D.Ore. 1886).

In certain other cases, however, it has been held that a charter remains executory until cargo is loaded. *Belvedere* v. *Compania Ploman de Vapores S.A.*, 189 F.2d 148, 1951 AMC 1217 (5th Cir. 1951) (the decision suggests, however, that it concerns a voyage charter); *Interocean Shipping Co.* v. *M/V Lygaria*, 1981 AMC 2244 (D.Md. 1981).

It is submitted, however, that at least in cases involving charter provisions such as Clause 18, the owner's and charterer's liens are intended to be rights which can be exercised when delivery is taken of the vessel and performance begins. There can be little doubt, for example, that a charterer who pays hire in advance commencing from the moment of delivery has a lien on the vessel under Clause 18. Since the owner's and charterer's liens are by nature reciprocal, the owner's lien on sub-freights under Clause 18 equally should operate from the time performance begins, whether or not cargo has yet been loaded. It must be recognized, of course, that ordinarily no sub-freights will be due and owing in any event until the cargo of which it is an incident has been loaded.

The law is well settled with respect to liens relating to cargo. In the case of the owner's lien on cargo owned by the charterer, the owner may not exercise the lien unless the goods are brought on board or otherwise within the vessel's control such that there is a union of ship and cargo. At the same time, a lien on the vessel for cargo loss or damage will not arise unless there has been a union of ship and cargo. *The Keokuk*, 76 U.S. (9 Wall.) 517, 519 (1870): *Osaka Shosen Kaisha* v. *Pacific Export Lbr. Co.*, 260 U.S. 490 (1923); *Krauss Brothers Lumber Co.* v. *Dimon Steamship Corp.*, 290 U.S. 117 (1933); *Diana Compania Maritima S.A. of Panama* v. *Subfreights of the S.S. Admiralty Flyer*, 280 F. Supp. 607, 1968 AMC 2093 (S.D.N.Y 1968); *Antria Shipping Co. Ltd.* v. *Triton Int'l Carriers Ltd.*, 1980 AMC 678, 680 (S.D.N.Y. 1976).

Shipowner's lien

American courts recognize the owner's right under the general maritime law to exercise a lien on the charterer's *own* cargo for hire due under the charter, unless there is a contrary provision in the charter. See *The Bird of Paradise*, 72 U.S. 545 (1867). Thus, even in the absence of Clause 18, the owner would have a lien on the charterer's own cargo for amounts due under the charter. See *Jebsen* v. *A Cargo of Hemp*, 228 F. 143 (D. Mass 1915). If the cargo is owned by a third party, the owner will not have a lien on the cargo but, under Clause 18 of the charter, will have a lien on sub-freights.

The shipowner's lien is said to come into existence upon the execution of the charter party. The lien remains inchoate, however, and cannot be enforced until the cargo has been loaded. *American Steel Barge Co.* v. *Chesapeake & Ohio Coal Agency Co.*, 115 F. 669 (1st Cir. 1902):

> . . . [T]he rights of the owner of the vessel under the clause in question reverted to the date of the execution of the charter, and did not accrue as of the date of the giving of the bill of lading, as now supposed by the owner of the cargo.
>
> As, therefore, on the broad rules of the admiralty, the owner of the vessel had a lien on this freight, which accrued as of the date of the charter, he stood, in the eyes of the admiralty, which requires no formal assignment, with all the rights of an assignee under a deed of assignment. (115 F. at 673.)

See also *Luckenbach Overseas Corp.* v. *Subfreights of the Audrey J. Luckenbach*, 232 F. Supp. 572, 1965 AMC 692 (S.D.N.Y. 1963), where the court stated

Under Clause 18 of the charter party, the owner of the vessel was given and had a lien on all freights earned by the vessel. This lien came into existence as an inchoate lien on the date of the charter party . . . .(1965 AMC at 694).

The scope of the shipowner's lien on cargo and sub-freights was explained in *The Freights of The Kate*, 63 F. 707 (S.D.N.Y. 1894), where the court stated:

The . . . charters gave a lien on "all cargoes and all subfreights for any amount due under this charter". This clause is a common one in time charters. The words "due" and "under this charter", are words limiting the extent of the lien given. They are used in their ordinary commercial sense, and mean sums which are "due" and payable at the time when any freights are due and collectible, and which might be then lawfully collected and applied to the sums then "due" in case of the charterers' default, as distinguished from future or contingent liabilities, not then payable; and also such sums as become due under the provisions of the charter.

This lien, will, therefore, include charter hire up to the time when the vessels were withdrawn from the company's service, and such other amounts also as were then actually "due" to the shipowners from the charterers, for advances made for charterers' account, for coal, provisions, port dues, and any other sums which the provisions of the charter required the company to pay; also any sums then due and payable on account of short delivery or damage to cargo, through the fault of the steamship company, for which the company, by the terms of the charter, was bound to indemnify the ship and owners. (63 F. at 722.)

As stated above, if the cargo is not owned by the charterer, but is owned by a third party, the owner has no lien on the cargo for hire due under the charter. *Goodpasture Inc.* v. *M.V. Pollux*, 602 F.2d 84, 1979 AMC 2515, reh. denied, 606 F.2d 321 (5th Cir. 1979) illustrates this principle very clearly. Goodpasture contracted with Empac to sell it a quantity of wheat under terms whereby title to the cargo remained with Goodpasture until payment was made. Empac chartered the vessel to carry the wheat. After the cargo was loaded, Empac failed both to pay Goodpasture for the wheat and hire to the owner. The owner then refused to issue freight prepaid bills of lading and later withdrew the vessel. Subsequently, the owner filed an *in rem* action against the cargo to recover the unpaid hire. The court held, however, that the arrest failed because the owner did not have a valid lien on the cargo, since title to the cargo never passed to Empac and there was no contract between the owner and Goodpasture. As the court stated:

Goodpasture had no contract with Negocios, only with Empac: did not care whether the wheat was carried to Colombia, to Timbuktu, or was consumed on board by mice so long as it was paid for; and owed no duties to the ship or Negocios except those exacted of all by the law in general. In particular, whatever rights to payment for use of the Pollux Negocios may have had against Empac, the charterer, did not run against Goodpasture or its wheat.

In a further blow to the owner, the court went on to hold that not only was there no basis for the arrest of the cargo, but the arrest constituted an unlawful conversion of the goods for which the owner was liable.

Although the owner will not have a lien on cargo owned by a third party, the owner can by contract acquire a right to a lien on sub-freights owing by a third party. Thus, Clause 18 gives the owner a lien on "all cargoes, and all sub-freights" for amounts due under the charter. See *The Kimball*, 70 U.S. 37 (1835); *American Steel Barge Co.* v. *Chesapeake & Ohio Coal Agency Co.*, above; *Larsen* v. 150 *Bales of Sisal Grass*, 147 F. 783 (S.D.Ala. 1906); *The Freights of The Kate*, above: *N. H. Shipping Corp.* v. *Freights of The Jackie Hause*, 181 F.Supp. 165 (S.D.N.Y. 1960); *The Pandora*, S.M.A. No. 1466 (Arb. at N.Y. 1980).

The shipowner's lien on sub-freights is deemed to arise by virtue of the contract, and is not, therefore, a lien "obtained by attachment, judgment, levy, or other legal or equitable process or proceedings" for purposes of the Bankruptcy Act. *In re North Atl. Gulf S.S. Co.*, 204 F.Supp. 899, 1963 AMC 871 (S.D.N.Y. 1962), aff'd 320 F.2d 628 (2d Cir. 1963). The owner's maritime lien on sub-freights owed to a bankrupt time charterer is not subject to the filing requirements of Article 9 of the Uniform Commercial Code. *In re Sterling Navigation Co. Ltd.*, 31 B.R. 619, 1983 AMC 2240 (S.D.N.Y. 1983); *In re Pacific Caribbean (U.S.A.) Inc.*, 1985 AMC 2045 (Bankr. N.D. Cal. 1984).

When the shipowner's lien can be exercised

The owner's lien on cargo and sub-freights may be exercised only if the charterer is in default in payment of hire or some other amount due under the charter. See, e.g., *Union Industrielle et Maritime* v. *Nimpex International Inc.*, 459 F.2d 926, 1972 AMC 1494 (7th Cir. 1972); *Marine Traders Inc.* v. *Seasons Navigation Corp.*, 422 F.2d 804, 1970 AMC 346 (2d Cir. 1970).

Furthermore, the lien may be exercised only if the cargo has not been unconditionally released to the consignee. *United States* v. *Freights of the Mt. Shasta*, 274 U.S. 466, 1927 A.M.C. 943 (1927); *Beverly Hills Nat. Bank & Trust Co.* v. *Compania de Navegacion Almirante S.A. Panama (The Searaven)*, 437 F.2d 301 (9th Cir. 1971), *cert.* denied 402 U.S. 966 (1971); *N.H. Shipping Corp.* v. *Freights of the Jackie Hause*, above. The owner may discharge the cargo and still retain his lien thereon, provided he retains control over it. Among the alternatives available to the owner is the method employed in *The Jackie Hause*, above. There the owner agreed to release the cargo on condition that the sub-freights be substituted for it and deposited in an escrow account.

The lien may be exercised on sub-freights up to the amount thereof, and only if the sub-charterer or shipper has notice of the shipowner's lien and has not yet paid the sub-freights to the charterer. See *American Steel Barge Co.* v. *Chesapeake & Ohio Coal Agency Co.*, above; *Akt. Dampsk. Thorbjorn* v. *Harrison & Co.*, 260 F. 287 (S.D.N.Y. 1918); *Larsen* v. 150 *Bales of Sisal Grass*, 147 F. 783 (S.D. Ala. 1906); *The Solhaug*, 2 F.Supp. 294, 300 (S.D.N.Y. 1931); *Hall Corp.* v. *Cargo Ex Steamer Mont Louis*,62 F.2d 603, 605 (2d Cir. 1933); *Marine Traders Inc.* v. *Seasons Navigation Corp.*, above; *Oceanic Trading Corp.* v. *The Freights of The Diana*, 423 F.2d 1 (2d Cir. 1970).

The lien on sub-freights is non-possessory, i.e., it does not depend for its validity upon any right the owner of the lien may have to proceed against the cargo or to take the cargo into possession. Thus, the owner is not required to bring an action against the cargo to enforce its lien on freights; rather, the lien may be asserted on its own directly against the party who owes the sub-freights. See *Tarstar Shipping Co.* v. *Century Shipline Ltd.*, 451 F.Supp. 317, 1979 AMC 1011 (S.D.N.Y 1978), aff'd 597 F.2d 837, 1979 AMC 1096 (2d Cir. 1979).

The lien on sub-freights may be exercised even if the amount due under the sub-charter or bills of lading is unliquidated or in dispute. See *United States* v. *Freights of the Mt. Shasta*, above.

Payment of sub-freights without notice of the owner's lien or the charterer's default will effectively discharge the lien. See *American Steel Barge Co.* v. *Chesapeake & Ohio Coal Agency Co.*, above, holding that the absence of knowledge of the owner's lien on cargo and sub-freights protected the holder of the bill of lading for amounts paid to the master on account of freight to become due; *Larsen* v. 150 *Bales of Sisal Grass*, above, holding that the owner's lien on sub-freights was discharged when the bill of lading freights were paid prior to a default by the charterer without knowledge of the terms of the charter or whether freights due thereunder had been paid; *Akt. Dampsk.* v. *Harrison & Co.* (*The Thorbjorn*), above, holding that a provision in a time charterparty giving a lien for charter hire on all cargoes and sub-freights did not entitle the owner to a lien on cargo owned by a sub-charterer who had paid hire without notice of any claim by the owner.

In *Union Industrielle et Maritime* v. *Nimpex International Inc.*, above, the court held that: "Payment by Nimpex to Midland before the lien arose, extinguished all claims by Union to any freights related to this cargo."

There have been cases, however, where the sub-charterer or shipper has been required to pay twice. Thus, where hire is due under the charter, and the sub-charterer makes payment of the sub-freights to the charterer *with notice* of the shipowner's lien, the owner may still be entitled to exercise his lien on the sub-freights.

In *Tarstar Shipping Co.* v. *Century Shipline Ltd.*, above, the sub-charterer was required to pay sub-freights twice. The owner had given the sub-charterer oral and written notice of its lien on sub-freights after the charterer defaulted. Prior to receiving the notice of lien, the sub-charterer had paid the sub-freights to a company which acted as its agent in making payment to the charterer. The sub-charterer received the notice of lien, however, *before* its agent actually made payment to the charterer, but failed to make any attempt to determine whether payment had been made or to hold it up. The court held that the sub-charterer was under a duty to make a prompt and good faith effort to ascertain the status of the freights in the hands of its agent. Since the sub-charterer could have stopped payment by its agent to the charterer, it was held liable to the owner for the entire sum due to the owner from the charterer.

See also *Antria Shipping Co. Ltd.* v. *Triton Int'l Carriers Ltd.*, 1980 AMC 681 (E.D.Pa. 1978), aff'd without opinion 609 F.2d 500 (3d Cir. 1979).

In *Jebsen* v. *A Cargo of Hemp*, 228 F. 143, 147–48 (D. Mass. 1915), Ore Company failed to pay hire under its charter with the owner. The vessel had been sub-chartered by Ore to Munson Line and Munson had paid Ore freights due under the sub-charter with Ore. The court nonetheless held (1) that the owner had a right to cause the judicial seizure of the cargo for freights due from Ore, and (2) as an incident to that right, could pursue the freight due from the cargo owner (Peabody) to Munson,

> not because he has a lien upon it, but because it represents the sum to be paid for the use of the ship in the carriage of the cargo, for which he has a lien on the cargo. He is entitled to be compensated, either by payment of the charter money, which represents the use of the ship, or, failing that, by resort to the sum agreed to be paid by the shippers as freight. (228 F. at 149.)

The court further held that, by virtue of its lien on the cargo, the owner's right to bill of lading freights had priority over Munson's right thereto. The court stated:

> It does not appear, if material, whether these payments [Munson to Ore] were before or after notice was given by the libelant of his intention to enforce his alleged lien; and no question has been raised as to the effect one way or the other of such payments . . . the Munson Line must be deemed to have taken with notice of and subject to the reservation of the lien on the cargo for the charter money due to the Owner, the libelant; and the insolvency of the Ore Company, far from divesting the libelant of the lien and entitling the Munson Line by subrogation or otherwise to the benefit of it, furnishes occasion for the resort by the libelant to the security afforded by the lien which he expressly reserved, and which it is not contended that he has ever done anything to waive.
>
> The fact that the claimant [Munson] has paid the Ore Company what was due from it to that company does not create an equity in its favor . . . The Munson Line was bound, as a matter of

prudent business conduct, to examine the charter of the Ore Company, and to govern itself by the provision therein reserving to the Owner a lien on "all cargoes" for the charter money . . . The payment by the Munson Line to the Ore Company must, I think, be deemed to have been made at its risk. (228 F. 145–46, 148.)

In *In re North Atlantic and Gulf Steamship Co.*, 204 F.Supp. 899, 904, 1963 AMC 871, 877 (S.D.N.Y. 1962), aff'd 320 F.2d 628 (2d Cir. 1963), the court stated:

. . . [T]he shipowner may at any time prior to payment of the subfreights by the shipper, assert his lien by giving notice to the shipper of its existence . . . Such notice of lien bars the shipper from discharging his liability for the subfreights by payment to the charterer.

Constructive notice of the owner's lien is sufficient to bind a sub-charterer or shipper. *The Solhaug*, 2 F.Supp. 294 (S.D.N.Y. 1931), provides another example of a situation where the sub-freights were held to be subject to the owner's lien even though payment already had been made to the charterer. The court held that the effect of the lien clause was to give the owner a valid lien upon all sub-freights for any amounts due under the head charter as and from the time the head charter was entered into. The lien, the court stated, was enforceable against all parties having actual or constructive notice of its terms. The shipper was held to have had at least constructive notice of the head charter and, therefore, of the owner's lien, and in paying sub-freights without making reasonable inquiry, did so at its peril.

In *East Asiatic Trading Co.* v. *Navibec Shipping Ltd.*, 1979 AMC 1043, 1046 (S.D.N.Y. 1978), the court stated that it is not required that the sub-charter recite or even acknowledge the existence of the shipowner's lien on sub-freights to put the sub-charterer on notice of the lien. The court observed that the mere reference in the sub-charter to the disponent owner's status as a charterer would suffice to give constructive notice of the head charter and its lien clause. See also *Sarma Navigation S.A.* v. *Navibec Shipping Ltd.*, 1979 AMC 1040 (S.D.N.Y. 1978).

"Freight pre-paid" bills of lading

If freight pre-paid bills of lading are issued by the owner or with his authority and are delivered to third parties, the owner may not assert his lien on the sub-freights or the cargo. In *Beverly Hills National Bank & Trust Co.* v. *Compania de Navegacion Almirante S.A. Panama* (*The Searaven*), 437 F.2d 301, 304 (9th Cir. 1971), *cert.* denied 402 U.S. 996 (1971), where the bills of lading were marked "Freight prepaid as per Charter Party", the court held that the "lien on freights is lost, however, if they are paid without notice of the shipowner's rights".

It is worthy of note that because prepaid bills of lading had been negotiated to purchasers for value before the lien was exercised in *Beverly Hills*, the posting of a bond for payment of freights by the consignee could not have preserved the owner's lien. The lien was discharged when the bills were negotiated to parties without notice of the lien, and could not have been restored by the posting of a bond or other security to substitute for the hire.

If the owner exercises his lien on the cargo of a third party, the shipper cannot set off any debts of the charterer to himself. See *American Steel Barge Co.*, above.

Moreover, since the owner's lien arises when the charter comes into effect, it will give him priority over the charterer's assignee of the sub-freights. See *Luckenbach Overseas Corp.* v. *The Subfreights of the Audrey J. Luckenbach*, 232 F.Supp. 572, 1965 AMC 692 (S.D.N.Y. 1963). In *Schilling* v. *A/S D/S Dannebrog*, 320 F.2d 628, 1964 AMC 678 (2d

Cir. 1963), the court held that the owner could assert a lien on sub-freights for the full amount of the installment due, where the time charterer returned the ship prematurely in breach of the charter. The court held that the owner was not obliged to pro-rate the amount of hire due on the period of actual use by the charterer.

See, generally, *Rainbow Line Inc.* v. *The Tequila*, 341 F.Supp. 459, 1972 AMC 1540 (S.D.N.Y. 1972), aff'd 480 F.2d 1024, 1973 AMC 1431 (2d Cir. 1973); *Diana Compania Maritima S.A.* v. *Subfreights of the Admiralty Flyer*, 280 F.Supp. 607, 1968 AMC 2093 (S.D.N.Y. 1968).

Self-help

A maritime lien on cargo can be perfected by bringing an *in rem* action against the goods. Under American procedure, such an action is known as an "arrest". If the underlying claim is not otherwise resolved, an arrest will result in a judicial sale of the goods. In some cases, the right to exercise a lien by refusing to deliver the cargo has been recognized. This "self-help" approach may be permitted if the owner has a valid lien on the goods. The holder of the lien has no right to convert the goods to his own use, however, and if owner's retention of the cargo fails to persuade the charterer to meet its obligations, an *in rem* action must be commenced to achieve a judicial sale of the goods.

In *The Lenoudis Kiki*, S.M.A. No. 2323 (Arb. at N.Y. 1986), the panel held that owner was justified in stopping discharge of the cargo to force charterer to make a final hire payment. The vessel was chartered for a trip to carry a cargo of rice from ports in Texas to Passau. Although charterer paid the initial installment of hire, it was consistently dilatory in making further payments. When the vessel arrived at the discharge port, hire remained outstanding. The cargo was carried under a bill of lading which stated that ocean freight would be paid by the U.S. Government. Because of that provision in the bill of lading, owner was uncertain about its right to exercise a maritime lien on the cargo for the hire due. In order to attempt to force charterer to make the final hire payment, owner stopped the discharge with cargo remaining on board. The vessel remained at the discharge port until the hire was paid. The panel sanctioned owner's conduct and rejected charterer's argument that the refusal to continue discharge constituted a withdrawal of the vessel from its service. According to the panel: " . . . as long as the ship remained in port, and was the custodian of the cargo, this action cannot be construed as a withdrawal, but should be considered as a notice of cure. Stopping the discharge was the only defense open to owners."

A similar ruling was issued in *The Sally Stove*, S.M.A. No. 2320 (Arb. at N.Y. 1986). There, the panel held that owner was justified in suspending the discharge of a cargo of steel pipes because of charterer's failure to pay overdue hire.

Charterer's liens

Under the general maritime law, the charterer has a lien on the vessel for breach of the charter by the owner, if the breach occurs after performance has begun. The leading case is *The Oceano*, 148 F. 131, 133 (S.D.N.Y. 1906), where the court stated:

> As soon as the performance of a charter party is commenced a lien exists on the vessel in favor of the shipper or charterer, and a suit *in rem* may be maintained for any liability of the master or owner arising therefor . . . Damages sustained by a charterer through breach of a charter contract constitute a lien on the vessel.

In *Rainbow Line Inc.* v. *The Tequila*, 480 F.2d 1024 (2d Cir. 1973), the court held that the charterer had a maritime lien on the vessel for the owner's breach of charter. The vessel was chartered on the New York Produce form for a term of six months with options to renew for two additional periods of six months. The owner prematurely withdrew the vessel from the charterer's service, and arbitrators awarded the charterer damages arising from the withdrawal. Subsequently, the charterer commenced an *in rem* action against the vessel to recover on the award. The court stated as follows in holding that the charterer had a maritime lien under the General Maritime Law:

> The American law is clear that there is a maritime lien for the breach of a charter party, and because the damages sought to be recovered by [charterer] are all of a maritime nature and flow directly from the breach of the charter, it has a maritime lien. (480 F.2d at 1027.)

See also *The Schooner Freeman* v. *Buckingham*, 59 U.S. 182, 190 (1856), stating that "charterparties, must, in the invariable regular course of . . . business, be made, for the performance of which the law confers a lien on the vessel".

Schilling v. *A/S D/S Dannebrog*, above, involved the question of whether a charterer had a maritime lien against the vessel for the amount of fuel remaining on board at the time of redelivery. Clause 3 of the charter provided that "the Owners, at the port of redelivery, shall take over and pay for all fuel remaining on board the vessel at the current prices in the respective ports . . . ". The court clearly indicated that if there were a default by the owner under Clause 3, the charterer would have a valid maritime lien on the vessel under Clause 18, which provided in part: "and the charterers to have a lien on the ship for all moneys paid in advance and not earned." On the facts before it, however, the court found that there was no default by the owner under Clause 3. Rather, the court held that by not making payment, the owner had in effect set off the amount due against even larger claims he had against the charterer for unpaid hire arising from the premature redelivery of the vessel.

In two cases, it has been held that the charterer does not have a lien on the vessel for prospective lost profits. *European-American Banking Corp.* v. *M/S Rosaria*, 486 F.Supp. 245 (S.D. Miss. 1978) and *Interocean Shipping Co.* v. *M/V Lygaria*, 1981 AMC 2244 (D.Md. 1981). In the latter case, the charterer sought to exercise a maritime lien for profits it would have made had the vessel been able to perform a sub-charter. The court held that even assuming that the vessel's unavailability resulted from the owner's failure to maintain her in a seaworthy condition in breach of its charter obligations, the charterer had no lien for prospective lost profits because none of the cargo that would have been carried was ever loaded.

In *Inter-American Shipping Enterprises Ltd.* v. *T.T. Tula*, 1982 AMC 951 (E.D. Va. 1981), it was held that charterer did not have a lien on the vessel for overpaid charter hire.

Priority of charterer's lien

Where the chartered vessel is the subject of a foreclosure proceeding, issues can arise relating to the relative priority of a charterer's claim against the vessel for breach of charter. As a general rule, maritime liens that arise as a result of the owner's breach of charter will only have the low priority of a contract lien. In *The Bold Venture*, 638 F. Supp. 87, 1987 AMC 182 (W.D. Wash. 1986), the charterer argued that its lien claim was entitled to the status of a tort. The court rejected this contention and held that the breach of charter claims sounded only in contract.

The usual rules of priority do not apply if preferred maritime lien claims are involved. Maritime liens which arise prior in time to a preferred ship mortgage or which have preferred status because they arise out of a tort such as a collision outrank preferred ship mortgages. Thus, a lien for breach of charter will outrank a preferred ship mortgage if it comes into existence prior to the filing of the mortgage. Maritime liens for breach of charter which arise after the filing of a ship mortgage will be subordinate to the mortgage. These rules were formerly provided for in the Ship Mortgage Act, 46 U.S.C. §953. The Act was amended on 23 November 1988 by Public Law 100–710. The relevant sections are now codified at 46 U.S.C. §§31301(5) and (6) and 31321–31330.

Liens for supplies ordered by charterer

Clause 18 was designed to preclude repair yards or suppliers who furnish goods or bunkers to the vessel under contracts with the charterer from obtaining a lien on the vessel for amounts due, and has been held effective for this purpose.

In *Schilling* v. *A/S D/S Dannebrog*, above, the court held that Clause 18 "is sufficient to preclude a lien in a supplier who knows or should know of its existence in the charter." (320 F.2d at 632.) In that case, it was claimed that the charterer had a maritime lien for the value of fuel on board when the vessel was returned to the owner. The court held that since the supplier of the fuel did not have a lien on the vessel for the fuel, the charterer likewise had no lien, since its claim arose by way of subrogation to the rights of the third-party supplier.

See also *Unites States* v. *The Lucie Schulte*, 343 F.2d 897 (2d Cir. 1965), holding that "the prohibition of lien clause in the instant charters was adequate to defeat lien claims of a material man who could have ascertained its existence by reasonable diligence"; *United States* v. *Carver*, 260 U.S. 482 (1923); *Damps. Dannebrog* v. *Signal Oil & Gas Co.*, 310 U.S. 268 (1940). See, generally, *Cardinal Shipping Corp.* v. *Seisho Maru*, 1985 AMC 2630, 744 F.2d 461 (5th Cir. 1984).

The effect of Clause 18 has been largely neutralized, however, by amendments to the Federal Maritime Lien Act, 46 U.S.C. §§971–975. The Act was adopted in 1910 for the purpose of providing a uniform law regulating suppliers' liens, and superseded the existing general maritime law and state laws to the extent it covers the creation of liens on vessels. As amended in 1971, Section 971 provided as follows:

> Any person furnishing repairs, supplies, towage, use of dry-dock or marine railway, or other necessaries, to any vessel, whether foreign or domestic, upon the order of the owner of such vessel, or of a person authorized by the owner, shall have a maritime lien on the vessel, which may be enforced by suit *in rem*, and it shall not be necessary to allege or prove that credit was given to the vessel.

The Federal Maritime Lien Act was amended on 23 November 1988 by Public Law 100–710. 46 U.S.C. §971 was amended such that the term "necessaries" is defined to include "repairs, supplies, towage, and the use of a dry dock or marine railway". 46 U.S.C. §31301(4). Although the phrase "or other necessaries" was deleted, the legislative history states that no change in substantive law was intended. See H.R. Rep. No. 100–918, 100th Cong., 2d Sess. 14, 15, 36 (1988).

A broad range of types of suppliers may obtain a lien for providing necessaries. In general, any items reasonably needed in the ship's business or to keep her out of or remove her from danger will be deemed "necessaries". As used in the Act, the term "necessaries" has been held to include stevedoring services. *Jan C. Uiterwyk Co. Inc.* v. *M.V. Mare Arabico*, 459 F.Supp. 1325 (D.Md. 1978); *Nacirema Operating Co. Inc.* v. *S.S. Al Kulsum*, 407 F.Supp. 1222 (S.D.N.Y. 1975); *John T. Clark* v. *S.S. Al Kulsum*, 1974 AMC 1489 (S.D.N.Y. 1974). Indeed, it has been held that a stevedore is entitled to assert a maritime lien not only for time worked by the stevedore but also for detention time and "guarantee time", both of which are periods for which stevedores must be paid pursuant to collective bargaining agreements even if no work is actually performed. See *Atlantic & Gulf Stevedores Inc.* v. *M/V Rosa Roth*, 587 F. Supp. 103, 1985 AMC 718 (S.D.N.Y 1984).

"Necessaries" also includes fuel and lubricating oil. *Gulf Trading & Transp. Co.* v. *The Hoegh Shield*, 658 F.2d 363, 1982 AMC 1138 (5th Cir. 1981); *In re Queen Ltd.*, 361 F.Supp. 1009 (E.D.Pa. 1973). Other "necessaries" include pilotage, food, repairs, seaman's wages, radar and any other equipment, drydocking and advertising. Even cigarettes have been held to be "necessaries". *Allen* v. *The Contessa* 196 F.Supp. 649, 1961 AMC 2190 (S.D. Tex. 1961).

Several courts have held that containers provided to a vessel under a lease agreement are necessaries. See, e.g., *Foss Launch & Tug Co.* v. *Char Ching Shipping U.S.A. Ltd.*, 808 F.2d 697, 1987 AMC 913 (9th Cir. 1987) and cases cited therein. In addition, insurance has been held to be a necessary, such that the issuer of a policy has a maritime lien for the payment of premiums. See *Equilease Corp.* v. *M/V Sampson*, 793 F.2d 598, 1986 AMC 1826 (5th Cir. 1986) (*en banc*).

General agents appointed by an owner to represent the vessel, however, ordinarily will not have a maritime lien for advances or disbursements. The reason for this is that general agents are not considered to act in reliance on the vessel as security. Rather, they are deemed to rely on the credit of the owner for whom they act. See *Savas* v. *Maria Trading Corp.*, 285 F.2d 336, 1961 AMC 260 (4th Cir. 1960); *P.T. Perusahaan Pelayaran Samudera Trikora Lloyd* v. *Salzachtal*, 373 F.Supp. 267 (S.D.N.Y. 1974). A "special agent", on the other hand, who is engaged by the owner to supply services or necessaries or to make cash advances to a supplier of necessaries will be entitled to exercise a maritime lien under the Act.

A maritime lien may be assigned or may be acquired by way of subrogation. In *Medina* v. *Marvirazon Compania Naviera, S.A.*, 709 F.2d 124, 1983 AMC 2113 (1st Cir. 1983), the court held that a person who advanced funds to discharge seamen's wage liens was subrogated to the seamen's rights so long as the party making the advances did not occupy "such a close relationship to the vessel and its Owners and exercised sufficient control over the ship that it would be inequitable to grant him a lien".

It appears that the same rule would apply with respect to a party who has made payment on behalf of the ship to a supplier of necessaries. In *Tramp Oil and Marine Ltd.* v. *M/V Mermaid I*, 630 F.Supp. 630, 1987 AMC 129 (D.P.R. 1986), a bunker fuel broker attempted to exercise a maritime lien for fuel supplied to the vessel. Broker A had been contacted by Broker B and had arranged for a fuel supplier to make the delivery. The court held that Broker A did not have a lien. Although Broker A had paid the fuel supplier, the charterer had paid Broker B the price of the fuel. Before paying Broker A, however, Broker B went into bankruptcy. The court noted case law in which parties have become subrogated to the rights of a lienor or have taken assignments of such rights but found that these rules did not apply to the case of the plaintiff. According to the court, Broker A could have protected itself by denying Broker B its credit or by requesting that the fuel supplier assign his lien. According to the court, it would not have been equitable to allow Broker A to become automatically subrogated to the lien of the fuel supplier since the charterer, on behalf of the vessel, had already paid for the fuel supplied and it was no fault of the charterer that the funds had not reached Broker A.

Section 972 provides that "the managing owner, ship's husband, master, or any person to whom the management of the vessel at the port of supply is intrusted" shall be presumed to have authority from the vessel owner to procure supplies, etc. Section 973 provides that those persons presumed to have authority to bind the vessel "shall be taken to include such officers and agents when appointed by a charterer, by an owner *pro hac vice*, or by an agreed purchaser in possession of the vessel".

Notwithstanding Section 973, however, if the supplier has actual notice of Clause 18, or knows facts which should put him on notice that the charterer lacks authority to create liens on the vessel, the presumption of authority provided in Section 972 can be overcome. The burden of proof on the owner, however, may prove to be a heavy one.

There are a number of cases in which Section 971 has been interpreted liberally in favor of the supplier and as allowing it to rely upon a presumption that a maritime lien exists. The supplier is under no duty to investigate the terms of the charter or to inquire as to the charterer's authority to bind the vessel.

The presumption in favor of the supplier may be overcome if the vessel owner can show that the supplier had actual knowledge of a "no-lien clause". See *Marine Fuel Supply & Towing Inc.* v. *The Ken Lucky*, 859 F.2d 1405, 1989 AMC 390 (9th Cir. 1988); *Gulf Oil Trading Co.* v. *M/V Caribe Mar*, 757 F.2d 743, 1985 AMC 2726 (5th Cir. 1985); *Lake Union Drydock Co.* v. *M/V Polar Viking*, 446 F.Supp. 1286, 1978 AMC 1477 (W.D. Wash. 1978), where the court held that the assertion of lien will be barred only if the materialman had actual knowledge of the prohibition of lien clause; *Gulf Trading* v. *M/V Tento*, 1979 AMC 753 (N.D. Cal. 1979); *Jan C. Uiterwyk Co. Inc.* v. *M/V Mare Arabico*, above.

Ramsay Scarlett & Co., Inc. v. *S.S. Koh Eun*, 462 F.Supp. 277 (E.D. Va. 1978) is representative of the post-1971 cases concerning Section 971. There the disponent owner attempted to avoid maritime liens asserted by stevedores on the grounds that since the stevedores knew the vessel was operating under a time charter, they should be presumed to have known about the prohibition of lien clause. The court rejected the argument stating:

> The Court finds the post-1971 law to be as follows: The supplier of necessities to a vessel has no duty or inquiry as to the existence of a charter or a prohibition of lien clause in a known charter. The supplier is entitled to rely upon the statutory presumption of 46 U.S.C. §971 *et seq*. Any prohibition of lien clause is thus ineffective against such a supplier of necessaries absent actual knowledge of a charter including a prohibition of lien clause. Knowledge of a charter alone does not bar a lien. (462 F.Supp. at 285.)

It is common for the vessel owner to instruct the master or its agents to stamp invoices or order forms from stevedores and other materialmen with a notice that the vessel is operating under a charter which contains a prohibition of lien clause. The stamping of invoices in this manner may be sufficient to put the suppliers on notice that the charterer does not have authority to create liens against the vessel.

It is clear, however, that to be effective, the supplier must have actual notice of the prohibition of lien clause at the time it provides services or supplies to the vessel. Thus, the stamping of a delivery receipt with a notice of the prohibition of lien clause *after* bunkers had already been supplied to the vessel was held to be ineffective in *Gulf Oil Trading Co.* v. *M/V Freedom*, 1985 AMC 2738 (D.Or. 1985). On the other hand, an oil company was refused a maritime lien for bunkers supplied to a vessel where it had received a letter giving notice of the prohibition of lien clause prior to the delivery of the bunkers. *Gulf Oil Trading Co.* v. *The Caribe Mar*, 757 F.2d 743, 1985 AMC 2726 (5th Cir. 1985).

It is possible for the supplier to waive its lien. Section 974 of the Federal Maritime Lien Act provides:

Nothing in this chapter shall be construed to prevent the furnisher of repairs, supplies, towage, use of dry dock or marine railway, or other necessaries, or the mortgagee, from waiving his right to a lien, or in the case of a preferred mortgage lien, to the preferred status of such lien, at any time by agreement or otherwise; and this chapter shall not be construed to affect the rules of law existing on June 5, 1920, in regard to (1) the right to proceed against the vessel for advances. (2) laches in the enforcement of liens upon vessels, (3) the right to proceed *in personam*, (4) the rank of preferred maritime liens among themselves, or (5) priorities between maritime liens and mortgages, other than preferred mortgages, upon vessels of the United States.

It would seem from Section 974, however, that a waiver of the lien will be found only where the supplier has clearly manifested an intention to forego the lien in favor of other security. See *Nacirema Operating Co.* v. *S.S. Al Kulsum*, above; *Lake Union Drydock Co.* v. *M/V Polar Viking*, above; *Ramsay Scarlett & Co. Inc.* v. *S.S. Koh Eun*, above. In *Jones Tug & Barge Co.* v. *S.S. Liberty Manufacturer*, 1978 AMC 1183 (C.D. Cal. 1976), the court held that the suppliers had waived their lien on the vessel when they agreed to render services in reliance upon the credit of the vessel's P. & I. Club.

In contrast, in *Gulf Trading & Transp. Co.* v. *The Hoegh Shield*, above, the court ruled that a supplier of bunkers had a maritime lien on the vessel even though it admittedly relied on the credit of the time charterer. According to the court, the supplier did not rely *solely* on the charterer's credit and took no action which indicated "the purposeful intention of foregoing its maritime lien in the vessel". (1982 AMC at 1145.)

It is clear that as between the vessel owner and the supplier of goods or services, it is the former who has the affirmative duty of informing the latter of the no-lien clause. However, as between the owner and the charterer, it is the latter who has the duty to give notice of the prohibition of lien clause. Under Clause 18, the charterer undertakes not to allow the creation of liens against the vessel, and there can be little doubt that this language would extend to supplier's liens. The charterer's failure to give notice of a prohibition of lien clause would constitute a breach of the charter, entitling the owner to indemnity from the charterer. The charterer's duty to indemnify the owner in this context would include costs incurred in posting a bond to obtain the release of the vessel if she is arrested. See, e.g. *The Irene's Grace*, S.M.A. No. 1213 (Arb. at N.Y. 1978); *The George Vergottis*, S.M.A. No. 1214 (Arb. at N.Y. 1978); *The Scotiacliffe Hall*, S.M.A. No. 1464 (Arb. at N.Y. 1980).

There are other types of liens the charterer must be wary of in dealing with third parties. For example, what of the situation where the cargo receiver causes the vessel to be arrested in exercising a maritime lien for cargo damage for which the charterer is liable? It would seem that if the cargo loss were the direct result of the charterer's acts, it properly could be said that the charterer was in breach of Clause 18 by causing the lien to come into existence. In *The Peerless*, 2 F.2d 395, 1923 AMC 236 (S.D.N.Y. 1923), the court held that the charterer's redelivery of the vessel subject to a lien for repairs for which it was responsible was a fundamental breach of the charter.

In *The Three Sisters*, S.M.A. No. 345 (Arb. at N.Y. 1969), the majority of the panel held that the owner was justified in withdrawing the vessel from the service of the charterer as the result of the charterer's breach of its promise under Clause 18 not to "suffer, nor permit to be continued, any lien or encumbrance incurred by them or their agents, which might have priority over the title and interest of the owners in the vessel". The vessel had been arrested by the shippers as the result of the charterer's failure to pay dockage, storage and stevedoring charges.

See also *The Wismar*, S.M.A. No. 1454 (Arb. at N.Y. 1980). There the charterer sub-chartered the vessel on a New York Produce form charter which contained terms identical with those of the head charter. The sub-charterer wrongfully cancelled the sub-charter and caused the vessel to be arrested in Canada to obtain security for claims it had against the registered owner. The arbitrators noted that the time chartered owner would have been in breach of Clause 18 and obliged thereunder "to procure the release of the vessel from arrest had the arrest resulted from its own actions or those of its agents". Since the arrest was in fact caused by the sub-charterer with respect to claims against the registered owner, the panel held that it was the registered owner's duty to take steps to release the ship from arrest. The panel observed that, for purposes of Clause 18, a sub-charterer is not deemed to be an agent of the charterer.

Obligation to free vessel from arrest

The issues of who as between the owner and charterer must bear the cost of releasing the vessel from an arrest and whether either party has any obligation to free the vessel must be determined on the facts of each case. In general, it seems correct to say that if the arrest arose from a breach of charter, the party in breach is obligated to bear the cost of securing the release of the vessel.

Thus, in *The Pandora*, S.M.A. No. 1466 (Arb. at N.Y. 1980), the charterer failed to pay hire due and owing, and the owner exercised its lien upon the cargo under Clause 18. The arbitrators stated that while Clause 18 is silent as to which party must pay for the costs involved in exercising the lien, since the necessity for such action arose from a failure of performance by the charterer, the charterer was liable for all expenses incurred by the owner in preserving and exercising the lien.

The situation presented in *The Wismar*, above, was considerably more complex. There the vessel was arrested in Canada by a sub-charterer for claims of tortious interference in the loading of the cargo which were directed at the owner. The panel noted that under Clause 18, the time charterer "would be obliged to procure the release of the vessel from arrest had the arrest resulted from its own action or those of its agents". But since the arrest was caused by the sub-charterer in connection with claims against the owner, the owner was held to be under an affirmative duty to release the ship, failing which the vessel was off-hire until she was freed.

In *The Scotiacliffe Hall*, S.M.A. No. 1464 (Arb. At N.Y. 1980), the arbitrators held that the charterer was in breach of Clause 18 and, therefore, under a duty to free the vessel from an arrest brought by the cargo receivers at the discharge port. The panel noted that the receivers were not agents of the charterer. The vessel was arrested, however, in connection with claims against the charterer, and for this reason, the detention of the vessel was held to be attributable to actions of the charterer.

The Ming Belle, S.M.A. No. 2043 (Arb. at N.Y. 1984) involved the grounding of a loaded vessel in the Red Sea. A salvage tug was called in to assist refloating the vessel and the salvors subsequently filed a claim for salvage security. Owner promptly posted security, but cargo security was not posted until 13 days later. Owner contended that the vessel was on hire during the period the vessel was detained due to the unsatisfied salvage lien because the charterer and subcharterer failed to post cargo's share of the security. The panel majority rejected owner's contention, finding no charter provision obligating charterer or subcharterer to post salvage security on behalf of the cargo owner.

One other arbitration award warrants mention. In *The Gabrielle Wesch*, 1981 AMC 1324 (Arb. at N.Y. 1981), the vessel was placed under arrest in legal proceedings brought in Guatemala by a third party seeking security for a cargo claim it had against the charterer. The cargo claim concerned an unrelated voyage on a different vessel. The owner and charterer made substantial efforts to attempt to lift the arrest, but both were unsuccessful. At the time the award was issued, the ship had been under arrest for more than a year and remained under arrest. The charterer contended that it was not responsible for the arrest under Clause 18 because it was "illegal" in that it was based on a false statement that the vessel was owned by the charterer. The panel majority rejected this argument, however, finding that even if the Guatemalan courts were ultimately to conclude that the arrest was improper, that would not make the arrest "illegal" since it was authorized by the Guatemalan court. The majority concluded that the arrest was the charterer's responsibility under Clause 18, because it existed by reason of causes attributable to the charterer and not because of any fault of the owner. The charterer, therefore, was held liable for hire and all expenses resulting from the arrest.

Seguros Banvenez S.A. v. *S.S. Oliver Drescher*, 761 F.2d 855, 1985 AM 2168 (2d Cir. 1985) involved, *inter alia*, the arrest of a vessel as security for a cargo claim. At the request of the owner, Drescher, the District Court ordered the charterer, Venline, to furnish Drescher with sufficient security so that Drescher, in turn, could post the bond necessary for the release of the vessel. The Second Circuit reversed the District Court on this issue, reasoning:

> Venline did not ask to be brought into court, and it did not concede liability over to Drescher. Indeed, that issue remains to be decided in arbitration. A shipowner is not compelled to furnish a bond to the person who has arrested his ship. Its *quid pro quo* for voluntarily furnishing security is the release of its ship. Depriving Venline of its property by compelling it to furnish a bond to Drescher without any similar *quid pro quo*, without any valid prior finding as to the parties' respective rights, and without any provision for protection of Venline's interests and expenses, smacks of a violation of due process. (761 F.2d at 863–64, 1985 AMC at 2179–80.)

Charterer's property subject to maritime lien

Equipment owned by the charterer and which is placed on board the vessel and is "an integral part of the vessel and essential to its navigation and operation" will be subject to maritime liens against the vessel. In *The Tropic Breeze*, 456 F.2d 137, 1972 AMC 1622 (1st Cir. 1972), cement equipment owned by the charterer which was essential to the vessel's operation as a bulk cement carrier was held to be subject to a maritime lien. In other cases, refrigeration equipment, diving bells, air pumps, nets, net lifters, oil tanks, and fishing gear have all been held to be subject to maritime liens even though owned by the charterer.

Salvage

"114. 19. That all derelicts and salvage shall be for the Owners' and Charterers' equal benefit after deducting Owners' and Charterers' expenses and

115. Crew's proportion." [The rest of Clause 19, up to and including Line 132, concerns general average: it is set out in the full text of the charter.]

Division of net salvage earned

The words "equal benefit" in Lines 114 and 115 of the New York Produce form suggest an intention to divide equally what is left of the salvage award after deducting that which the owners and the charterers have each contributed or sacrificed to enable it to be earned.

The *Pocklington* sustained damage while salving the *Dart*. While this damage was being repaired she was off-hire. Her owners paid for the repairs and incurred certain other expenses in connection with the salvage operations. The charterers claimed from the owners half of the gross salvage award, relying on a clause reading "All derelicts and salvage shall be for owners' and charterers' equal benefit". Bigham, J., held that all that was to be divided was the net amount after deducting on the one hand the owners' losses and expenses including hire lost during repairs and on the other hand the charterers' loss of time during the salvage itself and the cost of the extra fuel consumed (conceded by the owners as proper deductions). He said: " 'Equal benefit' cannot be accorded to shipowner and charterer without taking into account what each has contributed towards securing the benefit. Salvage in this clause does not mean the amount recovered in the suit in the Admiralty Court. It means the net pecuniary result of the salvage operations."

Booker v. *Pocklington Steamship* [1899] 2 Q.B. 690.

This decision suggests that a broad rather than a narrow interpretation should be given to the word "expenses", so as to allow before division of the net salvage the cost of repairs to the ship caused by the salvage operation, hire during the salvage and any subsequent repairs and also the cost of charterers' bunkers consumed. The corresponding clause in the Baltime form (19) is worded more fully and provides expressly for this result.

Fuel for Owners' Account

"133. 20. Fuel used by the vessel while off hire, also for cooking, condensing water, or for grates and stoves to be agreed to as to quantity, and the
134. cost of replacing same, to be allowed by Owners."

Fuel costs payable by owners

Clause 20 provides that fuel used by the vessel while off hire is to be for owners' account (see page 308 above). The remaining part of Clause 20, and in particular the phrase "Fuel . . . for grates and stoves" was considered by the courts in *The Sounion* [1987] 1 Lloyd's Rep. 230. The Court of Appeal, reversing Gatehouse, J., agreed with the majority view of the arbitrators that the pattern of the New York Produce form was that the cost of fuel for propelling the ship and for cargo work was intended to be for charterers' account and the cost of fuel used for the crew's domestic purposes for the owners' account. The court held that Clause 20 was intended to extend the owners' liability to all fuel used for the crew's domestic purposes, whether that was for lighting, heating, cooking or other crew facilities such as air-conditioning or power for televisions or personal electrical equipment; "grates and stoves" was not to be given a restrictive construction and confined only to heating as the owners had contended.

American Law

The rather archaic language of Clause 20 was considered by arbitrators in *The Ming Autumn*, S.M.A. No. 2189 (Arb. at N.Y. 1986). Charterer argued that all fuel consumed for domestic purposes was for owner's account and sought to include the modern equivalents of "grates and stoves" such as electricity and steam, as well as air conditioning and fans in the crew cabins. The panel agreed that charterer was entitled to a credit for diesel oil used for cooking which it calculated based on the estimated daily use of the ship's range. In addition, the panel awarded charterer a credit for fuel used to heat the vessel's accommodations. According to the panel, charterer was not entitled to any other fuel credit. Perhaps the most controversial item concerned air conditioning and it was the view of the arbitrators that this was not covered by Clause 20 as drafted. Based on this ruling, if it is the intent of the parties to allow charterer a credit for the cost of air conditioning aboard the vessel, an express amendment to that effect should be made.

In *The Mykali II*, S.M.A. No. 2240 (Arb. at N.Y. 1986), charterer claimed a credit for the cost of cooking while the vessel was in port. The panel noted, however, that Clause 20 states "to be agreed to as to quantity". There was no provision in the charter expressing an agreement as to quantity and in the arbitration the parties could not agree. Although charterer offered a calculation of the vessel's daily domestic consumption, the panel found it to be speculative. The panel declined to give any allowance for inport cooking and stated "the proper place for this claim to be quantified is in the fixture negotiations where the quantity should be agreed upon".

Drydocking and Gear

"135. 21. That as the vessel may be from time to time employed in tropical waters during the term of this Charter, Vessel is to be docked at a
136. convenient place, bottom cleaned and painted whenever Charterers and Captain think necessary, at least once in every six months, reckoning from
137. time of last painting, and payment of the hire to be suspended until she is again in proper state for the service.
138. ....
139. ....
140. 22. Owners shall maintain the gear of the ship as fitted, providing gear (for all derricks) capable of handling lifts up to three tons, also
141. providing ropes, falls, slings and blocks. If vessel is fitted with derricks capable of handling heavier lifts, Owners are to provide necessary gear for
142. same, otherwise equipment and gear for heavier lifts shall be for Charterers' account. Owners also to provide on the vessel lanterns and oil for
143. night work, and vessel to give use of electric light when so fitted, but any additional lights over those on board to be at Charterers' expense. The
144. Charterers to have the use of any gear on board the vessel.
145. 23. Vessel to work night and day, if required by Charterers, and all winches to be at Charterers' disposal during loading and discharging;
146. steamer to provide one winchman per hatch to work winches day and night, as required, Charterers agreeing to pay officers, engineers, winchmen,
147. deck hands and donkeymen for overtime work done in accordance with the working hours and rates stated in the ship's articles. If the rules of the
148. port, or labor unions, prevent crew from driving winches, shore Winchmen to be paid by Charterers. In the event of a disabled winch or winches, or
149. insufficient power to operate winches, Owners to pay for shore engine, or engines, in lieu thereof, if required, and pay any loss of time occasioned
150. thereby."

A reference to Clause 21 appears at page 85 above. On the question of bottom fouling see also pages 307 and 310 above.

Carriage of Goods by Sea Act

"151. 24. It is also mutually agreed that this Charter is subject to all the terms and provisions of and all the exemptions from liability contained
152. in the Act of Congress of the United States approved on the 13th day of February, 1893, and entitled "An Act relating to Navigation of Vessels;
153. etc.," in respect of all cargo shipped under this charter to or from the United States of America. It is further subject to the following clauses, both
154. of which are to be included in all bills of lading issued hereunder:
155. U.S.A. Clause Paramount
156. This bill of lading shall have effect subject to the provisions of the Carriage of Goods by Sea Act of the United States, approved April
157. 16, 1936, which shall be deemed to be incorporated herein, and nothing herein contained shall be deemed a surrender by the carrier of
158. any of its rights or immunities or an increase of any of its responsibilities or liabilities under said Act. If any term of this bill of lading
159. be repugnant to said Act to any extent, such term shall be void to that extent, but no further.
160. Both-to-Blame Collision Clause
161. If the ship comes into collision with another ship as a result of the negligence of the other ship and any act, neglect or default of the
162. Master, mariner, pilot or the servants of the Carrier in the navigation or in the management of the ship, the owners of the goods carried
163. hereunder will indemnify the Carrier against all loss or liability to the other or non-carrying ship or her owners in so far as such loss
164. or liability represents loss of, or damage to, or any claim whatsoever of the owners of said goods, paid or payable by the other or non-
165. carrying ship or her owners to the owners of said goods and set off, recouped or recovered by the other or non-carrying ship or her
166. owners as part of their claim against the carrying ship or carrier."

Incorporation of Harter Act and United States Carriage of Goods by Sea Act 1936

Harter Act

The Act of 1893 is known as the Harter Act. Both it and the United States Carriage of Goods by Sea Act are set out in Appendix A.

The Harter Act is now partially superseded by the United States Carriage of Goods by Sea Act 1936. The Harter Act remains effective for the period the carrier has charge of the goods prior to loading and after discharge until delivery. Where, as is sometimes the case, the U.S.A. Clause Paramount is deleted from Clause 24, but the clause is left otherwise unamended, Section 3 of the Harter Act in certain circumstances makes the owners' right to rely upon some of the exceptions in Clause 16 and certain other defences upon which the owners might otherwise be entitled to rely, conditional upon the exercise of due diligence to make the ship seaworthy in all respects. Thus, if the ship is unseaworthy and the exercise of due diligence cannot be established, it is no defence to the owners that the particular unseaworthiness was not the effective cause of the loss or damage suffered.

By the express words of Lines 151 to 153 of Clause 24, the Harter Act is applicable only in respect of all cargo shipped under the charter to or from the U.S.A. The incorporation of the United States Carriage of Goods by Sea Act is not restricted in this way; and on the authority of the decisions in the *Adamastos* case, below, and *The Satya Kailash* [1984] 1 Lloyd's Rep. 588, this Act applies to all trading under the charter without any geographical limitation.

The United States Carriage of Goods by Sea Act

It is suggested that the effect of the incorporation of the United States Act will normally be as follows:

(1) the express obligation of seaworthiness at the beginning of the charter period (see page 64 above) is reduced from an absolute obligation that the ship will be seaworthy to an obligation to exercise due diligence to make the ship seaworthy (see page 428 below);

(2) before and at the beginning of each voyage under the charter the owners will be obliged to exercise due diligence to make the ship seaworthy, in accordance with Section 3(1) of the Act (see page 428 below); and

(3) all the provisions of the Act are to be given effect to so as to regulate the rights and obligations of the owners and the charterers, to the extent that the provisions are capable of that treatment when notionally written out in full in the charter; this is particularly important so far as concerns the excepted perils listed in the Act (see page 429 below).

The *Saxon Star* was chartered for as many consecutive voyages as she could tender for within a period of 18 months. Delays occurred on voyages, including the ballast voyage to the first loading port, due to breakdowns of machinery caused by the incompetence of the engine room staff. They were incompetent despite the fact that the owners had exercised due diligence in their selection. Their incompetence made the ship unseaworthy. The charterers claimed that owing to that unseaworthiness the number of voyages completed within the charter period was less than it should have been.

The charter contained an absolute warranty of seaworthiness in these terms: "being tight, staunch and strong, and every way fitted for the voyage, and to be maintained in such condition during the voyage, perils of the sea excepted." It was also provided by a typewritten clause: "It is agreed that the . . . Paramount Clause . . . as attached [is] to be incorporated in this charter-party." The attached Paramount Clause was in the same terms as the U.S.A. Clause Paramount in Clause 24 of the New York Produce form.

The owners argued that the absolute warranty of seaworthiness in the charter was reduced to an undertaking to exercise due diligence to make the ship seaworthy by reason of the incorporation into the charter by the Paramount Clause of the United States Act.

It was held by the House of Lords unanimously that:

(1) It was plainly the intention of the parties to incorporate the Hague Rules into the charter and this intention should be given effect to; so the words in the Paramount Clause "This bill of lading" should be read as "This charter-party."

(2) Section 5 of the United States Act, which provides that the Act is not to apply to charter parties, was to be ignored.

And by a majority that:

(3) The charter being of world-wide scope, the limitation in the United States Act to voyages to and from the United States should be disregarded and voyages should be subject to the Act regardless of where they started or finished.

(4) The standards of obligation introduced by the United States Act—The Hague Rules—were applicable to all voyages whether these were in ballast or with cargo.

(5) The immunity given to the owners by Section 4(1) of the United States Act in respect of "loss or damage" extended beyond physical loss or damage to cargo and covered the loss here claimed, namely the loss to the charterers from the reduction in the number of voyages under the charter.

Adamastos Shipping v. *Anglo-Saxon Petroleum (The Saxon Star)* [1958] 1 Lloyd's Rep. 73.

The decisions of the House of Lords in the *Adamastos* case should, it is believed, be applied equally to charters on the New York Produce form. There are of course important differences between time charters and consecutive voyage charters. These differences are considered under "Seaworthiness obligation for each voyage" at page 428 below. But it is clear from the approach of the House of Lords in the *Adamastos* case that if the contract shows that the parties did intend the Hague Rules to apply to their charter the courts will strive to give effect to that intention as far as that can sensibly be done. It is not thought that the approach would be different under a time charter as opposed to a consecutive voyage charter, and the decisions of the courts since the *Adamastos* case tend to support this conclusion: see below.

In the New York Produce form it is made clearer than it was in the *Adamastos* case that the U.S.A. Clause Paramount is to apply to the charter itself as well as to bills of lading issued under it: see Lines 153 and 154.

The U.S.A. Clause Paramount in Lines 155 to 159 is the same clause as in the *Adamastos* case. Once the words "bill of lading" are read as "charter" (see *The Aliakmon Progress*, below) the wording of the clause is unambiguous; the provisions of the Act are incorporated and will prevail over conflicting terms elsewhere in the printed form. Whether the provisions of the Act will prevail over terms in typescript is a matter of construction of the contract as a whole: see below under "Other effects of the United States Act". Not all clauses incorporating the Hague Rules or Hague Rules legislation make the Rules "paramount" despite their being headed "Clause Paramount": see *Marifortuna Naviera* v. *Government of Ceylon* [1970] 1 Lloyd's Rep. 247. The stronger wording of the *Adamastos* clause was pointed out in that case; see also the comments of Goff, L.J., in *The Agios Lazaros* [1976] 2 Lloyd's Rep. 47, at page 53.

In cases relating to time charters for a trip, the courts have shown no hesitation in acknowledging that Clause 24 incorporates the Hague Rules into the charter. In *The Aliakmon Progress* [1978] 2 Lloyd's Rep. 499, under a trip charter on the New York Produce form, the Court of Appeal upheld the owners' defence of error in navigation (Section 4(2)(*a*) of the United States Carriage of Goods by Sea Act 1936) against a claim for damages following damage to the ship in a collision with a quay caused by a navigational error on board. Lord Denning, M.R., said: "It is plain on the decision of the House of Lords in the *Adamastos* case . . . that, although there is a clause saying 'This bill of lading shall have effect' &c. nevertheless it really meant, 'This charterparty shall have effect', &c. So the provisions of the Hague Rules apply to this time charter." The Court of Appeal gave effect in the owners' favour to the same defence under a trip charter in *The Aquacharm* [1982] 1 Lloyd's Rep. 7; see further below at page 430.

The decision of the House of Lords in the *Adamastos* case was again considered by the Court of Appeal in *The Satya Kailash*, below, where the court held that Clause 24 of the New York Produce form had the effect of incorporating the United States Carriage of Goods by Sea Act 1936 into a short-term time charter for lightening purposes in India and that the provisions of the Act in the context of the charter were not confined to voyages to or from the United States.

The *Oceanic Amity* was time chartered on the New York Produce form for a period of 20 to 40 days for the purpose of lightening the charterers' ship *Satya Kailash* off Tuticorin. The *Satya Kailash* suffered ranging damage due to the negligent navigation of the *Oceanic Amity*. The question arose whether the owners of the *Oceanic Amity* were exempted from liability for this damage either by Clause 24 of the charter or by the exceptions in Clause 16. It was held by the Court of Appeal (Robert Goff and Oliver, L.JJ.) that:

(1) Clause 24 effectively incorporated the United States Carriage of Goods by Sea Act into the charter and that its effect was not confined to voyages to or from United States ports.
(2) The damage suffered by the *Satya Kailash* was "loss or damage" arising from neglect in navigation within the meaning of Section 4(2)(*a*) of the United States Act, so that the owners of the *Oceanic Amity* were protected by that exception.
(3) The owners were not, however, protected by the exception "errors of navigation" in Clause 16 of the charter because those words were not wide enough to embrace negligent errors (see page 352 above).

The Satya Kailash [1982] 2 Lloyd's Rep. 465 and [1984] 1 Lloyd's Rep. 588 (C.A.).

Although certain language used by Robert Goff, L.J., in *The Satya Kailash* suggests that he would have accepted the proposition that the voyage by voyage obligations of seaworthiness of the United States Act are applicable to a period time charter on the New York Produce form, that question did not arise in the case. Thus, the extent to which the Hague Rules will be given effect in period time charters, particularly with regard to questions of seaworthiness (as to which see further below), still remains to be fully worked out by courts.

Manner of incorporating the United States Act

The Act is to be incorporated in the manner laid down by Lord Esher, M.R., in *Hamilton* v. *Mackie* (1889) 5 T.L.R. 677, for the incorporation of charter terms in a bill of lading and approved by the House of Lords in the *Adamastos* case: "the conditions of the charterparty must be read verbatim into the bill of lading as though they were there printed *in extenso*. Then if it was found that any of the conditions of the charterparty on being so read were inconsistent with the bill of lading they were insensible, and must be disregarded." Viscount Simonds adopted this passage in the *Adamastos* case and continued, [1958] 1 Lloyd's Rep. 73, at page 81: "It is obvious that there is much in the Act which in relation to this charter-party is insensible, or, as I would rather say, inapplicable, and must be disregarded." Lord Somervell said, at page 99: "The provisions of the Act are therefore to be incorporated as terms of the contract *as far as applicable*."

The United States Act applicable to all voyages under the New York Produce form

Following the *Adamastos* decision, the Act will apply to ballast as well as laden voyages and whether or not voyages begin or end in the United States. In the words of Viscount Simonds at [1958] 1 Lloyd's Rep. 73, page 82: "The contractual subject-matter was the whole period during which the vessel was under charter, and it is, in my opinion, to this whole period that the parties agreed that the statutory standard of obligation and immunity should relate". The incorporating words in the New York Produce form charter are in the same wide terms. See also *The Satya Kailash* [1982] 2 Lloyd's Rep. 465, [1984] 1 Lloyd's Rep. 588 (C.A.).

Seaworthiness obligation for each voyage

Without the incorporation of the United States Act there is under the New York Produce form no express or implied obligation of seaworthiness at the beginning of each of the voyages under the charter. There are only the obligations of seaworthiness at the beginning of the charter and the maintenance obligation in Lines 37 and 38, see pages 64 and 165.

But it is suggested that the incorporation of the United States Act creates an obligation before and at the beginning of each voyage to exercise due diligence to make the ship seaworthy. This is a step beyond the decision in the *Adamastos* case. There the charter was for consecutive voyages and thus there was already a seaworthiness obligation in respect of each voyage, although one that was held to be modified by the incorporation of the Act.

In *The Aquacharm* [1982] 1 Lloyd's Rep. 7, it was accepted by Lord Denning, M.R., and Griffiths, L.J., *obiter*, that Clause 24 of the New York Produce form had the effect of incorporating into a time charter for a trip with a single cargo the Hague Rules' obligation of due diligence to make the ship seaworthy at the beginning of the voyage. This again was little more than a modification of the existing obligation of seaworthiness at the time of delivery. In the case of a period time charter, the Act, if it has the effect suggested, is *creating* an obligation rather than modifying an existing one. But when the Act is notionally written out in full in the charter there seems no good reason to disregard as "insensible" or "inapplicable" the relevant provision, Section 3(1), nor to give "voyage" anything other than its ordinary meaning. Moreover Section 3 of the Harter Act which requires the exercise of due diligence to make the ship seaworthy is expressly incorporated by Lines 151 to 153 in respect of all cargo-carrying voyages to and from the United States.

This view of the impact of the *Adamastos* decision upon the New York Produce form of time charter should, however, be treated with some caution pending its full acceptance by the courts. In *The Hermosa* [1980] 1 Lloyd's Rep. 638, at page 647, Mustill, J., made the following, *obiter*, comments: "the difficulties created by the inclusion of the Hague Rules into a time charter have not yet been worked out by the Courts. The analogy with a consecutive voyage charter is not exact. For example, the charterer pays directly for the whole of the time while the ship is on hire, including ballast voyages; and there are in most time charters express terms as regards initial seaworthiness and subsequent maintenance which are not easily reconciled with the scheme of the Hague Rules, which create an obligation as to due diligence attaching voyage by voyage. It cannot be taken for granted that the interpretation adopted in [the *Adamastos* case] in relation to voyage charters applies in all respects to time charters incorporating the Hague Rules. It is, however, unnecessary to tackle this problem in the present case, for on the findings which I have made, there was a breach of the initial warranty of seaworthiness or (if that warranty is to be regarded as qualified by the Hague Rules) of the obligation to exercise due diligence to make the ship seaworthy."

Other effects of the United States Act

General

The provisions of the Act are notionally written out in the charter and only those which are in that context "insensible" or "inapplicable" or "inconsistent with the purpose of the charterparty" are disregarded. Lord Reid said in the *Adamastos* case, [1958] 1 Lloyd's Rep. 73 at page 91: "That leaves to be incorporated those parts of the Act which enact the rights and liabilities of carrier and shipper and which are capable of being applied to a charter-party if one reads owner and charterer for carrier and shipper." (Lord Reid was in the minority in the House of Lords as to the results which followed from this incorporation.)

Conflict with other clauses

Where there is a conflict between the provisions of the Act which are incorporated by Clause 24 of the New York Produce form and the other printed terms of the contract, the provisions of the Act will override. Where there is no conflict, the provisions of the Act will supplement those other terms. Shaw, L.J., in *The Agios Lazaros* [1976] 2 Lloyd's Rep. 47, said, at page 59: " . . . the terms of the specific contract and the Hague Rules are fused together. The combined terms interact between themselves. There is no line of demarcation or difference in quality or effect save that if the incorporated clause is also a paramount one the Hague Rules will not merely supplement the specific contract but will operate also to modify any incompatible clauses in it."

The Agios Lazaros was a case where the paramount clause was incorporated by an additional clause in typescript. The position may be different if there is a conflict between the provisions of the Act as incorporated by the printed Clause 24 and typescript additional clauses. This was the case in *The Satya Kailash* [1984] 1 Lloyd's Rep. 588, where there were typed additional clauses imposing certain absolute warranties of seaworthiness. Robert Goff, L.J., in giving the judgment of the Court of Appeal, said: "in our judgment, these clauses cannot affect the construction to be placed on cl. 24 as such. The most that could be said of these clauses is that, as typed clauses, they might be given precedence over the printed clause paramount in cl. 24 so as to override *pro tanto* the provisions of s.4(1) of the United States Act as incorporated into the charter. We cannot see that the fact that the parties have thought fit to provide for an absolute warranty of seaworthiness in these clauses can otherwise affect the incorporation of the United States Act into the charter by cl. 24. If anything, their presence pre-supposes that the qualified seaworthiness obligations under ss.3(1) and 4(1) of the United States Act would otherwise be applicable."

Exceptions in Section 4(2) of the United States Act

Subject to this the owners and, where appropriate, the charterers will be entitled, in addition to the exceptions set out in Lines 103 and 104, to the protection given by the exceptions in Section 4(2) of the United States Act, set out in full at page 501 above.

The owners of the *Aliakmon Progress* sued for hire due under a trip charter on the New York Product form. This action was brought against a firm which had guaranteed the obligations of the charterers. These guarantors sought to set off a claim for damages arising out of an incident at an Icelandic port. While berthing the master had given an astern order too late, rammed the quay and damaged the ship. Temporary repairs were done and a cargo loaded for Antwerp. After discharge permanent repairs were done in Antwerp, which caused the ship to lose her previous cargo arrangements and to have to wait 39 days for a replacement cargo. The Court of Appeal held that because the owners were entitled to rely on Section 4(2)(*a*) of the United States Act ("Act, neglect, or default of the master . . . in the navigation . . . of the ship") this cross-claim of the guarantors was not sustainable.

The Aliakmon Progress [1978] 2 Lloyd's Rep. 499.

The *Aquacharm* was time chartered for a trip on the New York Produce form to carry a cargo of coal from Baltimore to Japan. Having been ordered to load to maximum draft for a passage through the Panama Canal, the master negligently failed to take into account that in passing through a fresh water lake which forms part of the Canal, the ship's forward draft would increase. The ship was consequently refused entry to the Canal; after considerable delay part of the cargo had to be discharged, carried through the Canal on another ship and then reloaded. The Court of Appeal held that the ship remained on hire (see page 303 above) and that the alternative claim by charterers to recover as damages the hire they had to pay was defeated because that loss arose from neglect of the master in the management of the ship which was excepted under Section 4(2)(*a*) of the U.S. Act.

The Aquacharm [1980] 2 Lloyd's Rep. 237 and [1982] 1 Lloyd's Rep. 7 (C.A.).

Conversely, the exceptions set out in Lines 103 and 104 of the charter will be rendered ineffective by Section 3(8) to the extent that they give wider protection than the Act.

The extent to which the application of the United States Act (including Section 3(8), above) is restricted by the fact that Section 2 relates only to "the loading, handling, stowage, carriage, custody, care and discharge" of cargo has been a matter of debate. In the *Adamastos* case, Devlin, J., took the view that the words "loss or damage" in Section 4(1) and (2) of the Act, while not restricted to physical loss of or damage to the goods, were restricted to loss or damage "in relation to" or "in connection with" the operations listed in Section 2 as set out above. In the House of Lords, the majority agreed with Devlin, J., that "loss or damage" was not restricted to physical loss or damage and so could embrace the claim in that case, namely one for the loss of voyages under a consecutive voyage charter (whether or not, as Lord Somervell considered, that claim did arise in relation to the loading and carriage of goods). However, the Court of Appeal in *The Satya Kailash* [1984] 1 Lloyd's Rep. 588, 595, said that what had been decided by the House of Lords on this point in *Adamastos* was no more than that "where the subject matter of the contract is not merely the carriage of goods by sea but is voyages, the immunities in s.4 are, despite the express words of s.2, to be read as relating to the contractual voyages".

The Court of Appeal in *The Satya Kailash* went on to lay down the wider principle that where the Hague Rules are incorporated they give the owners protection not only against loss or damage in relation to the matters referred to in Section 2, but also in relation to other contractual activities performed by the owners under the charter. Robert Goff, L.J., said at page 596: "S.2 of the United States Act specifies the activities in relation to which the carrier, under any contract of carriage of goods by sea, shall be subject to the responsibilities and liabilities and entitled to the rights and immunities set forth in the Act. This range of activities is very comprehensive, and comprehends the full range of activities under the ordinary bill of lading contract to which the Act applies; so that, under any such contract, the carrier will be able, in respect of any such activities, to invoke the immunities in s.4. However, under a charter-party (whether a time or a voyage charter-party) the owner is required to perform a wider range of activities than those specified in s.2; for example, under a time charter there will be ballast voyages to be performed, and under a voyage charter the vessel will be required to proceed to a loading port as specified in the charter-party or as ordered by the charterers. The question arises: if the United States Act is incorporated into a charter-party, is the owner entitled to invoke the immunities in s.4 in respect of this wider range of activities? The answer given to that question by the majority of their Lordships in the *Adamastos* case is, in our judgment, in the affirmative . . . "

Consequently, it was held in *The Satya Kailash* that, as the loading of grain from a mother ship was a contractual activity to be performed under the charter, the owners of the lightening vessel were entitled to the immunities in Section 4 of the Act in respect of damage caused by the lightening vessel to the mother ship (which was owned by the charterers), even though that damage did not fall within any of the range of activities specified in Section 2 of the Act. (See page 427 above. See also *The Aliakmon Progress*, above, *Australian Oil Refining* v. *Miller* [1968] 1 Lloyd's Rep. 448, and the comments upon the latter case in *The Satya Kailash*.)

The immunities given by Section 3 of the Harter Act are not expressed as being subject to the same restriction as that imposed by Section 2 of the United States Carriage of Goods by Sea Act, described in the previous paragraphs. This may be thought to give Clause 24 of the New York Produce form a wider application than would be the case if reference were made only to the 1936 Act. But this must be doubtful in view of the fact that the words in Lines 151 to 153 which incorporate the Harter Act expressly do so "in respect of all cargo" shipped to or from United States ports, which may suggest a similar restriction.

Section 3(6) of the United States Act

The incorporation of the United States Act will give the owners the benefit of the one-year time limit provision in Section 3(6): see page 364 above and *The Agios Lazaros* [1976] 2 Lloyd's Rep. 47. But in *The Standard Ardour* [1988] 2 Lloyd's Rep. 159, Saville, J., construed "loss or damage" in the context of Section 3(6) as being limited to claims for loss or damage to, or of, or connected with the goods on board or to be put on board. He held that a claim by time charterers arising out of delay in the issue of bills of lading due to the failure of the owners to provide a ship properly equipped to measure the quantity loaded was not a claim relating to the goods loaded and was not therefore caught by the one-year time limit provision of Section 3(6).

For the effect on the time limit of the incorporation of the Inter-Club Agreement into a New York Produce form charter see page 253 above.

Sections 4(4) and 4(6) of the United States Act

The owners will also obtain the benefit of the limited right to deviate under Section 4(4) and of the rights in respect of dangerous goods given by Section 4(6), see page 127 above.

Section 4(3) of the United States Act

The wording of this Section appears at page 128 above. It was held by Mustill, J., in *The Athanasia Comninos* [1981] COM LR 132 (see page 240 above), that charterers could not use this provision as a defence to a claim by owners under the implied indemnity arising from Clause 8 of the New York Produce form. Indeed, the judge doubted whether it had any meaning at all in the charter. He said: "This is not the place for a full discussion of the difficult problems raised by the incorporation of the Hague Rules into the inapposite context of a Time Charter. I will merely say that whatever result the parties may have intended to achieve when including the Rules, and even if 'shipper' can be read as meaning 'charterer', they would need to use much clearer language than this to introduce the idea of fault into the shipowner's implied indemnity, where it has never been before. It may be that Article IV, Rule 3 [the equivalent provision in the Hague Rules to Section 4(3) of the Act] means nothing at all in the context of a time charter."

Division of operations between owners and charterers

The incorporation of the United States Act does not transfer from the charterers to the owners the responsibility for those operations which have been allocated to the charterers by the express provisions of the charter. For example, the charterers remain responsible for loading and stowing the cargo, as agreed in Line 78. What the Act does is to establish the standard to be applied to those operations which remain with the owners in accordance with the allocation in the charter. Devlin, J., said of the Hague Rules in *Pyrene* v. *Scindia* [1954] 1 Lloyd's Rep. 321, at page 328: "Their object . . . is to define not the scope of the contract service but the terms on which that service is to be performed . . . I see no reason why the Rules should not leave the parties free to determine by their own contract the part which each has to play."

Both-to-blame collision clause

This clause has been inserted into bills of lading to deal with a particular situation under American law whereby the carrier, although protected by the Hague Rules against direct suit by cargo on the carrying ship, may become liable to that cargo indirectly. This arises from American law allowing cargo lost or damaged in collision to recover in full from the non-carrying ship and for that ship to recover an indemnity from the carrying ship in accordance with its proportion of blame for the collision. Where both ships are to blame the carrier ends up with an indirect liability to his own cargo. The both-to-blame collision clause gives the carrier a contractual right to recover over against cargo and thus effectively restores the Hague Rules position. This is explained more fully in the American law section at page 437 below, where the validity of the clause is also considered.

American Law

Harter Act and COGSA

Although the Harter Act and COGSA do not by their own terms apply to charters, they may effectively be incorporated in whole or in part in the charter. See, e.g. *United States* v. *The Marilena P*, 433 F.2d 164, 1969 AMC 1155 (4th Cir. 1969); *The Marine Sulphur Queen*, 460 F.2d 89, 1972 AMC 1122 (2d Cir. 1972), *cert.* denied 409 U.S. 982 (1972).

Clause 24 of the New York Produce form expressly incorporates the Harter Act, at least for cargo shipped under the charter to and from the United States. It is not yet settled whether the mere reference to "U.S.A. Clause Paramount" without more effectively incorporates COGSA into the charter. The issue was raised but not decided in *Nissho-Iwai Co. Ltd.* v. *M/T Stolt Lion*, 617 F.2d 907, 913, 1980 AMC 867, 875 (2d Cir. 1980). COGSA can be incorporated by reference in the charter, however, either expressly or by a Clause Paramount which explicitly provides for incorporation or which otherwise indicates the intent of the parties that COGSA is to govern. The statement in Clause 24 of the New York Produce form that the charter "is subject to the following clauses . . . " and the reference to the U.S.A. Clause Paramount does effectively incorporate COGSA. *Hartford Fire Insurance Co.* v. *Calmar S.S. Corp.*, 404 F.Supp. 442, 1976 AMC 2636 (W. D. Wash. 1975). The most important effect of the incorporation of the Harter Act and COGSA in a charter is that the absolute warranty of seaworthiness is reduced to a duty to use due diligence to make the vessel seaworthy. See discussion above at page 167.

There are some significant differences between the Harter Act and COGSA. The most important one is that whereas both Acts apply to the time when the cargo is loaded on board the vessel until it is discharged, the Harter Act also applies to damage occurring between the time the cargo is discharged until proper delivery is made. *Caterpillar Overseas S.A.* v. *S.S. Expeditor*, 318 F.2d 720, 1963 AMC 1662 (2d Cir. 1963), *cert.* denied 375 U.S. 942 (1963); *Procter and Gamble Ltd.* v. *M/V Stolt Llandaff*, 1981 AMC 1880, 1885 (E.D. La. 1981).

Owner and charterer as carrier

Under the Carriage of Goods by Sea Act, it frequently happens that both the owner and the charterer will be a carrier insofar as cargo is concerned. This will occur, for example, where a bill of lading is issued by the charterer on its own form and is signed by the master. See, generally, *Trade Arbed Inc.* v. *S/S Ellispontos*, 482 F.Supp. 991, 994 (S.D. Tex. 1980) and cases cited therein.

We have discussed above at pages 255 to 260 the question of the rights and liabilities as between the owner and charterer where both are held liable for cargo damage. Even though the owner and charterer both may be carriers, it does not automatically follow from this that their rights and duties with respect to the cargo owner will be the same.

In *Hasbro Industries Inc.* v. *St. Constantine*, 1980 AMC 1425 (D. Haw. 1980), there was major cargo damage when a fire broke out in the vessel's engine room. Bills of lading had been issued by a sub-charterer and the cargo owner brought an action against both the owner and the sub-charterer. After a trial, the court found that the fire was caused by an unseaworthy condition of the vessel which was within the owner's actual privity and knowledge and for which the owner was held liable to cargo under Section 4(2)(*b*) of the Carriage of Goods by Sea Act. The charterer and sub-charterer, however, were exonerated from liability even though their duties to cargo were also governed by the Carriage of Goods by Sea Act. The court noted that the charterer had no direct control over the operation or maintenance of the vessel or the training of the crew. Thus, the charterer did not have "actual privity and knowledge" of the causes of the fire as required to establish the carrier's liability under Section 4(2)(*b*) of the Carriage of Goods by Sea Act.

According to the court, the charterer's obligation was to ensure that the owner carried out his duty to keep the vessel "in a thoroughly efficient state and classified in the highest class Norwegian Veritas". This obligation the charterer fulfilled by "requiring that the vessel be maintained to the classification standards and by monitoring the ship's inspection to insure that the standards were being maintained".

The *St. Constantine* involved a claim under the fire exception of COGSA which, as the discussion above indicates, imposes a burden on the cargo owner to prove that the cause of the fire was within the *actual* privity and knowledge of the carrier. The burden of proof under other sections of COGSA is not so great, however, and in the usual case where the owner is held liable because of cargo damage or loss caused by the failure to exercise due diligence to correct an unseaworthy condition, the charterer's direct liability to cargo is likely to be co-extensive with that of the owner.

Time to commence proceedings

In *Son Shipping Co.* v. *DeFosse & Tanghe*, 199 F.2d 687 (2d Cir. 1952), the court held that the incorporation of COGSA in the charter did not also result in the application of COGSA's one year time for suit provision to the commencement of arbitration proceedings. There the charterer demanded arbitration in connection with a claim for loss of cargo after the one year limitation period had run. The shipowner contended that the demand for arbitration was untimely, but the court rejected the defense, saying:

> Nor does the reservation to the carrier in the charter party of all rights it would have under [COGSA] make the demand for arbitration untimely. It is true that the demand was not made within the one year limitation upon suits, contained in §1303(6) of the above Act, but there is, nevertheless, no time bar because arbitration is not within the term "suit" as used in that statute. Instead, it is the performance of a contract providing for the resolution of controversy without suit . . . We are aware that the time within which arbitration may be demanded may be of great importance to the parties who have by contract agreed to have their differences so determined, especially to a shipowner. But unless they see fit to condition their agreement by an express time limitation, a demand within a reasonable time, as here, is not barred. (199 F.2d at 689.)

Where the charter contains an arbitration clause the question of whether a claim is time-barred is one for decision by the arbitrators. *Conticommodity Services Inc.* v. *Phillip & Lion*, 613 F.2d 1222 (2d Cir. 1980); *Office of Supply, Government of the Republic of Korea* v. *N.Y. Navigation Co. Inc.*, 469 F.2d 377, 1973 AMC 1238 (2d Cir. 1972). In very limited situations, however, the court will determine whether a demand for arbitration should be denied on grounds of laches. In *Conticommodity Services Inc.*, above, the court interpreted its previous ruling in *Reconstruction Finance Corp.* v. *Harrisons & Crosfield*, 204 F.2d 366 (2d Cir. 1953), *cert.* denied 346 U.S. 854 (1953) very narrowly, and held that the "court could determine only those questions of delay that relate to the two issues it is required to decide under Section 4 of the [Arbitration] Act—the making of an arbitration agreement and the failure, refusal, or neglect to arbitrate". (613 F.2d at 1226.) For example, if a party shows that its ability to present proof in relation to the demand for arbitration has been prejudiced by the delay of the other in making the demand, it would be within the court's power to determine whether the dilatory party should be permitted to use the Arbitration Act to compel an arbitration.

Despite the language of *Son Shipping* to the effect that an "arbitration" is not a "suit" as that word is used in COGSA, New York arbitration panels have generally followed the English rule and required strict adherence to the COGSA one-year statute of limitations with respect to the commencement of arbitration proceedings on claims for cargo damage arising under charters incorporating that Act. See *The Osrok*, S.M.A. No. 654 (Arb. at N.Y. 1971). In *The M/S Uranus*, 1977 AMC 586, 590–91 (Arb. at N.Y. 1977), the panel concluded that by including the "General Clause Paramount", the parties intended that the one-year time bar be a part of the charter, at least as to cargo claims. A similar result was reached in *The Silverhawk*, S.M.A. No. 1041 (Arb. at N.Y. 1976) and *The Prairie Grove*, 1976 AMC 2589 (Arb. at N.Y. 1976). In the latter case, the panel's strict application of the one-year time bar was approved by the District Court, which stated:

> The parties by contract agreed that the liability of the carrier and the ship for loss or damage should be discharged unless suit were brought within one year after delivery of the goods. No suit was so brought nor was a demand for arbitration made within one year. Arbitrators have ruled that the claim is time-barred and they could have (indeed should) rationally so decide. (1976 AMC at 2594.)

The incorporation of COGSA in the charter may also result in the application of the one-year time bar to cargo damage actions against stevedores. *United States* v. *The South Star*, 210 F.2d 44 (2d Cir. 1954) was a suit by the government against the vessel owner for cargo damage. The charter incorporated the COGSA one-year limitation provision as to suits for the loss of or damage to cargo. The suit was filed more than one year after the cargo was delivered, and as to the vessel owner, the suit was dismissed. The vessel owner had impleaded the ship's agent and stevedores, however, and the government contended the one-year limitation period did not apply to them. The court rejected this view, stating:

> As the vessel and the owner were under the duty of stowage in a proper manner, Judge Leibell held that the limitation provisions of the charter enured also to the benefit of the ship's agent and the stevedore, to whom the performance of such duty had been delegated. We agree with this view . . . (210 F.2d at 45).

See also *A. M. Collins & Co.* v. *Panama R. Co.*, 197 F.2d 893 (5th Cir. 1952), *cert.* denied 344 U.S. 875 (1952).

In cases where the owner or charterer is sued by a third-party cargo owner for the loss of or damage to cargo, he will often in turn seek indemnity from the other for amounts he may have to pay the cargo owner. In this situation, the owner's or charterer's claim for indemnity is not governed by the one-year limitation provision contained in COGSA, even if the underlying cargo claim is governed by COGSA. *Lyons-Magnus Inc.* v. *American Hawaiian S.S. Co.*, 41 F.Supp. 575, 1941 AMC 1550 (S.D.N.Y. 1941); *Spanish Amer. Skin Co.* v. *Buanno Transp. Co.*, 1975 AMC 910 (N.Y. Civ. 1975); *Francosteel Corp.* v. *S.S. Tien Cheung*, 375 F.Supp. 794, 1973 AMC 2370 (S.D.N.Y. 1973). Instead it is governed by the doctrine of laches, and the court or the arbitrators should look to the analogous state law governing indemnity claims to determine whether the action is timely. In New York, the analogous statute of limitations allows indemnity claims to be commenced within six years after payment has been made on the underlying cargo claim. See C.P.L.R. §213; *St. Paul Fire and Marine Ins. Co.* v. *United States Lines*, 258 F.2d 374, 1958 AMC 2385 (2d Cir. 1958).

This rule should apply even if the charter incorporates COGSA. As the court stated in *Francosteel Corp.*, above:

> In any event, the court finds the COGSA period of limitations inapplicable to suits for indemnity. The application of this statute to an indemnification claim would thwart the purpose of Rule 14 of the Federal Rules of Civil Procedure as well as the modern trend of authority. Any other conclusion would sanction a plaintiff to selectively sue an isolated defendant, and, by skillful manipulation of the limitations period, allow him to deny that defendant any claim for indemnity against a third-party defendant who may be subject to liability over. (For example, plaintiff brings suit one day before it is time-barred.) (1973 AMC at 2372.)

Similarly, in *Marubeni-Iida (A) Inc.* v. *Toko Kaiun Kabushiki Kaisha*, 327 F.Supp. 519 (S.D. Tex. 1971), the cargo owner brought an action against the charterer and shipowner for cargo damage. The charterer then commenced an action for indemnity against the stevedore. The stevedore contended that the indemnity action was time-barred under the one-year time for suit provision of COGSA, on the theory it was a third-party beneficiary of the bill of lading. The court noted that a stevedore could possibly be considered a third-party beneficiary of a bill of lading if the intent was expressly recited in the bill. The court held, however, that such a provision would only protect the stevedore in an action brought directly against it by the cargo owner, and not in an indemnity action by the charterer.

In earlier editions of this book, we made reference to an anomalous decision of the Fifth Circuit which held that the right of indemnity was governed by COGSA's one-year limitation period. *Grace Lines Inc.* v. *Central Gulf S.S. Corp.*, 416 F.2d 977 (5th Cir. 1969), *cert. denied*, 398 U.S. 939 (1970). That decision was consigned "to the briney deep" by the Fifth Circuit in *Hercules Inc.* v. *Stevens Shipping Co. Inc.*, 698 F.2d 726, 1983 AMC 1786 (5th Cir. 1983) (*en banc*), wherein the court adopted the majority rule that a cause of action for indemnity "arises separately from and after liability has been established" (698 F.2d at 735) and is governed by the doctrine of laches.

The difficulties which nonetheless may arise with respect to indemnity claims are illustrated by the decision of the arbitrators in *The Ruth*, S.M.A. No. 2426 (Arb. at N.Y. 1987). In that case, an intermediate charterer was held liable in a London arbitration for a cargo contamination claim. The cargo claim was governed by COGSA and although it was, in fact, put into arbitration in London more than one year after delivery, the English High Court of Justice found that the claim was not time-barred and permitted it to proceed. Having been held liable in the London arbitration for the cargo contamination claim, the intermediate charterer sought indemnity from the owner in New York arbitration under the head charter. However, the New York panel ruled against the intermediate charterer. According to the panel, by agreeing to New York arbitration with owner and London arbitration with the subcharterer, the intermediate charterer took the risk of a conflict of law between England and the United States. The New York panel was of the view that, had the contamination claim been asserted in New York, it would have been rejected because it was time-barred. The panel found that, notwithstanding the decision of the English court, had the claim been brought in New York, it would have been held time-barred. According to the panel, the risk of this conflict was to be borne by the intermediate charterer rather than owner.

Both-to-blame collision clause

The "both-to-blame" clause becomes operable in the context of claims for cargo damage resulting from a mutual fault collision. If the collision is the result of negligent navigation, the cargo interests usually will be unable to obtain any recovery from the carrying vessel because of the errors in navigation exception from liability contained in the United States Carriage of Goods by Sea Act. The cargo interests, however, can obtain a full recovery from the non-carrying vessel. *The Atlas*, 93 U.S. 302, 315 (1876). The non-carrying vessel, in turn, will seek indemnity from the carrying vessel for its proportional share of the liability to cargo. See *The Chattahoochee*, 173 U.S. 540 (1898). Under the both-to-blame clause, the carrying vessel is entitled to reimbursement from cargo for any amount it is required to pay the non-carrying vessel by way of indemnity for the cargo claim.

Thus, in a collision between vessel A and vessel B in which both vessels are at fault, cargo on A may recover its entire loss from B. Cargo's recovery against B becomes an element of B's damages, part of which is then recoverable from A in proportion to A's fault. The net result is that A will be indirectly liable for part of the cargo loss on A, even though A has no direct liability for this loss. It is the avoidance of this indirect liability which the both-to-blame clause is designed to achieve.

The both-to-blame clause has long been held invalid when used by common carriers in contracts of affreightment governed by the Harter Act or the United States Carriage of Goods by Sea Act. *United States* v. *Atlantic Mut. Ins. Co.*, 343 U.S. 236, 1952 AMC 659 (1952). In that case, the Supreme Court held that a shipowner engaged in the common carriage of goods may not, under the above Acts, exempt himself from liability for negligence for which he is responsible.

The clause has been held valid, however, when used in a private contract of charter. *American Union Transport Inc.* v. *United States*, 1976 AMC 1480 (N.D. Cal. 1976). In that case, the court stated:

> . . . the parties to a private carriage contract enjoy freedom to adjust the risk of loss or damage in any way they choose and may avoid liability for any cause, including liability for negligence.
>
> We also have in mind that the both-to-blame clause, as here used in a private carriage contract, does not really "exculpate" the carrying ship from a cargo claim of navigational negligence since it is the policy of the admiralty law . . . to exempt the carrying ship from such a claim by cargo in any event; nor does the clause operate to exempt the other non-carrying ship from paying the penalty for its negligence. The carrying ship merely seeks in a private carriage contract to make its statutory exemption from navigational negligence to cargo meaningful by requiring cargo to indemnify it for that part of cargo damage by which it has been indirectly burdened—notwithstanding its exemption.
>
> Whatever may be the public policy consideration of a both-to-blame clause in bills of lading arising out of common carriage, such considerations are not sufficiently applicable in contracts of private carriage to justify the overturning of a long-established maritime rule recognizing the legality of such arrangements in private carriage contracts. (1976 AMC at 1483–85.)

See also *Alamo Chemical Transportation Co.* v. *M/V Overseas Valdes*, 1979 AMC 2033, 469 F.Supp. 203 (E.D.La. 1979), holding that a both-to-blame clause is valid in a private contract.

The question remains whether the both-to-blame clause would be valid even in a charter if it is used in conjunction with a Clause Paramount. (The charter in *American Union Transport Inc.* apparently did not incorporate COGSA by any reference.) Since the Clause Paramount by its own terms purports to render invalid any clause inconsistent with COGSA, which would include the both-to-blame clause, it is arguable that the Clause Paramount nullifies that clause. As the cases discussed above indicate, however, there are persuasive reasons for concluding that the both-to-blame clause is valid in a private contract, even if COGSA is incorporated therein.

Nature of the Charter

"167. 25. The vessel shall not be required to enter any ice-bound port, or any port where lights or light-ships have been or are about to be with-
168. drawn by reason of ice, or where there is risk that in the ordinary course of things the vessel will not be able on account of ice to safely enter the
169. port or to get out after having completed loading or discharging.
170. 26. Nothing herein stated is to be construed as a demise of the vessel to the Time Charterers. The owners to remain responsible for the
171. navigation of the vessel, insurance, crew, and all other matters, same as when trading for their own account."

Ice clause

See under Clause 15 of the Baltime form, page 485 below.

Not a demise of the vessel

Line 170 of the New York Produce form emphasises what in any event results from the other provisions of the charter, namely that it is a "time" and not a "demise" charter. The same is true of the Baltime form despite the lack of an equivalent to Line 170. The basic distinction between time and other forms of charter is as follows.

Demise charters

Under a demise charter the owners lease their ship to the charterers for an agreed period of time in exchange for periodic payments of hire.

The charterers obtain possession and control of the ship. Indeed they become, at least in relation to third parties, the temporary owners of the ship: see *The Father Thames* [1979] 2 Lloyd's Rep. 364. Lord Herschell, L.C., said of such a charterer in *Baumwoll* v. *Furness* [1893] A.C. 8, that he had "become, pro hac vice and during the term of the charter, the owner of the vessel".

It is usual for the owners to tender their ship bare of officers and crew and leave it to the charterers to provide and pay for their own men, in which case the charter may correctly be called a "bareboat" charter, which expression is often used synonymously with "demise". In any event the officers and crew of a demise chartered ship are treated for most purposes as the servants not of the owners but of the charterers. Thus bills of lading signed by the master bind the demise charterers and not the owner: *Baumwoll* v. *Furness* [1893] A.C. 8. Similarly the demise charterers and not the owners will be liable for damages caused by collision as a result of the negligence of the officers or crew: *Fenton* v.

Dublin S.S. (1838) 8 A. & E. 835, and see also the judgment of Sheen, J., in *The Father Thames* [1979] 2 Lloyd's Rep. 364 with regard to the consequent creation of a maritime lien upon the ship.

Time charters

Under a time charter the owners provide services for the charterers with their ship, which they themselves officer and crew, for an agreed period of time in exchange for periodic payments of hire.

It is usual for the charterers to provide and pay for bunkers; but the officers and crew remain the servants of the owners, who retain responsibility for the navigation and general management of the ship. The owners do not part with possession of their ship. In *Port Line* v. *Ben Line* [1958] 1 Lloyd's Rep. 290, Diplock, J., said that a charter on the New York Produce form was a "time charter, not one by demise. It gave [the charterers] no right of property in or to possession of the vessel". This is emphasised in Line 170 of the New York Produce form.

A time charter is not a lease nor a contract for the hire of the ship. It is rather a contract for the provision of services, which services the owners provide through their officers, crew and ship. This is so despite the contrary implication of certain key words used in most standard forms of time charter, such as "let", "hire", "delivery" and "redelivery". As Lord Reid said in *The London Explorer* [1971] 1 Lloyd's Rep. 523, at page 526: "Under such a charter there is no hiring in the true sense. It is not disputed that throughout the chartered vessel remains in the possession of the owners, and the master and crew remain the owners' servants. What the charterer gets is a right to have the use of the vessel." See also the comments of Roskill, J., in *The Madeleine*, under Delivery, at page 88, above.

In *Sea & Land Securities* v. *Dickinson* (1942) 72 Ll.L.Rep. 159, MacKinnon, L.J., referred to the origin of these expressions as being in demise charters, predating the more modern form of time charter. He said, at page 162: "The modern form of time charter-party is in essence one under which the shipowner agrees with the time-charterer that during a certain named period the shipowner will render services as a carrier by his servants and crew to carry the goods which are put on board his ship by the time-charterer, and certain phrases surviving in the printed form now used are only pertinent to the older form of demise charter-party. Those phrases are, as in this one: 'The owners agree to let the steamer' and: 'The charterers agree to hire the steamer.' There is no 'letting' or 'hiring' of the steamer, or anything of the sort, here . . . 'Redelivery' is only a pertinent expression if there has been any delivery or handing over by the shipowners to the charterers. There never has been anything of that sort here; the ship has at all times been in the possession of the shipowners and they simply undertook to do services with their crew in carrying the goods of the charterers."

This, as stated above, is in contrast to a demise charter which is essentially a contract for hire and under which the owners do part with possession of the ship. In the same judgment quoted from above, MacKinnon, L.J., at page 163, emphasised this difference between demise and time charters: "there is all the difference between hiring a boat in which to row yourself about, in which case the boat is handed over to you, and contracting with a man on the beach that he shall take you for a row, in which case he merely renders services to you in rowing you about."

The time charter will specify the areas of the world in which the ship may be used (see under Trading Limits at page 105 above) and any types of cargo which may not be loaded (see under Lawful Merchandise at page 125 above).

For "time charters for a trip" see under voyage charters below.

Voyage charters

Under a voyage charter the owners agree that their ship, officered, crewed and bunkered by them, shall carry specified cargo on an agreed voyage in exchange for freight, characteristically a "single payment for the voyage calculated by reference to the quantity of cargo loaded or discharged".

Such a charter may cover more than one voyage, these voyages being separated either by the necessary ballast voyages (a "consecutive voyage" charter: see, for example, *The Saxon Star* [1958] 1 Lloyd's Rep. 73 and page 425 above) or by repositioning voyages upon which the owners may carry cargoes for others than the charterers (an "intermittent voyage" charter: see, for example *The Oakworth* [1975] 1 Lloyd's Rep. 581 and page 54 above). When, as is often the case, a consecutive voyage charter is expressed to be not for a specified number of voyages, but for as many voyages as can be completed within a certain period, it will share at least some of the attributes of a time charter: see the comments of Donaldson, J., in *The Berge Tasta* [1975] 1 Lloyd's Rep. 422, at page 424.

In very frequent use today is the "time charter for a trip". This is usually drawn up on one of the standard time charter forms, but specifies a particular voyage or voyages and is for the actual duration of this voyage(s) rather than for a period of years, months or days. If, nevertheless, the charterers' payments are to be of hire at periodic intervals, such a charter will be treated for almost all purposes as a time charter despite the initial uncertainty of its duration. (For a charter of this type, see *Temple Steamship* v. *Sovfracht* (1945) 79 Ll.L.Rep. 1; and comments at pages 95 and 96 above.)

The Law Reform (Frustrated Contracts) Act 1943 applies to demise and time charters but does not apply to voyage charters; see *The Eugenia* [1963] 2 Lloyd's Rep. 155 and 381, discussed at page 337 above.

Navigation

Even though the charterers "provide and pay for" pilotage under Clause 2, the pilot does not become the servant of the charterers so as to cause them to be vicariously liable for the pilot's negligence: *Fraser* v. *Bee* (1900) 17 T.L.R. 101, and the general comments at page 175 above.

Extent of insurance cover

Clause 26 of the New York Produce form, putting upon the owners the responsibility for insurance "same as when trading for their own account", when coupled with the obligation to pay for the insurance of the ship under Clause 1, requires the owners to insure against war risks, as well as against hull and machinery risks, within the trading limits laid down in the charter: see the judgment of Donaldson, J., in *World Magnate Shipping* v. *Rederi A/B Soya* [1975] 2 Lloyd's Rep. 498. The words "of the vessel" in Clause 1 are not to be construed narrowly, and may include appropriate ancillary cover, such as freight and disbursements: see *The Athos* [1981] 2 Lloyd's Rep. 74, below.

The way in which such insurance is effected, including the precise risks insured against and the value for which the ship is insured, are matters for the discretion of the owners; but that discretion is to be exercised according to the standards of a prudent owner: see *The Athos* below.

It does not follow from the words "same as when trading for their own account" that the owners are obliged to maintain during the charter insurance cover identical to that which they had been trading under prior to the beginning of the charter period: see the judgment of Robert Goff, J., in *The Antaios* [1981] 2 Lloyd's Rep. 284, and below.

Baltime form

Clause 3 of the Baltime form requires the owners "to provide and pay . . . for insurance of the Vessel". More specific provisions are then made so far as concerns war risks insurance in Clause 21; if the ship is traded to a dangerous zone as defined in part (A) of the clause then, by Lines 145 to 148 of part (B), the owners may "insure their interests in the Vessel and/or hire against any of the risks likely to be involved thereby on such terms as they shall think fit" for the ultimate account of the charterers. The equivalent provisions of the STB tanker form, in Lines 501 to 508, are more specific and more restrictive.

Effect on owners' claims against charterers for damage to ship

A provision that the owners are to pay for the insurance of their ship does not imply that they may not claim against the charterers for damage to the ship caused by the charterers or their servants: *Aira Force* v. *Christie* (1892) 9 T.L.R. 104.

Moreover, an agreement that the charterers may order the ship outside the charter trading limits in exchange for paying any extra premium required by the ship's underwriters does not relieve the charterers of their obligation as to the safety of the ports outside those limits to which they order the ship.

The New York Produce form charter for the *Helen Miller* contained an additional clause defining the trading limits as being "between safe ports within Institute Warranty Limits including St. Lawrence up to and including Montreal, but excluding Cuba . . . Guinea, and all unsafe ports, but Charterers have the liberty of breaking limits, they paying extra insurance, if any, . . . ". The charterers ordered the ship to ports outside the Institute Warranty Limits and she suffered ice damage on voyages to these ports, which were found to have been unsafe at the relevant time. Mustill, J., held that the charterers were liable for this damage. The owners had given general consent to trading outside the Limits but this did not detract from the charterers' duty to select ports which were safe, and this was not affected by the charterers' payment of extra insurance premium: "by paying the premium the charterer does obtain a benefit—the benefit of being able to send the ship on a voyage which the owner would not otherwise allow her to perform. But this is not at all the same as saying that the charterer thereby obtains the right to send her on such a voyage risk-free."

The Helen Miller [1980] 2 Lloyd's Rep. 95.

But in *The Evia (No. 2)* [1982] 2 Lloyd's Rep. 307, the House of Lords held that the war clause in the Baltime charter, Clause 21, which *inter alia* gives the owners the right to insure against the war risks it describes and charge the premium to the charterers, operates as a complete code and prevents the owners claiming under other provisions of the charter in respect of those described risks: see pages 146 above and 492 below.

Provisions for reimbursement of premiums by charterers

It is often provided in time charters, either by printed provisions such as Lines 145 to 148 of the Baltime form or by special additional clauses, that certain insurances are to be placed by the owners but paid for ultimately in whole or in part by the charterers. For extra insurance for breaking Institute Warranty Limits see *The Helen Miller*, above, and for a series of disputes concerning insurance against war risks in dangerous areas see below.

Discounts from premiums

The charterers are not obliged under such clauses to reimburse the owners more than they actually have to pay to their underwriters. Thus they are entitled to credit for any discounts against the gross premium which the underwriters allow to the owners: see *The Athos* [1981] 2 Lloyd's Rep. 74 and page 444 below, where Neill, J., said: "I am satisfied that *prima facie* a duty to reimburse imposes an obligation to repay that which the other party has expended and that therefore the paying party is entitled to the benefits of any discounts which the payee has received."

Premiums for war risks insurance

In a series of recent cases charterers have challenged the demands of owners for reimbursement of premiums for war risks insurance. Most of the cases have been on standard form charters with added provisions, varying in their detailed wording, requiring reimbursement of premiums by charterers.

One general principle emerging from the decisions in these cases is that the extent of the war risks cover that is to be arranged (and therefore paid for ultimately by the charterers to the degree provided for by the additional clause(s) in question) is a matter for the discretion of the owners, albeit that this discretion is to be exercised according to the standards of a prudent owner: see *The Athos* [1981] 2 Lloyd's Rep. 74 and below.

It also appears from these decisions that "insurance of the vessel" in Clause 1 of the New York produce form and other general expressions of a similar kind will not be narrowly construed and will extend to certain ancillary risks such as detention expenses, freight and disbursements which might not strictly be said to be insurances of the ship herself.

Otherwise, the extent of the charterers' obligation to reimburse the owners depends on the precise wording of the particular additional clause. Consequently it is with the construction of those precise words that the cases set out below are mainly concerned.

The New York Produce form charter for the *Athos* included an additional clause reading as follows: "35. War Risk Insurance is always be maintained . . . Charterers to reimburse Owners for . . . extra War Risk Insurance following receipt of invoices and supporting vouchers . . . "

In February 1980 the charterers ordered the ship to Iran, which at that time was a dangerous area. The owners were consequently obliged to pay an additional premium to their War Risks Association, the Hellenic. The full cover provided by the Hellenic was divided into the following parts:

Part A. (i) Hull, Machinery, etc.
(ii) Freight, Premiums, Disbursements, etc.
B. Detention or Diversion Expenses.
C. Protection and Indemnity cover.
D. Sue and Labour.

The additional premium paid was calculated on the ship's insured value, which included an element for freight and disbursements and had been maintained at the same level for several years despite a large drop in her market value. Moreover the percentage applied to this insured value to produce the premium payable was considerably increased by the owners' decision to maintain full cover with the Association including the part described as "Detention or Diversion Expenses", which they could have opted to exclude. This part of the cover provided running expenses if the ship were detained or diverted by reason of certain war risks and, in the event of detention exceeding 90 days, ten per cent of the insured value per annum pro rata to the period of detention. The charterers objected to the consequent size of the additional premium that the owners sought from them under Clause 35. They argued that by including cover for freight and disbursements and by opting for cover for "Detention or Diversion Expenses" the owners had gone beyond insurance "of the vessel" under Clause 1; also that the insured value on the ship should have been reduced. Neill, J., held that the whole additional premium paid by the owners was recoverable from the charterers. He said that "insurance of the vessel" in Clause 1 should not be narrowly construed; and that the extent of the cover was a "matter for the discretion of the owners though that discretion is to be exercised according to the standards of a prudent owner". The cover arranged by the owners satisfied this test and the additional premium paid was recoverable under Clause 35. In particular he held that the owners were entitled:

(a) to include in the insured value of the ship the element for freight and disbursements, as being part of "the sum which an owner requires to compensate him if the vessel becomes an actual or a constructive total loss",

(b) to maintain the insured value despite the substantial fall in market value, in accordance with general market practice,

(c) as prudent owners, to take out the optional cover for "Detention or Diversion Expenses", in view of the high degree of risk of the ship being trapped in Iran.

The Athos [1981] 2 Lloyd's Rep. 74; appealed on other grounds [1983] 1 Lloyd's Rep. 127.

The *Antaios* was chartered and sub-chartered under four charterparties, each on the New York Produce form and each containing an additional Clause 40 which read: "Any increase in war risk premiums for the vessel, officers and crew, after delivery to be notified immediately by the Owners to the Charterers and the latter to pay the increase, if vessel trading in areas where increase effective, however, increase as payable by Charterers not to exceed what would have been quoted if vessel was covered with Lloyd's London."

Each charter also provided for worldwide trading within Institute Warranty Limits (which could be broken on payment by the charterers of extra insurance) and for the ship to be entered in a P. & I. Club. When the ship was delivered under the head charter, in January 1979, the Arabian Gulf had not been declared an additional premium area by the Hellenic War Risks Association, in which the ship was entered. But it had become an additional premium area by the time of delivery under the sub-charters. The *Antaios* entered the Gulf on 17 September 1981, and the owners paid for the full cover of the Hellenic Association, including cover in respect of "Detention or Diverson Expenses" (see *The Athos*, above) and in respect of "Freight, Premiums, Disbursements".

Robert Goff, J., held that (1) the sub-charterers were liable only for the increased rate of premium over the rate current at the time of delivery and (2) Clause 40 was intended to apply to the whole cover offered by the Hellenic Association.

The Antaios [1981] 2 Lloyd's Rep. 284.

The *Oinoussian Virtue* was fixed for a trip to the Persian Gulf on the New York Produce form. Additional Clause 36(b) provided: "Any additional war risk insurance premiums over and above normal war risk insurance premiums and any war risk bonuses, if any, to be for Charterers' account." Robert Goff, J., held that everything depended on the wording of the particular clause and that the word "additional", when contrasted with "normal", naturally referred to the additional premium payable for entering an "additional premium area" under the ship's war risk insurance cover. He also upheld the arbitrator's decision that the charterers were liable for the premium payable by the owners for the full cover of the owners' War Risks Association, including cover for "Detention or Diversion Expenses" (see *The Athos*, above); the arbitrator had held that it was reasonable for the owners to take out such cover and Clause 36 (*b*) referred to "any" additional war risk premium.

The Oinoussian Virtue (No. 2) [1981] 2 Lloyd's Rep. 300.

The *Apex* was chartered on the New York produce form for a trip to the Arabian Gulf. An additional Clause 53 provided that: "Premium for basic war risk insurance on hull and machinery and crew always to be for Owners account but any additional premium and/or crew bonus in respect of these risks arising from the vessel proceeding at time charterers request to areas currently or subsequently designated as excluded areas by vessel's war risk underwriters to be for time charterers account who to pay to the Owners the amount due against presentation of underwriters'/brokers' original invoice(s)."

The owners paid additional premiums to the Hellenic Association to maintain cover for all risks under Parts A to D of its cover (see *The Athos*, above.) They sought to recover these from the charterers who disputed liability for premiums other than for cover under Part A (i), C and D.

It was held by Mustill, J., that the words "hull and machinery" in Clause 53 were not to be construed as defining the cover and meant no more than the ordinary war risks insurance in respect of the ship; accordingly the charterers were liable to pay the additional premiums in respect of the Part A (ii) and Part B covers, the latter being an integral part of the cover offered by the Hellenic Association (see *The Athos*, above).

The Apex [1982] 2 Lloyd's Rep. 407.

(See also *The Agathon*, below, in which Hobhouse, J., criticised the construction of "hull and machinery" in this case.)

The above cases all concerned charters on the New York Produce form. The cases which follow concern other forms of charter.

The *Taygetos* was chartered on the Beepeetime 2 form for a period of 10 years from August 1975. Clause 38 of the charter provided: "Any extra expenses which may be incurred by Owners if the vessel has to trade in areas where there is war (de facto or de jure) shall be borne by Charterers provided that before such expenses are incurred Charterers are given an opportunity to signify their approval. Any additional war risk insurance premiums on the vessel and/or crew imposed by vessel's war risk underwriters by reason of vessel being in breach of trading warranty limits and/or crew war bonus to be borne by Charterers." (The second sentence was added in typescript to the printed Clause 38). Disputes arose regarding the charterers' obligation to reimburse the owners for additional premiums for voyages into the Arabian Gulf in 1980 and 1981, the ship being entered in the Hellenic Association. It was held by Bingham, J., that the second sentence of Clause 38 was wide enough to include Part B cover (see *The Athos*, above), and a reasonable and prudent owner would not have opted out of the Part B cover.

The Taygetos [1982] 2 Lloyd's Rep. 272.

The *Agathon* was chartered on the Baltime form, the war clause, Clause 21 (see page 492 below) being unamended. In the course of the 12 month charter the ship was ordered to Basrah and in September 1980 became trapped. The ship was entered in the Hellenic Association with full cover (see *The Athos*, above). It was held by Hobhouse, J., that the words in Clause 21 (B) entitling the owners to " . . . insure their interests in the vessel and/or hire against any of the risks likely to be involved thereby on such terms as they shall think fit" were specific terms and were to be distinguished from the general terms considered in all previous cases except *The Apex*. Nevertheless on a proper construction of these words, they did apply to the full cover provided by the Hellenic Association.

The Agathon (No. 2) [1984] 1 Lloyd's Rep. 183.

The *El Champion* and two other ships were time chartered under separate charters for trips to the Persian Gulf. Two of the charters provided by Clause 68: "Basic War Risk Insurance Premium to be always for Owner's account. Any Extra War Risk Insurance premium on hull and machinery due to vessel's trading Persian Gulf to be for charterer's account . . . " In the third charter "Persian Gulf" was omitted from Clause 68. Between the dates of the charters and the dates the ships entered the Gulf there had been no increase in the war risks rates either generally or for the Gulf. The charterers argued that they were therefore not obliged to pay for the Gulf premiums, these being "Basic" and not "Extra". It was held by Staughton, J., that "Basic" war risk premiums referred to the rate payable for worldwide trading and that Clause 68 required the charterers to reimburse the owners for the "Extra" or additional premiums payable on entering an additional premium area. This was so whether or not "Persian Gulf" was included in Clause 68. He also held

that if the owners had effected policies on "Increased Value and/or Disbursements and/or Interest Values", premiums on such policies were also "on hull and machinery."
The El Champion [1985] 2 Lloyd's Rep. 275.

The *Discaria* was voyage chartered for the carriage of cargo from Qatar to Iran. The charter provided by Clause N. 4: "All additional was risk premiums and blocking and trapping insurance together with war risk bonuses payable to officers and crew to be for Charterers' account." Before the voyage the owners cancelled their existing war risks insurance, which did not include cover against loss of earnings, and took out a new package which did include this cover. It was held by Staughton, J., that the clause did not enable the owners to recover the premiums in respect of loss of earnings cover, because it was restricted to extra premiums required under an existing insurance (by contrast to extra insurance taken out in face of the danger) and it was not necessarily comprehended in "blocking and trapping."
The Discaria [1985] 2 Lloyd's Rep. 489.

American Law

Ice clause

Under the ice clause, the master may not be compelled to enter an icebound port or a port where, because of ice conditions, the vessel may be unable to safely enter or depart after having completed loading or discharging. *The Dirphys*, S.M.A. No. 283 (Arb. at N.Y.). It is incumbent on the master, however, to protest the port as inaccessible or potentially so. The master's failure to protest may result in a waiver of the owner's rights under the ice clause. *The Dirphys*, above; *The Leprechaun Spirit*, S.M.A. No. 1056 (Arb. at N.Y. 1976).

In a number of cases, it has been held that ice conditions may render a port or berth unsafe, such that the safe port/safe berth warranty discussed above at pages 156, 158 applies. This would seem to be correct, since the ice clause does not modify the safe port/ safe berth warranty. Indeed, the ice clause would appear to both reinforce and broaden the warranty by expressly stating the master's right to refuse to enter a port which may be dangerous because of ice conditions, or which the master reasonably may fear will become dangerous because of ice. It is certain that the mere expectation of ice conditions will not make a port unsafe. Under the ice clause, however, the master may still be entitled to refuse to go there if he has a realistic fear that the vessel may become trapped or exposed to danger because of ice. See *The Leprechaun Spirit*, above.

Time charterer's interest in the vessel

A time charter is simply a contract for the use of the vessel for any given period of time, and gives the time charterer no property interest in the ship. *Robins Dry Dock & Repair Co.* v. *Flint*, 275 U.S. 303 (1927); *The Bay Master*, 1969 AMC 359 (E.D.N.Y 1969); *Mondella* v. *The Elie V*, 223 F.Supp. 390 (S.D.N.Y. 1963); *Federal Commerce & Navigation Co.* v. *The Marathonian*, 392 F.Supp. 908 (S.D.N.Y. 1975), aff'd *per curiam* 528 F.2d 907 (2d Cir. 1975), *cert.* denied 425 U.S. 975 (1976).

In *Robins*, the vessel was damaged while in dry dock as the result of negligence of the yard's employees. The charterer attempted to recover damages from the dry dock yard for loss of the use of the vessel while she was repaired. The court held that the charterer had no property interest in the vessel, and could not recover for losses sustained as a result of a third party's negligent interference with the performance of the contract between the charterer and the vessel's owner.

This rule was challenged in *The Marathonian*, above, where the charterer sought to recover from the offending vessel for loss of use while the vessel was repaired following a collision. On the authority of *Robins*, the claim was denied. See also *Rederi A/B Soya* v. *Evergreen Marine*, 1972 AMC 1555 (E.D. Va. 1971).

An exception to *Robins* was made in *Venore Transportation Co.* v. *M/V Struma*, 583 F.2d 708, 1978 AMC 2146 (4th Cir. 1978). There the court held that *Robins* was inapplicable because of the nature of the charter arrangements. The *Oswego Liberty* was time chartered for a period of 13½ years. During the course of the charter, she was in collision with the *Struma* and was laid up for repairs for over one year. Under the terms of the charter, the charterer was required to pay hire while the vessel was undergoing repairs. The charterer brought an action against the *Struma* to recover the hire paid to the owner while she underwent repairs.

The court found that because there was no suspension of the charterer's obligation to pay hire while the vessel was being repaired, the charterer had standing to bring the claim. While recognizing that, in the technical sense, the charterer has no possessory interest in the vessel, the court held that "its interest in the vessel is sufficient to give it standing to claim damages, measured by charter hire paid when the owner has no claim for loss of use because its receipts of charter hire have been interrupted". (1978 AMC at 2150.)

See also *Standard Navigazione S.p.A.* v. *M/V K.Z. Michalos*, 1981 AMC 748 (S.D.Tex. 1981), holding that a time charterer who was contractually obligated to pay hire while the vessel was undergoing repairs following a collision was subrogated to the rights of the owner to the extent of the hire paid, and could bring an action against the owner of the other vessel.

The effect of *Robins* can be extremely significant in a variety of contexts. In *Riffe Petroleum Co.* v. *Cibro Sales Corp.*, 601 F.2d 1385, 1979 AMC 1611 (10th Cir. 1979), for example, the time charterer was a debtor in a Chapter XI proceeding in bankruptcy. The bankruptcy court had issued a general stay order which prohibited the commencing of any actions against the debtor. After the issuance of the stay order, a bunker supplier commenced an *in rem* action against the vessel to enforce a maritime lien for the furnishing of necessaries and fuel oil. The time charterer then sought to hold the bunkers supplier in contempt of the stay order by reason of its action against the vessel. The court held that the *in rem* action did not violate the bankruptcy order because it was not directed against any property of the debtor. As the court noted, "under a time charter, the shipowner agrees to carry goods in a ship in which the charterer has no property interest". (1979 AMC at 1615.)

"The owners to remain responsible . . . "

It is a basic feature of time charter that it is the responsibility of the owner to man and maintain the vessel. While the charterer undertakes responsibility for certain charges arising out of the employment of the ship, such as bunkers, a time charter is in no sense a demise of the vessel. Although the charterer has the right to employ the vessel as it wishes, within limits set by the charter, the responsibility for navigation, maintaining insurance, providing a crew, and all such other matters remains with the owner. See, generally, *Bergan* v. *Int'l Freighting Corp.*, 254 F.2d 231, 1958 AMC 1303 (2d Cir. 1958); *Riffe Petroleum Co.* v. *Cibro Sales Corp.*, 601 F.2d 1385, 1979 AMC 1611 (10th Cir. 1979).

In *H. Schuldt* v. *Standard Fruit & Steamship Co.*, 1979 AMC 2470, 2477 (S.D.N.Y. 1978), the vessel grounded while docking at Pier 42 of the East River, New York, as the result of negligence on the part of the docking pilot. The owner contended that since the charterer was obliged to pay for pilotage, it thereby assumed responsibility for any negligent acts of the pilot. The court disagreed, and held that under the demise clause, the owner remained responsible for the negligence of the docking pilot.

The charterer's interest in the vessel is such that, in the absence of any active negligence of its own, it is not liable to crew members for unseaworthiness or operating negligence. See *Morewitz* v. *Imbros Shipping Co. Ltd.*, 1979 AMC 1622 (E.D. Va. 1978). Thus, a time charterer ordinarily would not incur liability for any personal injuries suffered by crew members. Nonetheless, if the charterer performs any functions which put it in a position of owing a duty of care to crew members, it will be liable for losses resulting from its acts. *Mondella* v. *S.S. Elie V*, 223 F.Supp. 390, 393, 1965 AMC 2672, 2676 (S.D.N.Y. 1963).

Insurance

The owner's responsibility under this section to insure the vessel, "same as when trading for their own account", reinforces the language of Clause 1 under which it is obliged to pay for insurance for the vessel. These clauses would seem to impose a duty on the owner to carry insurance on the vessel that a reasonably prudent owner would be expected to have for trading within the charter limits, and should include hull and machinery, war risk and protection and indemnity insurance.

Although the charterer has no ownership interest in the vessel, it may, by contract, assume liability to indemnify the owner for insurance costs. This assumption of responsibility for insurance costs occurs most frequently when the owner is faced with additional costs because of the trade in which the charterer uses the vessel. Thus, in *Seas Shipping Co. Inc.* v. *United States*, 1951 AMC 503 (S.D.N.Y. 1951), the charterer agreed to reimburse the owner for the extra cost of marine insurance occasioned by the vessel's trading beyond the full limits of "American Institute trade warranties". (The owner's claim for additional premiums was denied, however, because the court found that the vessel did not go beyond the allowed trading limits.) See also *The Stuyvesant*, S.M.A. No. 1722 (Arb. at N.Y. 1982).

In *The Panagos D. Pateras*, S.M.A. No. 1566 (Arb. at N.Y. 1981), the charter contained a typewritten clause which provided:

> Any extra war risk insurance and/or officially imposed crew bonus to be for Charterers' account, including any additional war risk premiums for Suez Canal transit if any.

The owner had the vessel covered for war risks with the Hellenic Mutual War Risks Association (Bermuda) Limited. The Association's cover was divided into four parts, including (A) hull and machinery, disbursements, etc., (B) detention and diversion expenses, (C) protection and indemnity and (D) sue and labor. Under the rules of the Association, all of these items formed part of the standard cover. The charterer admitted liability for all extra premiums related to a passage through the Suez Canal, except those for item (B), which, it argued, were for the owner's account under Clause 1 of the New York Produce form. According to the charterer, the item (B) cover was in reality "blocking and trapping" insurance which, under standard war risk cover, is offered only as a separate form of coverage.

The arbitrator rejected this argument, and held that the owner was entitled to reimbursement for the item (B) cover. As he stated:

> Even if I were to find that the item of Blockage and Trapping is a separate item under the standard War Risks policy, I could not see any reason to make Owners change their basic coverage. The choice of where or which medium to use to obtain normal War Risks coverage lies solely with Owners. If by the selection of any specific Association or Underwriter, certain additional coverages are made available over and above those considered as 'standard' in an open market policy, but always within the described rules of coverage, the Charterers must accept the means determined by Owners to be in their best interests. It would be impractical for every underwriter or association all to have exactly similar terms, and even more so for a shipowner to have to change its chosen means of cover to suit the requests of every individual charterer, unless specifically contracted for under the Charter Party.

See also *The Olympic Armour*, S.M.A. No. 1840 (Arb. at N.Y. 1983), holding that charterer was obligated to informing owner for added premiums incurred in respect of the Hellenic War Risks Club's Part 2(B) cover for "detention and diversion expenses"; *The Capetan Costis I*, S.M.A. No. 1622 (Arb. at N.Y. 1981), holding that the owner was entitled to reimbursement for extra premiums for a passage through the Suez Canal.

In *The Crane Nest*, 1939 AMC 1186 (Arb. at N.Y. 1939), a time chartered owner was held liable for extra insurance costs under a sub-charter. The charterer admitted responsibility for extra insurance premiums, but contended that the sum charged was excessive. The arbitrator held that the sub-charterer had made a good faith effort to procure the lowest rate to be had, and that the charterer was liable.

Commissions

"172. 27. A commission of $2\frac{1}{2}$ per cent is payable by the Vessel and Owners to ....
173. ....
174. on hire earned and paid under this Charter, and also upon any continuation or extension of this Charter.
175. 28. An address commission of $2\frac{1}{2}$ per cent payable to ....
on the hire earned and paid under this Charter.
By cable authority from"

Although the broker, whose name is to be inserted into Line 173, is not himself a party to the charter contract, his right to commission may be enforced against the owners by the charterers, acting as his trustees for this purpose: *Les Affréteurs Réunis* v. *Walford* [1919] A.C. 801. If the charterers decline to do so, the broker may himself enforce his right, joining the charterers as co-defendants to his action.

Commission is payable under Clauses 27 and 28 only on hire which is both earned and paid under the charter or any extension of it. Thus if the charter is ended by agreement between the parties to it the broker will not be entitled to commission on the hire that would otherwise have become payable.

The *Clematis* was chartered for 18 months, the brokers being entitled to $2\frac{1}{2}$ per cent on the hire paid and earned. After four months the ship was sold to the charterers and the charter was cancelled by mutual agreement. The brokers sought commission for the remaining 14 months. The House of Lords held that they were not entitled to it. The brokers could succeed only if there were implied into the contract a term that the owners would not in any circumstances terminate it and their Lordships saw no reason for such an implication. Lord Buckmaster said: "The contract works perfectly well without any such words being implied, and, if it were intended on the part of the shipbroker to provide for the cessation of the commission which he earned owing to the avoidance of the charterparty, he ought to have arranged for that in express terms between himself and the shipowner."

French v. *Leeston Shipping* [1922] 1 A.C. 451.

The position might be otherwise where the premature termination of the charter was brought about, in the words of Lord Dunedin in the above case, "simply and solely to avoid payment of the commission". But it seems that nothing else—for example, a breach by the owners of their contractual obligations to the charterers—will entitle the broker either to commission on hire not paid and earned or to damages for preventing the earning of that commission: see also *White* v. *Turnbull, Martin* (1898) 3 Com. Cas. 183. (For the different position under the Baltime form, see page 496 below; for the willingness of the courts in certain other agency agreements to imply a term that the principal will not deprive the agent of his commission by breaking the main contract and thus releasing the other party to it, see *Alpha Trading* v. *DunnShaw-Patten* [1981] 1 Lloyd's Rep. 122; and see generally on this question *Bowstead on Agency* 15th edition, pages 233 to 238.)

Address commission

For comments on the usual practice with regard to this commission see *The Good Helmsman* [1981] 1 Lloyd's Rep. 377, at pages 419 to 421.

By cable authority from

See the cases cited at page 41 above.

American Law

Commissions

The services performed by a broker in arranging a charter are not considered maritime for jurisdictional purposes. Consequently, claims by brokers for commissions ordinarily are not maritime or admiralty causes and do not give rise to a maritime lien in favor of the broker. See *The Thames*, 10 F. 848 (S.D.N.Y. 1881); *Taylor* v. *Weir*, 110 F. 1005 (D.Or. 1901); *Andrews & Co.* v. *United States*, 124 F.Supp. 362, 1954 AMC 2221 (Ct. Cl. 1954), aff'd 292 F.2d 280 (Ct. Cl. 1954); *Marchessini & Co. (New York)* v. *Pacific Marine Co.*, 227 F.Supp. 17, 1964 AMC 1538 (S.D.N.Y. 1964); *European-American Banking Corp.* v. *M/S Rosaria*, 486 F.Supp. 245, 255 (S.D.Miss. 1978); and *Boyd, Weir & Sewell Inc.* v. *Fritzen-Halcyon Lijn Inc.*, 1989 AMC 1159 (S.D.N.Y. 1989).

But see *Naess Shipping Agencies Inc.* v. *SSI Navigation Inc.*, 1985 AMC 346 (N.D. Cal. 1984), where the court held that there was admiralty jurisdiction of a broker's claim for commissions. In that case, the broker had arranged contracts for the construction and subsequent charter of four container vessels. The court found that since the broker's duties were to extend throughout the period of performance of the construction contracts and charters, and because the broker was to be paid commissions over the 14-year life of the contracts, there was admiralty jurisdiction. The court distinguished other decisions holding that there is no admiralty jurisdiction over a broker's claim for commissions on the basis that, in the present case, it could not be said that the contracts were preliminary to a maritime contract; rather, because the broker's duties were to extend throughout the life of the contracts, the brokerage contract itself was deemed to be maritime in nature.

Since the broker ordinarily is not a party to the charter, he cannot claim a right of action under it to recover commissions. *Congress Coal and Transp. Co. Inc.* v. *International S.S. Co.*, 1925 AMC 701 (Penn. 1925). Moreover, a charterer's attempt to enforce the broker's rights in an action under the charter has been rejected. In two cases arbitrators held that they lacked jurisdiction to award broker's fees since the claim did not constitute a dispute between the parties to the charter. *The Caribbean Trader*, S.M.A. No. 41 (Arb. at N.Y. 1964) and *Jugotanker-Turisthotel* v. *Mt. Ve Balik Kurumu*, S.M.A. No. 1133 (Arb. at N.Y. 1977).

The broker's entitlement to commissions is entirely dependent upon the language of the contract authorizing the commissions. Unless the charter provides otherwise, the broker may recover commissions only to the extent that hire is actually paid under the charter. *Lougheed & Co. Ltd.* v. *Suzuki*, 216 App. Div. 487, 215 N.Y.S. 505, *aff'd.*, 243 N.Y. 648, 152 N.E. 642 (1926); *Caldwell Co.* v. *Connecticut Mills*, 225 App. Div. 270, 273, 232 N.Y.S. 625, *aff'd.*, 251 N.Y. 565, 168 N.E. 429 (1929); *Tankers Int'l Navigation Corp.* v. *National Shipping & Trading Corp.*, 499 N.Y.S. 2d 697, 1987 AMC 478 (A.D.I. 1986).

In *Lougheed*, above, the charter provided that a commission was due "on the monthly payment of hire". The charterer paid no hire because of the owner's failure to make a timely delivery of the vessel. The court dismissed the broker's claim for commissions and stated that the brokerage clause "indicated a clear intention to pay commissions only on the monthly payment of hire when received". (216 App. Div. at 492.) According to the court, "commissions were payable to [the broker] only as and when monthly hire for the steamship was received . . .". (*Id.* at 493.)

In *Tankers Int'l*, above, the broker claimed commissions on funds paid by the charterer to the owner to settle the latter's claim for unpaid hire. While the court stated that a factual question was raised as to whether the obligation to pay commissions survived charterer's default, the court observed that as a matter of law, the payment of settlement funds was not the equivalent of the payment of hire as earned under the charter. According to the court:

> Even had the shipowners recovered the full amount of hire sought by their claims, it is well settled that a broker is not entitled to recover commissions merely because his principal has secured a benefit equivalent to what he would have received had the contract been performed. (499 N.Y.S. 2d at 701.)

In *Roundtree Co.* v. *Dampskibs Aktieselskabet Oy II*, 1934 AMC 26 (Cty. Ct. N.Y. 1933) a broker's claim for commissions based on the earnings under a substitute charter entered into by the charterer in mitigation of damages under a charter which the broker had arranged and which the charterer had cancelled was denied.

Where a charterparty contains a provision that commissions are payable upon its execution, a broker is entitled to receive such commissions even if no hire is earned. See *Vellore S.S. Co. Ltd.* v. *Steengrafe*, 229 F. 394 (2d Cir. 1915).

The Baltime Form

THE BALTIC AND INTERNATIONAL MARITIME CONFERENCE

(Formerly The Baltic and White Sea Conference)

UNIFORM TIME-CHARTER

"IT IS THIS DAY MUTUALLY AGREED between .... Owners of the Vessel called .... of .... $\frac{\text{tons gross}}{\text{tons nett}}$ Register, classed .... of .... indicated horse power, carrying about.......................... tons deadweight on Board of Trade summer freeboard inclusive of bunkers, stores, provisions and boiler water, having as per builder's plan ....cubic-feet $\frac{\text{grain}}{\text{bale}}$ capacity, exclusive of permanent bunkers, which contain about.... tons, and fully loaded capable of steaming about.................knots in good weather and smooth water on a consumption of about .... tons best Welsh coal, or about .... tons oil-fuel, now .... and .... of...Charterers, as follows:"

Formation of the contract: See pages 21 to 27.

Parties to the contract: See pages 33 to 41.

Description of the ship: See generally pages 48 to 75.

When the ship must comply with the description: page 60.

Name of the ship: page 61.

Flag: page 64.

Statement as to class: page 69.

Deadweight capacity: page 69.

"About": page 70.

Speed and Consumption: page 72.

Misrepresentation: For a general discussion of statements made in the course of negotiations and of misrepresentation see pages 49 to 53.

Remedies for breach of contract: For a general discussion of conditions, warranties and intermediate terms and the remedies for breach see pages 54 to 59.

Period/Port of Delivery/Time of Delivery

"1. The Owners let, and the Charterers hire the Vessel for a period of.............................. calendar months from the time (not a Sunday or a legal Holiday unless taken over) the Vessel is delivered and placed at the disposal of the Charterers between 9 a.m. and 6 p.m., or between 9 a.m. and 2 p.m. if on Saturday, at.. .... in such available berth where she can safely lie always afloat, as the Charterers may direct, she being in every way fitted for ordinary cargo service.

The Vessel to be delivered.."

Let and hire: See pages 439 to 441.

Charter period (overlap/underlap): See generally pages 88 to 96.

Delivered and placed at the disposal of the Charterers

Delivery: page 88.

Delivery of ship not meeting her description: page 61.

Delivery of unseaworthy/seaworthy ship: page 65.

Readiness on delivery: page 113.

Readiness and fittedness for purposes of cancelling clause: pages 288 to 290 and pages 113 to 121.

Acceptance of delivery: page 121 and generally on waiver pages 59 to 60.

Time for delivery: page 287.

Remedies for breach of contract: See pages 54 to 59.

Available berth

The charterers must nominate a berth, on or before the ship's arrival at the port or place of delivery, to which the ship can proceed without delay.

The *Golfstraum* was chartered on the Baltime form with delivery at Sfax. When she arrived off that port it was congested and she had to wait four days before the charterers could obtain a berth for her. Mocatta, J., held that the charterers were in breach of an obligation to nominate, before or on arrival, a berth immediately available to the ship and the owners were entitled to hire for the waiting period.

The Golfstraum [1976] 2 Lloyd's Rep. 97.

Safely lie always afloat: See page 154.

In every way fitted for ordinary cargo service: See page 64.

Trade

"2. The Vessel to be employed in lawful trades for the carriage of lawful merchandise only between good and safe ports or places where she can safely lie always afloat within the following limits: ....

No live stock nor injurious, inflammable or dangerous goods (such as acids, explosives, calcium carbide, ferro silicon, naphtha, motor spirit, tar, or any of their products) to be shipped."

Lawful trades: See page 130.

Lawful merchandise: See pages 125 to 130.

Shipment of cargo excluded under the charter: page 125.

Dangerous cargo: page 126.

It is to be noted that the Baltime form, unlike the New York Produce form, expressly prohibits the shipment of dangerous cargo: see page 129.

Safe Ports: See pages 136 to 155; see also page 493 below.

Trading limits: See pages 105 to 107.

Owners to Provide

"3. The Owners to provide and pay for all provisions and wages, for insurance of the Vessel, for all deck and engine-room stores and maintain her in a thoroughly efficient state in hull and machinery during service.

The Owners to provide one winchman per hatch. If further winchmen are required, or if the stevedores refuse or are not permitted to work with the Crew, the Charterers to provide and pay qualified shore-winchmen."

Owners to pay for insurance of the vessel: See pages 441 to 446.

Maintain in a thoroughly efficient state: See page 165.

Charterers to Provide

"4. The Charterers to provide and pay for all coals, including galley coal, oil-fuel, water for boilers, port charges, pilotages (whether compulsory or not), canal steersmen, boatage, lights, tug-assistance, consular charges (except those pertaining to the Master, Officers and Crew) canal, dock and other dues and charges, including any foreign general municipality or state taxes, also all dock, harbour and tonnage dues at the ports of delivery and re-delivery (unless incurred through cargo carried before delivery or after re-delivery), agencies, commissions, also to arrange and pay for loading, trimming, stowing (including dunnage and shifting boards, excepting any already on board), unloading, weighing, tallying and delivery of cargoes, surveys on hatches, meals supplied to officials and men in their service and all other charges and expenses whatsoever including detention and expenses through quarantine (including cost of fumigation and disinfection).

All ropes, slings and special runners actually used for loading and discharging and any special gear, including special ropes, hawsers and chains required by the custom of the port for mooring to be for the Charterers' account. The Vessel to be fitted with winches, derricks, wheels and ordinary runners capable of handling lifts up to 2 tons."

Charterers to provide and pay: See pages 171 to 176.

Fuel: page 171.

Lights: page 173.

Pilotages: page 174.

Port charges:

It should be noted that under the Baltime form, unlike the New York Produce form, charterers are to pay all dock, harbour and tonnage dues at the ports of delivery and redelivery (unless incurred through cargo carried before delivery or after redelivery). See the comment on page 174 and *Scales v. Temperley Steam Shipping* (1925) 23 Ll.L.Rep. 312.

Agencies: page 175.

Loading, trimming, stowing, unloading and delivery of cargoes: page 245.

In *The Filikos* [1981] 2 Lloyd's Rep. 555, Lloyd, J., assumed (since it was unnecessary for him to decide the point) that the obligation in Clause 4 of the Baltime form to arrange and pay for loading, stowing and unloading of the cargo would have the effect of transferring the duty of and responsibility for loading, stowing and discharging the cargo to the charterers. See also the judgment of Donaldson, M.R. in the Court of Appeal, [1983] 1 Lloyd's Rep. 9, at page 11.

Off-hire periods: page 176.

Bunkers

"5. The Charterers at port of delivery and the Owners at port of re-delivery to take over and 43
pay for all coal or oil-fuel remaining in the Vessel's bunkers at current price at the respective ports. 44
The Vessel to be re-delivered with not less than ....tons and not exceeding ....tons of coal or 45
oil-fuel in the Vessel's bunkers. 46"

Bunkers on delivery and redelivery: See page 181.

Hire

"6. The Charterers to pay as hire: .... per 30 days, commencing in accordance with clause 1 until her re-delivery to the Owners.

Payment of hire to be made in cash, in .... without discount, every 30 days, in advance.

In default of payment the Owners to have the right of withdrawing the Vessel from the service of the Charterers, without noting any protest and without interference by any court or any other formality whatsoever and without prejudice to any claim the Owners may otherwise have on the Charterers under the Charter."

Payment of hire and withdrawal: See generally pages 194 to 219.

Payment

Cash: page 194.

Banker's drafts, payment orders and telex transfers: pages 194 to 197.

Payment of less than amount due: page 197.

Deductions from hire permitted by the terms of the charter: page 199.

Under Clause 14 of the Baltime form the charterers or their agents may advance necessary funds to the master for ship's disbursements and such advances may be deducted from the hire. Also, under Clause 11A (Lines 85 and 86), off-hire claims may be deducted from a subsequent hire payment by virtue of the words "Any hire paid in advance to be adjusted accordingly." See *The Nanfri* [1978] 2 Lloyd's Rep. 132 and page 199 above. Such deductions must, however, be quantified on a reasonable assessment made in good faith: *The Nanfri*, above.

Deductions from hire of claims for damages: equitable set-off: page 200.

Amount the charterers may deduct: page 203.

In advance: page 204.

Hire for last month: page 205.

Unlike the New York Produce form, there is no provision in the Baltime form for payment of less than a full month's hire when redelivery is expected within the following 30 days. The full 30 days' hire must nevertheless be paid and any overpayment left for adjustment after redelivery: see page 205 and *Tonnelier* v. *Smith* (1897) 2 Com.Cas. 258.

The right to withdraw: See pages 206 to 219.

In default of payment

It should be noted that the words in Lines 51 to 54 of the Baltime form differ somewhat from those in the New York Produce form. They provide for the right of withdrawal "In default of payment". In *The Georgios C.* [1971] 1 Lloyd's Rep. 7, the Court of Appeal held that these words meant "in default of payment and so long as default continues", so that a late payment or tender of hire by the charterers would extinguish the right of withdrawal if this right had not been exercised by the owners prior to that payment or tender. This construction, and the decision it led to, were overruled by the decision of the House of Lords in a case concerning the New York Produce form, *The Laconia* [1977] 1 Lloyd's Rep. 315; see page 208 above.

Lord Wilberforce there emphasised that the words "In default of payment" had to be related to the obligation in Line 50 of the Baltime form to pay hire instalments "in advance", saying: "The Court of Appeal have in effect construed the words 'in default of payment' not as meaning 'in default of payment in advance', but as meaning 'in default of payment whether in advance or later, so long as the vessel has not been withdrawn.' This is a reconstruction not a construction of the clause." This decision of the House of Lords brought the effect of the relevant words in the Baltime form into line with the effect of the corresponding words in the New York Produce form.

Re-delivery

"7. The Vessel to be re-delivered on the expiration of the Charter in the same good order as when delivered to the Charterers (fair wear and tear excepted) at an ice-free port in the Charterers' option in

....

....

between 9 a.m. and 6 p.m., and 9 a.m and 2 p.m. on Saturday, but the day of re-delivery shall not be a Sunday or legal Holiday.

The Charterers to give the Owners not less than ten days' notice at which port and on about which day the Vessel will be re-delivered.

Should the Vessel be ordered on a voyage by which the Charter period will be exceeded the Charterers to have the use of the Vessel to enable them to complete the voyage, provided it could be reasonably calculated that the voyage would allow re-delivery about the time fixed for the termination of the Charter, but for any time exceeding the termination date the Charterers to pay the market rate if higher than the rate stipulated herein."

Redelivery in same good order: See pages 188 to 190.

Fair wear and tear excepted: page 190.

Redelivery of damaged ship: page 189.

Failure to redeliver at port named: page 190.

Charter period (overlap/underlap): See pages 88 to 96.

Legitimate final voyage: page 88.

It should be noted that there is no equivalent in the New York Produce form to Lines 61 to 65 of the Baltime form. This last paragraph of Clause 7 has, however, no application in the case of a legitimate last voyage. If therefore the charterers send the ship on a final voyage which is legitimate in the sense that it may reasonably be expected to allow redelivery by the end of the charter period, hire continues to be payable at the charter rate until redelivery even if, as it turns out, the voyage overruns the charter period. Hire would only be payable for the excess period at the market rate, in such circumstances, if the overrun was caused by some separate breach on the part of the charterers.

The *Alex* was chartered on an earlier version of the Baltime form, Clause 6 of which was in substantially the same terms as Clause 7 of the present form. In that case, however, the proviso in the last paragraph was deleted so that the paragraph read: "Should steamer be ordered on a voyage by which the charter period will be exceeded charterers to have the use of the steamer to complete the voyage [. . .] but for any time exceeding termination date charterers to pay market rate if higher than rate stipulated herein." It was found by the umpire in arbitration proceedings that there was no breach by the charterers in regard to their orders for the last voyage, but that for reasons for which the charterers were not responsible the ship was delayed and was redelivered after the end of the charter period. The owners contended that they were entitled to the market rate for the excess period. Atkinson, J., held that Clause 7 had no application, saying:

> "It seems to me plain that the clause is dealing only with something which is *ex necessitate* a breach, namely an ordering of a voyage which the charterers have no right to order."

Hector Steamship v. *V/O Sovfracht* (1945) 78 Ll.L.Rep. 275.

Illegitimate last voyage: page 91.

Charter period extended by express or implied margin: page 91.

Redelivery after end of charter period

The last paragraph of Clause 7 allows the charterers to continue to use the ship at the market rate on a voyage which will on a reasonable calculation exceed the charter period by a small margin. The expectation must be of redelivery "about" the time fixed for the termination of the charter. In his (dissenting) judgment in *The Johnny* [1977] 2 Lloyd's Rep. 1, Lord Denning, M.R., expressed the view, *obiter*, that the word "about" in Line 63 allowed an overlap of only two or three days beyond the fixed maximum period of 13 months. But *obiter* comments of Parker, J., in *The Bunga Kenanga* [1981] 1 Lloyd's Rep. 518 are to the effect that this view is too restrictive. It may be that exactly the same considerations apply to the latitude given by the word "about" in this context as when it is used to define the charter period itself: as to which see page 93. It could, however, be argued that when considering this word in Line 63 no account should be taken of the length of the total charter period, but only of the time unexpired when the last voyage orders are given.

Market rate

It has been held by the Court of Appeal that the appropriate rate to adopt is the current rate for a time charter which corresponds as closely as possible with the actual time charter under which the voyage is performed.

The Johnny was chartered for minimum 11/maximum 13 calendar months under the Baltime form. The maximum 13 calendar months expired on 7 November. On 19 September the charterers fixed the ship for a voyage from U.K./Continent to Karachi. She loaded at Rotterdam between 2 and 18 October and was redelivered in Karachi on 7 December. The owners, who conceded that Clause 7 applied, argued that they were entitled to hire from 7 November to 7 December at the current market rate for a time charter trip from U.K./Continent to Karachi. The charterers contended that the appropriate rate was the current market rate for an 11/13 months time charter. It was held by a majority of the Court of Appeal that the use in Clause 7 of the words "if higher than the rate stipulated herein" pointed to a comparison between period charter rates at different times and not to a comparison between a rate for a period and a rate for a trip: accordingly the appropriate market rate was the current rate for a period charter as nearly as possible identical to the original charter.

The Johnny [1977] 2 Lloyd's Rep. 1.

Early redelivery: See page 94.

Definition of period of hire by reference to the duration of a specified trip or voyage: See page 95.

Cargo Space/Master

"8. The whole reach and burthen of the Vessel, including lawful deck-capacity to be at the Charterers' disposal, reserving proper and sufficient space for the Vessel's Master, Officers, Crew, tackle, apparel, furniture, provisions and stores.

9. The Master to prosecute all voyages with the utmost despatch and to render customary assistance with the Vessel's Crew . . . ."

Whole reach and burthen of the vessel

These words entitle the charterers to use all space which is cargo space, in the accepted sense of that term; space properly required for ballast is not included: see *Weir v. Union S.S.* [1900] A.C. 525. The words refer to the structural capacity of the ship at the time the charter is entered into, not at the time the ship was built: *Japy Freres v. Sutherland* (1912) 6 Ll.L.Rep. 381. See also *Noemijulia Steamship v. Minister of Food* (1950) 83 Ll.L.Rep. 500 and 84 Ll.L.Rep. 354.

Prosecution of voyage with utmost despatch: See page 231.

Application of Clause 13 exceptions (see also page 476).

If delay on the voyage is due to neglect or default of the master, the owners will generally be protected by Clause 13.

The *Istros* was chartered under the 1920 form of the Baltime charter and was ordered on a voyage from the Tyne. Although the weather on the voyage was bad there was nothing to justify the master putting into three ports of refuge en route. It was held that he was negligent in so doing and had failed to prosecute the voyage with utmost despatch. But since there was no evidence of any personal want of due diligence or default on the part of the owners, it was held that they were protected by the exceptions clause. Wright, J., said (the exceptions clause then being numbered 12 and the present Clause 9 being numbered 8):

"There has been in this case no want of due diligence on the part of the owners or their manager in making the ship seaworthy and fitted for the voyage, and there has been no other personal act or omission or default on their part. Any neglect or default that there has been has been that of the owners' servants. The arbitrator has found that there has been such neglect or default by the master and that has caused the delay. That seems to me to come within the precise words of Clause 12. It is not necessary here to consider whether every possible case that may arise under Clause 8 of a failure on the part of the captain to prosecute all voyages with utmost despatch is covered by Clause 12. I have not in my mind at this moment any specific type of case of a breach of Clause 8 by the act of the captain for which, notwithstanding Clause 12, the owner would be responsible. But there may be such cases. In any view, it seems to me that Clause 12 must receive effect where the case comes within its clear terms. If the effect of that is to render the owners free from any liability for loss or delay where there is a failure on the part of the captain to prosecute the voyage with the utmost despatch, then I think the owner is entitled to the full benefit of that clause."

Istros v. Dahlstrom (1930) 38 Ll.L.Rep. 84.

(This decision was approved by the House of Lords in *The TFL Prosperity* [1984] 1 Lloyd's Rep. 123, summarised at page 476 below.)

The owners will, it seems, also be protected if delay is attributable to the failure of the ship's engineers to run the engines properly.

The *Apollonius* was chartered on the Baltime form and was delayed on a voyage from Japan to the River Plate by the failure of the engineers to operate the main engines at full output at certain times. It was held by Mocatta, J., that this constituted a breach of the obligation under Clause 9 to prosecute the voyage with the utmost despatch, but that the owners were protected by Clause 13.

The Apollonius [1978] 1 Lloyd's Rep. 53.

(Views expressed by Mocatta, J., on other aspects of this case were criticised by the House of Lords in *The TFL Prosperity*, above.)

But the extent of the protection afforded by Clause 13 against breaches of Clause 9 has not yet been fully explored by the courts.

In *Suzuki v. Beynon* (1926) 24 Ll.L.Rep. 49, the view was expressed that if an exceptions clause "wiped out" the obligation to prosecute the voyage with the utmost despatch, the exceptions clause should not be given effect. But the weight of opinion in that case was that if there were matters to which the obligation to proceed with utmost despatch might apply, apart from neglect or default of the master, exceptions excluding liability for the master's negligence should be given full effect. (For a summary of this case see page 231 above.) Wright, J., in *Istros v. Dahlstrom*, above, thought that there might be some such matters but gave no examples: he thought that in any event Clause 9 had practical effect in recognising the duty of the master to act as stated, even if Clause 13 gave the owners a defence against claims for breach of that duty.

Where delay is the result of orders by the owners, they will obtain no protection from Clause 13: *International Bulk Carriers v. Evlogia Shipping* (*The Mihalios Xilas*) [1978] 2 Lloyd's Rep. 186.

Master (continued)

[Clause 9 continued]

“ . . . The Master to be under the orders of the Charterers as regards employment, agency, or other arrangements. The Charterers to indemnify the Owners against all consequences or liabilities arising from the Master, Officers or Agents signing Bills of Lading or other documents or otherwise complying with such orders, as well as from any irregularity in the Vessel’s papers or for overcarrying goods. The Owners not to be responsible for shortage, mixture, marks, nor for number of pieces or packages, nor for damage to or claims on cargo caused by bad stowage or otherwise.

If the Charterers have reason to be dissatisfied with the conduct of the Master, Officers, or Engineers, the Owners, on receiving particulars of the complaint, promptly to investigate the matter, and, if necessary and practicable, to make a change in the appointments.”

Employment and indemnity: See generally pages 236 to 242.

It should be noted that the Baltime form, unlike the New York Produce form, contains an express indemnity: See page 238.

Orders: page 236.

Employment: page 239.

Agency, or other arrangements

A similar clause to the employment and indemnity clause in the Baltime form was considered by the House of Lords in *Larrinaga Steamship* v. *The Crown* (1944) 78 Ll.L. Rep. 167, summarised at page 239 above. In that case Lord Wright said in regard to these terms:

“The shipowner is entitled in the ordinary course to decide to what firm or person in each port the ship in the course of the charter-party is to be consigned as agent. The selection is here left to the charterers. . . . ‘Arrangements’ is a wider term. It is also used in this charter-party [T.99A, a wartime version of the Baltime form] in Clause 3. There it refers to disbursements which have to be made for services in connection with operating the ship, and I think it has a similar scope in Clause 9.”

See also page 175 above.

Consequences or liabilities

It was held in *Royal Greek Government* v. *Minister of Transport (The Ann Stathatos*) (1950) 83 Ll.L.Rep. 228, summarised at page 240, that “consequences or liabilities” in Clause 9 were not limited to matters not covered by other provisions of thecharter. Devlin, J., said, at page 234: “I see nothing incongruous in the idea that the clause was intended to have, as it were, a life of its own and to be more than a bin for odds and ends left over from other clauses. Dangerous cargoes, trades, ports and places can all be prohibited by express provision; but many cases may arise which are outside the rigid framework of a prohibition clause, but where an owner, if he were free to choose, might prefer not to go to a particular place or take a particular cargo, not necessarily because he foresees any definite danger but because he feels it might lead to trouble. If he is to surrender his freedom of choice and put his master under the orders of the charterer, there is nothing unreasonable in his stipulating for a complete indemnity in return."

It was held in *Bosma v. Larsen* [1966] 1 Lloyd's Rep. 22 that the indemnity against "all consequences or liabilities" imposes the obligation to indemnify against the incurring of a liability and hence that the owners' cause of action under Clause 9 in respect of a liability for damage to cargo under bills of lading arose when that liability to cargo was created and not when the cargo claim was paid. But the decision was not followed in *County & District Properties v. Jenner* [1976] 2 Lloyd's Rep. 728, where it was held that the cause of action in a claim under a building contract did not, on the wording of the indemnity clause in that contract, arise until the underlying liability was ascertained. The court in *Green & Silley Weir v. British Railways Board* [1980] 17 B.L.R. 94, also declined to follow *Bosma v. Larsen*. Neill, J., in *The Caroline P* [1984] 2 Lloyd's Rep. 466 (see page 264 above) having analysed the authorities did not state whether he agreed with the decision in *Bosma v. Larsen* or not, but he observed that McNair, J., had not dealt separately with the words "all consequences" in construing the indemnity provision in Clause 9. *Bosma v. Larsen* must now, therefore, be regarded as very doubtful authority.

Such orders

In *The Ann Stathatos* (1950) 83 Ll.L.Rep. 228 it was held that "such orders" did not relate only to the signing of bills of lading or other documents: see under "Consequences or liabilities", above.

Causation: page 241.

Ordinary expenses and navigational risks: page 241.

Relationship with Clause 13

The owners may have a defence under Clause 13 to a claim by the charterers for damages caused by the wrongful refusal of the master to obey their employment orders if the claim can be categorised as a claim for delay during the currency of the charter, or if it is in respect of physical loss or damage to goods on board (see page 476 below). The question whether such a claim could be regarded as a claim for delay was left open by the Court of Appeal in *The Charalambos N. Pateras* [1972] 1 Lloyd's Rep. 1. The ground upon which that case was actually decided by the Court of Appeal (namely that the second sentence of Clause 13 covered financial loss as well as physical loss or damage) was held to be incorrect by the House of Lords in *The TFL Prosperity* [1984] 1 Lloyds' Rep. 123, see page 476 below.

Signing bills of lading: See generally pages 261 to 274.

It should be noted that the Baltime form does not expressly require the master to sign bills of lading "as presented". But the position is likely to be the same whether there words appear in the charter or not; see page 271 above.

American Law

Charterer's rights to issue bills of lading

In *The Penta*, S.M.A. No. 1603 (Arb. at N.Y. 1981), the panel majority ruled that under Clause 9 of the Baltime 1939 form, the charterer did not have the right to issue bills of lading or to order the master to authorize it, as agent, to sign bills of lading. The majority reasoned that a contrary decision could give the charterer the power to circumvent the owner's right to exercise its lien on sub-freights if it were to issue and sign bills of lading without having to advise the master of the identity of the sub-charterer or shipper. According to the panel majority, the express indemnity given to the owner in Clause 9 against all consequences by reason of the signing of bills of lading did not give the charterer the right to issue bills itself. Rather, if the charterer wished to have this right, it was necessary to obtain the express agreement of the owner.

Directions and Logs/Suspension of Hire etc./ Cleaning Boilers

"10. The Charterers to furnish the Master with all instructions and sailing directions and the Master and Engineer to keep full and correct logs accessible to the Charterers or their Agents.

11. (A) In the event of drydocking or other necessary measures to maintain the efficiency of the Vessel, deficiency of men or Owners' stores, breakdown of machinery, damage to hull or other accident, either hindering or preventing the working of the vessel and continuing for more than twenty-four consecutive hours, no hire to be paid in respect of any time lost thereby during the period in which the Vessel is unable to perform the service immediately required. Any hire paid in advance to be adjusted accordingly.

(B) In the event of the Vessel being driven into port or to anchorage through stress of weather, trading to shallow harbours or to rivers or ports with bars or suffering an accident to her cargo, any detention of the Vessel and/or expenses resulting from such detention to be for the Charterers' account even if such detention and/or expenses, or the cause by reason of which either is incurred, be due to, or be contributed to by, the negligence of the Owners' servants.

12. Cleaning of boilers whenever possible to be done during service, but if impossible the Charterers to give the Owners necessary time for cleaning. Should the Vessel be detained beyond 48 hours hire to cease until again ready."

Off-hire clause: See generally pages 295 to 310.

"Net loss of time" clause

It is suggested that this clause is a "net loss of time" clause rather than a "period" clause, in view of the words "no hire to be paid in respect of any time lost thereby": see the discussion at pages 269 to 300 above. But once the ship is again able to perform the service immediately required the hire becomes payable again: see by way of example *Court Line v. Finelvet (The Jevington Court)* [1966] 1 Lloyd's Rep. 683, at page 474 below, and part (3) of the judgment of Roskill, J.

From when full hire again becomes payable: page 297.

Partial inefficiency: page 299.

Deficiency of men: page 300.

Breakdown: page 301.

Or other accident, either hindering or preventing the working of the vessel

These words have been held not subject to the *ejusdem generis* rule (see page 306 above). They therefore have their full natural meaning and embrace, for example, grounding in a river: *Magnhild v. McIntyre* [1920] 3 K.B. 321 and [1921] 2 K.B. 97 (Court of Appeal), and *Court Line v. Finelvet* [1966] 1 Lloyd's Rep. 683. They have also been held to cover encrustation of a ship's bottom by molluscs in waters where this could not have been expected to happen: *The Apollonius* [1978] 1 Lloyd's Rep. 53 (but see *The Rijn* [1981] 2 Lloyd's Rep. 267 and page 307 above).

For the words to apply there must be an "accident". The Court of Appeal has held that the refusal of a crew to sail save in a convoy does not come within the words: *Royal Greek Government v. Minister of Transport (The Illissos)* (1949) 82 Ll.L.Rep. 196. An "accident" is something that happens out of the ordinary course of things: see the judgment of Mocatta, J., in *The Apollonius* [1978] 1 Lloyd's Rep. 53.

Working: pages 301 to 305.

Continuing for more than twentyfour consecutive hours

Once the 24 hours have been exceeded, they are counted in with the rest of the delay: *Meade-King, Robinson v. Jacobs* [1915] 2 K.B. 640.

Clause 11 (B)

Clause 11 (A) sets out the events in which the ship is to be off-hire. Clause 11 (B) is to the opposite effect and lists events in which the ship is to remain on hire, regardless of the negligence of the owners' servants. To the extent Clause 11 (B) overlaps in subject matter with 11 (A) it operates in effect as an exception clause upon an exception clause.

Situations may arise in which an event mentioned in 11 (A) causes or is caused by one mentioned in 11 (B). For instance, an "accident to her cargo" may result in "damage to hull". Where the detention is in fact caused by the damage to the hull, itself resulting from an accident to the cargo, the ship will be off-hire. Where, on the other hand, the detention is caused by the damage to the cargo then the ship will remain on hire, as where the ship puts into port to discharge the cargo which has shifted or heated as a result of the accident to it.

Following the explosion in the coal cargo of the *Ann Stathatos,* see page 240 above, her hull and superstructure were damaged and took some time to repair. There was, however, no material damage to the coal itself. Thus the detention of the ship was caused by repairs to hull damage, but the hull damage arose out of an accident to the cargo. Devlin, J., held that, as the detention was caused by the repairs to the hull damage, Clause 11(A) applied and the ship was off-hire under that part of the clause.

Royal Greek Government v. Minister of Transport (1950) 83 Ll.L.Rep. 228.

(See also *Burrell v. Green* [1914] 1 K.B. 293 (shifted deck cargo damaging ship).)

To bring themselves within Clause 11 (B) the owners must show that the effective (or "proximate") cause of the relevant detention or expense was one of the events described in that part of the clause. It is not enough to show that at the time the ship was, for example, trading to a river with a bar.

The *Jevington Court* was outward bound from Rosario with a part cargo of cereals when, as a result of negligence by the compulsory pilot and defects in the marking of a channel, she grounded in the area known as the Martin Garcia Bar. After nearly six weeks she was refloated. She was then fit to continue her voyage but further delay was caused by the necessity to discharge, cool and reload the heated cargo at Buenos Aires. At the time the ship was under time charter on the Baltime form. The owners claimed that hire (and certain expenses) were payable by the charterers during the grounding period, relying on Clause 11(B). Roskill, J., held (1) that the words "with bars" applied both to "ports" and to "rivers," and (2) that it was necessary for the owners to prove that the proximate cause of the detention (and expenses) was the trading of the ship to a river with a bar, which they could not do in the present case. With regard to the time at Buenos Aires he held (3) that the ship was on hire again because although there had been an "accident" under Clause 11(A) the ship was at all relevant times able "to perform the service immediately required", namely to unload and later reload the heated cargo.

Court Line v. Finelvet [1966] 1 Lloyd's Rep. 683.

With bars

It was decided in *Court Line v. Finelvet*, above, that the words "with bars" apply both to "ports" and to "rivers". In the earlier version of the clause which was in use at the time of *Magnhild v. McIntyre* [1921] 2 K.B. 97 ("shallow harbours, rivers, or ports where there are bars") this was not so and the words applied to "ports" only and not to "rivers". Roskill, J., in the former case remarked: "The Court must be careful, when construing a clause in a standard form of charter, not to have too much regard to other decisions on a clause which, although similar in some respects, is in crucial respects differently worded."

It appears from the judgment of Roskill, J., in the *Court Line* case, that a "bar" is a natural underwater bank of sand or silt, with deep water on either side, which ships cross on limited draft rather than sail around: it does not have to be at the mouth of a river and it does not necessarily cease to be a bar because it has a dredged channel or channels through it.

Incident caused by charterers' breach: page 307.

Other obligations during off-hire periods: page 308.

Effect on other remedies of owners and charterers: page 309.

Responsibility and Exemption

"13. The Owners only to be responsible for delay in delivery of the Vessel or for delay during the currency of the Charter and for loss or damage to goods onboard, if such delay or loss has been caused by want of due diligence on the part of the Owners or their Manager in making the Vessel seaworthy and fitted for the voyage or any other personal act or omission or default of the Owners or their Manager. The Owners not to be responsible in any other case nor for damage or delay whatsoever and howsoever caused even if caused by the neglect or default of their servants . . ."

[Clause 13 is continued below]

Clause 13 exceptions

The exceptions in Lines 95 to 100 of Clause 13 are restricted to cases of delay in delivery, delay during the currency of the charter and physical loss or damage to goods on board, not caused by personal want of due diligence to make the ship seaworthy, or personal default, on the part of the owners or their manager. The second sentence of Clause 13 (Lines 99 and 100) does not exempt the owners from liability for all other types of loss or damage and in particular does not extend the exemption to financial loss generally.

The *TFL Prosperity*, a "roll-on, roll-off" ship, was chartered on the Baltime form. An additional typed clause (Clause 26) specified in detail certain fixed structural attributes of the ship. In particular the free height under the main deck was stated to be 6.10 metres. In fact the height was only 6.05 metres which meant that a trailer double-stacked with containers could not be loaded into the main deck. The charterers claimed the financial losses they had suffered as the result of the misdescription. The owners relied on Clause 13, there having been no personal default on their part. It was held by the House of Lords, reversing the Court of Appeal and overruling that court's decision in *The Charalambos N. Pateras* [1972] 1 Lloyd's Rep. 1, that:

(i) the first sentence of Clause 13 (Lines 95 to 99) dealt only with the matters for which liability was accepted by the owners, namely delay in delivery, delay during the currency of the charter and loss or damage to goods on board (which necessarily meant physical loss or damage—as opposed to financial loss or damage) if due to the stated causes;

(ii) the second sentence of Clause 13 (Lines 99 and 100) was, as a matter of construction of Clause 13 read as a whole, linked to the first sentence and was also directed, and directed only, to the same types of delay and physical loss or damage to goods as the first sentence;

(iii) hence Clause 13 did not afford the owners a defence to the charterers' claim for financial losses suffered as a result of the owners' breach;

(iv) in any event, Clause 13 could not be construed so as to exempt the owners from liability for breach of a term as to description.

The TFL Prosperity [1984] 1 Lloyd's Rep. 123 (H.L.).

In reaching its decision in *The TFL Prosperity* the House of Lords disagreed with the decision of Walsh, J., in the Supreme Court of New South Wales in *Westfal-Larsen* v. *Colonial Sugar Refining* [1960] 2 Lloyd's Rep. 206, which had been accepted as correct by McNair, J., in *The Brabant* [1965] 2 Lloyd's Rep. 546 and by Mocatta, J., in *The Apollonius* [1978] 1 Lloyd's Rep. 53. In the *Westfal-Larsen* case, the owners claimed general average contribution from the charterers who defended on the ground of unseaworthiness. The owners were held entitled to defeat that defence by relying upon the exceptions in Clause 13. Lord Roskill, in criticising Walsh, J.'s decision, observed that the claim in the *Westfal-Larsen* case "was not one for loss of or damage to cargo, but arose because of the inability of the vessel to maintain proper steam by reason of bunker trouble which it seems was the fault of the chief engineer".

Delay in delivery

The clause will not protect the owner against all delays in the delivery of the ship, even if not caused by personal want of due diligence or personal default of the owners or their manager. In particular, it will not apply to delays arising out of prior contractual arrangements to which the charterers are not parties unless in the context of the charter as a whole it is clear that the intention was that the charterers should bear the risks of such delays. The clause, being for the benefit of the owners, will be construed in favour of the charterers.

The *Helvetia-S*, which was described in the charter as "the new building motor vessel to be named later . . . now in course of construction", was chartered on the Baltime form. By Clause 1 the ship was "to be delivered per 10th June, 1956 laydays"; the cancelling date (Clause 22) was 15 July. There was a delay in the construction of the ship and on 12 June the owners informed the charterers that she would not be ready before August. The question arose whether the owners were protected by Clause 13. It was argued for the owners that "delay in delivery" in Line 95 meant "postponement of delivery" and that any event which was outside the control of the owners and which occurred in the course of construction was within the scope of the clause if it caused delay. Pearson, J., held that the clause did not bear such a wide interpretation; delay in construction was not delay in delivery.

The Helvetia-S [1960] 1 Lloyd's Rep. 540.

(This decision was approved by the House of Lords in *The TFL Prosperity*, above.)

Delay during the currency of the charter

The clause will normally protect the owners against liability for delay during the charter period even where there has been a breach of the master's obligation to prosecute voyages with the utmost despatch (Clause 9), provided there has been no personal want of due diligence or personal default on the part of the owners or their manager: see *Istros* v. *Dahlstrom* (1930) 38 Ll.L. Rep. 84 and page 467 above. See also page 470 and *The TFL Prosperity*, above.

Personal want of due diligence

The owners are only liable under the clause for personal want of due diligence to make the ship seaworthy on their part or the part of their manager or for any other personal act or default. The effect of the clause is to cut down the liability which would otherwise result from a breach of the absolute warranty of seaworthiness implied at the beginning of the charter period or from a breach of the obligation to deliver the ship "in every way fitted for ordinary cargo service" in Line 16 (see pages 64 and 456). "Due diligence" in Line 97 is not construed as in the Hague Rules so as to include the failures of servants, agents and independent contractors (see *The Muncaster Castle* [1961] 1 Lloyd's Rep. 57), but is qualified by the word "personal" in Line 98.

The *Brabant* was chartered on the Baltime form for one round voyage for the carriage of woodpulp. The charter provided in an additional clause in typescript: "The decks and holds and other cargo spaces to be properly cleaned at Owners' risk and expense before loading." Woodpulp shipped at Swedish ports was damaged by residues of a previous cargo of coal. The owners incurred liability to bill of lading holders and sought an indemnity from the charterers under Clause 9. It was found that the presence of coal residues was due to the failure of the crew properly to clean the holds prior to loading but that there was no personal fault on the part of the owners or their managers. It was held by McNair, J., that the liability of the owners under Clause 13 was limited to personal want of due diligence; but that in the particular circumstance of the case the typescript clause putting upon the owners the risk of hold cleaning overrode Clause 13.

The Brabant [1965] 2 Lloyd's Rep. 546.
(See also *Westfal-Larsen* v. *Colonial Sugar Refining* [1960] 2 Lloyd's Rep. 206.)

Whose acts or omissions are to be regarded as the "personal" acts or omissions of the owner depends, it seems, on the constitution and organisation of the owners' concern, or if the operation of the ship has been delegated to managers, of the managers' concern (see *The Marion* [1984] 2 Lloyds Rep.1 (H.L.) and *The Ert Stefanie* [1989] 1 Lloyd's Rep. 349 (C.A.).) As Willmer, L.J., said in *The Lady Gwendolen* [1965] 1 Lloyd's Rep. 335, at page 345: "Where . . . the owners are a limited company it is almost inevitable that difficult questions will arise. It is necessary to look closely at the organisation of the company in order to see of what individual it can fairly be said that his act or omission is that of the company itself."

In that case the question of the owners' "personal" fault or privity arose in the context of their right to limit liability under Section 503 of the Merchant Shipping Act 1894. The owners were a brewery company whose shipping activities were subsidiary to their main business. The ships were run by a manager who was not a member of the board of directors but who was responsible to an assistant managing director. It was held by Hewson, J., and the Court of Appeal that the assistant managing director was, so far as concerned the shipping operations of the company, the owners' *alter ego* and that his defaults were defaults of the owners personally. Views were however expressed in the Court of Appeal that the omissions of the manager of the shipping department might also rank as personal omissions of the owners. Willmer, L.J., said, at page 345: "Where, as in the present case, a company has a separate traffic department, which assumes responsibility for running the company's ships, I see no good reason why the head of that department, even though not himself a director, should not be regarded as someone whose action is the very action of the company itself, so far as concerns anything to do with the company's ships."

But Lord Diplock, in *Tesco* v. *Nattrass* [1972] A.C. 153 disagreed with those views in so far as they suggested that a person who was not entrusted with the powers of the company itself could be the *alter ego* of the company. He considered that the question of which persons were to be treated under a *criminal* statute as being the company for the purpose of acts done in the course of its business, was to be answered by identifying those "who by the memorandum and articles of association or as a result of action taken by the directors, or by the company in general meeting pursuant to the articles, are entrusted with the exercise of the powers of the company". He then went on, at page 200: "There has been in recent years a tendency to extract from Denning, L.J.'s judgment in *H.L. Bolton (Engineering) Co. Ltd.* v. *T. J. Graham & Sons Ltd.* [1957] 1 Q.B. 159, 172, 173 his vivid metaphor about the 'brains and nerve centre' of a company as contrasted with its hands, and to treat this dichotomy, and not the articles of association, as laying down the test of whether or not a particular person is to be regarded in law as being the company itself when performing duties which a statute imposes on the company. In the case in which this metaphor was first used Denning, L.J., was dealing with acts and intentions of directors of the company in whom the powers of the company were vested under its articles of association. The decision in that case is not authority for extending the class of persons whose acts are to be regarded in law as the personal acts of the company itself, beyond those who by, or by action taken under, its articles of association are entitled to exercise the powers of the company. In so far as there are dicta to the contrary in *The Lady Gwendolen* [1965] P. 294 they were not necessary to the decision and, in my view, they were wrong."

It was, however, suggested by Mustill, L.J., giving the judgment of the Court of Appeal in *The Ert Stefanie* [1989] 1 Lloyd's Rep. 349, at page 352, that a person who was not on the board of the company might be treated as being among those persons who together constituted the governing mind and will of the company if he exercised a senior managerial function which, had it not been delegated to him, would have fallen within the competence of the directors. The addition of such a person to those persons whose actions are in effect those of the company itself accords with the view of Willmer, L.J., in *The Lady Gwendolen*, above, and it seems that it is this view that will prevail, at least in civil cases. But Mustill, L.J., went on to hold that, by contrast, it was not possible, other than in an exceptional case, to subtract someone from the corporate direction just because when doing the act which led to the liability he was performing a function which would ordinarily lie outside the sphere of the board. In the case of *The Ert Stefanie*, which concerned an owner's right to limit under Section 503 of the Merchant Shipping Act 1894, it was held by Hobhouse, J., and the Court of Appeal that the fault of a director of the managing company who was personally at fault in the exercise of functions ordinarily outside the sphere of a board (giving advice to a master about special requirements and precautions for the carriage of a particular cargo), was the "actual fault" of the owners.

It has also been held in cases relating to the right to limit under the Merchant Shipping Acts that owners or their managers are personally responsible for instituting and maintaining proper systems for the efficient management, operation and manning of their ships and that it is not enough for them merely to appoint competent subordinates: see *The Garden City* [1982] 2 Lloyd's Rep. 382 and *The Marion* [1984] 2 Lloyd's Rep. 1 (H.L.).

A fortiori the owners will not have the benefit of Clause 13 if the damage has been caused by the incompetence of a crew member who has been personally engaged by them without due enquiry into his capabilities, for the lack of such enquiry will amount to personal want of due diligence: *The Roberta* (1938) 60 Ll.L.Rep. 84 and *The Hongkong Fir* [1961] 2 Lloyd's Rep. 478.

Burden of proof

The burden of proof is on the owners to show how the delay, loss or damage complained of arose and that this is covered by Clause 13. As Greer, L.J., said of the clause (then numbered 12) in *The Roberta* (1938) 60 Ll.L.Rep. 84, above: "That, I think, means that if the shipowner can establish that the loss or damage was not caused by want of due diligence on his part, then he would bring himself within Clause 12, but if he does not establish that and he does not give an account of how he came to deliver damaged goods he does not bring himself within the exception."

Relationship between Clause 13 and other clauses

It has been seen above that Clause 13 will normally protect the owners from a breach of the obligation under Clause 9 to prosecute the voyage with the utmost despatch. It will also cut down the absolute warranty of seaworthiness which would otherwise be imposed by the obligation to deliver the ship "in every way fitted for ordinary cargo service".

Misdescription

But it seems that the clause will not ordinarily protect the owners against misdescription of the ship. In the following case the question arose in relation to the speed warranty, but was not decided.

The *Apollonius* was time chartered for a trip on the Baltime form. In the charter, she was described as "when fully loaded, capable of steaming about $14\frac{1}{2}$ knots in good weather and smooth water on a consumption of about 38 tons oil fuel". Clause 13 of the charter was amended to read: "The Owners only to be responsible for delay in delivery of the vessel or for delay during the currency of the charter and for loss or damage to goods on board, if such delay or loss or damage has been caused by want of due diligence on the part of the Owners or their servants or their Manager in making the vessel seaworthy and fitted for each voyage during the currency of the Charter, or any other personal act or omission or default of the Owners or their Manager." As the result of heavy fouling (not attributable to want of due diligence), the ship was not capable at the time of delivery of the speed warranted. As a result time was lost on the charter voyage from Japan to the Argentine. Time was also lost on that voyage by the failure of the engineers to work the engines at their full output.

Mocatta, J., took the view that the warranty as to speed applied at the time of delivery but left open the question whether the owners were protected by Clause 13 from liability for breach of that obligation. In dealing with this aspect of the case, Mocatta, J., said:

"[Counsel for the charterers] sought to say here that the word 'delay' in this clause was inapt to describe what had happened consequent upon the breach of the speed warranty or upon the failure of the engineers to work the main engine as it should have been worked, but I do not find this argument wholly convincing as regards delay due to breach of the speed warranty and in my opinion it fails as regards the engineers' conduct. It seems to me on the whole that the word 'delay' in its context may well be applicable to both events, but . . . it is unnecessary to decide this as regards the speed warranty."

The Apollonius [1978] 1 Lloyd's Rep. 53.

However, it was held by the House of Lords in *The TFL Prosperity* [1984] 1 Lloyd's Rep. 123 that Clause 13 would not, even if widely construed, protect the owners against a claim for misdescription where the parties had set out in the charter a detailed description of the ship which was built for, and to be employed in, a particular trade. (See page 476 above for a summary of the facts of the case.) Lord Roskill, with whom all other members of the House agreed, said at page 130: "In truth if cl. 13 were to be construed so as to allow a breach of the warranties as to description in cl. 26 to be committed or a failure to deliver the vessel at all to take place without financial redress to the charterers, the charter virtually ceases to be a contract for the letting of the vessel and the performance of services by the owners, their master, officers and crew in consideration of the payment of time charter hire and becomes no more than a statement of intent by the owners in return for which the charterers are obliged to pay large sums by way of hire, though if the owners fail to carry out their promises as to description or delivery, are entitled to nothing in lieu. I find it difficult to believe that this can accord with the true common intention of the parties and I do not think that this conclusion can accord with the true construction of the charter in which the parties in the present case are supposed to have expressed that true common intention in writing."

Furthermore if the ship has been misdescribed in the negotiations leading to the fixture and the misrepresentation has induced the charterers to enter into the contract, Clause 13 may afford no protection if it is held not to have been a fair and reasonable provision in the circumstances, under Section 3 of the Misrepresentation Act 1967, as amended by Section 8(1) of the Unfair Contract Terms Act 1977: see page 52 above for comments on this and other sections of the 1967 Act.

Construction of exceptions clauses

For commentary on the construction of exceptions clauses see pages 353 to 355.

Additional clauses in typescript

Where special provision has been made in an additional clause in typescript imposing responsibility on the owners for a particular matter, it may be held that the additional typescript clause is not overridden by Clause 13: see *The Brabant* [1965] 2 Lloyd's Rep. 546, page 478 above, approved to this extent by the House of Lords in *The TFL Prosperity*, above. In *The TFL Prosperity*, Lord Roskill, with whom the other members of the House agreed, considered that where a typed addendum clause was clearly intended to be in substitution for a printed clause it was not to be regarded as necessarily prevailing over a printed exceptions clause merely because it was in typescript. (See page 476 for a summary of the facts of this case.)

Paramount clause

Where a charter in the Baltime form is made subject to a Paramount clause, the effect of such a clause in relation to other terms of the charter will depend upon the words of incorporation and the words of the Paramount clause itself, but in general the provisions of Clause 13 will be overridden by the Hague Rules: see *Adamastos* v. *Anglo-Saxon Petroleum* [1958] 1 Lloyd's Rep. 73, *Marifortuna* v. *Government of Ceylon* [1970] 1 Lloyd's Rep. 247 and pages 425 to 426 above.

If a Paramount clause of the type incorporated into the New York Produce form by Clause 24 (see page 424 above) were to be incorporated into the Baltime form it seems that the general result would be the same as in the case of the New York Produce form. The wide exceptions of Clause 13 would be replaced so far as concerned physical loss of or damage to cargo by the narrower immunities of Section 4(2) of the United States Carriage of Goods by Sea Act. The initial seaworthiness obligation would become one to exercise due diligence and an obligation of the same type probably created in respect of each voyage under the charter: see page 428 above.

If an incorporating clause refers only to "Paramount clause" without identifying any particular enactment under which the Hague Rules have been given statutory force, the Hague Rules themselves are incorporated.

The *Agios Lazaros* was chartered under a voyage charter which provided: "New Jason clause, both to blame collision clause, P and I bunkering clause and Chamber of Shipping War Risks clauses Nos. 1 and 2 and also Paramount clause are deemed to be incorporated in this Charter Party."

The question arose whether a claim under the charter was subject to the one-year time limit in Article III, Rule 6, of the Hague Rules. It was contended that since there were many different forms of Paramount clause, the reference merely to "Paramount clause" was ineffective. It was held by the Court of Appeal that as the intention of the parties was clear from the reference to "Paramount clause" the charter should be subject to the Hague Rules, and that the Hague Rules in their original form should be incorporated. Lord Denning, M.R., said:

"What does 'paramount clause' or 'clause paramount' mean to shipping men? Primarily it applies to bills of lading. In that context its meaning is, I think, clear beyond question. It means a clause by which the Hague Rules are incorporated into the contract evidenced by the bill of lading and which overrides any express exemption or condition that is inconsistent with it . . . It seems to me that when the 'paramount clause' is incorporated [in a charter], without any words of qualification, it means that all the Hague Rules are incorporated. If the parties intend only to incorporate part of the rules (for example, art. IV), or only so far as compulsorily applicable, they say so. In the absence of any such qualification, it seems to me that a 'clause paramount' is a clause which incorporates all the Hague Rules."

The Agios Lazaros [1976] 2 Lloyd's Rep. 47.

Responsibility and Exemption (strikes etc.)

[Clause 13 continued]

"... The Owners not to be liable for loss or damage arising or resulting from strikes, lock-outs or stoppage or restraint of labour (including the Master, Officers or Crew) whether partial or general."

[Clause 13 is continued below]

General comment on Lines 101 and 102

"Loss or damage" in Line 101 includes financial as well as physical loss or damage: *The TFL Prosperity* [1984] 1 Lloyd's Rep. 123, at page 128. But these exceptions will afford no protection if what occurs is caused by negligence (see *Polemis* v. *Furness Withy* (1921) 8 Ll.L. Rep. 263 and 351), unless the claim can be categorised as a claim for delay within the first sentence of Clause 13 and there has been no personal want of due diligence or personal default on the part of the owners or their manager (see page 477 above.)

Strikes

"Strike" was defined by Lord Denning, M.R., in *The New Horizon* [1975] 2 Lloyd's Rep. 314, as; "a concerted stoppage of work by men done with a view to improving their wages or conditions, or giving vent to a grievance or making a protest about something or other, or supporting or sympathizing with other workmen in such endeavour. It is distinct from a stoppage which is brought about by an external event such as a bomb scare or by apprehension of danger."

The fact that other work goes on and that the action is confined to particular ships or even to one ship does not necessarily prevent the action constituting a strike.

The *Laga* was delayed by the refusal of port workers at Nantes to unload or assist vessels carrying coal, in support of French coal miners who were on strike. The port workers continued to work other ships as normal. It was held by McNair, J., that "strike" in the exceptions clause of the voyage charter under which the *Laga* was employed included a sympathetic or general strike and that the fact that other work continued was irrelevant. So far as the *Laga* was concerned there was a strike.

The Laga [1966] 1 Lloyd's Rep. 582.

Nor does the fact that the action involves no breach of the workers' contracts of employment, or that what is involved is merely a reduction of the hours of work, prevent the action being regarded as a strike.

The *New Horizon* was delayed by the refusal of certain workers at St. Nazaire to work a night shift. Normally the port worked throughout the 24 hours, the work being done in three shifts; but the workers were not obliged by their contracts to work a night shift. It was held by the Court of

Appeal that the refusal to work the night shift, which was aimed at improving conditions of work, amounted to a strike.

Tramp Shipping v. Greenwich Marine (The New Horizon) [1975] 2 Lloyd's Rep. 314.

Crew

Where there was a concerted refusal by crew members to sail because of fear of submarine action in time of war, it was held by Sankey, J., that the owners were protected by an exception against strikes: *Williams v. Naamlooze* (1915) 21 Com. Cas. 253. On the other hand, where crew members refused to permit stevedores to unload cargo in pursuance of a grievance against the owners, it was held that the resulting loss did not come within the exception in the charter against "strikes or stoppages of labour": *Compania Naviera Bachi v. Hosegood* (1938) 60 Ll.L.Rep. 236. Porter, J., said, at page 243: "Neither strike nor stoppage of labour, in my view, caused the loss; it was rather an interference with those endeavouring to discharge by an outside body than a withholding of labour by the workmen engaged in the discharge themselves."

Stoppage

"Stoppage" is not confined to interruptions caused by labour disputes. Thus, whereas the refusal of men to work because of a fear of disease may not constitute a strike (*Stephens v. Harris* (1887) 57 L.T. 618), such a refusal would, it seems, be a "stoppage": *The New Horizon*, above. When used on its own the word "stoppage" has been construed to mean a complete stoppage of work.

The *Mercedes de Larrinaga* was employed under a voyage charter which provided "in the event of any stoppage . . . continuing for the period of six running days from the time of the vessel being ready to load, this charter shall . . . become null and void." The vessel, although ready to load, did not receive any cargo over the six-day period. Over this period there was a rail strike which impeded but did not completely prevent cargo being brought to the loading berth. The evidence was that there was loading of other ships going on over the whole period although at a reduced rate. Roche, J., held this did not amount to a stoppage. His decision was upheld by the Court of Appeal.

Miguel de Larrinaga v. Flack (1924) 20 Ll.L.Rep. 268, and (1925) 21 Ll.L.Rep. 284.

(See also *Akt. Adalands v. Whittaker* (1913) 18 Com. Cas. 229.)

In Clause 13 the word "stoppage" is qualified by the words "whether partial or general" and so may include interruptions which are not complete. But it does not, it is suggested, cover a "go slow" or "work to rule".

Responsibility and Exemption (charterers' responsibilities)

[Clause 13 continued]

"The Charterers to be responsible for loss or damage caused to the Vessel or to the Owners by goods 103
being loaded contrary to the terms of the Charter or by improper or careless bunkering or loading, 104
stowing or discharging of goods or any other improper or negligent act on their part or that of 105
their servants. 106"

Charterers' responsibility for loss or damage to the ship

Lord Roskill in *The TFL Prosperity* [1984] 1 Lloyd's Rep. 123, at page 128, doubted whether the exceptions in Lines 103 to 106 imposed any greater liability on the charterers than would fall on them in any event either under the charter or at common law.

It was held in *The White Rose* [1969] 2 Lloyd's Rep. 52 that in order to recover under these Lines the owners must show that the "loss or damage" was caused by one of the three categories of event set out in Lines 104 to 106. "Loss" covers financial loss by settling a liability. Donaldson, J., said in *The White Rose*, above, at page 60: "The indemnity afforded by this clause is clearly wide enough to cover loss incurred by a reasonable settlement of a potential liability, as contrasted with physical loss of or damage to the vessel or financial loss by, for example, the detention of the vessel. However, it only operates if the loss is caused by either (a) improper or careless loading or stowing by whoever is performing those functions, whether or not they are independent contractors appointed by the time charterers or servants or agents of such contractors or (b) some other improper or negligent act of whatsoever nature on the part of the time charterers or their servants."

Goods loaded contrary to charter

The loading of the ship at an unsafe berth may involve the charterers in liability under this clause.

The *Terneuzen*, which was chartered under the Baltime form, was damaged owing to the unsafety of the berth at which she had been ordered to load at Leningrad. It was held by Greer, L.J., in the Court of Appeal, that if the ship was off-hire for the time lost the owners would be entitled to recover the same amount under this clause as damage caused to the owners by goods being loaded contrary to the terms of the charter.

Lensen Shipping v. Anglo-Soviet Shipping (1935) 52 Ll.L.Rep. 141.

Servants

It was suggested in *The White Rose* [1962] 2 Lloyd's Rep. 52, above, that "servants" in Line 106 would be restricted to that class of person for whom the charterers are vicariously responsible.

Dangerous cargo: See generally pages 125 to 130.

Advances/Excluded Ports

"14. The Charterers or their Agents to advance to the Master, if required, necessary funds for 107
ordinary disbursements for the Vessel's account at any port charging only interest at 6 per cent p.a., 108
such advances to be deducted from hire. 109
15. The Vessel not to be ordered to nor bound to enter: a) any place where fever or epidemics 110
are prevalent or to which the Master, Officers and Crew by law are not bound to follow the Vessel 111
b) any ice-bound place or any place where lights, lightships, marks and buoys are or are likely to 112
be withdrawn by reason of ice on the Vessel's arrival or where there is risk that ordinarily the Vessel 113
will not be able on account of ice to reach the place or to get out after having completed loading or 114
discharging. The Vessel not to be obliged to force ice. If on account of ice the Master considers it 115
dangerous to remain at the loading or discharging place for fear of the Vessel being frozen in and/or 116
damaged, he has liberty to sail to a convenient open place and await the Charterers' fresh instructions. 117
Unforeseen detention through any of above causes to be for the Charterers' account. 118"

Deductions from hire: See page 199.

Ice

Scrutton, L.J., in *Limerick v. Stott* [1921] 2 K.B. 613, said, at page 620, that the clause "enables the captain to refuse to go to an ice-bound port, and to refuse to force ice which he meets on his voyage, without being guilty of any breach of charter, and without prejudicing his owners' right to hire while he is waiting for proper orders, or for a sea free of ice. He is also allowed, but is not obliged, to leave a port which is likely to become icebound; that is . . . it cannot be said that the owner loses his right to hire, because the captain elects to stay when he might have escaped".

Icebound port

A port which, but for artificial measures, would naturally be icebound for certain months of the year is not an icebound port within the meaning of an ice clause if it is kept open by icebreakers.

The *Innisboffin* was chartered on an earlier version of the Baltime form for "one Baltic round" voyage. The ship was ordered to Abo which was kept open the whole winter by icebreakers. There was evidence that ships regularly ran six voyages a week between Abo and Stockholm. It was held by the Court of Appeal affirming Bailhache, J., that Abo was not an icebound port.

Limerick v. Stott [1921] 2K.B. 613.

Ordinarily

If the ship would not ordinarily be prevented by ice from reaching and departing from the port to which she is ordered, there is no breach of this clause; but the port may nevertheless be unsafe because of ice: *The Sussex Oak* (1950) 83 Ll.L.Rep. 297, below. But see the remarks of Lord Roskill in *The Evia* (*No.2*) [1982] 2 Lloyd's Rep. 307, at page 321.

Vessel not to be obliged to force ice

The master may refuse to force ice. But if he elects to force ice in order to reach a port to which he has properly been ordered the charterers will not be responsible for damage sustained by the ship.

In *Limerick v. Stott*, above, the ship encountered thick ice on the usual route to Abo, when she was some 200 miles from the port. The master instead of waiting for icebreaker assistance decided to try to force the ice. He failed and the ship became fast. An icebreaker was then called and for the rest of the voyage the ship had icebreaker assistance. It was held by the Court of Appeal that the charterers were not liable for the damage caused to the ship in trying to force the ice.

Damage from ice en route

In *Limerick v. Stott*, above, the ship could have reached her port of destination, Abo, in safety, had the master waited and called for icebreaker assistance straight away instead of attempting to force ice. But if, because of ice en route, the port of destination cannot be reached in safety and the master has to force ice, the charterers may be liable for the damage to the ship on the ground that the port is unsafe.

The *Sussex Oak* was chartered under the Baltime form and was ordered to proceed to Hamburg in January, 1947. On her passage up the Elbe ice was encountered but the pilots considered it safe to proceed. However, when the ship was nearing the approaches to Hamburg she was stopped by a large ice flow. The ship was then in a part of the river in which she could neither turn, go astern nor anchor in safety. On the advice of the pilots she forced her way through the ice, suffering damage in consequence. It was found as a fact that the master acted properly in proceeding without icebreaker assistance. It was held by Devlin, J., that the charterers were liable for the damage to the ship on the ground that Hamburg was then an unsafe port and the charterers were not entitled to order the ship to go there. Devlin J., said:

"It is immaterial in point of law where the danger is located, though it is obvious in point of fact that the more remote it is from the port the less likely it is to interfere with the safety of the voyage. The charterer does not guarantee that the most direct route or any particular route to the port is safe, but the voyage he orders must be one which an ordinarily prudent and skilful master can find a way of making in safety. In the present case, the only route to Hamburg was by the Elbe, and the arbitrator has found that this approach was unsafe by reason of ice."

The Sussex Oak (1950) 83 Ll.L.Rep. 297.

It was argued by the charterers in the above case that the owners could not rely on the safe port obligation under Clause 2 because Clause 15 gave an exclusive remedy for ice dangers. Devlin, J., dismissed this argument, but Lord Roskill in *The Evia* (*No. 2*) [1982]

2 Lloyd's Rep. 307, at page 321, expressly left open the question whether Devlin, J., was correct on this point.

Loss of Vessel/Overtime/Lien

"16. Should the Vessel be lost or missing, hire to cease from the date when she was lost. If the date of loss cannot be ascertained half hire to be paid from the date the Vessel was last reported until the calculated date of arrival at the destination. Any hire paid in advance to be adjusted accordingly.

17. The Vessel to work day and night if required. The Charterers to refund the Owners their outlays for all overtime paid to Officers and Crew according to the hours and rates stated in the Vessel's articles.

18. The Owners to have a lien upon all cargoes and sub-freights belonging to the Time-Charterers and any Bill of Lading freight for all claims under this Charter, and the Charterers to have a lien on the Vessel for all moneys paid in advance and not earned."

Loss of ship: See generally under "Frustration", pages 322 to 339.

Owners' lien upon cargoes: See pages 396 to 399.

All cargoes and sub-freights belonging to the Time-Charterers

In contrast to the New York Produce form, Clause 18 of the Baltime form makes it clear that a lien may be exercised only upon cargoes belonging to the charterers: see *International Bulk Carriers* v. *Evlogia Shipping (The Mihalios Xilas)* [1978] 2 Lloyd's Rep. 186 and page 397 above.

Where the lien may be exercised: page 398.

Owners' lien upon sub-freights: See pages 399 to 402.

Lien of charterers upon the ship: See page 404.

Salvage/Sublet

"19. All salvage and assistance to other vessels to be for the Owners' and the Charterers' 129
equal benefit after deducting the Master's and Crew's proportion and all legal and other expenses 130
including hire paid under the charter for time lost in the salvage, also repairs of damage and coal 131
or oil-fuel consumed. The Charterers to be bound by all measures taken by the Owners in order 132
to secure payment of salvage and to fix its amount. 133
20. The Charterers to have the option of subletting the Vessel, giving due notice to the Owners, but 134
the original Charterers always to remain responsible to the Owners for due performance of the Charter. 135"

Salvage: See page 420.

Liberty to sub-let: See pages 109 to 110.

War

"21. (A) The Vessel unless the consent of the Owners be first obtained not to be ordered nor continue to any place or on any voyage nor be used on any service which will bring her within a zone which is dangerous as the result of any actual or threatened act of war, war hostilities, warlike operations, acts of piracy or of hostility or malicious damage against this or any other vessel or its cargo by any person, body or State whatsoever, revolution, civil war, civil commotion or the operation of international law, nor be exposed in any way to any risks or penalties whatsoever consequent upon the imposition of Sanctions, nor carry any goods that may in any way expose her to any risks of seizure, capture, penalties or any other interference of any kind whatsoever by the belligerent or fighting powers or parties or by any Government or Ruler.

(B) Should the Vessel approach or be brought or ordered within such zone, or be exposed in any way to the said risks, (1) the Owners to be entitled from time to time to insure their interests in the Vessel and/or hire against any of the risks likely to be involved thereby on such terms as they shall think fit, the Charterers to make a refund to the Owners of the premium on demand; and (2) notwithstanding the terms of clause 11 hire to be paid for all time lost including any lost owing to loss of or injury to the Master, Officers, or Crew or to the action of the Crew in refusing to proceed to such zone or to be exposed to such risks.

(C) In the event of the wages of the Master, Officers and/or Crew or the cost of provisions and/or stores for deck and/or engine room and/or insurance premiums being increased by reason of or during the existence of any of the matters mentioned in section (A) the amount of any increase to be added to the hire and paid by the Charterers on production of the Owners' account therefor, such account being rendered monthly.

(D) The Vessel to have liberty to comply with any orders or directions as to departure, arrival, routes, ports of call, stoppages, destination, delivery or in any other wise whatsoever given by the Government of the nation under whose flag the Vessel sails or any other Government or any person (or body) acting or purporting to act with the authority of such Government or by any committee or person having under the terms of the war risks insurance on the Vessel the right to give any such orders or directions.

(E) In the event of the nation under whose flag the Vessel sails becoming involved in war, hostilities, warlike operations, revolution, or civil commotion, both the Owners and the Charterers may cancel the Charter and, unless otherwise agreed, the Vessel to be redelivered to the Owners at the port of destination or, if prevented through the provisions of section (A) from reaching or entering it, then at a near open and safe port at the Owners' option, after discharge of any cargo on board.

(F) If in compliance with the provisions of this clause anything is done or is not done, such not to be deemed a deviation."

War

The words in Line 136 "to be ordered" and in Line 137 "be used" do not only apply to the ordering of the ship by the charterers to ports or places of loading or discharge or to places for bunkering en route. Whether the charter be for a period or for a trip, the ship is subject to the charterers' orders throughout, even when following a customary route and if, with the full knowledge of the route to be followed, the charterers allow the ship to proceed into a dangerous zone, an implication that they ordered the ship to proceed into it will readily be drawn.

The words in Lines 136 and 137 "nor continue to any place or on any voyage" do not mean "continue in pursuance of an order", but mean that the charterers are not to allow the ship to continue when it is obvious that the ship is about to enter a zone which is dangerous.

The owners' remedy for breach by the charterers of Clause 21(A) is not confined to the rights given to the owners under sub-Clauses (B) and (C). Sub-Clauses (B) or (C) come into operation if the owners consent to the ship being brought within a dangerous zone, but if the owners do not consent, and the charterers are in breach of sub-Clause (A), the owners have a remedy in damages.

The *Eugenia* was time chartered under the Baltime form "for a trip out to India via Black Sea" from the time of delivery at Genoa. The charterers ordered the ship to load cargo at two Black Sea ports for discharge at ports on the East Coast of India, but did not give the master any express orders to proceed either via Suez or the Cape. However, at that time the Suez Canal was the customary route for such a voyage. On 29 October 1956, Israeli forces invaded Egypt and on 30 October the Canal became, as the umpire in arbitration proceedings found, a dangerous zone within the meaning of sub-Clause (A). The owners consented neither to the ship proceeding via Suez nor to her entering or continuing into the Canal after it became a dangerous zone. On 30 October the owners objected to the ship entering the Canal but the charterers took no action. On 31 October the ship entered the Canal and was subsequently blocked there. It was held by the Court of Appeal, affirming Megaw, J., on this point, that the charterers were in breach of Clause 21(A) and were liable in damages to the owners on the grounds that they impliedly ordered the ship, without the consent of the owners, to enter a dangerous zone or, alternatively, allowed the ship to continue into such a zone.

The Eugenia [1963] 2 Lloyd's Rep. 381.

Owners to be entitled to insure their interests in the vessel and/or hire

Under Clause 21(B)(1), Lines 146 and 147, the owners are entitled to insure their interests in the ship and/or the hire if the ship approaches or is brought or ordered within a dangerous zone as defined in Clause 21(A). And in these circumstances the charterers are obliged to refund the premium. In *The Agathon (No. 2)* [1984] 1 Lloyd's Rep. 183, Hobhouse, J., held that these words entitled the owners to recover the premium for the full cover provided by the Hellenic War Risks Association. See page 445 above for a summary of the facts of this case.

In *The Evia* (*No. 2*) [1982] 2 Lloyd's Rep. 307, the House of Lords held that, in respect of the war risks referred to in Clause 21(A), the charterers were relieved of their safe port obligation under Clause 2. One reason given by Lord Roskill was that, as by Clause 21(B)(1) the charterers were to refund the owners' war risk insurance premium, it would be unjust that they should remain exposed to a subrogated claim by the war risk underwriters under Clause 2. See page 146 above and below.

Hire to be paid for all time lost

Under Clause 21(B)(2), Lines 149 and 150, hire is to be paid for all time lost if the ship approaches or is brought or ordered within a dangerous zone as defined in Clause 21(A), notwithstanding the provisions of the off-hire clause. But it was held in the case which follows that this sub-clause did not exclude the operation of the doctrine of frustration. The sub-clause did not apply in circumstances which would, apart from the clause, have the effect of frustrating the charter.

The *Evia* was time chartered on the Baltime form for a period of 18 months, two months more or less in charterers' option. The ship was delivered on 20 November 1979, and therefore redelivery was due between 20 March and 20 July 1981. In March 1980 the charterers ordered the *Evia* to load cargo for Basrah and on 20 August 1980 (after a period waiting to discharge) she berthed at that port. On 22 September 1980 she completed discharge at Basrah but by this date hostilities had broken out between Iraq and Iran and the ship was unable to sail because of the danger to navigation in the Shatt-al-Arab waterway caused by the war. It was held by the umpire in arbitration proceedings that the charter was frustrated on 4 October 1980, but the owners argued that since Clause 21(B) made provision for the events which had occurred the doctrine of frustration did not apply. On appeal it was held by Robert Goff, J., and the Court of Appeal that Clause 21(B) was not intended to legislate for the consequences of frustration or to exclude frustration; it simply provided that if time was lost in the circumstances specified, hire was to continue to be paid notwithstanding the off-hire clause. The House of Lords agreed.

The Evia (No. 2) [1981] 2 Lloyd's Rep. 613, [1982] 1 Lloyd's Rep. 334 (C.A.) and [1982] 2 Lloyd's Rep. 307 (H.L.).

(For discussion of the nature of the safe port obligation see page 145.)

Any other Government

The words "any other Government" in Line 159 have been held, in the case of an almost identical provision in the War Risks Clause of the Gencon voyage charter, to mean any national government which exercised full executive and legislative power over an established territory irrespective of the fact that the charter was governed by English law and the British Government did not recognise the government in question either *de facto* or *de jure*.

The *Marilu*, flying the Italian flag, was chartered by a Czechoslovakian company for a voyage from North China ports to Europe under the Gencon form. The War Risks Clause provided:

"The ship shall have liberty to comply with any orders or directions as to departure, arrival, routes, ports of call, stoppages, destination, delivery or otherwise howsoever given by the Government of the Nation under whose flag the vessel sails or any department thereof, or by any other Government or any department thereof, or any person acting or purporting to act with the authority of such Government or of any department thereof, or by any committee or person having, under the terms of the war risks insurance on the ship, the right to give such orders or directions . . ."

Having loaded at Tsingtao and sailed for Europe, the ship was intercepted by a Formosan Government warship and taken to Keelung where, after discharge of her cargo, she was released. It was intimated by the British Foreign Office that, at the material time, the British Government had ceased to recognise the Formosan Government as being either the *de facto* or *de jure* government of the Republic of China, or to recognise that any government was located in Formosa. It was held by Sellers, J., that the reference to "any other Government" meant a national government (as opposed to a subservient authority such as a municipal or provincial government), which exercised full executive and legislative powers over an established territory. On the arbitrator's findings of fact, the Formosan Government was such a government and it was held that neither as a matter of construction nor as a rule of law was it relevant that the Formosan Government was not recognised by the British Government. Accordingly, the owners were held to have been entitled to comply with the orders of the Formosan Government warship to proceed to Keelung and discharge the cargo there.

Luigi Monta v. *Cechofracht* [1956] 2 Lloyd's Rep. 97.

Any discretion given to the owners or the charterers under a war clause must be exercised reasonably.

The *Hartbridge* was chartered for a voyage from the River Tyne to one of several named Spanish ports including Barcelona. The war clause in the charter provided that if any discharging port to which the ship might properly be ordered was blockaded or if, owing to any war, hostilities, warlike operations, civil war, civil commotions, revolutions, or the operation of international law, it was considered by the master or the owners in his or their discretion dangerous or impossible to reach the discharging port, the cargo should be discharged at another safe port. A week after the charter was signed a threat was made over the radio that Barcelona and the other ports named in the charter were to be blockaded, but in the event they never were and other ships continued to use the ports. Prior to the loading of any cargo the owners made it clear that they would not accept orders for Barcelona or any of the other named ports and finally the charterers nominated Oran, under protest, as an alternative. It was held that:

(1) "blockaded" meant blockaded in its legal sense and that Barcelona was never blockaded;

(2) the provisions of the war risks clause only applied after the cargo was loaded; and (*obiter*) that

(3) the discretion given to the owners under the war risks clause had to be exercised reasonably.

Lewis, J., said: "discretion must not be exercised in an arbitrary and unreasonable manner, and in this case there was really no exercise of discretion at all as the matter was not considered or no full or sufficient enquiry was made."

Government of the Republic of Spain v. *North of England Steamship* (1938) 61 Ll.L.Rep.44.

Furthermore, any option given to the owners or charterers must be exercised within a reasonable time.

The *Belpareil* was employed under a time charter which gave the owners and/or the charterers the option to cancel in the event of war between China and Japan. In September 1937, during the currency of the charter, war between China and Japan did break out and the war was still continuing in April 1938, when the charterers purported to exercise their option to cancel the charter. It was found as a fact by the umpire that a reasonable time for the exercise of the option had expired before April 1938. It was held by Branson, J., that the umpire had correctly directed himself and that the charterers were only entitled to a reasonable time in which to ascertain the relevant facts necessary to enable them to make up their minds.

Kawasaki K.K. v. *Belships* (1939) 63 Ll.L.Rep. 175.

In a war clause, "war" will probably be given its ordinary non-technical meaning; *Kawasaki K.K.* v. *Bantham* (1939) 63 Ll.L.Rep. 155. But contrast *Government of the Republic of Spain* v. *North of England Steamship* (1938) 61 Ll.L.Rep. 44, above, on the meaning given to "blockade" in a war clause.

American Law

War risk clauses

Even if the charter does not contain a war risk clause, the owner may abandon the voyage if war breaks out and the voyage would take the vessel to enemy territory. *The Kronprinzessin Cecilie*, 224 U.S. 12 (1917).

Where the charter contains a "restraint of princes" clause, it has been held that the owner may refuse to carry contraband consigned to one belligerent during war if there is a risk another belligerent may seize the cargo. *The Styria*, 186 U.S. 1 (1902); *The George J. Goulandris*, 36 F.Supp. 827, 1941 AMC 1804 (D.Me. 1941); *The Wildwood*, 133 F.2d 765, 1943 AMC 320 (9th Cir. 1943). In these cases, the courts held that it was reasonable for the master to abandon the voyage to protect both the ship and her cargo. The risk of seizure or danger to the vessel must be a real one, however, and where it is remote and speculative, the owner will not be justified in abandoning the voyage. See *Luckenbach S.S. Co.* v. *W. R. Grace & Co.*, 267 F. 676 (4th Cir. 1920).

In *The Trade Fortitude,* 1974 AMC 2195 (Arb. at N.Y. 1974), the owner withdrew the vessel in October 1973, at the time of the Yom Kippur War between Israel and the Arab countries when the charterer declined to name an alternative loading port. The charter contained the Chamber of Shipping War Risk Clauses (Tankers) 1952. When hostilities broke out into open war elsewhere in the Middle East, the owner refused to comply with the charterer's nomination of a loading port in the Persian Gulf, claiming it had become a "danger zone", even though there was no fighting there. It was found, however, that actual hostilities in Israel had ceased, and that United Nations observer teams were taking up positions. Although countries in the Persian Gulf were officially at war with Israel, there was no active fighting. Perhaps most importantly, the Persian Gulf had remained safe for vessels even while the war was raging throughout the preceding month. On these facts, the panel held that the Persian Gulf was not a "danger zone", and that the owner was not entitled to withdraw the vessel.

The panel summarized the factors to be considered in determining whether the owner was justified in withdrawing the vessel as follows:

> Each case turns upon its own particular facts; yet three guiding principles seem evident from the decided cases: (1) The fact situations to be considered in construing a war risks clause are those which are known and believed at the time in question, even if these are not the true facts and if later knowledge changes their significance. (2) An owner who refuses to go to a port, relying upon the provisions of a war risks clause, must have reasonable grounds to believe that one or more of the fact situations described in the clause actually exists, and (3) a charterer is not in breach of the charter if, at the time its orders are given to go to a specified port, there are no reasonable grounds to believe that any of the fact situations described in the clause actually exists. (1974 AMC at 2198.)

Cancelling

"22. Should the Vessel not be delivered by the .... day of.......................... 19...., the Charterers to have the option of cancelling.

If the Vessel cannot be delivered by the cancelling date, the Charterers, if required, to declare within 48 hours after receiving notice thereof whether they cancel or will take delivery of the Vessel."

Cancellation: See generally pages 287 to 292.

Declaration by charterers

The obligation on the charterers under the second paragraph of Clause 22 to declare within 48 hours of receiving notice whether they cancel or will take delivery arises only after the cancelling date has arrived: see the judgment of Pearson, J., in *The Helvetia-S* [1960] 1 Lloyd's Rep. 540, at page 552. For the facts of this case see page 477 above.

Arbitration

"23. Any dispute arising under the Charter to be referred to arbitration in London (or such other place as may be agreed) one Arbitrator to be nominated by the Owners and the other by the Charterers, and in case the Arbitrators shall not agree then to the decision of an Umpire to be appointed by them, the award of the Arbitrators or the Umpire to be final and binding upon both parties.

24. General Average to be settled according to York/Antwerp Rules, 1974. Hire not to contribute to General Average.

25. The Owners to pay a commission of .... to.......................... on any hire paid under the Charter, but in no case less than is necessary to cover the actual expenses of the Brokers and a reasonable fee for their work. If the full hire is not paid owing to breach of Charter by either of the parties the party liable therefor to indemnify the Brokers against their loss of commission.

Should the parties agree to cancel the Charter, the Owners to indemnify the Brokers against any loss of commission but in such case the commission not to exceed the brokerage on one year's hire."

Arbitration and governing law: See generally page 363.

Commission: See generally page 451. Under the Baltime form, the position of the brokers is better than it is under the New York Produce form in three ways:

(1) there is a minimum commission payable, enough to cover expenses plus a reasonable fee for work done (Lines 182 and 183);

(2) they are entitled to compensation if the full hire is not paid because of a breach of charter by either of the parties to it (Lines 183 to 185). The right is against the party in breach. Presumably where that party is the charterers, the owners will bring the action as trustees for the brokers;

(3) they are entitled to compensation of up to one year's commission if the parties agree to cancel the charter (Lines 186 and 187).

For a case in which the owners were held liable to the brokers under (2) above, where the owners had broken their obligation to deliver the ship by a stated date with the result that the charter had been cancelled, see *The Helvetia-S* [1960] 1 Lloyd's Rep. 540, page 477 above.

Appendix A

THE HARTER ACT 1893

§ 1. (46 U.S.C.A. § 190). Stipulations relieving from liability for negligence

It shall not be lawful for the manager, agent, master, or owner of any vessel transporting merchandise or property from or between ports of the United States and foreign ports to insert in any bill of lading or shipping document any clause, covenant, or agreement whereby it, he, or they shall be relieved from liability for loss or damage arising from negligence, fault, or failure in proper loading, stowage, custody, care, or proper delivery of any and all lawful merchandise or property committed to its or their charge. Any and all words or clauses of such import inserted in bills of lading or shipping receipts shall be null and void and of no effect.

§ 2. (46 U.S.C.A. § 191). Stipulations relieving from exercise of due diligence in equipping vessels

It shall not be lawful for any vessel transporting merchandise or property from or between ports of the United States of America and foreign ports, her owner, master, agent, or manager, to insert in any bill of lading or shipping document any covenant or agreement whereby the obligations of the owner or owners of said vessel to exercise due diligence [to] properly equip, man, provision, and outfit said vessel, and to make said vessel seaworthy and capable of performing her intended voyage, or whereby the obligations of the master, officers, agents, or servants to carefully handle and stow her cargo and to care for and properly deliver same, shall in any wise be lessened, weakened, or avoided.

§ 3. (46 U.S.C.A. § 192). Limitation of liability for errors of navigation, dangers of the sea and acts of God

If the owner of any vessel transporting merchandise or property to or from any port in the United States of America shall exercise due diligence to make the said vessel in all respects seaworthy and properly manned, equipped, and supplied, neither the vessel, her owner or owners, agent, or charterers, shall become or be held responsible for damage or loss resulting from faults or errors in navigation or in the management of said vessel nor shall the vessel, her owner or owners, charterers, agent, or master be held liable for losses arising from dangers of the sea or other navigable waters, acts of God, or public enemies, or the inherent defect, quality, or vice of the thing carried, or from insufficiency of package, or seizure under legal process, or for loss resulting from any act or omission of the shipper or owner of the goods, his agent or representative, or from saving or attempting to save life or property at sea, or from any deviation in rendering such service.

§ 4. (46 U.S.C.A. § 193). Bills of lading to be issued; contents

It shall be the duty of the owner or owners, masters, or agent of any vessel transporting merchandise or property from or between ports of the United States and foreign ports to issue to shippers of any lawful merchandise a bill of lading, or shipping document, stating, among other things, the marks necessary for identification, number of packages, or quantity, stating whether it be carrier's or shipper's weight, and apparent order or condition of such merchandise or property delivered to and received by the owner, master, or agent of the vessel for transportation, and such document shall be prima facie evidence of the receipt of the merchandise therein described.

§ 5. (46 U.S.C.A. § 194). Penalties; lien; recovery

For a violation of any of the provisions of sections 190–193 of this title the agent, owner, or master of the vessel guilty of such violation, and who refuses to issue on demand the bill of lading provided for, shall be liable to a fine not exceeding $2,000. The amount of the fine and costs for such violation shall be a lien upon the vessel, whose agent, owner, or master is guilty of such violation, and such vessel may be libeled therefor in any district court of the United States, within whose jurisdiction the vessel may be found. One-half of such penalty shall go to the party injured by such violation and the remainder to the Government of the United States.

§ 6. (46 U.S.C.A. § 195). Certain provisions inapplicable to transportation of live animals

Sections 190 and 193 of this title shall not apply to the transportation of live animals.

§ 7. (46 U.S.C.A. § 196). Certain laws unaffected

Sections 190–195 of this title shall not be held to modify or repeal sections 181, 182, and 183 of this title, or any other statute defining the liability of vessels, their owners, or representatives.

THE UNITED STATES CARRIAGE OF GOODS BY SEA ACT 1936

46 U.S.C.A. § 1300. Bills of lading subject to chapter

Every bill of lading or similar document of title which is evidence of a contract for the carriage of goods by sea to or from ports of the United States, in foreign trade, shall have effect subject to the provisions of this chapter.

§ 1. (46 U.S.C.A. § 1301). Definitions

When used in this chapter—

(a) The term "carrier" includes the owner or the charterer who enters into a contract of carriage with a shipper.

(b) The term "contract of carriage" applies only to contracts of carriage covered by a bill of lading or any similar document of title, insofar as such document relates to the carriage of goods by sea, including any bill of lading or any similar document as aforesaid issued under or pursuant to a charter party from the moment at which such bill of lading or similar document of title regulates the relations between a carrier and a holder of the same.

(c) The term "goods" includes goods, wares, merchandise, and articles of every kind whatsoever except live animals and cargo which by the contract of carriage is stated as being carried on deck and is so carried.

(d) The term "ship" means any vessel used for the carriage of goods by sea.

(e) The term "carriage of goods" covers the period from the time when the goods are loaded on to the time when they are discharged from the ship.

§ 2. (46 U.S.C.A. § 1302). Duties and rights of carrier

Subject to the provisions of section 1306 of this title, under every contract of carriage of goods by sea, the carrier in relation to the loading, handling, stowage, carriage, custody, care, and discharge of such goods, shall be subject to the responsibilities and liabilities and entitled to the rights and immunities set forth in sections 1303 and 1304 of this title.

§ 3. (46 U.S.C.A. § 1303). Responsibilities and liabilities of carrier and ship

Seaworthiness

(1) The carrier shall be bound, before and at the beginning of the voyage, to exercise due diligence to—

(a) Make the ship seaworthy;

(b) Properly man, equip, and supply the ship;

(c) Make the holds, refrigerating and cooling chambers, and all other parts of the ship in which goods are carried, fit and safe for their reception, carriage, and preservation.

Cargo

(2) The carrier shall properly and carefully load, handle, stow, carry, keep, care for, and discharge the goods carried.

Contents of bill

(3) After receiving the goods into his charge the carrier, or the master or agent of the carrier, shall, on demand of the shipper, issue to the shipper a bill of lading showing among other things—

(a) The leading marks necessary for identification of the goods as the same are furnished in writing by the shipper before the loading of such goods starts, provided such marks are stamped or otherwise shown clearly upon the goods if uncovered, or on the cases or coverings in which such goods are contained, in such a manner as should ordinarily remain legible until the end of the voyage.

(b) Either the number of packages or pieces, or the quantity or weight, as the case may be, as furnished in writing by the shipper.

(c) The apparent order and condition of the goods: *Provided*, That no carrier, master, or agent of the carrier, shall be bound to state or show in the bill of lading any marks, number, quantity, or weight which he has reasonable ground for suspecting not accurately to represent the goods actually received, or which he has had no reasonable means of checking.

Bill as prima facie evidence

(4) Such a bill of lading shall be prima facie evidence of the receipt by the carrier of the goods as therein described in accordance with paragraphs (3) (a), (b), and (c), of this section: *Provided*, That nothing in this chapter shall be construed as repealing or limiting the application of any part of sections 81–124 of Title 49.

Guaranty of statements

(5) The shipper shall be deemed to have guaranteed to the carrier the accuracy at the time of shipment of the marks, number, quantity, and weight, as furnished by him; and the shipper shall indemnify the carrier against all loss, damages, and expenses arising or resulting from inaccuracies in such particulars. The right of the carrier to such indemnity shall in no way limit his responsibility and liability under the contract of carriage to any person other than the shipper.

Notice of loss or damage; limitation of actions

(6) Unless notice of loss or damage and the general nature of such loss or damage be given in

writing to the carrier or his agent at the port of discharge before or at the time of the removal of the goods into the custody of the person entitled to delivery thereof under the contract of carriage, such removal shall be prima facie evidence of the delivery by the carrier of the goods as described in the bill of lading. If the loss or damage is not apparent, the notice must be given within three days of the delivery.

Said notice of loss or damage may be endorsed upon the receipt for the goods given by the person taking delivery thereof.

The notice in writing need not be given if the state of the goods has at the time of their receipt been the subject of joint survey or inspection.

In any event the carrier and the ship shall be discharged from all liability in respect of loss or damage unless suit is brought within one year after delivery of the goods or the date when the goods should have been delivered: *Provided*, That if a notice of loss or damage, either apparent or concealed, is not given as provided for in this section, that fact shall not affect or prejudice the right of the shipper to bring suit within one year after the delivery of the goods or the date when the goods should have been delivered.

In the case of any actual or apprehended loss or damage the carrier and receiver shall give all reasonable facilities to each other for inspecting and tallying the goods.

"Shipped" bill of lading

(7) After the goods are loaded the bill of lading to be issued by the carrier, master, or agent of the carrier to the shipper shall, if the shipper so demands, be a "shipped" bill of lading: *Provided*, That if the shipper shall have previously taken up any document of title to such goods, he shall surrender the same as against the issue of the "shipped" bill of lading, but at the option of the carrier such document of title may be noted at the port of shipment by the carrier, master, or agent with the name or names of the ship or ships upon which the goods have been shipped and the date or dates of shipment, and when so noted the same shall for the purpose of this section be deemed to constitute a "shipped" bill of lading.

Limitation of liability for negligence

(8) Any clause, covenant, or agreement in a contract of carriage relieving the carrier or the ship from liability for loss or damage to or in connection with the goods, arising from negligence, fault, or failure in the duties and obligations provided in this section, or lessening such liability otherwise than as provided in this chapter, shall be null and void and of no effect. A benefit of insurance in favor of the carrier, or similar clause, shall be deemed to be a clause relieving the carrier from liability.

§ 4. (46 U.S.C.A. § 1304). Rights and immunities of carrier and ship

Unseaworthiness

(1) Neither the carrier nor the ship shall be liable for loss or damage arising or resulting from unseaworthiness unless caused by want of due diligence on the part of the carrier to make the ship seaworthy, and to secure that the ship is properly manned, equipped, and supplied, and to make the holds, refrigerating and cool chambers, and all other parts of the ship in which goods are carried fit and safe for their reception, carriage, and preservation in accordance with the provisions of paragraph (1) of section 1303 of this title. Whenever loss or damage has resulted from unseaworthiness, the burden of proving the exercise of due diligence shall be on the carrier or other persons claiming exemption under this section.

Uncontrollable causes of loss

(2) Neither the carrier nor the ship shall be responsible for loss or damage arising or resulting from—

(a) Act, neglect, or default of the master, mariner, pilot, or the servants of the carrier in the navigation or in the management of the ship;

(b) Fire, unless caused by the actual fault or privity of the carrier;

(c) Perils, dangers, and accidents of the sea or other navigable waters;

(d) Act of God;

(e) Act of war;

(f) Act of public enemies;

(g) Arrest or restraint of princes, rulers, or people, or seizure under legal process;

(h) Quarantine restrictions;

(i) Act or omission of the shipper or owner of the goods, his agent or representative;

(j) Strikes or lockouts or stoppage or restraint of labor from whatever cause, whether partial or general: *Provided*, That nothing herein contained shall be constued to relieve a carrier from responsibility for the carrier's own acts;

(k) Riots and civil commotions;

(l) Saving or attempting to save life or property at sea;

(m) Wastage in bulk or weight or any other loss or damage arising from inherent defect, quality, or vice of the goods;

(n) Insufficiency of packing;

(o) Insufficiency or inadequacy of marks;

(p) Latent defects not discoverable by due diligence; and

(q) Any other cause arising without the actual fault or privity of the carrier and without the fault or neglect of the agents or servants of the carrier, but the burden of proof shall be on the person claiming the benefit of this exception to show that neither the actual fault or privity of the carrier nor the fault or neglect of the agents or servants of the carrier contributed to the loss or damage.

Freedom from negligence

(3) The shipper shall not be responsible for loss or damage sustained by the carrier or the ship arising or resulting from any cause without the act, fault, or neglect of the shipper, his agents, or his servants.

Deviations

(4) Any deviation in saving or attempting to save life or property at sea, or any reasonable deviation shall not be deemed to be an infringement or breach of this chapter or of the contract of carriage, and the carrier shall not be liable for any loss or damage resulting therefrom: *Provided, however*, That if the deviation is for the purpose of loading or unloading cargo or passengers it shall, prima facie, be regarded as unreasonable.

Amount of liability; valuation of cargo

(5) Neither the carrier nor the ship shall in any event be or become liable for any loss or damage to or in connection with the transportation of goods in an amount exceeding $500 per package lawful money of the United States, or in case of goods not shipped in packages, per customary freight unit, or the equivalent of that sum in other currency, unless the nature and value of such goods have been declared by the shipper before shipment and inserted in the bill of lading. This declaration, if embodied in the bill of lading, shall be prima facie evidence, but shall not be conclusive on the carrier.

By agreement between the carrier, master, or agent of the carrier, and the shipper another maximum amount than that mentioned in this paragraph may be fixed: *Provided*, That such maximum shall not be less than the figure above named. In no event shall the carrier be liable for more than the amount of damage actually sustained.

Neither the carrier nor the ship shall be responsible in any event for loss or damage to or in connection with the transportation of the goods if the nature or value thereof has been knowingly and fraudulently misstated by the shipper in the bill of lading.

Inflammable, explosive, or dangerous cargo

(6) Goods of an inflammable, explosive, or dangerous nature to the shipment whereof the carrier, master or agent of the carrier, has not consented with knowledge of their nature and character, may at any time before discharge be landed at any place or destroyed or rendered innocuous by the carrier without compensation, and the shipper of such goods shall be liable for all damages and expenses directly or indirectly arising out of or resulting from such shipment. If any such goods shipped with such knowledge and consent shall become a danger to the ship or cargo, they may in like manner be landed at any place, or destroyed or rendered innocuous by the carrier without liability on the part of the carrier except to general average, if any.

§ 5. (46 U.S.C.A. § 1305). Surrender of rights; increase of liabilities; charter parties; general average

A carrier shall be at liberty to surrender in whole or in part all or any of his rights and immunities or to increase any of his responsibilities and liabilities under this chapter, provided such surrender or increase shall be embodied in the bill of lading issued to the shipper.

The provisions of this chapter shall not be applicable to charter parties; but if bills of lading are issued in the case of a ship under a charter party, they shall comply with the terms of this chapter. Nothing in this chapter shall be held to prevent the insertion in a bill of lading of any lawful provision regarding general average.

§ 6. (46 U.S.C.A. § 1306). Special agreement as to particular goods

Notwithstanding the provisions of sections 1303–1305 of this title, a carrier, master or agent of the carrier, and a shipper shall, in regard to any particular goods be at liberty to enter into any agreement in any terms as to the responsibility and liability of the carrier for such goods, and as to the rights and immunities of the carrier in respect of such goods, or his obligation as to seaworthiness (so far as the stipulation regarding seaworthiness is not contrary to public policy), or the care or diligence of his servants or agents in regard to the loading, handling, stowage, carriage, custody, care, and discharge of the goods carried by sea: *Provided*, That in this case no bill of lading has been or shall be issued and that the terms agreed shall be embodied in a receipt which shall be a nonnegotiable document and shall be marked as such.

Any agreement so entered into shall have full legal effect: *Provided*, That this section shall not apply to ordinary commercial shipments made in the ordinary course of trade but only to other shipments where the character or condition of the property to be carried or the circumstances, terms, and conditions under which the carriage is to be performed are such as reasonably to justify a special agreement.

§ 7. (46 U.S.C.A. § 1307). Agreement as to liability prior to loading or after discharge

Nothing contained in this chapter shall prevent a carrier or a shipper from entering into any agreement, stipulation, condition, reservation, or exemption as to the responsibility and liability of the carrier or the ship for the loss or damage to or in connection with the custody and care and handling of goods prior to the loading on and subsequent to the discharge from the ship on which the goods are carried by sea.

§ 8. (46 U.S.C.A. § 1308). Rights and liabilities under other provisions

The provisions of this chapter shall not affect the rights and obligations of the carrier under the provisions of the Shipping Act, 1916, or under the provisions of sections 175, 181–183, and 183b–188 of this title or of any amendments thereto; or under the provisions of any other enactment for the time being in force relating to the limitation of the liability of the owners of seagoing vessels.

§ 9. (46 U.S.C.A. § 1309). Discrimination between competing shippers

Nothing contained in this chapter shall be construed as permitting a common carrier by water to discriminate between competing shippers similarly placed in time and circumstances, either (a) with respect to their right to demand and receive bills of lading subject to the provisions of this chapter; or (b) when issuing such bills of lading, either in the surrender of any of the carrier's rights and immunities or in the increase of any of the carrier's responsibilities and liabilities pursuant to section 1305 of this title; or (c) in any other way prohibited by the Shipping Act, 1916, as amended.

§ 10. [Repealed].

§ 11. (46 U.S.C.A. § 1310). Weight of bulk cargo

Where under the customs of any trade the weight of any bulk cargo inserted in the bill of lading is a weight ascertained or accepted by a third party other than the carrier or the shipper, and the fact that the weight is so ascertained or accepted is stated in the bill of lading, then, notwithstanding anything in this chapter, the bill of lading shall not be deemed to be prima facie evidence against the carrier of the receipt of goods of the weight so inserted in the bill of lading, and the accuracy thereof at the time of shipment shall not be deemed to have been guaranteed by the shipper.

§ 12. (46 U.S.C.A. § 1311). Liabilities before loading and after discharge; effect on other laws

Nothing in this chapter shall be construed as superseding any part of sections 190–196 of this title, or of any other law which would be applicable in the absence of this chapter, insofar as they relate to the duties, responsibilities, and liabilities of the ship or carrier prior to the time when the goods are loaded on or after the time they are discharged from the ship.

§ 13. (46 U.S.C.A. § 1312). Scope of chapter; "United States"; "foreign trade"

This chapter shall apply to all contracts for carriage of goods by sea to or from ports of the United States in foreign trade. As used in this chapter the term "United States" includes its districts, territories, and possessions. The term "foreign trade" means the transportation of goods between the ports of the United States and ports of foreign countries. Nothing in this chapter shall be held to apply to contracts for carriage of goods by sea between any port of the United States or its possessions, and any other port of the United States or its possessions: *Provided, however*, That any bill of lading or similar document of title which is evidence of a contract for the carriage of goods by sea between such ports, containing an express statement that it shall be subject to the provisions of this chapter, shall be subjected hereto as fully as if subject hereto by the express provisions of this chapter: *Provided further*, That every bill of lading or similar document of title which is evidence of a contact for the carriage of goods by sea from ports of the United States, in foreign trade, shall contain a statement that it shall have effect subject to the provisions of this chapter.

§ 14. [Concerns the power of the President of the United States to suspend provisions of the Act in certain circumstances]

§ 15 and § 16. [Concern the coming into effect and the name of the Act]

Appendix B

THE HAGUE-VISBY RULES

(The Hague Rules as amended by the Brussels Protocol 1968)

Article I

In these Rules the following words are employed, with the meanings set out below:—

(*a*) "Carrier" includes the owner or the charterer who enters into a contract of carriage with a shipper.

(*b*) "Contract of carriage" applies only to contracts of carriage covered by a bill of lading or any similar document of title, in so far as such document relates to the carriage of goods by sea, including any bill of lading or any similar document as aforesaid issued under or pursuant to a charter party from the moment at which such bill of lading or similar document of title regulates the relations between a carrier and a holder of the same.

(*c*) "Goods" includes goods, wares, merchandise, and articles of every kind whatsoever except live animals and cargo which by the contract of carriage is stated as being carried on deck and is so carried.

(*d*) "Ship" means any vessel used for the carriage of goods by sea.

(*e*) "Carriage of goods" covers the period from the time when the goods are loaded on to the time they are discharged from the ship.

Article II

Subject to the provisions of Article VI, under every contract of carriage of goods by sea the carrier, in relation to the loading, handling, stowage, carriage, custody, care and discharge of such goods, shall be subject to the responsibilities and liabilities, and entitled to the rights and immunities hereinafter set forth.

Article III

1. The carrier shall be bound before and at the beginning of the voyage to exercise due diligence to—

(*a*) Make the ship seaworthy.

(*b*) Properly man, equip and supply the ship.

(*c*) Make the holds, refrigerating and cool chambers, and all other parts of the ship in which goods are carried, fit and safe for their reception, carriage and preservation.

2. Subject to the provisions of Article IV, the carrier shall properly and carefully load, handle, stow, carry, keep, care for, and discharge the goods carried.

3. After receiving the goods into his charge the carrier or the master or agent of the carrier shall, on demand of the shipper, issue to the shipper a bill of lading showing among other things—

(*a*) The leading marks necessary for identification of the goods as the same are furnished in writing by the shipper before the loading of such goods starts, provided such marks are stamped or otherwise shown clearly upon the goods if uncovered, or on the cases or coverings in which such goods are contained, in such a manner as should ordinarily remain legible until the end of the voyage.

(*b*) Either the number of packages or pieces, or the quantity, or weight, as the case may be, as furnished in writing by the shipper.

(*c*) The apparent order and condition of the goods.

Provided that no carrier, master or agent of the carrier shall be bound to state or show in the bill of lading any marks, number, quantity, or weight which he has reasonable ground for suspecting not accurately to represent the goods actually received, or which he has had no reasonable means of checking.

4. Such a bill of lading shall be prima facie evidence of the receipt by the carrier of the goods as therein described in accordance with paragraph 3 (*a*), (*b*) and (*c*). However, proof to the contrary shall not be admissible when the bill of lading has been transferred to a third party acting in good faith.

5. The shipper shall be deemed to have guaranteed to the carrier the accuracy at the time of shipment of the marks, number, quantity and weight, as furnished by him, and the shipper shall indemnify the carrier against all loss, damages and expenses arising or resulting from inaccuracies in such particulars. The right of the carrier to such indemnity shall in no way limit his responsibility and liability under the contract of carriage to any person other than the shipper.

6. Unless notice of loss or damage and the general nature of such loss or damage be given in writing to the carrier or his agent at the port of discharge before or at the time of the removal of the goods into the custody of the person entitled to delivery thereof under the contract of carriage, or, if the loss or damage be not apparent, within three days, such removal shall be prima facie evidence of the delivery by the carrier of the goods as described in the bill of lading.

The notice in writing need not be given if the state of the goods has, at the time of their receipt, been the subject of joint survey or inspection.

Subject to paragraph 6*bis* the carrier and the ship shall in any event be discharged from all liability whatsoever in respect of the goods, unless suit is brought within one year of their delivery or of the date when they should have been delivered. This period may, however, be extended if the parties so agree after the cause of action has arisen.

In the case of any actual or apprehended loss or damage the carrier and the receiver shall give all reasonable facilities to each other for inspecting and tallying the goods.

6*bis*. An action for indemnity against a third person may be brought even after the expiration of the year provided for in the preceding paragraph if brought within the time allowed by the law of the Court seized of the case. However, the time allowed shall be not less than three months, commencing from the day when the person bringing such action for indemnity has settled the claim or has been served with process in the action against himself.

7. After the goods are loaded the bill of lading to be issued by the carrier, master, or agent of the carrier, to the shipper shall, if the shipper so demands, be a "shipped" bill of lading, provided that if the shipper shall have previously taken up any document of title to such goods, he shall surrender the same as against the issue of the "shipped" bill of lading, but at the option of the carrier such document of title may be noted at the port of shipment by the carrier, master, or agent with the name or names of the ship or ships upon which the goods have been shipped and the date or dates of shipment, and when so noted, if it shows the particulars mentioned in paragraph 3 of Article III, shall for the purpose of this article be deemed to constitute a "shipped" bill of lading.

8. Any clause, covenant, or agreement in a contract of carriage relieving the carrier or the ship from liability for loss or damage to, or in connection with, goods arising from negligence, fault, or failure in the duties and obligations provided in this article or lessening such liability otherwise than as provided in these Rules, shall be null and void and of no effect. A benefit of insurance in favour of the carrier or similar clause shall be deemed to be a clause relieving the carrier from liability.

Article IV

1. Neither the carrier nor the ship shall be liable for loss or damage arising or resulting from unseaworthiness unless caused by want of due diligence on the part of the carrier to make the ship seaworthy, and to secure that the ship is properly manned, equipped and supplied, and to make the holds, refrigerating and cool chambers and all other parts of the ship in which goods are carried fit and safe for their reception, carriage and preservation in accordance with the provisions of paragraph 1 of Article III. Whenever loss or damage has resulted from unseaworthiness the burden of proving the exercise of due diligence shall be on the carrier or other person claiming exemption under this article.

2. Neither the carrier nor the ship shall be responsible for loss or damage arising or resulting from—

(*a*) Act, neglect, or default of the master, mariner, pilot, or the servants of the carrier in the navigation or in the management of the ship.
(*b*) Fire, unless caused by the actual fault or privity of the carrier.
(*c*) Perils, dangers and accidents of the sea or other navigable waters.
(*d*) Act of God.
(*e*) Act of war.
(*f*) Act of public enemies.
(*g*) Arrest or restraint of princes, rulers or people, or seizure under legal process.
(*h*) Quarantine restrictions.
(*i*) Act or omission of the shipper or owner of the goods, his agent or representative.
(*j*) Strikes or lockouts or stoppage or restraint of labour from whatever cause, whether partial or general.
(*k*) Riots and civil commotions.
(*l*) Saving or attempting to save life or property at sea.
(*m*) Wastage in bulk or weight or any other loss or damage arising from inherent defect, quality or vice of the goods.
(*n*) Insufficiency of packing.
(*o*) Insufficiency or inadequacy of marks.
(*p*) Latent defects not discoverable by due diligence.
(*q*) Any other cause arising without the actual fault or privity of the carrier, or without the fault or neglect of the agents or servants of the carrier, but the burden of proof shall be on the person claiming the benefit of this exception to show that neither the actual fault or privity of the carrier nor the fault or neglect of the agents or servants of the carrier contributed to the loss or damage.

3. The shipper shall not be responsible for loss or damage sustained by the carrier or the ship arising or resulting from any cause without the act, fault or neglect of the shipper, his agents or his servants.

4. Any deviation in saving or attempting to save life or property at sea or any reasonable deviation shall not be deemed to be an infringement or breach of these Rules or of the contract of carriage, and the carrier shall not be liable for any loss or damage resulting therefrom.

5. (*a*) Unless the nature and value of such goods have been declared by the shipper before shipment and inserted in the bill of lading, neither the carrier nor the ship shall in any event be or become liable for any loss or damage to or in connection with the goods in an amount exceeding the equivalent of 10,000 francs per package or unit or 30 francs per kilo of gross weight of the goods lost or damaged, whichever is the higher.

(*b*) The total amount recoverable shall be calculated by reference to the value of such goods at the place and time at which the goods are discharged from the ship in accordance with the contract or should have been so discharged.

The value of the goods shall be fixed according to the commodity exchange price, or, if there be no such price, according to the current market price, or, if there be no commodity exchange price or current market price, by reference to the normal value of goods of the same kind and quality.

(*c*) Where a container, pallet or similar article of transport is used to consolidate goods, the number of packages or units enumerated in the bill of lading as packed in such article of transport shall be deemed the number of packages or units for the purpose of this paragraph as far as these packages or units are concerned. Except as aforesaid such article of transport shall be considered the package or unit.

(*d*) A franc means a unit consisting of 65·5 milligrams of gold of millesimal fineness 900. The date of conversion of the sum awarded into national currencies shall be governed by the law of the Court seized of the case.

(*e*) Neither the carrier nor the ship shall be entitled to the benefit of the limitation of liability provided for in this paragraph if it is proved that the damage resulted from an act or omission of the carrier done with intent to cause damage, or recklessly and with knowledge that damage would probably result.

(*f*) The declaration mentioned in sub-paragraph (*a*) of this paragraph, if embodied in the bill of lading, shall be prima facie evidence, but shall not be binding or conclusive on the carrier.

(*g*) By agreement between the carrier, master or agent of the carrier and the shipper other maximum amounts than those mentioned in sub-paragraph (*a*) of this paragraph may be fixed, provided that no maximum amount so fixed shall be less than the appropriate maximum mentioned in that sub-paragraph.

(*h*) Neither the carrier nor the ship shall be responsible in any event for loss or damage to, or in connection with, goods if the nature or value thereof has been knowingly mis-stated by the shipper in the bill of lading.

Note: By the 1979 Brussels Protocol, the provisions relating to "Poincaré Francs" in Article IV, Rule 5(a) and 5(d), were replaced by units of account defined in terms of the Special Drawing Right of member States of the International Monetary Fund.

6. Goods of an inflammable, explosive or dangerous nature to the shipment whereof the carrier, master or agent of the carrier has not consented with knowledge of their nature and character, may at any time before discharge be landed at any place, or destroyed or rendered innocuous by the carrier without compensation and the shipper of such goods shall be liable for all damages and expenses directly or indirectly arising out of or resulting from such shipment. If any such goods shipped with such knowledge and consent shall become a danger to the ship or cargo, they may in like manner be landed at any place, or destroyed or rendered innocuous by the carrier without liability on the part of the carrier except to general average, if any.

Article IV bis

1. The defences and limits of liability provided for in these Rules shall apply in any action against the carrier in respect of loss or damage to goods covered by a contract of carriage whether the action be founded in contract or in tort.

2. If such an action is brought against a servant or agent of the carrier (such servant or agent not being an independent contractor), such servant or agent shall be entitled to avail himself of the defences and limits of liability which the carrier is entitled to invoke under these Rules.

3. The aggregate of the amounts recoverable from the carrier, and such servants and agents, shall in no case exceed the limit provided for in these Rules.

4. Nevertheless, a servant or agent of the carrier shall not be entitled to avail himself of the provisions of this article, if it is proved that the damage resulted from an act or omission of the servant or agent done with intent to cause damage or recklessly and with knowledge that damage would probably result.

Article V

A carrier shall be at liberty to surrender in whole or in part all or any of his rights and immunities or to increase any of his responsibilities and obligations under these Rules, provided such surrender or increase shall be embodied in the bill of lading issued to the shipper. The provisions of these Rules shall not be applicable to charter parties, but if bills of lading are issued in the case of a ship under a charter party they shall comply with the terms of these Rules. Nothing in these Rules shall be held to prevent the insertion in a bill of lading of any lawful provision regarding general average.

Article VI

Notwithstanding the provisions of the preceding articles, a carrier, master or agent of the carrier and a shipper shall in regard to any particular goods be at liberty to enter into any agreement in any terms as to the responsibility and liability of the carrier for such goods, and as to the rights and immunities of the carrier in respect of such goods, or his obligation as to seaworthiness, so far as this stipulation is not contrary to public policy, or the care of diligence of his servants or agents in regard to the loading, handling, stowage, carriage, custody, care and discharge of the goods carried by sea, provided that in this case no bill of lading has been or shall be issued and that the terms agreed shall be embodied in a receipt which shall be a non-negotiable document and shall be marked as such.

Any agreement so entered into shall have full legal effect.

Provided that this article shall not apply to ordinary commercial shipments made in the ordinary course of trade, but only to other shipments where the character or condition of the property to be carried or the circumstances, terms and conditions under which the carriage is to be performed are such as reasonably to justify a special agreement.

Article VII

Nothing herein contained shall prevent a carrier or a shipper from entering into any agreement, stipulation, condition, reservation or exemption as to the responsibility and liability of the carrier or the ship for the loss or damage to, or in connection with, the custody and care and handling of goods prior to the loading on, and subsequent to the discharge from, the ship on which the goods are carried by sea.

Article VIII

The provisions of these Rules shall not affect the rights and obligations of the carrier under any statute for the time being in force relating to the limitation of the liability of owners of sea-going vessels.

Article IX

These Rules shall not affect the provisions of any international Convention or national law governing liability for nuclear damage.

Article X

The provisions of these Rules shall apply to every bill of lading relating to the carriage of goods between ports in two different States if:

(*a*) the bill of lading is issued in a contracting State, or

(*b*) the carriage is from a port in a contracting State, or

(*c*) the contract contained in or evidenced by the bill of lading provides that these Rules or legislation of any State giving effect to them are to govern the contract,

whatever may be the nationality of the ship, the carrier, the shipper, the consignee, or any other interested person.

[*The last two paragraphs of this article are not reproduced. They require contracting States to apply the Rules to bills of lading mentioned in the article and authorise them to apply the Rules to other bills of lading.*]

[*Articles 11 to 16 of the International Convention for the unification of certain rules of law relating to bills of lading signed at Brussels on 25th August 1924 are not reproduced. They deal with the coming into force of the Convention, procedure for ratification, accession and denunciation, and the right to call for a fresh conference to consider amendments to the Rules contained in the Convention.*]

Note: The 1968 Brussels Protocol was enacted in the United Kingdom by the Carriage of Goods by Sea Act 1971. The 1979 Brussels Protocol, replacing "Poincaré Francs" by units of account defined in terms of the Special Drawing Right of member States of the International Monetary Fund, was enacted in the United Kingdom by Section 2 of the Merchant Shipping Act 1981. Section 3 of the latter Act contains detailed provisions regarding the calculation of Sterling equivalents.

Appendix C

THE ARBITRATION ACT 1950

(As amended by the Arbitration Acts 1975 and 1979 and by the Administration of Justice Acts 1982 and 1985)

Part I: General Provisions as to Arbitration

Effect of Arbitration Agreements, &c.

Authority of arbitrators and umpires to be irrevocable

1. The authority of an arbitrator or umpire appointed by or by virtue of an arbitration agreement shall, unless a contrary intention is expressed in the agreement, be irrevocable except by leave of the High Court or a judge thereof.

Death of party

2.—(1) An arbitration agreement shall not be discharged by the death of any party thereto, either as respects the deceased or any other party, but shall in such an event be enforceable by or against the personal representative of the deceased.

(2) The authority of an arbitrator shall not be revoked by the death of any party by whom he was appointed.

(3) Nothing in this section shall be taken to affect the operation of any enactment or rule of law by virtue of which any right of action is extinguished by the death of a person.

Bankruptcy

3.—(1) Where it is provided by a term in a contract to which a bankrupt is a party that any differences arising thereout or in connection therewith shall be referred to arbitration, the said term shall, if the trustee in bankruptcy adopts the contract, be enforceable by or against him so far as relates to any such differences.

(2) Where a person who has been adjudged bankrupt had, before the commencement of the bankruptcy, become a party to an arbitration agreement, and any matter to which the agreement applies requires to be determined in connection with or for the purposes of the bankruptcy proceedings, then, if the case is one to which subsection (1) of this section does not apply, any other party to the agreement or, with the consent of the [creditors' committee established under Section 301 of the Insolvency Act 1986] the trustee in bankruptcy may apply to the court having jurisdiction in the bankruptcy proceedings for an order directing that the matter in question shall be referred to arbitration in accordance with the agreement, and that court may, if it is of opinion that, having regard to all the circumstances of the case, the matter ought to be determined by arbitration, make an order accordingly.

Note: The words in square brackets in sub-section (2) above were substituted by Section 439(2) of the Insolvency Act 1986.

Staying court proceedings where there is submission to arbitration

4.—(1) If any party to an arbitration agreement, or any person claiming through or under him, commences any legal proceedings in any court against any other party to the agreement, or any person claiming through or under him, in respect of any matter agreed to be referred, any party to those legal proceedings may at any time after appearance, and before delivering any pleadings or taking any other steps in the proceedings, apply to that court to stay the proceedings, and that court or a judge thereof, if satisfied that there is no sufficient reason why the matter should not be referred in accordance with the agreement, and that the applicant was, at the time when the proceedings were commenced, and still remains, ready and willing to do all things necessary to the proper conduct of the arbitration, may make an order staying the proceedings.

(2) *Repealed by the Arbitration Act 1975.*

Reference of interpleader issues to arbitration

5. Where relief by way of interpleader is granted and it appears to the High Court that the claims in question are matters to which an arbitration agreement, to which the claimants are parties, applies, the High Court may direct the issue between the claimants to be determined in accordance with the agreement.

Arbitrators and Umpires

When reference is to a single arbitrator

6. Unless a contrary intention is expressed therein, every arbitration agreement shall, if no other mode of reference is provided, be deemed to include a provision that the reference shall be to a single arbitrator.

Power of parties in certain cases to supply vacancy

7. Where an arbitration agreement provides that the reference shall be to two arbitrators, one to be appointed by each party, then, unless a contrary intention is expressed therein—

(*a*) if either of the appointed arbitrators refuses to act, or is incapable of acting, or dies, the party who appointed him may appoint a new arbitrator in his place;

(*b*) if, on such a reference, one party fails to appoint an arbitrator, either originally, or by way of substitution as aforesaid, for seven clear days after the other party, having appointed his arbitrator, has served the party making default with notice to make the appointment, the party who has appointed an arbitrator may appoint that arbitrator to act as sole arbitrator in the reference and his award shall be binding on both parties as if he had been appointed by consent:

Provided that the High Court or a judge thereof may set aside any appointment made in pursuance of this section.

Umpires

8.—(1) Unless a contrary intention is expressed therein, every arbitration agreement shall, where the reference is to two arbitrators, be deemed to include a provision that the two arbitrators [may appoint an umpire at any time] after they are themselves appointed [and shall do so forthwith if they cannot agree.]

(2) Unless a contrary intention is expressed therein, every arbitration agreement shall, where such a provision is applicable to the reference, be deemed to include a provision that if the arbitrators have delivered to any party to the arbitration agreement, or to the umpire, a notice in writ-

ing stating that they cannot agree, the umpire may forthwith enter on the reference in lieu of the arbitrators.

(3) At any time after the appointment of an umpire, however appointed, the High Court may, on the application of any party to the reference and notwithstanding anything to the contrary in the arbitration agreement, order that the umpire shall enter upon the reference in lieu of the arbitrators and as if he were a sole arbitrator.

Note: The words in square brackets in sub-section (1) above are those substituted and added by Section 6(1) of the Arbitration Act 1979.

Agreements for reference to three arbitrators

9. Unless the contrary intention is expressed in the arbitration agreement, in any case where there is a reference to three arbitrators, the award of any two of the arbitrators shall be binding.

Note: The words of this section are those substituted by Section 6(2) of the Arbitration Act 1979.

Power of court in certain cases to appoint an arbitrator or umpire

10.—(1) In any of the following cases—

(*a*) where an arbitration agreement provides that the reference shall be to a single arbitrator, and all the parties do not, after differences have arisen, concur in the appointment of an arbitrator;

(*b*) if an appointed arbitrator refuses to act, or is incapable of acting, or dies, and the arbitration agreement does not show that it was intended that the vacancy should not be supplied and the parties do not supply the vacancy;

(*c*) where the parties or two arbitrators are [required or are] at liberty to appoint an umpire or third arbitrator and do not appoint him;

(*d*) where an appointed umpire or third arbitrator refuses to act, or is incapable of acting, or dies, and the arbitration agreement does not show that it was intended that the vacancy should not be supplied, and the parties or arbitrators do not supply the vacancy;

any party may serve the other parties or the arbitrators, as the case may be, with a written notice to appoint or, as the case may be, concur in appointing, an arbitrator, umpire or third arbitrator, and if the appointment is not made within seven clear days after the service of the notice, the High Court or a judge thereof may, on application by the party who gave the notice, appoint an arbitrator, umpire or third arbitrator who shall have the like powers to act in the reference and make an award as if he had been appointed by consent of all parties.

[(2) In any case where—

(*a*) an arbitration agreement provides for the appointment of an arbitrator or umpire by a person who is neither one of the parties nor an existing arbitrator (whether the provision applies directly or in default of agreement by the parties or otherwise), and

(*b*) that person refuses to make the appointment or does not make it within the time specified in the agreement or, if no time is so specified, within a reasonable time,

any party to the agreement may serve the person in question with a written notice to appoint an arbitrator or umpire and, if the appointment is not made within seven clear days after the service of the notice, the High Court or a judge thereof may, on the application of the party who gave the notice, appoint an arbitrator or umpire who shall have the like powers to act in the reference and make an award as if he had been appointed in accordance with the terms of the agreement.]

[(3) In any case where—

(*a*) an arbitration agreement provides that the reference shall be to three arbitrators, one to be appointed by each party and the third to be appointed by the two appointed by the parties or in some other manner specified in the agreement; and

(*b*) one of the parties ("the party in default") refuses to appoint an arbitrator or does not do so within the time specified in the agreement or, if no time is specified, within a reasonable time,

the other party to the agreement, having appointed his arbitrator, may serve the party in default with a written notice to appoint an arbitrator and, if the appointment is not made within seven clear days after the service of the notice, the High Court or a judge thereof may, on the application of the party who gave the notice, appoint an arbitrator on behalf of the party in default who shall have the like powers to act in the reference and make an award (and, if the case so requires, the like duty in relation to the appointment of a third arbitrator) as if he had been appointed in accordance with the terms of the agreement.

[(4) Except in a case where the arbitration agreement shows that it was intended that the vacancy should not be supplied, paragraph (*b*) of each of subsections (2) and (3) shall be construed as extending to any such refusal or failure by a person as is there mentioned arising in connection with the replacement of an arbitrator who was appointed by that person (or, in default of being so appointed, was appointed under that subsection) but who refuses to act, or is incapable of acting or has died.].

Note: The words in square brackets in sub-section (1)(*c*) and sub-section (2) above were added by Section 6(3) and (4) of the Arbitration Act 1979. Sub-sections (3) and (4) above were added by Section 58 of the Administration of Justice Act 1985.

Reference to official referee

11. Where an arbitration agreement provides that the reference shall be to an official referee, any official referee to whom application is made shall, subject to any order of the High Court or a judge thereof as to transfer or otherwise, hear and determine the matters agreed to be referred.

Conduct of Proceedings, Witnesses, &c.

12.—(1) Unless a contrary intention is expressed therein, every arbitration agreement shall, where such a provision is applicable to the reference, be deemed to contain a provision that the parties to the reference, and all persons claiming through them respectively, shall, subject to any legal objection, submit to be examined by the arbitrator or umpire, on oath or affirmation, in relation to the matters in dispute, and shall, subject as aforesaid, produce before the arbitrator or umpire all documents within their possession or power respectively which may be required or called for, and do all other things which during the proceedings on the reference the arbitrator or umpire may require.

(2) Unless a contrary intention is expressed therein, every arbitration agreement shall, where such a provision is applicable to the reference, be deemed to contain a provision that the witnesses on the reference shall, if the arbitrator or umpire thinks fit, be examined on oath or affirmation.

(3) An arbitrator or umpire shall, unless a contrary intention is expressed in the arbitration agreement, having power to administer oaths to, or take the affirmations of, the parties to and witnesses on a reference under the agreement.

(4) Any party to a reference under an arbitration agreement may sue out a writ of subpoena ad testificandum or a writ of subpoena duces tecum, but no person shall be compelled under any such writ to produce any document which he could not be compelled to produce on the trial of an action, and the High Court or a judge thereof may order that a writ of subpoena ad testificandum or of subpoena duces tecum shall issue to compel the attendance before an arbitrator or umpire of a witness wherever he may be within the United Kingdom.

(5) The High Court or a judge thereof may also order that a writ of habeas corpus ad testificandum shall issue to bring up a prisoner for examination before an arbitrator or umpire.

(6) The High Court shall have, for the purpose of and in relation to a reference, the same power of making orders in respect of—

(*a*) security for costs;
(*b*) discovery of documents and interrogatories;
(*c*) the giving of evidence by affidavit;
(*d*) examination on oath of any witness before an officer of the High Court or any other person, and the issue of a commission or request for the examination of a witness out of the jurisdiction;
(*e*) the preservation, interim custody or sale of any goods which are the subject matter of the reference;
(*f*) securing the amount in dispute in the reference;
(*g*) the detention, preservation or inspection of any property or thing which is the subject of the reference or as to which any question may arise therein, and authorising for any of the purposes aforesaid any persons to enter upon or into any land or building in the possession of any party to the reference, or authorising any samples to be taken or any observation to be made or experiment to be tried which may be necessary or expedient for the purpose of obtaining full information or evidence; and
(*h*) interim injunctions or the appointment of a receiver;

as it has for the purpose of and in relation to an action or matter in the High Court:

Provided that nothing in this subsection shall be taken to prejudice any power which may be vested in an arbitrator or umpire of making orders with respect to any of the matters aforesaid.

Provisions as to Awards

Time for making award

13.—(1) Subject to the provisions of subsection (2) of section twenty-two of this Act, and anything to the contrary in the arbitration agreement, an arbitrator or umpire shall have power to make an award at any time.

(2) The time, if any, limited for making an award, whether under this Act or otherwise, may from time to time be enlarged by order of the High Court or a judge thereof, whether that time has expired or not.

(3) The High Court may, on the application of any party to a reference, remove an arbitrator or umpire who fails to use all reasonable dispatch in entering on and proceeding with the reference and making an award, and an arbitrator or umpire who is removed by the High Court under this subsection shall not be entitled to receive any remuneration in respect of his services.

For the purposes of this subsection, the expression "proceeding with a reference" includes, in a case where two arbitrators are unable to agree, giving notice of that fact to the parties and to the umpire.

Interim Awards

14. Unless a contrary intention is expressed therein, every arbitration agreement shall, where such a provision is applicable to the reference, be deemed to contain a provision that the arbitrator or umpire may, if he thinks fit, make an interim award, and any reference in this Part of this Act to an award includes a reference to an interim award.

Specific performance

15. Unless a contrary intention is expressed therein, every arbitration agreement shall, where such a provision is applicable to the reference, be deemed to contain a provision that the arbitrator or umpire shall have the same power as the High Court to order specific performance of any contract other than a contract relating to land or any interest in land.

Awards to be final

16. Unless a contrary intention is expressed therein, every arbitration agreement shall, where such a provision is applicable to the reference, be deemed to contain a provision that the award to be made by the arbitrator or umpire shall be final and binding on the parties and the persons claiming under them respectively.

Power to correct slips

17. Unless a contrary intention is expressed in the arbitration agreement, the arbitrator or umpire shall have power to correct in an award any clerical mistake or error arising from any accidental slip or omission.

Costs, Fees and Interest

Costs

18.—(1) Unless a contrary intention is expressed therein, every arbitration agreement shall be deemed to include a provision that the costs of the reference and award shall be in the discretion of the arbitrator or umpire, who may direct to and by whom and in what manner those costs or any part thereof shall be paid, and may tax or settle the amount of costs to be so paid or any part thereof, and may award costs to be paid as between solicitor and client.

(2) Any costs directed by an award to be paid shall, unless the award otherwise directs, be taxable in the High Court.

(3) Any provision in an arbitration agreement to the effect that the parties or any party thereto shall in any event pay their or his own costs of the reference or award or any part thereof shall be void, and this Part of this Act shall, in the case of an arbitration agreement containing any such provision, have effect as if that provision were not contained therein:

Provided that nothing in this subsection shall invalidate such a provision when it is a part of an agreement to submit to arbitration a dispute which has arisen before the making of that agreement.

(4) If no provision is made by an award with respect to the costs of the reference, any party to the reference may, within fourteen days of the publication of the award or such further time as the High Court or a judge thereof may direct, apply to the arbitrator for an order directing by and to whom those costs shall be paid, and thereupon the arbitrator shall, after hearing any party who may desire to be heard, amend his award by adding thereto such directions as he may think proper with respect to the payment of the costs of the reference.

(5) Section sixty-nine of the Solicitors Act 1932 (which empowers a court before which any proceeding is being heard or is pending to charge property recovered or preserved in the proceeding with the payment of solicitors' costs) shall apply as if an arbitration were a proceeding in the High Court, and the High Court may make declarations and orders accordingly.

Taxation of arbitrator's or umpire's fees

19.—(1) If in any case an arbitrator or umpire refuses to deliver his award except on payment of the fees demanded by him, the High Court may, on an application for the purpose, order that the arbitrator or umpire shall deliver the award to the applicant on payment into court by the applicant of the fees demanded, and further that the fees demanded shall be taxed by the taxing officer and that out of the money paid into court there shall be paid out to the arbitrator or umpire by way of fees such sum as may be found reasonable on taxation and that the balance of the money, if any, shall be paid out to the applicant.

(2) An application for the purposes of this section may be made by any party to the reference unless the fees demanded have been fixed by a written agreement between him and the arbitrator or umpire.

(3) A taxation of fees under this section may be reviewed in the same manner as a taxation of costs.

(4) The arbitrator or umpire shall be entitled to appear and be heard on any taxation or review of taxation under this section.

Power of arbitrator to award interest

[**19A.** (1) Unless a contrary intention is expressed therein, every arbitration agreement shall, where such a provision is applicable to the reference, be deemed to contain a provision that the arbitrator or umpire may, if he thinks fit, award simple interest at such rate as he thinks fit—

(*a*) on any sum which is the subject of the reference but which is paid before the award, for such period ending not later than the date of the payment as he thinks fit; and

(*b*) on any sum which he awards, for such period ending not later than the date of the award as he thinks fit.

(2) The power to award interest conferred on an arbitrator or umpire by subsection (1) above is without prejudice to any other power of an arbitrator or umpire to award interest.]

Note: This section was added by the Administration of Justice Act 1982, Section 15(6), Schedule I, Part IV.

Interest on awards

20. A sum directed to be paid by an award shall, unless the award otherwise directs, carry interest as from the date of the award and at the same rate as a judgment debt.

Special Cases, Remission and Setting aside of Awards, &c.

Statement of case

21. *Repealed by Sections 1(1) and 8(3) of the Arbitration Act 1979.*

Power to remit award

22.—(1) In all cases of reference to arbitration the High Court or a judge thereof may from time to time remit the matters referred, or any of them, to the reconsideration of the arbitrator or umpire.

(2) Where an award is remitted, the arbitrator or umpire shall, unless the order otherwise directs, make his award within three months after the date of the order.

Removal of arbitrator and setting aside of award

23.—(1) Where an arbitrator or umpire has misconducted himself or the proceedings, the High Court may remove him.

(2) Where an arbitrator or umpire has misconducted himself or the proceedings, or an arbitration or award has been improperly procured, the High Court may set the award aside.

(3) Where an application is made to set aside an award, the High Court may order that any money made payable by the award shall be brought into court or otherwise secured pending the determination of the application.

Power of court to give relief where arbitrator is not impartial or the dispute involves question of fraud

24.—(1) Where an agreement between any parties provides that disputes which may arise in the future between them shall be referred to an arbitrator named or designated in the agreement, and after a dispute has arisen any party applies, on the ground that the arbitrator so named or designated is not or may not be impartial, for leave to revoke the authority of the arbitrator or for an injunction to restrain any other party or the arbitrator from proceeding with the arbitration, it shall not be a ground for refusing the application that the said party at the time when he made the agreement knew, or ought to have known, that the arbitrator, by reason of his relation towards any other party to the agreement or of his connection with the subject referred, might not be capable of impartiality.

(2) Where an agreement between any parties provides that disputes which may arise in the future between them shall be referred to arbitration, and a dispute which so arises involves the question whether any such party has been guilty of fraud, the High Court shall, so far as may be necessary to enable that question to be determined by the High Court, have power to order that the agreement shall cease to have effect and power to give leave to revoke the authority of any arbitrator or umpire appointed by or by virtue of the agreement.

(3) In any case where by virtue of this section the High Court has power to order that an arbitration agreement shall cease to have effect or to give leave to revoke the authority of an arbitrator or umpire, the High Court may refuse to stay any action brought in breach of the agreement.

Power of court where arbitrator is removed or authority of arbitrator is revoked

25.—(1) Where an arbitrator (not being a sole arbitrator), or two or more arbitrators (not being all the arbitrators) or an umpire who has not entered on the reference is or are removed by the High Court, the High Court may, on the application of any party to the arbitration agreement, appoint a person or persons to act as arbitrator or arbitrators or umpire in place of the person or persons so removed.

(2) Where the authority of an arbitrator or arbitrators or umpire is revoked by leave of the High Court, or a sole arbitrator or all the arbitrators or an umpire who has entered on the reference is or are removed by the High Court, the High Court may, on the application of any party to the arbitration agreement, either—

(*a*) appoint a person to act as sole arbitrator in place of the person or persons removed; or

(*b*) order that the arbitration agreement shall cease to have effect with respect to the dispute referred.

(3) A person appointed under this section by the High Court as an arbitrator or umpire shall have the like power to act in the reference and to make an award as if he had been appointed in accordance with the terms of the arbitration agreement.

(4) Where it is provided (whether by means of a provision in the arbitration agreement or otherwise) that an award under an arbitration agreement shall be a condition precedent to the bringing of an action with respect to any matter to which the agreement applies, the High Court, if it orders (whether under this section or under any other enactment) that the agreement shall cease to have effect as regards any particular dispute, may further order that the provision making an award a condition precedent to the bringing of an action shall also cease to have effect as regards that dispute.

Enforcement of Award

26. An award on an arbitration agreement may, by leave of the High Court or a judge thereof, be enforced in the same manner as a judgment or order to the same effect, and where leave is so given, judgment may be entered in terms of the award.

Note: Certain provisions, not printed here, were added to this section by the Administration of Justice Act 1977 and the County Court Act 1984 in regard to County Court proceedings.

Miscellaneous

Power of court to extend time for commencing arbitration proceedings

27. Where the terms of an agreement to refer future disputes to arbitration provide that any claims to which the agreement applies shall be barred unless notice to appoint an arbitrator is given or an arbitrator is appointed or some other step to commence arbitration proceedings is taken within a time fixed by the agreement, and a dispute arises to which the agreement applies, the High Court, if it is of opinion that in the circumstances of the case undue hardship would otherwise be caused, and notwithstanding that the time so fixed has expired, may, on such terms, if any, as the justice of the case may require, but without prejudice to the provisions of any enactment limiting the time for the commencement of arbitration proceedings, extend the time for such period as it thinks proper.

Terms as to costs, &c.

28. Any order made under this Part of this Act may be made on such terms as to costs or otherwise as the authority making the order thinks just:

[Provided that this section shall not apply to any order made under subsection (2) of section four of this Act.]

Extension of s. 496 of the Merchant Shipping Act 1894

29.—(1) In subsection (3) of section four hundred and ninety-six of the Merchant Shipping Act 1894 (which requires a sum deposited with a wharfinger by an owner of goods to be repaid unless legal proceedings are instituted by the shipowner), the expression "legal proceedings" shall be deemed to include arbitration.

(2) For the purposes of the said section four hundred and ninety-six, as amended by this section, an arbitration shall be deemed to be commenced when one party to the arbitration agreement serves on the other party or parties a notice requiring him or them to appoint or concur in appointing an arbitrator, or, where the arbitration agreement provides that the reference shall be to a person named or designated in the agreement, requiring him or them to submit the dispute to the person so named or designated.

(3) Any such notice as is mentioned in subsection (2) of this section may be served either—

(*a*) by delivering it to the person on whom it is to be served; or

(*b*) by leaving it at the usual or last known place of abode in England of that person; or

(*c*) by sending it by post in a registered letter addressed to that person at his usual or last known place of abode in England;

as well as in any other manner provided in the arbitration agreement; and where a notice is sent by post in manner prescribed in paragraph (*c*) of this subsection, service thereof shall, unless the contrary is proved, be deemed to have been effected at the time at which the letter would have been delivered in the ordinary course of post.

Crown to be bound

30. This Part of this Act shall apply to any arbitration to which His Majesty, either in right of the Crown or of the Duchy of Lancaster or otherwise, or the Duke of Cornwall, is a party.

Application of Part I to statutory arbitrations

31.—(1) Subject to the provisions of section thirty-three of this Act, this Part of this Act, except the provisions thereof specified in subsection (2) of this section, shall apply to every arbitration under any other Act (whether passed before or after the commencement of this Act) as if the arbitration were pursuant to an arbitration agreement and as if that other Act were an arbitration agreement, except in so far as this Act is inconsistent with that other Act or with any rules or procedure authorised or recognised thereby.

(2) The provisions referred to in subsection (1) of this section are subsection (1) of section two, section three, section five, subsection (3) of section eighteen and sections twenty-four, twenty-five, twenty-seven and twenty-nine.

Meaning of "arbitration agreement"

32. In this Part of this Act, unless the context otherwise requires, the expression "arbitration agreement" means a written agreement to submit present or future differences to arbitration, whether an arbitrator is named therein or not.

Operation of Part I

33. This Part of this Act shall not affect any arbitration commenced (within the meaning of subsection (2) of section twenty-nine of this Act) before the commencement of this Act, but shall apply to an arbitration so commenced after the commencement of this Act under an agreement made before the commencement of this Act.

Extent of Part I

34. None of the provisions of this Part of this Act shall extend to Scotland or Northern Ireland.

NOTE: PART II OF THE ARBITRATION ACT 1950, WHICH IS NOT PRINTED HERE, DEALS WITH THE ENFORCEMENT OF CERTAIN FOREIGN AWARDS.

THE ARBITRATION ACT 1975

Effect of arbitration agreement on court proceedings

Staying court proceedings where party proves arbitration agreement

1.—(1) If any party to an arbitration agreement to which this section applies, or any person claiming through or under him, commences any legal proceedings in any court against any other party to the agreement, or any person claiming through or under him, in respect of any matter agreed to be referred, any party to the proceedings may at any time after appearance, and before delivering any pleadings or taking any other steps in the proceedings, apply to the court to stay the proceedings; and the court, unless satisfied that the arbitration agreement is null and void, inoperative or incapable of being performed or that there is not in fact any dispute between the parties with regard to the matter agreed to be referred, shall make an order staying the proceedings.

(2) This section applies to any arbitration agreement which is not a domestic arbitration agreement; and neither section 4(1) of the Arbitration Act 1950 nor section 4 of the Arbitration Act (Northern Ireland) 1937 shall apply to an arbitration agreement to which this section applies.

(3) In the application of this section to Scotland, for the references to staying proceedings there shall be substituted references to sisting proceedings.

(4) In this section "domestic arbitration agreement" means an arbitration agreement which does not provide, expressly or by implication, for arbitration in a State other than the United Kingdom and to which neither—

(*a*) an individual who is a national of, or habitually resident in, any State other than the United Kingdom; nor

(*b*) a body corporate which is incorporated in, or whose central management and control is exercised in, any State other than the United Kingdom;

is a party at the time the proceedings are commenced.

. . . . . .

General

Interpretation

7.—(1) In this Act—

"arbitration agreement" means an agreement in writing (including an agreement contained in an exchange of letters or telegrams) to submit to arbitration present or future differences capable of settlement by arbitration;

Note: The parts of this Act which are not printed relate to the enforcement of awards in accordance with the Convention on the Recognition and Enforcement of Foreign Arbitral Awards (the "New York Convention") adopted by the United Nations Conference on International Commercial Arbitration in 1958.

THE ARBITRATION ACT 1979

(As amended by Section 148 of the Supreme Court Act 1981)

Judicial review of arbitration awards

1.—(1) In the Arbitration Act 1950 (in this Act referred to as "the principal Act") section 21 (statement of case for a decision of the High Court) shall cease to have effect and, without prejudice to the right of appeal conferred by subsection (2) below, the High Court shall not have jurisdiction to set aside or remit an award on an arbitration agreement on the ground of errors of fact or law on the face of the award.

(2) Subject to subsection (3) below, an appeal shall lie to the High Court on any question of law arising out of an award made on an arbitration agreement; and on the determination of such an appeal the High Court may by order—

(*a*) confirm, vary or set aside the award; or

(*b*) remit the award to the reconsideration of the arbitrator or umpire together with the court's opinion on the question of law which was the subject of the appeal;

and where the award is remitted under paragraph (*b*) above the arbitrator or umpire shall, unless the order otherwise directs, make his award within three months after the date of the order.

(3) An appeal under this section may be brought by any of the parties to the reference—

(*a*) with the consent of all the other parties to the reference; or

(*b*) subject to section 3 below, with the leave of the court.

(4) The High Court shall not grant leave under subsection (3)(*b*) above unless it considers that, having regard to all the circumstances, the determination of the question of law concerned could substantially affect the rights of one or more of the parties to the arbitration agreement; and the court may make any leave which it gives conditional upon the applicant complying with such conditions as it considers appropriate.

(5) Subject to subsection (6) below, if an award is made and, on an application made by any of the parties to the reference,—

(*a*) with the consent of all the other parties to the reference, or

(*b*) subject to section 3 below, with the leave of the court,

it appears to the High Court that the award does not or does not sufficiently set out the reasons for the award, the court may order the arbitrator or umpire concerned to state the reasons for his award in sufficient detail to enable the court, should an appeal be brought under this section, to consider any question of law arising out of the award.

(6) In any case where an award is made without any reason being given, the High Court shall not make an order under subsection (5) above unless it is satisfied—

(*a*) that before the award was made one of the parties to the reference gave notice to the arbitrator or umpire concerned that a reasoned award would be required; or

(*b*) that there is some special reason why such a notice was not given.

(6A) Unless the High Court gives leave, no appeal shall lie to the Court of Appeal from a decision of the High Court—

(*a*) to grant or refuse leave under subsection (3)(*b*) or (5)(*b*) above; or

(*b*) to make or not to make an order under subsection (5) above.

(7) No appeal shall lie to the Court of Appeal from a decision of the High Court on an appeal under this section unless—

(*a*) the High Court or the Court of Appeal gives leave; and

(*b*) it is certified by the High Court that the question of law to which its decision relates either is one of general public importance or is one which for some other special reason should be considered by the Court of Appeal.

(8) Where the award of an arbitrator or umpire is varied on appeal, the award as varied shall have effect (except for the purposes of this section) as if it were the award of the arbitrator or umpire.

Determination of preliminary point of law by court

2.—(1) Subject to subsection (2) and section 3 below, on an application to the High Court made by any of the parties to a reference—

(*a*) with the consent of an arbitrator who has entered on the reference or, if an umpire has entered on the reference, with his consent, or

(*b*) with the consent of all the other parties,

the High Court shall have jurisdiction to determine any question of law arising in the course of the reference.

(2) The High Court shall not entertain an application under subsection (1)(*a*) above with respect to any question of law unless it is satisfied that—

(*a*) the determination of the application might produce substantial savings in costs to the parties; and

(*b*) the question of law is one in respect of which leave to appeal would be likely to be given under section 1(3)(*b*) above.

(2A) Unless the High Court gives leave, no appeal shall lie to the Court of Appeal from a decision of the High Court to entertain or not to entertain an application under subsection (1)(*a*) above.

(3) A decision of the High Court under subsection (1) above shall be deemed to be a judgment of the court within the meaning of section 27 of the Supreme Court of Judicature (Consolidation) Act 1925 (appeals to the Court of Appeal), but no appeal shall lie from such a decision unless—

(*a*) the High Court or the Court of Appeal gives leave; and

(*b*) it is certified by the High Court that the question of law to which its decision relates either is one of general public importance or is one which for some other special reason should be considered by the Court of Appeal.

Exclusion agreements affecting rights under sections 1 and 2

3.—(1) Subject to the following provisions of this section and section 4 below—

(*a*) the High Court shall not, under section 1(3)(*b*) above, grant leave to appeal with respect to a question of law arising out of an award, and

(*b*) the High Court shall not, under section 1(5)(*b*) above, grant leave to make an application with respect to an award, and

(*c*) no application may be made under section 2(1)(*a*) above with respect to a question of law,

if the parties to the reference in question have entered into an agreement in writing (in this section referred to as an "exclusion agreement") which excludes the right of appeal under section 1 above in relation to that award or, in a case falling within paragraph (*c*) above, in relation to an award to which the determination of the question of law is material.

(2) An exclusion agreement may be expressed so as to relate to a particular award, to awards under a particular reference or to any other description of awards, whether arising out of the same reference or not; and an agreement may be an exclusion agreement for the purposes of this section

whether it is entered into before or after the passing of this Act and whether or not it forms part of an arbitration agreement.

(3) In any case where—

(*a*) an arbitration agreement, other than a domestic arbitration agreement, provides for disputes between the parties to be referred to arbitration, and

(*b*) a dispute to which the agreement relates involves the question whether a party has been guilty of fraud, and

(*c*) the parties have entered into an exclusion agreement which is applicable to any award on the reference of that dispute,

then, except in so far as the exclusion agreement otherwise provides, the High Court shall not exercise its powers under section 24(2) of the principal Act (to take steps necessary to enable the question to be determined by the High Court) in relation to that dispute.

(4) Except as provided by subsection (1) above, sections 1 and 2 above shall have effect notwithstanding anything in any agreement purporting—

(*a*) to prohibit or restrict access to the High Court; or

(*b*) to restrict the jurisdiction of that court; or

(*c*) to prohibit or restrict the making of a reasoned award.

(5) An exclusion agreement shall be of no effect in relation to an award made on, or a question of law arising in the course of a reference under, a statutory arbitration, that is to say, such an arbitration as is referred to in subsection (1) of section 31 of the principal Act.

(6) An exclusion agreement shall be of no effect in relation to an award made on, or a question of law arising in the course of a reference under, an arbitration agreement which is a domestic arbitration agreement unless the exclusion agreement is entered into after the commencement of the arbitration in which the award is made or, as the case may be, in which the question of law arises.

(7) In this section "domestic arbitration agreement" means an arbitration agreement which does not provide, expressly or by implication, for arbitration in a State other than the United Kingdom and to which neither—

(*a*) an individual who is a national of, or habitually resident in, any State other than the United Kingdom, nor

(*b*) a body corporate which is incorporated in, or whose central management and control is exercised in, any State other than the United Kingdom,

is a party at the time the arbitration agreement is entered into.

Exclusion agreements not to apply in certain cases

4.—(1) Subject to subsection (3) below, if an arbitration award or a question of law arising in the course of a reference relates, in whole or in part, to—

(*a*) a question or claim falling within the Admiralty jurisdiction of the High Court, or

(*b*) a dispute arising out of a contract of insurance, or

(*c*) a dispute arising out of a commodity contract,

an exclusion agreement shall have no effect in relation to the award or question unless either—

(i) the exclusion agreement is entered into after the commencement of the arbitration in which the award is made or, as the case may be, in which the question of law arises, or

(ii) the award or question relates to a contract which is expressed to be governed by a law other than the law of England and Wales.

(2) In subsection (1)(*c*) above "commodity contract" means a contract—

(*a*) for the sale of goods regularly dealt with on a commodity market or exchange in England or Wales which is specified for the purposes of this section by an order made by the Secretary of State; and

(*b*) of a description so specified.

(3) The Secretary of State may by order provide that subsection (1) above—

(*a*) shall cease to have effect; or

(*b*) subject to such conditions as may be specified in the order, shall not apply to any exclusion agreement made in relation to an arbitration award of a description so specified;

and an order under this subsection may contain such supplementary, incidental and transitional provisions as appear to the Secretary of State to be necessary or expedient.

(4) The power to make an order under subsection (2) or subsection (3) above shall be exercisable by statutory instrument which shall be subject to annulment in pursuance of a resolution of either House of Parliament.

(5) In this section "exclusion agreement" has the same meaning as in section 3 above.

Interlocutory orders

5.—(1) If any party to a reference under an arbitration agreement fails within the time specified in the order or, if no time is so specified, within a reasonable time to comply with an order made by the arbitrator or umpire in the course of the reference, then, on the application of the arbitrator or umpire or of any party to the reference, the High Court may make an order extending the powers of the arbitrator or umpire as mentioned in subsection (2) below.

(2) If an order is made by the High Court under this section, the arbitrator or umpire shall have power, to the extent and subject to any conditions specified in that order, to continue with the reference in default of appearance or of any other act by one of the parties in like manner as a judge of the High Court might continue with proceedings in that court where a party fails to comply with an order of that court or a requirement of rules of court.

(3) Section 4(5) of the Administration of Justice Act 1970 (jurisdiction of the High Court to be exercisable by the Court of Appeal in relation to judge-arbitrators and judge-umpires) shall not apply in relation to the power of the High Court to make an order under this section, but in the case of a reference to a judge-arbitrator or judge-umpire that power shall be exercisable as in the case of any other reference to arbitration and also by the judge-arbitrator or judge-umpire himself.

(4) Anything done by a judge-arbitrator or judge-umpire in the exercise of the power conferred by subsection (3) above shall be done by him in his capacity as judge of the High Court and have effect as if done by that court.

(5) The preceding provisions of this section have effect notwithstanding anything in any agreement but do not derogate from any powers conferred on an arbitrator or umpire, whether by an arbitration agreement or otherwise.

(6) In this section "judge-arbitrator" and "judge-umpire" have the same meaning as in Schedule 3 to the Administration of Justice Act 1970.

Minor amendments relating to awards and appointment of arbitrators and umpires

6.—(1) In subsection (1) of section 8 of the principal Act (agreements where reference is to two arbitrators deemed to include provision that the arbitrators shall appoint an umpire immediately after their own appointment)—

(*a*) for the words "shall appoint an umpire immediately" there shall be substituted the words "may appoint an umpire at any time"; and

(*b*) at the end there shall be added the words "and shall do so forthwith if they cannot agree".

(2) For section 9 of the principal Act (agreements for reference to three arbitrators) there shall be substituted the following section:—

"9. Unless the contrary intention is expressed in the arbitration agreement, in any case where there is a reference to three arbitrators, the award of any two of the arbitrators shall be binding."

(3) In section 10 of the principal Act (power of court in certain cases to appoint an arbitrator or umpire) in paragraph (*c*) after the word "are", in the first place where it occurs, there shall be inserted the words "required or are" and the words from "or where" to the end of the paragraph shall be omitted.

(4) At the end of section 10 of the principal Act there shall be added the following subsection:—

"(2) In any case where—

(*a*) an arbitration agreement provides for the appointment of an arbitrator or umpire by a person who is neither one of the parties nor an existing arbitrator (whether the provision applies directly or in default of agreement by the parties or otherwise), and

(*b*) that person refuses to make the appointment or does not make it within the time specified in the agreement or, if no time is so specified, within a reasonable time,

any party to the agreement may serve the person in question with a written notice to appoint an arbitrator or umpire and, if the appointment is not made within seven clear days after the service of the notice, the High Court or a judge thereof may, on the application of the party who gave the notice, appoint an arbitrator or umpire who shall have the like powers to act in the reference and make an award as if he had been appointed in accordance with the terms of the agreement."

Application and interpretation of certain provisions of Part I of principal Act

7.—(1) References in the following provisions of Part I of the principal Act to that Part of that Act shall have effect as if the preceding provisions of this Act were included in that Part, namely,—

(*a*) section 14 (interim awards);

(*b*) section 28 (terms as to costs of orders);

(*c*) section 30 (Crown to be bound);

(*d*) section 31 (application to statutory arbitrations); and

(*e*) section 32 (meaning of "arbitration agreement").

(2) Subsections (2) and (3) of section 29 of the principal Act shall apply to determine when an arbitration is deemed to be commenced for the purposes of this Act.

(3) For the avoidance of doubt, it is hereby declared that the reference in subsection (1) of section 31 of the principal Act (statutory arbitrations) to arbitration under any other Act does not extend to arbitration under section 92 of the County Courts Act 1959 (cases in which proceedings are to be or may be referred to arbitration) and accordingly nothing in this Act or in Part I of the principal Act applies to arbitration under the said section 92.

Short title, commencement, repeals and extent

8.—(1) This Act may be cited as the Arbitration Act 1979.

(2) This Act shall come into operation on such day as the Secretary of State may appoint by order made by statutory instrument; and such an order—

(*a*) may appoint different days for different provisions of this Act and for the purposes of the operation of the same provision in relation to different descriptions of arbitration agreement; and

(*b*) may contain such supplementary, incidental and transitional provisions as appear to the Secretary of State to be necessary or expedient.

(3) In consequence of the preceding provisions of this Act, the following provisions are hereby repealed, namely—

(*a*) in paragraph (*c*) of section 10 of the principal Act the words from "or where" to the end of the paragraph;

(*b*) section 21 of the principal Act;

(*c*) in paragraph 9 of Schedule 3 to the Administration of Justice Act 1970, in sub-paragraph (1) the words "21(1) and (2)" and sub-paragraph (2).

(4) This Act forms part of the law of England and Wales only.

Appendix D

UNITED STATES ARBITRATION ACT

§ 1. "Maritime transactions" and "commerce" defined; exceptions to operation of title

"Maritime transactions", as herein defined, means charter parties, bills of lading of water carriers, agreements relating to wharfage, supplies furnished vessels or repairs to vessels, collisions, or any other matters in foreign commerce which, if the subject of controversy, would be embraced within admiralty jurisdiction; "commerce", as herein defined, means commerce among the several States or with foreign nations, or in any Territory of the United States or in the District of Columbia, or between any such Territory and another, or between any such Territory and any State or foreign nation, or between the District of Columbia and any State or Territory or foreign nation, but nothing herein contained shall apply to contracts of employment of seamen, railroad employees, or any other class of workers engaged in foreign or interstate commerce.

§ 2. Validity, irrevocability, and enforcement of agreements to arbitrate

A written provision in any maritime transaction or a contract evidencing a transaction involving commerce to settle by arbitration a controversy thereafter arising out of such contract or transaction, or the refusal to perform the whole or any part thereof, or an agreement in writing to submit to arbitration an existing controversy arising out of such a contract, transaction, or refusal, shall be valid, irrevocable, and enforceable, save upon such grounds as exist at law or in equity for the revocation of any contract.

§ 3. Stay of proceedings where issue therein referable to arbitration

If any suit or proceeding be brought in any of the courts of the United States upon any issue referable to arbitration under an agreement in writing for such arbitration, the court in which such suit is pending, upon being satisfied that the issue involved in such suit or proceeding is referable to arbitration under such an agreement, shall on application of one of the parties stay the trial of the action until such arbitration has been had in accordance with the terms of the agreement, providing the applicant for the stay is not in default in proceeding with such arbitration.

§ 4. Failure to arbitrate under agreement; petition to United States court having jurisdiction for order to compel arbitration; notice and service thereof; hearing and determination

A party aggrieved by the alleged failure, neglect, or refusal of another to arbitrate under a written agreement for arbitration may petition any United States district court which, save for such agreement, would have jurisdiction under Title 28, in a civil action or in admiralty of the subject matter of a suit arising out of the controversy between the parties, for an order directing that such arbitration proceed in the manner provided for in such agreement. Five days' notice in writing of such application shall be served upon the party in default. Service thereof shall be made in the manner provided by the Federal Rules of Civil Procedure. The court shall hear the parties, and upon being satisfied that the making of the agreement for arbitration or the failure to comply therewith is not in issue, the court shall make an order directing the parties to proceed to arbitration in accordance with the terms of the agreement. The hearing and proceedings, under such agreement, shall be within the district in which the petition for an order directing such arbitration is filed. If the making of the arbitration agreement or the failure, neglect, or refusal to perform the same be in issue, the court shall proceed summarily to the trial thereof. If no jury trial be demanded by the party alleged to be in default, or if the matter in dispute is within admiralty jurisdiction, the court shall hear and determine such issue. Where such an issue is raised, the party alleged to be in default may, except in cases of admiralty, on or before the return day of the notice of application, demand a jury trial of such issue, and upon such demand the court shall make an order referring the issue or issues to a jury in the manner provided by the Federal Rules of Civil Procedure, or may specially call a jury for that purpose. If the jury find that no agreement in writing for arbitration was made or that there is no default in proceeding thereunder, the proceeding shall be dismissed. If the jury find that an agreement for arbitration was made in writing and that there is a default in proceeding thereunder, the court shall make an order summarily directing the parties to proceed with the arbitration in accordance with the terms thereof.

§ 5. Appointment of arbitrators or umpire

If in the agreement provision be made for a method of naming or appointing an arbitrator or arbitrators or an umpire, such method shall be followed; but if no method be provided therein, or if a method be provided and any party thereto shall fail to avail himself of such method, or if for any other reason there shall be a lapse in the naming of an arbitrator or arbitrators or umpire, or in filling a vacancy, then upon the application of either party to the controversy the court shall designate and appoint an arbitrator or arbitrators or umpire, as the case may require, who shall act under the said agreement with the same force and effect as if he or they had been specifically named therein; and unless otherwise provided in the agreement the arbitration shall be by a single arbitrator.

§ 6. Application heard as motion

Any application to the court hereunder shall be made and heard in the manner provided by law for the making and hearing of motions, except as otherwise herein expressly provided.

§ 7. Witnesses before arbitrators; fees; compelling attendance

The arbitrators selected either as prescribed in this title or otherwise, or a majority of them, may summon in writing any person to attend before them or any of them as a witness and in a proper case to bring with him or them any book, record, document, or paper which may be deemed material as evidence in the case. The fees for such attendance shall be the same as the fees of witnesses before masters of the United States courts. Said summons shall issue in the name of the arbitrator or arbitrators, or a majority of them, and shall be signed by the arbitrators, or a majority of them, and shall be directed to the said person and shall be served in the same manner as subpoenas to appear and testify before the court; if any person or persons so summoned to testify shall refuse or neglect to obey said summons, upon petition the United States district court for the district in which such arbitrators, or a majority of them, are sitting may compel the attendance of such person or persons before said arbitrator or arbitrators, or punish said person or persons for contempt in the same manner provided by law for securing the attendance of witnesses or their punishment for neglect or refusal to attend in the courts of the United States.

§ 8. Proceedings begun by libel in admiralty and seizure of vessel or property

If the basis of jurisdiction be a cause of action otherwise justiciable in admiralty, then, notwithstanding anything herein to the contrary, the party claiming to be aggrieved may begin his proceeding hereunder by libel and seizure of the vessel or other property of the other party according to the usual course of admiralty proceedings, and the court shall then have jurisdiction to direct the parties to proceed with the arbitration and shall retain jurisdiction to enter its decree upon the award.

§ 9. Award of arbitrators; confirmation; jurisdiction; procedure

If the parties in their agreement have agreed that a judgment of the court shall be entered upon the award made pursuant to the arbitration, and shall specify the court, then at any time within one year after the award is made any party to the arbitration may apply to the court so specified for an order confirming the award, and thereupon the court must grant such an order unless the award is vacated, modified, or corrected as prescribed in sections 10 and 11 of this title. If no court is specified in the agreement of the parties, then such application may be made to the United States court in and for the district within which such award was made. Notice of the application shall be served upon the adverse party, and thereupon the court shall have jurisdiction of such party as though he had appeared generally in the proceeding. If the adverse party is a resident of the district within which the award was made, such service shall be made upon the adverse party or his attorney as prescribed by law for service of notice of motion in an action in the same court. If the adverse party shall be a nonresident, then the notice of the application shall be served by the marshal of any district within which the adverse party may be found in like manner as other process of the court.

§ 10. Same; vacation; grounds; rehearing

In either of the following cases the United States court in and for the district wherein the award was made may make an order vacating the award upon the application of any party to the arbitration—

(a) Where the award was procured by corruption, fraud, or undue means.

(b) Where there was evident partiality or corruption in the arbitrators, or either of them.

(c) Where the arbitrators were guilty of misconduct in refusing to postpone the hearing, upon sufficient cause shown, or in refusing to hear evidence pertinent and material to the controversy; or of any other misbehavior by which the rights of any party have been prejudiced.

(d) Where the arbitrators exceeded their powers, or so imperfectly executed them that a mutual, final, and definite award upon the subject matter submitted was not made.

(e) Where an award is vacated and the time within which the agreement required the award to be made has not expired the court may, in its discretion, direct a rehearing by the arbitrators.

§ 11. Same; modification or correction; grounds; order

In either of the following cases the United States court in and for the district wherein the award was made may make an order modifying or correcting the award upon the application of any party to the arbitration—

(a) Where there was an evident material miscalculation of figures or an evident material mistake in the description of any person, thing, or property referred to in the award.

(b) Where the arbitrators have awarded upon a matter not submitted to them, unless it is a matter not affecting the merits of the decision upon the matter submitted.

(c) Where the award is imperfect in matter of form not affecting the merits of the controversy.

The order may modify and correct the award, so as to effect the intent thereof and promote justice between the parties.

§ 12. Notice of motions to vacate or modify; service; stay of proceedings

Notice of a motion to vacate, modify, or correct an award must be served upon the adverse party or his attorney within three months after the award is filed or delivered. If the adverse party is a resident of the district within which the award was made, such service shall be made upon the adverse party or his attorney as prescribed by law for service of notice of motion in an action in the same court. If the adverse party shall be a nonresident then the notice of the application shall be served by the marshal of any district within which the adverse party may be found in like manner as other process of the court. For the purposes of the motion any judge who might make an order to stay the proceedings in an action brought in the same court may make an order, to be served with the notice of motion, staying the proceedings of the adverse party to enforce the award.

§ 13. Papers filed with order on motions; judgment; docketing; force and effect; enforcement

The party moving for an order confirming, modifying, or correcting an award shall, at the time such order is filed with the clerk for the entry of judgment thereon, also file the following papers with the clerk:

(a) The agreement; the selection or appointment, if any, of an additional arbitrator or umpire; and each written extension of the time, if any, within which to make the award.

(b) The award.

(c) Each notice, affidavit, or other paper used upon an application to confirm, modify, or correct the award, and a copy of each order of the court upon such an application.

The judgment shall be docketed as if it was rendered in an action.

The judgment so entered shall have the same force and effect, in all respects, as, and be subject to all the provisions of law relating to, a judgment in an action; and it may be enforced as if it had been rendered in an action in the court in which it is entered.

§ 14. Contracts not affected

[Not material]

§ 15. [1]Inapplicability of the Act of State doctrine

Enforcement of arbitral agreements, confirmation of arbitral awards, and execution upon judgments based on orders confirming such awards shall not be refused on the basis of the Act of State doctrine.

(Added Pub.L. 100–669, § 1, Nov. 16, 1988, 102 Stat. 3969.)

[1] So in original. See Codification note below.

Codification. Another section 15 was enacted by Pub.L. 100–702, Title X, § 1019(a), Nov. 19, 1988, 102 Stat. 4670, set out post.

§ 15. [1]Appeals

(a) An appeal may be taken from—

(1) an order—

(A) refusing a stay of any action under section 3 of this title,

(B) denying a petition under section 4 of this title to order arbitration to proceed,

(C) denying an application under section 206 of this title to compel arbitration,

(D) confirming or denying confirmation of an award or partial award, or

(E) modifying, correcting, or vacating an award;

(2) an interlocutory order granting, continuing, or modifying an injunction against an arbitration that is subject to this title; or

(3) a final decision with respect to an arbitration that is subject to this title.

(b) Except as otherwise provided in section 1292(b) of title 28, an appeal may not be taken from an interlocutory order—

(1) granting a stay of any action under section 3 of this title;

(2) directing arbitration to proceed under section 4 of this title;

(3) compelling arbitration under section 206 of this title; or

(4) refusing to enjoin an arbitration that is subject to this title.

(Added Pub.L. 100–702, Title X, § 1019(a), Nov. 19, 1988, 102 Stat. 4671.)

[1] So in original. See Codification note below.

Codification. Another section 15 was enacted by Pub.L. 100–669, § 1, Nov. 16, 1988, 102 Stat. 3969, and is set out ante.

Legislative History. For legislative history and purpose of Pub.L. 100–702, see 1988 U.S.Code Cong. and Adm. News, p. 5982.

CHAPTER 2—CONVENTION ON THE RECOGNITION AND ENFORCEMENT OF FOREIGN ARBITRAL AWARDS

§ 201. Enforcement of Convention

The Convention on the Recognition and Enforcement of Foreign Arbitral Awards of June 10, 1958, shall be enforced in United States courts in accordance with this chapter.

§ 202. Agreement or award falling under the Convention

An arbitration agreement or arbitral award arising out of a legal relationship, whether contractual or not, which is considered as commercial, including a transaction, contract, or agreement described in section 2 of this title, falls under the Convention. An agreement or award arising out of such a relationship which is entirely between citizens of the United States shall be deemed not to fall under the Convention unless that relationship involves property located abroad, envisages performance or enforcement abroad, or has some other reasonable relation with one or more foreign states. For the purpose of this section a corporation is a citizen of the United States if it is incorporated or has its principal place of business in the United States.

§ 203. Jurisdiction; amount in controversy

An action or proceeding falling under the Convention shall be deemed to arise under the laws and treaties of the United States. The district courts of the United States (including the courts enumerated in section 460 of title 28) shall have original jurisdiction over such an action or proceeding, regardless of the amount in controversy.

§ 204. Venue

An action or proceeding over which the district courts have jurisdiction pursuant to section 203 of this title may be brought in any such court in which save for the arbitration agreement an action or proceeding with respect to the controversy between the parties could be brought, or in such court for the district and division which embraces the place designated in the agreement as the place of arbitration if such place is within the United States.

§ 205. Removal of cases from State courts

Where the subject matter of an action or proceeding pending in a State court relates to an arbitration agreement or award falling under the Convention, the defendant or the defendants may, at any time before the trial thereof, remove such action or proceeding to the district court of the United States for the district and division embracing the place where the action or proceeding is pending. The procedure for removal of causes otherwise provided by law shall apply, except that the ground for removal provided in this section need not appear on the face of the complaint but may be shown in the petition for removal. For the purposes of Chapter 1 of this title any action or proceeding removed under this section shall be deemed to have been brought in the district court to which it is removed.

§ 206. Order to compel arbitration; appointment of arbitrators

A court having jurisdiction under this chapter may direct that arbitration be held in accordance with the agreement at any place therein provided for, whether that place is within or without the United States. Such court may also appoint arbitrators in accordance with the provisions of the agreement.

§ 207. Award of arbitrators; confirmation; jurisdiction; proceeding

Within three years after an arbitral award falling under the Convention is made, any party to the arbitration may apply to any court having jurisdiction under this chapter for an order confirming the award as against any other party to the arbitration. The court shall confirm the award unless it finds one of the grounds for refusal or deferral of recognition or enforcement of the award specified in the said Convention.

§ 208. Chapter 1; residual application

Chapter 1 applies to actions and proceedings brought under this chapter to the extent that chapter is not in conflict with this chapter or the Convention as ratified by the United States.

Convention on the Recognition and Enforcement of Foreign Arbitral Awards

Article I

1. This Convention shall apply to the recognition and enforcement of arbitral awards made in the territory of a State other than the State where the recognition and enforcement of such awards are sought, and arising out of differences between persons, whether physical or legal. It shall also apply to arbitral awards not considered as domestic awards in the State where their recognition and enforcement are sought.
2. The term "arbitral awards" shall include not only awards made by arbitrators appointed for each case but also those made by permanent arbitral bodies to which the parties have submitted.
3. When signing, ratifying or acceding to this Convention, or notifying extension under article X hereof, any State may on the basis of reciprocity declare that it will apply the Convention to the recognition and enforcement of awards made only in the territory of another Contracting State. It may also declare that it will apply the Convention only to differences arising out of legal relationships, whether contractual or not, which are considered as commercial under the national law of the State making such declaration.

Article II

1. Each Contracting State shall recognize an agreement in writing under which the parties undertake to submit to arbitration all or any differences which have arisen or which may arise between them in respect of a defined legal relationship, whether contractual or not, concerning a subject matter capable of settlement by arbitration.
2. The term "agreement in writing" shall include an arbitral clause in a contract or an arbitration agreement, signed by the parties or contained in an exchange of letters or telegrams.
3. The court of a Contracting State, when seized of an action in a matter in respect of which the parties have made an agreement within the meaning of this article, shall, at the request of one of the parties, refer the parties to arbitration, unless it finds that the said agreement is null and void, inoperative or incapable of being performed.

Article III

Each Contracting State shall recognize arbitral awards as binding and enforce them in accordance with the rules of procedure of the territory where the award is relied upon, under the conditions laid down in the following articles. There shall not be imposed substantially more onerous conditions or higher fees or charges on the recognition or enforcement of arbitral awards to which this Convention applies than are imposed on the recognition or enforcement of domestic arbitral awards.

Article IV

1. To obtain the recognition and enforcement mentioned in the preceding article, the party applying for recognition and enforcement shall, at the time of the application, supply:

(a) The duly authenticated original award or a duly certified copy thereof;

(b) The original agreement referred to in article II or a duly certified copy thereof.

2. If the said award or agreement is not made in an official language of the country in which the award is relied upon, the party applying for recognition and enforcement of the award shall produce a translation of these documents into such language. The translation shall be certified by an official or sworn translator or by a diplomatic or consular agent.

Article V

1. Recognition and enforcement of the award may be refused, at the request of the party against whom it is invoked, only if that party furnishes to the competent authority where the recognition and enforcement is sought, proof that:

(a) The parties to the agreement referred to in article II were, under the law applicable to them, under some incapacity, or the said agreement is not valid under the law to which the parties have subjected it or, failing any indication thereon, under the law of the country where the award was made; or

(b) The party against whom the award is invoked was not given proper notice of the appointment of the arbitrator or of the arbitration proceedings or was otherwise unable to present his case; or

(c) The award deals with a difference not contemplated by or not falling within the terms of the submission to arbitration, or it contains decisions on matters beyond the scope of the submission to arbitration, provided that, if the decisions on matters submitted to arbitration can be separated from those not so submitted, that part of the award which contains decisions on matters submitted to arbitration may be recognized and enforced; or

(d) The composition of the arbitral authority or the arbitral procedure was not in accordance with the agreement of the parties, or, failing such agreement, was not in accordance with the law of the country where the arbitration took place; or

(e) The award has not yet become binding on the parties, or has been set aside or suspended by a competent authority of the country in which, or under the law of which, that award was made.

2. Recognition and enforcement of an arbitral award may also be refused if the competent authority of the country where recognition and enforcement is sought finds that:

(a) The subject matter of the difference is not capable of settlement by arbitration under the law of that country; or

(b) The recognition or enforcement of the award would be contrary to the public policy of that country.

Article VI

If an application for the setting aside or suspension of the award has been made to a competent authority referred to in article V(1)(e), the authority before which the award is sought to be relied upon may, if it considers it proper, adjourn the decision on the enforcement of the award and may also, on the application of the party claiming enforcement of the award, order the other party to give suitable security.

Article VII

1. The provisions of the present Convention shall not affect the validity of multilateral or bilateral agreements concerning the recognition and enforcement of arbitral awards entered into by the Contracting States nor deprive any interested party of any right he may have to avail himself of

an arbitral award in the manner and to the extent allowed by the law or the treaties of the country where such award is sought to be relied upon.

2. The Geneva Protocol on Arbitration Clauses of 1923 and the Geneva Convention on the Execution of Foreign Arbitral Awards of 1927 [27 LNTS 157; 92 LNTS 301] shall cease to have effect between Contracting States on their becoming bound and to the extent that they become bound, by this Convention.

Article VIII

1. This Convention shall be open until 31 December 1958 for signature on behalf of any Member of the United Nations and also on behalf of any other State which is or hereafter becomes a member of any specialized agency of the United Nations, or which is or hereafter becomes a party to the Statute of the International Court of Justice [T.S. 993; 59 Stat. 1055], or any other State to which an invitation has been addressed by the General Assembly of the United Nations.

2. This Convention shall be ratified and the instrument of ratification shall be deposited with the Secretary-General of the United Nations.

Article IX

1. This Convention shall be open for accession to all States referred to in article VIII.

2. Accession shall be effected by the deposit of an instrument of accession with the Secretary-General of the United Nations.

Article X

1. Any State may, at the time of signature, ratification or accession, declare that this Convention shall extend to all or any of the territories for the international relations of which it is responsible. Such a declaration shall take effect when the Convention enters into force for the State concerned.

2. At any time thereafter any such extension shall be made by notification addressed to the Secretary-General of the United Nations and shall take effect as from the ninetieth day after the day of receipt by the Secretary-General of the United Nations of this notification, or as from the date of entry into force of the Convention for the State concerned, whichever is the later.

3. With respect to those territories to which this Convention is not extended at the time of signature, ratification or accession, each State concerned shall consider the possibility of taking the necessary steps in order to extend the application of this Convention to such territories, subject, where necessary for consitutional reasons, to the consent of the Governments of such territories.

Article XI

In the case of a federal or non-unitary State, the following provisions shall apply:

(a) With respect to those articles of this Convention that come within the legislative jurisdiction of the federal authority, the obligations of the federal Government shall to this extent be the same as those of Contracting States which are not federal States;

(b) With respect to those articles of this Convention that come within the legislative jurisdiction of constituent States or provinces which are not, under the constitutional system of the federation, bound to take legislative action, the federal Government shall bring such articles with a favourable recommendation to the notice of the appropriate authorities of constituent States or provinces at the earliest possible moment;

(c) A federal State Party to this Convention shall, at the request of any other Contracting State transmitted through the Secretary-General of the United Nations, supply a statement of the law and practice of the federation and its constituent units in regard to any particular provision of this Convention, showing the extent to which effect has been given to that provision by legislative or other action.

Article XII

1. This Convention shall come into force on the ninetieth day following the date of deposit of the third instrument of ratification or accession.

2. For each State ratifying or acceding to this Convention after the deposit of the third instrument of ratification or accession, this Convention shall enter into force on the ninetieth day after deposit by such State of its instrument of ratification or accession.

Article XIII

1. Any Contracting State may denounce this Convention by a written notification to the Secretary-General of the United Nations. Denunciation shall take effect one year after the date of receipt of the notification by the Secretary-General.

2. Any State which has made a declaration or notification under article X may, at any time thereafter, by notification to the Secretary-General of the United Nations, declare that this Convention shall cease to extend to the territory concerned one year after the date of the receipt of the notification by the Secretary-General.

3. This Convention shall continue to be applicable to arbitral awards in respect of which recognition or enforcement proceedings have been instituted before the denunciation takes effect.

Article XIV

A Contracting State shall not be entitled to avail itself of the present Convention against other Contracting States except to the extent that it is itself bound to apply the Convention.

Article XV

The Secretary-General of the United Nations shall notify the States contemplated in article VIII of the following:

(a) Signatures and ratifications in accordance with article VIII;
(b) Accessions in accordance with article IX;
(c) Declarations and notifications under articles I, X and XI;
(d) The date upon which this Convention enters into force in accordance with article XII;
(e) Denunciations and notifications in accordance with article XIII.

Article XVI

1. This Convention, of which the Chinese, English, French, Russian and Spanish texts shall be equally authentic, shall be deposited in the archives of the United Nations.

2. The Secretary-General of the United Nations shall transmit a certified copy of this Convention to the States contemplated in article VIII.

Done at New York June 10, 1958.

Appendix E

ASBATIME

1981 Revision of New York Produce Exchange Form (Code name: Asbatime)

November 6th, 1913—Amended October 20th, 1921; August 6th, 1931; October 3rd, 1946; June 12th, 1981.

THIS CHARTER PARTY, made and concluded in ...... day of ...... 19......

Owners

between ...... Owners of the good ...... Steamship/Motorship ......

Description of Vessel

of ...... of ...... tons gross register, and ...... tons net register, having engines of ...... horsepower and with hull, machinery and equipment in a throughly efficient state, and classed ...... of about ...... cubic feet grain/bale capacity ......, and about ...... long/metric tons deadweight capacity (cargo and bunkers, including fresh water and stores not exceeding ...... long/metric tons) on a salt water draft of ...... no summer freeboard, inclusive of permanent bunkers, which are of the capacity of about ...... long/metric tons of ...... fuel oil and ...... long/metric tons of ......, and capable of steaming, fully laden, under good weather conditions about ...... knots on a consumption of about ...... long/metric tons of ...... now ...... and

Charterers

...... Charterers of the City of ......

Duration

The Owners agree to let and the Charterers agree to hire the vessel from the time of delivery for about ...... within below mentioned trading limits.

Sublet

Charterers shall have liberty to sublet the vessel for all or any part of the time covered by this Charter, but Charterers shall remain responsible for the fulfillment of this Charter.

Delivery

Vessel shall be placed at the disposal of the Charterers ...... in such dock or at such berth or place (where she may safely lie, always afloat, at all times of tide, except as otherwise provided in Clause 6) as the Charterers may direct. If such dock, berth or place be not available, time shall count as provided in Clause 5. Vessel on her delivery shall be ready to receive cargo with clean-swept holds and tight, staunch, strong and in every way fitted for ordinary cargo service, having water ballast and with sufficient power to operate all cargo-handling gear simultaneously (and with full complement of officers and crew for a vessel of her tonnage), to be employed in carrying lawful merchan-

Dangerous Cargo

Cargo Exclusions

dise excluding any goods of a dangerous, injurious, flammable or corrosive nature unless carried in accordance with the requirements or recommendations of the proper authorities of the state of the vessel's registry and of the states of ports of shipment and discharge and of any intermediate states or ports through whose waters the vessel must pass. Without prejudice to the generality of the foregoing, in addition the following are specifically excluded: livestock of any description, arms, ammunition, explosives ....

Trading Limits

The vessel shall be employed in such lawful trades between safe ports and places within .... excluding ....

as the Charterers or their agents shall direct, on the following conditions:

Owners to Provide

1. The Owners shall provide and pay for the insurance of the vessel and for all provisions, cabin, deck, engine-room and other necessary stores, including boiler water; shall pay for wages, consular shipping and discharging fees of the crew and charges for port services pertaining to the crew; shall maintain vessel's class and keep her in a thoroughly efficient state in hull, machinery and equipment for and during the service.

Charterers to Provide

2. The Charterers, while the vessel is on hire, shall provide and pay for all the fuel except as otherwise agreed, port charges, pilotages, towages, agencies, commissions, consular charges (except those pertaining to individual crew members or flag of the vessel), and all other usual expenses except those stated in Clause 1, but when the vessel puts into a port for causes for which vessel is responsible, then all such charges incurred shall be paid by the Owners. Fumigations ordered because of illness of the crew shall be for Owners' account. Fumigations ordered because of cargoes carried or ports visited while vessel is employed under this Charter shall be for Charterers' account. All other fumigations shall be for Charterers' account after vessel has been on charter for a continuous period of six months or more.

Charterers shall provide necessary dunnage and shifting boards, also any extra fittings requisite for a special trade or unusual cargo, but Owners shall allow them the use of any dunnage and shifting boards already aboard vessel.

Bunkers on Delivery and Redelivery

3. The Charterers on delivery, and the Owners on redelivery, shall take over and pay for all fuel and diesel oil remaining on board the vessel as hereunder. The vessel shall be delivered with: .... long/metric* tons of fuel oil at the price of .... per ton; .... tons of diesel oil at the price of .... per ton. The vessel shall be redelivered with: .... tons of fuel oil at the price of .... per ton; .... tons of diesel oil at the price of .... per ton ....

(*Same tons apply throughout this clause)

Rate of Hire

Redelivery Areas and Notices

4. The Charterers shall pay for the use and hire of the said vessel at the rate of .... daily, or .... United States Currency per ton on vessel's total deadweight carrying capacity, including bunkers and stores, on .... summer freeboard, per calendar month, commencing on and from the day of her delivery, as aforesaid, and at and after the same rate for any part of a month; hire shall continue until the hour of the day of her redelivery in like good order and condition, ordinary wear and tear excepted, to the Owners (unless vessel lost) at .... unless otherwise mutually agreed. Charterers shall give Owners not less than .... days notice of vessel's expected date of redelivery and probable port ....

Hire Payment and Commencement

5. Payment of hire shall be made so as to be received by Owners or their designated payee in New York, i.e. .... in United States Currency, in funds available to the Owners on the due date, semi-monthly in advance, and for the last half month or part of same the approximate amount of hire, and should same not cover the actual time, hire shall be paid for the balance day by day as it becomes due, if so required by Owners. Failing the punctual and regular payment of the hire, or on any breach of this Charter, the Owners shall be at liberty to withdraw the vessel from the service of the Charterers without prejudice to any claims they (the Owners) may otherwise have on the Charterers.

Time shall count from 7 A.M. on the working day following that on which written notice of readiness has been given to Charterers or their agents before 4 P.M., but if required by Charterers, they shall have the privilege of using vessel at once, in which case the vessel will be on hire from the commencement of work.

Cash Advances

Cash for vessel's ordinary disbursements at any port may be advanced, as required by the Captain, by the Charterers or their agents, subject to $2\frac{1}{2}$ percent commission and such advances shall be deducted from the hire. The Charterers, however, shall in no way be responsible for the application of such advances.

Berths

6. Vessel shall be loaded and discharged in any dock or at any berth or place that Charterers or their agents may direct, provided the vessel can safely lie always afloat at any time of tide, except at such places where it is customary for similar size vessels to safely lie aground.

Spaces Available

7. The whole reach of the vessel's holds, decks, and usual places of loading (not more than she can reasonably and safely stow and carry), also accommodations for supercargo, if carried, shall be at the Charterers' disposal, reserving only proper and sufficient space for ship's officers, crew, tackle, apparel, furniture, provisions, stores and fuel.

Prosecution of Voyages

8. The Captain shall prosecute his voyages with due despatch, and shall render all customary assistance with ship's crew and boats. The Captain (although appointed by the Owners) shall be under the orders and directions of the Charterers as regards employment and agency; and Charterers are to perform all cargo handling at their expense under the supervision of the Captain, who is to sign the bills of lading for cargo as presented in conformity with mate's or tally clerk's receipts. However, at Charterers' option, the Charterers or their agents may sign bills of lading on behalf of the Captain always in conformity with mate's or tally clerk's receipts.

Bills of Lading

All bills of lading shall be without prejudice to this Charter and the Charterers shall indemnify the Owners against all consequences or liabilities which may arise from any inconsistency between this Charter and any bills of lading or waybills signed by the Charterers or their agents or by the Captain at their request.

Conduct of Captain

9. If the Charterers shall have reason to be dissatisfied with the conduct of the Captain or officers, the Owners shall, on receiving particulars of the complaint, investigate the same, and, if necessary, make a change in the appointments.

Supercargo and Meals

10. The Charterers are entitled to appoint a supercargo, who shall accompany the vessel and see that voyages are prosecuted with due despatch. He is to be furnished with free accommodation and same fare as provided for Captain's table, Charterers paying at the rate of .... per day. Owners shall victual pilots and customs officers, and also, when authorized by Charterers or their agents, shall victual tally clerks, stevedore's foreman, etc., Charterers paying at the rate of .... per meal for all such victualling.

Sailing Orders and Logs

11. The Charterers shall furnish the Captain from time to time with all requisite instructions and sailing directions, in writing, and the Captain shall keep full and correct deck and engine logs of the voyage or voyages, which are to be patent to the Charterers or their agents, and furnish the Charterers, their agents or supercargo, when required, with a true copy of such deck and engine logs, showing the course of the vessel, distance run and the consumption of fuel.

Ventilation

12. The Captain shall use diligence in caring for the ventilation of the cargo.

Continuation

13. The Charterers shall have the option of continuing this Charter for a further period of ....

Laydays/ Cancelling

14. If required by Charterers, time shall not commence before .... and should vessel not have given written notice of readiness on or before .... but not later than 4 P.M. Charterers or their agents shall have the option of cancelling this Charter at any time not later than the day of vessel's readiness.

Off Hire

15. In the event of the loss of time from deficiency and/or default of officers or crew or deficiency of stores, fire, breakdown of, or damages to, hull, machinery or equipment, grounding, detention by average accidents to ship or cargo unless resulting from inherent vice, quality or defect of the cargo, drydocking for the purpose of examination or painting bottom, or by any other similar cause preventing the full working of the vessel, the payment of hire and overtime, if any, shall cease for the time thereby lost. Should the vessel deviate or put back during a voyage, contrary to the orders or directions of the Charterers, for any reason other than accident to the cargo, the hire is to be suspended from the time of her deviating or putting back until she is again in the same or equidistant position from the destination and the voyage resumed therefrom. All fuel used by the vessel while off hire shall be for Owners' account. In the event of the vessel being driven into port or to anchorage through stress of weather, trading to shallow harbors or to rivers or ports with bars, any detention of the vessel and/or expenses resulting from such detention shall be for the Charterers' account. If upon the voyage the speed be reduced by defect in, or breakdown of, any part of her hull, machinery or equipment, the time so lost, and the cost of any extra fuel consumed in consequence thereof, and all extra expenses shall be deducted from the hire.

Total Loss

16. Should the vessel be lost, money paid in advance and not earned (reckoning from the date of loss or being last heard of) shall be returned to the Charterers at once.

Exceptions

The act of God, enemies, fire, restraint of princes, rulers and people, and all dangers and accidents of the seas, rivers, machinery, boilers and steam navigation, and errors of navigation throughout this Charter, always mutually excepted.

Liberties

The vessel shall have the liberty to sail with or without pilots, to tow and to be towed, to assist vessels in distress, and to deviate for the purpose of saving life and property.

Arbitration

17. Should any dispute arise between Owners and the Charterers, the matter in dispute shall be referred to three persons at New York, one to be appointed by each of the parties hereto, and the third by the two so chosen; their decision, or that of any two of them, shall be final and for the purpose of enforcing any award this agreement may be made a rule of the Court. The arbitrators shall be commercial men conversant with shipping matters.

Liens

18. The Owners shall have a lien upon all cargoes and all sub-freights for any amounts due under this Charter, including general average contributions, and the Charterers shall have a lien on the ship for all monies paid in advance and not earned, and any overpaid hire or excess deposit to be returned at once. Charterers will not suffer, nor permit to be continued, any lien or encumbrance incurred by them or their agents, which might have priority over the title and interest of the Owners in the vessel.

Salvage

19. All derelicts and salvage shall be for Owners' and Charterers' equal benefit after deducting Owners' and Charterers' expenses and crew's proportion.

General Average

General average shall be adjusted, according to York-Antwerp Rules 1974, at such port or place in the United States as may be selected by the Owners and as to matters not provided for by these Rules, according to the laws and usage at the port of New York. In such adjustment disbursements in foreign currencies shall be exchanged into United States money at the rate prevailing on the dates made and allowances for damage to cargo claimed in foreign currency shall be converted at the rate prevailing on the last day of discharge at the port or place of final discharge of such damaged cargo from the ship. Average agreement or bond and such additional security, as may be required by the Owners, must be furnished before delivery of the goods. Such cash deposit as the Owners or their agents may deem sufficient as additional security for the contribution of the goods and for any salvage and special charges thereon, shall, if required, be made by the goods, shippers, consignees or owners of the goods to the Owners before delivery. Such deposit shall, at the option of the Owners, be payable in United States money and remitted to the adjuster. When so remitted the deposit shall be held in a special account at the place of adjustment in the name of the adjuster pending settlement of the general average and refunds or credit balances, if any, shall be paid in United States money.

York-Antwerp Rules

Charterers shall procure that all bills of lading issued during the currency of the Charter will contain a provision to the effect that general average shall be adjusted according to York-Antwerp Rules 1974 and will include the "New Jason Clause" as per Clause 23.

Drydocking

20. The vessel was last drydocked .... The Owners shall have the option to place the vessel in drydock during the currency of this Charter at a convenient time and place, to be mutually agreed upon between Owners and Charterers, for bottom cleaning and painting and/or repair as required by class or dictated by circumstances. Payment of hire shall be suspended upon deviation from Charterers' service until vessel is again placed at Charterers' disposal at a point not less favorable to Charterers than when the hire was suspended. ....

....

....

Cargo Gear

21. Owners shall maintain the cargo-handling gear of the ship which is as follows: ....

....

....

providing gear (for all derricks or cranes) capable of lifting capacity as described. Owners shall also provide on the vessel for night work lights as on board, but all additional lights over those on board shall be at Charterers' expense. The Charterers shall have the use of any gear on board the vessel. If required by Charterers, the vessel shall work night and day and all cargo-handling gear shall be at Charterers' disposal during loading and discharging.

Stevedore Stand-by

In the event of disabled cargo-handling gear, or insufficient power to operate the same, the vessel is to be considered to be off hire to the extent that time is actually lost to the Charterers and Owners to pay stevedore stand-by charges occasioned thereby. If required by the Charterers, the Owners are to bear the cost of hiring shore gear in lieu thereof.

Crew Overtime

22. In lieu of any overtime payments to officers and crew for work ordered by Charterers or their agents, Charterers shall pay Owners $.................... per month or pro rata.

Clauses Paramount

23. The following clause is to be included in all bills of lading issued hereunder:

This bill of lading shall have effect subject to the provisions of the Carriage of Goods by Sea Act of the United States, the Hague Rules, or the Hague-Visby Rules, as applicable, or such other similar national legislation as may mandatorily apply by virtue of origin or destination of the bills of lading, which shall be deemed to be incorporated herein and nothing herein contained shall be deemed a surrender by the carrier of any of its rights or immunities or an increase of any of its responsibilities or liabilities under said applicable Act. If any term of this bill of lading be repugnant to said applicable Act to any extent, such term shall be void to that extent, but no further.

This Charter is subject to the following clauses all of which are to be included in all bills of lading issued hereunder:

New Both-to-Blame Collision Clause

If the ship comes into collision with another ship as a result of the negligence of the other ship and any act, neglect or default of the master, mariner, pilot or the servants of the carrier in the navigation or in the management of the ship, the owners of the goods carried hereunder will indemnify the carrier against all loss or liability to the other or non-carrying ship or her owners insofar as such loss or liability represents loss of, or damage to, or any claim whatsoever of the owners of said goods, paid or payable by the other or non-carrying ship or her owners to the owners of said goods and set off recouped or recovered by the other or non-carrying ship or her owners as part of their claim against the carrying ship or carrier.

The foregoing provisions shall also apply where the owners, operators or those in charge of any ships or objects other than, or in addition to, the colliding ships or objects are at fault in respect to a collision or contact.

New Jason Clause

In the event of accident, danger, damage or disaster before or after commencement of the voyage resulting from any cause whatsoever, whether due to negligence or not, for which, or for the consequences of which, the carrier is not responsible, by statute, contract, or otherwise, the goods, shippers, consignees, or owners of the goods shall contribute with the carrier in general average to the payment of any sacrifices, losses, or expenses of a general average nature that may be made or incurred, and shall pay salvage and special charges incurred in respect of the goods.

If a salving ship is owned or operated by the carrier, salvage shall be paid for as fully as if salving ship or ships belonged to strangers. Such deposit as the carrier or his agents may deem sufficient to cover the estimated contribution of the goods and any salvage and special charges thereon shall, if required, be made by the goods, shippers, consignees or owners of the goods to the carrier before delivery.

War Clauses

(a) No contraband of war shall be shipped. Vessel shall not be required, without the consent of Owners, which shall not be unreasonably withheld, to enter any port or zone which is involved in a state of war, warlike operations, or hostilities, civil strife, insurrection or piracy whether there be a declaration of war or not, where vessel, cargo or crew might reasonably be expected to be subject to capture, seizure or arrest, or to a hostile act by a belligerent power (the term "power" meaning any de jure or de facto authority or any purported governmental organization maintaining naval, military or air forces).

(b) If such consent is given by Owners, Charterers will pay the provable additional cost of insuring vessel against hull war risks in an amount equal to the value under her ordinary hull policy but not exceeding a valuation of .... In addition, Owners may purchase and Charterers will pay for war risk insurance on ancillary risks such as loss of hire, freight disbursements, total loss, blocking and trapping, etc. If such insurance is not obtainable commercially or through a government program, vessel shall not be required to enter or remain at any such port or zone.

(c) In the event of the existence of the conditions described in (a) subsequent to the date of this Charter, or while vessel is on hire under this Charter, Charterers shall, in respect of voyages to any such port or zone assume the provable additional cost of wages and insurance properly incurred in connection with master, officers and crew as a consequence of such war, warlike operations or hostilities.

Ice

24. The vessel shall not be required to enter or remain in any icebound port or area, nor any port or area where lights or lightships have been or are about to be withdrawn by reason of ice, nor where there is risk that in the ordinary course of things the vessel will not be able on account of ice to safely enter and remain in the port or area or to get out after having completed loading or discharging.

Navigation

25. Nothing herein stated is to be construed as a demise of the vessel to the Time Charterers. The Owners shall remain responsible for the navigation of the vessel, acts of pilots and tug boats, insurance, crew, and all other similar matters, same as when trading for their own account.

Commissions

26. A commission of .... per cent is payable by the vessel and Owners to .... on hire earned and paid under this Charter, and also upon any continuation or extension of this Charter.

Address

27. An address commission of .... percent is payable to .... on hire earned and paid under this Charter.

Rider

Rider Clauses .... as attached hereto are incorporated in this Charter.

Rider of Suggested Additional Clauses

(None of these Clauses apply unless expressly agreed during the negotiations and enumerated in line 362)

Extension of Cancelling

28. If it clearly appears that, despite the exercise of due diligence by Owners, the vessel will not be ready for delivery by the cancelling date, and provided Owners are able to state with reasonable certainty the date on which

the vessel will be ready, they may, at the earliest seven days before the vessel is expected to sail for the port or place of delivery, require Charterers to declare whether or not they will cancel the Charter. Should Charterers elect not to cancel, or should they fail to reply within seven days or by the cancelling date, whichever shall first occur, then the seventh day after the expected date of readiness for delivery as notified by Owners shall replace the original cancelling date. Should the vessel be further delayed, Owners shall be entitled to require further declarations of Charterers in accordance with this Clause.

Grace Period

29. Where there is failure to make "punctual and regular payment" of hire, Charterers shall be given by Owners two clear banking days (as recognized at the agreed place of payment) written notice to rectify the failure, and when so rectified within those two days following Owners' notice, the payment shall stand as regular and punctual. Payment received by Owners' bank after the original due date will bear interest at the rate of 0.1 percent per day which shall be payable immediately by Charterers in addition to hire.

At any time while hire is outstanding the Owners shall be absolutely entitled to withhold the performance of any and all of their obligations hereunder and shall have no responsibility whatsoever for any consequences thereof in respect of which the Charterers hereby indemnify the Owners and hire shall continue to accrue and any extra expenses resulting from such withholding shall be for the Charterers' account.

Cargo Claims

30. Damage to and claims on cargo shall be for Owners' account if caused by unseaworthiness of the vessel, but shall be for Charterers' account if caused by handling and stowage, including slackage. Claims for shortage ex ship shall be shared equally between Owners and Charterers.

War Cancellation

31. In the event of the outbreak of war (whether there be a declaration of war or not) between any two or more of the following countries: The United States of America, the United Kingdom, France, the Union of Soviet Socialist Republics, the People's Republic of China, ……

……

……

or in the event of the nation under whose flag the vessel sails becoming involved in war (whether there be a declaration of war or not), either the Owners or the Charterers may cancel this Charter. Whereupon the Charterers shall redeliver the vessel to the Owners in accordance with Clause 4; if she has cargo on board, after discharge thereof at destination, or, if debarred under this Clause from reaching or entering it, at a near open and safe port as directed by the Owners; or, if she has no cargo on board, at the port at which she then is; or, if at sea, at a near open and safe port as directed by the Owners. In all cases hire shall continue to be paid in accordance with Clause 4 and except as aforesaid all other provisions of this Charter shall apply until redelivery.

War Bonus

32. Any war bonus to officers and crew due to vessel's trading or cargo carried shall be for Charterers' account.

Requisition

33. Should the vessel be requisitioned by the government of the vessel's flag during the period of this Charter, the vessel shall be deemed to be off hire during the period of such requisition, and any hire paid by the said government in respect of such requisition period shall be retained by Owners. The period during which the vessel is on requisition to the said government shall count as part of the period provided for in this Charter.

If the period of requisition exceeds …… month, either party shall have the option of cancelling this Charter and no consequential claim may be made by either party.

On/Off-hire Survey

34. Prior to delivery and redelivery the parties shall each appoint surveyors, for their respective accounts, who shall conduct joint on-hire/off-hire surveys. A single report shall be prepared on each occasion and signed by each surveyor, without prejudice to his right to file a separate report setting forth items upon which the surveyors cannot agree. If either party fails to have a representative attend the survey and sign the joint survey report, such party shall nevertheless be bound for all purposes by the findings in any report prepared by the other party. On-hire survey shall be on Charterers' time and off-hire survey on Owners' time.

Stevedore Damage

35. Any damage caused by stevedores during the currency of this Charter shall be reported by Captain to Charterers or their agents, in writing, within 24 hours of the occurrence or as soon as possible thereafter. The Captain shall use his best efforts to obtain written acknowledgement by responsible parties

causing damage unless damage should have been made good in the meantime.

Stevedore damages involving seaworthiness shall be repaired without delay to the vessel after each occurrence in Charterers' time and shall be paid for by the Charterers. Other minor repairs shall be done at the same time, but if this is not possible, same shall be repaired while vessel is in drydock in Owners' time, provided this does not interfere with Owners' repair work, or by vessel's crew at Owners' convenience. All costs of such repairs shall be for Charterers' account. Any time spent in repairing stevedore damage shall be for Charterers' account.

Charterers shall pay for stevedore damages whether or not payment has been made by stevedores to Charterers.

Charterers' Colors

36. Charterers shall have the privilege of flying their own house flag and painting the vessel with their own markings. The vessel shall be repainted in Owners' colors before termination of the Charter. Cost of time of painting, maintaining and repainting those changes effected by Charterers shall be for Charterers' account.

Return Premium

37. Charterers shall have the benefit of any return insurance premium receivable by Owners from their underwriters as and when received from underwriters by reason of vessel being in port for a minimum period of 30 days if on full hire for this period or pro rata for the time actually on hire.

Water Pollution

38. The vessel shall be off hire during any time lost on account of vessel's non-compliance with government and/or state and/or provincial regulations pertaining to water pollution. In cases where vessel calls at a U.S. port, Owners warrant to have secured and carry on board the vessel a Certificate of Financial Responsibility as required under U.S. law.

Appendix F

AMERICAN LAW COMMENTARY ON TANKER TIME CHARTERS BASED ON STB FORM

IT IS THIS DAY MUTUALLY AGREED between .... as Owner/Chartered Owner (herein called "Owner") of the .... (herein called "Vessel") and .... (herein called "Charterer") that the Owner lets and the Charterer hires the use and services of the Vessel for the carriage of ...., in bulk, and such other lawful merchandise as may be suitable for a vessel of her description, for the period and on the terms and conditions hereinafter set forth.

The type of petroleum or other liquid products to be carried is customarily described by a general categorization, to which viscosity and other characteristics are sometimes added. Thus, the description may be "crude and/or dirty petroleum products" or "clean petroleum products". The nature of the cargoes carried is, of course, highly important to the owner insofar as it relates to the condition of the vessel's tanks, pumping capacity and safety gear. The loading of cargo not within the described category would be a breach and would expose the charterer to a claim for damages. See *The Witfuel*, S.M.A. No. 1381 (Arb. at N.Y. 1979), where the loading of a distillate clean petroleum product was held to be a breach of the charter which restricted the charterer to crude and/or dirty petroleum products. On the other hand, the owner would be in breach if the chartered vessel was incapable of carrying the specified cargo safely. (See above, page 131.)

TERM

1. (a) The term of this Charter shall be for a period of about (hereinafter "Original Period") plus any extensions thereof as provided in (b) below. The Original Period shall commence at the time when the Vessel is placed at the Charterer's disposal as provided in Clause 5. The word "about" as used above shall mean "14 days more or less" and shall apply to the term of this Charter consisting of the Original Period plus any extensions as hereinafter provided.

The STB form fixes at 14 days the amount of "underlap" or "overlap" permitted, i.e., redelivery may be made not more than 14 days before or after expiration of the flat period. In New York this would probably be considered a strict requirement, following the decisions in *The Romandie*, S.M.A. No. 1092 (Arb. at N.Y. 1977), *The M.V. Scaldia*, S.M.A. No. 905 (Arb. at N.Y. 1975) and *The Elizabeth Entz*, S.M.A. No. 588 (Arb. at N.Y. 1971). However, in England, the principle of *The Dione* [1975] 1 Lloyd's Rep. 115, might entitle the charterer to redeliver beyond the 14-day leeway under circumstances beyond the charterer's control.

EXTENSIONS

(b) Charterers shall have the option of extending the term of this Charter for a period of .... (hereinafter "Extended Period") by written notice to Owner at least 30 days previous to the expiration of the Original Period. The term of this Charter may be extended by Charterer also for periods (hereinafter "Off-Hire Extenions") of all or any part of the time the Vessel is off hire during the Original Period and/or Extended Period, if any, by giving written notice to Owner at least 30 days before the expiration of the Original Period or Extended Period, as the case may be, and, if Charterer so elects and gives a further written notice to Owner at least 30 days before the expiration of any such Off-Hire Extension, all or any part of the time the Vessel is off hire following the previous notice shall be added to the term of this Charter.

The option to extend the charter term for a fixed period which would be given the charterer by the first sentence of this clause is, in practice, granted only infrequently; in most instances the sentence is deleted.

More importantly, the second sentence grants the charterer the option of "tacking" all or any part of the aggregate "off-hire" time to the charter time. In the absence of such a provision, there would be no right to "tack" off-hire periods.

VESSEL PARTICULARS

2. The following are particulars and capacities of the Vessel and her equipment:

A. Cargo Carrying Capacity

I. Total cargo tank capacity when 100% full .... US Barrels
II. Weight of stores, etc., permanently deducted from cargo carrying capacity .... L.T.
III. a. Fresh water consumption per day .... L.T.
b. Capacity of evaporators per day .... L.T.
c. Quantity of fresh water deductible from cargo carrying capacity on a daily basis .... L.T.
IV. Estimated loss of cargo carrying capacity due to "sag" when fully loaded with light, medium, heavy cargo
Light .... L.T.
Medium .... L.T.
Heavy .... L.T.
V. The vessel can carry .... tons (of 2,240 lbs.) total deadweight (as certified by Classification Society) of cargo, bunkers, water, and stores on an assigned summer mean draft of .... ft. .... in. and an assigned freeboard of .... ft. .... in.

B. Other Tank Capacities

I. Total capacity of fuel tanks for propulsion .... US Barrels
II. Total capacity of fresh water tanks .... L.T.
III. Total capacity of segregated ballast tanks .... L.T.

C. Capacity of Pumps

I. Cargo Pumps
a. Number ....
b. Make ....
c. Type ....
d. Design rated capacity of each pump in U.S. Barrels per hour and corresponding head in feet .... US Bbls/Hr. .... Feet/Head

II. Stripping Pumps
a. Number ....
b. Design capacity of each pump in U.S. Barrels per hour for the guaranteed discharge head of .... US Bbls/Hr. .... Feet/Head

III. Segregated Ballast Pumps
a. Number ....
b. Design capacity each pump .... US Bbls/Hr.

D. Cargo Loading/Discharge Manifold

The whole manifold is made of steel or comparable material and is strengthened and supported to avoid damage from loading and discharge equipment and to withstand a maximum load from any direction equivalent to the safe working load of the cargo hose lifting equipment.

I. a. Number of manifold connections ....
b. Diameter of manifold connections ....
c. Distance from centers of manifold connections ....
d. Distance from manifold connections to ship's side ....

e. Distance center of manifold connections to deck ....

f. Distance bow/center of manifold ....

g. Safe working load of cargo hose lifting equipment .... tons.

II. Cargo Manifold Reducing Pieces

Vessels from 16 to 60 MDWT are equipped with a sufficient number of cargo manifold reducing pieces of steel or a comparable material to permit presenting of flanges of 8″, 10″ and 12″ (ASA) cargo hoses/arms at all manifold connections on one side of the vessel.

Vessels over 60 MDWT are equipped with a sufficient number of cargo manifold reducing pieces of steel or a comparable material to permit presenting of flanges of 10″, 12″ and 16″ (ASA) cargo hose/arms at all manifold connections on one side of the vessel.

E. Heating Coils

I. Type of coils and material of which manufactured ....

II. Ratio heating surface/volume

a. Center Tanks Ft.²/40 Ft.³

b. Wing Tanks Ft.²/40 Ft.³

F. Cargo Loading/Performance

Vessel can load homogeneous cargo at maximum rate of .... B/H.

G. Vessel Particulars

I. Length overall .... ft. .... In.

II. Fully loaded summer draft in salt water of a density of 1.025 .... ft. .... inches on an assigned freeboard of ....

III. Fresh Water allowance .... In.

IV. Light ship draft Forward .... Ft. .... In.
Aft .... Ft. .... In.
Mean .... Ft. .... In.

V. Moulded Depth ....

VI. Light ship freeboard .... Ft. .... In.

VII. TPI on light ship draft ....

VIII. TPI on summer draft ....

IX. Extreme beam ....

X. Gross Reg. Tons ....

XI. Net Reg. Tons ....

XII. Suez Canal Tonnage ....

XIII. Panama Canal Tonnage ....

XIV. Flag of Registry ....

XV. Call letters ....

XVI. Classification Society ....

XVII. Maximum bunkers aboard when vessel is placed at Charterer's disposal to be ....

XVIII. Owner shall provide Charterer with copies of the Vessel's plans upon Charterer's request therefor, provided, in the case of a newbuilding, that Owner need not provide same until such plans are available to him from the building yard.

XIX. Vessel is equipped with a fresh water evaporator which will be maintained in good operating condition. Owners warrant that this evaporator is capable of making sufficient fresh water to supply the vessel's needs.

XX. Owner warrants vessel is capable of heating cargo to 135°F. and of maintaining same throughout entire discharge. Should vessel fail to heat cargo in accordance with Charterer's instructions, Charterer shall have the option to:

a) Delay discharge of the cargo

b) Delay berthing of the Vessel

c) Discontinue discharge and remove vessel from berth until cargo is heated in accordance with Charterer's instructions.

All time lost to be considered as off-hire and for Owner's account. In addition, any expenses incurred in moving vessel from berth will be for Owner's account.

A detailed description of the chartered vessel is not uncommon in tanker charters, although the foregoing is unusually comprehensive. Many forms merely incorporate by reference a separate schedule of particulars.

The described capacities would no doubt be construed as "intermediate obligations" under English law, and as "warranties" under American law. Thus, failure of the vessel to comply with the description in some particulars would represent a breach of charter, but would not justify termination of the charter unless the consequences were sufficiently serious. (See above, pages 57–59, 76).

Several points should be noted with respect to the particulars described. The capacity of each of the pumping systems (cargo, stripping, and segregated ballast) is the "design" capacity. In the case of older vessels, actual capacity will obviously be substantially less. Yet under Clause 4 of the STB form (below, page 549) the owner warrants that the vessel "shall fulfill the . . . capabilities . . . in Clause 2", and exercise "due diligence" that such capabilities are maintained throughout the charter period. Pumping capacity is further modified by Clause 8 (below, page 551), under which the owner warrants that the vessel is capable of discharging a given quantity of product per hour at specified temperatures.

Clause 2 (G. XX) also contains an express warranty that the vessel can heat cargo to 135°F. The provision then gives the charterer three options in the event of any failure to maintain this temperature. In essence, the charterer may simply suspend discharging operations and put the vessel off-hire until she is able to achieve the required heating.

It must be noted, however, that where the time charter is for the carriage of a variety of petroleum products that do not all require heating, the vessel's heating warranty cannot be construed as an undertaking to heat indiscriminately all cargoes to the warranted temperature continuously and uniformly. *The London Confidence*, S.M.A. No. 1257 (Arb. at N.Y. 1978).

HIRE

3. (a) The Charterer shall pay hire for the use of the Vessel at the rate of .... in .... currency per ton (of 2,240 lbs.) on Vessel's deadweight as shown in Clause 2. A. per calendar month, payment to be made in advance monthly at .... by check without discount commencing with the date and hour the Vessel is placed at Charterer's disposal hereunder and continuing to the date and hour when the Vessel is released to Owner at the expiration of this Charter except as otherwise expressed in this Charter. Any hire paid in advance and not earned shall be returned to the Charterer at once. In no event will initial payment of hire be made until Charter Party is signed and Vessel placed at Charterer's disposal as herein provided.

Unlike older charter forms, hire under this clause is payable by "check" rather than "cash"—a reflection of modern commercial practices.

The last sentence provides that the first installment of hire need not be paid until the charter is "signed" and the vessel delivered to the charterer. A charter, of course, need not be in writing to be valid and binding, but when a written charter is contemplated, as it almost invariably is, the actual signing may not take place until weeks or even months after delivery. Hire, of course, is due in any event when the vessel is placed at charterer's disposal.

DEDUCTIONS

(b) The Charterer shall be entitled to deduct from hire payments: (1) any disbursements for Owner's account and any advances to the Master or Owner's agents, including commissions thereon, (2) layup savings calculated in accordance with Clause 17, (3) any previous overpayments of hire including offhire and including any overpayments of hire concerning which a bona fide dispute may exist but in the latter event the Charterer shall furnish an adequate bank guarantee or other good and sufficient security on request of the Owner, (4) any Clause 8 and 9 claims, and (5) any other sums to which Charterer is entitled under this charter. The Charterer shall be entitled to $2\frac{1}{2}\%$ commission on any sums advanced or disbursements made for the Owner's account. However, the Owner shall have the option of making advances to the Charterer or its designated agent for disbursements (provided such advances are deemed adequate and reasonable by the Charterer), and, in such event, no commissions shall be paid.

The STB form approaches the troublesome issue of deductions from hire by giving the charterer fairly extensive liberty to deduct. Thus, the charterer may deduct an overpayment of hire resulting from the vessel going off-hire, even if the off-hire is disputed. The sole check on this is an obligation to furnish security to the owner on request in the case of "bona fide disputes".

The same is presumably true for off-hire and other allowances to the charterer for performance deficiencies measured by Clauses 8 and 9. The above language permits a deduction for "any Clause 8 and 9 claims". This suggests that so long as there is a bona fide "claim" a deduction may be made, even though the "claim" ultimately may be reduced or eliminated. Thus, the charterer need not fear a withdrawal for under-payment (i.e., nonpayment) of hire in the case of disputed deductions made in good faith.

Finally, there is a catch-all provision allowing deductions for "any other sums to which charterer is entitled under this charter". Since this is restricted to amounts to which the charterer is "entitled", as opposed to mere "claims", the charterer probably makes disputed deductions (other than for off-hire and Clause 8 and 9 claims) at his peril, i.e., if he ultimately fails to substantiate his right to the sums involved, the deduction *ipso facto* would constitute at least partial nonpayment of hire and therefore justify a withdrawal. (See above, pages 220–221).

FINAL VOYAGE

(c) Should the Vessel be on her final voyage at the time a payment of hire becomes due, said payment shall be made for the time estimated by Charterer to be necessary to complete the voyage and effect release of the Vessel to Owner, less all deductions provided for in sub-paragraph (b) of this Clause which shall be estimated by Charterer if the actual amounts have not been received and also less the amount estimated by Charterer to become payable by the Owner for fuel and water on release as provided in Clause 19. (b). Upon redelivery any difference between the estimated and actual amounts shall be refunded to or paid by the Charterer as the case may require.

This paragraph simply provides for the deduction of estimated disbursements, fuel on redelivery, etc., from the final month's hire, a practice widely followed under all forms of time charter, whether or not expressly authorized.

LOSS OF VESSEL

(d) Should the Vessel be lost or be missing and presumed lost, hire shall cease at the time of her loss or, if such time is unknown, at the time when the Vessel was last heard of. If the Vessel should become a constructive total loss, hire shall cease at the time of the casualty resulting in such loss. In either case, any hire paid in advance and not earned shall be returned to the Charterer. If the Vessel should be off hire or missing when a payment of hire would otherwise be due, such payment shall be postponed until the off-hire period ceases or the safety of the Vessel is ascertained, as the case may be.

A question may arise as to the meaning of "constructive total loss" in this context. If the usual stipulation in a hull insurance policy were followed (i.e., that the insured vessel should be considered a "CTL" if the cost of recovery and repair would exceed her insured value), some incongruity might result. For example, a vessel could have an insured value of \$10 million and be worth only \$5 million in a depressed market. If, after a casualty, it would cost \$7 million to repair her, she would not be a CTL for insurance purposes, yet it would be wholly impractical for the owner to spend \$7 million to repair a vessel worth \$5 million after repairs. See discussion in chapter on Frustration above, page 322.

On the other hand, if the provision is construed as meaning the vessel will be deemed a CTL only if the cost of recovery and repairs exceed her value when repaired, the question then arises as to whether "value" should be determined with or without reference to the vessel's charter.

One final comment might be made on Clause 3(d). The last sentence of the clause provides that payment of hire is to be deferred if the vessel is off-hire when a payment of hire would otherwise be due. This avoids the sometimes difficult task of the charterer forecasting how much off-hire may properly be deducted if the vessel is, for example, under repair on the due date. By postponing payment until the off-hire has ceased the charterer need pay in advance only for such part of a hire period for which he knows he will have the use of the vessel.

REDUCTION IN HIRE

(e) If the Vessel shall not fulfill the Owner's Warranty or any other part of her description as warranted in Clause 4, Charterer shall be entitled without prejudice to a reduction in the hire to correct for the deficiency and to any other rights the Charterer may have.

This clause appears to be a "catch all" clause to cover breaches of warranty, such as cubic capacity not covered by express off-hire provisions in Clauses 8, 9 and 11.

DEFAULT

(f) In default of punctual and regular payment as herein specified, the Owner will notify .... at .... whereupon the Charterer shall make payment of the amount due within ten (10) days of receipt of notification from the Owner, failing which the Owner will have the right to withdraw the Vessel from the service of the Charterer without prejudice to any claim the Owner may otherwise have against the Charterer under this Charter.

This is a modification of the traditional "withdrawal" clause permitting termination for any delay in payment. By requiring notice of default and allowing a grace period, the provision averts the well known hardships resulting from a withdrawal in a high market.

INCREMENT

(g) The rate of hire set forth in sub-paragraph (a) of this Clause includes an increment of $........................ to cover in full any expenses for Charterer's account for extra victualling by the Master, telephone calls, radio messages, telegrams and cables and all overtime worked by the Vessel's officers and crew at Charterer's request.

(h) The rate of charter hire set forth in this Clause 3 is equivalent to $........................ per hour.

This provision expands the usual stipulation of a lump sum increment for crew overtime so as to include a variety of minor expenses often charged separately to the charterer.

WARRANTIES

4. Owner warrants that at the time the Vessel is placed at Charterer's disposal, the Vessel shall fulfill the descriptions, particulars and capabilities set forth in Clause 2 above, and shall be tight, staunch, and strong, in thoroughly efficient order and condition and in every way fit, manned, equipped, and supplied for the service contemplated, with holds, cargo tanks, pipelines, and valves clear, clean, and tight and with pumps, heating coils, and all other equipment in good working order. Such description, particulars, and capabilities of the Vessel shall be maintained by Owner throughout the period of the Vessel's service hereunder so far as possible by the exercise of due diligence.

The STB form here makes both the stated particulars of the vessel and her seaworthiness matters of express warranty as of the date of delivery. Thereafter the warranty is reduced to one of "due diligence", although any performance shortfall would of course make operative the off-hire provisions of Clauses 8, 9 and 11 regardless of how much "due diligence" the owner might have exercised.

HIRE

5. (a) The use and services of the Vessel shall be placed at the disposal of the Charterer at .... (hereinafter "Port of Delivery") at such readily accessible dock, wharf, or other place as the Charterer may direct. Charter hire shall commence when the Vessel is at such dock, wharf, or place and in all respects ready to perform this Charter and ready

for sea and written notice thereof has been given by the Master to the Charterer or its Agents at the Port of Delivery.

The requirement that the vessel be "ready for sea" on delivery, in addition to being ready to load, probably avoids the result of those cases that hold that hire runs if a vessel can load, even if some repair of certain equipment (e.g., radar) may be necessary before the vessel can sail. (See above, page 122.) After delivery, the temporary failure of equipment needed only for sea would probably not cause off-hire during loading, since there would be no "time lost".

LAYDAYS

(b) Hire shall not commence before ...., except with Charterer's consent, and the Vessel shall be placed at Charterer's disposal in accordance with the provisions hereof no later than .... in default of which Charterer shall have the option to cancel this Charter declarable not later than the day of the Vessel's readiness. Cancellation by Charterer or acceptance of the use of the Vessel's services shall be without prejudice to any claims for damages Charterer may have for late tender of the Vessel's services.

The first sentence of this provision is quite similar to other standard "laydays/cancelling" clauses, such as Clause 14 of the New York Produce form. The final sentence is *not* found in most such clauses, but it probably does no more than avoid a finding of waiver of any claim on account of mere acceptance or cancellation. Thus, the owner would not be liable for late delivery unless occasioned by his default in proceeding to the delivery port with the utmost dispatch (e.g., by making an unwarranted intermediate voyage) or unless he had misrepresented the position or expected readiness of the vessel at the time of fixing. (See above, page 293.)

USE OF VESSEL

(c) The whole reach and burthen of the Vessel (but not more than she can reasonably stow and safely carry) shall be at the Charterer's disposal, reserving proper and sufficient space for Vessel's Officers, Crew, Master's cabin, tackle, apparel, furniture, fuel, provisions, and stores.

This is a standard provision found in time charter forms and no comment is required.

TRADING LIMITS

6. (a) The Vessel may be employed in any part of the World trading between and at ports, places, berths, docks, anchorages, and submarine pipe-lines in such lawful trades as the Charterer or its agents may direct, subject to Institute Warranties and Clauses attached hereto but may be sent to ports and places on the North American Lakes, the St. Lawrence River and tributaries between May 15 and November 15 and through the Straits of Magellan and around Cape Horn and The Cape of Good Hope at any time of the year without payment of any extra premium. Notwithstanding the foregoing restrictions, the Vessel may be sent to Baltic Sea ports not North of Stockholm, and to Helsingfors and Abo, Finland, and other ports and places as set forth in the Institute Warranties and Clauses, provided, however, that Charterer shall reimburse Owner for any additional premia properly assessed by Vessel's underwriters and payable by Owner for breach of such trade warranties.

It has become an almost universal practice to limit a vessel's trading under a time charter to "Institute Warranty limits", which are the trading limits set by the Institute of London Underwriters, for sailing beyond which extra hull insurance premiums are charged. The above provision contemplates that the particular Institute Warranty clauses will be attached to the charter, and permits the charterer to order the vessel to certain specified areas which may be outside warranty limits without payment of any extra premiums required under the vessel's hull insurance. The charterer can order the vessel outside other specified Institute Warranty limits only by paying the additional premiums which may be charged by underwriters.

BERTHS

(b) The Vessel shall be loaded, discharged, or lightened, at any port, place, berth, dock, anchorage, or submarine line or alongside lighters or lightening vessels as Charterer may direct. Notwithstanding anything contained in this Clause or any other provisions of this Charter, Charterer shall not be deemed to warrant the safety of any port, berth, dock, anchorage, and/or submarine line and shall not be liable for any loss, damage, injury, or delay resulting from conditions at such ports, berths, docks, anchorages, and submarine lines not caused by Charterer's fault or neglect or which could have been avoided by the exercise of reasonable care on the part of the Master or Owner.

This is a modification of the usual "safe port" and "safe berth" warranties. The STB form expressly disclaims a warranty of safety and, instead, limits the charterer's liability to loss caused by his "fault or neglect". Additionally, the provision makes it explicit that the owner must bear the loss if it could have been avoided by reasonable care on his part or that of the master. See, for example, *The Athenoula*, S.M.A. No. 1410 (Arb. at N.Y. 1980), in which the panel pointed out that safe berth Clause 16 of the MOBILTIME form did not warrant the safety of a berth but rather obligated the charterer to exercise due diligence in ensuring that the vessel be employed between safe berths. The provision appears to leave open the possibility of a "divided damages" result if both the charterer and the owner contributed to a casualty. Thus the trend in admiralty to allocate damages on a proportionate fault theory is not negated, although the basis of the charterer's responsibility has been changed from strict liability to actual fault. But see *The Halekulani*, S.M.A. No. 1633 (Arb. at N.Y. 1981).

The problem of safety in loading is particularly acute for tanker owners today, since many of the "ports" and "berths" to which their vessels may be ordered consist of nothing more than mooring buoys, with little or no protection from weather and seas heretofore associated with the notion of a "harbor". Moreover, much of the crude originates in areas where there is need for concern over the "political" safety of the port. Under the STB form these additional risks appear to have been shifted to the owner.

FUEL

(c) The Charterer shall accept and pay for all fuel in the Vessel's bunkers at the time the vessel is placed at Charterer's disposal not exceeding the maximum quantity stated in Clause 2 above. Any excess quantity shall be removed by the Owner at its expense before such time unless the Charterer elects to accept such excess at the price determined as hereinafter provided or at such other price as may be mutually agreed. Payment for such fuel shall be in accordance with The Esso International Contract Price List current for the date when and the port or place where the vessel is placed at Charterer's disposal under the Charter or the nearest port to which such list applies.

The STB language avoids most of the difficulties associated with payment for bunkers on delivery by specifying the precise penalty for excess bunkers (i.e., removal at the owner's expense) and the precise standard for determining the value of the bunkers.

CARGO

7. The Charterer shall have the option of shipping any lawful dry cargo in bulk for which the Vessel and her tanks are suitable and any lawful merchandise in cases and/or cans and/or other packages in the Vessel's forehold, 'tween decks, and/or other suitable space available, subject, however, to the Master's approval as to kind and character, amount and stowage. All charges for dunnage, loading, stowing, and discharging so incurred shall be paid by the Charterer.

This clause simply reserves to the charterer the right to ship dry cargo otherwise suitable for a tanker. Thus, for example, it permits the carriage of grain during periods when the demand for tankers for the carriage of crude oil or petroleum products is limited.

SPEED, FUEL AND PUMPING WARRANTIES

8. The Owner warrants that the Vessel is capable of maintaining and shall maintain throughout the period of this Charter Party on all sea passages from Seabuoy to Seabuoy a guaranteed average

speed under all weather conditions of .... knots in a laden condition and .... knots in ballast (speed will be determined by taking the total miles at sea divided by the total hours at sea as shown in the log books excluding stops at sea and any sea passage covered by an off-hire calculation) on a guaranteed daily consumption of .... tons (of 2,240 lbs.) of Diesel/Bunker C/High Viscosity Fuel Oil maximum .... seconds Redwood No. I at 100 degrees F. for main engine, and .... tons (of 2,240 lbs.) of Diesel for auxiliaries for propulsion.

For each day that heat is applied to cargo the guaranteed daily consumption is .... bbls. of Diesel/Bunker C/High Viscosity Fuel Oil maximum .... seconds Redwood No. I at 100 degrees F. per tank day. For each hour that tank cleaning is required, the guaranteed consumption is .... bbls. of Diesel/Bunker C/High Viscosity Fuel Oil maximum .... seconds Redwood No. I at 100 degrees F. per machine hour.

The Charterer is entitled to the full capabilities of the Vessel and the Owner warrants that the Vessel is capable of discharging a cargo of petroleum at the following minimum rates:

Light petroleum (viscosity less than 320 SSU at 100°F.) .... bbls/hr
Medium petroleum (viscosity of 320 to 3200 SSU at 100°F.) .... bbls/hr
Heavy petroleum (viscosity above 3200 SSU at 100°F.) .... bbls/hr
or of maintaining a pressure of 100 PSI at ship's rail should the foregoing minimum rates not be met.

Charterer is to be compensated at $.................... per hour or pro rata for each part of an hour that Vessel takes in excess of the pumping rates as stipulated above. The owner understands and agrees that he will receive no credit or compensation if the Vessel is able to discharge at a rate greater than those specified above. Any delay to Vessel's discharge caused by shore conditions shall be taken into account in the assessment of pumping performance. Pumping performance shall be reviewed in accordance with Clause 9.

Here we have one of the salient differences between a typical tanker time charter form and the New York Produce and Baltime forms. Under the usual dry cargo charters speed performance is measured under "good" or "ordinary" weather conditions. Tanker time charters such as the STB form utilize the "guaranteed" or "all weather" speed concept, under which such external factors as wind, seas, currents and fog are all ignored. This approach has the virtue of simplicity, and if a vessel is engaged over a long period of time in standard trades, these factors should average out fairly well. However, the provision has not been applied literally in a number of New York arbitrations. Thus, in *The Golar Kansai*, S.M.A. No. 1263 (Arb. at N.Y. 1978), the speed warranty and hire adjustment provisions of the MOBILTIME form were held geared to "moderate (Beaufort 1-5)" weather. See also *The Athenoula*, S.M.A. No. 1410 (Arb. at N.Y. 1980) and *The Efplia*, S.M.A. No. 1359 (Arb. at N.Y. 1979), where speed performance under the MOBILTIME and TEXACOTIME forms was measured under "moderate" weather also.

In *The Ionic*, SMA No. 2519 (set at N.Y. 1988), a dispute arose under a Texacotime charter concerning responsibility for reduced speed in various circumstances. The panel majority ruled that it is not proper to exclude from the performance calculation time lost as a result of restricted visibility caused by weather conditions unless speed was reduced to comply with the International Collision regulations. The panel was unanimous in ruling that periods of reduced engine speed are to be excluded from performance calculations where the vessel has to transmit restricted sea lanes and engine speed was reduced to comply with either international or local laws. The panel noted, however, that it was a prerequisite to owner's rights under the performance clause that it demonstrate the ability of the vessel to meet and maintain its guaranteed speed and consumption under all weather conditions. As stated by the panel: "Specifically, the vessel must have been capable of meeting the performance requirements throughout the period of the charter on a seabuoy-to-seabuoy basis."

An unresolved issue is the extent to which the performance guarantees of speed and consumption apply to periods of deliberately slow steaming. One possible solution to the problem of claims for excess consumption is to stipulate in advance a "curve" or scale of consumption at various speeds.

Still another issue may be generated by the use of VLCC's virtually as storage facilities by keeping them at loading or discharge ports for weeks or months. If this results in bottom fouling there may be a dispute as to whether any loss of speed is the owner's sole responsibility.

In *The Stolt Capricorn*, S.M.A. No. 2359 (Arb. at N.Y. 1987), owner's failure to show that the vessel's cargo pumps were in good working condition and complied with the provisions of Clause 8 led to its being found liable for charterer's damages. The arbitrators stated that, had owner shown that the vessel complied with the provisions of Clause 8, it would have been absolved from any performance claims. One of the issues raised in the case related to back pressure from the shore. The panel ruled that "the Master had a duty to the court and/or protest any delays which might have been caused from shoreside to the performance of his vessel". In the absence of such protest or records, the panel concluded that owner could not show that prevailing shore conditions were such that they adversely affected the discharge.

ADJUSTMENT OF HIRE

9. (a) The speed and consumption guaranteed by the Owner in Clause 8 will be reviewed by the Charterer after three calendar months counting from the time of delivery of the Vessel to the Charterer in accordance with this Charter Party and thereafter at the end of each three (3) calendar month period. If at the end of each twelve (12) calendar month period (or at any time during the term of this charter) it is found that the Vessel has failed to maintain as an average during the preceding twelve (12) calendar month period (or for any other twelve month period during the term of this Charter) the speed and/or consumption warranted, the Charterer shall be retroactively compensated in respect of such failings as follows:

(b) Speed — Payment to Charterer of $.................................... per hour or pro rata for each part of an hour that Vessel steams in excess of the equivalent time Vessel would have taken at the guaranteed speed warranted in Clause 8 as calculated in accordance with Attachment I — "Performance Calculations".

(c) Consumption — the Owner to reimburse the Charterer for each ton of 2,240 lbs. or pro rata for part of a ton in excess of the guaranteed daily consumption for main engine and/or auxiliaries and/or heating and/or tank cleaning including any excess not borne by the Owner in accordance with the off hire clause of this Charter Party at the average price for the particular grade of oil as set forth in the then current Esso International Contract Price List at .... for the total period under review provided that Vessel's actual speed is in accordance with Clause 8. To the extent the Vessel's speed is less than that warranted, fuel consumption allowed will be determined in accordance with Attachment I — "Performance Calculations".

(d) The basis for determining the Vessel's performance in (a) and (b) above shall be the statistical data supplied by the Master in accordance with Clause 14. (b).

(e) Owner to have similar privileges under this Clause for receiving compensation as Charterers do should Vessel performance as concerns speed be in excess or consumption for propulsion be below the descriptions outlined herein.

(f) The Charterer shall provide Owner with an opportunity to review any claim submitted by Charterer under this Clause, and the Owner shall complete such review, and provide Charterer with the results thereof within 30 days from the date such claim was mailed by Charterer to Owner. Charterer may deduct from hire any amount to which it is entitled under this Clause after the expiration of 40 days from the date of Charterer's mailing of a claim relating thereto to Owner.

In the event of Charterer having a claim in respect of Vessel's performance during the final year or part of the Charter period and any extension thereof, the amount of such claim shall be withheld from hire in accordance with Charterer's estimate made about two months before the end of the Charter period and any necessary adjustment after the end of the Charter shall be made by the Owner to the Charterer or the Charterer to the Owner as the case may require.

This clause is one of the more sophisticated attempts to provide a method for adjusting hire in the event of underperformance. It should be noted that in the case of speed and consumption, the owner is entitled to extra compensation if performance of the vessel *exceeds* the guaranteed rates. See *The Golar Kansai*, S.M.A. No. 1263 (Arb. at N.Y. 1978); *The Northern Star*, S.M.A. No. 1494 (Arb. at N.Y. 1980). In *The Golar Kansai*, however, a case involving the MOBILTIME form, the owner was held not entitled to credit for underconsumption of fuel which resulted from the vessel's failure to maintain her minimum speed.

The Northern Star decision illustrates the difficulty of applying the hire adjustment clause in certain circumstances. The vessel demonstrated superior speed performance and lower fuel consumption capability during the first two years of the charter, and the issue arose in subsequent years during periods of "slow steaming" ordered by the charterer. In an interim ruling, the panel decided that

> any periods of slow steaming or lay up should be evaluated for hire purposes on the basis of actual daily hire rate established during the last preceding quarter year in which the vessel performed at speeds unimpeded by Charterer's orders. Daily allowances to Owner for proven underconsumption of fuel and diesel oils at full speed should also be due to Owner, during slow steaming and/or lay up periods on the same basis as was allowed during the last preceding quarter in which the vessel performed at speeds unimpeded by Charterer's orders.

In so holding, the panel pointed out that the hire adjustment clause compensated either owner or charterer for proven speed capability and consumption characteristics of the vessel, and to construe it otherwise would be to allow the clause to work only in favor of one party. Thus, once the vessel had established a speed capacity in excess of that warranted, then the charterer could simply order the vessel not to steam at greater than the warranted speed and effectively prevent the owner from earning any additional hire. See also *The Columbia Liberty*, S.M.A. No. 2220 (Arb. at N.Y. 1986).

Pursuant to the last provision of Clause 8, no extra compensation is payable for any excess in pumping rates above the minimum guaranteed.

Under Clause 9(f) the charterer may deduct underperformance claims 40 days after mailing to the owner a statistical claim, apparently without regard to whether or not the claim is disputed.

Finally, it might be noted that hire adjustment under such a clause does not involve ordinary contract law concepts of damages and mitigation. Therefore, a refusal by charterer to accept a substitute vessel in mitigation of damages for speed deficiency, in the absence of a substitution provision, is a proper exercise of his rights and does not affect the adjustment of hire. *The Golar Kansai*, above.

LIENS

10. The Owner shall have a lien on all cargoes for all amounts due under this Charter, and the Charterer shall have a lien on the Vessel for all moneys paid in advance and not earned, all disbursements and advances for the Owner's account, for the value of any of Charterer's fuel used or accepted for Owner's account, for all amounts due to Charterer under Clause 9, and other provisions of this Charter and for any damages sustained by the Charterer as a result of breach of this Charter by the Owner.

This language is similar to Clause 18 of the New York Produce form. Ordinarily, the lien will not extend to cargo owned by third parties. (See above, page 408.) Unlike Clause 18 of the New York Produce form, however, there is no express grant of a lien on "subfreights" so that the owner's position regarding security is uncertain if the cargo has been sold to a third party. Of course, if the bill of lading incorporated the terms of the time charter by reference, the consignee could well be said to have purchased cargo subject to a lien. However, this is not a common practice in the tanker trade.

The charterer's lien on the vessel is express and quite broad. Under American law, this would be clearly enforceable and subject the vessel to *in rem* proceedings in the United States District Court.

OFF HIRE

11. (a) In the event of loss of time from breakdown of machinery, interference by authorities, collision, stranding, fire, or other accident or damage to the Vessel, not caused by the fault of the Charterer, preventing the working of the Vessel for more than twelve consecutive hours, or in the event of loss of time from deficiency of men or stores, breach of orders or neglect of duty by the

Master, Officers, or Crew, or from deviation for the purpose of landing any injured or ill person on board other than any person who may be carried at Charterer's request, payment of hire shall cease for all time lost until the Vessel is again in an efficient state to resume her service and has regained a point of progress equivalent to that when the hire ceased hereunder; cost of fuel consumed while the Vessel is off hire hereunder, as well as all port charges, pilotages, and other expenses incurred during such period and consequent upon the putting in to any port or place other than to which the Vessel is bound, shall be borne by the Owner; but should the Vessel be driven into port or to anchorage by stress of weather or on account of accident to her cargo, such loss of time, shall be for Charterer's account. If upon the voyage the speed of the Vessel be reduced or her fuel consumption increased by breakdown, casualty, or inefficiency of Master, Officers, or Crew, so as to cause a delay of more than twenty-four hours in arriving at the Vessel's next port or an excess consumption of more than one day's fuel, hire for the time lost and cost of extra fuel consumed, if any, shall be borne by the Owner. Any delay by ice or time spent in quarantine shall be for Charterer's account, except delay in quarantine resulting from the Master, Officers, or Crew having communications with the shore at an infected port, where the Charterer has given the Master adequate written notice of infection, which shall be for Owner's account, as shall also be any loss of time through detention by authorities as a result of charges of smuggling or of other infraction of law by the Master, Officers, or Crew.

(b) If the periods of time lost for which hire does not cease to be payable under the foregoing provisions of this Clause because each such period or delay is not of more than twelve (12) hours duration exceed in the aggregate one hundred and forty-four (144) hours in any charter party year (and pro rata for part of a year), hire shall not be payable for the excess and any hire overpaid by the Charterer shall be repaid by the Owner.

(c) In the event of loss of time by detention of the Vessel by authorities at any place in consequence of legal proceeding against the Vessel or the Owner, payment of charter hire shall cease for all time so lost. Cost of fuel and water consumed as well as all additional port charges, pilotages, and other expenses incurred during the time so lost shall be borne by the Owner. If any such loss of time shall exceed thirty consecutive days, the Charterer shall have the option to cancel this Charter by written notice given to the Owner while the vessel remains so detained without prejudice to any other right Charterer may have in the premises.

There are several important differences between the STB off-hire provisions and those of dry cargo forms, such as the New York Produce form. Thus, under the STB form the vessel will go off-hire for delays caused by "interference by authorities". This is not the case under the New York Produce off-hire clause.

In order for off-hire to accrue under the first part of the clause (i.e., for breakdowns of machinery, collision, etc.) the delay must be for at least 12 hours. Once the 12-hour minimum is met, however, the vessel will be off-hire for the entire period of the delay, including the 12-hour "franchise" period. Furthermore, paragraph "(b)" requires the addition of all periods of delay under 12 hours, and if they aggregate more than 144 hours in a year (or pro rata for part of a year) the vessel will be off-hire for the excess.

The clause also provides that the vessel is off-hire for any deviation to land sick or injured "persons", except those carried at the charterer's request. This would usually mean deviating to land disabled crewmen. Again, this is a category of off-hire not within Clause 15 of the New York Produce form. Moreover, for the second group of delays subject to off-hire (i.e., deficiency of men, deviation, etc.) there is no minimum "franchise" period.

The off-hire is measured not by the period of the vessel's incapacity, but rather by the time the use of the vessel has been effectively lost to the charterer, i.e., from the commencement of the breakdown or deviation until the vessel is again in a position equivalent to that she was in when the breakdown occurred or the deviation began. This contrasts with the line of cases interpreting Clause 15 of the New York Produce form, treating the vessel as off-hire only for the period of actual incapacity. See above, page 311).

One difference in the STB form in favor of the owner is the provision that time lost putting into a port of refuge by reason of an "accident" to cargo is for the charterer's account. Under the New York Produce form the vessel is off-hire for loss of time occasioned by "average accident . . . to cargo".

In the case of loss of speed or excess bunker consumption, there is a "franchise" period of one day.

All the off-hire provisions must be read in conjunction with Clause 8. Thus, even if there is no off-hire because the applicable two-hour or 24-hour minimum has not been met, the loss of time will of course "count" insofar as computation of the vessel's average speed is concerned. By the same token, actual off-hire periods are excluded from the calculations of speed and consumption under Clause 8.

The final sentence of paragraph "(a)" allocates off-hire for quarantine delays. Under the corresponding New York Produce form, there is no specific mention of quarantine, and numerous disputes have arisen as to whether the circumstances of the quarantine gave rise to a "deficiency of men" for which the vessel was off-hire.

Paragraph "(c)" settles in the charterer's favor the issue of whether the vessel is off-hire if she is arrested or attached (although it is silent with respect to the situation where the vessel is arrested or attached in connection with claims for which the charterer bears ultimate responsibility). It also grants the charterer the option to cancel if the arrest continues for 30 consecutive days. Thus, an owner who lacks the resources to post the required security risks losing a valuable charter if the vessel is subjected to prolonged legal restraint. See discussion above, page 317.

DRYDOCKING

12. (a) Owner, at its expense, shall drydock, clean, and paint Vessel's bottom and make all overhaul and other necessary repairs at reasonable intervals not to exceed twenty-four (24) months for which purpose Charterer shall allow Vessel to proceed to an appropriate port. Owner shall be solely responsible therefor, and also for gasfreeing the Vessel, upon each occasion. All towing, pilotage, fuel, water and other expenses incurred while proceeding to and from and while in drydock, shall also be for Owner's account. Fuel used during such drydocking or repair as provided in this Clause or Clause 15 or in proceeding to or from the port of drydocking or repair, will be charged to Owner by Charterer at the price charged to Charterer by its bunker supplier at such port if bunkers are obtained there or at the next replenishment port.

(b) In case of drydocking pursuant to this Clause at a port where Vessel is to load, discharge or bunker, under Charterer's orders, hire shall be suspended from the time the Vessel received free pratique on arrival, if in ballast, or upon completion of discharge of cargo, if loaded, until Vessel is again ready for service. In case of drydocking at a port other than where Vessel loads, discharges, or bunkers, under Charterer's orders, the following time and bunkers shall be deducted from hire: total time and bunkers including repair port call for the actual voyage from last port of call under Charterer's orders to next port of call under Charterer's orders, less theoretical voyage time and bunkers for the direct voyage from said last port of call to said next port of call. Theoretical voyage will be calculated on the basis of the seabuoy to seabuoy distance at the warranted speed and consumption per Clause 8.

Clause 12 is a fairly straightforward provision requiring the vessel to be drydocked at least every two years on the owner's time and at his expense. As indicated in the comment under Clause 8, however, disputes may arise if the charterer's use of the vessel requires exceptional bottom cleaning to avoid loss of speed.

Paragraph "(b)" represents an effort to make off-hire for drydocking concomitant with the charterer's loss of trading time. It may not always be apparent just what "theoretical voyage" should be deducted from the time spent in deviating to the dry dock, since the location of the dry dock may cause a change in orders. In practice, however, the owner and the charterer usually cooperate in arranging a drydocking so as to minimize the charterer's loss of use of the vessel and the period of off-hire.

OWNER PROVIDES

13. The Owner shall provide and pay for all provisions, deck and engine room stores, galley and cabin stores, galley and crew fuel, insurance on the Vessel, wages of the Master, Officers, and Crew, all certificates and other requirements necessary to enable the Vessel to be employed throughout the

trading limits herein provided, consular fees pertaining to the Master, Officers, and Crew, all fresh water used by the Vessel and all other expenses connected with the operation, maintenance, and navigation of the Vessel.

This section is similar to Clause 1 of the New York Produce form. It should be noted, however, that under the above wording the owner undertakes to provide all "certificates" necessary to employ the vessel within the permissible trading limits. This would no doubt include the "certificates of financial responsibility" required under United States oil pollution regulations and similar documents which may now or hereafter be required in other jurisdictions.

MASTER'S DUTIES

14. (a) The Master, although appointed by and in the employ of the Owner and subject to Owner's direction and control, shall observe the orders of Charterer in connection with Charterer's agencies, arrangements, and employment of the Vessel's services hereunder. Nothing in this Clause or elsewhere in this Charter shall be construed as creating a demise of the Vessel to Charterer nor as vesting Charterer with any control over the physical operation or navigation of the Vessel.

(b) The Master and the Engineers shall keep full and correct logs of the voyages, which are to be patent to the Charterer and its agents, and abstracts of which are to be mailed directly to the Charterer from each port of call.

(c) If the Charterer shall have reason to be dissatisfied with the conduct of the Master or Officers, the Owner shall, on receiving particulars of the complaint, investigate it and if necessary, make a change in the appointments.

These provisions are quite similar to the comparable ones of the New York Produce form and require no comment. See discussion above, page 243.

In *The Zacharia T*, S.M.A. No. 2224 (Arb. at N.Y. 1986), the vessel was chartered to carry a cargo of crude oil from Esmeraldas, Ecuador to Corpus Christi, Texas. The charter provided that the vessel was to load a full cargo of crude oil, "consistent with safe transit draft for the Panama Canal of 39' 6" tropical fresh water". The safe draft instruction was later amended by charterer to a maximum transit draft of 38' 11" TFW. The vessel loaded at a single-point mooring buoy and because prevailing swell conditions made it virtually impossible to obtain an accurate draft reading, the master requested that the loading master advise him when 51,000 long tons had been pumped aboard. When loading was finished, it was established by surveyors that the quantity loaded was 53,435 long tons. Because the excess tonnage put the ship at a draft which would have prevented her from transiting the Panama Canal, the master registered a protest. It was not feasible to off-load any of the cargo at Esmeraldas and, instead, the vessel lightered at Balboa and reloaded the excess cargo after the ship and the lightering vessel had passed through the Panama Canal. A dispute arose between owner and charterer as to liability for the lightering expenses and off-hire. The panel held that owner was liable because it was the master's responsibility to ensure that the vessel was not overloaded. According to the panel:

> [I]t always remains the Master's duty to see to it that the vessel is loaded and trimmed in such a manner as to safely prosecute the intended voyage. If the intended passage involves transit through a draft limiting channel or canal, as here, it is incumbent on the Master to take this into account and load the vessel in such a manner as to accomplish the voyage without delay or extra expense.

FUEL, PORT CHARGES, ETC.

15. (a) The Charterer (except during any period when the Vessel is off hire) shall provide and pay for all fuel except for galley and Crew as provided in Clause 13. The Charterer shall also pay for all port charges, light dues, dock dues, Panama and other Canal dues, pilotage, consular fees, (except those pertaining to Master, Officers, and Crew), tugs necessary for assisting the Vessel in, about, and out of port for the purpose of carrying out this Charter, Charterer's agencies and commissions incurred for Charterer's account and crew expense incurred for connecting and disconnecting cargo

hoses and arms. The Owner shall, however, reimburse the Charterer for any fuel used or any expenses incurred in making a general average sacrifice or expenditure, and for any fuel consumed during drydocking or repair of the Vessel.

This provision is consistent with the usual allocation of fuel costs to the charterer. It may be noted that fuel consumed as part of a general average sacrifice is for the owner's account, which is logical since the vessel and cargo will then share this cost in accordance with established rules governing apportionment of general average expenses. Under Clause 23 the cost of fuel consumed during salvage operations is to be deducted from any recovery. If there is a salvage effort but no recovery, there is no provision to alter the basic principle that the cost is to be borne by the charterer.

TUGS AND PILOTS

(b) In engaging pilotage and tug assistance, Charterer is authorized by Owner to engage them on behalf of Owner on the usual terms and conditions for such services then prevailing at the ports or places where such services are engaged, including provisions there prevailing, if any, making pilots, tug captains, or other personnel of any tug the borrowed servants of the Owner.

(c) Neither the Charterer nor its agents nor any of its associated or affiliated companies, nor any of their agents or employees, shall be under any responsibility for any loss, damage, or liability arising from any negligence, incompetence, or incapacity of any pilot, tug captain, or other personnel of any tug, or arising from the terms of the contract of employment thereof or for any unseaworthiness or insufficiency of any tug or tugs, the services of which are arranged by Charterer on behalf of Owner, and Owner agrees to indemnify and hold Charterer, its agents, associated and affiliated companies and their employees harmless from and against any and all such consequences.

(d) Charterer shall have the option of using its own tugs or pilots, or tugs or pilots made available or employed by any associated or affiliated companies, to render towage or pilotage services to the Vessel. In this event, the terms and conditions relating to such services prevailing in the port where such services are rendered and applied by independent tugboat owners or pilots, shall be applicable, and Charterer, its associated or affiliated companies and their pilots shall be entitled to all exemptions from and limitations of liability, applicable to said independent tugboat owners or pilots and their published tariff terms and conditions.

Paragraph "(b)" of Clause 15 is obviously aimed at towage and pilotage conditions such as the so-called "U.K. Towing Conditions". These are standard contract terms that make the vessel owner responsible not only for damage caused by errors on the part of the vessel, but also for errors on the part of the tug. Such contracts are void in the United States as against public policy. However, they are valid in England and elsewhere. By this clause the charterer is authorized to bind the owner to these terms, if they are customary or required at the particular port or terminal where the services are needed.

Paragraph "(c)" expresses what is in all probability the general rule in any event, i.e., the charterer engages the tug or pilot on behalf of the owner and assumes no responsibility for the safe navigation of the vessel. However, this provision should be read in conjunction with the limited "safe port" and "safe berth" obligations of Clause 6. These would seem to preclude the charterer from directing the vessel to a port or berth which he knows or should know lacks adequate towage facilities. See *The Agia Erini II*, S.M.A. No. 1602 (Arb. at N.Y. 1981).

In *Scholl* v. *Chuang Hui Marine Co. Ltd.*, 646 F. Supp. 137, 1987 AMC 1162 (D.Conn. 1986), the charter contained a clause similar to STB Clause 15(c). Charterer and owner were sued by a petroleum inspector who claimed that he was injured when he slipped on an oily substance on the deck of the tanker. The court granted summary judgment in favor of charterer and dismissed the petroleum inspector's claim, holding that the charterer had no duty to the inspector to maintain the deck in a safe condition.

The final provision of Clause 15 [paragraph "(d)"] is an effort to have the charterer's affiliated towing companies treated as separate and independent entities for purposes of determining liability in the event of a casualty. It is conceivable that claims involving such tugs would be held subject to New York arbitration under the charter, in which case the owner could urge that the towing conditions could not be enforced. Since such conditions would presumably be valid where they were promulgated, some rather difficult conflict of laws issues would be raised.

ADDITIONAL EQUIPMENT

16. The Charterer, subject to the Owner's approval not to be unreasonably withheld, shall be at liberty to fit any additional pumps and/or gear for loading or discharging cargo it may require beyond that which is on board at the commencement of the Charter, and to make the necessary connections with steam or water pipes, such work to be done at its expense and time, and such pumps and/or gear so fitted to be considered its property, and the Charterer shall be at liberty to remove it at its expense and time during or at the expiry of this Charter; the Vessel to be left in her original condition to the Owner's satisfaction.

The addition of equipment such as pumps may complicate the evaluation of the vessel's performance under Clause 8. Moreover, notwithstanding the assertion that the equipment remains the charterer's property, it may be subject to maritime liens against the vessel. See *Payne v. The Tropic Breeze*, 412 F.2d 707 (1st Cir. 1969).

LAY-UP

17. The Charterer shall have the option of laying up the Vessel for all or any portion of the term of this Charter, in which case hire hereunder shall continue to be paid, but there shall be credited against such hire the whole amount which the Owner shall save (or reasonably should save) during such period of layup through reduction in expenses, less any extra expenses to which the Owner is put as a result of such layup.

Should the Charterer, having exercised the option granted hereunder, desire the Vessel again to be put into service, the Owner will, upon receipt of written notice from the Charterer to such effect, immediately take steps to restore the Vessel to service as promptly as possible. The option granted to the Charterer hereunder may be exercised one or more times during the currency of this Charter or any extension thereof.

Lay-up is a frequently utilized privilege when the tanker market is depressed. The basic formula for apportioning savings and expenses is simple and fair, although it may prove quite complicated in practice. For example, calculating "savings" in insurance and maintenance may be difficult if the vessel is part of a large fleet. Similarly, the effects of long term lay-ups on a vessel's subsequent performance are difficult to gauge, and there no doubt will be disputes as to just what degree of "restoration" the charterer is responsible for.

REQUISITION

18. (a) In the event that title to the Vessel shall be requisitioned or seized by any government authority (or the Vessel shall be seized by any person or government under circumstances which are equivalent to requisition of title), this Charter shall terminate automatically as of the effective date of such requisition or seizure.

(b) In the event that the Vessel should be requisitioned for use or seized by any government authority on any basis not involving, or not equivalent to, requisition of title, she shall be off hire hereunder during the period of such requisition, and any hire or any other compensation paid in respect of such requisition shall be for Owner's account, provided, however, that if such requisition continues for a period in excess of 90 days, the Charterer shall have the option to terminate this Charter upon written notice to the Owner. Any periods of off-hire under this Clause shall be subject to the Charterer's option for off-hire extension set forth in Clause 1 (b) hereof.

Even without a provision such as this clause, requisition of title to a vessel has traditionally been held to "frustrate" a charter. (See above, page 332.)

Insofar as requisition of use is concerned, the application of the doctrine of frustration is less certain. Paragraph "(b)" is framed in terms of an option given to the charterer to terminate if the requisition lasts 90 days or more. There is no provision as to when the option must be exercised, so that the clause would probably be read as continuing the option for the duration of the requisition. No comparable option is given to the owner, although in the case of a sufficiently lengthy requisition he could presumably declare the charter "frustrated" under general legal principles (assuming, of course, that the charterer had elected not to exercise his option).

It should be noted that all off-hire during a period of requisition of use may be added to the term of the charter at the charterer's option.

REDELIVERY

19. (a) Unless the employment of the Vessel under this Charter shall previously have been terminated by loss of the Vessel or otherwise, the Charterer shall release the Vessel to the Owner's use, free of cargo, at the expiration of the term of this Charter stated in Clause I (including any extension thereof provided in said Clause or elsewhere in this Charter), at .... (herein called "Port of Redelivery") and shall give written notice of the date and hour of such release. At the Charterer's option, the vessel may be released to the Owner with tanks in a clean or dirty condition.

(b) The Owner shall accept and pay for all fuel in the Vessel's bunkers when this Charter terminates. Payment for such fuel shall be made in accordance with the Exxon International Company Contract Price List current for the date when and the port or place where the Vessel is redelivered by Charterer to Owners under this Charter, or the nearest port to which such list applies.

It is customary to provide for redelivery within a range of ports rather than at a particular port, thereby giving the charterer flexibility during the final period of trading under the charter.

BILLS OF LADING

20. (a) Bills of Lading shall be signed by the Master as presented, the Master attending daily, if required, at the offices of the Charterer or its Agents. However, at Charterer's option, the Charterer or its Agents may sign Bills of Lading on behalf of the Master. All Bills of Lading shall be without prejudice to this Charter and the Charterer shall indemnify the Owner against all consequences or liabilities which may arise from any inconsistency between this Charter and any bills of lading or other documents signed by the Charterer or its Agents or by the Master at their request or which may arise from an irregularity in papers supplied by the Charterer or its Agents.

(b) The carriage of cargo under this Charter Party and under all Bills of Lading issued for the cargo shall be subject to the statutory provisions and other terms set forth or specified in subparagraphs (i) through (vi) of this Clause and such terms shall be incorporated verbatim or be deemed incorporated by the reference in any such Bill of Lading. In such subparagraphs and in any Act referred to therein, the word "carrier" shall include the Owner and the Chartered Owner of the Vessel.

(i) *Clause Paramount*. This bill of lading shall have effect subject to the provisions of the Carriage of Goods by Sea Act of the United States, approved April 16, 1936, except that if this Bill of Lading is issued at a place where any other Act, ordinance, or legislation gives statutory effect to the International Convention for the Unification of Certain Rules relating to Bills of Lading at Brussels, August 1924, then this Bill of Lading shall have effect subject to the provisions of such Act, ordinance, or legislation. The applicable Act, ordinance, or legislation (hereinafter called "Act") shall be deemed to be incorporated herein and nothing herein contained shall be deemed a surrender by the Owner or Carrier of any of its rights or immunities or an increase of any of its responsibilities or liabilities under the Act. If any term of this Bill of Lading be repugnant to the Act to any extent, such term shall be void to that extent but no further.

(ii) *New Jason Clause*. In the event of accident, danger, damage, or disaster before or after the commencement of the voyage, resulting from any cause whatsoever, whether due to negligence or not, for which, or for the consequences of which, the Carrier is not responsible, by statute, contract or otherwise, the cargo shippers, consignees, or owners of the cargo shall contribute with the Carrier in General Average to the payment of any sacrifices, losses, or expenses of a General Average nature that may be made or incurred and shall pay salvage and special charges incurred in respect of the cargo. If a salving ship is owned or operated by the Carrier, salvage shall be paid for as fully as if the said salving ship or ships belonged to strangers. Such deposit as the Carrier or its Agents may deem sufficient to cover the estimated contribution of the cargo and any salvage and special charges thereon shall, if required, be made by the cargo, shippers, consignees or owners of the cargo to the Carrier before delivery.

(iii) *General Average*. General Average shall be adjusted, stated, and settled according to York/Antwerp Rules 1950, as amended, and, as to matters not provided for by those rules, according to the laws and usages at the Port of New York. If a General Average statement is required, it shall be prepared at such port by an Adjuster from the Port of New York appointed by the Carrier and approved by the Charterer of the Vessel. Such Adjuster shall attend to the settlement and the collection of the General Average, subject to customary charges. General Average Agreements and/or security shall be furnished by Carrier and/or Charterer of the Vessel, and/or Carrier and/or Consignee of cargo, if requested. Any cash deposit being made as security to pay General Average and/or salvage shall be remitted to the Average Adjuster and shall be held by him at his risk in a special account in a duly authorized and licensed bank at the place where the General Average statment is prepared.

(iv) *Both to Blame*. If the Vessel comes into collision with another ship as a result of the negligence of the other ship and any act, neglect or default of the Master, mariner, pilot, or the servants of the Carrier in the navigation or in the management of the Vessel, the owners of the cargo carried hereunder shall indemnify the Carrier against all loss or liability to the other or noncarrying ship or her owners in so far as such loss or liability represents loss of, or damage to, or any claim whatsoever of the owners of said cargo, paid or payable by the other or recovered by the other or noncarrying ship or her owners as part of their claim against the carrying ship or Carrier. The foregoing provisions shall also apply where the owners, operators, or those in charge of any ships or objects other than, or in addition to, the colliding ships or object are at fault in respect of a collision or contract.

(v) *Limitation of Liability*. Any provision of this Charter to the contrary notwithstanding, the Carrier shall have the benefit of all limitations of, and exemptions from, liability accorded to the Owner or Chartered Owner of vessels by any statute or rule of law for the time being.

(vi) *Deviation Clause*. The Vessel shall have liberty to sail with or without pilots, to tow or be towed, to go to the assistance of vessels in distress, to deviate for the purpose of saving life or property or of landing any ill or injured person on board, and to call for fuel at any port or ports in or out of the regular course of the voyage.

The STB form follows the usual practice by providing that the master is to sign bills of lading "as presented", but that such bills are to be "without prejudice" to the charter. In essence, this means that the form and provisions of the bill should create no obligation on the part of the owner, as a "carrier", greater than the obligations created by the terms of the charter itself. Of course, paragraph "(b)" goes on to provide for the application of COGSA to all carriage under the charter, thus effectively making the owner liable to cargo to the same extent as he would be if COGSA governed *ex proprio vigore*. Hence, only in the event of the charterer issuing a bill of lading increasing the carrier's obligation to cargo would paragraph "(a)" come into play.

Paragraph "(b)" provides for a far clearer incorporation of COGSA by reference than does the New York Produce form. See discussion above, page 432. Thus, in cases where the charterer is the shipper, COGSA nevertheless governs the parties' rights and immunities by agreement. This provision also requires the inclusion of a "Clause Paramount" in all bills of lading issued under the charter, together with the clauses enumerated as subparagraphs "ii" through "vi".

The meaning of the statement that such clauses shall be "deemed" incorporated by reference in all bills of lading is not clear, since any third party holder of a bill would not be bound to the terms of the charter unless they were incorporated in the bill by reference. As far as cargo owned by the charterer at all stages is concerned, the bill would be a mere receipt and document of title, and the charter itself would evidence the terms of the contract of carriage.

The "New Jason Clause" is, of course, the traditional means of eliminating the carrier's fault as a bar to recovery in general average. In accordance with the decision of the United States Supreme Court in *The Jason*, 225 U.S. 32 (1912), carriers are permitted to eliminate fault as a bar to recovery in general average, but only to the extent that they may validly exonerate themselves by contract from liability for cargo loss or damage. Thus, in practice, cargo will be liable for its proportion of general average expenses occasioned by "errors in navigation", but not for general average expenses occasioned by the carrier's lack of "due diligence" to make the vessel seaworthy.

See, e.g., *The Argo Merchant*, S.M.A. No. 2101 (Arb. at N.Y. 1985), wherein charterer was held liable to make a general average payment.

Under the present STB form general average is to be stated in accordance with the York-Antwerp Rules of 1950, rather than the revised York-Antwerp Rules of 1974. However, since these do not have the force of treaty or statute, the parties are free to contract for the application of any particular version of the Rules. Care should be taken, however, to assure that bills of lading issued under the charter incorporate by reference whatever version of the York-Antwerp Rules is prescribed in the charter.

The "Both-to-blame Collision Clause" is designed to require cargo on the carrying vessel to indemnify her owner against the consequences of cargo's right to recover in full from the non-carrying vessel in a mutual fault collision case. Thus, if vessel A collides with vessel B, and both vessels are at fault, cargo on A may recover its loss from B on a straight tort theory. (Cargo on A of course may not recover from A in the usual both-to-blame case, where A's fault is negligent navigation, since "errors in navigation" is a defense under COGSA.) However, cargo's recovery against B becomes part of B's damages, part of which are then recoverable from A in proportion to A's fault. The net result is that A will be indirectly liable for part of the cargo loss on A, even though A is under no direct liability for such loss. It is the avoidance of this indirect liability at which the clause is directed.

The both-to-blame Clause has long been held invalid under COGSA. See discussion above, page 436. However, in *American Union Transport Inc.* v. *United States*, 1976 AMC 1480 (N.D.Cal. 1976), the court upheld its validity in private carriage. The question remains whether the both-to-blame Clause would be considered valid when used in conjunction with a "Clause Paramount", since the latter by its own terms would render invalid any clause inconsistent with COGSA, which would include the both-to-blame Clause. The STB incorporation of COGSA does not, however, expressly purport to make invalid all clauses inconsistent with COGSA, but only those clauses which reduce the *carrier's* rights. Hence, it is arguable that the both-to-blame Clause in the STB form is valid for carriage of cargoes owned by the charterer.

Under United States law, the right of limitation of liability is available only to owners and bareboat charterers, and not to time or voyage charterers. 46 U.S.C.§§183, 186. Even an owner or bareboat chartered owner may not be entitled to limitation in respect of a liability arising under a "personal" contract, such as a charterparty. *Pendleton* v. *Benner Line*, 246 U.S. 353 (1918). Thus, since no United States statute or rule of law gives the owner the right to limit his liability under the charter, paragraph "(b) (v)" would appear to be ineffectual in a case where the owner is the "carrier" and the charterer is the cargo owner; in such a case the owner would be liable to the charterer without the benefit of a right of limitation for any cargo loss or damage resulting from a cause not excepted under the terms of the charter.

Where, however, the governing contract of carriage is evidenced by a bill of lading which has been negotiated to a holder in due course, the owner will be entitled to limit his liability to the holder for cargo loss or damage not caused with his "privity or knowledge". But if the bill of lading is issued by the charterer, the holder will be entitled to recover in full for cargo loss or damage resulting from a cause not excepted under COGSA, which would govern the bill of lading evidencing the contract of carriage between the charterer, as a "carrier", and the holder of the bill. If the cause of the loss is a failure to exercise due diligence to make the vessel seaworthy, or some other cause for which ultimate liability rests on the owner under the terms of the charter, the charterer will of course be entitled to indemnity, and since the right to indemnity arises out of a "personal" contract (the charter), the owner will not be entitled to limit his liability vis-à-vis the charterer. The end result will be that the owner will, indirectly, be liable in full for the loss or damage. Paragraph "(b) (v)" of Clause 20 therefore appears to have no effect other than to make it clear that nothing in the charter is to be construed as depriving the owner of any legal right he would otherwise have to limit his liability to third parties.

As with the both-to-blame Clause, there may be some inconsistency between COGSA's restrictions on deviation and a "liberties" clause such as 20(b)(vi) of the STB form, when the cargo is being carried for a third party under a bill of lading. However, when the carriage is performed for the charterer pursuant to the terms of the charter there would appear to be no reason why the provisions of the liberties clause should not be given full force.

21. *War Risks.* (a) No contraband of war shall be shipped, but petroleum and/or its products shall not be deemed contraband of war for the purposes of this Clause. Vessel shall not, however, be required, without the consent of Owner, which shall not be unreasonably withheld, to enter any port or zone which is involved in a state of war, warlike operations, or hostilities, civil strife, insurrection or piracy whether there be a declaration of war or not, where it might reasonably be expected to be subject to capture, seizure or arrest, or to a hostile act by a belligerent power (the term "power" meaning any de jure or de facto authority or any other purported governmental organization maintaining naval, military, or air forces).

(b) For the purposes of this Clause it shall be unreasonable for Owner to withhold consent to any voyage, route, or port of loading or discharge if insurance against all risks defined in Article 21 (a) is then available commercially or under a Government program in respect of such voyage, route or port of loading or discharge. If such consent is given by Owner, Charterer will pay the provable additional cost of insuring Vessel against Hull war risks in an amount equal to the value under her ordinary hull policy but not exceeding .... In addition, Owner may purchase war risk insurance on ancillary risks such as loss of hire, freight disbursements, total loss, etc., if he carries such insurance for ordinary marine hazards. If such insurance is not obtainable commercially or through a Government program, Vessel shall not be required to enter or remain at any such port or zone.

(c) In the event of the existence of the conditions described in Article 21 (a) subsequent to the date of this Charter, or while vessel is on hire under this Charter, Charterer shall, in respect of voyages to any such port or zone assume the provable additional cost of wages and insurance properly incurred in connection with Master, Officers and Crew as a consequence of such war, warlike operations or hostilities.

Under the New York Produce and other time charter forms the owner usually has a right to refuse to proceed to a port where hostilities are under way which might threaten the vessel or her cargo. The owner's right in such cases derives not from an express "war risks" provision but rather from the charterer's obligation to nominate "safe ports". To be "safe", a port must be "politically" safe as well as safe for navigation, and a port where a substantial risk of capture or damage from war-like operations exists does not satisfy the obligation. However, as noted, Clause 6(b) of the STB form disclaims any warranty of "safe port" and limits the charterer's obligation to the exercise of reasonable care. Clause 21 goes even further, and in effect obligates the owner to send the vessel even to a war zone, provided war risk insurance is available.

Paragraph "(a)" is broadly worded, covering as it does not only hostile acts of *de jure* and *de facto* governments, but also those of any "purported governmental organization maintaining naval, military, or air forces". This would appear to include certain guerrilla or terrorist groups. On the other hand, acts of saboteurs and rioters not engaged by such an organization would not be covered.

Under paragraph "(b)" the charterer is obligated to pay the additional cost of war risk hull insurance, if it is available, in which case the owner is required to permit the vessel to undertake a voyage or enter loading or discharging ports where hostilities are in progress. The owner is also permitted to purchase war risk insurance against "ancillary risks", including loss of hire, freight, disbursements, and total loss. If he carries marine risk insurance against such risks, and while the paragraph does not expressly so state, the plain inference is that the additional cost of such war risk insurance, like the additional cost of war risk hull insurance resulting from the charterer ordering the vessel to a zone where hostilities are in progress, will be for the charterer's account. See above, page 449.

EXCEPTIONS

22. (a) The Vessel, her Master and Owner shall not, unless otherwise in this Charter expressly provided, be responsible for any loss or damage to cargo arising or resulting from: any act, neglect, default or barratry of the Master, Pilots, mariners or other servants of the Owner in the navigation or management of the Vessel; fire, unless caused by the personal design or neglect of the Owner; collision, stranding, or peril, danger or accident of the sea or other navigable waters; or from explosion, bursting of boilers, breakage of shafts, or any latent defect in hull, equipment or machinery. And neither the Vessel, her Master or Owner, nor the Charterer, shall, unless otherwise in this Charter expressly provided, be responsible for any loss or damage or delay or failure in performing hereunder arising or resulting from: act of God; act of war; perils of the seas; act of public enemies, pirates or assailing thieves; arrest or restraint of princes, rulers or people, or seizure under legal process provided bond is promptly furnished to release the Vessel or cargo; strike or lockout or stoppage or restraint of labor from whatever cause, either partial or general; or riot or civil commotion.

Under the first sentence of Clause 22 (a) the owner and her master, *in personam*, and the vessel, *in rem*, are exonerated from liability for cargo loss or damage resulting from certain specified causes, including errors in navigation or management, fire not caused by the owner's personal design or neglect, perils of the sea, and latent defects.

The second sentence is a "mutual" exceptions clause shielding both the owner and the charterer against liability for "any loss or damage or delay or failure in performing" under the charter, resulting from a list of causes considerably broader than the list contained in the corresponding provision of the New York Produce form (Clause 16, second sentence). As interpreted by the American courts, a "mutual" exceptions clause excuses only the party whose performance is affected by the occurrence of one of the excepted causes. Thus, if the owner is unable to follow the charterer's sailing instructions because of a tugboat strike, the owner will not be liable in damages. But as the strike does not affect the charterer's ability to pay hire, and as nothing in the off-hire clause (Clause 11) provides for off-hire for time lost on account of a tugboat strike, the charterer will not be relieved of the obligation to pay hire during the delay. See *Clyde Commercial S.S. Co.* v. *West India S.S. Co.*, 169 Fed. 275 (2d Cir. 1909).

Conversely, if a bank strike makes it impossible for the charterer to pay hire when due, the charterer will be excused so long as the strike continues to have that effect, but the owner will remain obligated to follow the charterer's orders with respect to sailing, loading, discharging, etc.

NUMBER OF GRADES

(b) The Owner warrants the Vessel is constructed and equipped to carry .... grades of oil. If for any reason the Vessel, upon arrival at a loading port, is unable to load the required number of grades, the Charterer will do its utmost to provide a suitable cargo consistent with Vessel's capabilities. However, if this is not possible the Vessel is to proceed to the nearest repair port in ballast and will there repair all bulkhead leaks necessary, any time and expense being for Owner's account.

(c) The exceptions stated in subparagraph (a) of this Clause shall not affect the Owner's undertakings with respect to the condition, particulars and capabilities of the Vessel, or the provisions for payment and cessation of hire or the obligations of the Owner under Clause 20 in respect of the loading, handling, stowage, carriage, custody, care and discharge of cargo.

The first sentence of paragraph "(b)" is a warranty that the vessel is capable of carrying a specified number of grades of oil. The second sentence, however, is in effect a modification of the off-hire provisions of Clause 11; if the vessel cannot, "for any reason", comply with the warranty, she will not necessarily go off-hire, since the charterer will then be obligated to "do its utmost" to provide a cargo which the vessel will be able to load. Only if this proves impossible will the owner be obligated to send the vessel to the nearest repair port in ballast, and there effect the necessary repairs. In that case the time lost and the expenses will be for the owner's account.

23. All salvage moneys earned by the Vessel shall be divided equally between the Owner and the Charterer after deducting Master's, Officers' and Crew's share, legal expenses, hire of Vessel during time lost, value of fuel consumed, repairs of damage, if any, and any other extraordinary loss or expense sustained as a result of the service, which shall always be a first charge on such money.

This provision is very clear and requires no special comment.

OIL POLLUTION

24. Owner warrants that the Vessel is entered in TOVALOP and will remain so entered during the currency of this Charter, provided, however, that if Owner acquires the right to withdraw from TOVALOP under Clause VIII thereof, nothing herein shall prevent it from exercising that right.

When an escape or discharge of oil occurs from the Vessel and threatens to cause pollution damage to coastlines, Charterer may, at its option, and upon notice to Owner or Master, undertake such measures as are reasonably necessary to prevent or mitigate such damage, unless Owner promptly undertakes same. Charterer shall keep Owner advised of the nature of the measures intended to be taken by it. Any of the aforementioned measures actually taken by Charterer shall be at Owner's expense (except to the extent that such escape or discharge was caused or contributed to by Charterer), provided that if Owner considers said measures should be discontinued, Owner may so notify Charterer and thereafter Charterer shall have no right to continue said measures under the provisions of this Clause and all further liability to Charterer thereunder shall thereupon cease.

If any dispute shall arise between Owner and Charterer as to the reasonableness of the measures undertaken and/or the expenditure incurred by Charterer hereunder, such dispute shall be referred to arbitration as herein provided.

The provisions of this Clause are not in derogation of such other rights as Charterer or Owner may have under this Charter, or may otherwise have or acquire by law or any International Convention.

A tanker owner who is a party to the TOVALOP agreement undertakes to reimburse governments for their oil pollution cleanup costs, within specified monetary limits, unless the owner can prove absence of fault, and further undertakes to carry insurance against the contractual liability thus assumed. TOVALOP was revised in 1988 to provide for substantially increased coverage and limits of liability.

Under the second and third sentences of Clause 24, the charterer is authorized to undertake cleanup measures, at the owner's expense, following an oil spill, if they are not promptly undertaken by the owner. The latter may, however, request the charterer to discontinue such measures, in which case any further steps undertaken by the charterer will be for its own account.

The final sentence of Clause 24 simply preserves any rights either party may have under the charter, or under any law or international Convention. Thus, where the International Convention on Civil Liability for Oil Pollution Damage is in force, under Article III, liability for oil pollution is channeled through the vessel owner, who has a right of indemnity from a charterer or other third party who may be responsible for the spill.

CLEAN SEAS

25. The Owner agrees to participate in the Charterer's program covering oil pollution avoidance. Such program aims to prevent the discharge into the sea anywhere in the world of all oil, oil water or ballast, chemicals or oily waste material in any form if the said material is of a persistent nature, except under extreme circumstances whereby the safety of the Vessel, cargo or life would be imperiled.

The Owner agrees to adhere to the oil pollution avoidance instructions provided by the Charterer in the Charterer's Vessel Instruction Manual together with any amendments which may be issued in writing or by radio to cover special cases or changes in International and National Regulations or Laws. The Master will contain on board the Vessel all oily residues from consolidated tank washings, dirty ballast, etc. Such residues shall be contained in one compartment after the separation of all possible water has taken place by safe methods employing the use of settlement and decanting or mechanic separation to approved and recognized standards.

The oily residue will be pumped ashore at the loading or discharge terminal either as segregated oil, dirty ballast, commingling with cargo or as is possible for Charterer to arrange with each cargo.

If the Charterer requires that demulsifiers be used for the separation of oil and water, the cost of such demulsifiers will be at the Charterer's expense.

Owner will also arrange for the Vessel to adhere to Charterer's oil pollution program during off-hire periods within the term of this Charter including the preparing of cargo tanks for drydocking and repairs. In the latter cases, the Charterer agrees to bear costs for the disposal of oil residues.

Vessel will take all necessary precautions while loading and discharging cargo or bunkers as well as ballast to ensure that no oil will escape overboard.

Nothing in the Charterer's instructions shall be construed as permission to pollute the sea by the discharge of oil or oily water etc. The Owner agrees to instruct the Master to furnish Charterer with a report covering oil pollution avoidance together with details of the quantity of oil residue on board on arrival at the loading port.

This clause requires the owner to follow "load on top" and other systems adopted by the oil companies in their efforts to minimize pollution of the sea by oil if so directed by the charterer.

PRODUCTS

26. Owner hereby agrees to receive sales representatives of affiliates of Charterer which market marine products. However, Owner is under no obligation to purchase from said affiliates, and said affiliates are under no obligation to sell to Owner any of such products. Owner designates the following as the appropriate persons or organizations with whom said affiliates should deal:

Name ....

Address ....

This clause is obviously intended simply to allow the charterer to make a "sales pitch" in efforts to sell lubricating oil and other petroleum products produced by the charterer.

CHANGE OF OWNERSHIP

27. Owner's rights and obligations under this Charter are not transferable by Sale or Assignment without Charterer's consent. In the event of the Vessel being sold without its consent in addition to its other rights, Charterer may, at its absolute discretion, terminate the Charter, whereupon the Owner shall reimburse Charterer for any hire paid in advance and not earned, the cost of bunkers, for any sums to which Charterer is entitled under this Charter, and for any damages which Charterer may sustain.

By this clause the STB form sharply limits the owner's ability to profit from a high rate charter by selling the vessel "with charter". Although it may be argued that the charterer would not be entitled to withhold consent to a sale to a reputable purchaser unreasonably, nevertheless the severe penalty of termination in the event of a transfer without its consent would make any prudent owner hesitate before attempting such a sale without first obtaining the charterer's express approval.

Nothing in the clause would appear to prohibit the beneficial owner of a vessel registered in the name of a corporation from disposing of his interest indirectly by a sale of his shares of corporate stock.

ARBITRATION

28. Any and all differences and disputes of whatsoever nature arising out of this Charter shall be put to arbitration in the City of New York pursuant to the laws relating to arbitration there in force, before a board of three persons, consisting of one arbitrator to be appointed by the Owner, one by the Charterer, and one by the two so chosen. The decision of any two of the three on any point or points shall be final. Until such time as the arbitrators finally close the hearings either party shall have the right by written notice served on the arbitrators and on an officer of the other party to specify further disputes or differences under this Charter for hearing and determination. The arbitrators may grant any relief which they, or a majority of them, deem just and equitable and within the scope of the agreement of the parties, including, but not limited to, specific performance. Awards pursuant to this Clause may include costs, including a reasonable allowance for attorney's fees, and judgment may be entered upon any award made hereunder in any Court having jurisdiction in the premises.

There are several important differences between the arbitration clause of the STB form and that of the New York Produce form. Under the latter the arbitrators must be "commercial men", a term which in New York is understood to exclude practising lawyers. However, under the STB form the parties may choose either lawyers or commercial men, and frequently the panel will be comprised of a mixture of lawyers and non-lawyers.

The STB arbitration clause gives the arbitrators wide powers, including the right to order specific performance. Absent express authorization, it is doubtful that such an award would be valid and enforceable. American courts have held that arbitrators may grant equitable relief, however, if the arbitration clause is sufficiently broad to give them express authority to do so.

Finally, the STB arbitration clause expressly authorizes the awarding of attorneys' fees, a point on which the New York Produce form is silent. Without such express authorization an award of attorneys' fees has been held outside the scope of the arbitrators' power while such an award would be clearly valid under the STB form. *Transvenezuelian Shipping Co. S.A.* v. *Czarnikow-Rionda Co. Inc.*, 1982 AMC 1458 (S.D.N.Y. 1982). In practice, however, New York arbitrators do not always award attorneys' fees, even when the arbitration clause gives them discretion to do so.

ASSIGNMENT SUBLET

29. (a) Charterer, upon notice to Owner, may assign this Charter Party to any of its affiliates.

(b) Charterer shall also have the right to sublet the Vessel, but in the event of a sublet, Charterer shall always remain responsible for the fulfillment of this Charter in all its terms and conditions.

These provisions expressly give the charterer the right to assign the charter and to "sublet" the vessel—rights it would have under American law, even without such express provisions, unless the charter provided otherwise.

LAWS

30. The interpretation of the Charter and of the rights and obligations of the parties shall be governed by the laws applicable to Charter Parties made in the City of New York. The headings of Clauses are for convenience of reference only and shall not affect the interpretation of this Charter. No modification, waiver or discharge of any term of this Charter shall be valid unless in writing and signed by the party to be charged therewith.

Charters, being maritime contracts, are not subject to State or local law, as such, but are governed by the "general maritime law" of the United States, which is a set of judicially fashioned rules with antecedents in English admiralty law and operating uniformly throughout the country. (See above.) To a large extent the substantive law of carriage of goods under ocean bills of lading has been modified by federal statutes (e.g., the Harter

Act and COGSA) but carriage under charterparties remains relatively free of statutory regulation. Thus, in the main, by Clause 30 the parties merely accept the applicability of the general maritime law of the United States, rather than the law of any other country.

IN WITNESS, WHEREOF, THE PARTIES HAVE CAUSED THIS CHARTER TO BE EXECUTED IN DUPLICATE THE DAY AND YEAR HEREIN FIRST ABOVE WRITTEN.

....

WITNESS TO SIGNATURE OF

....

WITNESS TO SIGNATURE OF

Index

Numbers in italic refer to American Law pages

Numbers in italic refer to American Law pages

Numbers in italic refer to American Law pages

Numbers in italic refer to American Law pages

Numbers in italic refer to American Law pages

Numbers in italic refer to American Law pages

Numbers in italic refer to American Law pages

Numbers in italic refer to American Law pages

Numbers in italic refer to American Law pages

Numbers in italic refer to American Law pages